Colonial Families of the Eastern Shore of Maryland

Volume 2

Robert W. Barnes
and
F. Edward Wright

HERITAGE BOOKS
2018

HERITAGE BOOKS
AN IMPRINT OF HERITAGE BOOKS, INC.

Books, CDs, and more—Worldwide

For our listing of thousands of titles see our website
at
www.HeritageBooks.com

Published 2018 by
HERITAGE BOOKS, INC.
Publishing Division
5810 Ruatan Street
Berwyn Heights, Md. 20740

International Standard Book Number
Paperbound: 978-1-58549-342-5

CONTENTS

iii

iv

INTRODUCTION

Kent County is first mentioned in the records in 1642. At that time the Governor and Council appointed Commissioners for the Isle and County of Kent.[1] On 16 May 1631 King Charles I granted a license to William Clayborne to trade along the shores of the Chesapeake, and the same year Clayborne established a trading post on Kent Island. The Marylanders who came in 1634 claimed authority over Kent Island, and after many legal disputes with Clayborne, Lord Baltimore appealed to the Committee of Trade and Plantations, and in 1638 they issued a report in favor of Lord Baltimore.[2] As early as 1638 Kent Isle had sent two delegates to the General Assembly: Nicholas Brown and Christopher Thomas.[3] Baltimore County was carved out of Kent County in 1659 and Talbot County was erected in 1662.[4]

Cecil County, extending from the mouth of the Susquehanna and down the eastern side of the Bay to Swan point and from there to Hell Point, and so up Chester River, to its head, was established in 1674. Kent Island was removed from the jurisdiction of Kent County by an Act of the Legislature passed 22 May 1695.[5]

An Act of 19 April 1706 stated that after 1 May 1706, Kent County would be bounded by a line drawn from the south point of Eastern Neck, up the Bay to Sassafras river, up the said river to the south end of Long Horse Bridge, thence by a line drawn by east and by south to the exterior bounds of the Province and with the exterior bounds [south?] to the line of Queen Anne's County, and with said County down Chester River to Eastern Neck.[6] This same Act provided for the erection of Queen Anne's County.[7]

A variety of sources was used in putting together this secoond volume of Kent County Family Histories, and are described below.

Land Records were combed looking for statements that provided clues to marriages, descents of property, and places of origin. Sometimes rather complicated family relationships are unraveled on the pages of land records.

Criminal Proceedings were found to be full of information on what our ancestors were really like.

Probate Records, including wills, inventories, administration accounts, and balances of final distributions of estates, are one of the staple resources of genealogical research. All categories of records were searched in order to build as a complete a picture of the family as possible. In the case of William Johnson, his will written 5 March 1748, designated his wife as executrix, but did not name her. Fortunately the inventory named the executrix as Beatrice Johnson.[8]

Frequently a succession of probate records in the settlement of an estate established the remarriage of the widow.

Depositions, sworn testimony by witnesses, called deponents, are found in a variety of places. Land records, land commissions, ejectment papers are just a few of the sources for these items, which usually give the name of the deponent and his or her age, and often contain references to other family members.

Ejectment Papers referred to cases involving landlords and tenants and ownership of land. The documents in these cases often contain much helpful family history.

Bonds and Indentures were other types of records, frequently overlooked, that were checked. A bond is a promise, backed by a financial consideration to perform a certain action. Trustees would post a bond that they would pay the minor children of a decedent their fair share of their father's estate when the child reached majority. Grantors would post a bond that they would convey certain property. Executors and administrators posted bond they would well and truly perform their duties in settling an estate.

Indentures are written agreements and may apply to conveyances of land, but may also be a form of contract between two persons involving matters other than real estate.

Chattel Records are documents concerning the transfer of movable property, such as cattle, slaves, furniture or farming implements from one person to another. They contained many examples of parents conveying such movable property to their children or grandchildren.

Several publications have already appeared making research on Kent County families easier. Perhaps the first to appear was George A. Hanson's *Old Kent: The Eastern Shore of Maryland*.[9] First published in 1876, it has been reprinted many times. The next work to appear was Frederick G. Usilton's *History of Kent County, Maryland, 1630-1916*.[10]

In recent years Henry Peden has compiled two books dealing with the people of Kent County: *Revolutionary Patriots of Kent County*,[11] and *Inhabitants of Kent County, Maryland, 1637-1787*.[12] Regional sources include a number of volumes from Family Line Publications: *Sketches of Maryland Eastern Shoremen*,[13] *Citizens of the Eastern Shore of Maryland, 1659-1750*,[14] 5 volumes of *Maryland Eastern Shore Vital Records*, covering the years 1648-1825, and 8 volumes of *Maryland Eastern Shore Newspaper Abstracts*, dealing with the period from 1790 to 1834. The Maryland State Archives has published *A Guide to Maryland State Archives Holdings of Kent County Records on Microform*.[15]

It is a myth that colonial Maryland was populated only by British subjects. In Kent County, as in the rest of the Province, a variety of ethnic groups were found. For example, the Ricaud family had ties to England, but may have been of French descent. John Hendrickson and Cornelius Comegys were from the Netherlands. Hans Hanson was of Swedish descent, while John Peter Zenger and Francis Ludolph Bodien were from Germany.

The English no doubt made up the bulk of Kent County's colonial population. Land records and depositions often provided a clue to the origins of the settlers.

There seems to have been at least one person of Spanish birth or descent living in Kent County: Andrew Ellenor, who was so designated in one of the records. Colonial Kent County had at least one free African-American. Edmund Coy, formerly a slave to Philip Kennard, died leaving a will dated 23 December 1737 and proved 25 January 1737/8. His will states he was set free by will of the said Kennard. To Philip Kennard (merchant), he left the testator's share of grain, etc., made on plantation of Dr. Thomas William, in trust for use of son Edmund, now a slave to the said Philip Kennard, and granddaughter, Lene, also a slave.[16]

This is the second in a series of volumes of family histories pertaining to the colonial families of the Eastern Shore. Any additional material concerning the families in this second volume will be published in subsequent volumes.

END NOTES

1. *Maryland Manual: A Guide to Maryland State Government, 1994-1995.* Ed. by Diane P. Frese. Annapolis: Maryland State Archives. 1994.

2. Edward B. Mathews, "The Counties of Maryland: Their Origin, Boundaries, and Election Districts," in *Maryland Geological Survey: Volume VI* (Baltimore: The Johns Hopkins Press, 1906), p. 511.

3. *Biographical Directory of the Maryland Legislature.* Ed. by Edward C. Papenfuse, et al. (New York: The Johns Hopkins University Press, 2 Vols., 1975-1985), I, 16.

4. Mathews, *op. cit.*, p. 512.

5. Mathews, *op. cit.*, p. 512.

6. Mathews, *op. cit.*, p. 514, cites Acts of Maryland 1706: Ch. 3.

7. Mathews, *op. cit.*, p. 534.

8. Maryland Wills, Liber 28:149; Maryland Inventories, Liber 45:63.

9. *Old Kent: The Eastern Shore of Maryland*, by George A. Hanson (1876). Reprint: Baltimore, Clearfield Co.

10. *History of Kent County, Maryland, 1630-1916*, by Frederick G. Usilton (1916). Reprint: Bowie, Heritage Books.

11.	Family Line Publications, Westminster, Maryland.

12.	Family Line Publications, Westminster, Maryland.

13.	Published in 1898, condensed and reissued in 1992.

14.	This work includes tax lists, petitions, levy records and militia records.

15.	Annapolis: Maryland State Archives.

16.	Maryland Will Book 21:868.

SOURCES AND ABBREVIATIONS

(Source of entry is followed by volume and page number.)

AACR: *Anne Arundel County Church Records of the 17th and 18th Centuries.* By F. Edward Wright. Westminster: Family Line Publications, 1989.

AALR: Anne Arundel County Land Records.

ARMD: *Archives of Maryland* (published series).

BDML: *Biographical Dictionary of the Maryland Legislature.* By Edward C. Papenfuse et al. 2 vols. Baltimore: The Johns Hopkins University Press, 1979, 1985.

BFD: Balances of Final Distributions (now abstracted by Moxey and Skinner).

BMGS: *Maryland Genealogical Society Bulletin.*

CECH: *Early Anglican Church Records of Cecil County.* By Henry C. Peden, Jr. Westminster: Family Line Publications, 1990.

CEMM: Cecil Monthly Meeting (Quakers); Register 1678-1820; Marriages 1698-1784; Special Collections MSA M908.

ESVR: *Eastern Shore Vital Records.* Comp. by F. Edward Wright. 5 vols. Westminster: Family Line Publications, 1982-1986.

INAC: Inventories and Accounts (now abstracted by Skinner).

INKE: *Inhabitants of Kent County, Maryland, 1637-1787.* By Henry C. Peden, Jr. Westminster: Family Line Publications, 1994.

KEAD: Kent County Administration Accounts.

KECH: Kent County Chancery Records.

KECP: Kent County Court Proceedings.

KECR: Kent County Criminal Records.

KECT: Kent County Chattel Records.

KEEJ: Kent County Ejectment Papers, MSA.

KELR: Kent County Land Records.

KELR A: Kent County Land Records, Liber A, 1648-1679, Transcript, on MSA MF CR 50,062-1.

KELR B: Kent County Land Records, 1679-1692, Transcript, on MSA MF CR 50,062-2.

KELR C: Kent County Court Land Records, 1692-1706, on MSA MF CR 50,063-1. The first part of Liber C is a

	transcript of Liber I. "The first part of Liber I is in a Book marked Liber B for transcribing old records.
KELR G:	Kent County Land Records, Liber G, was transcribed into Liber A, beginning at folio 465, with these words: "In the beginning of a book marked Lib: G was the part of a conveyance the first parts being wanting what remains is here inserted as followeth viz."
KELR K:	Kent County Land Records, 1681 - 1685, on MSA MF CR 50,062-3.
KELR M:	Kent County Land Records, 1694-1701, on MSA MF CR 50,063-2.
KELR JD#1:	Kent County Land Records, 1701-1704, on MSA MF CR 50,063-3.
KELR GL#1:	Kent County Land Records, 1704-1707, on MSA MF CR 50,063-4. Also contains Bonds and Indentures, 1694-1706.
KELR JSN:	Kent County Land Records, 1707-1714, on MSA MF CRE 50,064-1.
KELR BC#1:	Kent County Land Records, 1714-1718, on MSA MF CR 50,064-2.
KELR JS#W:	Kent County Land Records, 1719-1726, on MSA MF CR 50,064-3.
KELR JS#X:	Kent County Land Records, 1726-1730, on MSA MF CR 50,065-1.
KELR JS#16:	Kent County Land Records, 1730-1734, on MSA MF CR 50,065-2.
KELR JS#18:	Kent County Land Records, 1734-1738, on MSA MF CR 50,0661-1.
KELR JS#22:	Kent County Land Records, 1738-1740, on MSA MF CR 50,066-2.
KELR JS#23:	Kent County Land Records, 1740-1742, on MSA MF CR 50,067-1.
KELR JS#25:	Kent County Land Records, 1744-1747, on MSA MF CR 50,068-1.
KELR JS#26:	Kent County Land Records, 1747-1751, on MSA MF CR 50,068-2.
KELR JS#27:	Kent County Land Records, 1751-1754, on MSA MF CR 50,068-3.
KELR JS#28:	Kent County Land Records, 1754-1758, on MSA MF CR 50,069-1.

KELR JS#29:	Kent County Land Records, 1758-1761, on MSA MF CR 50,069-2.
KELR DD#1:	Kent County Land Records, 1761-1765, on MSA MF CR 50,070-1.
KESH:	Shrewsbury Parish Register, Kent County.
KESP:	St. Paul's Parish Register, Kent County.
KEWB:	Kent County Will Books.
MCW:	*Maryland Calendar of Wills* (from Prerogative Court). By Jane Baldwin Cotton (Volumes 1-8) and F. Edward Wright (Volumes 9-16).
MDAD:	Maryland Administration Accounts; originals are at MSA.
MDTP:	Maryland Testamentary Proceedings; originals are at MSA.
MHM:	*Maryland Historical Magazine.*
MHS:	Maryland Historical Society, Baltimore.
MINV:	Maryland Inventories (now abstracted by Skinner).
MSA:	Maryland State Archives, Annapolis.
MWB:	Maryland Will Book.
(N):	Name unknown.
PCLR:	Provincial Court Land Records; originals are at MSA.
QALR:	Queen Anne's County Land Records.
THMM:	Third Haven Monthly Meeting.
WCMN:	Wyand, Jeffrey A., and Florence L. Wyand. *Colonial Maryland Naturalizations.* Baltimore: Genealogical Publishing Co., 1975.

OTHER ABBREVIATIONS

a.	acre(s)
AA Co.	Anne Arundel County
adj.	adjoining
admin.	administrator or administered
admx(s).	administratrix (administratices)
afsd.	aforesaid
b.	born
BA Co.	Baltimore County
bapt.	baptized
BC	Baltimore City
bro(s).	brother(s)

bur.	buried
c	circa (about)
CE Co.	Cecil County
cont.	containing
conv.	conveyed
CV Co.	Calvert County
dau(s).	daughter(s)
dec.	deceased
dep.	deposed
dist.	distributed
DO Co.	Dorchester County
dwell. plant.	dwelling plantation
e.	east
exec(s).	executor(s)
extx(s).	executrix (executrices)
FR Co.	Frederick County
inv.	inventoried
KE Co.	Kent County
m.	married or month
n.	north
nunc.	nuncupative
plant.	plantation
QA Co.	Queen Anne's County
s.	south or shilling(s)
sd.	said
s.p.	died without issue
TA Co.	Talbot County
T.P.	Testamentary Proceedings
Test:	Testes (meaning witnesses)
tob.	tobacco
v.p.	during father's lifetime
w.	west
wit.	witness

ADDITIONS, CORRECTIONS, and COMMENTS

TO

Historic Families of the Eastern Shore, *Volume I*

The compilers are indebted to Mr. Chris Christou of Baltimore, Mr. Rennie Stavely of Silver Spring, Mr. William J. Utermohlen of Alexandria, VA, and Dolores Crouch Youngman of Tallahassee, FL, for their submissions.

(CC)	- submitted by Christ Christou.
(RS)	- submitted by Rennie Stavely.
(WU)	- submitted by William J. Utermohlen.
(DCY)	- submitted by Dolores Crouch Youngman.

TO SOURCES AND ABBREVIATIONS
KEEJ: Kent Co. Ejectment Papers, MSA.

TO TEXT

p. 1:   Moses Alford and Mary (Stavely) were the parents of Mary. The other children were apparently by a former marriage. (RS)

p. 3:   Line 22: Abraham <u>Evans</u> was the father of Abraham: Abraham ... should read Abraham <u>Ambrose</u> was the father of ...

p. 5:   Frances Blackiston did not m. Thomas Ambrose in 17<u>63</u> (he d. in 1740). (CC) She m. Abram Ambrose on 31 Aug 1763.{KESP}

p. 11:   William Ashby's inventory was filed on 1 June 17<u>67</u>. It must be another William Ashby whose will was dated 1785. (CC)

p. 23:   The unplaced Rachel Barney was the widow of Thomas Medford (See p. 259). She m. Barney after Medford's death in 1719. Rachel was the dau. of George Mackall, whose will of 1675, was proved in SM Co. By this will he gave his dau. Rachel 400 a. *Hepburn's Choice* and *Magy's Jointure*, the first of which was mentioned in Rachel's will and the second in her husband's will. Thomas and Rachel had other children in addition to the ones listed on p. 259. Dau. Rachel Medford m. William Moore. Anne Medford who m. Richard Kennard. (Both were daus. of Medford, and not of Barney). Rachel Moore was named in her father's will, and Ann was not. However, Ann was a grandmother by the will of her own mother, and other deeds show her as a Medford. The Medford name was passed as a first name to her descendants. (CC)

p. 26:   Edward Beck m. Ann Queeney, dau. of the widow Ann Queeney, who m. 2nd, Richard Pullen. (CC)

p. 27:   John Beck (#3) d. after 1732 (not after 1723), since he gave a deposition in 1732. (CC)

p. 30:   The unplaced Alexander and Elizabeth Beck are children of #11, Alexander Beck and his wife Susanna. Susanna m. 2nd, Vincent Blackiston and he named his son-in-law Alexander Beck (see p. 40). (CC)

p. 31:   The unplaced Edward Beck, uncle of Sutton Queeney, is the same as #2, Edward Beck on p. 26. (He was an uncle because Edward Beck m. Sutton's aunt Ann.) (CC)

p. 32:   The unplaced Samuel Beck who d. in 1749 m. Elizabeth Wilkinson on 19 June 1729 at St. Luke's Parish, QA Co. She d. and had a will proven in KE Co. on 13 Jan 1778. She named her children Margaret Rue, Frances Wroth, Samuel Beck, and John Beck. Margaret and John signed the inventory of Samuel Beck as next of kin. (CC)

p. 32:   The unplaced Samuel Beck who m. Sarah Davis was the son of Samuel Beck and Elizabeth Wilkinson. Samuel is listed in DAR Lineage Books as having served in the Revolutionary War. Samuel Beck, Jr., d. leaving a will dated 1790, naming his bro. John. (CC)

p. 38:   William Blackiston also m. Ann Moore, dau. of John Moore and Elizabeth Dowland. By her, he was the father of: ROSAMOND; and HANCE BLACKISTON. Hance is the unnamed child Ann Moore Blackiston was carrying when William made his will. Hance's own will had Moores as witnesses, and William Blackiston signed the inventory of John Moore as next of kin. William must have been m. twice as the range of children's ages is too great for one woman: dau. MARY was b. c1711/2, while ROSAMOND was b. c1730, and there was an unborn child in 1737. (CC)

p. 45:   The Ebenezer Blackiston bur. 1709 was the son of George and Barbara (Lawson) Blackiston (#4. Ebenezer on p. 37). (CC)

p. 117:   Joyce Finch m. Sutton Queeney, Sr. See their children's birth records. The unplaced Joyce Queeney was Joyce Finch wife of Sutton Queeney. She m. John Toas in 1699 after Sutton Queeney, Sr., d. (CC)

           Mary Pearce was the sister of Joyce Finch, not of Sutton Queeney, and thus was the aunt of Sutton's children. She was the widow Mary Caulk whose husband Isaac d. in 1704, and she m. 2nd, Daniel Pearce. (CC)

p. 122:   Arthur Foreman was living as late as 1756 (not 1746), when his will was dated. (CC)

p. 128:   Hannah Boh was Hannah Burke. She m. Thomas Burke, and left a will dated 2 Feb 1761 and proved 2 April 1761. (CC)

p. 133:   John Gale, Jr., d. 6 Dec 1775.{CEMM} (CC)

p. 142:   Hannah(retta) Mahon (Mahawn) m. 1st, Bartholomew Garnett, 2nd, Ebenezer Blackiston, and 3rd, Matthew Richardson. She d. after 1794 when, as Hannahretta Richardson, she deeded land that had belonged to her father Thomas Mahawn, to her son Joseph Blackiston. (CC)

p. 146: 1. Jacob Alexander Glenn, Sr., b. 27 Feb 1686 in Schenectady, NY, m. Ann Hanson, dau. of Hans Hanson. She was b. 17 Feb 1689. See *Bible Records, 1581-1917*, pp. 94-96, and *Early Settlers of Schenectady, NY.* (CC)

p. 147: 4. Jacob Alexander Glenn, Jr., was b. 2 Oct 1718 in KE Co., and m. Rebecca Miller, b. 20 June 1725 in KE Co. (CC)

p. 194: 5. THOMAS HEBRON - m. by 6 Nov 1711, Katherine, extx. of Richard Unitt of KE Co. Rennie Stavely suggests that this is probably Katherine Bowdie who m. Richard Unit. (RS)

p. 203: Mary Pullen was m. four times: 1st, Nathaniel Howell; 2nd, after 1693, Richard Kennard; 3rd, on 19 June 1701 George Browning; and 4th, on 26 Oct 1714, Matthew Howard. (CC)

p. 206: 2. JOSEPH HULL m. 1st Hannah Stavely not Shapely. Rennie Stavely believes that the reference to a second marriage is incorrect and that the Frances given as the second wife is in fact the first wife Hannah. (RS)

p. 259: THE MEDFORD FAMILY. (RS)
1. BULMER MEDFORD d. 1665 in SM Co.
2. THOMAS MEDFORD m. Rachel Mackall, dau. of George MacKall (or Macall) of SM Co. Following the death of Thomas Medford she m. (N) Barney. She d. leaving a will dated 24 Oct 1731 and proved 6 July 1733. In it she mentioned sons: Balmour Midford, George Midford; daus.: Ann Kennard and Rachell Moore; grandson Richard son of Ann Kennard, grandson Thomas Midford and grandson John Moore.
Thomas, son of Thomas and Rachel Medford d. before 1733; was a Vestryman at Shrewsbury Parish Church, 1726.
Ann, dau. of Thomas and Rachel Medford m. (N) Kennard; they had a son Richard.

Rachell, dau. of Thomas and Rachel Medford m. William Moore and had issue: John, Asenath, Thomas, Martha (m. Rasin Gale) and George.
3. BULMER MEDFORD - Bulmer m. Sarah Unit (b. 20 Jan 1725), dau. of Richard Unit who was bro. of Mary Unit Stavely.
Change name of the son of Bulmer and Sarah from Michael to Macall (b. 10 Oct 1738). [RS]

p. 259:   See comments by CC under p. 23.

p. 282:   John Moore, son of Richard and Rebecca Moore of Kilworth, Ireland (mentioned as unplaced on p. 286) is included in a well documented genealogy of the family which appeared in *The Colonial Genealogist* 4 (3) 172. Although Richard's will did not name his children, the settlement of his estate did. His sons were: THOMAS; and JOHN, who m. Grace Dowland, dau. of William and Amy (Erickson) Dowland. (CC)

p. 286:   The unplaced Mary More, extx. of Stephen Whetstone, was previously m. to Thomas More, son of Richard. Her maiden name was Mary Browne. (CC)

p. 296:   Mary Pearce was the sister of Joyce Finch, not of Sutton Queeney, and thus was the aunt of Sutton's children. She was the widow Mary Caulk whose husband Isaac d. in 1704, and she m. 2nd, Daniel Pearce. (CC)

p. 298:   The unplaced Joyce Queeney was Joyce Finch, wife of Sutton Queeney. Ann Gilbert, dau. of Richard and Rosamond Gilbert, m. 1st, Mr. Queeney (possibly a Sutton Queeney also) in Westmoreland Co., and 2nd, Richard Pullen. Mary Pearce was the sister of Joyce Finch, not of Sutton Queeney. She was the widow Mary Caulk whose husband d. in 1704. Mary Caulk m. Daniel Pearce on 4 Feb 1704. (CC)

p. 301:   2. ABRAHAM REDGRAVE, Jr. Line 2 should read ... ; he d. before <u>1740</u>. (RS)

p. 301:	Abraham Redgrave, Jr., m. three times: 1st, Elizabeth, widow of Philip Rasin; 2nd, Elizabeth (N); and 3rd, Alice Wilson. (CC)
p. 303:	Line 10. By his wife Damosel (N), ... This unusual name suggests that this may be Damlin (Damsel) Cole, dau. of John and Elizabeth Cole, who was baptized at Shrewsbury in Jan 1715. (RS)
p. 304:	Isaac Redgrave had only one child by Mary: JOSEPH. All the other children were by Elizabeth Corse. (CC)
p. 304:	7. William Redgrave, b. 1727, is mentioned in a deed as William, son of John. (CC)
p. 307:	NB: repeats what is in the footnote. (CC)
p. 312:	Edward and Hannah (Smith) Scott had two sons: EDWARD, b. 29 Aug 1726; and JOHN, b. 10 Oct 1726 [sic]. A memorandum in KE Co. Ejectment Papers states that JOHN was b. 10 Oct 1728. The 1730 date probably refers to his baptism.
p. 314:	David Scott had a dau. Martha, wife of Isaac Freeman. (CC)
p. 319:	The same sentence is repeated for Rebecca, bapt. 1712. (CC)
p. 334:	George Vansant m. Rebecca Wilson, dau. of John Wilson, whose will proved in KE Co. in 1732, named his dau. Rebecca Vansant. (CC)
p. 335:	Last paragraph. Joshua and Catherine had the following children: CHRISTOPHER; JOSHUA; JOHN; RACHEL, m. 8 da., 6 mo., 1750, Gershom Mott, Jr.; SARAH, m. 9 da., 5 mo., 1753, Writson Browning. (CEMM)
	His dau. Ann Smith m. 1st, Joseph Mann, whose will, proved in KE Co. in 1748 named his wife Anne, son George Vansant Mann and his wife's bro. Cornelius

Vansant. Ann m. 2nd, Nicholas Smith who d. 1770. She d. 1775 and as Ann Smith had a will proved in which she named her son George Vansant Mann. He later d. in QA Co. in 1802.

p. 339:   Judith Wedge (Crouch) (later Draper) had another son by Richard Crouch: Richard, Jr., who was almost certainly a sibling of Wedge. Richard Crouch and Wedge Crouch owned land about the same time.{INKE} Moreover, Wedge and Mary (Hurtt) Crouch, and Richard and Ann Crouch both had sons named Thomas, born only months apart.{ESVR 2:17, 18}

THE ACKLAND FAMILY

1. WILLIAM ACKLAND d. in KE Co. by Oct 1741. He m. Mary (N).
On 16 Oct 1705 William Acklin witnessed the will of Margaret
Triggs, of TA Co.{MWB 12:1}
William was in KE Co. by 10 June 1734, when he patented two
tracts: 13 a. *Ackland's Lot,* and 47 a. *Stepney Fields.*{MPL EI#1:393,
EI#2:30 and EI#3:177, 178}
William d. leaving a will dated 24 Sep 1741 and proved 10 Oct 1741.
The heirs named were wife Mary (to have a life interest in dwell. plant.
and at her death to pass to children John and Sarah); dau. Mary Ann
(to have *Ackling's Lot* on the n. side of Chester River). The execs.
were wife Mary and son John. The will was witnessed by William
Harbson, Richard Ryley, and Jeremiah Spencer.{MWB 22:406}
On 29 Nov 1742 his estate was appraised by Cornelius Comegys and
E. Comegys, and valued at £163.2.1. No creditors or next of kin listed.
Unnamed execs. filed the inventory mentioning William Salsbury,
James Steel, Sarah Acland, and Christopher Williams on 26 Feb 1743.
{MINV 27:313}
On 25 Nov 1743 his estate was admin. by extx. Mary.{MWB 22:406;
MDAD 20:36}
William and Mary were the parents of the following children, born
in Shrewsbury Parish{KESH}: WILLIAM, b. 4 Sep 1706; SARAH, b. 8
Nov 1708, m. Michael Raiman on 24 Nov 174-; MARY, b. 18 Sep 1711;
and JOHN, b. 15 Sep 1713.

2. JOHN ACKLAND, son of William and Mary, was b. 15 Sep
1713.{KESH} He is probably the John "Acklind" who m. Anne Lattemore
on 30 March 17-- in St. Luke's Parish, QA Co.{ESVR 2:53}
KE Co. Debt Books list John Ackland as the owner of *Stepney
Fields* from 1752 to 1769.{INKE:1}
On 9 Sep 1765 he witnessed the will of William Herbison, of KE Co.
{MWB 33:412}

THE ALLABY FAMILY

1. PETER ALLABY was b. c1651, and gave his age as c80 when he
dep. in 1731.{CE Co. Land Commissions 1:195}
He was in KE Co. by 18 Feb 1694/5 when he registered a cattle
mark.{ESVR 1:5}
Peter Allaby, miller, on 22 Nov 1697 purchased from Mary Plumm,
alias Medford, of KE Co., land formerly belonging to John Plumm, part
of a tract formerly taken up by Wm. Hemsley, 100 a.{KELR M:74a}

1

On 22 July 1698 Peter Allaby and his wife Ann, of KE Co., conv. to Charles Tilden and Elias King, a tract called *P...lidge*.{KELR M:76a}

On 25 Sep 1708 Charles Wright and his wife Katharine, of QA Co., extx. of last will of Robert Norrest, conv. to Peter Allaby, of KE Co., miller, a tract called *Norrests Desire*, 18 a., part of a tract called *Marton* cont. 20 a. and part of another tract called *Philips Neglect* cont. 200 a., on the s. side of Sassafras River.{KELR JSN:86}

On 31 Aug 1726 William Soolison and his wife Rodah, of KE Co., conv. to Peter Allaby of the same place, a tract called *Henn Roost*, on the w. side of Herring Creek.{KELR JS#X:34}

On 3 May 1728 Peter Allaby, miller, of KE Co., and his wife Ann, conv. to James Talbott (actually Tibbot), of afsd. county, a tract called *Noriss's Desire*, on a branch of Herring Creek, 18 a.{KELR JS#X:230}

On 17 June 1730 Peter Allaby, of KE Co., millright, conv. to Hannah Brook, widow and relict of John Brook of afsd. county, dec., a parcel of land called *Henns Roost*, being the upper part of sd. land which was given by Philip Pryer to his [sic] George Thomas Pryer.{KELR JS#X:449}

Anne Allaby d. leaving a will dated 21 Jan 1731/2 and proved 10 March 1731 (1731/2). She left her entire estate to William Gudson, exec.{MWB 20:549}

Peter and Ann (N) Allaby were the parents of{KESP}: HANNAH, b. Sep ----; JOHN, b. 30 Jan 1690; and SARAH, b. 1 March 1694.

THE ALLIBONE FAMILY

EDWARD ALEBONE was in KE Co. by 7 Nov 1700 when he patented 52 a. known as *Allibone's Addition*.{MPL DD#5:552 and IL#B:116} He m. Jane (N), and d. by 17 Nov 1725.

On 7 da., 9 mo., 1724, it was recorded that Ed. Allibone was not able to come to Cecil meetings because of old age.{CEMM}

He d. leaving a will dated 13 Oct 1725 and proved 17 Nov 1725. To grandson John Davis he devised a tract bought of William Haywood and part of *Hilling's Adventure*. To grandson Robert Davis 2 s., 6 p. To grandson Edward Hailes and granddau. Jane Hailes personalty. To son-in-law Roger Hailes and dau. Ann, his wife, execs., residue of estate.{MWB 19:307}

Edward Alibone and his wife Jane were the parents of at least two daus.{CEMM}: MARY, b. 21 da., 2 mo., 1697; and ANNE, b. 21 da., 8 mo., 1692, m. Roger Hailes.

2

THE ARNOLD FAMILY

1. **JOHN ARNOLD** m. 1st, by 6 July 1733, Martha (N), and 2nd, on 10 June 1736, Hannah Debruler.{KESP}

John Arnold and wife Martha on 6 July 1733 joined Simon Wilmer, of KE Co., Gent., in conving to Henry Evans of the same town of Chester, Gent., the moiety or half part of a lot in Chester Town, No. 93, where sd. John Arnold dwelt.{KELR JS#16:393}

On 17 Nov 1747 John Arnold, of KE Co., and his wife Hannah, conv. to Thomas Bowers, one moiety of a part of a tract called *Essex* which had been devised by William Debruler, late of sd. county, to his bro. Peter Debruler, father of the sd. Hannah Arnold by his last will, 12½ a.{KELR JS#26:78}

John Arnold and wife Hannah had at least one son: JOHN.

2. **JOHN ARNOLD**, son of the above John, on 26 Nov 1746 was bound to Samuel Massey, hatter, as an apprentice to learn the trade of hatter, until age 21.{KEBI JS#20:242}

John Arnold, of Chester Town, d. leaving a will dated 10 Dec 1763 and proved 28 March 1767. The heirs named were wife Rebecca Arnold, to whom was devised the dwelling house, during son James Arnold's minority. Wife Rebecca was extx. The will was witnessed by Alexr. Cummings, Wm. Man, and Jno. Hynson.{MWB 35:323}

John and Rebecca were the parents of: JAMES.

Unplaced

ARNOLD, AMANIA, and Elizabeth Baswassick were m. 16 Jan 1706.{KESP}

ARNOLD, LAWRENCE, m. by 10 April 1674, Ann, dau. of Andrew Ellenor.{ARMD LI:113}

On 27 June 1676 it was ordered by the court that Thomas Arnoll, son of Lawrence Arnoll, live with Michaell Miller until the sd. Thomas arrived at the age of 21.{ARMD LIV:341, Liber C:71}

THE FRANCIS BARNES FAMILY

1. **FRANCIS BARNES** immigrated to MD c1666. With him came his children Francis Barnes, Jr. (and his wife Isabel and dau. Mary), Dorothy Barnes, Alice Barnes, and Thomas Barnes.{MPL 10:116, 117}

Francis Barnes was the father of: FRANCIS, Jr., DOROTHY, ALICE, and THOMAS.

2. FRANCIS BARNES, Jr., son of Francis, was transported with his wife Isabella and dau. Mary, by his father Francis before 1666.

On 30 April 1667 Francis was bound for England, when he appointed his wife Esabella Barnes and his son-in-law John Stevens as his attorneys. {ARMD LIV:236, Liber C:2}

Francis Barnes was the father of: MARY (to whom Henry Gott acknowledged on 1 Oct 1658 his gift of a calf). {ARMD LIV:145, Liber B:45}

Unplaced

BARNES, (N), m. by 20 March 1740, Mary, dau. of James Evans of KI, QA Co. {MWB 27:415}

BARNES, ABRAHAM, on 6 March 1750 was named as a bro.-in-law in the will of Edward Lloyd of TA Co. {MWB 37:474}

BARNES, ANN, at June Court 1687 was ordered that with the consent of her mother Ann Barns she was to live with Michaell Russell until age 16. {TAJU NN6}

BARNS, ELIZABETH, of KE Co., d. leaving a will dated 10 April 1757 and proved 2 Dec 1757. The heirs named were children Ann, James, and Alley Barns. The exec. was Hercules Coutes. The will was witnessed by Hugh Morrison, Caleb Gattery, and George Garnett. {MWB 30:462}

BARNES, FRANCIS, was b. c1679. He was age 68 when he dep. April 1747 that Elizabeth Foreman, an old woman living some years ago, was said to have been the dau. of one Ellis. Barnes stated that he knew Elizabeth Foreman personally, and she had several children, but she left the (Kent?) Island. {QAEJ: Blunt, Samuel}

BARNES, FRANCIS, of KI, carpenter, and wife Elleanor, on 18 Sep 1706 conv. to Edward Browne of Kent Island, 100 a., part of *Bellsher* on Kent Island, on s. side of Lovepoint Creek. {TALR 10:51}

He is prob. the Barnes who m. by 14 March 1702, Ellinor, dau. of John Wilson of TA Co. {MWB 3:465}

BARNES, FRANCIS, m. by 8 Sep 1724, Jane, widow of Philip Connor of Kent Island, QA Co. {MDAD 6:112, 357}

On 28 June 1726 Francis Barnes and his wife Jane conv. to Valentine Carter, Gent., 100 a., part of *Barnes' Satisfaction*. {QALR IKC:55}

4

On 13 Feb 1729 Francis Barnes gave to his son Thomas Barnes of Kent Island 323 a. called *Barneses Satisfaction* on Kent Island. {QALR IKC:275}

On 3 April 1741 Francis Barnes and his wife Jane conv. to Thomas Barnes 323 a. called *Barnes' Satisfaction* on Kent Island. {QALR RTB:341}

BARNES, GEORGE, m. by 13 July 1723, Mary, extx. of Charles Baker, of KE Co.{MDAD 5:227}

BARNES, JAMES, m. Ann Brown on 12 Sep 1733. {TAPE} On 6 May 1745 Ann Barnes, wife of James, age c60, dep., mentioning her former husband Thomas Brown. {TALC:297}

BARNES, JOHN, of the Isle of Kent claimed land for service in 1663.{MPL 9:155} As John Barnes, of TA Co., he d. leaving a will dated 18 Nov 1669 and proved 19 Nov 1670. To Edward Fowler, he left personalty. To John Curtis, ex. and residuary legatee of estate, real and personal, including 200 a. on Broad Creek. The will was witnessed by Thos. Blether and Jas. Murphey. {MWB 1:404}

At June Court 1668, Isabell Barnes [widow? of Jno. Barnes] shewed that Tho: Hynson, Anthony Griffin, John Morgan and Anthony Purse, all dec., stood indebted to her. {ARMD LIV:422, Liber BB No. 2:84}

At July Court 1671, Jno. Curtis shewed that Jno. Barnes died in his house and that he [Curtis] had looked to the deceased's cattle two winters, for which he demanded charges. {ARMD LIV:500, Liber BB No. 2:180}

BARNES, JOHN, of TA Co. d. by 10 April 1675 when his estate was admin. by Henry Parker. An inv. of 2980 lbs. tob. was mentioned, and payments were made to John Edmundson and John Hunt. {INAC 1:216}

BARNES, JOHN, of TA Co. d. by 15 Nov 1675 when his estate was admin. by Dr. Richard Tilghman. An inventory of 1672 lbs. tob. was mentioned. {INAC 1:462}

BARNES, JOHN, petitioned the March 1705 Court. He said he had married the relict of William Viney, dec., and David Arey retains Godfrey Viney, son of sd. William Viney, dec. in his service and refuses to deliver him to the petitioner and his mother. Ordered discharged. {TAJU RF10:}

BARNES, JOHN, m. Mary (N). They were the parents of{KESP}: JOHN, b. 15 Nov 172-.

BARNES, JOHN, on 17 Nov 1731, with his wife Rebekah and Elizabeth Smith, his mother, conv. to Edward Barwick of TA Co., 50 a., part of *Jump's Choyce*. {QALR RTA:98}

BARNES, JOHN, acknowledged his disorderly marriage on 9 da., 7 mo., 1747.{CEMM}

BARNS (or BARNES), JOHN, of KE Co., d. by 23 March 1752, when his estate was appraised by Arthur Miller and Abraham Milton, and valued at £42.15.0. James Smith and Jeames Reid signed as creditors. Mary Tayler and William Tayler signed as next of kin. Hannah Barnes, admx., filed the inventory on 3 Feb 1753.{MINV 53:77}

BARNES, JOHN, was duly enlisted in the company of Capt. John Milbourn and received the sum of 5 on 30 Oct 1740 (recorded 3 June 1743).

BARNES, JOHN, QA Co., d. leaving a will dated 3 June 1775 and proved 31 July 1775. He named his sister Mary Barns (to have £20, and all my shirts), bro. Joseph Barnes (to have horse, saddle), James Conner, wearing apparel, father Thomas Barnes (to have 1 shilling), bro. Thomas Barnes, Jr. (to have 1 shilling). Brother-in-law, William Earickson, and brother James Barnes, execs. (to have the residue of estate, equally). The will was witnessed by James Earickson; Samuel Kirby; Benja. Teakle. {MWB 40:449}

BARNES, JOSEPH, of KE Co., d. (date unknown), when his estate was appraised by Christopher Bellicon and Mil. Bellicon, and valued at £5.2.6. No creditors or next of kin listed. Daniel Fox, admin., filed the inventory on 7 Jan 1764.{MINV 82:237}

BARNES, MARY, and John Cornine were charged at March Court 1705 that on 10 Oct 1704 at Tuckahoe Hundred they cohabited together. He was fined. {TAJU RF10:}

BARNES, MARY At June Court 1705 the petition of Thomas Taylor of Kings Creek was heard. He stated that about 4 or 5 Dec last a distempered lame woman named Mary Barnes was brought and set down at his door. She was ordered to be transferred to the house of Daniell Sherwood. {TAJU RF10:}

BARNES, ROSAMOND, spinster, of St. Paul's Parish, at June Court 1732, was found guilty of committing fornication on 10 June 1731, and begetting a bastard child. She was ordered to receive 5 lashes.{KECR JS#WK:299}

BARNES, SARAH, d. by 11 Jan 1727, when her estate was appraised by John Tilden and Thomas Medford. Francis Bodien and William Hume signed as creditors. Sarah Deal and Elisabeth Deall signed as next of kin. Griffith Jones filed the inventory on 5 July 1728.{MINV 13:230}

BARNES, THOMAS, d. by 2 March 1676.{INAC 6:494}

BARNES, THOMAS, m. Mary (N). He may be the Thomas Barnes who d. by 23 March 1712, when his estate was admin.{INAC 34:143} Thomas and Mary were the parents of one son{KESP}: JOHN, b. 10 March 1711.{KESH}

BARNES, THOMAS, age 60, dep. Sep 1769 that Ralph Distance owned *Isaac's Chance*, when the deponent was a small boy. Distance d. leaving two daus. Anne (who m. 1st, John Dailey by whom she had 4 or 5 children, and 2nd, Edmund Kelly), and Mary. At the time of her father's death, Mary was the widow of Timothy Matthews, and after her father's death, she m. 2nd, John Gilbert, by whom she had several children. {QAEJ: Hutchens, James}

BARNES, THOMAS, m. by 6 Feb 1773, Martha, widow of Thomas Newcomb, Jr., of KE Co.{MDAD 67:416}

BARNES, WILLIAM, of KE Co. on Delaware, farmer, on 6 Oct 1748 with Abraham Falconar, of KE Co., MD, conv. to Richard Bennett, of QA Co., merchant, a tract called *Goose Haven*, lately the land of Gilbert Falconar, dec., 600 a.{KELR JS#26:186}

THE BATHERSHALL FAMILY

1. HENRY BATHERSHALL and Rachell Rusk were m. Dec ----.{KESP} He may be the Henry Bathurshell who m. by 29 Oct 1711, (N), legatee of George Smith, of KE Co.{INAC 33A:10}
   Henry d. leaving a will dated 4 Jan 1713/14 and proved 28 April 1714. He left to sons William and John, a tract called *Arcadia*; in event of their deaths, to pass to Thos. and Susannah Russh. Sons to be sent to school when they were 10 or 11 years of age. In event of marriage of wife to a unkind person, afsd. sons to live with their godfather ----, or with their bro. Rush. To his wife Rachell, extx., and two afsd. sons, he left personalty.{MWB 13:715}
   Battershall's estate was admin. 3 May 1715, and again on 7 Jan 1716. Legatees were Dr. Glen, Thomas Ruth and Susannah Ruth. The extx. was Rachell Battershell.{INAC 36C:125 and 38B:73}

On 13 June 1718, his estate was admin. again by Joseph Gerard. Mentioned in the acount were Michael Taney and Thomas Taney, sons of Michael Taney (dec.). Payments were made to Capt. Schee and Arthur Miller. Legatees were Thomas Rush and Susanna Rush. {MDAD 1:77}

Rachell Battershall was bur. 26 Feb 1717. {KESP} Henry and Rachel were the parents of two sons, and possibly one dau. {KESP}: WILLIAM, b. 8 June 1709; JOHN, b. 28 Feb 1711; and MARY, bur. 22 Jan 1713.

2. WILLIAM BATHERSHALL, son of Henry and Rachel, was b. 8 June 1709. {KESP} William Mackey and James Smith, of KE Co., posted bond on 25 June 1720 giving security that they would pay William Battershell, one of the orphans of Henry Battershell, dec., £9.12.2 as a filial portion of the estate of Henry Battershell. {KEBI JS#W:72A}

3. JOHN BATHERSHALL, son of Henry and Rachel, was b. 28 Feb 1711{KESP}, and d. in KE Co. by 2 Feb 1762, having m. Elizabeth (N). Thomas Rush, Robert Green and William Mackey, of KE Co., posted bond they would pay John Batershell, one of the orphans of Henry Battershell, dec., £9.12.2 when he arrived at the age of 21. The bond was recorded 30 July 1720. {KEBI JS#W:76A}

John Battershill, of KE Co., d. leaving a will dated 10 Sep 1757 and proved 2 Feb 1762. Sons William and Henry Battershill were devised land; in the event of their deaths without issue the land was to pass to next youngest bro. Other heirs were step-son Freeman Gimmerson, and daus. Rachel and Mary Battershill. The execs. were wife Elizabeth Battershill and friend John Smith, Jr. The will was witnessed by Aaron Underhill, Caleb Jacson, and Wm. Smith. {MWB 31:511}

On 5 March 1762, his estate was appraised by Joseph Wickes and William Dunn, and valued at £113.3.1. Thomas and William Ringgold and B. Hands signed as creditors. William Battershall and Henry Battershall signed as next of kin. John Smith, exec., filed the inventory on 22 May 1762. {MINV 77:200}

In Sep 1763, his estate was appraised again by John Wickes and Das. Dunn, and valued at £27.2.4. John Sutton, exec., filed the inventory mentioning William Battershill and Henry Battershill on 7 July 1764. {MINV 84:6}

John Battershall was the father of: WILLIAM; HENRY; RACHEL; MARY; and perhaps others.

THE BORDLEY FAMILY

Refs.: A: *Bordley Pedigree* (Chart). By Bryden Bordley Hyde. Gibson Island: The Author, 1990.

Hyde states that the Bordley family originated in Bordley, in Craven, West Yorkshire. By 1379, Johannes de Bordley was paying a poll tax on lands of Fountain Abbey in Wigglesworth, located some 10 miles from the Abbey.{A: cites *Domesday Book*, 1086, and *Fountains Abbey Rental Book*, 1495}

1. WILLIAM BORDLEY of Wigglesworth d. in 1547. In his will[1] he left money for the town of Rathmell. He m. Margaret (N), by whom he was the father of{A}: JOHN; and JANE.

2. JOHN BORDLEY of Wigglesworth, son of William and Margaret, d. testate in 1579. He is bur. at Long Preston.{A}
By his unidentified first wife he was the father of{A}: WILLIAM. By his second wife, Margaret (N), he was the father of{A}: RICHARD; JOHN; HARRY; and MARY.

3. WILLIAM BORDLEY of Cockley Bank, Rathmell, West Yorkshire, eldest son of John Bordley of Wiggglesworth, d. leaving a will dated 1610, proved 1611. He m. at Giggleswick on 18 Feb 1600, Elizabeth, bapt. 29 March 1588, dau. of Richard Foster and Isabella Browne (dau. of John). After William Bordley's death, Elizabeth m. 2nd, Richard Key.
William and Elizabeth (Foster) Bordley were the parents of{A}: JOHN, bapt. 19 April 1601, d. 1630; WILLIAM, bapt. 6 Jan 1605 at Giggleswick; and THOMAS of Cockeram and Thornham, Lancashire.

4. WILLIAM BORDLEY, 2nd son of William and Elizabeth (Foster) Bordley, was bapt. 6 Jan 1605 at Giggleswick, and was bur. 1669 at Hawkeshead, Lancashire. He m. 1st, on 4 June 1630, Susannah Smithies, dau. of (N) Smithies of Tunstall, Lancashire. She was bur. 16 April 1661 at Hawkeshead, and William m. 2nd, on 17 Nov 1664 at Hawkeshead, Agnes Burrow, who was bur. 25 Dec 1714 at Lancaster.{A}
William's father left money for his education, so William probably attended Giggleswick School and Christ's College, Cambridge University. William was Master of Tunstall School, Lancashire, 1630-1647, Headmaster at Hawkshead Grammar School, 1647-1669.{A; see also "History of Tunstall," by Col. C. H. Chippendell, *Chetham Society*, 1940, pp. 13-14}
William and Susannah (Smithies) Bordley were the parents of{A}: ELIZABETH, 1630-1632; MARGARET, 1632-1636; WILLIAM, 1635-1638; and STEPHEN, b. 1637.

---

[1] Wills of the first three generations of Bordley are at the Borthwick Institute, University of York.

William and Agnes (Burrow) Bordley were the parents of{A}:
BRIDGET, 1665-1666; and Rev. WILLIAM, bapt. 29 Jan 1666/7.

5. Rev. STEPHEN BORDLEY, son of William and Susanna, was bapt.
1 Jan 1636/7 at Tunstall, and d. at St. Mary's, Newington, Surrey, in
1695. Administration was granted by the Prerogative Court of Canterbury on 30 Sep 1695. He m. Margaret Colston, b. c1640, d. at Newcastle, in 1720. Her will of 1718, probated at Newcastle in 1720, is at
the Dept. of Palaeography and Diplomatic, University of Durham.
Margaret was a dau. of William and Margaret (Proctor) Colston.
Through the Proctors, the Bordleys of Maryland descend from the
Ogles and Greys of Northumberland, England.{A: cites Surtees Society,
CXI:173 and Northumberland County History, by Edw. Bateson, 2:192}
    Stephen Bordley took his B.A. and M.A. at Christ's College,
Cambridge. He was ordained a Deacon at Lincoln Cathedral in March
1660/1, and in Sep 1661 was ordained a Priest at Durham Cathedral.
He was curate at Ryton, Durham until 1664, and until 1689 was Vicar
at St. Hilda's, South Shields, Durman (where his children were born).
From 1689 to 1695 he was Rector of St. Mary's, Newington, Surrey.
He was made a Prebendary (Willesden) of St. Paul's Cathedral, London.{A}
    Stephen and Margaret were the parents of{A}: MARGARET, bapt.
16 Aug 1666, m. George Lumley in 1691, at London; WILLIAM, bapt.
25 Aug 1671 (blind); Rev. STEPHEN, bapt. 24 Aug 1674, came to MD;
MARY, (bapt.?) 24 Sep 1672; Hon. THOMAS, bapt. 26 May 1677, came
to MD; ELIZABETH, b. c1680; and JOHN, bapt. 16 June 1681, m. and
had issue.{A: cites Register of All Saints, Newcastle Upon Tyne}

6. Rev. WILLIAM BORDLEY, son of William and Agnes (Burrow)
Bordley, was bapt. 29 Jan 1666/7, and d. 1741. He m. Anne Furthergill
of Tunstall, Lancashire. William Bordley was educated at Sedbergh
Grammar School, and admitted sizar, at age 18, to St. John's College,
Cambridge, in 1685. He received his B.A. and M.A. in 1689. He was
Headmaster of Lancaster Grammar School, 1690-1708, and Vicar at
Hawkeshead Church from 1720 to 1741. William and Anne had a son
WILLIAM, a son JOHN, and four daus.{A: cites The Royal Grammar
School, Lancaster, by A. L. Murray, Cambridge: Heffer Co., 1951}

7. Rev. STEPHEN BORDLEY, son of Rev. Stephen and Margaret
(Colston) Bordley, was bapt. 24 Aug 1674, and was bur. 25 Aug
1709.{KESP} He m. Ann, dau. of John Hynson, on 14 Oct 1700.
    At age 17 he was admitted sizar at Christ's College, Cambridge, in
1690 and took his B.A. in 1694/5. He was ordained a deacon in Sep
1695 and priest on 20 Sep 1696. Henry Compton, Bishop of London,
sent him to MD where he was assigned to St. Paul's Parish, KE Co.{A}

On 27 Nov 1707, George Lumley and his wife Elizabeth, of KE Co., confirmed ½ part of a tract called *Bounty*, made over by John Hynson to Stephen Bordley and his wife Ann and by them made over to afsd. George Lumley and his wife Elizabeth, conv. to Thomas Tolley.{KELR JSN:12}

On 31 Nov 1719, John Davis and his wife Mary, of KE Co., conv. to Thomas Slipper, part of a tract called *Bounty* being part of 100 a. formerly given by Coll. John Hynson, dec., to his dau. Ann, the then wife of Stephen Boardly, but now the wife of Alexander William-son.{KELR JS#W:88}

Rev. Stephen Bordley, d. by 17 Nov 1709 when his estate was admin.{INAC 31:198} It was also admin. by Ann, wife of Rev. Alexander Williamson, on 27 Feb 1711, 25 Aug 1713, and 21 Nov 1716.{INAC 33A:171, 34:72 and 38B:74}

Stephen and Ann (Hynson) Bordley were the parents of{KESP}: MARGRETT, b. July 1701, bur. 13 Dec 1702; ANN, b. 22 Oct and bur. 27 Oct 170-; THOMAS, b. 22 Oct 1704; MARY, b. 22 July, bapt. 10 Aug 1708; and STEPHEN, b. 13 Jan 1709.

8. Hon. THOMAS BORDLEY, of Annapolis, son of Rev. Stephen and Margaret (Colston) Bordley, was b. 16 May 1677 at South Shields, Durham, England, and d. 1726 in MD. He came to MD with his bro., Rev. Stephen Bordley, in 1696, and m. 1st, c1708, Rachel, dau. of Richard Beard of Annapolis. She d. in 1722, and Thomas m. 2nd, in 1723, Ariana Vanderheyden, dau. of Mathias Vanderheyden of NY and MD.{A}

Thomas probably read law in England, and in MD was admitted to practice before the Provincial Court, AA Co. Court, and PG Co. Court, as well as the Court of Chancery. He served in the Legislature, and was a member of the Council and was Attorney General of MD, 1718-1721, and Commissary General, 1718-1721.{A}

On Oct 1720 Thomas was granted 100 a. called *Steventon* on the w. side of a branch of Langfords Bay. In a deed he stated that Thomas, the son of the late Rev. Stephen Bordley, of KE Co., dec., is seised in fee of the land called *Kindness*. For the affection he had and bore for his nephews Thomas and Stephen Bordly, sons of the sd. Stephen, dec., he gave to Thomas Bordley his nephew the northernmost 60 a. called *Steventon* and to the sd. Stephen, his nephew, the remaining part of the tract *Steventon*.{KELR JS#W:152}

At his death he owned 19 slaves, 6 servants, 100 law books and over 7500 a. of land.{A}

By Rachel Beard, Thomas Bordley was the father of{A}: Hon. STEPHEN, b. 1709; WILLIAM, b. 1716, d. 1762; ELIZABETH; and JOHN.

By Ariana Vanderheyden, Thomas was the father of{A}: THOMAS, b. 1724; MATTHIAS, b. 1725; and Judge JOHN BEALE, b. 1727.

9. THOMAS BORDLEY, son of Stephen and Anne (Hynson) Bordley, was b. 22 Oct 1704. Thomas Bordley and Mary Smithers were m. 19 Dec 1727. Mary Bordley, wife of Thomas Bordley, d. 31 July 1729. Thomas Bordley m. on 21 Feb 1731 as his 2nd wife, Ann Miller.{KESP}

On 15 Sep 1733, Arthur Miller, of KE Co., Gent., conv. to Ann Bordley, wife of Thomas Bordley and dau. of afsd. Arthur Miller, the remainder of *East Huntington*.{KELR JS#16:387}

On 1 April 1734, Thomas Bordley and his wife Ann, of KE Co., conv. land to Alexander Williamson: Whereas a patent was granted on 15 July 1695 to Audry Lewellin of AA Co. for a tract called *Residue* and whereas William Taylard of AA Co. contracted marriage with sd. Audry the sd. William Taylard by agreement with sd. Audry his wife investing himself with a right to the before mentioned land *Kindness* and whereas William Taylard with Audry his wife by deed dated 11 Oct 1700 conv. to Stephen Bordley, of KE Co., clergr. of the afsd. tract *Kindness* and sd. Stephen Bordley dying without will the land became the right of Thomas Bordley, eldest son to afsd. Stephen dec.{KELR JS#16:442}

Thomas Bordley, of KE Co., d. leaving a will dated 24 April 1751 and proved 7 Nov 1752. The heirs named were son William Bordley to whom was devised land on the e. side of the road leading from Farley to Chestertown; son Arthur Bordley, to whom land was devised known as *Kindness*; son Stephen; dau. Sarah; son William; son Arthur Bordley. The extx. was wife Anne. The will was witnessed by Richard Porter, Jr., Phi. Milton, and James Thomas.{MWB 28:399}

On 16 March 1753, Thomas Bordley's estate was appraised by James McClean and W. Hynson, and valued at £1100.18.3. Edward Lloyd and Thomas Ringgold for D. Cheston signed as creditors. J. Bordley (bro.) and J. Wrightson (who m. a dau. of dec.) signed as next of kin. Ann Bordley, extx., filed the inventory on 20 June 1753.{MINV 56:95}

On 1 Feb 1756, his estate was appraised again by James McClean and W. Hynson, and valued at £126.16.0. Thomas Ringgold and Joseph Nicholson signed as creditors. J. Bordley and Ja. Wrightson signed as next of kin. Anne Bordley, extx., filed the inventory on 17 June 1756.{MINV 60:716}

Thomas Bordley was the father of (by Martha): (N), dau., bur. 22 Aug 1729; (by Anne): (N), dau., b. 31 Dec 17--; (N), dau., b. 31 Dec 17-; (N), b. 13 Jan 1732; (N), b. 22 Nov 17--; THOMAS, b. ---, d. 3 Nov 1749; WILLIAM, b. 18 Sep 1741; ARTHUR, b. 2 Jan 1743; MARY, b. 1 July 1746{KESP}; STEPHEN; SARAH.

10. STEPHEN BORDLEY, son of Stephen and Anne (Hynson) Bordley, was b. 13 Jan 1709. He m. 1st, Priscilla Murphy on 22 April 1731.{KESP} He m. 2nd, by 11 March 1744, Sarah Harris. They were named in the administration account of James Harris, of KE Co.{MDAD 21:159, 163}

On 18 Jan 1736, Stephen Bordley, of QA Co., and his wife Prissilla, conv. land to Alexander Williamson, of KE Co. The land, patented on 8 Oct 1720 to Thomas Bordley, late of the City of Annapolis, Esq., dec., was called *Steventon* in KE Co., 100 a., and sd. Thomas Bordley, Esq., by deed of gift dated 16 May 1721 granted same to above sd. Stephen Bordley with the proviso that Thomas should make over to his younger bro. the afsd. Stephen when he came to age certain property.{KELR JS#18:345}

At March Court 1748, it was presented that Stephen Bordley, Gent., on 10 March 1748, assaulted John Thompson. Bordley was fined 2 s., 6 p.{KECR JS#25:30B}

Stephen Bordley, age c50, on 16 July 1762, dep.{KEEJ: John Carville}

On 24 June 1763, Stephen Bordley of the City of Annapolis, Esq., conv. land to Samuel Griffith, son of George, of KE Co., Gent. The deed stated that John Bordley, of KE Co., Gent., lately dec., in his lifetime did enter into bond to the afsd. George Griffith, Gent., dec., on 14 May 1753 in the penal sum of £250 conditioned that he, the sd. John Bordley, convey to George Griffith part of a tract called *The Adventure* and of that part adjoining Edward Worrell's land which was adjudged to be equal in value to 60 a. of *Providence*, then lately surveyed in the presence of sd. George Griffith and John Bordley and whereas in 1753 it was adjudged that sd. George Griffith with his wife Elizabeth should convey to sd. John Bordley and that John Bordley and his then wife Isabella should convey to George Griffith 70⅔ a. of tract called *The Adventure*.{KELR DD#1:431}

Stephen Bordley d. leaving a will dated 19 Aug 1776 and proved 7 Sep 1776. Heirs named were Robert Cruickshank, exec.; Dr. William Bordley; goddau. Mary Cruickshank; Mrs. Ann Carvill, widow of John Carvill, Jr.; Jane Carvill, dau. of afsd. Ann Carvill; Col. Richard Lloyd and James his son; and Mary and Ann, daus. of Priscilla Brewer. The will was witnessed by John Whaland, Sarah Burk, and A. Glenn.{MWB 41:135}

Stephen and Priscilla were the parents of: MARGRETT, b. Feb, 1731.{KESP}

11. JOHN BORDLEY, son of Hon. Thomas and Rachel (Beard) Bordley, was b. 1721 and d. 1761. He m. Isabella, dau. of James Conner of Philip. She m. 2nd William Stevenson, Jr.

John Bordley of Chester Town, and wife Isabella, on 28 May 1759, conv. to Joshua Vansant, yeoman, a tract called *Bordleys Gift*.{KELR JS#29:107}

On 22 June 1759 John Bordley of Chester Town, merchant, and his wife Isabella, late Isabella Conner, dau. of John Connor of Chester Town, dec., conv. to James Nicols, of QA Co., Gent., ½ lot in Chester Town, No. 50.{KELR JS#29:116}

John Bordley, merchant, of KE Co., d. leaving a will proved 31 March 1761. The heir named was wife Isabella, to whom was devised lands called *The Fancy, Bordley's, Beginning, Partnership, The Grumble, The Adventure*, and pt. of *Providence*. If at the death of his wife there were not heirs, then the land would pass to Mathias Bordley of CE Co. or to Beal Bordley of BA Co. Also mentioned were bros. Stephen and William, sister Elizabeth, half-bro. Mathias, and Beal Bordley. The extx. was his wife. The will was witnessed by Richard Porter, and Thomas and Geo. Garnett.{MWB 31:212}

On 8 June 1761, John Bordley's estate was appraised by John Chapple and Richard Graves, value unknown. James Anderson and Thomas Smith signed as creditors. Elisabeth Bordley and Beale Bordley signed as next of kin. Mrs. Isabella Bordley, wife of Mr. William Stevenson, extx., filed the inventory on 9 Aug 1762.{MINV 78:182}

On 15 April 1761 his estate was appraised again, value unknown. The widow, who m. Mr. William Stevenson, extx., filed the inventory cont. a list of debts on 14 March 1764.{MINV 82:312}

Another appraisal totalling £1146.4.3 was filed by Mr. William Stevenson, on 14 March 1764.{MINV 82:317}

John Bordley was the father of: STEPHEN.

12. JOHN BEALE BORDLEY, son of Hon. Thomas and Ariana Vanderheyden, was b. 1727 and d. 1804. He m. Margaret, dau. of Samuel Chew and Henrietta Maria (Lloyd) Chew.{A}

Beale Bordley, of BA Co., and his wife Margarett, on the 3rd Tues. of Nov 1759 petitioned to examine the evidences of the bounds of a tract called *Bennets Bridge*.{KELR JS#29:201}

13. WILLIAM BORDLEY, son of Thomas and Anne, was b. 18 Sep 1741. He m. Elizabeth, and they were the parents of at least three children, whose births are recorded at Cecil Monthly Meeting: SARAH, b. 5 da., 3 mo., 1770; THOMAS, b. 26 da., 4 mo., 1772; and ELISABETH, b. 22 da., 6 mo., 1773.{CEMM}

14. STEPHEN BORDLEY, Jr., son of Thomas and Ann, was b. 13 Jan 1732, and d. 22 Aug 1771. He m. Hannah Bowers, of KE Co., dau. of William Bowers, whose distribution mentioned a grandson William Bordley, son of Stephen.{BFD 6:202}

In 1772, his estate was appraised by James McClean and James Piner (dec. by 14 March 1772), appraised by James McClean and Emory Sudler (on 14 March 1772), and valued at £830.1.6. John Cadwalader and Richard Lloyd for James Anderson signed as creditors. Henry Bordley (uncle) and Arthur Miller (uncle) signed as next of kin. William Bordley and Anthony [Arthur] Bordley, admins., filed the undated inventory.{MINV 110:257}

Another inventory was made when his estate was appraised, value unknown. William Bordley and Arthur Bordley, admins., filed the inventory cont. a list of debts on 28 Jan 1775.{MINV 120:117}

Stephen and Hannah (Bowers) Bordley were the parents of{A}: WILLIAM, b. 1769, m. 1769; and ARTHUR.

THE BOWDY (BOUDY, BOWDAY, BOWDIE) FAMILY

1. RICHARD BOUDY, m. by 8 June 1709 Elisabeth, widow and extx. of John Cracknell of CE Co.{INAC 29:320}

Richard Boudy d. leaving a will dated 5 Oct 1705 and proved 17 Oct 1706. He named eldest son Richard, (personalty); son Henry, (1s); son Solomon, (1s. for disobedience); and dau. Katharine, wife of Richard Unitt (extx., all lands and ½ personalty); and dau. Rosamond, (residue of estate).{MWB 12:171}

On 22 Oct 1708, the estate of Richard Boudy was admin. by Richard Knitt, exec. The account mentioned a son Richard Boudy.{INAC 29:231}

Elizabeth Bowdy (Bowday), d. leaving a will dated 10 Dec 1711 and proved 7 Jan 1711. She named eldest son John Cracknell at 21 years (personalty); son Thomas Cracknell (at 21 years, 50 a., part of tract called *Drevitt*, purchased from Philip Rasin; if he died without issue land was devised to John Kearly during life). John Kearly was named exec., and joint residuary legatee with afsd. children, of whom he was guardian.{MWB 13:377}

Elizabeth Bowdy's estate was inv. on 1 Jan 1711 and filed on 5 March 1711.{INAC 33A:148} Her estate was admin. 19 Feb 1714 by exec. John Kersley.{INAC 36B:139}

Richard Boudy was the father of: RICHARD; HENRY; SOLOMON; KATHERINE, wife of Richard Unick or Unitt; and ROSAMOND.

2. HENRY BOWDY, son of Richard, on 12 June 1710, gave bond to Elizabeth Bowdy, spinster, regarding a tract which Richard Bowdy, the late husband of the sd. Elizabeth, purchased from Philip Rasin, of KE Co.{KELR JSN:216}

3. SOLOMON BOWDY, son of Richard, and Kath. Eads were m. 13 April 17--.{KESP}

BOWDY, (N), m. by 6 Nov 1711, Rosamond, heir of Richard Unitt, of KE Co.{INAC 33A:164}

BOWDIE, JOHN, of St. Paul's Parish, labourer, at March Court 1729, was found guilty of stealing property of Isaac Perkins worth 400 lbs. of tob., on 10 Feb 1729, and fined £10.{KECR JS#WK:118}

John m. (1st?) Sarah (N). They were the parents of{KESP}: RACHEL, b. Jan ----; (N), son b. 3 Nov ----. He m. (2nd?) Mary (N). They were the parents of{KESB}: JOHN, b. 9 Feb 1735; HENRY, b. 9 June 1737; and SARAH, b. 7 Jan 1739.

THE THOMAS BOWERS FAMILY

1. THOMAS BOWERS was b. c1698, giving his age as c44 on 12 Aug 1742 when he dep.{KELR JS#24:122} He m. by 24 July 1725, Ann, widow and extx. of William Debruler, of KE Co., and a granddau. of Isabella Pearce, who in her will dated 21 Feb 1728, left personalty to granddau. Anne, wife of Thomas Bowers.{MWB 19:742; MDAD 7:49}

On 27 Feb 1724 Gideon Pearce, of KE Co., Gent., and his wife Ann, conv. to Thomas Bower of the same county, a tract called *Heading*, 150 a.{KELR JS#W:423} On 17 Nov 1747 John Arnold, of KE Co., and his wife Hannah, conv. to Thomas Bowers, one moiety of a part of a tract called *Essex*, 12½ a.{KELR JS#26:78}

Thomas Bowers, of KE Co., d. leaving a will dated 6 Dec 1768 and proved 18 Nov 1771. Mentioned were children Pearce, William, Thomas, Isabella Vansant, Ann Gilbert, and Martha Jordan; grandsons James Corse, son of David and Mary Corse; Thomas Corse, son of David and Mary Corse; William Bordley, son of Stephen and Hannah Bordley; and granddau. Anne Corse, dau. of David and Mary Corse. The exec. was son Thomas. The will was witnessed by William Cowarden and Alexander Cameron.{MWB 38:425}

On 21 Nov 1771, Thomas Bowers' estate was appraised by Charles Groom and St. Leger Everett, and valued at £302.13.11. John Weitman and William Bordley signed as creditors. Pearce Bowers and William Bowers signed as next of kin. Thomas Bowers, exec., filed the inventory on 7 Dec 1771.{MINV 107:393}

On 26 Oct 1772, his estate was again appraised by Charles Groome and St. Leger Everett, and valued at £235.5.8. John Weir and William Bordley signed as creditors. Pearce Bowers and William Bowers signed as next of kin. Thomas Bowers, exec., filed the inventory on 6 Nov 1772.{MINV 110:263}

Another inventory was taken and valued at £50.6.11. Thomas Bowers, exec., filed the inventory mentioning cash received on 29 Dec 1772.{MINV 110:407}

On 29 Dec 1772 distribution of Thomas Bowers' estate was made by Thomas Bowers, exec. Legatees were sons Pearce and William. Residue in eight parts equally to son Thomas; son Pearce; son William; dau. Isabella Vansant; dau. Ann Gilbert; dau. Martha Jordan; grandchildren James, Ann, and Thomas Corse; and grandson William Bordley, son of Stephen.{BFD 6:202}

Thomas Bowers, member of Cecil Meeting, an Elder, d. 7 Nov 1771. Thomas and Ann were the parents of the following children, whose births were recorded in Cecil Monthly Meeting{CEMM}: THOMAS, b. 26 Oct (or Dec 1725 - his birth is also recorded in Shrewsbury Parish); ISABELLA, b. 28 July 1727 (she and Joshua Vansant, also of KE Co., with consent of parents, were m. 10 Nov 1749 at Cecil Meeting House); ANN, b. 10 Dec 1729/30; MARY, b. 29 Nov 1731/2 (with the consent of their parents, she m. David Corse on 9 Nov 1757); JOHN, b. 11 Dec 1733; HANNAH, 23 Dec 1736; MARTHA, b. 23 May 1738 (with the consent of their parents, she and Emanuel Jenkinson were m. at Cecil Meeting House on 14 March 1759); PEARCE, b. 3 Jan 1741/2; and WILLIAM, 28 Dec 1743.

2. THOMAS BOWERS, son of William and Ann, was b. 26 Oct (or Dec) 1725, his birth is also recorded in Shrewsbury Parish). He is probably the Thomas Bowers, age c38, who dep. c1773.{KEEJ: Samuel Griffith}

Thomas Bowers m. 1st, by 2 Jan 1758, Mary (N). On 2 Jan 1758 Thomas Lewis, of KE Co., conv. to Mary Bowers, wife of Thomas Bowers and dau. of afsd. Thomas Lewis, part of the tract *Arcadia*, released out the original tract called *Arcadia* by the present Thomas Lewis' father (?) old Arthur Miller, 50 a., where sd. Thomas Lewis' mother dwelled at the time of her death and the deeds from the sd. Miller to the father of the sd. Lewis will more at large make appear [sic].{KELR JS#28:400}

Thomas Bowers m. 2nd, Ann (N). He d. 29 Nov 1784. Thomas and Ann were the parents of the following children, born in Cecil Monthly Meeting{CEMM}: ANN, b. 18 Nov 1762; THOMAS, b. 27 Nov 1764; JOHN, b. 20 Nov 1766; MARTHA, b. 4 Aug 1768 and d. 21 Oct; MARY, b. 19 June 1771; MARTHA, Aug 1773; ELISABETH, 10 Aug 1775; and WILLIAM, b. 12 Jan 1778.

3. PEARCE BOWERS, son of William and Ann, was granted a certificate by Cecil Monthly Meeting on 8 da., 11 mo., 1758.{CEMM}

THE WILLIAM BOWERS FAMILY

1. WILLIAM BOWERS, d. c1747. He m. on 21 April 1731 Jane Canaday who d. by Feb 1758.{KESP}
   William Bowers, of KE Co., d. leaving a will written 7 Oct 1747 and proved c1747. In his verbal will he stated that his two sons should be at their own disposing at age 18. The will was witnessed by James Roberts and William Cannady.{MWB 25:193}
   On 15 June 1748, the estate of William Bowers was appraised by Ra. Page and Samuel Miller, and valued at £146.12.3. William Murray signed as creditor. Edward Kennardy signed as next of kin. Jane Bowers (Quaker), admx., filed the inventory mentioning Benjamin Riend on 31 Aug 1748.{MINV 37:139}
   Jane Bowers, of KE Co., d. leaving a will dated 31 Aug 1757 and proved 13 Feb 1758. The heirs named were children Thomas Bowers, Dean Canady, Wm. Canady, and Stephen Canady. The exec. was son Thomas Bowers. Mentioned was the tract *Dean's Adventure*. The will was witnessed by Ralph Page, James Roberts, and Sarah Roberts.{MWB 30:460}
   William and Jane were the parents of (recorded in St. Paul's Parish){KESP}: THOMAS; JAMES; and WILLIAM.

2. JAMES BOWERS, son of William and Jane, d. leaving a will dated 18 Aug 1757 and proved 17 Feb 1758. The heirs named were mother Jane Bowers and bro. Thomas Bowers. The will was witnessed by John Wilson, Sarah Goodwin (formerly Sarah Canady), and Sarah Robert. {MWB 30:459}

Unplaced

BOWERS, MARY, in March 1723, was indicted for stealing a suit of women's muslin head cloaths of Joseph Young, but seems to have d. before her case came to trial. The sureties, John Bowers and Samuel Gooding, were both discharged from their recognizances.{KECR JS#22:6}

THE BOWLES FAMILY

1. ISAAC BOWLES, was the father of: JOHN, d. by 6 May 1704; ISAAC, d. by 1709; and JAMES, d. by 6 Nov 1753.

2. JOHN BOWLES, son of Isaac (1), d. by 6 May 1704. On 6 March 1690 he purchased from Cornelius Comegys and his wife Rebecca 300 a., called *Comeggys Farms*.{KELR B:185}

On 7 May 1691, John Bowles, of KE Co., conv. to his bro. Isaac Bowles and Mary his wife of the same county, and after their decease to Isaac Bowles, Jr., the son of James and Mary Bowles, 2/3 of a tract of 300 a. called *Comeggys Farm*, lately in the occupation of Cornelius Comegys, of KE Co., Gent., and now in the occupation of Isaac Bowles. {KELR B:289}

John Bowles and Margrett McNieu (McNiell?/McNiett?) m. 4 Sep 170-.{KESP} John Bowles was bur. 6 May 1704.{KESP}

John Bowles settled in TA Co., where he d. leaving a will dated 11 Jan 1702, proved Aug 1703. He named his grandson Bowles Green, granddau. Catherine Green, and granddau. Ann Green, as well as mentioning his bro. Isaac and the latter's son, Isaac Bowles. He named his son-in-law Peter Green as exec. and residuary legatee.{MWB 3:253}

John Bowles (Bowls) d. by 10 Sep 1706, when his estate was admin. by Peter Green.{INAC 25:409} The estate of Margrett Bowles was admin. on Nov 1710 and 6 Nov 1711 by Francis Meeks.{INAC 32B:103 and 33A:152}

3. ISAAC BOWLES, Sr., son of Isaac (1), m. Mary Rease on 20 Sep ----.{KESP} Isaac d. leaving a will dated 23 Aug 1701 and proved 7 June 1709. To wife Mary, extx. and sole legatee, she to give same to children Isaac (Bowles) and Ann Higley at her decease.{MWB Part 2, 12:104}

Mary, wife of Isaac Bowles, was a dau. of Thomas Kear, and on 7 July 1708 was mentioned in the account filed by William Dixon, admin. of Thomas Kear.{INAC 28:160}

Isaac Bowles patented 200 a. called *Green Bank* on 10 Jan 1706.{MPL CD#4:300}

Isaac's estate was inv. on 8 April 1710. Next of kin was Michael Hacket.{INAC 31:426} His estate was admin. on 28 May 1711 by Mary Bowles, extx.{INAC 32C:53}

The estate of Isaac Bowles, Jr., was admin. on 12 May 1710 and 10 May 1711 by the admx. Mary Hacket, wife of Michael Hacket.{INAC 31:233 and 32C:52}

On 3 Aug 1714, Mary Bowles, of KE Co., widow of Isaac, conv. to George Hastings and his wife Mary, granddau. of Mary Bowles, for love and affection, part of a tract called *Green Bank*, 200 a.{KELR BC#1:28}

Mary Bowles, widow, and relique of Isaac Bowles, dec., confirmed to her granddau. Mary Hastens and her husband, George Hastens, all the straw that was on her plant., her bed stead and all the furniture, a green rugg, blanketts and one pillow, a small iron pott, a pewter dish, 4 hoggs, two flitches of bacon and all the hoggs fatt, one brass bridle, Peter the Negro and his bed, until Isaac Bowles arrived to the age of 21.{KEBI JS#W:4A}

Mary Bowles, widow, d. leaving a will dated 12 Jan 1715 and proved 20 Nov 1717. To grandson Isaac Bowles, and grandchildren George and

Mary Hastins, personalty. Michael Hackett and Simon Wilmore were execs.{MWB 14:546}

On 20 March 1719, Mary Bowles' estate was admin. by Michael Hackett. Legatee mentioned was George Hastings. Payments were made to Vivian Beck, William Bladen, Esq., Thomas Bordley, Esq., Thomas Smyth, Esq. and James Harris.{MDAD 2:6}

On 11 Aug 1720 Mary Bowles' estate was again admin. by Michaell Huckell. George Hastings was mentioned as a legatee.{MDAD 3:65}

Isaac and Mary were the parents of: ISAAC, b. -- Aug ----; and ANN, m. (N) Higley.{KESP}

4. JAMES BOWLES, son of Isaac (1), m. Mary (N). They were the parents of: ISAAC, Jr., mentioned in a deed dated 1691.

5. ISAAC BOWLES, son of Isaac (3) and Mary, was evidently a ward of Michael Hackett. On 4 Jan 1717 a valuation was made of the land and plantations of an orphan Isaac Bowles, under the guardianship of Michael Hackett, 1200 lbs. of tob.{KEBI JS#W:45B}

Unplaced

BOWLES, JAMES. *In the following entry of KE Co. land records is a reference to a James Bowles who d. by 1753, leaving three daus. This may refer to James Bowles of the distinguished family of Southern Maryland.*

On 6 Nov 1753 George Plater of SM Co., Esq., conv. to Nicholas Smith, of KE Co., the tract *Grantham*, 500 a.; defending against other claims including Elinor, Mary and Jane, daus. and coheirs of James Bowles, Esq., dec., and against Kenelm Cheseldine.{KELR JS#27:361}

THE THOMAS BOYER FAMILY

Refs.: A: Data generously made available by John M. Gibson of Drumore, PA.

1. THOMAS BOYER, son of (N), and possibly bro. of William (1), m. by 24 Aug 1725, Anne, dau. of Thomas and Mary Christian, of KE Co., who on that date conv. to Thomas and Anne 60 a. part of a tract called *Morton,* on Herring Branch, 60 a.{KELR JS#W:482 (462)}

Thomas d. leaving a will dated 23 Jan 1728/9 and proved 27 April 1730. To his wife Ann, he left ⅓ of estate. To son Nathaniel, dwell. plant. ----. To dau. Hannah, a parcel of land. Wife Ann and bro. William were named execs.{MWB 20:37}

Thomas and Ann were the parents of: THOMAS, b. c1696; NATHANIEL, minor in 1728; and HANNAH.

2. THOMAS BOYER, son of Thomas and Ann, was b. c1696 (but probably earlier) and d. by 10 April 1733. He m. Mary (N).{A}
In 1713 William Boyer conv. 150 a. of *Partner's Addition.* {KELR BC#1:1}
On 7 June 1726, Thomas Boyer, of KE Co., and his wife Mary, conv. to John Rogers, part of a tract called *Partners Addition* on w. side of Swan Creek, 100 a. {KELR JS#W:544}
He d. leaving a will dated 27 Oct 1732, proved 20 April 1733. To wife Mary, he left his dwell. plant., and at her decease to pass to two sons Richard and Nicolas: son Richard to have 90 a.; son Nicolas 60 a. Execs. were wife and son Richard. {MWB 20:768}
Thomas was the father of: RICHARD; NICHOLAS; and probably ISAAC.

3. NATHANIEL BOYER, son of Thomas and Ann, was a minor in 1728, and d. 1785. He m. Ruth Terry, b. 23 Dec 1730, d. 1804, dau. of Hugh and Sara (Christian) Terry.
Nathaniel and Ruth were the parents of{A}: NATHANIEL, d. 1817; TERESA, d. c1844/5; RUTH, d. 1817; ANNE, m. (N) Martin; (N), dau., m. (N) Pell; HUGH; and HENRIETTA, m. (N) Harmon.

4. RICHARD BOYER, son of Thomas and Mary, was b. c1709. Richard Boyer, age 49, dep. in April 1759. {KEEJ: Thomas Harris}
On 19 March 1727, Gideon Pearce, of KE Co., Gent., and his wife Ann, conv. to Thomas Williams, practitioner in physick, part of a tract called *The Addition*, taken up by Richard Boyer and Mathw. Adams and Thomas. Boyer and his wife Mary and sold to afsd. Gideon Pearce on 10 Feb 1724. {KELR JS#X:221}
On 12 Feb 1761, Richard Boyer, inspector, age c52, dep. regarding the bounds of a tract called *Adams Choice.* {KELR JS#29:350}
Boyer d. by 2 Dec 1761, when his estate was appraised by Peter Massey and John Massey, and valued at £132.14.7. Giles Cooke and Samuel Black signed as creditors. John Wallace and Isaac Boyer signed as next of kin. Thomas Boyer, admin., filed the inventory on 19 Feb 1762. {MINV 75:235}
The estate of Richard Boyer, of KE Co., was appraised again on 1 Nov 1763 by Peter Massey and William --aley, and valued at £166.4.9. George Pearce and Giles Cooke signed as creditors. Isaac Boyer and Rachel Boyer signed as next of kin. Thomas Boyer, admin., filed the inventory on 3 Nov 1763. {MINV 82:37}
Richard Boyer m. Margrett (N). They were the parents of{KESP; KESB}: JOHN, (named in the will of William Boyer, Jr.); THOMAS, b.

14 Aug 1737; MARY, b. 21 Feb 1739; RACHEL, 15 May 1742, m. Ebenezer Reyner; REBECCA, b. 18 Aug 1744; RICHARD, b. 20 Oct 1746; STEPHEN, b. 10 Feb 1748/9; BENJAMIN, b. 11 da., 11 mo., 1751; JAMES, b. 11 da., 1 mo., 1754; and DANIEL. b. 5 da., 12 mo., 1756.

5. NICHOLAS BOYER, son of Thomas and Mary, was alive on 18 March 1745, when he conv. to his bro. Richard Boyer of the same county, 60 a. of tract called *Headings*. The deed stated that Thomas Boyer, father of the afsd. Richard and Nicholas, made his last will and devised his then dwell. plant. being a tract called *Headings*, 90 a., to Richard and 60 a. to Nicholas.{KELR JS#25:345}

6. ISAAC BOYER, prob. son of Thomas and Mary - *so placed because he signed the inventory of Richard Boyer as one of the next of kin.* Isaac Boyer m. Rebecca McCay on 1 Oct 1746. They were the parents of{KESH}: LAMBERT, b. 6 Nov 1748; SARAH, b. 22 da., 10 mo., 1751; MILLESSON, b. 14 da., 4 mo., 1754; JEMIMA, b. 18 da., 1 mo., 1757; KEZIAH, b. 9 da., 7 mo., 1759; FANNAH, b. 11 da., 7 mo., 1762; and JESSE, b. 20 da., 1 mo., 1765.

4-x. STEPHEN BOYER, son of Richard and Margaret, was b. 10 Feb 1748/9, and d. by 18 Feb 1774, when his estate was appraised by Peter Massey and Robert Maxwell, and valued at £24.10.0. William Henry and Isaac Spencer signed as creditors. Thomas Boyer and Richard Boyer signed as next of kin. Mary Boyer, admx., filed the inventory on 5 May 1774.{MINV 115:347}

On 24 June 1774 his estate was appraised and valued at £7.12.5. Margaret Boyer, admx., filed the undated inventory.{MINV 121:262}

THE WILLIAM BOYER FAMILY

Refs.: A: Data generously made available by Mr. John M. Gibson of Drumore, PA.

1. WILLIAM BOYER was b. c1667, and d. 1732. He and Philiss Holeoger were m. in St. Stephen's Parish, CE Co., on 26 Dec 1688. Phillis d. by 1720.{A; CECH:1}

At age 58, on 10 June 1725, he dep. regarding the bounded tree of a tract called *The Forrest*.{KELR JS#W:486 (466)} At age c62 on 2 May 1728/9, William Boyer, of KE Co., dep. regarding the bounds of a tract called *Adventure;* he recalled riding along the road called Sassafras Main Road near to Wilson's Creek on the s. side of sd. creek and about

300 yards to the s. of a bridge called Long Bridge (later called Windals) in company with William Pearce and Philip Holeager. {KELR JS#X:383}

On 1 March 1713, William Boyer, of KE Co., and his wife Phillis, conv. to Thomas Boyer, carpenter, a tract called *Partners Addition*, on the w. side of Swan Creek, 150 a.{KELR BC#1:1}

On 16 Aug 1720, William Boyer, of KE Co., conv. to his son William Boyer, a parcel of land, standing at the dividing of two roads which led from the head of Sassafras, the one leading to Mr. James Heath's and the other unto Duck Creek, 100 a.{KELR JS#W:117}

On 13 April 1731, William Boyer, Sr., age c64, dep. regarding the bounds of a tract called *The Adventure*; he recalled riding in company with Col. William Pearce and Philip Holegder and coming up a hill on the w. side of a Windall's Branch, formerly Wilson's Creek.{KELR JS#16:127}

William Boyer, Sr., d. leaving a will dated 1 Feb 1732 and proved 27 June 1733. To son Aug't, exec.; dau. Mary Nowland; dau. Elizabeth Mecay; wife ----; daus. Sarah and Rachel he left personalty. To son-in-law Robert Mecay, personalty; two boys to remain on the plant. during their servitude in case wife ---- thinks fit to stay on same.{MWB 20:772}

The estate of Mr. William Boyer, of KE Co., was appraised on 14 Aug 1733, by John Rogers and Simon Wilmer, Jr., and valued at £130.8.0. Jo. Young and John Gresham signed as creditors. A son and dau. who refused to sign were next of kin. Augustine Boyer, exec., filed the inventory on 20 March 1733.{MINV 18:23}

His estate was inv. on 14 Aug 1733. Next of kin were son and dau. who refused to sign. Exec. Augustine Boyer filed the inventory on 20 March 1733/4.{MINV 18:23}

William and Phillis were the parents of the following children, born in CE Co.{CECH: 1, 15, 24, 49}: MARY, b. 13 Sep ----, m. Sylvester Nowland; AUGUSTINE, b. 15 Dec 1691, d. 1766; WILLIAM, b. 23 Aug 1695, bapt. 3 Oct 1697, d. 1754; ELIZABETH, m. Robert Mecay; SARAH; and RACHEL.

2. AUGUSTINE BOYER, son of William and Phillis, was b. in CE Co. on 15 Dec 1691, and d. 1766.{A} On 26 Aug 1740, Augustine Boyer, of KE Co., age c50 years, dep. regarding the bounds of a tract called *Larkins Addition;* he recalled that many years earlier he heard his father, William Boyer, and Dennis McCarty say ... there stood a bounded tree which his father and old Eliza. Hill, relict of Samuel Hill, proved that they differed a little about the particular place ...(?).{KELR JS#23:43}

Augustine Boyer, Sr., of KE Co., d. leaving a will dated 9 Oct 1766 and proved 9 Jan 1767. Mentioned were grandchildren and son Augustine Boyer, Jr. The will was witnessed by Thomas Price Smith, Healy/Haley Pell, and Micle/Michael Chambers.{MWB 35:163}

The estate of Augustine Boyer, of KE Co., was appraised on 4 April 1767 by Alexander Baird and Samuel Davis, and valued at £471.8.10. No creditors listed. Nathel Boyer and Thomas Boyer signed as next of kin. Augustine Boyer, exec., filed the inventory on 28 April 1767.{MINV 92:132}

The estate of Augusteen/Augustine Boyer, of KE Co., was appraised on 16 March 1768 by Alexander Baird and Samuel Davis, and valued at £51.15.0. No creditors listed. Nathaniel Boyer and Thomas Boyer signed as next of kin. Augustine Boyer, exec., filed the inventory on 18 May 1768.{MINV 97:189}

Distribution of the estate of Augustine Boyer, of KE Co., was made on 22 March 1769 by Augustine Boyer, admin. Legatees were all his grandchildren. Residue to son Augustine.{BFD 5:182}

Augustine Boyer was the father of the following children, named in the will of his bro. William, Jr.: AUGUSTINE, Jr., b. 29 Oct 1721; PHYLLIS; REBECCA; WILLIAM, d. 1766; PHILIP, d. 1761; THOMAS; and MARY.

3. WILLIAM BOYER, son of William and Phillis, was born 23 Aug 1695 and bapt. 3 Oct 1697 in St. Stephen's Parish, CE Co.{CECH:24, 49}

On 11 June 1725, Jane Holledger, of KE Co., spinster, relict and widow of Philip Holledger, dec., conv. to her "cuzin" William Boyer, Jr., and his wife Penelope, a parcel of land which her afsd. husband sold to William Boyer, Sr., except 25 a. that already belonged to her cousin Augustine Boyer.{KELR JS#W:422}

William Boyer, of KE Co., d. leaving a will dated 20 Nov 1754 and proved 13 Jan 1755. The heirs named were wife Penelopy Boyer; William and Phillip Boyer, sons of Augustine Boyer, Sr.; and John Boyer, son of Richard Boyer, to whom he devised land called *Phillip's Neglect* (495 a.). Land was also given to Thomas Boyer, son of Augustine Boyer, Jr. (100 a.); Thomas Boyer, son of Nathaniel Boyer (100 a. of tract called *Indian Range*); black Michael (50 a. of land in *Indian Range*), he to be free from servitude when age 24, if wife Penelopy be then dec. To the parish of Shrewsbury was devised a 35 a. tract called *Mill Fork*, for a school. He mentioned bro. Augustine Boyer, Phyllis and Rebecca Boyer, daus. of bro. Augustine Boyer, Sr. and Susanna Mercer. The execs. were wife Penelopy Boyer, Wm. Reason, Esq., and Augustine Boyer, Jr. The will was witnessed by Wm. Caulk, Robert Webb, and John Pell.{MWB 29:355}

On 17 Jan 1755, William's estate estate was appraised by Cornelius Comegys and Alexander Baird, and valued at £899.2.1. John Boyer and John Shaw signed as creditors. Augustine Boyer, Rachel Boyer,

Penelope Boyer, and William Rasin signed as next of kin. Augustine Boyer, Jr., exec., filed the inventory on 16 May 1755.{MINV 60:244}

The estate of William Boyer, of KE Co., was appraised on 18 Oct 1755 by Cornelius Comegys (also C. Comegys) and Alexander Baird, and valued at £33.7.11. No creditors or next of kin listed. Penelope Boyer, William Rasin, and Augustine Boyer, Jr., execs., filed the inventory on 17 June 1756.{MINV 60:723}

On 29 Dec 1755, Penelope Boyer and Augustine Boyer, Jr., execs. of William Boyer, late of KE Co., conv. to John Williams, carpenter of the same county. Whereas John Howard and his wife Ann conveyed to afsd. William Boyer all that tract called *Norris Design Resurveyed*, 55 a. with a grist mill thereon and several houses and appurtenances with the claus if Howard repaid or caused to be repaid to Boyer at the same amount with interest, then the deed would be void.{KELR JS#28:226}

William's estate, with balance of £1338.10.5, was distributed on 23 Aug 1757 by admins. Penelope Boyer, Augustine Boyer, and William Rasin. Reps. were unknown to the office.{BFD 2:66}

Another estate with balance of £826.17.0 was to be distributed by same admins. on 29 May 1759. The representatives were unknown. {BFD 3:4}

4. AUGUSTINE BOYER, son of Augustine and Rebecca, was b. 29 Oct 1721, and d. 1772. He m. Elizabeth Everett who d. 1774.

Augustine Boyer, Sr., of KE Co., d. leaving a will dated 10 Jan 1771. Mentioned were sons Thomas and Augustine Boyer, Jr., dau. Mary and granddau. Elizabeth, dau. of son Thomas. Tracts mentioned were *The Adventure, Phillips Neglect, Eades, Rich Level, Boyers Adventure, The Forrest, Mill Fork, Heiths Range,* and land in Sussex Co., DE. The will was witnessed by John Veazey 3rd, Thomas Pryce Smith, and Augustine Price.{MWB 38:736}

The estate of Augustine Boyer, of KE Co., was appraised on 6 Nov 1772 by Daniel Massey and Alexander Baud, and valued at £1285.9.7. Nathaniel Boyer and Thomas Boyer signed as next of kin. Thomas Boyer and Augustine Boyer, Jr., execs., filed the undated inventory.{MINV 110:400}

The estate of Augustine Boyer, of KE Co., was again appraised and valued at £266.11.10. Thomas Boyer and Augustine Boyer, Jr., execs., filed the inventory cont. a list of debts on 9 Jan 1773.{MINV 111:193}

The estate of Mr. Augustine Boyer, of KE Co., was appraised on 4 Nov 1773 by Daniel Massey and Alexander Baird, and valued at £335.12.2. Thomas Boyer signed as next of kin. Thomas Boyer and Augustine Boyer, Jr., execs., filed the inventory on 9 Dec 1773.{MINV 114:210}

Elizabeth Boyer, of KE Co., d. leaving a will dated 6 Nov 1773 and proved 5 May 1774. The heirs named were son Thomas Boyer, to whom was devised a tract on the Delaware in Slauter Neck, Sussex Co., DE, cont. 370 a. now rented and in the possession of John Ricords; dau. Mary Shewel; granddau. Elizabeth Boyer (minor), dau. of son Thomas Boyer; and son Augustin Boyer, exec. The will was witnessed by Augustine Price, Thomas Pryce, and Hugh McKinnie.{MWB 39:663}

The estate of Elisabeth Boyer, of KE Co., was appraised on 28 June 1774 by Samuel Davis and Daniel Massey, and valued at £272.17.0. No creditors listed. Nathaniel Boyer and Thomas Boyer signed as next of kin. Augustine Boyer, exec., filed the inventory on 11 Aug 1774.{MINV 116:278}

Augustine and Elizabeth (Everett) Boyer were the parents of{A}: THOMAS, b. 14 March 1743, d. 1778; AUGUSTINE, m. Mary Montgomery; and MARY, d. after 1770, m. (N) Shewell or Sewell.

5. WILLIAM BOYER, son of Augustine and Rebecca (Christian), d. c1766. He m. Catherine (N).

William Boyer, of KE Co., d. leaving a will dated 21 Sep 1766 and proved 8 Oct 1766. Mentioned were children Rebecca and Eleanor. The will was witnessed by Thos. Ellis, James Watson, and John Tore.{MWB 34:298}

His estate was appraised on 19 Nov 1766 by Solomon Semans and William Semans, and valued at £224.3.6. Benjamin Canby and Thomas Ellis signed as creditors. Augustine Boyer and Thomas Boyer signed as next of kin. Katharine Boyer, extx., filed the inventory on 7 May 1767.{MINV 94:9}

The estate of William Boyer, of KE Co., was appraised on 10 Feb 1768 by Solomon Semans and William Semans, and valued at £29.0.2. Benjamin Canby and Thomas Ellis signed as creditors. Augustine Boyer and Thomas Boyer signed as next of kin. Katharine Boyer, extx., filed the inventory on 2 June 1768.{MINV 97:195}

Distribution of the estate of William Boyer, of KE Co., was made on 27 Aug 1768 by Catharine Boyer, extx. Distribution was made to widow Catharine and two daus. Rebeccah and Eleanor.{BFD 5:110}

William and Catherine were the parents of: REBECCA; and ELEANOR.

6. PHILIP BOYER, son of Augustine, d. by 13 June 1761, when his estate was appraised by Samuel Davis and Samuel Dickinson, and valued at £219.11.8. Joseph Boyer, Jr., and William Boyer. Elisabeth Boyer, admx., filed the inventory on 15 Aug 1761.{MINV 76:58}

His estate, with balance of £219.11.8, was to be distributed on 27 Jan 1763. Elizabeth Boyer was admx. The representatives "were unknown to the office."{BFD}

Unplaced

BOYER, AGNES, on 6 Nov 1738 gave her son John Boyer a mare, a cow and yearling.{KEBI JS#18:186}

BOYER, BENJAMIN, of KE Co., d. by 18 June 1775, when his estate was appraised by Christopher Hall and Joseph Boot, and valued at £35.17.10. Isaac Spencer and W. Rogers signed as creditors. Richard Boyer and Mary Boyer signed as next of kin. Thomas Boyer, admin., filed the inventory on 22 Aug 1775.{MINV 122:77}

BOYER, ELIZABETH, on 25 May 1764, was named as a dau. in the distribution of the estate of Henry Semans, of KE Co.{BFD 4:35}

BOYER, JAMES, of Shrewsbury Parish, at November Court 1732, was found guilty of committing fornication on 10 Jan 1731, with Rachel Bostick and begetting a bastard child. He was fined £3. Deposition was made by Rachel Bostick, age c18.{KECR JS#WK:330}
   James Boyer, of KE Co., d. by 14 April 1747, when his estate was appraised by Ja. Caulk and Lambert Wilmer, Jr., and valued at £65.1.0. Gideon Pearce and James Bayard signed as creditors. Benjamin Marley, Sr., and Mary Bast signed as next of kin. The admx. (name not given) filed the inventory on 6 June 1747.{MINV 35:38}

BOYER, JOHN, m. Sarah Smythers on 24 Feb 1744/5. They were the parents of{KESH}: MARY, b. 8 Aug 1745; ELISABETH, b. 7 Dec 1747; STEPHEN, b. 20 Feb 1748/9; and JOHN, b. 29 June 1750.

BOYER, RICHARD, at August Court 1745, was charged on 15 June 1745, with assaulting Mary Crompton. He was fined 20 s.{KECR JS#24:210}

BOYER, SARAH, of Shrewsbury Parish, at June Court 1732, was found guilty of committing fornication on 10 June 1731, and begetting a bastard child. She was fined 30 s.{KECR JS#WK:296}

BOYER, SARAH, at June Court 1761, it was presented that Benjamin Chrisfield committed fornication with Sarah Boyer, spinster, and begot a base born child. Each was fined 30 s.{KECR DD#1:6A}

BOYER, THOMAS, was b. c1718. Thomas Boyer, age c36, dep. on 17 April 1754.{KEEJ: Isaac Freeman}

BOYER, WILLIAM, of KE Co., d. by 10 April 1747, when his estate was appraised by Lambert Wilmer, Jr., and John Falconer, Jr., and valued at £68.15.3. James Bayard and H. Wilmer signed as creditors. Merty Best and Benjamin Marley signed as next of kin. Margaret Boyer, admx., filed the inventory on 25 July ----.{MINV 35:356}

BOYER, WILLIAM, PHILIP BOYER, and JOHN BOYER, on 7 June 1760, were conv. property by Alexander McCay of Salem Co., West New Jersey, eldest son and heir of Alexander McCay, late of KE Co., MD.{KELR JS#29:278}

THE BREWARD (BREWER, BROORD, BROWARD) FAMILY

The original spelling seems to have been Broord. Later some family members used the spelling Broward.

1. JAMES BROORD, of KE Co., and his sons James, John, and Solomon were naturalized on 25 March 1702.{WCMN}
   James Broward (Brouard) d. leaving a will dated 3 March 1708/9 and proved 7 June 1709. He named his wife Anne, to have ½ dwell. plant. during lifetime; son James, residue of sd. plant.; son John and Solomon, 200 a. of *James Bruars Reserve*. To three sons afsd. the *Marshy Island* adjacent dwell. plant. If wife m. during minority of sd. children, Francis Collins to have charge of their estate.{MWB Part 2, 12:124}
   James Broward's estate was admin. on 30 July 1709, 6 June 1710 (Francis Collins and Ann Breward were execs.), and again on 2 Aug 1710. Ann Breward had m. 2nd, Hayden, and John Picket was a legatee.{INAC 30:96, 31:243, and 32A:40}
   James was the father of: JAMES; JOHN; and SOLOMON.

2. JAMES BREWER, son of James, was b. c1690 and is almost certainly the James who d. by 7 Nov 1753. On 27 April 1730, James Brewer, of KE Co., age c40, dep. regarding the bounds of a parcel of land called *Darnels Lott*.{KELR JS#16:19}
   James Breward, of KE Co., d. leaving a will dated 15 Oct 1753 and proved 7 Nov 1753. The heirs named were grandson John Breward, son of John Breward, to whom was devised a tract called *Prices Pair*; son James Breward, to whom was devised a tract called *Breward Industry*; dau. Mary, to whom was devised land on which son John lived, until son James arrived at age 21. The execs. were dau. Mary Breward and son-in-law Clemons Flenton. The will was witnessed by Solomon Breward, James Breward, Jr., and John Connolin.{MWB 28:552}
   On 14 Nov 1755, his estate was appraised by William Smith and W. Comegys, Jr., and valued at £192.2.4. Isaac Willson and William Boots signed as creditors. Solomon Bruce and Hannah Mackintouch signed as

next of kin. Clement Flinton, the surviving exec., filed the inventory on 8 March 1755.{MINV 60:188}

James Breward was the father of: JOHN; MARY; and JAMES, not yet 21.

3. JOHN BREWARD, son of James, d. by 31 Jan 1754, when his estate was appraised by William Smith and W. Comegys, Jr., and valued at £21.7.4. No creditors or next of kin were listed. Clement Flinton and Mary Bruard, admins., filed the inventory mentioning Solomon Brouard and Hannah Brouard on 28 Oct 1754.{MINV 58:261}

4. SOLOMON BREWARD, son of James, was b. c1700. On 1 April 1746, Solomon Breward, of KE Co., age c46, dep. regarding the bounds of a tract called *Webby.*{KELR JS#25:364} In November Court 1724, Solomon Breward was ordered to answer a charge of hog stealing. James Broward and George Gleaves, of KE Co., were sureties.{KECR JS#22:42}

Solomon m. by 1 June 1725, Isabella, who on that day, joined him in conveying to Samuel Norriss of afsd. county, a tract called *Browards Reserve*, 200 a.{KELR JS#W:476 (456)}

Solomon Breward, of KE Co., d. leaving a will dated 5 Dec 1754 and proved 5 June 1755. The heirs named were: son Robert Breward, son Joseph Breward, son James Breward, dau. Anne Breward, (grand?) son Asell Cosden (begotten of dau.) in return for maintaining the testator during his natural life, was to have 50 a. in FR Co., called *Rattle Snake Denn*. The exec. was son Asell Cosden. The will was witnessed by William Wilshier, Edward Clemens, and Clemmons Flintkem.{MWB 29:450}

Solomon and Isabel were the parents of{KESB}: SARAH, b. 13 Nov 1724; ROBERT; JOSEPH; JAMES; and ANN.

Unplaced

BREWERD, CHARLES (also Charles Broward), of KE Co., d. by 27 May 1751, when his estate was appraised by John Wallis and Samuel Mansfield, and valued at £172.13.8. James Undrill and Thomas Ringgold for Sedgley & Cheston signed as creditors. George Denning and John Denning signed as next of kin. Catharine Broward, admx., filed the inventory on 20 July 1751.{MINV 47:161}

On 5 Aug 1752, his estate was again appraised, by John Wallis and Samuel Mansfield, and valued at £68.9.11. H. Callister for Foster Cunliffe & Sons signed as creditor. George Denning and John Denning signed as next of kin. Catharine Daugherty (late Catharine Broward), wife of John Daugherty, admx., filed the inventory on 24 Feb 1753. {MINV 53:76}

BREWER, JAMES, age c30, on 24 March 1774, dep. that he heard his uncle James Brewer say ....{KEEJ: John Comegys}

BREWAR, PRISCILLA, at November Court 1756, confessed to fornication but refused to name the father; she was fined £3.{KECR JS#25:166A}

THE BRISCOE FAMILY

1. JOHN BRISCOE, on 20 June 1709, conv. to his son Alexander Briscoe, 60 a. adjoining his (John Briscoe's) plant.; also cattle.{KELR JSN:153}

On the same day he dated his will, proved 27 June 1715. To eldest son Alexander and to son John, each, 100 a., being part of *Providence*. To dau. Rachell Ford, a tract called *Chance*, cont. 65 a.; if she d. before husband Robert Ford, he was to have sd. land. To wife Mary, personalty, and joint exec. with son Alexander.{MWB 14:71}

John Briscoe was the father of: ALEXANDER; JOHN; and RACHEL, wife of Robert Ford.

2. ALEXANDER BRISCO, son of John, and his wife Elizabeth, was b. c1696. On 7 June 1735, he conv. to Robert Ford and his wife Rachel of the afsd. county, a tract called *Chance*, 65 a.{KELR JS#18:142}

On 11 Aug 1757, Alexander Brisco, of KE Co., age c61, dep. regarding the bounds of the tract called *Green Oak*.{KELR JS#28:370}

On 14 Jan 1763, Alexander Brisco, of KE Co., and his wife Elizabeth, conv. to Isaac Briscoe of afsd. county, part of a tract called *Providence*, 106 a.{KELR DD#1:192}

Alexander Briscoe, of KE Co., d. leaving a will dated 19 April 1765 and proved 2 June 1766. Mentioned were children John and Joseph Briscoe; Sarah March; and heirs of son William. The exec. was Joseph Briscoe. The will was witnessed by J. and Robert Maxwell, Jr., and Wm. Dick.{MWB 34:50}

On 10 June 1766 his estate was appraised by Jonathon Turner and Joshua Lamb, and valued at £ 262.18.0. Isaac Morrison and J. Nicholson signed as creditors. John March and Isaac Briscoe signed as next of kin. Joseph Briscoe, exec., filed the inventory on 21 Nov 1766.{MINV 90:361}

On 2 Feb 1767 distribution of the estate was made by Joseph Briscoe, exec., to children (equally), Joseph and Sarah March. Legatees were son John and heirs of son William.{BFD 5:77}

Alexander and Elizabeth were the parents of{KESH}: JOHN, b. 12 May 1712; and WILLIAM, b. 11 July 1714; JOSEPH; and SARAH, m. (N) March.

3. JOHN BRISCO, son of John, m. by 13 July 1725, Hannah, widow and admx. of John Miers, of KE Co.{MDAD 6:424}

On 19 March 1756, John Brisco, of KE Co., and his wife Hannah, conv. to William Salsbury of the same county, blacksmith, part of a tract called *Chance*, 100 a.{KELR JS#28:230}

John and Hannah were the parents of three children, born in Shrewsbury Parish: REBEKAH, b. 21 Feb 1723; HANNAH, b. 24 May 1726; and JOHN, b. 8 Sep 1728.

4. JOHN BRISCO, son of Alexander and Elizabeth, was b. 12 May 1712. He and Hannah Corse were m. 23 July 1739.{KESH} He is placed as John Brisco, Jr., because John Briscoe, bro. of his father was still living.

On 20 March 1752, John Brisco, Jr., of KE Co., and his wife Hannah, conv. to John Hicks of the same place, farmer, part of a tract called *Howards Lott Resurveyed*, 92 a.{KELR JS#27:187}

On 31 March 1757, John Brisco, Jr., dep. regarding the bounds of the tracts called *Yapp, Mangys Joynture,* and *Howells Farm Henham* (no age given).{KELR JS#28:376}

5. WILLIAM BRISCO, son of Alexander and Elizabeth, was b. 11 July 1714. He m. Mary Ann Jones 29 April 1739 in Shrewsbury Parish, where the births of their children were recorded.

William Briscoe, of KE Co., d. by 15 April 1763, when his estate was appraised by Roger Hales and Jonathon Turner, and valued at £163.8.10. B. Hands and Andrew Ronald for James McLachlan signed as creditors. William Briscoe and Elisabeth Stavely signed as next of kin. Mary Ann Briscoe, admx., filed the inventory on 15 June 1763. {MINV 80:411}

On 12 April 1764 his estate was appraised by Jonathon Turner and Roger Hales, and valued at £27.18.6. No creditors or next of kin listed. Ann Briscoe, admx., filed the inventory mentioning James McLachlan, William Briscoe and Elisabeth Stavely on 11 May 1764.{MINV 83:210}

On 22 June 1764 distribution of the estate was made by Mary Ann Briscoe, admx.{BFD 4:36}

William and Mary were the parents of: SARAH, b. 18 Jan 1739/40;[2] WILLIAM, b. 24 March 1740/1; NATHANIEL, b. 5 Dec 1742; ELISABETH, b. 29 Oct 1744; MARY, b. 30 Oct 1748; JACOB, b. 14 Aug 1746; and JOSEPH, b. 11 May 1750.

---

[2] She may be the Sarah Briscoe charged at November Court 1761 with having committed fornication and begetting a base born child. She was fined £3.{KECR DD#1:13B}

6. JOSEPH BRISCOE, son of Alexander and Ann, m. by 29 March 1762, Ann, admx. of John Terry, of KE Co.{MDAD 47:368}

Mr. Briscoe, of KE Co., d. by 13 Sep 1768, when his estate was appraised by H. Maxwell and Jonathon Turner, and valued at £1198.3.10. Donaldson Yeates and John March signed as creditors. Benjamin Briscoe and William Briscoe signed as next of kin. Ann Briscoe, admx., filed the inventory on 23 June 1769.{MINV 100:175}

His estate was again appraised by J. Maxwell and Jonathon Turner, and valued at £3.5.10. Ann Briscoe, admx./extx., filed the inventory on 28 Feb 1771.{MINV 106:105, 106}

Unplaced

BRISCO, MARY, on 3 March 1757 confessed to fornication but refused to name the father. She was fined £3.{KECR JS#25:172A}

BRISCO, THOMAS, m. Ann (N). The births of their children were recorded in Shrewsbury Parish: JOHN, b. 29 Sep 1737; ELISABETH, b. 17 Nov 1739; and MARGARET, b. 11 Nov 1741; JACOB, b. 12 Dec 1745.

THE EDWARD BROWN FAMILY

Refs.: A: "Brown (formerly Browne), sometime of Betchworth," *Burke's American Families with British Ancestry* (1939). Reprinted: Baltimore, Genealogical Publishing Co., 1977, 2583-2584.

1. EDWARD BROWNE and Sarah Williams were m. 28 Oct 1668.{ARMD LIV:187, Liber B:75} Edward d. c1678.{A:2584}

An unidentified deposition dated 23 March 1720 stated that: "My father William Trew and William Davis did joyntly and severally buy of Cornelius Comegys a tract called *Comegys Choice* in 1671 and William Davis sold his part to Edward Brown grandfather to old Morgan Brown, dec., and Edward Brown gave his moiety of land to his grandson Morgan Brown being the lower part of the sd. tract. This is to make a division in the land (establish the boundaries).{KELR JS#W:150}

Edward and Sarah (Williams) Brown were the parents of{A:2584}: MORGAN, b. 11 Oct 1669{ARMD LIV:188, Liber B:76}; and EDWARD, b. c1678.

2. MORGAN BROWN, son of Edward and Sarah, was b. 11 Oct 1669.

On 24 Jan 1684 Morgan Williams, of KE Co., made a will leaving to his grandson Morgan Brown 175 a. of *Comages' Choice*.{MWB 4:156}

This is probably the same Morgan Browne who d. by 10 Aug 1704 when his estate was inv., showing servants and a list of debts. The inventory was filed on 30 Aug 1704.{KE Inv. from Wills, 3:290}

Morgan Brown was probably the father of: MORGAN, b. c1694.

3. EDWARD BROWN, son of Edward and Sarah (Williams) Brown, was b. 1678 and d. 1716. He m. Mary, dau. of John Erickson.{A:2584}

Edward Brown settled on Kent Island, QA Co., where he d. leaving a will dated 6 Nov 1713 and proved 9 June 1716. Son John was to have the tracts *Belshew* and *Scilla*. Son Matthew was also to have 100 a. of *Scilla*. Daus. Mary and Rachel were left personalty. Dau. Sarah was also named. Sons were to be of age at 18, and daus. at 16 or marriage. Wife Mary was named extx. and was to have use of the dwell. plant. during widowhood. The will was witnessed by B. Ball, B. Wickes, and Wm. Rakes.{MWB 14:201}

Edward and Mary (Erickson) Brown were the parents of{A:2584}: Major JOHN, b. 1699; MATTHEW; MARY; RACHEL; and SARAH.

4. MORGAN BROWN, probably son of Morgan (2), was b. c1694 and was a member of Cecil Meeting on 9 da., 9 mo., 1715, when he requested a certificate of his clearness of marriage.{CEMM} Morgan Brown, of KE Co., and Rebecca Durden of TA were m. 7 da., 10 mo., 1715 at Third Haven Meeting.{Carroll, Quakerism of the Eastern Shore: 225} On 13 da., 7 mo., 1732 he was disowned because of his excessive drinking and quarrelling.{CEMM} On 30 Oct 1750, Morgan Brown, Quaker, age c56, affirmed regarding the bounds of a tract called *Utrick* alias *Sewell*. {KELR JS#26:417}

Morgan Brown, of KE Co., d. by 11 Dec 1751, when his estate was appraised by Edward Comegys and Henry Hosier, and valued at £1150.15.6. James Williamson for Foster Cunliffe, Esq. & Sons and Thomas Ringgold for Sedgley & Cheston signed as creditors. Edward Brown, Sr., and Ed. Brown signed as next of kin. Rebecca Brown (Quaker), admx., filed the inventory on 7 Feb 1753.{MINV 53:80}

On 7 Feb 1753 distribution of the estate was made by Rebecca Brown, admx.{BFD 1:66}

Morgan and Rebecca may have been the parents of: MORGAN.

5. Major JOHN BROWN, son of Edward and Mary (Erickson) Brown, was b. 1699, and d. 1747. He m. Jane, dau. of Capt. Thomas de Coursey, who d. by Dec 1771.{A:2584}

Major John Brown, of KE Co., d. by 11 Aug 1747, when his estate was appraised by Samuel Tovey and Alexander Williamson, and valued at £257.3.3. James Bryan signed as creditor. Edward Brown, Thomas Coursey Brown and Walter Dougherly signed as next of kin. Jane Brown, admx., filed the inventory on 14 April 1748.{MINV 35:540}

On 10 March 1754, Jane Brown, of KE Co., widow, conv. to her son
Thomas Browne, part of a tract called *Trumpingtown*, 366 a.
{KELR JS#26:447}

On 10 April 1761 distribution of the estate of John Brown was
made by Joan (Jane?) Brown, admx. Distribution was made to widow
and nine representatives equally, children of Edward Brown (son dead),
Thomas, John, William, Mathew, Joseph, Mary Ann, Rachel, and
Dorothy. {BFD 3:62}

Jane Brown, widow, of KE Co., d. leaving a will dated 1 Feb 1763
and proved 26 Dec 1771. Mentioned were children William, Joseph, and
Dorothy Hodges. She referred to her four children, "now alive." She
also mentioned her grandsons William and Zachariah Smith. Tracts
mentioned were *Trumpingtown*, *Smith's Meadows*, and *Coursey's
Choice* (in QA Co.). The will was witnessed by Thomas Slipper, William
Holls, and John Williamson. {MWB 38:440}

John and Jane were the parents of: THOMAS COURSEY, b. 8 May
1726; EDWARD, b. Oct ----, d. by 1761; THOMAS COURSEY, b. 5 May
----; ANN, b. 30 April ----{KESP}; JOSEPH; DOROTHY, m. (N) Hodges;
RACHEL, m. (N) Smith; MATTHEW; JOHN; and WILLIAM, b. 1738.
{A:2584}

6. MORGAN BROWN, possibly son of Morgan (4) and Rebecca,
"having removed out of the Province," on 9 da., 10 mo., 1754, requested
a certificate. {CEMM}

At November Court 1771, it was presented that Morgan Brown, on
17 Aug 1771, assaulted Henry Wannell. He was fined £6. {KECR
DD#1:140B}

At March Court 1772, it was presented that Morgan Brown assaulted Ann Jackson. He was fined 50 s. {KECR DD#1:144A}

7. THOMAS COURSEY BROWN, son of Major John (5) and Jane
(Coursey) Brown, d. c1755.

Thomas Coursey Brown, of KE Co., d. leaving a will dated 17 May
1755. The heirs named were wife Casandra; dau. Martha, who was left
in the care of her Aunt Welty Ann Course; son Thomas, to whom was
devised "land I have interest in," *Parell*, lying in the Eastern Neck,
called *Trumping Town*. Son Thomas was to be bound to Charles Tilden
to the trade of a joiner after he was educated at school until he was
educated sufficiently for country business; bro. John Brown, was to
have part of *Trupintown*, where the testator lived with his mother.
The extx. was his wife. The will was witnessed by Alexander Williamson, Martha Brown, and Margaret MacDonald. {MWB 29:507}

On 2 Dec 1755 his estate was appraised by Thomas Smith and
William Hodges, and valued at £169.4.4. Thomas Ringgold and Thomas
Spencer for MM Luxon & Kenney signed as creditors. John Brown and

34

Mathew Brown signed as next of kin. Cassandra Rogers, wife of Nathaniel Rogers, extx., filed the inventory on 8 April 1756. {MINV 60:479}

On 21 June 1761 distribution of the estate was made by Cassandra Rogers, extx., wife of Nathaniel Rogers. Distribution was made to widow and children, Martha and Thomas. {BFD 3:98}

Thomas Coursey Brown was the father of: MARTHA; and THOMAS.

8. JOHN BROWN, son of Major John Brown (5) and Jane, d. by 17 Sep 1760.

John Brown, of KE Co., d. leaving a will dated 17 April 1760 and proved 17 Sep 1760. Mentioned were bro. Mathew Brown, bro. William Brown, bro. Joseph Brown, mother Jane Brown, sisters Dorothy Brown and Rachel Smith, and niece Mary Gibbons. He referred to the will of his dec. bro. Thomas Coursey Brown. The exec. was friend Alexr. Williamson. The will was witnessed by Draper Lusby, and John and William Hynson. {MWB 31:103}

The estate of John Brown, of KE Co., was appraised by William Ringgold, Jr. and William Hodges, and valued at £482.15.9. Thomas Ringgold, Jr. and Dennis Connway signed as creditors. William Brown and David Brown signed as next of kin. Mathew Brown, exec., filed the inventory on 30 Sep 1761. {MINV 76:62}

Distribution of the estate of John Brown, of KE Co., was made by Matthew Brown, admin. on 10 May 1762. {BFD 3:129}

9. MATTHEW BROWN, son of Major John Brown (5) and Jane, d. c1766. He m. Martha (N).

Matthew Brown, of KE Co., d. leaving a will dated 23 July 1764 and proved 23 July 1766. Mentioned were wife Martha, and his father's estate in possession of "my mother." The will was witnessed by Richard Jones, John Smythe, and Martha Ann Jones. {MWB 34:39}

10. THOMAS BROWN, son of Thomas Coursey Brown (7), is probably the Thomas who d. by 16 Nov 1773, when his estate was appraised by James Smith and Nathaniel Beding, and valued at £39.9.10. Thomas Smith and Smyth & Ringgold signed as creditors. William Brown and Joseph Brown signed as next of kin. Martha, wife of William Crabbin, admx., filed the inventory on 10 March 1774. {MINV 115:346}

THE JOHN AND SARAH BROWN FAMILY

1. JOHN BROWN, d. by 24 Aug 1759. He m. Sarah (N).

On 14 Sep 1754, John Browne of KE Co., farmer, and his wife Sarah, conv. to Philip Rickets of the same place, farmer, the tract called *Browns Level*, 40 a.{KELR JS#28:78}

John Brown d. by 24 Aug 1759, having m. Sarah (N). They had issue: GEORGE; and SARAH.

2. GEORGE BROWN, son and heir of John and Sarah, was mentioned in an indenture made 24 Aug 1759, between George Brown of KE Co., son and heir of John Brown, dec., of one part, and Sarah Brown, widow of sd. John Brown of the other part, and William Rasin of the other part.{KELR JS#29:140}

3. SARAH BROWN, Jr., dau. of John and Sarah, on 14 May 1759, was conv. by William Hamlin of KE Co., a parcel of land called *Hamlins Lott* on the n. side of Steel Pone Creek, 2½ a.{KELR JS#29:167}

THE PEREGRINE BROWN FAMILY

Refs.: A: Brown entries in the Internatioanl Genealogy Index, 1994 ed. B: KELR BC#1:295. C: Coldham, *American Wills and Administrations in the Prerogative Court of Canterbury*. D: Wright, *Maryland Eastern Shore Vital Records*. E: Sherwood, *American Colonists in English Records*.

1. PEREGRINE BROWNE of London, m. 1st, Mary (N), and 2nd on 25 Dec 1692, Margaret Brock. On 8 Dec 1703 Peregrine Browne of St. Catherine Cree Church dep. that he had m. the sister of James Frisby of CE County, who d. leaving a will dated 10 Sep 1702, and that he (Browne) had arranged for the education of Frisby's sons Thomas, James, and Peregrine.{C:83}

On 1 April 1709 Peregrine Browne conv. to John Moll, innholder, all of Browne's right, title and interest in a certain lot of land in the Town of Chester on Chester River, No. 9, formerly taken up by Peregrine Metcalfe, and now in my occupation as exec. of sd. Metcalfe.{KELR BC#1:150}

On 30 Sep 1712 Peregrine Browne, Sr., was granted admin. of the goods of Peregrine Brown, Jr., who d. in MD, a bachelor.{E:167}

Peregrine Browne of the City of London, merchant, d. leaving a will dated 23 Feb 1711/2, proved 10 Aug 1713. He left all his plantations in MD called *Turkey Point* and *Ratcliffe Cross* to his wife Margaret, and named his children Peregrine, Joseph, John, and Margaret Brown, and

Elizabeth Duddlestone. His father-in-law, Joseph Brocke, was to be overseer. The will was witnessed by Wh. Kennett, John Nottingham, and Tho. Kilner.{E:167}

On 17 Oct 1713, administration on the estate of Peregrine, Jr. was granted to Margaret, the widow and extx. of Peregrine Brown, Sr.

Peregrine Brown was the father of the following children, all bapt. at St. Dunstan's, Stepney{A}: (by Mary), JAMES, bapt. 22 March 1681; MARY, bapt. 27 Feb 1683; FRISBY, bapt. 6 Feb 1688; PEREGRINE, bapt. 30 April 1689; JOHN, bapt. 8 Oct 1690; (by Margaret Brock), JOSEPH, bapt. 20 Sep 1694; ELIZABETH, bapt. 1 Jan 1695; and MARGARET, bapt. 14 July 1697.

2. PEREGRINE BROWN, son of Peregrine Brown and his first wife Mary was bapt. 30 April 1689. (He was bur. in St. Paul's Parish, KE Co., MD, on 14 Feb 1711.){D1:15} He probably d. in MD a bachelor. In Sep 1712 admin. was granted to his father Peregrine Brown, but the elder Peregrine Brown d., and in Oct 1713, admin. was granted to Margaret, widow of the father of Peregrine, Jr.{C:42} Peregrine Brown, Jr.'s estate was admin. on 19 April 1713 by Col. Thomas Smith, of KE Co., and Richard Bennett, of QA Co.{INAC 36A:187} His estate was admin. again c1717 by the same admins.{INAC 38B:112}

3. JOHN BROWN, son of Peregrine Brown and his first wife Mary, was bapt. 8 Oct 1690, and stated he was "of the Kingdom of England," when he m. in Shrewsbury Parish, KE Co., Mrs. Rachel Scott, widow of Col. Edward Scott, on 28 Oct 1726.{D2:2} He d. in Shrewsbury Parish, KE Co., on 9 Jan 1728/9.

John Brown's estate was inv. on 3 June 1729. Next of kin were James Cruckshank and Gideon Pearce. Rachel Brown, admx. and extx., filed the inventory on 13 Aug 1729.{MINV 15:158}

On 15 Dec 1729 Rachel Brown of KE Co., widow, conv. to Samuell Wright, the dower or third part of a tract left by Col. Edward Scott in his last will to his son William Scott called *Stepney Heath Manner*, and Samuell Wright the possessor of the other 2/3 parts, as it was allotted by Edward Scott admin. of the sd. Col. Edward Scott to the afsd. Rachel Brown.{KELR JS#X:399}

On 28 Oct 1730 Rachel Brown of KE Co., widow, John Tilden, Gent., and his wife Katherine, and Isabella Blay, spinster, conv. land to William Pearce, Gent. This was land which William Blay, late of afsd. county, Gent., dec., was seized of: *Blays Parke* resurveyed as *William...*, *Howells Addition* and *James' Inspection*, 880 a., and one other tract in BA Co., called *Dale Town*, 300 a. and including within the survey 400 a. out of a patent formerly surveyed by Thomas Howell called *Howells Out Lands* of 700 a., ... and other land.{KELR JS#16:73}

On 15 Nov 1731 Henry Knock of KE Co., and his wife Susanna, conv. to Mrs. Rachel Brown of the same county, widow, 11 a. of a tract formerly called *Bennetts Hope*, now called *Rachel's Farm*, part of a tract called *Childs Harber* but now called *Hamshore*, 11 a. {KELR JS#16:185}

On 23 June 1732 Aquilla Paca of BA Co., Gent., and his wife Rachel, conv. to Peregrine Brown, son of the same Rachel by her late husband John Brown, late of SO Co., Esq., dec., a tract called *Bennets Hope* and now upon a resurvey thereof in the name of the same Rachel called *Rachel Farm*, 345 a.; also a tract called *Blays Rainge*, 100 a.; also part of a tract called *Childs Harbour* now *Hampshire* which the same Rachel purchased of Henry Knock; also the tract called *Philips Neglect*, 400 a., excepting 89 a. sold to Henry Knock out of the tract called *Rachels Farm*. {KELR JS#16:237}

John and Rachel were the parents of: PEREGRINE, b. 1 Oct 1727.

4. JOSEPH BROWN, son of Peregrine and Margaret (Brock), was bapt. 20 Sep 1694 in London, and was in Philadelphia by 1731.

On 22 May 1718 Maurice Birchfield, Surveyor General of His Majesty's Customs, and Joseph Browne, late of the City of London, son and heir of Peregrine Brown, late of the City of London, merchant, conv. to Thomas Smith of Chester River 500 a. called *Ratcliffe Cross*. {B}

On 3 March 1731 Jos. Brown of the City of Philadelphia, Gent., to Nicholas Riley of KE Co., the sd. Jos. Browne as heir-at-law to his father Peregrine Browne, late of the City of London, merchant, agent to Mrs. Margt. Brown of London, relict and extx. of sd. Peregrine Brown, a tract called *Plum Park*. {KELR JS#16:235}

5. PEREGRINE BROWN, son of John and Rachel, was b. 1 Oct 1727, and was living c1750.

Mary Denning of KE Co., widow, one of the daus. of Christopher Hall, late of the sd. county, dec., (c1750) conv. to Peregrine Browne, Gent., ¼ of a tract which was the late dwell. plant. of Christopher Hall, father of afsd. Mary. {KELR JS#26:336}

On 17 April 1752 Peregrine Brown of KE Co., Gent., conv. land to George Wilson of the same county, Gent. Whereas Christopher Hall late of afsd. county, dec., was seized of two tracts, one called *Tibbals* and the other called *Castle Cary*, together cont. 300 a., which were devised by sd. Christopher Hall to his dau. Rachel Hall in tail who d. without issue and the land reverted equally to her four sisters: Elizabeth Conn---dy (Kennedy), Sarah Woodland, Mary Denning, and Margret Wilson. And whereas Peregrin Brown had heretofore purchased of Elizabeth Kennedy and Mary Denning their fourth parts. {KELR JS#27:121}

At June Court 1752, it was charged that Peregrine Brown of Shrewsbury Parish, Gent., on 10 Feb 1752, committed fornication with Elizabeth Eldridge and begot a bastard child. Each was fined 30 s. {KECR JS#25:95B, 96A} At June Court 1757, Elizabeth Eldridge was fined 30 s. for committing fornication; she named Mr. Peregrine Brown as the father of her base born child. (It appears that the name of the child was also Peregrine Brown.){KECR JS#25:175B}

THE CAMPBELL FAMILY

1. JOHN CAMPBELL, d. in SM Co., MD, by 4 Nov 1695. He m. Catherine (N).
   Campbell d. leaving a will dated 6 Dec 1684 and proved 4 Nov 1695. He named his wife Catherine who was to have his plant. for life, and was to be residuary legatee. He named his eldest son Thomas as co-exec. with the testator's wife. Youngest sons Richard and James were to have 350 a. *Campbell's Farm* in CE Co., and 100 a. *The Forest of Dean*. John Campbell also named his daus. Faith, wife of Henry Taylor, Rachel wife of John Russell, and Dorothy. The will was witnessed by William Husband, Jno. Woodward, and Jas. Blan.{MWB 7:190}
   John Campbell was the father of: THOMAS; RICHARD; JAMES; FAITH, m. Henry Taylor; RACHEL, m. John Russell; and DOROTHY.

2. RICHARD CAMPBELL, of KE Co., son of John of SM Co., d. by Oct 1715. He m. Sarah (N), who may have m. 2nd, Nathaniel Pearce, and 3rd, (N) Hicks.
   Richard and wife Sarah, on 18 Nov 1708, conv. to David Young of same county, the parcel called *Cambells Farm*, 76 a.{KELR JSN:89}
   Richard d. by 6 Oct 1715 when his estate was appraised. Next of kin were James Campbel, Abraham Redgiaux (probably Redgrave), and Edward Crew.{INAC 37A:38}
   His estate was admin. on 20 March 1716. Payments were made to Edward Crew and his bro. Samuel Crew for their portion of their father's (unnamed) estate (the dec. was exec.). Nathaniel Pearce was admin. and exec.{INAC 39B:56} His estate was admin. again on 21 Aug 1716 by the admx., Sarah Pearce, wife of Nathaniel Pearce.{INAC 38B:72}
   Nathaniel Pearce, Gideon Pearce and William Redden, of KE Co., were bound to John Campbell, Mary Campbell and Sarah Campbell, orphans of Richard Campbell, dec., on 27 July 1720, to pay them £10.8.8½ when of age.{KEBI JS#W:76B, 77A}
   Richard and Sarah (N) Campbell were the parents of{KESH}: JOHN, b. 17 June 1706; RICHARD, b. 22 March 1707; SARAH, b. 13 March 1709; JAMES, b. 9 Nov 1711; and MARY, b. 16 Sep 1713.

3. JAMES CAMPBELL, son of John, m. by 31 Jan 1708, Margaret, extx., of Lovering Millward of KE Co.{INAC 29:77}

James Campbell, of KE Co., and wife Margret, on 8 June 1711, conv. to David Young, a tract called *Cambles Farm* on Jacobus Creek, 76 a.{KELR JSN:257}

4. JOHN CAMPBELL, son of Richard (2) and Sarah, was b. 17 June 1706. On 23 March 1752 he was named as a son of Sarah Hicks in a deposition made that day by William Pearce, age c34, another son of Sarah Hicks, regarding the bounds of a tract called *Friendship;* he declared that his mother Sarah Hicks told him that her son John Camble ....{KELR JS#27:150}

He may be the John Campbell who m. Mary (N), and had a dau.: ELIZABETH, b. 18 July 1739.{KESH}

Unplaced

CAMMELL, JOHN, m. by 30 Oct 1682, Elisabeth, relict and admx. of William Savin of CE Co.{INAC 8:282}

CAMBELL, JOHN, d. by 14 May 1712, when his estate was admin. by the extx., Rebecca, wife of Cornelius Comegys. Legatee was widow (unnamed).{INAC 33A:244}

CAMPBELL, JOHN, sadler, at August Court 1763, was charged on 10 March 1763, with assaulting Rebecca Cozens. He was fined 20 s. {KECR DD#1:36A}

CAMPBELL, JOHN,, of KE Co., d. by 3 Dec 1766, when his estate was appraised by John Chapple and Abraham Miller, and valued at £71.10.3. No creditors or next of kin were listed. James Piner, admin., filed the inventory mentioning Lowing Merritt, John Gilbert, Thomas Smyth and Thomas Ringgold on 20 Dec 1766.{MINV 92:55}

THE CARROLL FAMILY

1. EDWARD CARROLL, of KE Co., d. by 19 March 1710 when his estate was admin. by Francis Collins.{INAC 32C:103} It was admin. again on 5 Aug 1712.{INAC 3B:117}

Edward Carroll m. Mary (N). They were the parents of{KESP}: PHILLIP, b. 2 Oct 1695; MARY, b. 2 Oct 1696; and (probably) EDWARD.

2. PHILIP CARROLL, son of Edward and Mary, was b. 2 Oct 1695.
Phillip Carroll, of KE Co., on 24 June 1721, conv. to Richard Davice
of the same place, a parcel of land on Morgans Creek being part of a
tract bought by his father, Edward Carrell.{KELR JS#W:175}
At June Court 1731, Philip Carrol, of Shrewsbury Parish, was found
guilty of committing fornication on 10 April 1729 with Margaret
Falconar and begetting a bastard child. He was fined 600 lbs. of
tob.{KECR JS#WK:207}

3. EDWARD CARROLL is placed as a son of Edward, because he was
an orphan in 1718.
John Fanning of KE Co., carpenter, on 6 Oct 1718 assigned to
Thomas Gideons an orphan boy named Edward Carrill who had been
bound to him (Fanning) by the KE Co. Court. Edward Carroll still had
to serve for an additional 3 years.{KEBI JS#W:89B}
EDWARD, m. Honour (N). They were the parents of: PHILLIP, b.
1 Dec 1727.{KESP}

4. PHILIP CARROLL, son of Edward and Honour, was b. 1 Dec 1727.
{KESP}
He is probably the Philip Carroll, charged at August Court 1766,
with assaulting William Copper on 10 May 1766. He was fined 50
S.{KECR DD#1:81A}

Unplaced

CARROLL, JAMES, and Margrett Miller were m. 12 Jan 1707.{KESP}

CARROLL (or CARROL), NEAL, of KE Co., d. by 1 Oct 1753, when
his estate was appraised by John Graham and William Kitinly, and
valued at £5.15.0. No creditors or next of kin listed. Neal Shirky,
admin., filed the inventory on 20 Nov 1753.{MINV 56:18}

THE DENNIS CARTER FAMILY

1. DENNIS CARTER was in KE Co. by June 1712 when James Heath,
of QA Co., Gent. and his wife Mary, conv. to Dennis and and his wife
Alice, and after their decease unto James Carter, son of the sd. Dennis
and Alice, part of a tract called *the Holt(?)*, in CE and KE Cos., 105
a.{KELR JSN:301}
Dennis and Alice were the parents of: JAMES.

3. JAMES CARTER, son of Dennis and Alice, inherited *The Holt* from his father. KE Co. Debt Books for 1733-1735 and 1769 show that he owned the tract, but by 1769 John Francis owned the tract.{INKE:6, 13}

2. DENNIS CARTER, of KE Co., d. leaving a will dated 7 Nov 1754 and proved 3 Feb 1755. The heirs named were wife Rhode Carter and dau. Sarah Carter, who was to have the plant. called *New Dissin*, when of age. The will was witnessed by John Kennedy, Wm. Caulk, and William Heverin.{MWB 29:359}

Dennis and his wife Rhoda were the parents of: SARAH (under age in 1754).

THE HENRY CARTER FAMILY

1. HENRY CARTER was transported in 1652.{MPL 6:159} He m. Mary (N).

Henry and Mary were the parents of: ELIZABETH, b. 25 March 1669.{ARMD LIV:187, Liber B:76} On c28 June 1670, Robert Dunn recorded a cattle mark for a calf given by him to Elizabeth, dau. of Henry Carter.{ARMD LIV:291, Liber C:38}

2. HENRY CARTER, probably a different Henry from the one above, d. by Jan 1706/7. He and his wife Sarah, relict of John Evans, of the afsd. county, dec., on 25 Aug 1684 bound James Evans the son of the sd. John Evans, apprentice to Thomas Davis of the county afsd., taylor, to learn his art, to serve him for a term of 11 years.{KELR K:75, 105}

On 10 Aug 1695 Henry patented 50 a. *Chance*.{MPL 40:10}

He may be the Henry Carter who, at November Court 1696, was was permitted to keep a public ferry at the wading place at the north end; he was to proved a sufficient boat. He was to received 3500 lbs. of tobacco per year. {TAJU AB8: 1} At October Court 1697 Henry Carter who kept a ferry on Kent Island requested an increase in allowance. The court allowed him an additional 500 lbs. of tobacco per year. {TAJU AB8: 441}

Henry Carter of TA Co., died leaving a will dated 17 June 1706 and proved 21 Jan 1706/7. The heirs named were eld. son Valentine and hrs., all real estate. To son John and dau. Elizabeth Elliot, personalty. The execs. were 2 sons afsd. The will was witnessed by Jno. Stevens, Elizabeth Enger and Alexander Forbes. {MWB 12:92}

Henry Carter was the father of: VALENTINE; JOHN; and ELIZABETH, m. (N) Elliott.

3. VALENTINE CARTER, son of Henry, was named in his father's will, and d. by Oct 1726. He m. Rebecca (N) by March 1711. She

admin. his estate and m. 2nd, by 28 Oct 1731, John Collins. {QALR RTA:104}

On 26 March 1711 Valentine Carter and wife Rebecka of Kent Island, conv. to Isaac Hudson, weaver, 100 a. on Long Creek, east side of Kent Island called *Ashford*. {QALR ETA: 84}

Valentine Carter of QA Co., died leaving a will dated 12 Sept 1726 and proved 13 Oct 1726. The heirs named were son Richard and hrs., plantation where he now lives (for desc. see will) and 50 a. bou. of Frances Barnes. To dau. Elizabeth, dwelling plantation, and 50 a. bou. of Frances Barnes after decease of wife Rebecca. The will was witnessed by John Carter, James Sudler and Joseph Sudler. {MWB 18:548}

Valentine Carter was the father of: HENRY, named in the will, made 11 Aug 1701, of Richard Huchins of KI, TA Co. {MWB 12:17}; RICHARD; and ELIZABETH.

4. JOHN CARTER, son of Henry, was named in his father's will, and d. on KI, QA Co., by March 1740. He m. Mary (N).

On Aug 28 1711 John Carter and wife Mary of Kent Island conv. to Valentine Carter all claims to *Co-Partnership* and *Jones his Plott* on Kent Island. {QALR ETA: 90}

On 7 Dec 1727 Edward Cockey and his wife Sarah conv. to John Carter, Gent., 98 a. called *Mattapex Neck* and 187 a. called *The Ridge*. {QALR IKC:157}

John Carter of Kent Island, QA Co., died leaving a will dated 15 May 1740 and proved 25 March 1740. The heirs named were daus. Elizabeth Earukson, Susanna Elliott and Ruth Wells, personalty. To son John, dwelling plantation, 170 a. *"Cranny Neck"* and part of *"Coppdeges Range."* To son Jacob, 200 a. *"Oyormines."* To son Vallentine, 187 a. *"The Ridge."* To son Henry, 130 a. *"Matepax."* To child., viz., John, Jacob, Vallentine, Henry and Mary, residue of estate. The execs. were sons John and Jacob. The will was witnessed by George Moor, Jacob Winchester and Samuel Hunter. {MWB 22:321}

John Carter was the father of: ELIZABETH, m. (N) Earickson; SUSANNA, m. (N) Elliott; RUTH, m. (N) Wells; HENRY; JOHN; JACOB, b. c1720; and VALENTINE.

5. HENRY CARTER, son of Valentine, was named in the 1701 will of Richard Huchins, and was probably the Henry who had been living about one year earlier, according to a 1738 dep. made by Jerom Coventon, age c42.{KELR JS#22:288} On 21 April 1741 a valuation was made of the plant. of Henry Carter; Jacob Carter, guardian. {QALR RTB:351}

6. RICHARD CARTER, son of Valetine, was living as late as June 1759.

On 4 June 1759 Richard Carter and his wife Sarah conv. to John Legg, planter and inspector at Kent Island Warehouse, 20 a., part of *Donn's Hazard Corrected*, at the head of Eastern Creek. {QALR RTE:344}

On 27 Aug 1760 Richard Carter conv. to Thomas Ringgold, Gent., a bond for *Carter's Addition, Copartnership* and 50 a. devised to Richard Carter by his father, Valentine Carter, part of *Barnes's Satisfaction*. {QALR RTF:98}

7. JACOB CARTER, son of John, was b. c1720. Jacob Carter, age 50, dep. March 1770 and mentioned his bro. Henry Carter. {QAEJ: Carter, Henry}.

On 23 Aug 1758 Andrew Cox and his wife Ruth conv. to Jacob Carter 250 a., part of *Winsor's Forrest* or *Forrest of Winsor*. {QALR RTE:280}

8. VALENTINE CARTER, son of John, was named in his father's will, and was living on 21 April 1741 when a valuation was made of his plantation; John Elliott, Sr., guardian. {QALR RTB:351}

THE RICHARD CARTER FAMILY

1. RICHARD CARTER, of TA Co., immigrated in 1665.{MPL 9:50} He m. Elizabeth, sister of Thomas Raizin.

On 20 July 1684 Richard Carter of London, merchant, conv. to Timothy Dunnavon, cooper, and his wife Mary, 200 a. in St. Michael's River. {TALR 1:358}

On 17 June 1691 John Browne of Wye River and his wife Elizabeth conv. to Richard Carter of St. Michael's River, merchant, part of the land laid out for Thomas Williams called *The Addition* on Williams' Branch, Back Wye River; part of *Partnership*, 350 a. adj. {TALR 5:298}

On 1 May 1698 Timothy Dunavan of St. Michaels River, cooper, and his wife Mary conv. to Richard Carter, merchant, a parcel of land called *Long Branch* between Marshy Branch and Long Branch. {TALR 6:30}

In 1702 Richard Carter, of TA Co., merchant, and wife Elizabeth, on 23 Nov 1702, conv. to Flower Walter, of KE Co., 400 a., called *Price's Hill*.{KELR JD#1:108}

On 20 Nov 1705 George Dehorty and his wife Amey conv. to Richard Carter 100 a., part of *Stevensfields* on Tuckahoe Creek bequeathed to George Dehorty by James Markes in his last will. {TALR 9:366}

On 22 Feb 1715 Elizabeth Carter, widow and relict of Richard Carter, dec., granted to her bro. Thomas Rasin of KE Co., MD, power of attorney to recover debts owed to her or to the estate of her dec. husband. {TALR 12:371}

On 28 Nov 1723 Mrs. Elizabeth Carter, formerly of MD but now of the Parish of St. Andrews Holborne in County Middlesex, widow, confirmed to William Lampson of London, Gent. power of attorney. Shortly to proceed to Maryland to take from and turn out Mr. Thomas Raizin of Maryland, merchant, her bro., from the possession of her plantatation or plantations, in or near Miles River and by due course of law recover from him all increase of all Negroes, cattle, effects and tobacco as belongs to the plantation - not to turn out Elizabeth Carter's overseer without her consent. {TALR 13:129}

Richard Carter died without issue, and his nephews and nieces in England inherited his estate.

On 15 April 1710 Samuel Cockayne, County of Yorke, England, Gent., conv. to Elizabeth Carter, relict of Richard Carter of TA Co., merchant, dec. - Samuel Cockayne for himself and his wife Ann; for Christopher Tisdell and his wife Mary, the surviving daus. of the elder bro. of Richard Carter and co-heirs of the same Richard, in full compensation of the dower and third part of the real estate of Richard Carter due to her - grant to Elizabeth Carter all that plant, dwell. houses, tobacco houses, etc. where the afsd. Richard Carter lately dwelt and all the land adj. extending as far as the Mill Bridge and the Great Road which leads from the head of St. Michaels River towards Choptank River and all that plant. called the *Swamp Plantation* and the dwell. house, tobacco houses, etc. and and all lands contiguous to the said plant. being all the lands in the neck, the whole cont. 1000 a. To hold during her natural life. {TALR 11:136}

On 8 June 1717 Ann Cockayne, widow and relict of Samuel Cockayne, Gent., dec., conv. to William Cockayne, son of Samuel and Ann, part of the inheritance of Richard Carter, late of TA Co., Gent. which now are or heretofore were in the occupation of Elizabeth Carter, widow and relict of Richard Carter as her dower. {TALR 12:292}

On 18 May 1719 Ann Cockayne of TA Co., widow, the oldest dau. of William Carter of Gilling in Yorkshire, Great Britain, merchant, who was the oldest bro. of Richard Carter of TA Co., merchant; and Thomas Cockayne, the oldest son, William and Samuel Cockayne, the other sons of the afsd. Anne, all of TA Co., Gents., conv. to Norton Knatchbull of QA Co., merchant, Lambeth Fields, purchased by William Carter of William Jones and his wife Sarah, being made over to them by Thomas Yewell who purchased it form Henry Costyne in whose name the land was originally surveyed, lying about 1 miles from the head of Wye River. {QALR IKA:224}

THE WILLIAM CARTER FAMILY

1. **WILLIAM CARTER** was a servant in the (c1702) inventory of Michael Miller of (KE) Co.{INAC 1:660} He d. by May 1736.

He m. Elizabeth Tilden m. 19 May 1725.{KESP} She was actually Elinor Tilton, dau. of Humphrey Tilton. See the indenture Tripartite made 28 Dec 1748.{KELR JS#26:174}

William Carty (actually Carter), of KE Co., and wife Elenor, on 29 Aug 1727, conv. to Phillip Kennard, a tract called *Lynn*, formerly belonging to John James, grandfather to the afsd. Elenor now wife to sd. William Carty.{KELR JS#X:165}

William Carter d. leaving a will dated 22 March 1736 and proved 22 May 1736. He named son George to have tract called *Thomas' Desire*, and ⅓ personal estate, and dau. Mary to have residue of personal estate. Children afsd. in care of David Hull, exec.{MWB 21:579}

William and Elinor (Tilton) Carter were the parents of: GEORGE; and MARY.{MINV 21:484}

2. **GEORGE CARTER**, son of William (1) and Elinor, was living on 15 March 1755, when he conv. land to Thomas Chandlor of afsd. county, farmer. The deed stated that John James in his lifetime had surveyed for him a tract called *The Grange* cont. 900 a. in BA Co., and now KE Co. on Steel Pone Creek and on Jacobus Creek, and the afsd. John James conv. same to Benjamin Blackleach 100 a. of the sd. land, and Benjamin Blackleach sold the same to Humphry Tilton which they then called *Broockhill* in 1687. Humphry Tilton in his will devised to his dau. Elenor the same land, and she afterwards m. William Cartor by whom she had the afsd. George Cartor. George Reed m. Mary, another dau. of the afsd. Humphry Tilton, and by him had a son Tilton Reed. Humphry Tilton by his last will devised to his son James lands which he formerly had from his maternal grandfather, John James, and immediately after the decease of his sd. father the afsd. James Tilton, son of Humphrey, d. leaving no issue, and his lands became the right of the afsd. George Cartor and the afsd. Tilton Reed, who were the only surviving heirs of the afsd. Humphry Tilton by his afsd. dau. The land that was the right of the afsd. James Tilton the son became the right of the afsd. George Cartor and Tilton Reed equally and the afsd. George Cartor makes sale of the afsd. 100 a.{KELR JS#28:87}

Unplaced

CARTER, (N), m. by 20 Feb 1737, Sarah, sister of Mary Ann Sudler, who made a will on 20 feb 1737, naming her sister Sarah Carter and the latter's dau. Mary Ann Carter. {MWB 21:899}

CARTER, (N), m. by 24 Oct ---, Sarah, dau. of James Ringgold of KI, QA Co. {MWB 22:161}

CARTER, (N), m. by 20 March 1748, Rebecca, dau. of James Evans of KI, QA Co. {MWB 27:415}

CARTER, BENJAMIN, of TA Co., died leaving a nuncupative will dated --- Feb 1733 and proved 23 April 1733. The exec. was David Robinson. The will was witnessed by Peter Stevens and Thomas Allin. {MWB 20:623}

CARTER, EDWARD, m. Isabella Hamilton 17 Nov 1709. {TAPE}

CARTER, ELIZABETH, m. William Camper on 11 June 1727. {TAPE}

CARTER, JOHN, d. by Dec 1751. On 18 Dec 1751 a valuation was made of the land of John Carter, son of John Carter, dec.; William Price, guardian. {QALR RTD:69}

CARTER, MARY, at November Court 1705 was charged that she had been was delivered of a bastard child. She named the father as John Burk. She was fined. {TAJU RF10:}

CARTER, MARY, of KI, QA Co., d. leaving a will dated 20 Jan 1768, and proved 15 June 1768. She named her cousin, Mary Richardson, dau. of Benjamin Richardson; her bro. John Carter; her sisters Martha Carter, Elizabeth and Sarah Price, and mentioned her mother. The exec. was John Carter. Martha Hutchings and Anne Wilson witnessed the will. {MWB 36:444}

CARTER, SAMUEL, was b. c1679, and d. 11 Feb 1708. {TAPE}
He was age c26 when he dep. in c1705 concerning a servant boy by him sold to John Alexander named Thomas Hughes, who was bound to Nathaniel Hughes of Liverpool, England for 5 years and after their arrival in Maryland --- 1704 he (Carter) sold Thomas Hughes for 5 years and did deliver him to John Alexander per indenture which was for 5 years. {TALR 9:348}

CARTER, WILLIAM, m. Margaret (N).
On 4 Nov 1742 Alice Collier, widow, gave to her dau., Margaret Carter, 100 a., part of *Bishop's Addition* and *Bishop's Outlett* on Corsica Creek. {QALR RTB:506}
William and Margaret were the parents of: MARY, b. 18 Feb 1732. {TAPE}

THE CARTY (CARTEY, CARTHY) FAMILY

1. **MAURICE CARTY**, innholder, d. by Dec 1726.

At March Court 1724, was ordered to answer charges of breaking the sabbath day.{KECR JS#22:68} At November Court 1724, he was charged with keeping a disorderly publick house. Wm. Murphy said that on Friday night he was at Maurice's house and played cards with Wm. Carman and lost some money and the sd. Maurice went Carman's halves.{KECR JS#22:46}

On 30 May 1724 Thomas French and his wife Ann conv. to Morres Carty of KE Co., innholder, 150 a. called *Malton*, formerly taken up by Robert Smith. {QALR IKB:250}

Maurice (Morris) Carty, innholder, d. leaving a will dated 2 Dec 1726 and proved 8 Dec 1726. To son Maurice he left a tract in KE Co. To dau. Margt. he left a tract called *Smith's Range* in QA Co. To dau. Susannah he left a tract in Quaker Neck, formerly belonging to John and Joseph Everett. To dau. Mary he left a tract at head of Chester, QA Co., formerly John French's. To servants Jonathan Whitworth and Mary his wife, and William Stanley, he left the remainder of their time. To wife Susannah, extx., he left the residue of estate.{MWB 19:27}

His estate was appraised on 26 March 1726 and on 12 May 1727, his widow Susannah, extx., and now wife of John Harris, filed the inventory.{MINV 12:11} A list of debts was filed 25 May 1728 by John Harris and his wife Susanna Harris (widow of the dec.).{MINV 13:99}

Maurice and Susanna were the parents of: MAURICE, bapt. 15 April 1724 at St. Paul's Parish; KATHERINE, m. William Pope; MARGARET,[3] m. Henry Ellars; and MARY, m. Alexander Kelley.{KELR JS#26:124}

2. **KATHERINE CARTY**, dau. of Maurice, m. William Pope. On 30 May 1748, William Pope, of KE Co. on Delaware, and his wife Katharine, conv. land to Alexander Kelley, of KE Co., MD. Whereas Maurice Cartey, of KE Co., dec., was seized of a tract formerly called *Sewell*, 249 a. and 156 perches; he d. intestate whereby the land became the right of his three daus., the afsd. Katharine, Margret the wife of Henry Ellars, and Mary, dec., lately the wife of the afsd. Alexander Kelley.{KELR JS#26:124}

---

[3] On 20 July 1731 a valuation was made of the plantation on the e. side of Elliott's Branch, belonging to Margaret Cartee, orphan of Morris Cartee of KE Co.; James Kersey, guardian. {QALR RTA:104}

Unplaced

CARTY (or CARTER), DENNIS, of KE Co., d. by 9 Feb 1755, when his estate was appraised by Augustine Boyer, Jr. and Frederick Hanson, and valued at £56.19.6. James Read and John Elgin signed as creditors. Charles Carty and Catherin Dunahow signed as next of kin. John Dunnahow and Rhoda Carter, execs., filed the undated inventory. {MINV 60:305}

CARTY, EDMUND, of KE Co., d. by 1 March 1762, when his estate was appraised by James McClean and John Browning, and valued at £367.13.6. Thomas and William Ringgold and B. Hands signed as creditors. No next of kin listed. Joseph Maynor, admin., filed the inventory on 20 May 1762.{MINV 77:204} On 4 Dec 1762 distribution of the estate was made by Joseph Magnor, admin.{BFD 3:161}

CARTEE, ELINOR, servant to Dennis Hopkins, at June Court 1698 was judged to be 17 years old. {TAJU AB8: 573}
    At November Court 1705 it was presented that Elinor Cartee, on 3 May 1705, at Lower Hundred on Kent Island, was delivered of a bastard child. She refused to name the father. {TAJU RF10:}

THE CARVILLE FAMILY

Refs.: A: Barnes; *Baltimore County Families, 1659-1759*, pp. 99-100.

1. (N) CARVILLE was the father of at least two sons{A}: ROBERT; and THOMAS.

2. ROBERT CARVILLE, son of (N), and bro. of Thomas, was b. c1636 and d. by 1705. He immigrated to MD c1669 with his wife Johanna, dau. of Alexander D'Hinozossa, who was the Dutch Governor of Delaware.{A}
    He held many public offices including that of Delegate to the Assembly from SM Co., 1674-75, 1676-82, and 1682-84. He never held any office after 1689 as he was a Roman Catholic.{A}
    Robert and Johanna were the parents of{A}: MARGARET, d. by 1721, m. Cecil Butler.

3. THOMAS CARVILLE, son of (N), and bro. of Robert (2), was transported to MD by 1669. He resided in SM and CV Cos. until 1682 when he moved to KE Co.{A}
    Thomas m. Susanna (N) by Nov 1702 when he and his wife were legatees in the will of John Eyres of CH Co.{MWB 11:362}

49

Thomas and his wife had one son{A}: JOHN, d. 1709.

3. JOHN CARVILLE, son of Thomas and Susanna, d. by 6 Sep 1709. He m. Mary, dau. of James and Susanna Phillips. After Carville's death she m. 2nd, Richard Smithers.{A}

Carville was a delegate to the Assembly from KE and CE Cos.{A}

He left a will dated 20 May 1709 and proved 6 Sep 1709. He named wife Mary, (extx., to have his dwell. plant., and Gunpowder Island during life); son John (to have all lands except those given to his mother); and four daus., unnamed (to have personalty and lands afsd. should son John die without issue).{MWB Part 2, 12:253}

The estate of John Carville was appraised on 30 Sep 1709 and the inventory was filed on 28 Oct 1709. Mary Carville, the extx., admin. the estate on 23 Feb 1710. His estate was admin. again on 30 Dec 1712. Richard Smithers, the exec., admin. the estate on 28 May 1713.{INAC 30:398, 32C:103 and 34:186, 225}

On 6 May 1718 his estate was admin. by Mary Smithers, wife of Richard Smithers. Payments were made to Samuell Sloats and John Johnson, James Harris, James Butler as exec. of Edward Warner, Benjamin Brain, Mr. Boardley, Mr. Macnemara and Thomas Carvil.{MDAD 1:147}

John Carville was the father of{A}: JOHN; AVARILLA, m. 31 Oct 1717, Edward Hall; SUSANNA, m. (N) Johnson, by whom she had a dau. Mary; PHOEBE, m. Charles Hynson; and BLANCHE, m. 1st, Parker Hall, and 2nd Luke Griffith.

4. Capt. JOHN CARVILLE, son of John and Mary, was b. c1705/7, as shown by the following depositions. On 22 Sep 1747, Mr. John Carvil, age c40, dep. regarding the bounds of a tract called *Great Oak*.{KELR JS#26:101} In Oct 1753, John Carvill, age c48, dep. regarding the bounds of a tract called *Cornwallis's Choice*.{KELR JS#28:38} On 19 Aug 1755, John Carville, age c49, dep. regarding the bounds of a tract called *Cornwallis Choice*.{KELR JS#28:160} On 4 Oct 1756, Captain John Carville, age c50, dep. regarding the bounds of a tract called *Great Oak*.{KELR JS#28:294} John Carvill, of KE Co., age 56, dep. on 30 Aug 1763.{KEEJ: Isabella Barclay}

John Carvill and Jane Harris were m. 25 Nov 1732.{KESP} She admin. the estate of James Harris on 11 March 1744.{MDAD 21:163}

On 30 March 1752, John Carvil, Gent., of KE Co., conv. to his son John Carvil, Jr., part of two tracts, 100 a.{KELR JS#27:106}

On 6 Sep 1762, John Carvill of KE Co., Gent., and his wife Jane, conv. to Jervis James of the same county, part of a tract called *Packerston*, 23 a.{KELR DD#1:162}

John Carvill, Jr., of KE Co., d. by 23 May 1771, when his estate was appraised by Bartus Wilkens and James Piner, and valued at £89.0.6.

Beale Bordley and Edward Loyd signed as creditors. Robert Cruckshank and W. Hynson, Jr. signed as next of kin. John Carvill, admin., filed the inventory on 6 Aug 1771.{MINV 106:388}

John and Jane (N) Carville were the parents of the following children, whose births were recorded at St. Paul's Parish{A}: JOHN, b. 9 Sep 1733; and MARY, b. 4 Aug 1736.

5. JOHN CARVILLE, son of John and Jane, was b. 9 Sep 1733.{KESP} He m. Anne (N), who survived him.

John Carvil, son of John, was a legatee in the distribution made 29 Jan 1759 of the estate of Richard Johnson of KE Co.{BFD 2:116}

He is probably Capt.(?) John Carvil, of KE Co., whose estate was appraised on 27 March 1773 by John Wickes and James Dunn, and valued at £859.10.8. Thomas Ringgold and James Anderson signed as creditors. J. C. Hynson and Richard Hynson signed as next of kin. Ann Carvill, admx., filed the inventory on 3 June 1773.{MINV 111:421}

His estate was appraised again on 1 April 1773 by John Wickes and James Dunn, and valued at £1042.11.1. Thomas Ringgold and Morgan & Slubey signed as creditors. Thomas Hynson and Richard Hynson signed as next of kin. Ann Carvil, admx., filed the inventory on 3 June 1773.{MINV 114:237}

His estate was again appraised and valued at £8.16.1. No creditors or next of kin listed. Ann Carvill, admx., filed the inventory cont. a list of debts on 11 May 1774.{MINV 115:414}

On 3 March 1774 the estate was appraised by John Wickes and James Dunn, and valued at £136.3.0. Morgan & Slubey and Thomas Ringgold signed as creditors. J. C. Hanson and Richard Hynson signed as next of kin. Ann Carvill, admx., filed the inventory on 11 May 1774.{MINV 115:415}

The estate of John Carvill, Jr., of KE Co., was appraised and valued at £2.2.10. No creditors or next of kin listed. Ann Carvill, admx., filed the inventory cont. a list of debts on 11 May 1774.{MINV 115:417}

On 29 Aug 1774 his estate was again appraised by John Wickes and James Dunn, and valued at £22.0.5. Morgan & Slubey and Thomas Ringgold signed as creditors. No next of kin listed. Ann Carvil, admx., filed the inventory on 18 Oct 1774.{MINV 118:25}

His estate was again appraised and valued at £2.0.0. No creditors listed or next of kin listed. Ann Carvell, admx., filed the inventory cont. a list of debts on 18 Oct 1774.{MINV 118:253}

THE CHANCELLOR FAMILY

1. WILLIAM CHANCELLOR, of the City of Philadelphia, sail maker, and his wife Mary, on 18 Oct 1737 conv. 800 a. *Town Relief* to Charles Hynson of the Town of Chester, merchant. The land was devised by

Edward Scott in his will dated 28 Oct 1725 to his dau. Mary, wife of William Chancellor.{KELR JS#18:491}

William and Mary were the parents of: WILLIAM; and ELIZABETH.

2. WILLIAM CHANCELLER, (practitioner of physick) of the City of Philadelphia, heir of William Chanceller and his wife Mary, late of the same place, dec., and Abraham Stedman and his wife Elizabeth, extx. of the sd. William Chanceller, on 29 July 1756, conv. to James Roberts of KE Co., part of a tract called *Town Relief*, 200 a. Salome, wife of afsd. William Chanceller, acknowledged the indenture.
{KELR JS#28:271}

3. ELIZABETH CHANCELOR, dau. of William Chancellor, on 11 July 1748 was conv. certain land by Francina Hynson of KE Co., widow and devisees of Charles Hynson, late of the same county, merchant, dec. The deed stated that: Whereas in and by a certain indenture dated 18 Oct 1737 made between sd. William Chancellor and his wife Mary confirmed to Charles Hynson 600 a. being the residue of a tract called *Town Reliefe* over and above the 200 a. in the same indenture mentioned to have been devised to George Lumley, the whole tract cont. 800 a.{KELR JS#26:128}

THE CHANDLER FAMILY

1. THOMAS CHANDLER, was b. c1683, as shown by the following deposition. On 24 March 1743, Thomas Chandler, age c60, dep. regarding the bounds of a tract called *Intermixt*.{KELR JS#25:97}

Thomas Chandler, Sr. d. 11 March 1745/6.{KESH}

Thomas m. Mary (N), by whom he had at least one son: THOMAS, Jr., b. 14 July 1712.{KESH}

2. THOMAS CHANDLER, Jr., son of Thomas and Mary, was b. 14 July 1712.{KESH} He m. Mary (N).

Thomas Chandler, of KE Co., d. leaving a will dated 13 Sep 1762 and proved 20 Oct 1762. The heirs named were eldest son Michael to whom was left part of the tract called *Ray Cote*, son Thomas, son Nathaniel, and dau. Hannah to whom was devised the land on Steel Pone called *The Grance*. The exec. was son Thomas Chandler. The will was witnessed by John Crow, Andrew Toalson, and Jonas Crow.{MWB 31:743}

On 1 Nov 1762 his estate was appraised by Joseph Rasin and Abraham Rasin, and valued at £606.5.8. John Duyer and Jane Medford signed as creditors. Michael Chandler and Nathaniel Chandler signed as next of kin. Thomas Chandler, exec., filed the inventory on 14 Dec 1762.{MINV 79:432}

His estate was again appraised and valued at £186.0.3. No creditors listed or next of kin listed. Thomas Chandler, exec., filed the inventory cont. a list of debts on 22 Dec 1762.{MINV 79:425}

On 1 Dec 1763 his estate was appraised by Joseph Rasin and Abraham Rasin, and valued at £223.9.8. John Duyer and Thomas Redford signed as creditors. Michael Chandler and Nathaniel Chandler signed as next of kin. Thomas Chandler, exec., filed the inventory on 14 Jan 1764.{MINV 82:252}

On 23 Dec 1767 distribution of the estate was made by Thomas Chandler, exec. Legatees were Nathaniel and Hannah Chandler. {BFD 5:76}

Thomas and Mary were the parents of the following children, whose births are recorded in Shrewsbury Parish: MICHAL, b. 27 Jan 1734; PHEBE, b. 2 May 1736; THOMAS, b. 19 Oct 1738; ANN, b. 30 Jan 1740; MARY (NB: Her mother was named as Rachel), b. 23 Nov 1742;[4] NATHANIEL, b. 26 Dec 1744; SARAH, b. 1 March 1747; and HANNAH, b. 26 Sep 1749.

3. MICHAEL CHANDLER, son of Thomas and Mary, was b. 27 Jan 1734.{KESH} He m. Tapenah (N).

Michael Chandler, of KE Co., d. by 21 May 1772, when his estate was appraised by Joseph Rasin and John Dyer, and valued at £202.14.1. Donaldson Yates and Abraham Cannell signed as creditors. Thomas Chandler and Nathaniel Chandler signed as next of kin. Tahponah Chandler, admin., filed the inventory on 9 Aug 1772.{MINV 110:275}

On 27 March 1773 his estate was appraised by John Dyer and Joseph Rasin, and valued at £44.5.6. Donaldson Yeates and Isaac Camull (?) signed as creditors. Thomas Chandler and Nathaniel

---

[4] She may be the Mary Chandler who was presented at August 1764 Court for having committed fornication and begetting a base born child. She was fined £3 and ordered to give security to keep the county from any charge that might accrue by means of the afsd. bastard child called Nathaniel.{KECR DD#1:52A}

At August Court 1766 it was presented that Mary Chandler, spinster, on 1 March 1765, committed fornication and begot a base born child. She was fined £3 and ordered that she give security to indemnify the county from any charge that might accrue by means of her bastard child called Spencer.{KECR DD#1:82B}

At November Court 1771 it was presented that Mary Chandler committed fornication and begot a base born child. Fined £3.{KECR DD#1:141B}

Chandler signed as next of kin. Tahpenah Chandler, admx., filed the inventory on 17 June 1773.{MINV 114:196}

Michael had at least one son: THOMAS, named in the will of his uncle Nathaniel Chandler.

4. NATHANIEL CHANDLER, son of Thomas and Mary, was b. 26 Dec 1744.{KESH}

Nath'l. Chandler, of KE Co., d. leaving a will dated 20 July 1773 and proved 4 Aug 1773. The heirs named were bro. Thomas Chandler, sister Sarah Chandler and nephew Thomas Chandler, son of bro. Michael Chandler. The exec. was bro.-in-law, Marmaduke Medford. The will was witnessed by Abraham Rasin, Macall Medford, and Thomas Rasin.{MWB 39:491}

On 10 Aug 1773 his estate was appraised by Joseph Rasin and John Duyer, and valued at £81.1.10. Donaldson Yeates and Isaac Cannell signed as creditors. Thomas Chandler and Phebe Gale signed as next of kin. Marmaduke Medford, exec., filed the inventory on 18 Nov 1773.{MINV 114:221}

On 9 May 1775 his estate was appraised and valued at £475.11.9. Donaldson Yates and Jerom Cannel (admin. of A. Cannell) signed as creditors. Thomas Chandler and Charles Gale signed as next of kin. Marmaduke Medford, exec., filed the inventory on 15 May 1775. {MINV 119:332}

His estate was appraised again and valued at £20.2.6. No creditors listed or next of kin listed. Marmaduke Medford, exec., filed the inventory cont. a list of debts on 15 May 1775.{MINV 119:360}

Unplaced

CHANDLER, ABEL, and wife Hannah, on 31 Dec 1763, were conv. by William Beck of KE Co., a tract called *Addition to Ki[lli]ngsworthmoor* near Chester River, 50 a., and part of *Partnership*, 11½ a.{KELR DD#1:349}

CHANDLER, JANE, spinster, at March Court 1768, was presented on 1 Jan 1766 for committing fornication and begetting a base born child. She was fined 30 s.{KECR DD#1:99A}

At November Court 1769, it was presented that Isaac Parsons, on 1 March 1766, committed fornication with Jane Chandler and begot a base born child. He was fined £3.{KECR DD#1:112A}

CHANDLER, JOHN, Jr., d. by 14 Feb 1714, when his estate was admin.{INAC 36B:244}

CHANDLER, JOHN, was bur. 13 March 1716.{KESP}

THE CHRISFIELD FAMILY

1. **PHILIP CHRISFIELD**, d. by 6 March 1740. He m. Rosamond Burgan, dau. of Philip Burgan.{MWB Part 2 12:129}

On 24 March 1739 Philip, and his wife Rossamond of KE Co., conv. to John Burgan, Sr., a tract called *Ivingo*, being that part of the tract which the same Phillip Chrisfield and Rossamond his wife were entitled to by virtue of the last will of Phillip Burgan, late of KE Co., dec.{KELR JS#22:555}

Philip Chrisfield d. leaving a will dated 3 Jan 1740 and proved 6 March 1740. He named sons Philip and Richard (to have 1 s. each), son John (to have 60 a. called *Jones Neglect* lying next to land of Daniel Perkins; should he die to pass to his bro. Arthur), son Arthur, and wife Rosamond (to have residue of estate). The exec. was not named. {MWB 22:387}

On 1 Jan 1742/3, Rosamond Christfield, of QA Co., let to George Harrington of KE Co., her former dwell. plant.{KELR JS#24:332} On 27 Nov 1745, Rosamond Christfield, late Smith, of KE Co., widow, conv. to John Gleaves of the afsd. place, part of a tract called *Broad Neck* on Morgans Creek.{KELR JS#25:321}

Phillip and Rosamond Chrisfield were the parents of: PHILIP; RICHARD; JOHN; ARTHUR; and ABSALOM (he was b. 17 Nov 1740{KESH}).

2. **JOHN CHRISFIELD**, probably son of Philip, and wife Ellinor were the parents of: MARY, b. 30 da., 6 mo., 1759; SARAH, b. 25 da., 10 mo., 1761; JOHN, b. 25 da., 5 mo., 1764; and ARTHUR, b. 13 da., 10 mo., 1768.{KESH}

3. **ARTHUR CHRISFIELD**, son of Philip and Rosamond, was named by Sarah Sullivan, at March Court 1759, as the father of her child. {KECR JS#25:221A, 222B}

Arthur Christfield, of KE Co., d. leaving a will proved 14 May 1767. The heir named was wife Ann Christfield. The will was witnessed by Jno. Ambrose and Mary Crouch.{MWB 35:397}

On 11 June 1767, the estate of Anton (or Arthur) Chrisfield was appraised by Edward Dyer, Sr. and John Shield, and valued at £47.11.1. Thomas Smyth and Morgan & Slubey signed as creditors. John Christfield and Abraham Chrisfield signed as next of kin. Ann Christfield, extx., filed the inventory on 1 Oct 1767.{MINV 95:77}

On 18 March 1769 distribution of the estate was made by Hans Blackiston and his wife Anne Blackiston, execs. Distribution was made to the widow (unnamed).{BFD 5:175}

CHRISFIELD, BENJAMIN, at June Court 1761, was presented for having committed fornication with Sarah Boyer (q.v.) and begetting a base born child. He was fined 30 s.

CHRISFIELD, EDWARD, d. in the field while reaping at William Harris's 4 July 1699.{KESP}

THE CHRISTIAN FAMILY

1. LAWRENCE CHRISTIAN, immigrated in 1665.{MPL 9:489} On 14 Aug 1683, John Larkin, and Catharine his wife, conv. to Laurance Christian of CE Co. a parcel called *Worton* in CE Co., now in KE Co., 600 a.{KELR JS#18:94}
   Lawrence was the father of: THOMAS.

2. THOMAS CHRISTIAN, son of Lawrence, and Thomas' wife Mary, on 24 Aug 1725, conv. to their son and dau. Thomas Boyer and his wife Anne, part of a tract called *Morton (Worton?)*, on Herring Branch, 60 a. {KELR JS#W:482 (462)}
   Thomas Christian, yeoman, d. leaving a will dated 24 Nov 1728 and proved 3 Jan 1728. To wife Mary, he left ⅓ of his estate; to son Thomas, he left part of dwell. plant; to son James he left plant. whereon William Goodson now lives, including 200 a. of dwell. plant. afsd. and personalty; to son-in-law John Yorkson called *Round Stone*; to son-in-law Hugh Terry, daus. Elizabeth, Rebecca and Ann, personalty. To children, viz., Thomas, James, Rachell, and Mary, he left residue of personalty. Execs. were wife and Thomas Yorkson.{MWB 19:555}
   His estate was inv. on 15 Jan 1729 and 30 Nov 1734. Next of kin were August Boyer and John Yorkson. Execs. Mary Gale and Thomas Yorkson filed the inventory on 30 Nov 1734.{MINV 20:530}
   Thomas and Mary were the parents of: THOMAS; JAMES; ELIZABETH; REBECCA; ANNE, m. by 24 Aug 1725, Thomas Boyer; JAMES; RACHEL; MARY; and SARAH, m. by 9 Nov 1734, Hugh Terry (q.v.).

3. THOMAS CHRISTIAN, late of KE Co., but now of CE Co., son of Thomas, on 14 March 1742, conv. to Hugh Terry of CE Co., a tract called *Moreton*, 600 a., and 97 a. of a tract called *Larkins Addition* sd. to contain 800 a.{KELR JS#24:158}

4. JAMES CHRISTIAN, son of Thomas, and James' wife Rachel, on 30 April 1742, conv. to William Ellis of CE Co., part of a tract at the head

of Sassafrass River whereon Thomas Christian, father of the sd. James lately dwelt called *Worton*, 200 a., devised to James Christian by the last will of Thomas Christian. {KELR JS#23:399}

Unplaced

CHRISTIAN, CHRISTIAN, and Margrett Wessells were m. 16 April 1707.{KESP} Christian d. by 24 Aug 1709 when his estate was admin.{INAC 30:200} It was admin. again on 22 Nov 1710 by Elisabeth Ladimore, the admx.{INAC 32B:252}

THE CHURCH FAMILY

1. THOMAS CHURCH was bur. 6 June 1709.{KESP} He m. Mary (N) who m. 2nd, William Pott.
   Thomas left a will dated 26 May 1709 and proved 1 Aug 1709. He named eldest son Philemon to have dwell. plant. and lands; dau. Tabitha Pearce (Church) to have all lands on s. side of Worton Creek; and wife Mary, extx., to have personal estate.{MWB Part 2, 12:164}
   Thomas' estate was inv. on 29 Sep 1709. Named as next of kin was William Pearce.{INAC 30:377} His estate was admin. on 29 June 1711 by the extx., Mary Pott, wife of William Pott.{INAC 32C:17}
   On 22 June 1720, Gidn. Pearce, Michll. Hackett and William Graves were bound to Philemon Church and Tabitha Church, orphans of Thomas Church, to pay each £100, their legacy by the will of William Pott, when they are of age.{KEBI JS#W:72B, 73A}
   Thomas Church was the father of: PHILEMON; and TABITHA, m. (N) Pearce.

2. PHILEMON CHURCH, son of Thomas, and Philemon's wife Katherine, on 14 March 1726 conv. to Gideon Pearce, a tract called *The Exchange*, on Wortons Creek, 100 a.{KELR JS#W:526} On 21 April 1726, Philemon and wife Katharine of KE Co., conv. to Gideon Pearce of the same county, a tract called *St. Andrews Crosse*, 350 a.{KELR JS#W:524}
   At August Court 1728, Philemon Church, Shrewsbury Parish, labourer, was charged with stealing on 10 May 1727 a barrow hog worth 200 lbs. of tob. belonging to John Wrightson. He was pardoned by the Governor.{KECR JS#22:18}

Unplaced

CHURCH, SAMUEL, of KE Co., d. leaving a will dated 28 Nov 1758 and proved 12 Dec 1758. Mentioned were wife Margaret; children

Samuel, William, Sarah, and Elizabeth; and sister Jane, wife of Thomas Broowick, paper merchant, on Ludgate Hill, London. The execs. were Margaret Church and McGeorge Garnett, Sr. The will was witnessed by Thos. Bourk, Daniell Norris, and George Wm. Forrester.{MWB 30:679}

On 26 April 1759 his estate was appraised by Richard Willson and Nicholas Smith, and valued at £647.5.9. William Rasin and James Louttit signed as creditors. No next of kin listed. Margaret Church, extx., filed the inventory on 17 Nov 1759.{MINV 69:49}

His estate was again appraised and valued at £200.17.0. Margaret Church, extx., filed the inventory cont. a list of debts on 1 April 1763.{MINV 80:221}

His estate was again appraised and valued at £438.12.1. No creditors listed. Margaret Church, extx., filed the inventory cont. a list of debts on 1 April 1763.{MINV 80:223}

On 11 Feb 1760, when his estate was appraised by Richard Willson and Nicholas Smith, and valued at £2.17.6. James McLachlan and Samuel Sloss signed as creditors. Margaret Church, extx., filed the inventory on 1 April 1763.{MINV 80:190}

On 5 April 1763 distribution of the estate was made by Margaret Church, acting extx.{BFD 3:179}

Widow Margaret may be the Margaret Church charged at the June Court 1761 with having committed fornication and begotten a base born child. She was fined £3.{KECR DD#1:9A}

THE DENNIS CLARK FAMILY

1. DENNIS CLARK, of KE Co., was bur. 27 Dec 1716. He m. Mary (N) who m. as her 2nd husband, Samuel Clark.

Dennis Clark, shoemaker, and wife Mary, on 19 June 1716, conv. to William Pope, 107 a., part of a tract called *Riser(?)*.{KELR BC#1:142}

On 18 Dec 1716 Dennis Clarke of KE Co., and his wife Mary, conv. to William Dicas of the same county, a parcel of land called *Kemps*, 320 a., which Dennis Clarke purchased of Griffith Jones.{KELR BC#1:169}

Dennis Clark was bur. 27 Dec 1716.{KESP} He d. leaving a will dated 11 Dec 1716 and proved 24 Jan 1716. He named dau. Mary Wilde (to have personalty and unsold portion of *Kemp's Beginning* on Muddy Creek); dau. Rebecca (to have 100 a. of *Viana* near head of Chester River); son William (to have 150 a., upper part of *Viana*); daus. Mary and Sarah (to have 100 a. each of sd. tract, *Viana*.); son Dennis (to have upper part of dwell. plant.); wife Mary, extx. (to have ⅓ of dwell. plant. during life; also ⅓ personal estate, remaining part to six youngest children); son John (to have remaining part of dwell. plant. at age 21 years. To grandson John Wilde, personalty. Testator states that having purchased 150 a. of Cornelius Comegys Sr., and not having had the full complement, sd. Cornelius bequeathed to him a piece of the same tract called *The Release*); Edw. Comegys (to have 20s. for writing will).{MWB 14:350}

The estate was inv. on 31 May 1717; listed as next of kin were William True (Trew) and John True (Trew).{INAC 37B:226} It was admin. on 2 July 1717 by extx.: Mary Clarke.{INAC 39B:55}

On 25 Feb 1719, his estate was admin. by Mary Clark, now wife of Samuell Clark.{MDAD 3:39} On 9 May 1719 his estate was admin. by Mary Clerk, wife of Samuel Clerk.{MDAD 2:257}

On 15 Jan 1721, his estate was admin. again by Mary Clark, now wife of Samuell Clark. Legatees were James Smith, John Wild, paid to his mother Mary Delahuntre.{MDAD 4:151}

Dennis Clarke was the father of: MARY, m. 30 July 1714 Joseph (or John) Wilde by whom she had a son John b. 27 Jan 1714 {KESP}; REBECCA, m. 1st, James Smith, and 2nd, Robert Farrell (q.v.); WILLIAM; MARTHA, m. John Alley (q.v.); SARAH, m. Joseph Mason; DENNIS; and JOHN.

2. WILLIAM CLARK, son of Dennis, may be the William, who was b. c1704 and was living as late as 1750. At age c45, on 15 March 1749, he dep. regarding the bounds of a tract called *Sewell* alias *Utrick*. {KELR JS#26:243}

On 11 June 1750, William Clark age c47, dep. regarding the bounds of a tract called *Tulleys Fancy*.{KELR JS#26:414}

William Clark, son of Dennis, m. Rachel (N). In 1725 William Clark of KE Co., and his wife Rachel, gave 150 a. to his sisters, Martha Clark and Sarah Clark.{KELR JS#W:408}

On 7 March 1728/9, William and wife Rachel, and James Smith and wife Rebecca, conv. to William Smithers of the same county, a tract called *Viena*, 31 a.{KELR JS#X:335}

At November Court 1729, it was ordered that Rachel Clarke wife of William Clarke give security for her appearance in court.{KECR JS#WK:98}

On 14 Jan 1734, William Clark of KE Co., and his wife Rachel, conv. to Joseph Mason of the same county, carpenter, ½ of the tract called *Clarks Conveniency* on Philips Creek, 77 a.{KELR JS#18:91}

On 3 June 1751, William Clark of KE Co., and his wife Rachel, conv. to John Woodall of the same county, a tract called *Viana*, 128 a.{KELR JS#27:8}

On 18 Aug 1763, William Clark of KE Co., and his wife Rachel, and Thomas Ringgold of Chester, merchant, conv. to John Woodall of the same county, part of a tract called *Viana*, 128 a.{KELR DD#1:400}

William Clark, of KE Co., d. leaving a will dated 26 July 1765 and proved 9 Sep 1765. Mentioned were wife Rachel; children William, Mary Woodall, Sarah Cloud, Mathew (dau.) Clark, Rachel Clark, and

John and Charles Clark; and grandchildren, sons and daus. of Charles Clark, dec. Youngest daus. are Mathew and Rachel. The tracts *Clark's Addition* and *Ellise's Chance* were mentioned. The extx. was wife Rachel Clark. The will was witnessed by Wm. and George Blackiston, and John Beck.{MWB 33:405}

His estate was appraised by William Blackiston and John Blackiston, and valued at £212.10.0. Frances Meredith and George Blackiston signed as creditors. John Clarke and Mathias Clarke signed as next of kin. Rachel Clarke, extx., filed the inventory on 19 Nov 1766.{MINV 90:359}

William Clark, of KE Co., d. before 25 Jan 1767, when distribution of the estate was made by Mrs. Rachell Clark, extx., to the widow and the two youngest children Mathew and Rachel. The legatees were widow (accountant), William Clark, Mary Woodall, Sarah Cloud, Mathew Clark, and Rachel Clark.{BFD 5:77}

William Clark was the father of: WILLIAM; MARY, m. (N) Woodall; SARAH, m. (N) Cloud (or Clovos); MARTHA (or MATHEW), m. Abraham Parsons; RACHEL, m. Benjamin Fowler; JOHN and CHARLES (d. by 1767).

3. DENNIS CLARK, son of Dennis, and his wife Mary were the parents of: REBECCA, b. Nov 1719.{KESP}

4. JOHN CLARK, son of William (2) and Rachel, of KE Co., d. in his youth leaving a will dated 27 Sep 1770 and proved 28 Oct 1770. Mentioned were mother; sister Rachel, m. to Benjamin Fowler; sister Martha Parsons; and sister Sara Clovos. The will was witnessed by James Hurlock, James Garlan, and Francis Meredith.{MWB 38:90}

On 2 Dec 1771, his estate was appraised by William Blackiston and Gilbert Falconer, and valued at £229.3.5. Benjamin Fowler, Thomas Gilpin and Thomas Gilpin & Co. signed as creditors. Benjamin Fowler for self and wife and Abraham Parsons for self and wife signed as next of kin. William Clark, of QA Co., admin., filed the inventory on 12 Dec 1771.{MINV 107:212}

A list of debts was appraised and valued at £0.8.8. William Clark, admin., filed the list of debts on 9 Aug 1774.{MINV 116:264}

5. CHARLES CLARK, son of William (2) and Rachel, d. by Sep 1762.

On 1 Sep 1762, his estate was appraised by John Falconer (also John Falconah) and John Watson, and valued at £123.12.5. Thomas Gilpin signed as creditor. William Clark and John Clerk signed as next of kin. Rachele Clark, admx., filed the inventory on 19 March 1763. {MINV 80:187} On 18 Feb 1764 distribution of the estate was made by Rachel Clark, admx.{BFD 4:84}

Charles Clark was the father of children, mentioned in the will of his father William.

THE GEORGE CLARK (GLAZIER) FAMILY

1. GEORGE CLARK, glazier and plummer, and wife Mary, on 21 Jan 1737, conv. to James Read of the county afsd., whitesmith, 1/8 of a lot in Chester Town, No. 60.{KELR JS#18:550}

On 21 Sep 1740, George Clark, of KE Co., glazier, and his wife Mary, conv. to Samuel Read, of DO Co., joyner, Lot No. 60 in Chester Town.{KELR JS#23:51}

On 17 Feb 1748, George Clarke, of KE Co., glaysier, conv. to Daniel Clarke of the same place, glaysier, son of the afsd. George Clarke, Lot No. 60 in Chester Town.{KELR JS#26:184}

George Clark, of KE Co., d. leaving a will dated 20 Aug 1752 and proved April 1756. His children, Daniel and William, were named. The will was witnessed by George Shervin, Christopher Bateman, and St. Leager James.{MWB 30:62}

On 28 June 1756 his estate was appraised by James Cann and James Hastings, and valued at £24.6.0. Kinum Wroth signed as creditor. D. Clarke signed as next of kin. Jerom Conell and George Skirvin, admins., filed the inventory on 11 Jan 1757.{MINV 62:228}

George Clark and wife Mary were the parents of: DANIEL; JOSHUA FOSTER, b. 4 Jan 1729-30; MARTHA, b. 21 Sep 1738; THOMAS, b. 1 April 1741; and WILLIAM.

2. DANIEL CLARK, son of George and Mary, m. Elizabeth (N).

Jeremiah Burchinall and his wife Ann made oath that on 30 Jan 1731 Daniel Clark being at the dwelling house of the sd. Jeremiah Burchnall had part of the helix of his left ear bitt off by a mare. 4 July 1739.{KEBI JS#18:248}

At March Court 1748, it was presented that Daniel Clark of St. Paul's Parish, glazier, assaulted Catharine Hammond. He was fined 5 s. {KECR JS#25:31A}

Daniel Clark, a hatter, of Chester Town, on 17 July 1751, he conv. to Samuel Massey, of QA Co., innholder, ¼ of Lot No. 66 in Chester Town. His wife Elizabeth consented.{KELR JS#27:66}

At August Court 1758, it was presented that Daniel Clark, glazier, in Nov 1757, assaulted John Jones. He was fined 10 s.{KECR JS#25:196A}

THE GEORGE CLARK (PLANTER) FAMILY

1. **GEORGE CLARK**, d. by 28 Feb 1767. He m. Elizabeth (N) who m. 2nd, Woolman Spencer.

At November Court 1745, he was presented for dealing with Joseph Nicholson's Negro, Felix, to the value of 9 s. The case was continued to the next court.{KECR JS#24:234, 245}

At June Court 1746, he was charged with stealing two bushels of Indian corn of Samuel Massey. On 1 Nov 1745 he was ordered to stand in the pillory for ½ hour and receive 25 lashes.{KECR JS#24:283}

George Clark, of KE Co., d. leaving a will dated 18 Dec 1766 and proved 28 Feb 1767. The heirs named were wife Elizabeth Clark and her children sons George, John, Thomas, and James Clark. The extx. was wife. The will was witnessed by Mathew Hazell and Wm. Dille.{MWB 35:161}

George Clark's estate was appraised by George Pressbury and James Ringgold, and valued at £115.4.6. Thomas Ringgold & Co. signed as creditors. Elisabeth Yardsley and John Clark signed as next of kin. Woolman Spencer and his wife, Elisabeth Spencer, execs., filed the inventory on 3 April 1769.{MINV 98:285B}

A list of debts was appraised again and valued at £7.7.16. Woolman Spencer and Elisabeth Spencer, execs., filed the list on 29 Sep 1770. {MINV 104:106}

On 29 Sep 1770 distribution of the estate was made by Elisabeth Spencer, extx., wife of Woolman Spencer, extx., to wife Elisabeth and her children. Legatees were George Clark, Thomas Clark, and James Clark.{BFD 6:7}

George Clark, and wife Elizabeth were the parents of: GEORGE; JOHN; THOMAS; and JAMES.

THE JOHN CLARK FAMILY

1. **JOHN CLARKE**, yeoman, d. leaving a will proved 8 Jan 1725/6. He named: sons Henry and John (to have real estate; four daus. Mary, Jane, Margrett and Elinor (to have residue of personal estate); dau. Mary, wife of William Ellis; elder son Henry to be bound as apprentice to John Aurdell. Execs. were John Aurdell and Roger Hicks.{MWB 18:484}

On 2 May 1726 his estate was appraised by John Rogers and William Simcock. Creditor was Edward Michall. Next of kin were Thomas Jones and Jane Jones. Mary Clark, accountant, filed the inventory on 30 Aug 1726.{MINV 11:544} An additional inventory was filed on 22 April 1727. John Rogers and William Simcoke were appraisers.{MINV 12:106}

John Clark was the father of: HENRY; JOHN; MARY, m. William Ellis; JANE; MARGARET; and ELEANOR.

2. HENRY CLARK, son of John, was living on 23 Jan 1758, when he and wife Esabella, conv. land to John Falconar of the same place. Whereas sd. Henry with his bro. John Clarke joined in a deed of conveyance to sd. John Falconar for part of a tract called *London Bridge*, 50 a. which since has been found to be vacant and taken up by Daniel Massy and again conv. to sd. Henry.{KELR JS#28:424}

3. JOHN CLARK, son of John, d. by 8 May 1749, when his estate was appraised by Daniell Bryan and C. Comegys, and valued at £76.5.1. Daniell Bryan and Daniell Massy signed as creditors. George Vansant, Jr. and Mary McDougall signed as next of kin. Henry Clarke, admin., filed the inventory on 20 June 1749.{MINV 41:25}

Unplaced

CLARK, ALEXANDER d. before 10 Oct 1713 when his sons John Clark and William Clarke his bro., of KE Co., yeomen, conv. to William Blay, part of a tract called *Cocks Stall*, being all the land that their father Alexander Clarke claimed a right to and lived on when he d., on the s. side of Sassafras River, 50 a.{KELR JSN:347}

CLARK, BENJAMIN, and Jane Gray were m. 1729.{KESP}
    Benjamin Clarke d. by 9 Aug 1744, when his estate was appraised by John Carvill and Paul Whiche, and valued at £92.16.0. Hugh Campbell and James Anderson signed as creditors. No next of kin listed. Jane Clark, admx./extx., filed the inventory on 5 Jan 1744. {MINV 30:186}
    Benjamin and Jane had at least one son: JOHN; on 21 Aug 1744 as John Clark, son of Benjamin Clark, dec., an orphan, was bound to Robert White, until age 21.{KEBI JS#20:134} On 21 June 1745 John Clark, orphan, was bound to Thomas Warcope, barber, as an apprentice, until age 21, to the trade of a barber.{KEBI JS#20:191}

CLARK, DANIEL, at March Court 1744, was charged on 1 March 1744, with assaulting John Atkins. He was fined 5 s.{KECR JS#24:192}

CLARK, ELIZABETH, of Shrewsbury Parish, spinster, at November Court 1726, was found guilty of committing fornication on 1 Oct 1725 and begetting a bastard child; she was fined 30 s. She declared that the father of her base born child was Jacob Vanbeber of CE Co. {KECR JS#22:228}

On 27 April 1733, Elizabeth Bond, wife of James Bond of KE Co., formerly known as Elizabeth Clarke, dep. that about 5 years earlier, last Feb, Patrick Fitzgarroll of St. Paul's Parish of the afsd. county had carnal knowledge of her body and begot a bastard child. He was fined 30 s. {KECR JS#WK:386}

CLARK, ELIZABETH, at August Court 1750, was presented that on 1 June 1749, she committed fornication and begot a bastard child. She was fined 30 s. {KECR JS#25:62B}

CLARK, GEORGE, and Jane (N) were the parents of: JAMES, bapt. 12 May 171-; and GEORGE, b. 22 Jan 1712. {KESP}

CLARK, GEORGE, was bur. 27 Nov 1716. {KESP}

CLARK, GILBERT, of SM Co., patented *Killins Worth More*, 500 a., on 1 Oct 1683. {MPL 25:69}

CLARKE, HENRY, was transported in 1674. {MPL 15:353}

CLARK, HENRY (HENERY), and Sarah (N) were the parents of: ELIZABETH, bapt. 16 June 1699. {KESP}

CLARK, JAMES, of St. Paul's Parish, weaver, at November Court 1726, was found guilty of assaulting Bartholomew Collins on 26 Sep 1726 and was fined 50 lbs. of tob. {KECR JS#22:219}

CLARK, JOHN, of CE Co., on 6 April 1706, assigned to William Taylor all his right to a parcel of land called *Stand Off* formerly taken up by his father, 33⅓ a. near the head of the Mill Branch and near the head of Sassafras River. {KELR JSN:161}

CLARK, JOHN, d. leaving a will dated 2 March 1713 and proved 29 June 1718. To John Reed and Robert Randall, he left personalty. The exec. was Richard Campbell. {MWB 14:637}
His estate was inv. on 30 July 1718 and again on 4 Sep 1719. {MINV 2:226 and 3:168}
On 5 Dec 1719, his estate was admin. by George Dashiel. {MDAD 3:40}

CLARK, JOHN, at June Court 1740, was charged that on 10 June 1740, he assaulted Thomas Chin. He was fined £5. {KECR JS#23:88}
At November Court 1742, it was presented that John Clark, on 1 Jan 1741, and often before and since, committed fornication with Mary Marcey and begot a bastard child. He was fined 30 s. {KECR JS#24:72}

His estate was appraised by Benjamin Blaxton and Benjamin Hazel, and valued at £150.19.5. William White signed as creditor. Thomas Clark signed as next of kin. Ann Clark, admx., filed the inventory on 24 March 1758.{MINV 65:133}

CLARKE, JOHN, at August Court 1759, was presented that on 10 June 1759 he assaulted Hugh Hall. He was fined 2 s., 6 pence.{KECR JS#25:228B}

CLARK, MARY, was bapt. 25 Sep 1717.{KESP}

CLARK, MARY, spinster, at August Court 1745, was charged that on 1 June 1744, and at diverse times as well before as since, she committed fornication and begot a bastard child. She was fined 30 s.{KECR JS#24:210}
    At March Court 1746, was presented that on 1 Aug 1745, and at diverse times as well before as since, she committed fornication and begot a bastard child. She was fined 30 s.{KECR JS#24:341}
    On 6 March 1754, Mary Clark was convicted of having been delivered of a base born child begotten by Richard Earle. She was fined 30 s.{KECR JS#25:206A}
    At November Court 1756, Mary Clark confessed to fornication but refused to name the father; she was fined £3.{KECR JS#25:166A}
    In April 1758 Mary Clark confessed to committing fornication and named the father. She was fined 30 s. John Trew entered into security to pay the fine and fees.{KECR JS#25:193A}
    Mary Clarke, white woman, was charged on 10 June 1764 with committing fornication with a Negro man and begetting a base born child which was delivered on 10 Feb 1765. She was ordered into seven years of servitude, sold to Joseph Nicholson, Jr., and the child, called Hannah, to serve until age 31.{KECR DD#1:58A}

CLARK, PATRICK, was the victim of a plot by Walter Freestone. At August Court 1728, Freestone was charged with intended murder against Patrick Clark.{KECR JS#22:26}
    Patrick Clarke, of St. Paul's Parish, blacksmith, at August Court 1734, was found guilty of assaulting William Graves on 21 March 1733. He was fined 2 s., 6 pence.{KECR JS#WK:537}

CLARK, PETER, d. by 26 Aug 1698.{INAC 16:136}

CLARKE, REBECCAH, spinster, at March Court 1764, was charged that on 10 Nov 1762, she committed fornication and begot a base born child. She was fined £3. She was ordered to give security to keep the county from any charge that might accrue by means of the afsd.

bastard child, called Joseph. John Clarke acknowledged himself as security.{KECR DD#1:45B}

CLARK, ROBERT, d. by 28 Feb 1740 when his estate was inv. Cornelius Hawkins, admin., filed the account on 6 March 1740.{MINV 25:472}

CLARK, SAMUEL, of St. Paul's Parish, at the November Court 1730, was found guilty of assaulting John Griffith on 1 Aug 1730 and fined 200 lbs. of tob.{KECR JS#WK:161}
    Samuell Clark and Mary (Clark, widow of Dennis Clark) were m. 25 Sep 1717.{KESP}
    Samuel Clark d. intestate before 3 July 1734, leaving one dau., Esther. An indenture Tripartite made 3 July 1734 between Simon Willmore, KE Co., and Ester Lee, widow of the same county and Margaret Shippen of the same county. Whereas Simon Wilmore by deed of bargain and sale on 28 Aug 1730 conveyed to Samuel Clarke of afsd. county, a lot in Chester Town, No. 85 (but was not paid). The lot is now conveyed by Willmore to Margaret Shippen for the same amount offered to Clarke and with the agreement of Ester Lee, only surviving child of Samuel Clarke who d. intestate.{KELR JS#18:42}
    Samuel and Mary were the parents of: ESTHER, b. 27 July 1718; and SAMUELL, b. 3 March 1720.{KESP}

CLARK, WILLIAM, son of Mary Clark, was b. 6 Feb 1734-5.{KESB}

CLARKE, WILLIAM, als. Massy, at November Court 1767, was charged that on 19 Aug 1767, he assaulted Sarah Parsons, wife of Isaac Parsons. He was fined £3.{KECR DD#1:96B}

THE CLEAVER FAMILY

1. JOHN CLEAVER, on 25 Nov 1728, conv. to his wife Elizabeth, a tract, adjoining a tract possessed by the heirs of Charles Hynson, dec., the tract to be called *Lords Gift*, originally surveyed for John Hynson, dec.{KELR JS#X:310}
    On 18 Sep 1759, his estate was appraised by Alexander Williamson and James Ringgold, and valued at £112.9.7. John Moore signed as creditor. John Cleaver and Darcus Hollis signed as next of kin. Elisabeth Cleaver, admx., filed the inventory on 5 Dec 1759.{MINV 69:55} On 2 Oct 1760 distribution of the estate was made by Elisabeth Clever, admx.{BFD 3:48}
    John and Elizabeth were the parents of: (probably) JOHN, Jr., b. c1702; BENJAMIN, b. 2 March 1712; and REBECCA, bur. 12 Aug 1729.{KESP}

2. JOHN CLEAVER, Jr., probably son of John and Elizabeth, was b. c1701/2, as shown by the following depositions. On 19 May 1752, John Cleaver, Jr., age c50, dep. regarding the bounded tree of a tract called *Stepney Heath Manner.*{KELR JS#27:147} On 12 June 1753, John Cleaver, Jr., age c51, dep. regarding the bounds of a tract called *Broadnox.*{KELR JS#27:287} On 27 Feb 1755, John Cleaver, Jr., age c52, dep. regarding the bounds of a tract called *Stanaway;* he recalled going to John Pryers who lived on Vincent Hatchinson's land.{KELR JS#28:97}

John Cleaver (or Clean), of KE Co., d. by 19 March 1765, when his estate was appraised by Charles Copper and Charles Hynson, and valued at £24.2.7. Nathan Hutchison and John Page for Thomas Smith signed as creditors. John Cleaver and Mary Cleaver signed as next of kin. William Cleaver, admin., filed the inventory on 5 April 1765.{MINV 86:234}

A list of debts, appraised and valued at £13.3.3, was filed by William Cleaver, admin., on 20 Nov ----.{MINV 90:352} Another list of debts was filed by William Cleaver on 27 June 1767.{MINV 92:152}

On 2 May 1768, his estate was appraised by Charles Hynson and Charles Copper, and valued at £130.11.11. John Page and Thomas Ringgold & Co. signed as creditors. William Cleaver and Benjamin Cleaver signed as next of kin. Mary Cleaver, admx., filed the inventory on 30 June 1768.{MINV 97:205}

On 9 Feb 1769, his estate was appraised by Charles Hynson and Charles Copper, and valued at £14.13.10. John Page and Thomas Ringgold & Co. signed as creditors. William Cleaver and Benjamin Cleaver signed as next of kin. Mary Cleaver, admx./extx., filed the inventory on 24 March 1769.{MINV 98:283}

On 31 May 1769 distribution of the estate was made by Mrs. Mary Cleaver, admx.{BFD 5:243}

John Cleaver m. Mary (N), by whom he had at least two children: WILLIAM, b. 17 March 1733; and JOHN.

3. BENJAMIN CLEAVER, son of John and Elizabeth, was b. 2 March 1712. At the August Court 1734, Benjamin Cleaver of St. Paul's Parish, was found guilty of committing fornication on 1 July 1733, with Elizabeth Evans and begetting a bastard child. He was fined 30 s.{KECR JS#WK:539}

4. WILLIAM CLEAVER, son of John and Mary, was b. 17 March 1733. He m. Ann (N), who m. 2nd, John Frazier.

William Cleaver d. by 28 April 1770, when his estate was appraised by Hezekiah Dunn and Charles Copper, and valued at £39.3.3. John Timms and John Page signed as creditors. Benjamin Cleaver and Mary Cleaver signed as next of kin. Ann Cleaver, admx., filed the inventory on 14 July 1770.{MINV 107:19}

On 14 Nov 1772, when his estate was appraised by Charles Copper and Hezekiah Dunn, and valued at £22.14.3. Charles Copper and Elisabeth Cain signed as creditors. Benjamin Cleaver and Mary Cleaver signed as next of kin. Ann Cleaver, wife of John Frazier, admx., filed the inventory on 2 Dec 1772.{MINV 110:264, 265}

On Dec 1772, distribution of his estate was made by Ann Frazier (late Ann Cleaver), admx., now wife of John Frazier.{BFD 6:153}

William and Ann had a son: (N), b. 4 July 1768.{KESP}

Unplaced

CLEAVER, DORCUS, of St. Paul's Parish, spinster, at March Court 1732, Dorcus Cleaver, St. Paul's Parish, spinster, was found guilty of committing fornication on 10 Aug 1732, and begetting a bastard child. She was fined 30 s. She named James Ringgold, the son of Charles Ringgold, as the father, the same James Ringgold being one of the Grand Jury.{KECR JS#WK:352}

CLEVER, MICHAEL, of KE Co., d. (date unknown), when his estate was appraised by N. Ricketts and Daniel Farrell, and valued at £12.19.8. Morgan & Slubey , Jr. and Thomas Smyth signed as creditors. William Hodges and Stephen Hodges signed as next of kin. Thomas Dullahuntee, admin., filed the inventory on 2 July 1768.{MINV 95:277}

CLEAVER, WALTER, labourer, at March Court 1756, was charged that on 10 Nov 1756, assaulted Elizabeth Cousins. He was fined 5 S.{KECR JS#25:156B}

THE CODD FAMILY

1. ST. LEGER CODD (information on whose English Ancestry will appear in Volume 3 of this series) was bur. 9 Feb 1707.{KESP} His will, dated 19 Sep 1704, was proved in CE Co. on 8 June 1705. He left his son James all lands in the Parishes of Wateringbury, Lenham, and Witchlin, County Kent, England. Son Berkeley was to have land in Lancaster Co., VA. Son St. Leger was to have land in CE Co. He also named his daus. Beatrix and Mary Peddison (Pattison).{MWB 12:195}

His estate was admin. on 9 Feb 1707, and 18 April 1709. Execs. were Berkley Codd and St. Leger Codd.{INAC 28:246 and 29:225; Chancery}

St. Leger Codd was the father of: JAMES; BERKELEY, d. by 28 April 1733 in Sussex Co., DE; ST. LEGER; BEATRIX; and MARY, m. Thomas Pattison of DO County.{MD Chancery, 28 April 1733:175}

2. ST. LEGER CODD, son of St. Leger, the testator of 1704, may be
the St. Leger who m. c1697 Ann, widow of Maj. Joseph Weekes.{INAC
15:217} St. Leger Codd m. 8 Oct 1700 Mary, dau. of Hans Hanson of
CE Co.{INAC 25:86; Chancery Court 20 May 1729:275}
    At June Court 1725, the Grand Jury presented St. Leager Codd of
St. Paul's Parish for assaulting Phil. Kenard, Jr. and violently taking
his cane on 23 Dec 1724. To offer evidence were Phil. Kenard, Jr.,
Nathl. Kenard, and Richd. Kenard.{KECR JS#22:93} Another presentment
stated that Edward Harris, of St. Paul's Parish, Gent., on 10 April
1726 the clerk of the Hon. Roger Woolford and St. Leadger Codd,
Esqs., falsely, coruptly, and extortiously receive and taken of a George
Copper, of KE Co., 160 lbs. of tob. for a fee from him to be due for two
copies of one indictment against the sd. George whereas in truth no
such fee was due.{KECR JS#22:286}
    St. Leger Codd was also charged with an adulterous affair, even
though he had a lawful wife. On 6 March 1726 having been admonished
by the vestrymen of his parish on 1 July 1727 and at diverse other
times adulterously frequent the company of Jane Kennard then and
yet being the wife of Nathaniel Kennard. Whereas St. Leger Codd
producing a noli prosequi from his Excellency. (Proceeding ordered to
cease by Leonard Calvert, asserting the case appeared to derive from
prejudice and malice.){KECR JS#22:344}
    Presented that Jane Kennard, wife of Nathaniel Kennard, on 1
June 1728 at St. Paul's Parish, assaulted Mary Codd, wife of St. Leger
Codd, Esq. She was fined 250 lbs. of tob.{KECR JS#WK:16}
    On 20 May 1729, Mary Codd, wife of St. Ledger Codd, of KE Co.,
stated in a bill of complaint that on 8 Oct 1700 she m. St. Ledger Codd
in the Church of England, and that for 20 years she had suffered cruel
treatment. Her husband left and built another house in which he lived;
he denied her support, refusing to cohabit with her. St. Ledger Codd
answered that he married under age and against the wishes of his
father.{MD Chancery, 20 May 1729:275}
    St. Leger Codd, Esq., d. leaving an inventory taken 25 June 1730
and filed 23 June 1732. Servants mentioned were John Annen
(shoemaker), Mary Ryley. Next of kin were Mary Codd and Beatrice
Codd.{MINV 16:528} A second inventory was taken 12 July 1730; and
filed 23 June 1732. Next of kin were Mary Codd, Frederick Hanson.
Admins. were James Stout and his wife Ann Stout.{MINV 16:535} A third
inventory was taken 27 Aug 1733 and filed 6 Dec 1735. Next of kin
were Benjamin Hopkins and Gideon Pearce. Admins. were James Stout
and his wife Ann Stout.{MINV 22:128}
    After St. Leger Codd's death, an indenture Tripartite on was made
on 3 July 1736, between James Stout, of KE Co., and his wife Ann, one
of the daus. of Saint Leger Codd late of the same county, Esq., dec., of
the first part and Mary Hopkens of the same county widow, lately

called Mary Codd another dau. of sd. Saint Leager of the second part and Gideon Pearce, Jr. of the same county, mariner and Batrix his wife another dau. of the same Saint Leiger of the third part. Whereas the afsd. Saint Leiger Codd was seized in his lifetime of 250 a., part of a tract called *Worton Manor* and d. intestate and sd. land descended to the same Ann, Mary and Beatrix as his heirs, since whose death sd. Ann m. James Stout, the afsd. Mary (m.) Benjamin Hopkens since deceased and Beatrix the same Gideon Pearce.{KELR JS#18:255} On 22 July 1736 James Stout, of KE Co., and his wife Anne, to Gideon Pearce, Jr., mariner. Whereas the same James and Anne together with Mary Hopkins, widow, and the afsd. Gideon (Pearce) and Beatrix his wife in right of Anne, Mary and Beatrix, daus. of Saint Leiger Codd, dec., were seized of 250 a., part of a tract called *Morton McCannor* by deed of partition on 3 July last past made a division of the land ....{KELR JS#18:268}

On 24 Feb 1763 Mary Watkins of KE Co., widow, one of the daus. of St. Ledger Codd of KE Co., Gent., dec., conv. to Edward Lloyd, of TA Co., part of Worton Mannor. St. Leger Codd d. leaving issue three daus.: Ann later the wife of James Stout, the sd. Mary party to these presents later the wife of Benjamin Hopkins and Beatrice later the wife of Gideon Pearce the younger to whom the land descended. The sd. James Stout and his wife Ann, the sd. Mary after the death of sd. Benjamin her husband and the sd. Gideon Pearce and his wife Beatrice in 1736 made a partition of the sd. land.{KELR DD#1:104}

Saint Leager Cood and Mary Francis were m 18 Oct 1700. They were the parents of{KESP}: MARTHA, bapt. 19 Sep 1708; SAINT LEAGER, bapt. 15 June 1712; ANN, m. James Stout; MARY, m. Benjamin Hopkins; and BEATRICE, m. Gideon Pearse, Jr. on 6 June 1734 in St. Paul's Parish.

3. BERKLEY CODD, son of St. Leger (1), the testator of 1704, was conv. land in Sussex Co., DE, by Richard Perrot on 29 Oct 1718. By his will dated 29 Sep 1723 Berkley Codd devised the land to his wife Mary who by her will dated 26 Sep 1733, devised the same to her great grandson, Thomas Till who in Oct 1760 d. intestate leaving a wife Gertrude (dau. of Rev. George Ross) and an only child named William who d. 11 Dec 1762 at the age 5 years. Gertrude later m. George Read. She and George Read were living in the town of New Castle, DE on 21 April 1773.{Sussex Co., DE, deeds Liber L#11:301, 320} Gertrude and George Read were the parents of: JOHN, bapt. in Immanuel Church New Castle Co., c1764. Gertrude was bur. at Immanuel Church.{F. Edward Wright, *Early Church Records of New Castle County*: 12, 74}

CODD, BALTASAR, Irishman, no known relation of the above, immigrated Aug 1638.{MPL 1:19, 71} Baltasar Codd demandeth 5 a. of town land due to him by conditions of plant. for transporting himself at his own charge into the Province in the month of August 1638. And was allowed. The sd. Baltasar assigned all his right and interest unto the sd. 5 a. unto Robert Clark." 25 July 1640.{MPL ABH:81}

CODD, BARTHOLOMEW, was transported into the Province in 1660/1.{MPL 4:590}

THE COLE/COLES FAMILY

1. JOHN COLE (COLES), son of Peter, m. 1st, Elizabeth (N), and 2nd, Katherine (N). He d. leaving a will dated 18 Dec 1723 and proved 11 Jan 1723/4. To wife Katherine, he left his dwell. plant. during life; at her decease to son Peter. To son John, he left 60 a. bought of Henry Ward. To wife and children, residue of estate. Execs. to bind sons John, David, Mathew, and Daniel to trades as they saw fit. Wife and son Peter were execs.{MWB 18:218}
    On 17 Sep 1740, Mr. George Wilson, age c43, dep. regarding the bounds of a tract called *Postern Hole;* he recalled hearing John Cole, KE Co., dec., tell his father, James Wilson, dec., that the sd. John's father, Peter Cole, told him that ... and that Daniel Pearce, of KE Co., dec., showed him ....{KELR JS#23:between 116 and 134}
    His estate was inv. on 1 April 1724. Next of kin were Catherine Cole, Peter Cole, George Hall.{MINV 9:410} A second appraisal was made on 11 May 1724. Next of kin were Catherine Cole and Peter Cole. The extx. was Katherine Cole.{MINV 10:304} A third inventory was taken 1 April 1724 and filed 10 Sep 1726. Next of kin: Catherine Coll, Peter Coll and George Hall.{MINV 11:525}
    On 3 July 1725, his estate was admin. by Katherine and Peter Cole, execs.{MDAD 6:410}
    John and Elizabeth Cole were the parents of the following children, all bapt. by Rev. James Williamson{KESH}: POTTER (PETER), b. 16 Nov 1700; ANN, b. 9 Oct 1702; ELLINOR, b. 26 Jan 1704; SARAH, b. 8 April 1707; JOHN, b. 31 May 1709; DAVID, b. 4 Aug 1711; DAMLIN (dau.), b. -- Jan 1715; MATTHEW, b. 17 Feb 171-;{KESH} and DANIEL.

2. PETER COLE, son of John and Elizabeth was b. 16 Nov 1700. On 2 May 1728/9, Peter, age c28 years, dep. regarding the bounds of a tract called *Adventure;* he stated about 15 years earlier he was in company with his father, John Cole who described a bounded tree.{KELR JS#X:383}

On 24 Oct 1749, Peter Cole, age c50, dep. regarding the bounds of a tract called *Philips Choice*.{KELR JS#26:269} On 8 Feb 1759, Peter Cole, age c57, dep. regarding the bounds of a tract called *Bridge Point*.{KELR JS#29:79} Peter Cole was age c57 on 3 April 1759.{KEEJ: Thomas Harris}

Peter Cole, of KE Co., d. leaving a will dated 30 Sep 1763 and proved 26 Oct 1763. The heirs named were children Peter, George, John, Benjamin, Rebecca, and Ann Cole; dau. Elizabeth's child, Mary; dau. Sarah Murphy wife of John Murphy; wife, Elizabeth Cole; and dau. Frances. The execs. were wife and son Peter Cole. The will was witnessed by John Eglin, Thos. Newcomb, and Edward Holeman.{MWB 31:1004}

On 3 Nov 1763 his estate was appraised by John Wilson and Peter Massy, and valued at £106.13.10. William Salisbory and James Black signed as creditors. George Cole and Frane (Frances) Sinah Cole signed as next of kin. Elisabeth Cole, extx., filed the inventory on 19 Dec 1763.{MINV 82:238}

On 2 Jan 1764, a list of debts was appraised and valued at £5.15.11. Elisabeth Cole, extx., filed the list on 21 Dec 1764.{MINV 86:123}

On 14 Aug 1766 distribution of the estate was made by Mrs. Elisabeth Cole, extx. Legatees were George Cole, John Cole, Benjamin Cole, Rebecca Cole, Ann Cole, Mary Cole, and Sarah Murphy. Residue to wife Elisabeth and dau. Frances.{BFD 5:1}

Peter Cole was the father of: PETER; GEORGE; JOHN; BENJAMIN; REBECCA; ANN; ELIZABETH; SARAH, m. John Murphy; and FRANCES.

3. DAVID COLE, son of John and Elizabeth, was b. 4 Aug 1711. At March Court 1731, David Cole of St. Paul's Parish was found guilty of committing fornication on 10 June 1731, with Elizabeth Beale. He was fined 30 s.{KECR JS#WK:281}

4. DANIEL COLE, son of John and Elizabeth, was named in his father's will. He and Mary Mansfield were m. 24 April 1743.{KESH}

Cole d. by 6 Feb 1769, when his estate was appraised by George Medford and Augustine Boyer, and valued at £448.14.3. William Semans and Thomas Ellis signed as creditors. Sary Cole and Elisabeth Cole signed as next of kin. Cuthbert Cole, admin., filed the inventory on 5 June 1769.{MINV 100:161}

On 12 Nov 1770, his estate was appraised again, by George Medford and Augustine Boyer, and valued at £86.0.6. William Semans and Thomas Ellis signed as creditors. Sarah Cole and Elisabeth Cole signed as next of kin. Cuthbert Cole, admin., filed the inventory on 19 Nov 1770.{MINV 104:123}

Daniel and Mary (Mansfield) Cole were parents of: JOHN, b. 19 June 1743; CUTHBERT, b. 16 May 1746; SARAH, b. 4 Aug 1748; and ELIZABETH, b. 22 Nov 1750.{KESH}

5. PETER COLE, Jr., possibly son of Peter, was b. c1726 and may be the Peter who d. by 25 March 1767. On 11 Aug 1757, at age c31, dep. regarding the bounds of the tract called *Green Oak*. (He mentioned that the creek called Fishing Creek was now called Lloyds Creek.){KELR JS#28:370}

Peter Cole's estate was appraised by Thomas Bowers and Joseph Rasin, and valued at £99.18.10. James McLachlen and Thomas Smyth signed as creditors. John Coles and Frances Sinah Cole signed as next of kin. Martha Cole, admx., filed the inventory on 18 Aug 1766.{MINV 90:170} A list of debts, appraised and valued at £2.6.8, was filed by Martha Cole, admx., on 25 March 1767.{MINV 91:206} On 8 May 1767 distribution of the estate was made by Martha Cole, admx.{BFD 5:51}

Martha Cole, widow, of KE Co., d. leaving a will dated 26 July 1773 and proved 14 Aug 1773. Heirs named were dau. Martha Cole and son John Mitchell, exec. The will was witnessed by Jno. March, Chas. Ford, John Murphy, and Martha Ford.{MWB 39:374}

On 11 Oct 1773, her estate was appraised by Robert Maxwell and Jonathon Turner, and valued at £830.19.4. Donaldson Yeates and Bouldin & Hoard signed as creditors. John Mitchell, Jr. and Fs. Sinah Cole signed as next of kin. John Mitchell, exec., filed the inventory on 6 May 1774.{MINV 115:402}

Martha Cole, of KE Co., d. before 15 March 1775 when distribution of the estate was made by John Mitchell, exec. Legatee: dau. Martha with residue to son John Mitchell.{BFD 7:32}

Peter and Martha were the parents of: MARTHA.

6. GEORGE COLE, son of George, m. Jane (N), possibly widow of (N) Mitchell.

On 30 Aug 1766, when his estate was appraised by John Wilson and Cornelius Vansant, and valued at £325.2.6. Benjamin Parsons and James Black signed as creditors. Sarah Murphy and Frances Sinah Cole signed as next of kin. Jane Cole, admx., filed the inventory on 14 Nov 1766.{MINV 90:349}

George Cole of KE Co., d. by April 1767, when his estate was appraised by John Wilson and Cornelius Vansant, and valued at £64.4.0. No creditors or next of kin listed. Jane Cole, admx., filed the inventory mentioning Mary Jones, Martha Cole and An. Many on 22 June 1767.{MINV 92:97}

On 22 June 1767 a list of debts, appraised and valued at £5.4.8. was filed by Jane Coal, admx.{MINV 92:150}

On 22 June 1767 distribution of the estate was made by Jane Cole, admx.{BFD 5:52} On 11 Aug 1768 another distribution of the estate was made by Jane Cole, admx.{BFD 5:86}

Jane Cole, widow, of KE Co., d. leaving a will dated 23 April 1774 and proved 29 April 1774. The heirs named were son George Cole and son John Mitchell, exec. The will was witnessed by James McClure and John Reed.{MWB 39:664}

On 6 May 1774, her estate was appraised by Macall Medford and Jonathon Turner, and valued at £301.11.1. George Vincent Newcomb and Elisabeth Cop signed as creditors. John Mitchell, Jr. and Elisabeth Cop signed as next of kin. John Mitchell, exec., filed the inventory on 13 June 1774.{MINV 115:391}

Jane Cole's estate was appraised again and valued at £4.3.0. John Mitchell, exec., filed the inventory cont. a list of debts on 18 May 1775.{MINV 119:361}

George and Jane were the parents of: GEORGE.

Unplaced

COLE, DANIEL, m. Elizabeth, possibly widow of (N) Watson. Elizabeth Cole d. leaving a will dated 16 March 1707 and proved 24 April 1710. To her husband Daniel Cole, she left dwell. plant. part of *Hide Parke*. To sons William and James Watson and Nathaniel Cole, she left the residue of *Hide Parke*.{MWB 13:71}

COLE, DANIEL, of KE Co., d. leaving a will dated 4 March 1760 and proved 24 May 1760. The exec. and residuary legatee was friend John Shawhan, Sr. The will was witnessed by Grace Kitts, Daniel Shawn, and Jno. March.{MWB 31:37}

On 10 June 1760, his estate was appraised by James Hart and Jonathon Turner, and valued at £3.6.6. John Shahawn, exec., filed the inventory.{MINV 70:156}

COLE, JOHN, d. by 4 Feb 1691, when his estate was admin.{INAC 12:1}

COLE, RICHARD, of the KE Co., son of John Cole, dec., on 24 March 1715 was placed as an apprentice and servant to afsd. John Clove, to be taught and kept to house labour, to serve until age 21, he now being c17 years old.{KEBI JS#W:10A}

COLE, Mr. THOMAS, age c50, dep. on 1 Feb 1655.{ARMD LIV:61, Liber A:120} He may be the Thomas Cole who immigrated in 1649.{MPL Q:47} "Thomas Cole demandeth 200 a. of land for transporting himself and Priscilla his wife into this province the last year at his own charge. Warrt. to lay out 200 a. for Thomas Cole at Parson's Neck upon the

Isle of Kent County or in any part of that or Ann Arundell County ret. by Michas next." 17 May 1650.{MPL ABH:40; 2:614}

COLE, THOMAS, of KE Co., d. leaving a will dated 7 July 1756 and proved 29 July 1756. The heirs named were: wife Margaret and cousin Morgan Conneway. The extx was Margaret Cole. The will was witnessed by George Fountain, Nicholas Boyer, and Jacob Linegar. {MWB 30:126}

COLE, WILLIAM, and Ann Beck were m. 14 Dec 1741.{KESH}

THE CONNER/CONNOR FAMILY

Refs.: A: BDML I:229.

1. PHILIP CONNER was b. c1615 and d. 1660. He immigrated to MD c1636 as a free adult, and settled in KE Co., where he was a Justice from 1647 to 1660. He was present at the Assembly in 1641/2, 1647/8, 1649, and 1658. He m. Mary, widow of John Philips. She m. 3rd, by 1667, John Wright.{A}

On 17 Sep 1640 Phillip Conner of the Isle of Kent, demandeth 100 a. by Conditions of Plantation for Transporting himself into the Province. On 25 Sep 1640 was laid out for Phillip Conner "one Neck of Land bounding on the n. with the Great Creek called Broad Creek on the w. with Chesapeak Bay, on the e. with a meridian line drawn from the head of Conners Creek for the length of 45 perches or thereabouts on the s. with a Paralell line drawn from the End of the 45 perches to Chesapeak Bay cont. in the whole 100 a. or thereabouts."{MPL ABH:84}

An entry dated 1 Aug 1650 refers to land laid out for Phillip Conner on the Isle of Kent called the *Woodyard Thickett.*{MPL ABH:105}[5]

Mary Conner m. as her 3rd husband, John Wright prior to 9 June 1667.{MPL 11:265 and MPL 4:63}

Philip and Mary were the parents of{A}: PHILIP; and SARAH, d. 1666.

2. PHILIP CONNER, son of Philip and Mary, was b. c1653 and d. 1703. He was a Justice of KE Co. from 1680 to 1685, and in 1694.{A}

On 28 Jan 1667 Phillip, son of Phillip Connor of KE Co., dec., age c14, chose Mr. John Wright as his guardian.{ARMD LIV:238, Liber C:3} On 28 Nov 1670 he was named as a legatee in the will of John Lawrence.{MWB 1:405}

---

[5] Omitted by Skordas in *Early Settlers of Maryland.*

Philip Conner patented *Little Neck*, 55 a., on 16 Aug 1680.{MPL 28:28} On 22 Aug 1687 Phillip Conner and Mary his wife, of KE Co., conv. to Thomas Smyth of the same county, a parcel of land called *Trumpington* being (a third) part of a divident of land formerly belonging to Thomas South and conv. by him to Anthony Purcee(?) to John Hynson and since then purchased by Nathaniel Evetts.{KELR B:245}

Philip Conner of Kent Island, TA Co., d. leaving a will dated 26 May 1701 and proved 7 June 1703. He named his wife Mary, to have personalty; son Philip, to have 290 a. *Conner's Neck*, sons Nathaniel and Charles, to have 410 a. *Woodyard Thickett*. The execs. were wife Mary and Thomas Smith. The will was witnessed by Thos. Braisier, Henry Monk, and Ellice Burk.{MWB 11:350}

On 5 June 1704, a tract on Kent Island called *Wood Yard*, was divided between Nathaniel and Charles Conn[er] as directed by the will of their father, Phillip Conn[er], late of Kent Island, dec.{KELR GL#1:new p. 37}

Philip and Mary were the parents of: PHILIP; NATHANIEL; and CHARLES.

3. SARAH CONNER, dau. of Philip and Mary, was transported prior to 1665, and d. by 1666.{MPL 10:2} She evidently m. (N) Shaw, and had a son: JOHN SHAW. On 29 March 1699 John Shaw of KE Co., conv. to Geffery Power of Bedeford, England, merchant, a tract formerly in TA Co., now KE Co., on the e. side of Morgans Creek called *Maydens(?) Lott*, laid out for 600 a. granted to Sarah Conner, mother of sd. John Shaw (in whose right he is seized) by patent, one moiety or one-half.{KELR M:86a}

On the back of another deed was written: "The within named part of *Maidens Lott* originally granted to Sarah Conner, dau. of Phillip Conner and sold by John Shaw, son and heirs-at-law to the sd. Sarah, and sold by the sd. Shaw to Robert Ingram Sr., and sold by Robert Ingram, Jr., son and heir to Ingram, Sr., to John Radford and by the sd. Radford sold to James Moore - Septembr. 14th 1725." {KELR JS#W:501}

4. PHILIP CONNER, son of Philip and Mary, d. in QA Co. leaving a will dated 16 April 1722 and proved 7 June 1722. He named his wife Jane (to be extx. and to have personal estate), and his sons James, Nathaniel, and Charles (to have land in KE Co. near Morgan's Creek). The will was witnessed by Nath'l. and Charles Conner, and Elin Murphy.{MWB 17:196}

Phillip Connor and Jane Harris were m. 4 March 1700.{KESP} They were the parents of: JAMES; NATHANIEL; and CHARLES.

5. CHARLES CONNER, son of Philip (4) is probably the Charles Conner, of QA Co., who, on 19 April 1749 conv. to Nathaniel Conner, of TA Co., joyner, a moiety or ½ of a tract formerly laid out for Sarah Conner, dau. of Philip Conner of Kent Island, and called *Maidons Lott* in KE Co. on Morgans Creek, 600 a. {KELR JS#26:210}

Unplaced

CONNOR, JAMES, and Elinor Flanagan were m. 1 Jan 1705. They were the parents of: ELIZABETH, dau. of Elynor Conner, b. 12 June 1709. {KESH}

CONNER, JAMES, and wife Catherine, were the parents of: JAMES, b. 2 June 1740. {KESH}

CONNER, JAMES, d. 5 April 1740. {KESH}
On 17 June 1743 his estate was appraised by George Medford and John Williams, and valued at £5.15.7. No creditors or next of kin named. Unnamed admx., filed the inventory on 18 June 1743. {MINV 28:215}

CONNER, JAMES, Quaker, of KE Co., d. by 9 Feb 1767, when his estate was appraised by Ebenezar Massy and Gilbert Falconar, and valued at £23.7.4. John Wright and William Anderson signed as creditors. Hannah Conner and John Wright signed as next of kin. John Vansant, admin., filed the inventory on 1 March 1769. {MINV 98:160}

CONNER, JOHN, of Newtown, KE Co., merchant, was conv. a lot and house, and Lot No. 49 in Newtown, by Laughlin O'Bryan of Newtown in KE Co., joyner, and his wife Mary.
At June Court 1738, John Conner of St. Paul's Parish, Gent., was found guilty of assaulting William Trulock on 8 May 1738. He was fined 5 s. {KECR JS#22:15}
John Conner, of Chester Town, merchant, sends greeting. Whereas by a deed dated 19 July 1740 between John Earl, then of Chester Town afsd., saddler of the one part and James Conner son of the afsd. John Connor of the other part the same John Earle confirmed to the same James Conner a half lot in Chester Town, No. 50. {KELR JS#26:226}
John Conner d. by 1 May 1740 when his estate was inv. It was filed 19 July 1740, by Henry Trulock, admin. The inventory mentioned Daniel Perkins, John Jones. {MINV 25:201}

CONNOR, JOHN, of KE Co., d. leaving a will dated 22 April 1747 and proved 14 Sep 1751. The heirs named were son James Connor, wife Elizabeth and dau. Isabella Connor. The exec. were wife Elizabeth,

Wm. Dames and son James Connor. The will was witnessed by Thomas
Bordley and James Smith, Jr. Probate showed that dau. Isabella
Connor was the only child of the testator alive at the time of his
death.{MWB 28:153}

On 5 Nov 1751 his estate was appraised by Joseph Nicholson and
Charles Scott, and valued at £1526.0.5. James Anderson and B. Hands
signed as creditors. John Bordley signed as next of kin. Elisabeth
Zuille, late Elisabeth Connor, wife of Matthew Zuille, extx., filed the
inventory on 29 Jan 1753.{MINV 52:104}

John Conner had at least two children: JAMES, d. young; and
ISABELLA, m. by 22 June 1759, John Bordley.[6]

CONNER, JOHN, m. by 11 March 1744, Elizabeth Harris, in admin.
account of James Harris of KE Co.{MDAD 21:163}

CONNOR, SUSANNA, on 20 March 1715(?) was the admx. of Francis
Spearman doe (pay) the sume of £3 ... 7 p., it being due to one of the
daus. of the sd. Francis a filial portion of the sd. Francis Estate and I
the subscriber have interm. with Prudence, one of the daus. of the
afsd. Francis do by the presents acknowledge to have received the sum
afsd. and also do release the afsd. admin. from the afsd. sume as also
from a certain obligation passed by the sd. admx. with sureties, viz.,
Wm. Spearman ... witness by hand the day above afsd. Robert Darby
(his marke).{KEBI JS#W:12A}

CONNOR, THOMAS, and wife Honor were the parents of: JAMES,
born 13 Sep 1706.{KESH}

THE COOLEY/COLEY/COLLEY FAMILY

1. DANIEL COOLEY, d. Oct 1729. He m. Elizabeth (N), who may
have m. 2nd, Edward Cousins.

On 5 Jan 1718, Daniel Coolley and his wife Elizabeth of KE Co.,
conv. to James Watson of afsd. county, part of a tract called *High
Park*, 300 a.{KELR JS#W:31} Elizabeth m. 2nd, Edward Couzens.

Daniell Cooley was bur. 22 Oct 1729.{KESP} He d. leaving a will
dated 30 Aug 1729 and proved 6 Feb 1729. To his six unnamed
children, he left personal estate; his wife was to be extx. and to have
her thirds. To son Benjamin, 80 a. called *Bristow*.{MWB 20:3}

---

[6] On 22 June 1759 John Bordley of Chester Town, merchant, and
his wife Isabella, late Isabella Conner, dau. of John Connor, late
of Chester Town, dec., conv. to James Nicols of QA Co., Gent., a
half lot in Chester Town, no. 50.{KELR JS#29:116}

Daniel Cooley (Cowley/Cowly)'s estate was appraised 10 July 1730. Next of kin were Nathaniel Cooley and Martha Cooley. Execs. were Edward Couzens and his wife Elisabeth Couzens.{MINV 15:549}

Daniell Cooley and Elizabeth Watson were m. 23 Oct ----. They were the parents of: NATHANIEL, b. April 1706; DANIEL, bapt. 24 March 1708; MARTHA, b. Oct 171-, m. Thomas Stalker; MARDY (MARY?), b. 10 Nov 1713, as Mary Cooley she was bur. 14 June 1714; BENJAMIN, 12 May 1719; RICHARD, b. 18 April 1722; and JOHN, b. 27 March 1727.{KESP}

2. NATHANIEL COOLEY, son of Daniel (1) and Elizabeth, was b. April 1706, and d. by Aug 1748. He m. 1st, Elizabeth (N), and 2nd, Anne. Elizabeth Cooley, wife of Nathaniel Cooley, was bur. 20 March 17--. Nathaniell Cooley and Ann Rogers m. 31 March 1729.{KESP}

On 2 May 1740, Nathaniel Cooley of KE Co., and his wife Anne, conv. to Thomas Stalker, part of a tract called *High Park*, 33 a.{KELR JS#23:172}

Nathaniel Cooley (Coley), of KE Co., d. by 22 Aug 1748, when his estate was appraised by Benjamin Wickes and Thomas Maslin, and valued at £146.19.9. Thomas Ringgold and William Murray signed as creditors. Richard Coley signed as next of kin. Anne Coley, admx., filed the inventory on 25 Oct 1748.{MINV 37:156}

On 2 Oct 1749 his estate was appraised again by Thomas Slipper and Thomas Maslin, and valued at £55.11.2. Richard Cooley and Thomas Ringgold signed as creditors. No next of kin named. Anne Cooley, admx., filed the inventory on 4 Jan 1749.{MINV 43:413}

Nathaniel and Ann Cooley were the parents of: DANIELL, b. 15 Feb 1730; MARTHA, b. 6 Feb 1730; NATHANIEL, b. 13 Jan 1732; and EDWARD, b. 9 Nov 1734.{KESP}

3. DANIEL COOLEY, son of Daniel (1) and Elizabeth, was bapt. 24 March 1708, and d. by 14 Dec 1747. He m. Mary (N), who m. 2nd, Nehemiah Jones.

Edward Cozens, William Crow, and Thomas Stalker, of KE Co., gave bond on 23 Aug 1735 they would pay Daniel Cooly £13.12.2 as his filial portion of the estate of Daniel Colly, his dec. father.{KEBI JS#18:22}

On 24 May 1746, Benjamin Cooley, Daniel Cooley and Richard Cooley, conv. to Martha Browne of the same county, widow, part of a tract called *High Park*, 33 a.{KELR JS#25:377}

Daniel Colley d. by 14 Dec 1747, when his estate was appraised by Isaac Freeman and Lambert Wilmer, Jr., and valued at £84.11.10. Daniell Bryane and Jam Vumfros signed as creditors. Benjamin Coley and John Coley signed as next of kin. Mary Jones, wife of Nehemiah Jones, admx., filed the inventory on 12 Oct 1750.{MINV 44:125}

By his wife Mary he was the father of: MARY, b. 27 March 1746.{KESP}

4. MARTHA COOLEY, dau. of Daniel (1) and Elizabeth, was b. Oct 171-. She m. Thomas Stalker who d. 1741. She may have m. 2nd, (N) Brown, and 3rd, (N) Hurt.

Thomas Stalker of KE Co., d. leaving a will dated 17 Nov 1741 and proved 12 Dec 1742. The heirs named were wife Martha, to whom all real estate descended, viz., 200 a. and 33 a., part of *High Rock*, 520 a. on Mill Creek, Orange Co., VA. At her decease the tract of 200 a. was to pass to John Scott and land in VA to be divided between wife's four bros., Benjamin, Dan., Rich. and Jno. Coley and 100 a. of *High Park* already belonging to John Nemio, Sr., and his son Jno. Nemio, Jr., to pass to heirs of Robt. Green, dec., should Jno. Nemio, Jr., afsd. d. without heirs. The will was witnessed by Peter Coner, Wm. Brown, and Mary Morgan.{MWB 22:457}

5. BENJAMIN COOLEY, son of Daniel (1) and Elizabeth, was b. 12 May 1719 and d. by Dec 1750. He probably m. Hannah (N) who admin. his estate, and who m. 2nd, James Kelley.

On 23 Aug 1735 Edward Cozens, William Crow, and Thomas Stalker, of KE Co., gave bond they would pay Benjamin Cooly £13.12.2 as his filial portion of the estate of Daniel Colly, his dec. father.{KEBI JS#18:23}

Benjamin Cooley (or Cealley), of KE Co., d. by 1 Dec 1750, when his estate was appraised by Christopher Bateman and Philip Milton, value unknown. William Kenney and Esau Watkins signed as creditors. Richard Coley and John Coley signed as next of kin. Hannah Cooley, admx., filed the inventory on 27 May 1751.{MINV 47:125}

On 23 Feb 1754 distribution of his estate was made by James Kelley and his wife Hannah, admx.{BFD 1:118}

6. RICHARD COOLEY, son of Daniel (1) and Elizabeth, was b. 18 April 1722.

Edward Cozens, William Crow, and Thomas Stalker, of KE Co., were bound to Richard Cooly, on 23 Aug 1735, to pay him £13.4.4, his filial portion of the estate of Daniel Colly, his dec. father.{KEBI JS#18:21}

Richard Coley of KE Co., d. leaving a will dated 24 Feb 1752 and proved 16 March 1752. The heirs named were dau. Martha, to whom was devised the plant. *Spalding*; dau. Frances; and bro. John Coley. Servant man John Askworth was to be free the Christmas after he had served five years. Bro.-in-law Simon Worrell, exec., was appointed to act as guardian to testator's children. The will was witnessed by Thomas Ringgold, Benjamin Everit, and Wm. Worrel.{MWB 28:286}

On 20 April 1752 his estate was appraised by Benjamin Everett and James Poiner (also James Piner, Jr.), and valued at £353.11.1. Mathew Hazel and Lovring Merritt signed as creditors. John Coley and Mary Worrell signed as next of kin. Simon Worrell, exec., filed the inventory on 15 June 1752.{MINV 50:50}

On 24 Feb 1753 his estate was appraised again by Benjamin Everett and James Piner, Jr., value unknown. Matthew Hazel and Low Merrit signed as creditors. John Caley and Mary Worrell signed as next of kin. Simon Worrell, exec., filed the inventory on 7 March 1753.{MINV 53:60}

On 20 Sep 1753 distribution of the estate was made by Simon Worrell, exec.{BFD 1:88}

Richard had at least two children, who were minors in 1752: MARTHA; and FRANCES.

7. JOHN COOLEY, son of Daniel (1) and Elizabeth, was probably the John who was b. 27 March 1727. He m. Jane, dau. of Ruth Gaitskill.

Edward Cozens, William Crow, and Thomas Stalker, of KE Co., were bound to John Cooly, on 23 Aug 1735, to pay him £13.12.2, his filial portion of the estate of Daniel Colly, his dec. father.{KEBI JS#18:20}

On 16 Aug 1749, John Cooley, of KE Co., to Martha Hurt, widow, his right to a parcel of land being part of a tract called *Hyde Park* which was conv. to sd. Martha by his bros. Benjamin, Daniel, and Richard by their deed dated May 1746, 33 a.{KELR JS#26:237}

John Coley, and wife Jane, one of the daus. of Ruth Gaitskill, late of KE Co., dec., on 8 March 1762, conv. to Hannah Wallis, widow, a part formerly devised to afsd. Ruth Gaitskill then Ruth Wallis by her father, part of a tract called *The Agreement*, 157 a.{KELR DD#1:58}

On 31 Jan 1763, Hannah Wallis of KE Co., widow, conv. to her son Francis Wallis, land which she purchased of John Cooley and his wife Jane, being part of a tract called *Agreement*, and an undivided part of a tract which Hannah purchased of Edward Holliday and Ruth Gatskill alias Holliday his wife.{KELR DD#1:177}

2-d. EDWARD COLEY, of KE Co., son of Nathaniel (2), was b. 1734, and d. by June 1774. He m. Rebecca (N).

On 4 Aug 1762, he conv. to James Dunn, Gent., part of a tract called *High Park*, 199 a.{KELR DD#1:110}

Edward Coley d. by 14 June 1774, when his estate was appraised by Samuel Griffith and Thomas Crew, and valued at £160.9.8. James Maslin and Thomas Smyth signed as creditors. John Coley and Wolman Spencer signed as next of kin. John Wales, admin., filed the inventory on 8 Aug 1774.{MINV 116:279}

Edward Coley and wife Rebecca were the parents of: NATHANIEL, b. 1 Oct 1762; JAMES, b. 1 June 1764; WOLMON (or SOLOMON) SPENCER, b. 27 March 1766; and JOHN, b. 11 April 1768.{KESP}

COOLEY, BENJAMIN, and wife Elizabeth were the parents of: BENJAMIN, b. 15 May 1715.{KESP}

COOLEY, MARTHA, on 30 Dec 1753 confessed herself guilty of fornication and having a bastard child. William Spencer confessed being the father.{KECR JS#25:112B}

COOLEY, SAMUEL, of KE Co., and wife Elizabeth, on 16 Nov 1714, conv. to Samuel Wallis and William Comegys ... both of the same county, 100 a., part of land called *Killingsworth*, that Daniel Cooley bought of Thomas Usher, dec.{KELR BC#1:}

THE COPPEDGE (COPING) FAMILY

1. EDWARD COPPEDGE (or Copping) immigrated by 1650. On 16 July 1651, Edward Copping demanded 100 a. of land for transporting himself into this Province Anno 1650. A warrant to lay out 100 a. for Edward Copping upon the Isle of Kent to be (or was) returned by November.{MPL ABH:157} (This is probably Edward Coppedge. The entry has John Coping marked out and Edward inserted.)

Edward Copping assigned 100 a. to Robert Dun for transporting a manservant named Richard Norton in 1649. (Signed Edward Coppeidg).{MPL ABH:247}

Edward d. by 8 April 1676 when his estate was admin.{INAC 2:141} It was admin. again on 10 Feb 1679, and again c1680 by admins. William Rawles and his wife Elisabeth Rawles.{INAC 6:641 and 7A:33}

Elizabeth, wife of Edward Copedg, d. 9 Sep 1669.{ARMD LIV:268, Liber C:22} Edward and Elizabeth Coppedge were the parents of: ELIZABETH, b. 7 July 1654; SARAH, b. 1 Jan 1656; JOHN, b. 31 March 1660; PHILLIP, b. 11 Nov 1663.{ARMD LIV:267, Liber C:21}

2. Capt. JOHN COPPEDGE, son of Edward, was b. 31 March 1660.

Capt. John Copedge gives to Charles Eareckson son of Matthew and Dorothy Eareckson a yearling heifer, 28 Aug 1695.{KELR GL#1:2A}

John Copedge, of TA Co., m. by 2 Sep 1698, Mary, relict and admx. of Allan Smith, of KE Co.{INAC 16:171}

On 1 June 1690 John Coppidge and his wife Mary, of Kent Island, conv. to Michael Miller of the same county, Gent., *Forest Lodge* in Coursey's Creek, late the property of Disborow Bennett of the Island, dec.{TALR 5:257}

THE COPPER FAMILY

1. GEORGE COPPER, was b. c1668/70, as shown by the following depositions: On 3 March 1725/6, George Copper, aged c56 years, dep. regarding the bounds of a tract called *Langfords Neck;* he said that he was sent by his master, Col. Hance Hanson on an errand to Capt. John Derricutt and going down to *Ship Neck* to call aboard of Capt. Derricutt's ship he saw a bounded tree newly cut down.{KELR JS#W:543} On 26 Feb 1746, George Copper, age c78, dep. regarding the bounds of the tract *Bounty.*{KELR JS#26:32} On 25 Aug 1746, George Copper, Sr., age c77, dep. regarding the bounds of a tract called *Providence.*{KELR JS#25:438} George Copper, age 87, dep. 31 July 1753.{KEEJ: Matthias Harris}

On 10 March 1714, George Copper and his wife Mary, conv. to John Cleaver, 50 a., part of a tract called *Lords Gift* of 300 a., between Graysing Creek and Langfords Bay.{KELR BC#1:56}

At March Court 1724, George Copper was ordered to appear to answer charge of making a false oath (before Thomas Ringgold 20 June 1724 in Langford Bay, Lower Hundred in St. Paul's Parish).{KECR JS#22:70}

George Copper, Sr., of KE Co., d. leaving a will dated 7 Jan 1746. Land was devised to sons William Copper, Charles Copper and George Copper. Slaves were bequeathed to daus. Rachell Glann, and Mary Gleaves (at age 16) and to granddau. Sarah Gleaves (at age 16). Grandson Joseph Copper was given stock. The execs. were son Charles Copper and Mary Gleaves. The will was witnessed by Vincent Hutcheson, Vincent Hutcheson, W. Hynson, and Chas. Hynson, Jr. {MWB 29:353}

On 28 Nov 1754 his estate was appraised by Ra. Page and Samuel Miller, and valued at £652.5.7. John Williamson and Rachel Bennet signed as creditors. George Copper and William Copper signed as next of kin. Son William Copper, son George Copper, dau. Rachel Copper, Sarah Gleaves, dau. Mary Copper and son Charles Copper signed as legatees. Charles Copper and Mary Gleaves, wife of Jonathon Leatherbury, execs., filed the inventory on 5 May 1755.{MINV 60:250}

George and Mary Copper were the parents of: WILLIAM, b. 31 Aug 1702; GEORGE, b. 12 Dec 1704; RACHELL, b. 3 April 1707, m. (N) Glann; SARAH, b. 1 May 1711, bur. 13 Feb 1714; MARTHA, b. 15 May 1714; JOSEPH, b. 22 Dec 1718; MARY, b. 18 April 1722; bapt. 5 Sep 1725, m. (N) Gleaves; and CHARLES.{KESP}

2. WILLIAM COPPER, son of George (1) and Mary, was b. 31 Aug 1702. William Copper, age 4-, mentioned his father, possibly c1750.{KEEJ: Isaac and Thomas Crown}

At June Court 1730, William Copper of St. Paul's Parish, was found guilty of assaulting John Tillard on 10 Feb 1729 and fined 5 s.{KECR JS#WK:134}

On 9 March 1756, William Copper of KE Co., and his wife Margret, conv. to his son William Copper the eldest of that name, and if he should die without heirs then to his sister Sarah Copper, 100 a., bounds as expressed in the last will of George Cooper late of afsd. county, dec., father of afsd. William.{KELR JS#28:228}

William Copper's estate was appraised by John Carvill and James Thomas, and valued at £285.18.1. Thomas Ringgold and Christopher Brown signed as creditors. Charles Copper and Charles Ringgold signed as next of kin. George Copper, admin., filed the inventory on 30 Jan 1760.{MINV 68:223}

On 21 June 1760 his estate was appraised by John Carvill and James Thomas, and valued at £26.0.0. George Copper, admin., filed the inventory mentioning Christopher Brown, Charles Ringgold and Charles Copper on 10 Nov 1763.{MINV 82:56}

William Copper, of KE Co., d. before 13 March 1764, when distribution of the estate was made by George Copper, admin.{BFD 4:30}

William and Mary Copper were the parents of: SARAH, b. 22 July 1736; MARY, b. 13 July 1735; GEORGE, b. 13 Sep 1726; REBECCA, b. 16 Aug 1729; and WILLIAM, b. 13 Aug 1732.{KESP}

3. GEORGE COPPER, son of George (1) and Mary, was b. 12 Dec 1704.

At March Court 1729, Geo. Copper, Jr., St. Paul's Parish, was found guilty of committing fornication on 10 June 1729 with Rebecca Davis and begetting a bastard child. He was fined 30 s., as was Rebecca.{KECR JS#WK:102, 105}

At November Court 1744, it was presented that George Copper, Jr., on 1 Nov 1744, assaulted William Slipper. Cooper was fined 2 s., 6 p.{KECR JS#24:182}

On 19 July 1748, George Copper, Jr. of KE Co., age 43, dep. regarding the bounds of a tract called *Blackhals Hermitage.*{KELR JS#26:145}

At March Court 1754, it was presented that George Copper, Jr., on 10 Jan 1754, assaulted George Bennett. He was fined 2 s., 6 p.{KECR JS#25:124B}

George Copper, of KE Co., d. leaving a will dated 20 Oct 1758 and proved 9 Dec 1758. Mentioned were wife Rebecca and children Philip, Cyrus, George, and Rebecca. The tract *Wedge's Recovery* was mentioned. The execs. were Rebecca and George Cooper. The will was witnessed by Thomas Slipper, Charles Ringold, and John Amol(?).{MWB 30:678}

On 14 Nov 1759 his estate was appraised by Ra. Page and John Wickes, and valued at £407.19.2. Richard Brice and James Claypoole signed as creditors. Rebecca Arnold and Philip Copper signed as next of kin. Rebecca Copper signed as legatee. Rebecca Copper, extx., filed the inventory on 25 Jan 1760.{MINV 68:233}

On 28 July 1760 his estate was appraised by Robert Ages and John Wickes, and valued at £75.2.11. Richard Price and James Claypool signed as creditors. Philip Copper and Rebecah Arnold signed as next of kin. Rebecah Copper (widow), extx., filed the inventory on 6 Sep 1760.{MINV 70:134}

George Copper, of KE Co., d. before 6 May 1761 when distribution of the estate was made by Rebecca Copper, extx., to widow and children Joseph, Rebecca, Samuel, Norris, Gustavus, Cyrus, and Benjamin.{BFD 3:97}

He probably m. Rebecca (N), by whom he had: SAMUEL, b. 9 Jan 1741; NORRIS, b. 19 Jan 1743; GUSTAVUS, b. 9 Feb 1745; CYRUS, b. 14 Dec 1747; BENJAMIN, b. 21 March 175-; PHILIP; GEORGE; and REBECCA.{KESP}

4. JOSEPH COOPER, son of George (1) and Mary, was b. 22 Dec 1718. He is probably the Joseph Cooper, labourer, who on 14 Dec 1758 confessed he committed fornication with Kezia Tillard on 6 Sep last and was fined 30 s.{KECR JS#25:219B, 220A}

Joseph Cooper m. Martha, dau. of George Foxon whose distrbution, made 25 July 1764, named dau. Martha wife of Joseph Copper.{BFD 4:60}

Joseph and Martha were the parents of: CHARLES, b. 4 April 1761; JOSEPH, b. 15 May 1763; NATHANIEL, b. 6 April 1766; and ALEXANDER, b. 15 March 1769.{KESP}

5. CHARLES COPPER, son of George (1) and Mary, was named in his father's will. He is probably the Charles Copper, of KE Co., who d. leaving a will dated 11 Feb 1775 and proved 20 March 1775. The heirs named were nephew William Copper, Jr., son of bro. William Copper and Elizabeth Ringgold; sister Mary Leatherbury, widow; nephew Charles Copper, son of bro. William Copper; nephew Philip Copper, son of bro. George Copper; son of nephew George Copper and son of bro. William Copper; niece Sarah Pinner; Mary Pinner, dau. of Thos. and Sarah Pinner; Elizabeth Pinner, dau. of Thos. and Sarah Pinner; Sarah Pinner, dau. of Thos. and Sarah Pinner; nephew William Hoges; nephew Charles Copper; Sarah Body, niece of wife Rachel, dec.; nephew Peregrine Leatherbury; nephew William Copper, Jr., son of bro. William Copper and Elizabeth Ringgold; Mary Pinner, Elizabeth Pinner, Sarah Pinner daus. of Thos. and Sarah Pinner. The extx. was niece Sarah Pinner. The will was witnessed by Chas. Hynson, H. Hynson, and Samuel Crouch.{MWB 40:304}

On 28 March 1775 his estate was appraised by James Dunn and Richard Spencer, and valued at £1118.11.10. James Anderson and William Bordley signed as creditors. William Copper and Charles Copper signed as next of kin. Sarah Piner, extx., filed the inventory on 7 Nov 1775.{MINV 120:343}

6. GEORGE COPPER, son of William (2) and Mary, was b. 13 Sep 1726.

At March Court 1756, it was presented that George Copper, Jr., son of William Copper, on 10 May 1751, committed fornication with Araminta Box and begot a bastard child.{KECR JS#25:156A}

At March Court 1758, it was presented that George Copper, son of William, of St. Paul's Parish, on 26 Oct 1756, committed fornication with Liney Keys and begot a bastard child. He was fined 30 s.{KECR JS#25:185A}

At November Court 1759, George Copper, of Worton, was presented for unlawfull cohabitation with Liner Key. He was fined 30 s.{KECR JS#25:231B} At August Court 1765, it was presented that George Copper committed fornication with Liner Key. He was fined 30 s.{KECR DD#1:52A}

George, of William, may be the George who m. Patience (N). They were the parents of: SAMUEL, bapt. 27 June 176-.{KESP}

7. WILLIAM COPPER, son of William (2) and Mary, was b. 13 Aug 1732.{KESP} William Copper, of KE Co., age c42, dep. on 24 March 1774.{KEEJ: John Comegys}

Unplaced

COOPER, THOMAS, on 13 March 1754, age c26, dep. regarding the bounds of a tract called *Yapp*.{KELR JS#27:255}

THE CORSE FAMILY

See also The Coursey Family Below.

1. JAMES CORSE, an overseer of Cecil Meeting was removed by death as noted on 8 da. 4 mo., 1720. He d. leaving a will dated 4 March 1720 and proved 22 April 1720. To eldest son James, he left 100 a. of *Heath's Chance*; to son William, residue of afsd. tract; dwell. plant., and 200 a. called *Middleneck*; son William was to make over to sons John and Michael, his title in 150 a. called *Hebron's Farm*; sons John and Michall, were to have tracts *Corse's Meadows* and *Greeres Range*.

To dau. Hannah, £100 and personalty. Sons John and Wm. were mamed execs.{MWB 16:39}

The inventory of his estate was taken on 6 May 1720, and filed on 24 July 1720. Next of kin were James Corse, Hannah Corse.{MINV 4:21}

On 22 March 1720, the estate was of James Course was admin. by William Course.{MDAD 3:314}

James Corse was the father of: JAMES; WILLIAM; JOHN, b. c1701; MICHAEL; and HANNAH.

2. JAMES CORSE, son of James (1), was b. c1688, and was that James Corse, Jr., of KE Co., who m. Ann Beck of the same place, single woman, on 23 da. 3 mo., 1710.{CEMM} On 10 Sep 1735, James Course, age c45 made an affirmation regarding the bounds of a tract called *Sims Farm.*{KELR JS#18:195} On 21 Feb 1743, James Course, Quaker, age c55, made an affirmation regarding the bounds of a tract called *Brotherly and Friendly Agreement.* {KELR JS#25:33}

On 17 Aug 1721, James and his wife Anna, planter, conv. to John Gale of the afsd. county, part of a parcel called *Ridmores Supply* at the head of a branch running out of Steelpone Creek.{KELR JS#W:170}

On 3 Oct 1743 Anne Corse, age c50, made an affirmation regarding the bounds of a tract called *Beckworth;* referred to her brother Caleb Beck and to Nicholas Barefoot servant of Edward Beck.{KELR JS#25:192} In Oct 1753, Ann Corse, age c60, Quaker, dep. regarding the bounds of a tract called *Cornwallis's Choice;* she stated that the creek leading eastward from Worton Creek was formerly called Back Creek and sometimes as Muddy Cove and sometimes Barneys Creek; she never heard it called Cornwallis Creek.{KELR JS#28:48}

On 5 da. 8 mo., 1729, a committee was appointed to visit James Course and his wife to enquire whether or not they were accessary in the disorderly marriage of their dau. with a man not of our Society.{CEMM}

James Corse, a member of Chester and Cecil Meetings d. 17 da. 2 mo., 1747. He d. leaving a will written 22nd day, 1st month, 1747, and proved 8 July 1747. The heirs named were wife Ann, son James, son Michael Course, son David, dau. Rachel Redgrave, dau. Ann England, dau. Elizabeth Howard, dau. Hannah Briscoe, dau. Offley, dau. Mary Curry and son Caleb. The exec. was son James. The will was witnessed by Michael Corse, John Dunn, Peter Ball and John Corse.{MWB 25:188}

On 31 May 1748 his estate was appraised by George Medford and John Williams, and valued at £56.9.5. John Dunn and Howell Buckinham signed as creditors. John Corse and Michael Corse signed as next of kin. James Course, exec., filed the inventory on 17 June 1748.{MINV 37:124}

87

On 13 March 1753, Ann Course, widow, age c59, Quaker, affirmed regarding the bounds of a tract called *Yapp;* she declared that her husband James Course, dec. told her ... and that John Hepbourn since dec. told her he was glad that Col. Maxfield was dead or else Edwd. Price would have lost his land.{KELR JS#27:254} Anne Corse wife of James Corse d. 1765.{CEMM}

James and Ann (Beck) Corse were the parents of{CEMM}: RACHEL, b. c1711, m. 1st, John Redgrave, and 2nd, by 13 March 1753, (N) Van Sant;[7] JENNETT, d. by 1753; ELIZABETH, reported on 11 da. 12 mo., 1735 as having taken a man not of our Society to be her husband{CEMM}; and JAMES, Jr., reported on 9 da. 3 mo., 1744, as having "gone out in marriage."

3. WILLIAM CORSE, son of James (1), d. by May 1738. He m. Barbara (N), who m. 2nd, Howell Buckingham.

On 12 Nov 1720, conv. to [his brothers] John and Michael Corse of the same county, his dwelling plantation left to him by his father, James Corse, dec., part of the tract called *Hepborns Farm*, 150 a.{KELR JS#W:133}

On 11da. 8 mo., 1727 William Corse was condemned for publick scandal by being proved guilty of fornication with a certain Alice Brown.{CEMM}

William Corse d. by 1 May 1738 when his estate was appraised (it was filed on 31 July 1738). Next of kin were James Corse, John Corse. The admx. was Barbary Corse.{MINV 23:390}

An additional inventory was taken 7 Feb 1739 and filed 9 Feb 1739, by the admx. Barbary Buckingham, wife of Howell Buckingham. {MINV 24:477}

4. JOHN CORSE, son of James (1), was b. c1701, and d. 7 da. 1 mo., 1763.{CEMM}. On 31 March 1757, John Corse, age c56, Quaker, affirmed regarding the bounds of the tracts called *Yapp, Mangys Joynture* and *Howells Farm Henham.*{KELR JS#28:375}

On 8 da. 10 mo., 1725 Jno. Corse requested a certificate to signify his clearness of marriage to be directed to Friends of Duck Creek Meeting in New Castle Co.{CEMM}

---

[7] On 13 March 1753 at age 42, she affirmed regarding the bounds of a tract called *Yapp;* recalled being on the opposite of the marsh with her father James Corse, since dec., and her sister Jennett, dec., a sawing locust posts; refers to John Redgraves her since dec. husband. 13 March 1753. {KELR JS#27:253} On 31 March 1757, Rachel Vansant, dau. of James Corse, dep. regarding the bounds of the tracts called *Yapp, Mangys Joynture* and *Howells Farm Henham* [no age given]. {KELR JS#28:379}

On 14 Dec 1733, with consent of his wife Susannah, he conv. to Michael Corse, carpenter, plantation called *Crows Farme* and a tract called *Greer's Range* adjoining, the land being left by the last will of our father James Corse.{KELR JS#18:4}

On 14 Dec 1744 a memorandum between John and Michael Course stated: Whereas James Course of KE Co., late dec., has by his last will 3 tracts to be equally divided between his two sons John and Michael Course and they agree that a line drawn from the ssw line of a parcel called *Groers Range* and .... [reference to land conveyed by John Corse and his wife Susannah to afsd. Michael Course. The memorandum or acknowledgement signed by Michael Corse on 14 Dec 1744.{KELR JS#18:12}

Susannah Corse wife of John Corse, a member of Cecil Meeting d. 8 da. 1 mo., 1747/8. On 11 da. 10 mo., 1752, it was noted that John Corse has taken a wife who is not of our Society. On 10 da., 7 mo., 1754, John Corse, Sr., was disowned for "marrying out." [*i.e.,* contrary to the rules of the Society of Friends].{CEMM}

John Corse, yeoman of KE Co. d. leaving a will dated 18 Nov 1762, and proved 16 March 1763. The heirs named were: children John, William, Timothy, Samuel, Hannah, Withyann, Thomas Hynson, Martha and Mary Corse, and dau. Susannah Lamb, leaving the youngest children under care of son John. Mentioned was Wethyann Corse. The exec. was son John Corse. The will was witnessed by Griffith Jones, Michael Corse and Elizabeth Walls.{MWB 31:875}

On 29 March 1763 his estate was appraised by Thomas Bowers and Rasin Gale, and valued at £471.9.10. Thomas Smyth and James Anderson signed as creditors. Hannah Corse and Joshua Lamb signed as next of kin. John Corse, exec., filed the inventory on 24 May 1763.{MINV 80:406}

The estate of John Corse, Quaker, of KE Co., was appraised again by Thomas Bowers and Rasin Gale, and valued at £51.9.8. James Anderson and Thomas Smith signed as creditors. Samuel Corse and Hannah Corse signed as next of kin. John Corse, exec., filed the inventory on 21 Jan 1764. {MINV 82:256} A list of debts was appraised and valued at £64.7.3. John Corse, exec., filed the list of debts on 21 Jan 1764.{MINV 82:265}

John and Susanna Corse were the parents of the following children{CEMM}: WILLIAM, b. 5 da. 12 mo., 1727; JOHN, b. 18 da. 9 mo., 1729, d. 17 da. 2 mo., 1807; SUSANNAH, b. 18 da. 9 mo., 1731 and d. 4 da. 9 mo., 1731; SUSANNAH, the second of that name of above, b. 18 da. 10 mo., 1733; TIMOTHY, b. 15 da. 7 mo., 1734; SAMUEL, b. 27 da. 12 mo., 1735; REBECCAH, b. 25d. 2 mo., 1738; SAMUEL, b. 7 da. 8 mo., 1740 and d. 26 da. 3 mo., 1770; HANNAH, b. 22 da. 6 mo., 1744 and [as] Hannah Leaburn d. 5 da. 6 mo., 1770;

REBECCAH Corse, second dau., b. 23 da. 12 mo., 1746 and d. 25 da. 12 mo., 1746.

5. MICHAEL CORSE, son of James (1), d. 26 da. 4 mo., 1749.{CEMM}

On 14 da. 9 mo., 1733, Michael Corse declared that he had an intention of marriage with Mary England, dau. of Isaac England of KE Co., Maryland, dec., and he now belonged to a monthly meeting in KE Co., Pennsylvania, so he requested a certificate.{CEMM}

On 13 da. 7 mo., 1749, Cecil Meeting noted that Michel Corse having departed this life who had the register of births, burials and marriages, Samuel Wallis was appointed in his place.{CEMM}

Michael Corse of KE Co., d. leaving a will dated 13 April 1749, and proved 1 Sep 1749. Sons Michael Corse and Daniel Corse were devised all the land including the dwell. plant., and part of the tract called *Friendship* and the tract, *Corse's Meadows*. His personal estate was to be divided among his children Isaac, Elizabeth, Jacob and Rebecca Corse. The execs. was wife Mary and bro. John Corse. The will was witnessed by James Price, Thomas Bowers and Rebecca Angers.{MWB 27:120}

On the 11th da., 11th mo., 1749 his estate was appraised by Samuel Wallis and William Rasin, and valued at £1084.9.11. Thomas Perkins and Thomas Bowers signed as creditors. John Corse and James Corse signed as next of kin. Mary Jones (late Mary Corse), wife of Griffeth Jones, extx., filed the inventory on 19 Dec 1750.{MINV 44:261}

On 3 May 1751 distribution of the estate of Michael Bowers was made by Griffith Jones and his wife Mary, acting extx. Distributions were made to six children: Michael, Daniel, Isaac, Elizabeth, Jacob and Rebecca Corse. {BFD 1:1}

On 15 Dec 1756 distribution of the estate was made by Mary Jones, acting extx., wife of Griffith Jones. Distribution was made to widow and to children: Michael, Daniel, Isaac, Elisabeth, Jacob and Rebecca. {BFD 2:45} Another distribution was made 19 July 1757 by Mary Jones, extx., wife of Griffith Jones.{BFD 2:71} A third distribution was made 24 April 1762 by the widow and extx. [Mary], now wife of Griffith Jones. Distribution was made to widow (1/3) and residue to Michael Course, Daniel Course, Isaac, Elisabeth, Jacob and Rebecca. {BFD 3:116}

Michael and Mary Corse were the parents of the following children{CEMM}: RACHEL, b. 19 da. 9 mo., 1734 and d. 17 da. 10 mo., 1734; ISAAC, b. 8 da. 1 mo., 1735/6; ELIZABETH, b. 19 da. 12 mo., 1737/8; MICHL., b. 12 da. 2 mo., 1740; DANIEL, b. 9 da. 8 mo., 1741; JACOB, b. 8 da. 1 mo., 1742/3; REBEKAH, b. 5 da. 12 mo., 1744.

6. JAMES CORSE, Jr., son of James (2) and Anne (Beck) Corse, d. by June 1750. He m. Susanna Perkins, who m. 2nd, John Day, and 3rd, Bartus Piner.

James Corse, Jr., was reported on 9 da. 3 mo., 1744, as having "gone out in marriage."{CEMM} On 9 da. 7 mo., 1747, James Corse and Susannah Perkins announced their intention to marry; however prior to the next meeting James Corse accomplished his marriage by a priest.{CEMM} On 8 da. 4 mo., 1748, Cecil Meeting issued a letter of testification against James Corse, son of James and Ann Corse, disowned for marrying out.{CEMM}

On 20 June 1750 his estate was appraised again by George Medford and Thomas Chandler, and valued at £197.9.0. Robert Guy and David Hall signed as creditors. Michael Corse and Rachel Vansant signed as next of kin. Susanna Corse, admx., filed the inventory on 15 Dec 1750.{MINV 44:257}

His estate was appraised again and valued at £7.0.0. Susanna Day, admx., filed the inventory containing a list of debts on 6 Oct 1762.{MINV 79:69}

A third inventory was taken on 7 Oct 1762, when his estate was appraised by Mathew Zuille and James Claypoole, and valued at £28.0.0. David Course and Rachel Talbot signed as creditors. David Course and Rachel Talbot signed as next of kin. Susanna Day, admx., filed the inventory on 13 Oct 1762.{MINV 79:69}

On 9 April 1763 distribution of the estate of James Corse, Jr., was made by Susannah Piner, admx., wife of Bartus Piner.{BFD 4:7}

7. WILLIAM CORSE, son of John (4) and Susannah, was b. 5 da. 12 mo., 1727. By 14 da. 10 mo., 1748, he had settled in KE Co., DE, when John Corse requested a certificate for his son William Corse who had moved there.{CEMM}

8. SAMUEL CORSE, son of John (4) and Susannah, was b. 7 da. 8 mo., 1740 and d. 26 da. 3 mo., 1770.

On 1 Aug 1770 his estate was appraised by Rasin Gale and Roger Hales, and valued at £10.15.6. John Parsons signed as creditor. George Leyburn and Joshua Lamb signed as next of kin. John Corse, admin., filed the inventory on 18 June 1771. {MINV 105:289}

9. ISAAC CORSE, son of Michael (5) and Mary, was b. 8 da. 1 mo., 1735/6.{CEMM}

On 28 March 1757 Isaac Corse of Philadelphia, house joyner, conv. to Francis Lamb of KE Co., planter, 57 a. called Friendship, 80 called Wetherills Hope and 13 a. called Corses Meadows.{KELR JS#28:371}

Unplaced

CORSE, DAVID, and Mary Bowers, both of KE Co., were m. with consent of parents on 9 da. 11 m., 1757.{CEMM} Mary Corse wife of

David Corse d. 28(20?) d. 3 mo., 1762.{CEMM} David and Mary Corse were the parents of JAMES, b. 10 da. 8 mo., 1758; ANN, b. 24 da. 8 mo., 1760 and Thomas, b. 23 da. 12 mo., 1761.{CEMM}.

David Corse, of KE, m. 2nd Elizabeth Fairbank on 31 Aug 1765, at James Fairbank.{TATH} On 25 da., 12 mo., 1766, a certificate was produced for Elizabeth Corse directed to the monthly meeting in KE Co.{TATH}

CORSE, ELIZABETH, declared on oath on 14 May 1755, that Pearce Lamb confessed fornication and entered into security to keep the child of the afsd. Elizabeth called Rebekah from becoming any charge to the county. Elizabeth was fined 30 shillings.{KECR JS#25:145A, 145B}

COURSE, ELISABETH, now Hart was reported in 7 mo., 1756, for having gone out in marriage.{CEMM}

CORSE, JAMES, ANN CORSE, and THOMAS CORSE, were named as grandchildren in the dist. of the estate of Thomas Bowers of KE Co., made 29 Dec 1772.{BFD 6:202}

CORSE, JOHN, on 11 da. 4 mo., 1753, was reported as being the reputed father of a base born child by a woman near Duck Creek. [She later acquitted him in writing.]

CORSE, JOHN, was charged at November Court 1769 that he did not give in his Negroe woman named Dido as a taxable. He was fined 50 shillings.{KECR DD#1:111A}

CORSE, JOHN, and wife Casandra were the parents of the following children: SARAH, b. 5 da. 11 mo., 1771 between 9 and 10 o'clock in the morning; JAMES RIGBY, b. 6 da. 3 mo., 1774; JOHN, b. 27 da. 7 mo., 1777.{CEMM}

CORSE, THOMAS, of Third Haven Creek, was the father of{TAMI}: JANE, b. 3 Aug 1699, bapt. 12 June 1703.

CORSE, THOMAS, son of John and Welthy Corse, KE Co., and Rosamond Lamb, dau. of George and Sarah Lamb of the same place, m. at Cecil Meeting House, 8 da. 6(?) mo., 1778. Rosamond d. 1 da. 3 mo., 1787.{CEMM}

CORSE, THOMAS, son of Thomas Corse and --- his wife d. 30 da. 2 mo., 1809.{CEMM}

CORSE, Wm., of KE Co. d. leaving a will dated 25 Sep 1765, and proved 6 Aug 1766. Mentioned were children: George, James, Daniel and Ann. Tracts named were *Middle Neck* and *Heath's Chance*. The extx. was his wife. The will was witnessed by Griffith Jones, John Gale, Jr. and McCall Medford.{MWB 34:209}

On 12 Aug 1766 his estate was appraised by Joshua Lamb and Macall Medford, and valued at £318.11.10. Abraham Canner and James Anderson signed as creditors. John Corse and Samuel Corse signed as next of kin. Elisabeth Corse, extx., filed the undated inventory.{MINV 92:43}

The estate of William Corse, of KE Co., was appraised and valued at £25.1.0. Elisabeth Everitt, wife of Hales Everitt, extx., filed the inventory containing a list of debts on 18 March 1767. {MINV 91:188}

On 18 March 1767 distribution of the estate was made by Elisabeth Everet, extx., wife of Hales Everet. Distribution was made to George Corse, Daniel Corse, James Corse and Ann Corse. {BFD 5:76}

THE COURSEY FAMILY

See also The Corse Family, above.

Refs.: A: BDML.

1. HENRY COURSEY was the father of{A}: HENRY, b. c1626/9; JOHN, d. c1661; WILLIAM, d. c1685; JAMES, of Lincoln's Inn, Mddx; JANE; CATHERINE (Katherine Coursey, sister of Henry, was transported by 1653{MPL ABH:313}); ANN, m. Tristram Thomas; JULIANA (was transported by 1661 by William{MPL 4:565}), m. John Russell.

2. HENRY COURSEY, son of Henry (1), was b. c1626/9, and d. 1695. He m. 1st, in 1658, Mary, widow of Richard Harris who d. 1657; 2nd, Elizabeth, d. 1702, widow of Simon Carpenter who d. 1670. Henry Coursey was a commander of foot in CE and KE Cos., 1681.{A}

Henry Cowrsey, age c29, dep. on 3 Oct 1657.{ARMD LIV:131, Liber B:35}

On 18 April 1653 "Mr. Henry Coursey demanded land due to him within this province for the transportation of himself and Messrs. John and William Coursey his Bros. and Katheren his sister. A warrant was issued same day to lay out for Mr. Henry Coursey for 200 a. upon Putuxent River or in any other place not formerly taken up ret. ... Jan."{MPL ABH:313}

On 6 Sep 1653 "Mr. Henry Coursey demanded land upon the Eastern Shore for the transportation of three servants, viz., Mary

93

Coursey his wife, Thomas Walton, Edward Dexter, Robert Price, Elizabeth Langford, Jane Kirkley, Mary Cole alias Bramson, John Mudbury, John Ferrick, Thomas Foster, Ann Fordum, William Lidle, David Hatch (Fizt.) 100 a. per pole (poll), and 200 a. more remaining due upon his demands made 18th Aprilis de Anno 1653. A warrant was issued to the Surveyor to lay out for Mr. Henry Coursey 1500 a. of land according to demand ret: 6 Aprilis next ut Supra."{ABH:313} Mary Coursey, wife of Henry, was transported prior to 1658.{MPL Q:183}

On 25 Oct 1662 Henry Coursey brought his servants Henry Cooper and John Hisok for the court to judge their ages . It was ordered that Cooper serve 9 years and Hissok 6 years. {ARMD LIV: 356, Liber BB No.2:4}

Henry Coursey of TA Co., d. leaving a will dated 17 June 1695 and proved 30 Oct 1695. The heirs named were: son Thomas, to have "*Trampington*" in Kent Co. To grandchild. James and Eliza: Earle and Carpenter and James Lillingston, personalty. To son John, 600 a., "*Coursey's Range*," w. side of Morgan's Creek on Wye River. To son James and dau. Jane 1000 a., "*Coursey's Choice*," equally. Either dying during minority survivor to inherit deceased's portion. To son Henry, 1000 a., "*Lord's Gift*," and 225 a., "*Burton;*" "*Black Walnut Neck*" to be reserved for use of wife during life. To cousin Eliza: Ustice and to Henry Fuler, personalty. To wife (unnamed), personalty including that formerly belonging to Simon Carpenter. Wife and 4 children by her, residuary legatees. The joint execs. were wife, dau. Jane, and son Thomas. Overseers: Jno. Henson, Sr., Thos. Smithson and Wm. Coursey. The will was witnessed by Chas. Blake, Rich'd. Macklin, Wm. Coursey and M. Earle.{MWB 7:184}

At February Court 1697 Madam Elizabeth Coursey, widow of Coll. Henry Coursey, was charged with having detained a parcel of 8 geese and ganders which did not properly belong to her. The geese were supposed to be Andrew Price's.{TAJU ABB: 524}

Eliza: Coursey, widow of Henry Coursey, of TA Co., d. leaving a will dated 14 Dec 1702 and proved 13 Jan 1702. The heirs named were grandsons Carpenter Lillingston and Carpenter Earle, personalty, part of which belonged to dec. husband, Henry Coursey, and part to first husband. To dau. Ann Earle, personalty which belonged formerly to son William Carpenter. To granddau. Eliza: Earle, personalty which formerly belonged to dau. Eliza. To granddaus. Jane, Mary and Frances Lillingston, personalty. The execs. and residuary legatees of estate were sons John and James Coursey. Rich'd. Macklyn and Rich'd. Tilghman requested to assist execs. in managing estate. The will was witnessed by Chas. Fitzgarrett, Wm. Fitzgarrett and Rich'd. Tilghman. {MWB 11:262}

Henry Coursey was the father of{A}: THOMAS, d. 1700/1, m. Ann Harris; JANE, d. by Feb 1696[8]; (poss.) ANNE, m. (N) Earle; HENRY, b. 1662; JAMES, d. 1714; and JOHN, d. 1713, m. Mary, dau. of Michael Turbutt.

3. JAMES COURSEY, son of Henry (1), was of Lincolns Inn in the County of Middlesex, Gent., when he sold to Dr. Richard Tilghman of MD a tract of land on Chester River, 400 a., which he acquired by will of his bro., John C. Coursey, dec., 20 July 1663.{MPL 10:447} He may be James Coursey, of TA Co., who immigrated 1677.{MPL 15:420}

4. JOHN COURSEY, son of Henry (1), d. 1661. He was Sheriff of KE Co. in 1657.{A} John Coursey was transported in 1653 and was named as a bro. to Henry; in 1658 he was named as a bro. to William. {MPL 4:538, 204; ABH:313 and Q:348}

5. WILLIAM COURSEY, son of Henry (1), d. 1685. He m. 1st, Juliana, widow of John Russell, and 2nd, Elizabeth.
   William immigrated in 1649 with his bros., probably from VA. He was a justice in KE Co. in 1661, and was also active in TA Co., as a Justice and a Delegate to the Assembly.{A} William Coursey, bro. of Henry, was transported by 1653.{MPL ABH:313} William Coursey, immigrated by 1651.
   On 3 Sep 1655 William Coursey demanded 100 a. of land for transporting himself into this province in May 1651. A warrant was issued the same day to lay out for William Coursey 100 a. upon or near St. Jerome's Creek or a branch thereof betwixt the fresh pound Neck and Barren Neck or in any other part of the province not formerly taken up ret: 1 Jan.{MPL ABH:424}
   On 10 Nov 1670 William Coursey conv. to his brother-in-law Tristram Thomas, Gent., land called *Trustram* where he lived on Wye River, 400 a.{TALR 1:126}

---

[8] Jane Coursey, of TA Co., died leaving a will dated 23 Dec 1695 and proved 5 Feb 1696. The heirs named were sister Ann Earle, sister Mary Lillingston and brother-in-law --- Lillingston, niece Jane and neph. Carpenter Lillingston, cous. Eliza: Ewestis, neph. James Earle, niece Eliza: Earle, brother-in-law Michael Earle, and to Richard Machlin, personalty. To mother (unnamed) during widowhood, personalty including slaves to be purchased with money left testatrix by Capt. Otho Southcoat of Ireland. To brothers John and James, sd. slaves in event of mother's marriage. To brother James at 21 yrs. of age, estate, real and personal, bequeathed testatrix by her father. To brother John, sd. estate in event of death of brother James afsd. without issue; to pass in turn to brother Thomas and hrs. The execs. were mother (unnamed) and brother Thomas Coursey. The will was witnessed by M. Earle, Anna Earle, Wm. Smith and Ruth Smith. {MWB 7:229}

95

On 17 Aug 1671, John Wells about to marry Ann Beedle, dau.-in-law to Wm. Coursey and sister to Henry Beedle entered a marriage contract; 500 a. on Chester River to be paid if the marriage did not take place before 10 Oct next. {TALR 1:163}

On 2 June 1673 William Coursey and his now wife, Juliana, relict and extx. of the last will of John Russell, Gent., of KE Co., conv. to Henry Beedle of AA Co. a gift of 250 a. called *Russendall* in Morgan's Creek. {TALR BB No.2:99, 104}

On 27 March 1680, William Coursey, of TA Co., and his wife Elizabeth conv. to William Smith of KE Co., 200 a., part of 1000 a. granted to William Coursey on 16 Sep 1668. {KELR B:16}

On 20 July 1681, William Coursey, of TA Co., Gent. and Elizabeth his wife conv. land to Abraham Ambrose, of KE Co. {KELR K:7A}

On 7 Dec 1682, William Coursey, of TA Co., and Elizabeth his wife conv. to Hans Hanson, of KE Co., 300 a., granted to William Coursey by patent on 16 Sep 1668. {KELR K:37}

William and his wife Elizabeth were the parents of{A}: WILLIAM, d. c1717/8, m. but d. s.p.

6. THOMAS COURSEY, son of Henry (2), and Ann Harris were m. 17 Oct 1699. {KESP} Thomas was bur. 28 Jan 1700. {KESP} Ann Harris Coursey m. 2nd, John Wells.

Thomas Coursey d. leaving a will dated 14 Feb 1700 and proved 31 July 1701. He named wife Ann during widowhood, leaving dwell. plant. called *Trumperton*. Execs. were his wife and two bros. John and James Coursey. {MWB 11:140}

His estate was admin. on 1 July 1701. Legatee named was Mrs. Rebecca Willmer. {INAC 21:277} The estate of Capt. Thomas Coursey was admin. again on 21 Dec 1702. Legatee was Mrs. Elisabeth Coursey. The admx. was Anne Wells, wife of John Wells. {INAC 23:118} The estate was admin. again on 24 Nov 1705. The admin. and exec. was John Wells. {INAC 26:166} The estate was admin. yet again on 5 Nov 1707. The account mentioned Henry Coursey, father. The extx. was Anne Wells, wife of John Wells. {INAC 27:200}

7. HENRY COURSEY, son of Henry (2) and Mary (Harris), was b. 24 May, and bapt. 16 July 1662{TA Court. VR; ARMD LVI:601, Liber BB#2:1} and d. 1707. He lived in TA Co. He m. Elizabeth, d. 1729, dau. of Elizabeth Desmyniers of Dublin. Henry was a delegate to the Assembly from TA Co.{A}

Elizabeth Coursey, widow, of QA Co., died leaving a will dated 27 Nov 1727 and proved 29 March 1729. The heirs named were sons Otho and William and dau. Arraminta, personalty. To daus. Elizabeth Cummins, Juliana and Mary, 20s. each. To son Henry, exec., residue of estate, either in Maryland, Ireland or Great Britain; and £160 bequeathed by mother Mrs. Elizabeth Desmyniers, late of Dublin, dec'd., with 1 moyety of residue of her estate; sd. bequests testator has ordered to be remitted to Philip Smith, mcht., London. The will was witnessed by John Emory, Robert Hassitt and John Fling. {MWB 19:644}

By his wife Elizabeth, he was the father of{A}: HENRY, b. 1693; OTHO; WILLIAM, b. 1703, d. 1769, m. Rachel, dau. of Solomon Clayton; ARAMINTA; ELIZABETH, m. William Cumming; JULIANA and MARY.

8. JAMES COURSEY, son of Henry (2), d. by May 1714.

At November Court 1712 James Coursey was appointed constable of Worrell Hundred instead of Thomas Lewis.{QAJU ET No.B:200}

James Coursey of TA Co., d. leaving a will dated 1 Jan 1703 and proved 5 May 1714. Brother John, was named exec., and heir of the entire estate, real and personal. He was to pay testator's debts and those of deceased mother, ---. The will was witnessed by W. Clayland, Wm. Fisher and Joana Wood. {MWB 13:717}

8. JOHN COURSEY, son of Henry (2), d. c1713. He m. Mary, dau. of Michael Turbutt.

On 23 Aug 1709 John Coursey of QA Co., Gent., and his wife Mary, conv. to Robert Ungle, GEnt., a claim to 400 a., part of *Four Square* near the freshes of Kings Creek.{TALR 11:86}

At March Court 1711 it was presented that John Coursey of Worrell Hundred, Gent., on 25 March being Sunday, gott drunk. Fined 100 lbs. of tobacco.{QAJU ET No.B:130}

John Coursey of QA Co., d. leaving a will dated 30 Dec 1712 and proved 21 May 1713. Son John received 1/2 "Coursey's Range." To son Thomas, residue of "Coursey's Range." To wife and 4 children, born of her, personal estate. In event of death of any dau. during minority or unmarried, deceased's portion to be divided among surviving children. Cousin Wm. Coursey and brother James Coursey to divide estate among children. The execs. were wife --- and bro.-in-law Samuell Turbutt. The will was witnessed by Charles Young, Jr., James Coursey and Matthew Smyth, Jr. {MWB 13:581}

John Coursey was the father of: JOHN; THOMAS; and one or more daughters.

9. WILLIAM COURSEY, prob. son of William (5), d. c1717/8.

On 3 April 1694 William Coursey, Gent., and his wife Elizabeth, conv. to John Salter, joyner, 600 a. called *Coursey's Towne*, patented 15 Feb 1659 to John and William Coursey on n. side of eastern branch of Chester River.{TALR 7:61}

On 23 Jan 1696, John Hawkins, of KE Co., and his wife Judith, and William Coursey and his wife Elizabeth, of TA Co., conv. to John King, of TA Co., tract called *Hawkins Pharsalia*, 200 a.{KELR M:48B}

On 23 Jan 1696, John Hawkins, of KE Co., and William Coursey, of TA Co., conv. to William Scott, of TA Co., part of a tract called *Hawkins Pharsalia*, 100 a.{KELR M:52A}

On 16 Aug 1703, William Carsey (Coursey), of TA Co., and his wife Elizabeth, conv. to Robert Smith land which Vincent Lowe of afsd. county, dec., by his last will devised several tracts to be sold by his execs., 3000 a., which was paid for by sd. Robert Smith, but the sd. execs. both d. before they had conv. the lands whereupon William Coursey and his wife Elizabeth were appointed by Act of Assembly in 1698 to sell the land.{KELR JD#1:145}

On 24 March 1713 William Coursey, Esq., and his wife Elizabeth, conv. to John Holson 300 a., part of *Hawkins' Pharsalia* on Milson's Branch.{QALR IKA:4}

Wm. Coursey of QA Co., d. leaving a will dated 29 May 1714 and proved 3 Feb 1717. The heirs named were wife Elizabeth, extx., dwelling plantation and tract called "*Cheston*," also 800 a. of adj. tract called "*Coursey Upon Wye*," lying on w. side of Carrolls Cove, during life. At her death afsd. lands to pass to kinsman Wm. Coursey (son of Henry Coursey). The remaining part of "*Coursey on Wye*" and a tract called "*Long Week*," on e. side of sd. Carroll's Cove, cont. in all 1,000 a., also 200 a., "*Hawkins Pharsalia*" on fork of Tuckahoe, and remaining part of "*Whitfield*" in KE Co., at head of Langford Bay, cont. 300 a., to wife Elizabeth, with personal estate of testator. The will was witnessed by Jacob Covington, Wm. Turbett, Elizabeth Bennett and Jane Evans. {MWB 14:472}

On 25 June 1718 Elizabeth Coursey, widow and relict of William Coursey, conv. to William Turbutt 400 a. called *Long Neck* on Wye River on e. side of Carroll's Cove; also 200 a., part of *Hawkins' Pharsalia* on the Tuckahoe.{QALR IKA:183}

On 16 March 1721 William Turbutt, Gent. mortgaged to Richard Bennett 600 a., part of *Coursey upon Wye*, by the will of Coll. William Coursey lately dec., bequeathed to his wife Elizabeth.{QALR IKB:144}

Elizabeth Coursey, widow of William Coursey of Wye River, QA Co., d. leaving a will dated 25 March 1725 and proved 6 Oct 1726. The heirs named were kinswoman Mary, wife of Thomas Hynson Wright; sister Sarah, wife of Jacob Covington; kinswomen Sarah, wife of Arthur Emory, Jr.; Elizabeth, wife of Thomas Wilkinson; Thomas, son of Thomas Marsh, of Kent Island, dec., personalty. To servant Elizabeth Willington, nine months of her time. To kinsman William Turbutt, remaining lands had of dec. husband not already sold or devised. To Michael, Anna and Mary, children of sd. William Turbutt; and John, Thomas and Mary, child. of John Coursey, dec., residue of personal estate at age of 21 or day of marriage. The execs. were William Turbutt, Thomas Hynson Wright and Mary his wife. The will was witnessed by Vincent Hemsley, David Lesage and Elizabeth Willington. Codicil dated 15 Aug 1726 gave to Elizabeth, wife of Thomas Wilkinson, personalty.{MWB 19:38}

10. OTHO COURSEY, son of Henry (7) and Elizabeth, was living on 26 May 1723 when he mortgaged to Richard Bennett, merchant, two tracts surveyed for Henry, father of Otho Coursey: The *Neglect,* 400 a. on w. side of Back Wye River; and *Coursey's Addition,* 150 a.{QALR IKB:216}

On 5 March 1719 Otho Coursey, Gent., conv. to Richard Bennett, merchant, land originally surveyed for Henry Coursey, grandfather of Otho Coursey for 1000 a. on e. side of Morgains Creek now called Back Wye River.{QALR IKB:13}

11. WILLIAM COURSEY, son of Henry (7) and Elizabeth, was b. 1703, d. 1769, m. cOct 1738, Rachel, dau. of Solomon Clayton. William Coursey, age 64, dep. 2 Oct 1767.{QAEJ: Downe: OS}

He may be the William Coursey of St. Paul's Parish, who at June Court 1727, was found guilty of committing fornication on 10 April 1726 with Alice Brown and begetting a bastard child. He was fined 30 S.{KECR JS#22:274}

On 4 Oct 1738 William Coursey, Gent., gave to Rachell Clayton, Gentlewoman, a gift in recognition of their intended marriage 800 a., all of *Cheston* on Wye River; also 290 a. adj., part of *Coursey Upon Wye.*{QALR RTB:204}

On 27 Oct 1741 Mary Clayton, widow, gave to her niece, Sarah Coursey, dau. of William Coursey, a mulatto girl called Doll, age 4 years.{QALR RTB:377}

On 27 Jan 1746/7 William Coursey, Gent. and his wife Rachel leased to John Holden *Sleeford* and *Sheppard Hook* for 15 years.{QALR RTC:204}

He may be the William Coursey, Gent., who, on 14 Oct 1747, gave to his dau. Rachel Coursey, a Negro named Nann.{QALR RTC:297}

William Coursey, of QA Co., d. leaving a will dated 2 March 1769 and proved 28 March 1769. He named his children Edward, Henry, William, Sarah and Mary Downs, and granddau. Mary Sewell. He referred to land which belonged to his last wife, and mentioned the tracts *Chester* and *Sheath.* The exec. was to be his son William. The will was witnessed by Jacob Seth, Wm. Kent, Jr., Joseph Blunkall, John Carty.{MWB 37:125}

William and Rachel (Clayton) Coursey were the parents of: EDWARD; HENRY; WILLIAM; SARAH; RACHEL (may have d. young); and MARY, m. (N) Downs.

12. THOMAS COURSEY, son of John (8), d. after Nov 1729.

Thomas Coursey of QA Co., died leaving a will dated 12 Nov 1729 and proved 24 Nov ---. The heirs named were nephew Solomon Coursey Wright, personal estate at age of 21; he dying during minority, to pass to nephew Solomon Wright at age of 21. The will was witnessed by Thomas Hynson Wright, William Norman and John Murray. Probate to above will taken at request of Mary Wright. {MWB 20:137}

Unplaced

CORSEY, HENRY, m. by 14 May 1742, Elizabeth, dau. of Elizabeth Ricketts of KE Co., widow, who conv. to her dau. Elizabeth Corsey, wife of Henry Coursey, of QA Co., a tract called *Bluff Point* on Morgans Creek. {KELR JS#23:416}

COURSEY, JOHN, and Margaret Downes, were named in the will (made 15 July 1759) of Nathaniel Wright, Jr., of QA Co., as being the parents of{MWB 37:604}: HENRY; and ELIZABETH.

CORSEY, WILLIAM, m. by 12 Nov 1764 Frances (N). On that day William Coursey and his wife Frances of QA Co., but late of TA Co., conv. to Thomas Tennant of TA Co., house carpenter, 40 a., part of *Venture.* {QALR RTG:97} On the same day Thomas Tennant of TA Co., carpenter, and his wife Mabell, conv. to William Coursey of QA Co. 168 a., part of *Satterfield's Luck.* {QALR RTG:93}

William and Frances were the parents of the following children, whose births were recorded in St. John's Parish, Caroline Co. {CAJO}: WILLIAM, b. 17 Aug 1759; FRANCES, b. 12 Dec 1761; MARY, b. 1 April 1764; and THOMAS, b. 10 Aug 1766.

COURSEY, William, m. by 18 Aug 1769, Anne, sister of William Jacobs of QA Co. {MWB 37:313}

COURSEY, WILLIAM, son of William (brother-in-law of Joseph DeRochbrune), on 15 Oct 1773 was named as nephew in the will of Joseph DeRochbrune of KI, QA Co., and left the rent from the tract Ashford. His sister Elizabeth Coursey was also named. {MWB 39:423}

THE COUSINS (COUSANS/COZENS) FAMILY

1. EDWARD COUSINS, and Elizabeth Fisher m. 27 April 170-. Elizabeth Cozens, wife of Edward Cozens, bur. 13 Nov 1729. {KESP}

On 4 March 1712, Edward Cosens and his wife Elizabeth, conv. to John Magner, 100 a., being part of a tract called *Providence*.{KELR JSN:319}

Edward Cousins (Cousands, Cosons, Cozens) d. leaving a will proved 17 March 1735. To son Edward he left his entire real estate. To wife Elizabeth he left ½ estate. Execs. were wife and son afsd.{MWB 21:567}

His estate was inv. on 26 March 1736; the inventory was filed 3 July 1736. Execs. were wife Elisabeth and son Edward.{MINV 21:478}

Edward and Elizabeth were the parents of: WILLIAM, bapt. 4 Nov 1708; and EDWARD, b. c1710.

2. EDWARD COUSANS, son of Edward and Elizabeth was b. c1710. On 21 March 1750, Edward Cousans, age c40, dep. regarding the bounds of a tract called *Boonly*.{KELR JS#27:27} He m. Elizabeth, dau. of Robert Green.

At March Court 1732, Edward Cozens, Jr., of St. Paul's Parish, was found guilty of assaulting Elizabeth, wife of Thomas Aires on 10 Oct 1732. He was fined 1000 lbs. of tob.{KECR JS#WK:367}

Edward Cousens of KE Co., for 3,500 lbs. of tob., on 8 Aug 1737 assigned to William Harris, Gent., a Negro woman named Judey, formerly appraised in the estate of his father Edward Couzans.{KEBI JS#18:96}

On 1 Aug 1739, Edward Couzans (Cozans) and his wife Elizabeth of KE Co., conv. to William Bradsha, of afsd. county, a parcel on a branch of Swan Creek called *Cuckolds Point*, 55 a.{KELR JS#22:398} On 22 Aug 1740, Edward Cousans, and his wife Elizabeth Cousans, conv. to William Yearly of afsd. county, part of a tract called *Hynson's Haven*, 50 a., called *Parker's Rest* and a parcel called *Cousans's Lott*, 100 a.{KELR JS#23:108}

At November Court 1739, it was presented that Edward Couzans, on 10 Nov 1739, stole a saddle of Phillip Davis.{KECR JS#23:18}

On 25 May 1743, Edward Couzens of KE Co., and his wife Elizabeth, conv. 24 a. to Edward Dyer of afsd. county, carpenter. {KELR JS#24:between folios 407 and 415}

On 5 Oct 1745, Edward Cozens of KE Co., and his wife Elizabeth, conv. to William Yearly, Sr., a tract called *Parkes's Rest* on Swan Island Creek, 50 a. and the tract called *Couzens's Lott*, 100 a., and a tract called *Couzens's Chance*, 68 a.{KELR JS#25:303}

On 8 May 1758 Elizabeth Couzens confessed to committing fornication and named the father. She was fined 30 s., and John Higgins entered into security for the fine and fees.{KECR JS#25:193A}

On 23 June 1758 St. Leger James, on the oath of Elizabeth Couzens, confessed to committing fornication and was fined 30 s. and entered into security with John Chappell for fines, fees and to keep the child of sd. Elizabeth Couzens from becoming any charge to the county.{KECR JS#25:195A}

Unplaced

COZENS, MARY, spinster, at August Court 1767, was charged that on 1 May 1766 she committed fornication and begot a base born child. She was fined 30 s. She was ordered to give security to keep the county from any charge by means of her bastard child called Rebecca.{KECR DD#1:92B}

THE COVINGTON FAMILY

1. THOMAS COVINGTON, was bur. 24 Jan 1708.{KESP} He m. Rachel (N) who m. 2nd, Robert Hannah or Harman.

On 5 March 1710, his estate was admin. The accountant named his son Thomas Covington, and the admx. Rachall Hannah, wife of Robert Hannah (Hanna).{INAC 32B:251} The estate was admin. again on 17 June 1710. The admx. was named as Rachell Harman, wife of Robert Harman.{INAC 31:235} Thomas and Rachel were the parents of: THOMAS, Jr.; JEREMIAH, b. c1696; and NEHEMIAH, bapt. 2 Dec 1708.{KESP}

2. JEREMIAH COVINGTON, son of Thomas, of KE Co., was b. c1696. On 22 Aug 1718, conv. to Michael Hackitt, 100 a., part of a tract called *Broadneck*; the deed stated that Jeremiah Covinton was seized of a parcel of land on the w. side of Morgans Creek called *Broad Neck*, but formerly of TA Co., which was purchased by Thomas Covinton, dec., who was father to sd. Jeremiah Covinton who is now seized of afsd. land.{KELR BC#1:306}

On 20 Nov 1721, Jeremiah Covinton of KE Co., conv. to John Blackston and his wife Hanah, ½ part of a parcel on Morgans Creek.{KELR JS#W:199}

On 19 Dec 1738 Jerom [sic] Coventon, age c42, dep. regarding the bounds of a tract called *the Dining Room*.{KELR JS#22:288}

Jeremiah Covington and Cassandra Wyath m. 19 Sep 1737.{KESP}

Jeremiah Covington of KE Co., d. by 25 July 1754, when his estate was appraised by George Skirven and John Brookes, and valued at £53.6.1. James Anderson and Richard Lloyd signed as creditors. Richard Wroth and Priscillah Wroth signed as next of kin. Thomas Covington, admin., filed the inventory on 21 Dec 1754.{MINV 60:194}

Jeremiah "Coventree" and wife Mary were the parents of: HANNAH, b. 23 March 1723; THOMAS, b. 16 May 1726; RACHELL, b. 27 Feb 1728; and PRISCILLA, b. 14 Feb 1731.{KESP}

3. NEHEMIAH COVINGTON, son of Thomas and Rachel, was bapt. 2 Dec 1708.{KESP} He m. Rachel (N) who admin. the estate.

Nehemiah Covington of KE Co., d. by 7 Feb 1764, when his estate was appraised by Nicholas Smith and William Smith, and valued at £242.1.11. Thomas Gilpin and Thomas & William Ringgold signed as creditors. William Downs and Rachel Covington signed as next of kin. Rachel Covington, admx., filed the inventory on 2 April 1764. {MINV 83:97}

He is probably the "Jeremiah Covington" of KE Co., whose list of debts were appraised and valued at £4.5.3 and filed by Rachel Covington, admx., on 11 Dec 1764.{MINV 86:126}

On 11 Dec 1764 distribution of the estate was made by Rachel Covington, admx.{BFD 4:81}

4. THOMAS COVINGTON, son of Jeremiah and Mary, was b. 16 May 1726. By Sep 1756 he m. Mary (N).

On 14 Sep 1756 Thomas "Coventry" (or Coventon) of KE Co., and his wife Mary, conv. to John Gleaves of afsd. county, farmer, part of a tract called *Broad Neck* and part of a tract called *Friendship,* 130 a.{KELR JS#28:279}

Unplaced

COVENTON, HENRY, of QA Co., and Rachel Roe were m. 19 da., 1 mo., 1738, with consent of their parents at QA Co. Meeting House.{CEMM}

Henry and Rachel were the parents of: SARAH, b. 14 da., 10 mo., 1741; MARY, b. 3 da., 11 mo., 1743; REBECCA, b. 1 da., 4 mo., 1746; RACHAEL, b. 27 da., 12 mo., 1750; and EDWARD, b. 22 da., 11 mo., 1754.{CEMM}

COVINGTON, MARY, was m. by a priest,[9] for which she was disowned by Cecil Meeting on 8 da., 6 mo., 1757.{CEMM}

COVINGTON, PHILLIP, was bur. 21 May 1709.{KESP}

THE COWARDING FAMILY

1. THOMAS COWARDING (CARWARDING) d. by 10 July 1722 when his estate was inv. Next of kin were Thomas Carwarding and John Carwarding. John Young signed as approver.{MINV 7:249}

On 2 July 1722 his estate was admin. by Edward Cowarden.

---

[9] Quakers referred to ministers of other denominations as priests or hireling ministers.

Thomas was probably the father of: THOMAS; and JOHN.

2. THOMAS COWARDING, son of Thomas (1), was b. c1681, and d. by Dec 1753. On 5 Nov 1745, Thomas Cowarden, age c63, dep. regarding the bounds of a tract called *Howards Gift*. {KELR JS#25:398}

Thomas Cowardin (Cowarden), of KE Co., d. leaving an estate which was appraised by P. Whichcote and John Reid, and valued at £22.1.10. No creditors listed. Ambross Cowardin and Elenor Cowarden signed as next of kin. Abraham Cowarden, admin., filed the inventory on 4 Dec 1753.{MINV 57:101}

Thomas Cowarden and Frances Ambrose were m. 12 April 1716.{KESP} They were the parents of: ABRAHAM.

3. JOHN COWARDING (CARWARDING), son of Thomas (1), m. Ann (N) and d. by 22 March 1750, when James Meeks of KE Co., and his wife Mary, conv. to Josias Ringgold, part of a tract called *Queen Charleton* which formerly belonged to John Cowarden son of Thomas of the afsd. county, dec., and the right of dower of which sd. John Cowarden's widow, the same James Meeks, purchased.{KELR JS#28:437}

John Cowarding, of KE Co., d. leaving a will dated 9 May 1752 and proved 13 June 1752. The heirs named were son Edward Cowarding; dau. Ann Strong, wife of James Strong; dau. Martha Willson, wife of James Willson; son Ebenezar Cowarding; and dau. Frances Cowarding. A proviso was made if Ebenezer should die of the smallpox "which he is now stricken with." The execs. were son Ebenezar and dau. Frances. The will was witnessed by Joseph Nicholson and Roseannah Thomas.{MWB 28:365}

John and Ann Cowarding were the parents of: EDWARD, b. 11 Nov 1723; ANN, b. 27 July 1725, m. James Strong; MARTHA, b. 26 May 1728, m. James Willson; EBENEZER, b. 6 Sep 1730; and FRANCIS, b. 25 Jan 1733.{KESP}

4. ABRAHAM COWARDEN, of KE Co., son of Thomas (2) , m. Mary (N).

At June Court 1744, Abraham Cowardine was presented for selling liquor, and was fined £5.{KECR JS#24:156}

At March Court 1745, it was presented that Abraham Cowarden, assaulted Joseph Thomas on 20 Nov 1745. He was fined 10 s.{KECR JS#24:241}

As Abraham Cowarden, heir of Frances Cowardine of afsd. county, dec., and devisee of Evan Evans of afsd. county, dec., he and his wife Mary on 8 June 1754, conv. land to Thomas Ringgold of Chester Town, merchant. The deed stated that whereas at the last Provincial Court the afsd. Abraham Cowardine did suffer a common recovery wherein the sd. Thomas Ringgold was demandant for the cutting off and baring all demandant estates tail and in a certain parcel of land of 100 a. being part of land called *Queen Charlton* which sd. Abraham's father Thomas possessed in right of his wife Frances and d. possessed of, and whereas the afsd. Evan Evans by his last will devised to the sd. Abraham in fee all that parcel of land of 106 a., part of a tract called *Poplar Farme*, which the afsd. Evan before that time had bought of James Harris, Esq. Now Abraham Cowardine grants to sd. Thomas Ringgold the afsd. two parcels, the one part of *Queen Charlton* of 100 a. which was given by deed from Abraham Ambrose to his wife Elenor Ambrose for life remainder to his son Thomas Ambrose in tail remainder to his dau. Frances (afterwards Frances Cowardin) and mother of the same Abraham in tail the other the sd. 106 a. which the sd. James Harris sold to the afsd. Evan Evans, part of a tract called *Poplar Farm*.{KELR JS#27:457}

Abraham Cowarden and Mary Joce m. 2 Nov 1738.{KESH}
They were the parents of: JOHN, b. 1 Dec 1739; MARTHA, b. 2 July 1741; PASCO, b. 25 Sep 1744; SARAH, b. 29 June 1747; and ABRAHAM, b. 2 da., 10 mo., 1751.{KESH}

3-a. EDWARD COWARDING, son of John (3) and Ann, was b. 11 Nov 1723.{KESP} He m. Anne (N), who m. 2nd, Thomas Lynch.

Edward Cowarding (Cowarden), cordwainer, and his wife Ann of KE Co., on 12 Nov 1741, conv. to John Pasko of KE Co., part of a tract which John Salsbury and his wife Mary sold to Sutton Quinny and his son Sutton Quinny sold to Edward Cowardine, being part of a manner called *Cornwallis His Choice*, on Worton Branch between Aquilla Beck's dwell. plant. and William Savory's and a parcel of land called *Doe Neck*.{KELR JS#23:307}

Edward Corwardine d. leaving an estate which was appraised by Paul Whichcot and George Griffith, and valued at £35.17.7. James Anderson and W. Hynson signed as creditors. John Cowarden and Thomas Cowarden signed as next of kin. Thomas Lynch and Ann Lynch, admins., filed the inventory on 5 Jan 1746.{MINV 34:175}

Edward d. by 18 March 1745 leaving issue: REBECCA.[10]

Unplaced

COWARDEN, DORCAS, and John Arthur, were charged, at August Court 1752, that on 10 May 1751, they committed fornication and begot a bastard child.{KECR JS#25:101A}

---

[10] On 18 March 1745 Rebecca Cowardine, orphan, dau. to Edward Cowardine of KE Co., dec., was bound to William Graves, Gent., as an apprentice, until age 16 or day of marriage.{KEBI JS#20:214}

COWARDEN, JOHN, and wife Frances were the parents of: JOHN, b. 19 Jan 1716.{KESP}

COWARDING, JOHN, of KE Co., d. leaving a will dated 21 Aug 1753 and proved 4 Sep 1753. The heirs named were bro. Peter Cowarding, to whom was devised the dwell. plant., being part of a tract called *Queen Charlton* (100 a.); and sister Elinor Cowarding. The extx. was wife. The will was witnessed by Joseph Wickes, William Cowarden, and James Meeks.{MWB 28:524}

On 22 Sep 1753 his estate was appraised by Paul Whichcote and John Wickes, and valued at £7.4.10. No creditors or next of kin listed. Mary Cowardin, extx., filed the inventory on 1 Aug 1754, mentioning James Meeks, Peter Cowardin, Elinor Cowardin and David Griffith.{MINV 57:376}

COWARDEN, MARY, spinster, at March Court 1745, was presented that on 20 Nov 1745 with assaulting Joseph Thomas; she was fined 10 s.{KECR JS#24:242}

THE GEORGE CROUCH FAMILY

1. GEORGE CROUCH immigrated c1640, with his wife (N), formerly a servant to Richard Hawlyn or Howbyn.{MPL 3:19} On 18 Aug 1650 George Crouch demanded 200 a. of land (100 a. for his own transportation about 10 years since, 50 a. in right of his wife who was servant to Richard Hawlyn of Kent, and 50 a. for the transportation of Mary his dau. since that time). A warrant was issued to lay out 200 a. for George Crouch upon the Western Shore of Chesapeak Bay over against Kent or thereabouts.{MPL ABH:45}

George "Croutch" was bur. 2 da., 10 mo., 1655.{ARMD LIV:38, Liber A:107}

Isacke Ilive dep. on 1 Jan 1655 that George Croutch before his death, in his time of sickness, desired to make his will and intended to give his son George two guns and cattle, and his dau. Marie a heifer, a sow and pigs, and the rest of the movables to his wife.{ARMD LIV:47, Liber A:113}

George Crouch was the father of: GEORGE; and MARY (transported since 1640).{MPL ABH:45, 3:19 and 5:531}

2. GEORGE CROUCH, son of George, was a ward of Nicholas Pickard, who on 20 July 1658 with Mary Baxter moved the court to have George Crouch, son of George Crouch, dec., left in the custody of Nicolas Pickard.{ARMD LIV:137, Liber B:40}

THE RICHARD CROUCH FAMILY

1. RICHARD CROUCH m. Judith, dau. of John Wedge. He d. by 23 Jan 1738, when his widow Judith had m. (N) Draper.

On 23 Jan 1739, Judith Draper of KE Co., widow, conv. to her son Wedge Crouch of the same county, a tract called *Wedges Resurvey*, on the eastern side of Graysins Creek, 100 a.{KELR JS#22:549}

Richard and Judith had at least two sons{KELR JS#23::251}: WEDGE; and RICHARD

2. WEDGE CROUCH, son of Richard (1) and Judith, was b. c1688 and d. by July 1755. On 26 Feb 1746, he dep. regarding the bounds of the tract *Bounty*.{KELR JS#26:32}

Wedge Crouch and Mary Hurtt were m. 24 Dec 1713.{KESP}

Wedge and his wife Mary, on 20 Nov 1722, conv. to James Smith of afsd. county, part of a tract called *Folly Land* at the head of Duns Creek, 425 a.{KELR JS#W:260}

On 21 June 1743 Wedge Crouch of KE Co., and his wife Mary, conv. to Richard Gresham of the same county, Gent., the moiety of a tract formerly laid out for John Wedge of afsd. county called *Wedges Recovery*, 100 a. plus the surplusage added by a resurvey and now called *Wedges Recovery Resurveyed*.{KELR JS#24:441}

Wedge Crouch, of KE Co., d. by 29 July 1755, when his estate was appraised by Samuel Groome and James Smith, and valued at £31.10.0. Sarah Graves, admx., filed the inventory 7 Sep 1756, mentioning Richard Lloyd, Alexander Corbett, Richard Crouch and Nicholas Crouch.{MINV 62:34}

Wedge and Mary were the parents of: THOMAS, b. 11 Nov 1722; CATHERINE, b. 30 Jan 1726;[11] and JOHN WEDGE, b. 13 Oct 1728.{KESP}

3. RICHARD CROUCH (probably the son of Richard (1) and Judith), was b. c1694, and was age c41 on 7 April 1735, when he dep. regarding the bounds of the tract *Chance*.{KELR JS#18:121}

On 26 Feb 1746, Richard Crouch, age c53, dep. regarding the bounds of the tract *Bounty;* he said that John Huff told him about 30-

---

[11] She may be the Catharine Crouch, spinster, charged at November Court 1750 that on 10 July 1749 she committed fornication and begot a bastard child. She was fined £3.{KECR JS#25:67A}

At March Court 1752, it was presented that Catharine Crouch, spinster, on 10 Jan 1750, committed fornication and begot a bastard child. She was fined 30 s.{KECR JS#25:88A} At the same court Stephen Brown, planter, was charged that on 10 Jan 17--, he committed fornication with Catharine Crouch and begot a bastard child. He was fined 30 s.{KECR JS#25:87B}

40 years earlier that his (Huff's) father-in-law, Henry Morgan, told him ....{KELR JS#26:32}

On 9 Oct 1761, Richard Crouch, age c67, dep. regarding the bounds of a tract called *Huntingfield*. (Wedge Crouch was mentioned as the bro. of Mr. Ringgold.){KELR DD#1:618}

Richard and Ann Crouch were the parents of: (possibly) RICHARD, b. c1715; MARY, b. 25 July 1720; THOMAS, b. 26 Feb 1722; REBECCA, b. 25 July 1725;[12] ANN, b. 5 Aug 1728; RACHELL, b. 13 Nov 1730; and SUSANNA, b. 12 March 1732.{KESP}

4. RICHARD CROUCH, possibly son of Richard (3) and Anne, was b. c1715. He was c40 years old on 27 Feb 1755, when he dep. regarding the bounds of a tract called *Stanaway;* about 8 years earlier he had been an overseer for Mary Hanson, lately dec., at her Swan Creek plant. and riding with her on a Sunday to Church along Swan Creek Main Road.{KELR JS#28:99}

At June Court 1753, it was presented that Richard Crouch, on 21 April 1753, assaulted Ann Joce. He was fined 5 s.{KECR JS#25:114B}

On 20 June 1757, Richard Crouch, Jr., age 42 or 43, dep. regarding the bounds of the tract called *Arcadia.*{KELR JS#28:426}

5. THOMAS CROUCH, son of Richard and Ann, was b. 26 Feb 1722. He is probably the Thomas Crouch who m. Mary Ambrose on 11 May 1754.

Thomas Crouch d. by 21 June 1774, when his estate was appraised by Jacob Glenn and Richard Miller, and valued at £329.19.9. J. Page and Thomas Ringgold signed as creditors. Rachel Clark signed as next of kin. Mary Crouch, admx., filed the inventory on 10 Sep 1774.{MINV 118:249}

A list of debts, appraised and valued at £5.13.1, was filed by Mary Crouch, admx., on 13 Dec 1775.{MINV 122:264}

On 13 Dec 1775 distribution of the estate was made by Mrs. Mary Crouch, admx.{BFD 7:53}

Thomas and Mary were the parents of: ANN, b. 17 Oct 17--; and JAMES, b. 16 May 1757.{KESP}

Unplaced

CROUCH, BLANCH, on 8 March 1754 confessed being guilty of fornication and having a base born child. She refused to identify the father.{KECR JS#25:125B}

---

[12] She may be the Rebecca Crouch, spinster, charged at August Court 1742 that on 1 July 1741 committed fornication and begot a bastard child. She was fined 30 shillings.{KECR JS#24:42}

CROUCH, JOHN, d. leaving a widow (N), who m. 2nd, William Elmes, who in obedience to an order of court dated 10 March 1709, was to give proof relating to the southern most bounds of a tract called *Coventry,* now in the possession of Major William Harris. To certify that he, William Elmes, having m. the widow of John Crouch (who owned the contiguous tract bounding s. upon the afsd. *Coventry)* had seen a bounded tree. 25 March 1710.{KELR JSN:267}

CROUCH, JOSIAS and wife Joan were the parents of: ELIZABETH, bapt. 21 May 1699.{KESP}

CROUCH, MARCH [sic], at June Court 1761, was charged with having committed fornication, begetting a base born child.{KECR DD#1:8A}

CROUCH, NICHOLAS, of KE Co., d. by 15 April 1760, when his estate was appraised by Jarvis James and John Hynson, Jr., and valued at £8.0.0. Thomas Ringgold signed as creditor. Mary Crouch and Martha Crouch signed as next of kin. William Murray, admin., filed the inventory on 7 April 1764, mentioning Richard Crouch and Nicholas Crouch.{MINV 83:108}

On 7 April 1764 distribution of the estate was made by William Murray, admin.{BFD 4:31}

THE WILLIAM CROW FAMILY

1. WILLIAM CROW was b. c1675. In Aug 1726, William Crowe, age c51, dep. regarding the bounds of a tract called *Arcadia;* he stated that the branch that comes on the e. side of St. Paul's Church and running to the Old Plantation of Capt. Ebenezar Blackstone where his father lived, had been called the n. branch of Langfords Bay by some, and others have called it the n.w. branch.{KELR JS#X:39}

William Crow and Mary Urick (actually Unick) were m. 24 May 1702.{KESP} On 10 March 1704 William Crowe and wife Mary rendered an account made up by William Crowe and his wife Mary as admx. of the estate of John Unick.{KELR GL#1:27/49; see also INAC 24:177}

On 24 June 1727 William Fowle, mariner, gave bond to William Crowe of KE Co., in the sum of £50, that he would get a sufficient deed to William Crowe from the heirs of William Treggo, late of the Kingdom of England, dec., for a tract formerly owned by Joseph Weeks and commonly called *Middle Plantation* between Northwest Branch and Northeast Branch of Langfords Bay. 41 May 1726.{KELR JS#W:528}

William Crow, of KE Co., d. leaving a will written 20 Nov 1745 and proved 7 Jan 1745. The heirs named were son William, Jr., son Isaac, son Thomas and dau. Martha Jackson. Mentioned was tract *Crow's*

Chance. The will was witnessed by John Smith, Stephen Canady, and Amos Adderton.{MWB 24:288}

On 9 Jan 1745, his estate was appraised by W. Hynson and Joseph Ringgold, and valued at £286.15.6. Edward Dyer and L. Wilmer signed as creditors. Thomas Crow and Marthar Jeappon signed as next of kin. Isaac Crow, admin., filed the inventory on 11 March 1745.{MINV 33:97}

On 18 Aug 1746 his estate was appraised by W. Hynson and Joseph Ringgold, and valued at £55.19.7. The unnamed admin. filed the inventory on 14 Oct 1746.{MINV 33:336}

William and Mary were the parents of: WILLIAM; ANN; MARY (probably d. young);[13] MARTHA, m. (N) Jackson (or Jeappon); ISAAC, b. c1707; THOMAS, b. c1708; and JAMES, b. 12 May 1714 (probably d. young).{KESP}

2. WILLIAM CROW, son of William and Mary, was named in his father's will. He d. soon after his father.

William Crow, of KE Co., d. leaving a will written 8 Oct 1746 and proved 19 Nov 1746. The heirs named were bros. Isaac Crow and Thomas Crow. The will was witnessed by John Smith and James Smith.{MWB 24:533}

3. ISAAC CROW, son of William and Mary, was b. c1707. On 29 Sep 1762, Isaac Crow, age c55; dep. regarding the tract *Sweetmans Addition;* he recalled about 40 years earlier when he was with his father Wm. Crow, now dec.{KELR DD#1:310}

On 20 Sep 1762, Isaac Crow of KE Co., and his eldest son William Crow, conv. to Henry Hurt of the same county, a tract called *Middle Plantation*, 350 a., and a tract called *Crows Chance*, 100 a.{KELR DD#1:131}

Isaac Crow m. 1st, Mary (N), by whom he was the father of: WILLIAM, b. 4 Feb 1737-8; EDWARD, b. 10 March 1739; JAMES, b. 29 Oct 174-; ANN, b. 17 Sep 1750.{KESP} He may have been the Isaac Crow who m. 2nd Sarah (N). Isaac and Sarah were the parents of: HANNAH, b. 1 Dec 17--; ISAAC, b. 10 April 1757; SARAH, b. 29 May 1758; SUSANNA, b. 6 Jan 1760; and MARY, b. 9 May 1762.{KESP}

4. THOMAS CROW, son of William and Mary, was b. c1708. On 17 Nov 1749, Thomas Crow, age c41, dep. regarding the bounds of the tract called *Hilstone.*{KELR JS#26:302}

---

[13] On 3 Aug 1713, Thomas Smyth, of KE Co., for love and respect for Mary Crow, dau. of William and Mary Crow of afsd. county, conv. to her 100 a. of a tract called *Killingsworth*, given to him by Robert Smith of TA Co., dec.{KELR JSN:334}

On 16 Jan 1755, Thomas Crow of KE Co., and his wife Sarah, and George Skirven of the same county, wheelwright, conv. to William Ringgold of Chester Town, Gent., the moiety of a tract between the branches of Fairy and Morgan Creek called *Comegys Farm*, granted to Cornelius Comegys for 370 a. and by him devised to his two daus., one of them the wife of Thomas Wilkins, the other the afsd. Sarah the now wife of sd. Thomas Crow, formerly wife of George Skirven.{KELR JS#28:72}

On 4 Feb 1760, Thomas Crow of KE Co., and his wife Sarah, and George Skirven of the same county, wheelwright, conv. to Thomas Wilkins of KE Co., moiety of a tract called *Comegys Farm Addition*, formerly granted to Cornelius Comegys for 320 a. and by him devised to his two daus., one of them the wife of Thomas Wilkins, dec., the other the afsd. Sarah the now wife of sd. Thomas Crow.{KELR JS#29:223}

Thomas Crow d. by 12 Jan 1771, when his estate was appraised by George Presbury and Samuel Griffith, and valued at £108.13.0. Thomas Smyth and J. Nicholson signed as creditors. Martha Crow signed as next of kin. Thomas Crow, admin., filed the inventory on 13 May 1772.{MINV 109:114}

Unplaced

CROW, MARY, was bur. 26 June 1727.{KESP}

CROW, SARAH, dau. of John Crow, dec., on 15 March 1742 was bound to James Woodland, until age 16 or day of marriage.{KEBI JS#20:1}

THE CRUMP FAMILY

1. WILLIAM CRUMP, d. by 11 Sep 1695, leaving a widow and extx. Frances. William Crump, of TA Co., immigrated Feb 1665, with Frances, his wife.{MPL 16:463} William Crump immigrated in 1663. With him came his wife Frances, son William, and also Elizabeth and John Crump.{MPL 6:135, 136}

On 11 Sep 1695, John Loyd of Chester, of TA Co., stated he had received from Frances Crump, widow and extx. of the last will of William Crump of Chester River, dec., legacy or part of the personal estate in right of Hannah his wife by the will of afsd. William. {KELR GL#1:2c}

William left issue: (probably) WILLIAM; (probably) JOHN; ROBERT; HANNAH, m. 1st, by 11 Sep 1695, John Loyd, and 2nd, by 12 Oct 1702, James Heath; MARY, m. by 11 Sep 1695, John Meriday of Chester River.{KELR GL#1:3A}

2. ROBERT CRUMP, son of William, was in KE Co. on 13 Aug 1702, when he and his wife Elizabeth conv. to James Heath, 200 a. of *Crumps Forrest* now in KE Co., 200 a., originally patented to William Crump, father of Robert.{KELR JD#1:34}

3. HANNAH CRUMP, dau. of William, m. 1st, John Loyd, and 2nd, by 12 Oct 1702, James Heath.
   On 12 Oct 1702, James Heath, of KE Co., and his wife Hannah, one of the daus. of William Crump, dec., and sister of Robert Crump then living, conv. to John Loyd of same county, 300 a. of a tract called *Crumps Forrest*, which William Crump by his last will devised to sd. Robert and Hannah.{KELR JD#1:93}

Unplaced

CRUMP, ELIZABETH, widowed mother of Mary Saul, who on 4 June 1703 bound herself an apprentice and servant to sd. Elizabeth Cramp for the space of 5 years ... "These are to certifie that the within Mary Cramp (came) in the ship called the *Concord*, Capt. Roger Beore commander, came to anchor in Virginia 28 May last. Last day of Feb 1703."{KELR GL#1:17A}

THE BENJAMIN DAWES FAMILY

1. BENJAMIN DAWS, of KE Co., tanner, was in KE Co. by 16 Sep 1756 when he and his wife Hannah, conv. to Thomas Gilpin of the same county, merchant, part of a tract which Benjamin purchased from Simon Wilmer called *Rich Levell* at the head of Sassafras River beginning at a locust post on the w. side of the main road which passes from Simon Wilmer's mill on the Herring Runn Branch to Robert Lewis's mill at the head of Sassafrax River ..., ½ a.{KELR JS#28:305}
   Benjamin Dawes, of KE Co., d. leaving a will dated 1 April 1760 and proved 18 Nov 1761. The heirs named were oldest son Isaac Daws, son Benjamin Daws, son Edward Daws, daus. Mary, Temperance and Sarah. The execs. were wife Hannah and Lewis Clothier. The will was witnessed by Frederick Hanson, Solomon Semans, and Healey Pett.{MWB 31:479}
   On 27 Nov 1761 his estate was appraised by Augustine Boyer, Jr. and Alexander Baird, and valued at £68.11.1. Benjamin Dawes, admin., filed the inventory mentioning William Marcer, Jr., Mary Dawes, Daniel Jackson and Thomas Canby on 18 Feb 1762.{MINV 75:230}
   Benjamin was the father of: ISAAC; BENJAMIN; EDWARD; MARY; TEMPERANCE; and SARAH.

2. BENJAMIN DAWS, son of Benjamin (1), d. by 10 Aug 1773, when his estate was appraised by Samuel Dickinson and Solomon Semans, and valued at £23.16.2. William Wood and James Davis signed as creditors. Margaret Daws, admx., filed the undated inventory.{MINV 113:6}

Unplaced

DAWS, GEORGE, at November Court 1763, was charged that on 20 June 1763 he assaulted James Skuse (Scuse). He was fined 2 s., 6 p.{KECR DD#1:41B}

DAWS, THOMAS, of KE Co., d. by Sep 1750. His wife was probably Margaret (N), who d. by 18 Dec 1759.
    Thomas Daws' estate was appraised by John Thorp and William Copper, Jr., and valued at £110.1.3. Richard Gresham and William Murray signed as creditors. Margaret Daws, admx., filed the inventory on 27 Sep 1758.{MINV 66:59}
    Margaret Daws, of Chester Town, KE Co., d. leaving a will dated 3 Nov 1759 and proved 18 Dec 1759. Mentioned were friends Alexander and Margaret McIntosh. The exec. was Alexander McIntosh. The will was witnessed by Wm. Cargile and Elizabeth Husbands.{MWB 30:803}

THE MATTHIAS DAY FAMILY

Some of the following information was based on the research of S. Eugene Clements and his wife Elsie and is furnished by his widow, Elsie Clements.

1. MATTHIAS DAY d. by 11 Dec 1742. He m. by 1723 Anne, sister of John March.{KE Wills, Lib. 18, folio 281}[14] Matthias Day was in KE Co. by 10 Oct 1709 when an unpatented certificate No. 121, Kent Manor, was recorded.{MdHR 40,038-121, 1-25-5-34, MSA #51224} Ann d. by Dec 1742.
    At August Court 1742, it was presented that Matthias Day did not clear the main road according to the Act of Assembly. He was fined 50 s.{KECR JS#24:51}

_____

[14] John March, physician of KE Co. d. leaving a will dated 23 Oct 1723. In it he named sisters Elizabeth Lockeet, Mary Wilks, Hannah March and Ann Day (which Jane Baldwin in her *Maryland Calendar of Wills* has read as Ann Doyn from the wills of the Prerogative Court - MWB 18:219). He referred to Mary Harper, dau. of sister Ann Day.

Mathias Day, of KE Co., d. leaving a will dated 23 Oct 1742 and proved 11 Dec 1742. The heirs named were wife Ann, son Mathias, son John, dau. Milcah, dau. Mary, wife of John Denning, son Stephen Marsh. Tracts mentioned were *Mathias, St. Johnsfield,* and *Sherwood Forest.* The execs. were wife and Christopher Hale. The will was witnessed by James Straham, Richard Benthame, and James McCabe.{MWB 23:53}

His estate was appraised by Nicholas Smith and Gideon Pearce, Jr. on 1 Jan 1742 and valued at £336.9.2. No creditors listed. Matthias Day and John Day signed as next of kin. The unnamed exec. filed the inventory on 16 March 1742.{MINV 27:320} On 16 June 1744, his estate was appraised by Nicholas Smith and Gideon Pearce, and valued at £25.6.6. The unnamed exec. filed the inventory on 20 June 1744.{MINV 29:446} Later his estate was appraised and valued at £9.15.0. Chris. Hall, admin. and exec., filed the inventory.{MINV 29:447}

The plantations of the orphans of Matthias Day, dec., viz., John, Malichiah, and Stephen March Day, were valued as follows: the plant. or real estate of John Day to be worth 600 lbs. of tob. per annum clerk of quit rents; the plant. of Malichiah Day worth 300 lbs. of tob. per annum; and the land of Stephan March Day (104 a. of which 40 a. may be cleared by his guardian).{KEBI JS#20:144}

Ann Day, widow, KE Co., d. leaving a will dated 31 Oct 1742 and proved 18 Dec 1742. The heirs named were Henry James, Peter Kinhead, Samuel Mains, Mary Shegs (widow), John McDaniel, and debts due testator. Children named were Mathias, John, Stephen, Mary Denning, wife of John, Milcah, and granddau. Mary Denning. The execs. were John Denning and son Mathias. The will was witnessed by Ebenezer Reyner, William Sappington, and John Wallace. {MWB 23:57}

Matthias Day was the father of: MATHIAS; JOHN; MILCAH (or MALACHI); MARY, d. 2 Feb 1738/9, m. 1st --- Harper and m. 2nd on 24 Dec 1737 John Denning{KESB}; and STEPHEN MARSH.

2. MATTHIAS DAY, of KE Co., son of Matthias and Anne, was mentioned in his father's will. He d. by 23 July 1751, when his estate was appraised by John Haley and John Graham, and valued at £149.16.5. William Haley and John Burgin signed as creditors. Thomas Sappington and John Denning signed as next of kin. John Day, admin., filed the inventory on 2 Sep 1751.{MINV 47:197}

His estate was again appraised by John Kelley and John Graham, and valued at £13.19.9. John Burgin and William Haley signed as creditors. Thomas Sappington and John Denning signed as next of kin. John Day, admin., filed the inventory of 13 June 1752.{MINV 50:40}

On 1 Sep 1756 distribution of the estate was made by John Day, admin.{BFD 2:42}

3. JOHN DAY, son of Mathias (1), was probably under age in 1742. He d. by 23 July 1762. He m. ca. 1750 Susannah Perkins, dau. of Daniel and Susannah (Stanton) Perkins. Susannah was b. 3 Dec 1723. {KESP} She m. 1st James Corse. Following the death of John Day, Susannah m. 3rd Bartus Piner; she d. 10 Jan 1778.{Day Family Bible at Archives of Delaware}

The plant. of John Day, son of Mathias Day was valued at 600 lbs. of tob. per year on 10 Nov 1745.{KEBI JS#20:19}

John Day, of KE Co., d. leaving a will dated 10 May 1762 and proved 23 July 1762. The heirs named were son John Day, to whom was devised a tract called *Addition to Matthias and St. Johns Field* (250 a.) and part of *Sherwood Forrest*; dau. Araminta Day; and wife Susannah. The will was witnessed by Bartus Piner, Stephen Denning, and John March.{MWB 31:689}

On 29 Sep 1762 his estate was appraised by John Maxwell and John Graham, and valued at £194.1.3. James Loulitt and Robert Maxwell, Jr. signed as creditors. Thomas Sappington and Stephen Marsh Day signed as next of kin. Susanna Day, extx., filed the inventory on 23 Oct 1762.{MINV 79:70}

On 8 Aug 1763 his estate was appraised by J. Maxwell and John Graham, and valued at £90.0.4. Robert Maxwell, Jr. signed as creditor. No next of kin listed. Susannah Piner, wife of Bartus Piner, extx., filed the inventory mentioning Thomas Sappinton, James Black and Stephen Mark Day on 16 Nov 1763.{MINV 82:108}

On 19 April 1764 his estate was appraised and valued at £43.12.6. No creditors or next of kin listed. The wife of Bartus Piner, extx., filed the inventory cont. a list of debts on 7 May ----.{MINV 83:208}

On 8 Sep 1764 distribution of the estate was made by Susannah Piner, extx., wife of Benjamin Piner. Distribution was made to widow (⅓) with residue to children, John and Araminta equally.{BFD 4:60}

On 22 April 1772 distribution of the estate was made by Bartus Piner and his wife Susanna Piner, execs. Distribution was made to widow (⅓) with residue to John Day and Aramintha Day.{BFD 6:124}

John and Susanna Day were the parents of{KESH, Day Family Bible at the Delaware Archives}: JOHN, b. 4 March 1754, m. 1st 8 Jan 1776, Rachel Wilson, dau. of James Wilson who d. 25 Aug 1779 and m. 2nd Mary Maxwell, dau. of William Maxwell; and ARAMINTA, b. 29 Dec 1756, m. 27 Jan 1778 James Wilson.

4. STEPHEN MARCH DAY, son of Matthias, was living as late as 20 Feb 1762, when he conv. to Thomas Sappington of the same place, his right in two parcels of land, one called *Matthias*, 100 a. and the other called the *Addition to the Matthias and St. Johns Fields*, 250 a.{KELR DD#1:77}

THE DEERE FAMILY

1. JOHN DEERE, of the Isle of Kent, having transported himself and his wife into the Province in 1647, was granted 200 a. on Kent Island on 20 Aug 1650.{ARMD LIV:82, Liber B:4} Christian Deere was bur. 14 July 1658.{ARMD LIV:129, Liber B:34} She may have been John Deere's first wife.

John Deere and Elizabeth Robinson were m. 22 Aug 1658.{ARMD LIV:129, Liber B:34} She may have been Elizabeth Hayling, whom he transported into MD, and whom he m. prior to July 1659. Elizabeth, his widow, later m. Thomas Hill.{MPL 10:272 and 4:60}

In his will written 21 July 1659, John Deere mentioned his dau. Christian Deere and his wife Eleasebeth whom he appointed extx. (exhibited in court 1 April 1662).{ARMD LIV:216, Liber B:96}

After John Deere's death, his widow Elizabeth m. Thomas Hill. On 28 April 1661 Thomas Hill of the Isle of Kent, and his wife Elesabeth, extx. of John Deere, sold cattle of John Deere, dec., to James Ringgould.{ARMD LIV:217, Liber B:97}

John was the father of: GEORGE; CHRISTIAN, b. 6 mo., 1655.{ARMD LIV:38, Liber A:107}

2. GEORGE DEERE, son of John, was not named in his father's will. However, the court ordered on 1 May 1661 that John Winchester take into possession the cattle that belonged to George Deere, son of dec. John Deere, until George Deere should come of age.{ARMD LIV:217 and 284, Liber B:97, C:34}

3. CHRISTIAN DEERE, dau. of John, was b. 6 mo., 1655, and was named as extx. of her father's will. On 30 June 1668 the court ordered that Christian Deare, the dau. of John Deare, dec., serve Robert Dunn for a term of four years or until married.{ARMD LIV:247, Liber C:9}

Unplaced

DEAR, RICHARD, at March Court 1742, was charged that on 1 May 1742 he stole 15 s. of James Barnes. He was found not guilty.{KECR JS#24:81}

At June Court 1745, it was presented that Richard Dear, labourer, on 1 March 1744, stole a swine of William Wilmore. He was ordered to stand in the pillory for ½ hour and receive 25 lashes.{KECR JS#24:197}

THE DORAN/DEORAN/DORIN FAMILY

1. **JAMES DORAN (DEORAN, DORIN)** d. in KE Co. on 29 Oct 1738.{KESH} He m. Jane (N), who m. 2nd, William Salst or Salisbury.

James Doran d. leaving a will dated 17 Sep 1738 and proved 22 Jan 1738/9. To son William, he left £53, 10 s., then in hands of Samuel Hyde (merchant) of London. To son James, 150 a. called *The New Beginning*; if sd. son d., to pass to dau. Elizabeth; residue of estate to be divided between sd. son James and daus. Mary and Elizabeth. To dau. Margrett Stevens, £30 paper money. To wife Jane, her thirds. Wife Jane and son James were execs.{MWB 22:16}

The inventory of Doran's estate was taken on 16 March 1739 and proved 10 Jan 1740. William Deoran was given mention. William Salst (Salsbury), his wife Jane, and Samuel Doran were execs.{MINV 25:465} A second inventory was taken 29 Sep 1740 and filed 10 Jan 1740. William Deoran was given mention. William Salsbury, his wife Jane Salsbury, and James Deoran were execs.{MINV 25:468}

James Doran was the father of the following children, whose births were recorded in St. Mary Ann's Parish, CE Co.{CECH:57}:
MARGARET, m. (N) Stevens; WILLIAM, b. 18 Sep 1718; JAMES, b. 15 Aug 1721; MARY, b. 9 Oct 1725; and ELIZABETH, b. 16 May 1729.

2. **JAMES DORAN**, son of James, m. by 12 Feb 1753, Sarah (N).

On 12 Feb 1753, James Doran of KE Co., innholder, and his wife Sarah, conv. to Hugh Wallis of KE Co., Lot No. 81 of Chester Town. {KELR JS#27:239}

James and Sarah were the parents of: WILLIAM, b. 28 Feb 1746/7.{KESH}

THE DARBY DULANY FAMILY

1. **DARBY DULANY** was in QA Co. by 30 Oct 1709 when he witnessed the will of John Copedge of Kent Island, QA Co.{MWB 14:76}

He m. by 11 Oct 1711, Katherine, extx. of Edmond Goodman of KE Co.{INAC 32C:79}

He d. in TA Co., leaving a will dated 30 Nov 1721 and proved 23 Dec 1723. The heirs named were his son-in-law Thomas Mooth or Nooth, and Matthew Delany, son of Margaret Tobin (if he was still living, and would come into the country). If both d. his property was to pass to Catherine Elston and Catherine Grace. Mark Hardcasin was left £20. The exec. was his wife Catherine. The will was witnessed by Thomas Douglas, Roger Scott, John Kersey, and William Elston. {MWB 18:273}

2. DARBY DULANY, no proven relationship to the above, was in KE Co. by 21 Feb 1754 when he was convicted of committing fornication by the oath of Frances Armstrong, having begot a child on the body of sd. Frances.{KECR JS#25:205B}

He d. by 7 May 1762, when his estate was appraised by John Campbell and James Claypoole, and valued at £13.12.11. D. Hands and Thomas Smith signed as creditors. Elijah Bishop, admin., filed the inventory on 10 March 1764.{MINV 82:360}

His estate was appraised again and valued at £6.5.0. Elijah Bishop, admin., filed the inventory cont. a list of debts on 11 March 1764.{MINV 82:364}

Unplaced

DULANY, EDMOND of KE Co., physician, at June Court 1739, was found guilty of assaulting Phil. Christfield on 1 March 1738, and fined £3.{KECR JS#22:166}

DULANY, JOHN, and Mary Wilkinson were m. 7 Sep 1718.{KESP}

THE ELLENOR FAMILY

1. ANDREW ELLENOR, d. prior to 1666, leaving an heiress, Margaret Hanson, who m. Alex. Waters.{MPL 10:311-312} Andrew Ellenor and Anicake Hanson were m. 5 da., 3 mo., 1656.{ARMD LIV:38, Liber A:107}

In Sep 1650, at a court held at Kent, Andrew Elina, Andrew Hanson, Anikeck Hanson, Margarett Hanson, Hance Hanson, Frederick Hanson, Catherine Hanson, were made to appear in Court. On 17 Sep 1650, a certificate of survey was granted, and land was laid out for Andrew Elina of the Province, a parcel of land lying on the e. side of a river running out of the Eastern Bay called Chester River and on the n. side of a creek in the river called Corsica Creek next adjoyning unto the land lately laid out for Henry Coursey ... (bounds described) 350 a. ... all that parcel called *Sintra* ....{MPL Q:365}

On 30 Oct 1657 Margrett Anderson agreed, with the consent of her father and mother, to serve Capt. Robert Vaughan until 1 Jan 1661. The indenture was witnessed by Thomas Wetherill, John Salter, Andrew Anderson, and Annecke Elinor. Reference was made to the father-in-law of Margrett Anderson, Andrew Elinor.{ARMD LIV:124, Liber B:19}

On 10 April 1674 the jury declared that Andrew Ellenor (a Spaniard) d. seized of ½ of the land called *Stoopley Gibson* held in the Manor of Baltimore and he d. June 1660; his two daus., Sarah, wife of William Joyner, was age c17, and Ann, wife of Lawrence Arnold, is age c15. After Ellenor's death his widow possessed his land, and m. 2nd, Macom Mehenny, and 3rd. m. John Dabb.{ARMD LI:113 cites Liber CD, folio 124}

Andrew and Annicake were the parents of{ARMD LIV:129, Liber B:34}: SARAH, b. 11 Aug 1658, m. William Joyner; and ANN, m. Lawrence Arnold.

THE FANNING FAMILY

It should be noted that there was an early Fanning family in CH Co. No relationship to the Eastern Shore family of that name has been established.

1. JOHN FANNING, was b. c1676, and d. by April 1735. He m. 1st, in Dec ----, Mary (N) Davies, extx. of David Davies.{KESP} She may have been a dau. of Robert Foreman, whose will, dated 22 Sep 1711, named a dau. Mary Fanning.{MWB 15:341} He m. 2nd, Jane (N), who was mentioned in his will.

On or about 15 Sep 1726, John Fannen, age c50, dep. regarding the bounds of a tract called *Arcadia*.{KELR JS#X:45}

On 26 Feb 1702/3 Mary Price, widow of William Price and not in a condition or capable of maintaining herself and child by reason of her lameness, she gave her child, Joseph Price, age 4 years on the 18 July following, to John Fannen and his wife Mary until age 21.{KELR GL#1:12}

On 9 June 1703, John Faning, of KE Co., and his wife Mary, sole extx. of the last will of David Davies, of KE Co., dec., conv. to Edward Scott, 200 a. of a tract called *Killy Longford*, which was devised to Mary by David Davies.{KELR JD#1:101}

In July 1704, came Joh: Fannen's uxor (wife) (Majr: Morr's account?), dau. to John Moor: and prayed to have the marke of her cattle ... recorded.{KELR GL#1:40}

On 18 Feb 1710 David Williams, of KE Co., made a will. Among the bequests was one of personalty to John and Mary Fanning. Mary Fanning witnessed the will.{MWB 13:292}

Fanning d. leaving a will dated 30 Jan 1731 and proved 21 April 1735. To wife Jane, extx., and dau. Mary, he left personal estate divided equally; should wife die, Thomas Maun to act as exec.
{MWB 21:405}

The inventory of his estate was taken 20 May 1735 and filed 4 Aug 1735. Next of kin were William Moore and John More. Exec. was Thomas Manan.{MINV 22:130}

An additional inventory was taken 30 July 1736 and filed 22 July 1736. Exec. was Thomas Mohone.{MINV 21:481}

John Fanning was the father of: MARY.

2. JAMES FANNING, no known relation to the above, m. Mary (N), who seems to have m. as her 2nd husband John Twigg.

James Fanning d. by 3 Nov 1727 when his estate was inv. by W. Graves and John Reed. Edward Scott signed as creditor. The inventory was filed on 21 Aug 1728 by John Twigg and his wife Mary Twigg.{MINV 13:280}

James and Mary were the parents of: ANN, b. 16 Dec 1705; MARY, b. 17 Dec 1709 [sic]; MILDERT, b. 19 Dec 1709 [sic]; MARGRETT, b. 6 Dec 1711; ROBERT, b. 5 March 1720; ARTHUR, b. 5 March 1723; and FRANCIS, b. 20 Feb 1725.{KESP}

3. JAMES FANNING, of KE Co., d. by 8 March 1762, when his estate was appraised by William Wilmer and James Smith, and valued at £2.9.10. Robert Cruckshanks, admin., filed the inventory on 13 March 1764.{MINV 83:93}

4. NICHOLAS FANNING, at March Court 1748, was presented on charges that on 1 Aug 1748, and at diverse times as well before as since, committed fornication with Margaret Oliver and begot a bastard child. Margaret was fined 30 s.{KECR JS#25:27B, 28A}

On 20 April 1756 Nicholas Fanning confessed of begetting a base born child on the body of Hannah Beck and was fined 30 s. Richard Willis entered into security to pay the fine, fees and to keep the base born child of Hannah Beck, called George Beck, from becoming any charge to the county.{KECR JS#25:212A}

5. RICHARD FANNING and Alse Welsh were m. 27 Jan 170-.{KESP}

THE FIDDIS FAMILY

1. JOHN FIDDIS and Elizabeth Mitchell were m. 7 Jan 170-.{KESP} He may have m. 2nd, Isabell, by whom he was the father of at least two children.

John Feddis, of KE Co., d. by 19 March 1723, when his estate was admin. by William Dicus.{MDAD 5:402} On 29 June 1723 his estate was admin. by William Davis.{MDAD 5:225}

John Fiddis and Isabel were the parents of: ALEXANDER, b. 3 Oct 1714; and JOHN, b. 3 July 1717.{KESP}

2. JOHN FIDDIS, son of John and Isabel, was b. 3 July 1717. He is probably the John Fiddis who m. by 3 March 1752, Sophia, dau. of Jonathan Garnett.

Between 1747 and 1760 John Feddis was listed in the KE Co. Debt Books as owning a part of Stratford Manor, which had been surveyed for George Garnett in 1735.{INKE:12, 68}

On 3 March 1752, John Fiddis (Fidies) of KE Co., and his wife Sophia, conv. to Abraham Milton, part of a tract called *Stratfords Mannor*, 66 a.{KELR JS#27:125}

On 22 Jan 1759, John Fiddis of KE Co., and his wife Sophia, conv. land to Joseph George of the same place. The deed states that Jonathan Garnett d. seized of 100 a. leaving 3 daus., Sophia, Martha and Mary, and whereas (N) George, father of the afsd. Joseph, purchased from afsd. Martha her third part and sd. Mary d. intestate and without issue by which her third part descended to sd. Sophia and Martha, and whereas the afsd. John Fiddis who married the sd. Sophia did afterwards purchase of the sd. Martha her half of the third part belonging to the sd. Mary.{KELR JS#29:129}

Unplaced

FIDDIS, MARTHA, was bur. 3 Jan 1715.{KESP}

THE FIELDS FAMILY

1. CHRISTOPHER FIELDS d. by 13 Nov 1718 when his estate was appraised by Christopher Higgs and Thomas Hopkins at a value of £20.5.6.{MINV 3:206}

He was probably the father of: CHRISTOPHER; and JAMES.

2. CHRISTOPHER FIELD, probably son of Christopher, m. 1st, Rachel (N). They were the parents of: CATERINA CHESTERMONY CORNELIUS, b. 12 April 1741 (this unusual name is also found in the Everett Family); and BENJAMIN, b. 13 April 175-.{KESH}

By his 2nd wife Elizabeth, Christopher had a son: CHRISTOPHER, b. Dec 1743.{KESH}

Christopher m. 3rd, Rebecca Hull on 23 July 1746.{KESH}

3. JAMES FIELD, probably son of Christopher, m. Mary (N), and d. by Dec 1766.

On 24 Dec 1766 his estate was appraised by Andrew Hynson and Isaac Freeman, and valued at £38.4.10. James Black and Samuel Thompson signed as creditors. James Fields and Joseph Fields signed as next of kin. Christopher Fields, admin., filed the inventory on 18 March 1767.{MINV 91:248}

James and Mary were the parents of: CHRISTOPHER, b. 21 Jan 1736/7; JAMES, b. 7 July 1739; JOSEPH, b. 12 Dec 1741; JOHN, b. 5 Sep 1744; WILLIAM, b. 28 Feb 1746/7; and WILLIAM, b. 27 Oct 1748.{KESH}

3. JAMES FIELDS, son of James and Mary, was b. 7 July 1739.{KESH} He may be the James Fields who d. by 20 July 1773. His estate was appraised by Thomas Croome and William Cowarden, and valued at £9.19.0. Christopher Fields and Coter Griffith signed as creditors. Christopher Fields and James Fields signed as next of kin. Joseph Fields, admin., filed the inventory on 25 Aug 1773.{MINV 113:7}

A list of debts was appraised and valued at £5.0.3. Joseph Field, admin., filed the inventory cont. a list of debts on 21 March 1774.{MINV 115:369}

Unplaced

FIELDS, RACHEL, at March Court 1765, was presented with having committed fornication and begetting a base born child. She was fined 30 s.{KECR DD#1:56A}

At November Court 1770, it was presented that Rachel Fields committed fornication and begot a base born child. She was fined £3.

She was ordered to give security to keep the county from any charge by means of her bastard child called MILICENT.{KECR DD#1:121B}

THE FLINTHAM FAMILY

1. WILLIAM FLINTHAM was in KE Co., DE, by 19 Feb 1732/3 when he witnessed the will of Adam Latham. On 5 Sep 1738 he was granted administration on the estate of Benjamin Flintham.{Kent Co., DE, Will Book H:78, 152}

He m. by 17 Jan 1737, Sarah, dau. of John Ball. On that day they were named in the will of John Ball. William may have been married earlier because Ball stipulated that the land that he had been devised by Daniel Norris should go to Sarah, but "in no case [should] pass to the heirs of William Flintham."{MWB 22:506}

By his unidentied 1st wife, William may have been the father of: CLEMENT.

By Sarah, William had at least one son: JOHN.

2. CLEMENT FLINTHAM, of KE Co., possibly son of William (1) by an unidentified 1st wife, d. by 22 May 1769, when his estate was appraised by John Eccleston and Isaac Spencer, and valued at £11.9.9. John Wallis and Jonathon Fowler signed as creditors. John Flinthin and Sarah Flintham signed as next of kin. Joseph Ireland, admin., filed the inventory on 20 June 1769.{MINV 100:172}

3. JOHN FLINTHAM (FLINTON), of KE Co., weaver, son of William (1) and heir of (his mother) Sarah, one of the daus. of John Ball, late of KE Co., dec., by the dau. and heir of Daniel Norris of KE Co., also dec., d. by Jan 1771.

On 16 Sep 1762, he conv. to Thomas Ringgold of Chester Town, merchant, part of several tracts, *Norris's Forrest*, *Tilghmans Farm*, and *Wilmer's Gift*, 50 a., in Quaker Neck.{KELR DD#1:148}

Thomas d. by 18 Jan 1771, when his estate was appraised by Charles Groome and Nathaniel Redding, and valued at £11.7.3. Thomas Ringgold & Sons signed as creditors. James Duncan and Abraham Milton signed as next of kin. James Ward, exec., filed the inventory on 10 Dec 1774.{MINV 119:60}

A list of debts was appraised at £42.13.6. John Ward, exec., filed the inventory cont. a list of debts on 10 Dec 1774.{MINV 119:61}

Unplaced

FLINTHAM, MARGARET, spinster, at November Court 1745, was charged that on 10 Nov 1745 she stole 2½ yards of line of Richard

Tittle. She was ordered to stand in the pillory ½ hour and receive 10 lashes.{KECR JS#24:228}

THE ROBERT FORD FAMILY

1. ROBERT FORD, m. Rachel (formerly O'Brine or O'Brien?).
   On 17 June 1735, Alexander Brisco and his wife Elizabeth, both of KE Co., conv. to Robert Ford and his wife Rachel of the afsd. county, a tract called *Chance*, 65 a.{KELR JS#18:142}
   On 13 May 1755, Robert Ford of KE Co., conv. to his son William Ford, part of Broomfield, 86 a.{KELR JS#28:114}
   On 25 July 1758, Robert Ford of KE Co., MD, and his son John Ford of KE Co., on Delaware, conv. to William Ford, son of afsd. Robert, part of a tract called *Chance* which the sd. Robert Ford was in right of his wife Rachel, formerly called Rachel Obrine(?), and the sd. John Ford was possessed of and lately dwelled. Mary Ford, wife of afsd. John, acknowledged the indenture.{KELR JS#29:37}
   Robert Ford and wife Rachel were the parents of: RICHARD, b. 28 Jan 1706; ROBERT, b. 13 Oct 1708; JOHN, b. 21 Sep 1710; CHARLES, b. 14 May 1712; REBEKAH, b. 25 Jan 1713; RACHEL, b. 2 March 1715; and ELIZABETH, b. 4 Feb 1727/8.{KESH}

2. RICHARD FORD, son of Robert and Rachel, was b. 28 Jan 1706.{KESH} On 24 Dec 1742, Gideon Pearce, Gent., and Richard Ford (Foard), and his wife Mary, of KE Co., conv. to Joseph Man, bricklayer, part of a tract called *The Forrest*, 60 a.{KELR JS#24:174}

3. JOHN FORD, son of Robert and Rachel, was b. 21 Sep 1710. He may be the John Ford who m. 1st, Elizabeth (N), and 2nd, on 8 Nov 1744 Mary Sewell.{KESH}
   John Ford was the father of (by Elizabeth): RACHEL, b. 25 Dec 1737; ELIZABETH, b. 9 Sep 1745; JAMES, b. 15 Jan 1747-8.{KESH}

4. CHARLES FORD, son of Robert and Rachel, was b. 14 May 1712. He m. Ann (N). They were the parents of: JOHN, b. 24 Aug 1739; CHARLES, b. 10 May 1737; ROBERT, b. 15 Sep 1738; and MARTHA, b. 28 Sep 1744.{KESH}

Unplaced

FORD, FERDINANDO, of KE Co., was conv. by Solomon Wright, attorney appointed by James Edmondson and William Edmondson, execs. of the last will of John Edmondson, of TA Co., dec., of TA Co., to make over part of two tracts of land, 150 a., part of tract called

Bluff Point to Fardenando Ford, of KE Co., also 150 a. being part of a tract called *Broad Neck*. These parcels were conv. to Edward Carroll and Edward Mahan.{KELR M:117B}

Ferdinando Ford d. by 13 Dec 1703 when his estate was inv.{MWB 3:286}

FORD, GEORGE, and Elizabeth Wilson were m. 3 May 1725.{KESP}

FORD, MARY, spinster, at March Court 1747, was charged that, on 1 May 1747, and at diverse times as well before as since, committed fornication and begot a bastard child. She was ordered to receive 6 lashes.{KECR JS#25:1B}

FORD, ROBERT, was b. c1722. On 7 Aug 1764, Robert Ford, age c42, dep. regarding the bounds of a tract called *Drecute*.{KELR DD#1:572}

FORD, Thomas, and his wife Ann, of KE Co., in 1704, conv. to Walter Lodge of the same county, a tract of 150 a. called *South Hampton*, originally laid out for William Hackett.{KELR JD#1:175}

FORD, THOMAS, of KE Co., and wife Hannah, on 8 April 1763, conv. to Kinvin Wroth of the same place, part of a tract called *The Hermitage*, 100 a.{KELR DD#1:360}

FORD, WILLIAM, and Elizabeth Groves were m. 6 Dec 1697. William was bur. 24 March 1716.{KESP}

THE FOREMAN FAMILY

1. ROBERT FOREMAN d. March 1719/20. He m. Margaret (N), b. c1681, who may have been a second wife. Margaret Foreman, widow, on 15 April 1724, was assaulted by James Watson, who was charged at June Court 1724 and fined 1 s.{KECR JS#22:15}

On 4 Jan 1741, Margaret Foreman, age c60, dep. regarding the bounds of a tract called *Dollington;* she recalled a statement by her husband Robert Foreman.{KELR JS#24:296}

On 21 June (1684?) Thomas Seward and his wife Lucy (also referred to as Lucretia) conv. to Robert Foreman of KE Co., a parcel of land, 100 a., part of a tract called *Blackhall Hermitage*.{KELR K:85}

Robert Foreman of (undesignated) Co., d. leaving a will dated 22 Sep 1711 and proved 15 March 1719/20. He left to his son Robert 50 a. of *Swestern* (in all 200 a.), to his younger sons Charles, William, and John, each 50 a. of the same tract. He left his youngest dau. Elizabeth personalty, and 1 s. each to his daus. Milderatt (Mildred?) Hendrickson and Mary Fanning. Son Arthur was to have 100 a. *Calead*, being the upper part of *Blackhall's Hermitage*. Wife Margaret was to have the use of the dwell. plant. for widowhood and the residue of the estate absolutely. She and son Arthur were named execs. The will was witnessed by Thomas Winn and Michael Haskell.{MWB 15:41}

Robert was the father of: ARTHUR, b. c1680; ROBERT, b. c1688; CHARLES; WILLIAM; JOHN; MILDERATT (MILDRED?), m. (N) Hendrickson; MARY, m. (N) Fanning; and ELIZABETH, m. by 8 Feb 1733 Richard Chaddock.

2. ARTHUR FOREMAN, son of Robert, was b. c1680, and was living as late as 1746. He m. 1st, Mary, and 2nd, Honour Miller.

On 19 June 1716, Arthur Foreman of KE Co., and his wife Honnor, conv. to Philip Rasin, their half of 50 a. of *Gibbs Choice*, part of a tract of 200 a., patented to John Gibbs called *Gibbs Choyce*, and 50 a. of sd. 200 a. conv. by John Gibbs to John Miller.{KELR BC#1:151}

On 13 Nov 1738 Arthur Foreman, aged c58, dep. regarding the bounds of a tract called *The Dineing Room;* he stated that about four years earlier being in company of John Wright and after some discourse he said to sd. Wright, "If you know anything concerning the bounds of Robert Roberts' land, you ought to discover it."{KELR JS#22:289}

On 22 May 1732, Arthur Foreman, age c53, dep. regarding the bounds of a tract *Viavan*. He heard his father say that Maj. Comegys told him that Boullay had cheated his son Cornelius, for which reason Boullay should never know where the land lay.{KELR JS#16:248}

On 8 Feb 1733, an agreement was made among Arthur Foreman of KE Co., of the first part, John Foreman of the same county, and his wife Mary of the second part, Richard Chaddock of the same county, and his wife Elizabeth of the third part, and James Calder, of Chester Town, in the county afsd., attorney-at-law of the fourth part executed the following indenture.

Whereas Robert Foreman, dec., father of the afsd. Arthur, John and Elizabeth, by virtue of the letters patented on 10 Oct 1707 was seized of a tract called *Swestern* on the lower most main branch of Morgans Creek, 200 a. Robert Foreman in his last will devised to his son Robert Foreman 50 a. of the afsd. land at the n.e. end thereof, and to his son Charles Foreman 50 a. of the same land adjoining to the sd. land of Robert, and to his son William Foreman 50 a. of the same land adjoining to the land of Charles, and to his son the afsd. John the last 50 a. of the same land adjoining to the land of William, and in case of any of the afsd. devisees should die without heirs the same land whould be equally devised amongst the survivors and his dau. the afsd. Elizabeth so that Elizabeth should have the same equal share thereof.

William, after the death of his father, d. without issue. Yet, for as much as the same will is attested only by two witnesses, it is presumed that the same lands did not pass thereby, but that the estate in fee thereof hath descended to the afsd. Arthur as heir-at-law to the afsd. Robert, the father whereupon Arthur [?] has consented to the request and for the benefit of the afsd. John and Mary and the afsd. Richard and Elizabeth and in order to accomplish the intent and design of the afsd. testator to convey to the afsd. James Calder the right of 100 a. being the two parcels thereof so as afsd. devised to the afsd. William and John. {KELR JS#16:429}

At June Court 1743, Arthur Foreman, age c64, dep. regarding the bounds of the tract called *The Chance*. {KELR JS#24:407}

On 19 May 1746, Arthur Foreman of KE Co., heir of Robert Foreman, late of sd. county, dec., conv. part of the tract *Swestern* to Charles Foreman of afsd. county, son of afsd. Robert, dec. {KELR JS#25:401}

On 19 Aug 1746, Arthur Foreman, age c66, dep. regarding the bounds of a tract called *Richards Adventure*. He stated that about 16-17 years earlier Mr. Pollard with several others came here to the s. side of Chinnapin Branch at which time John Wright came to them and said that he burnt a tree belonging to Booleys land; that he, the sd. Wright, and one Turlor, seeing Thomas Gwinn coming over the afsd. branch they concealed themselves behind a tree. The deponent said that John Wright was a person of a mean character. {KELR JS#25:429}

Arthur Forman, of KE Co., d. leaving a will dated 26 Jan 1756 and proved 7 Nov 1757. The heirs named were wife Elizabeth and child Francis Forman, exec. The will was witnessed by Arthur and Elizabeth Forman, and John Holt. {MWB 30:414}

Arthur Foreman m. 1st, on 13 May 1699, Mary Reed. Mary was bur. 10 March 1713. Arthur m. 2nd, on 2 June 1715, Honour Miller. Arthur was the father of (by Mary): ARTHUR, b. 3 Nov 1706; FRANCIS, b. 28 Oct 1707; MARY, b. 19 June and bapt. 2 Sep 1711; (by Honour): SARAH, b. 27 Aug 1715; HONOUR, b. 30 June 1721; and ROBERT, b. 12 Jan 1723. {KESP}

3. ROBERT FOREMAN, son of Robert (1), was b. c1688. On 19 July 1748, Robert Foreman of KE Co., age c56, dep. regarding the bounds of a tract called *Blackhals Hermitage*. {KELR JS#26:142} At age c64, on 1 March 1757, he dep. regarding the bounds of a tract called *Town Relief*. {KELR JS#28:323}

Robert Foreman, of KE Co., d. leaving a will dated 22 April 1762 and proved 27 July 1762. The heirs named were wife Elizabeth and son Walter Foreman. The execs. were Walter Foreman and wife of testator. The will was witnessed by Joseph Gray and John Tuckwell. {MWB 31:688}

Robert was the father of: WALTER.

6. JOHN FOREMAN, son of Robert (1), is probably the John Foreman who d. by Dec 1754.

John Forman, of KE Co., d. leaving a will proved 14 Dec 1754. The heirs named were two daus., Sarah and Beatrice, and two sons John and Fredrick (minors), to be bound to trades. The exec. was son-in-law Joseph Butcher. The will was witnessed by Benjamin Mackrill, Elizabeth Younger, and Jno. Younger.

On 11 Jan 1755 his estate was appraised by Richard Kinword and William Browning, and valued at £46.8.10. James Weir for James Sempile & Co. and William Coburn signed as creditors. Robert Foreman and Charles Foreman (bro.) signed as next of kin. Benjamin Foreman, admin., filed the inventory on 2 June 1755.{MINV 60:303}

John Foreman was the father of: JOHN; FREDERICK; SARAH; and BEATRICE.

2-a. FRANCIS FOREMAN, son of Arthur (2) and Mary, was b. 28 Oct 1707. He d. by 19 June 1763, leaving at least one son: ARTHUR.

2-aa. ARTHUR FOREMAN, son of Francis (2-a), was living in QA Co. on 19 June 1763, when an indenture tripartite was made by the sd. Arthur Foreman, of QA Co., son and devisee of Francis Foreman of the same county, dec., of the first part, and William Ringgold of Chester Town, merchant, of the second part, and Thomas Ringgold of Chester Town, merchant, of the third part, concerning 100 a., part of a tract near Chester Town called *Black Hall Hermitage* which Robert Foreman, great grandfather of sd. Arthur formerly purchased of Thomas Seward.{KELR DD#1:378}

Unplaced

FOREMAN, ARTHUR, m. Rebecca (N), by whom he had: JAMES, b. 11 Feb 1743/4.{KESH}

FOREMAN, ARTHUR, m. Elizabeth (N). They were the parents of: MARY, b. 22 Dec 1745; JACOB, b. 25 May 1748; and SARAH, b. 6 Aug 1750.{KESH}

FOREMAN, BENJAMIN, of KE Co., d. by 25 March 1768, when his estate was appraised by Charles Groome and Henry Trulock, and valued at £36.8.2. Rasin Gale and Thomas Smyth signed as creditors. Charles Foreman and Charles Foreman, Sr. signed as next of kin. Abraham Cowarden, admin., filed the inventory on 31 July 1769.{MINV 100:350}

A list of debts was appraised, value unknown, and filed by Ann Cowarden, admx. on 3 July 1769.{MINV 100:321}

On 31 July 1769 distribution of the estate was made by Abraham Cannell (Cowarden?), admin.{BFD 5:233}

FOREMAN, DEBORAH, was b. c1719 (or earlier). On 19 Aug 1755, Deborah Foreman, age c36, dep. regarding the bounds of a tract called *Cornwallis Choice*. She recalled that about 17-18 years earlier there was a difference between Thomas Williams and her husband about a division fence.{KELR JS#28:166}

In Oct 1753, Mrs. Deborah Foreman, age c55 or 56, dep. regarding the bounds of a tract called *Cornwallis's Choice*. She stated that soon after Dr. Thomas Williams was married to Mrs. Mary Hopkins there was a dispute between the deponent's husband, Willm. Powell and the afsd. William about a division fence.{KELR JS#28:46}

FOREMAN, JOHN, at August Court 1771, was charged that he committed fornication with Priscilla Rouse and begot a base born child. He was fined 30 s.{KECR DD#1:135A}

FOREMAN, MARGARET, at November Court 1757, swore that on 10 Oct 1757 John Dunlop appeared on a charge of bastardy and entered into security with George Skirven and Jeremiah Cannall for the payment of the fine and charges to keep the county indemnified from the bastard child of Margarett Foreman called Temperance Foreman.{KECR JS#25:183A}

FOREMAN, MARY, committed fornication with James Moore, and bore him a bastard child. At November Court 1760, James Moore, mariner, being a single man, was charged on 10 Nov 1759 and fined 30 s.{KECR JS#25:246B}

At November Court 1762, it was presented that Mary Foreman committed fornication and begot a base born child. She was fined 30 s.{KECR DD#1:27A}

FOREMAN, SARAH, spinster, at March Court 1769, was charged that on 10 March 1767, with committing fornication and begetting a base born child. She was fined £3 and ordered to give security to keep the county from any charge by means of her bastard child called PRISCILLA.{KECR DD#1:105A}

FOREMAN, WILLIAM, of AA Co., on 16 May 1687 bought from Charles Whitehead and Sarah his wife of the same county, tract called *the Friendship* near the head of Turtles Creek, land called *Turtle*, 200 a.{KELR B:234}

On 24 Nov 1691 William Foreman and his wife Elizabeth of AA Co. conv. to Lewis Derochbourn of the same county, tract called *The Friendship* near the head of Tarkell Creek, 200 a.{KELR B:304}

THE FORRESTER FAMILY

1. Rev. GEORGE WILLIAM FORRESTER settled in KE Co. by 1738, and d. 12 Nov 1774.{KESB} He m. 1st, Elizabeth (N), and 2nd, Mrs. Mary (Wilmer) Clay, dau. of Simon Wilmer, on 30 Oct 1746 by Rev. Hugh Jones of CE Co.{KESB} He m. 3rd, Catherine (N), who was named in his will.

An Indenture Tripartite was made 7 Aug 1751 between James Calder of KE Co., Gent., of one part, and George William Forester of the same place, clerk, and his wife Mary, of the second part, and Thomas Ringgold of the same place, Gent., of the third part. It stated that the sd. Mary Forester heretofore had devised to her by the last will of her father Simon Wilmer a water lot in Chester Town, No. 18, and sd. Mary Forester, while she was sole by the name of Mary Clay, sold and conv. the same to Samuel Massey, who sold the same to afsd. Thomas Ringgold and whereas doubts have arisen that the will might not create an estate tail in the sd. Mary Forester ....{KELR JS#27:51}

On 1 June 1754, George William Forrester of KE Co., clerk, and his wife Mary, dau. and devisee of Simon Wilmer, late of the afsd. county, dec., conv. to Thomas Ringgold of Chester Town, merchant, ¾ of a lot in Chester Town, No. 7, devised to Mary by the last will of her father.{KELR JS#28:57}

Madam Elisabeth Forester, wife of Rev. Mr. Forester, d. 1 Feb 174-, about 5 o'clock in the morning.

In 1752 George William Forrester patented 23½ a. called *Tobin's Folly*.{INKE:69}

George William Forrester, of KE Co., d. leaving a will dated 11 Nov 1774 and proved 21 Dec 1774. The heirs named were wife Catharine; three daus. by his dec. wife Mary, Mary Elizabeth, Anna and Charlotta Forrester; son George William Forrester; and dau. Francies Dorcas Henghes. Reference is made to five daus. Mentioned were 23 a. in George Town, called *Tobens Folly*. The execs. were wife Catharine, son George William Forrester, and James Pearse. The will was witnessed by Jas. Anderson, William Henry, and John Miller.{MWB 40:59}

On 9 Jan 1775, his estate was appraised by Peter Massey and Oliver Smith, and valued at £387.5.3. John Voorhees and William Henry signed as creditors. George William Forrester, exec., filed the inventory on 11 Oct 1775.{MINV 120:423}

Rev. George William Forrester was the father of (by Elizabeth): MARY, b. 28 Dec 1738; (by Mary): GEORGE WILLIAM, b. 11 March 1749/50; MARY ELIZABETH; ANNA; CHARLOTTA; FRANCES DORCAS, b. 10 March 1755, m. Thomas Hughes of CE Co. on 25 Aug 1774; and CATHERINE MARGARETTA, m. John Hamilton on 2 July 1772 in St. Mary Anne's Parish, CE Co.{KESH; CECH:68}

2. GEORGE WILLIAM FORRESTER, son of Rev. George William and Mary Forrester, was b. 11 March 1749/50, and on 29 Aug 1779 m. Temperance Redgrave.{KESH}

George William was a Lieut. in the Minute Company of KE Co. on 29 Jan 1776.{RPKE:96, cites ARMD 18}

George William and Temperance were the parents of: MARY WILMER, b. 8 June 1780.{KESH}

THE FOXON FAMILY

1. GEORGE FOXON, possible son to Richard Foxon of BA Co., d. in KE Co. leaving a will dated 18 April 1709 and proved 23 Dec 1710. To son John and unborn child, he left his entire estate. His unnamed wife was to be extx. In event of her death during minority of children, Charles Hynson was appointed guardian.{MWB 13:188}

Foxon's estate was admin. c1710, again in Feb 1713 by admx. Ann, wife of Henry Davis, whom she m. on 24 Aug 1711{KESP}, and again on 24 March 1715 by Henry Davis.{INAC 32B:101, 35A:137, and 37A:105}

George and Ann Foxon were the parents of: RACHEL, bapt. 13 Jan 1702{KESP; ESVR 1}; JOHN, b. 14 Nov 1704; GEORGE, Jr., b. 6 May 1709; and possibly MARTHA, m. (N) Green.

2. GEORGE FOXON, son of George, was b. 6 May 1709. He d. by March 1764.

On 5 Aug 1745 he conv. to John Mackrackin of Chester Town, tailor, and his wife Judith, certain land. The deed stated that on or about last day of June 1671 Richard Foxon, then of BA Co., (to which same Richard the same George party to these presents is now heir-at-law) sold to Edward Skidmore in fee all that tract called *Bluntville*, 125 a. However, before any deed for the conveyance was executed, the same Richard d., whereupon the same Edward Skidmore exhibited his bill in the High Court of Chancery against the heir-at-law of the sd. Richard being then an infant and against Susanna the relict and admx. of sd. Richard and William Chadbourn her then husband who then possessed the sd. tract of land. It was decreed that the heir or heirs of Richard Foxon should, when they arrive at lawful age, convey the land to sd. Edward or his heirs but in the meantime the afsd. William

Chadbourn and Susannah his wife should deliver up possession thereof to him the same Edward. And sd. Edward Skidmore in his will devised the same with other lands to his two sons Edward and Michael Skidmore and by a division between them the land called *Bluntville* became the part and share of the same Michael unto whom the sd. Judith is the sole surviving heir.{KELR JS#25:282}

George Foxen, of KE Co., d. leaving a will dated 25 Feb 1764 and proved 7 March 1764. The heirs named were sister Martha Green, widow, and dau. Martha Copper, wife of Joseph Copper. The exec. was son-in-law Joseph Copper, afsd. The will was witnessed by Jno. Crawford and John Timms.{MWB 31:1077}

On 27 May 1764 his estate was appraised by Gustavas Hanson and Thomas Hanson, Jr., and valued at £74.9.1. Joseph Copper, exec., filed the inventory mentioning Richard Brice, Mathew Green and William Murray on 2 July 1764.{MINV 84:250}

George Foxon, of KE Co., d. before 25 July 1764. Distribution of the estate was made by Joseph Copper, exec. Distribution was made to sister Martha Green and dau. Martha, wife of Joseph Copper.{BFD 4:60}

George was the father of: MARTHA, m. Joseph Copper.

THE FREEMAN FAMILY

Much of the information on this family was generously made available by Mr. Chris Christou of Baltimore, MD.

1. WILLIAM FREEMAN was b. c1668, and d. Feb 1737/8 in CE Co. He m. Ann (N), b. c1670, d. after 1737. Ann m. 2nd William Hutchinson.

William Freeman, Sr. of CE Co., conv. to his son Isaac Freeman of KE Co., part of a tract called *Verrina*, 200 a.{KELR JS#16:272}

William and Ann were the parents of: ISAAC, b. c1698, d. Feb 1756; JACOB, b. c1700; WILLIAM, Jr., b. c1703; THOMAS, b. c1705; RICHARD, b. c1707; and MARY, b. c1710, m. William Abbot on 7 May 1731.

2. ISAAC FREEMAN, son of William (1) and Ann, was b. c1698, and d. Feb 1756 in KE Co. He m. Hannah Comegys by Aug 1733. She was b. 10 Feb 1711 in KE Co., dau. of William and Mary (Vinett or Unett) Comegys. Hannah m. 2nd, Thomas Burke after 1756, and d. 1761 in KE Co.

William Comegys, Sr., of KE Co., to his son Isaac Freeman and Hannah, dau. of sd. William Comegys, a tract called *Timber Level*, taken up by Solomon Wright called *The Forrest*, 140 a.{KELR JS#16:376}

132

On 4 April 1738, Isaac Freeman of KE Co., and his wife Hannah, conv. to George Wilson of the same county, part of a tract called *Verinor*, 50 a.{KELR JS#22:151}

On 24 Oct 1749, Isaac Freeman, age 51, dep. regarding the bounds of a tract called *Philips Choice*.{KELR JS#26:269}

On 15 Aug 1750, Isaac Freeman of KE Co., Gent., and his wife Hannah, conv. to Giles Cooke of the same place, merchant, a lot in George Town, No. 16.{KELR JS#26:353}

Isaac Freeman, of KE Co., d. leaving a will dated 27 Jan 1756 and proved 1 March 1756. The heirs named were wife Hannah; children William, Abraham, Isaac, Jacob, and Mary; and son-in-law Wm. Wood. The execs. were Hannah Freeman and Abraham Freeman. The will was witnessed by Wm. Lovelin, John Falconer, and John Scott.{MWB 30:49}

On 10 March 1756 his estate was appraised and valued at £1010.15.1. Hannah Freeman and Abraham Freeman filed the inventory on 27 May 1756, mentioning Richard Wilson, Edward Piner, James McLachlan, John Scott, Isaac Freeman and Jacob Freeman.{MINV 60:734}

On 12 Nov 1756 his estate was appraised again by Richard Wilson and Edward Piner, and valued at £51.13.6. James McLachlan and John Scott signed as creditors. Isaac Freeman and Jacob Freeman signed as next of kin. Abraham Freeman and Hannah Boh (late Hannah Freeman, widow), execs., filed the inventory on 9 March 1758.{MINV 65:139}

A list of debts, appraised and valued at £309.5.5, was filed by Abraham Freeman, exec., filed the list of debts on 9 March 1758.{MINV 65:107}

On 1 Oct 1760 distribution of the estate was made by Abraham Freeman, acting exec., to the widow and three children, Abraham, Isaac, and Jacob. Legatees were son William and dau. Mary.{BFD 3:49}

Isaac and Hannah were the parents of: ABRAHAM, b. c1731; ISAAC, b. c1733, d. Dec 1795; JACOB, b. c1735, d. cMarch 1761, m. Jemima; WILLIAM, b. c1737, d. cFeb 1773; and MARY, b. 1740.

3. ABRAHAM FREEMAN, son of Isaac (2) and Hannah, was b. c1731, and by 7 Jan 1757 had m. Hannah (N).

On 7 Jan 1757, Abraham Freeman of KE Co., and son and heir of Isaac Freeman, late of sd. county, dec., conv. to Jacob Freeman, bro. of sd. Abraham, part of a tract called *Broad Oak*, which their father purchased of Benjamin and William Jones, 210 a. Acknowledged by Hannah, wife of Abraham Freeman.{KELR JS#28:340}

Freeman, age c29, made a dep. in March 1759 in which he mentioned his father, now dec.{KEEJ: Thomas Harris}

Abraham Freeman d. by 1 March 1773, when his estate was appraised by Robert Maxwell and Barten Piner, and valued at £1167.3.4. John Voorhees and Mary Freeman signed as creditors. Isaac Freeman and Mary Freeman signed as next of kin. Avarilla Freeman and John Sutton, admins., filed the inventory on 11 May 1773. {MINV 114:224}

4. ISAAC FREEMAN, Jr., son of Isaac (2) and Hannah, was b. c1733 and d. Dec 1795. About 1753 he m. Martha Scott, b. c1733, dau. of David Scott. She m. 2nd, Lambert Wilmer, c1749.

Isaac and Martha (Scott) Freeman were the parents of: SARAH, b. c1753, m. William Rasin; HANNAH, b. c1735, m. 1st, Philip Rasin, and 2nd, John Gleaves; EDWARD, b. c1758, m. Isabella Pearce; ISAAC, b. c1765; JAMES WILMER, b. c1760; and MARTHA, b. c1770, m. William T. Ringgold.

5. JACOB FREEMAN, son of Isaac (2) and Hannah, was b. c1735.

On 7 Jan 1757, Jacob Freeman of KE Co., conv. to Abraham Freeman, bro. to the same Jacob of the same county, ½ of tract called *Timber Levell*, 140 a., another called *Addition to Timber Levels*, 46 a., another called *Change(?)*, 28 a. and the other called *Peters Forrest*, 34 a., which Isaac Freeman left in his last will to be divided between the sd. Abraham and Jacob Freeman. {KELR JS#28:338}

Jacob Freeman, of KE Co., d. leaving a will dated 28 Dec 1760 and proved 25 March 1761. Mentioned as heirs were wife Jemimah Freeman, son Jacob (minor), bro. William Freeman, sister Mary Freeman, bro. Isaac Freeman, bro. Isau and second son Edward Freeman. The will was witnessed by Elizabeth Watkinson, John Eglin, and Wm. Rasin. {MWB 31:207}

On 27 March 1761 his estate was appraised by Peter Massey and John Wilson, value unknown. William Raisen and Robert Maxwell, Jr. signed as creditors. W. Freeman and Isaac Freeman signed as next of kin. Jemima Freeman, admx. and extx., filed the inventory on 20 June 1761. {MINV 76:5}

Jacob Freeman was the father of: JACOB; and EDWARD.

6. WILLIAM FREEMAN, son of Isaac (2), and Hannah, was b. c1737, and d. by Feb 1773.

William Freeman, of KE Co., d. leaving a will dated 17 Oct 1772 and proved 16 Feb 1773. The heirs named were bro. Isaac Freeman, exec., to whom was devised the tract *Verina*; sister Mary Freeman; and Stephen Boddy. The will was witnessed by Geo. Wilson, Wm. Piner, and W. Rogers. {MWB 39:40}

On 5 March 1773 his estate was appraised by Robert Maxwell and William Merritt, and valued at £693.11.7. William Henry and James Jones signed as creditors. Ann Freeman and Mary Freeman signed as next of kin. Isaac Freeman, exec., filed the inventory on 28 July 1773.{MINV 114:191}

Unplaced

FREEMAN, ANN (MRS.), of KE Co., d. by 9 Jan 1764, when her estate was appraised by Thomas Morton and Thomas Letchworth and valued at £30.0.0. No creditors or next of kin listed. Thomas Freeman, exec., filed the inventory on 10 Jan 1764.{MINV 82:225}

FREEMAN, JUDITH, spinster, at November Court 1746, was presented that, on 1 May 1745, and at diverse times as well before as since, she had committed fornication and begot a bastard child. She was ordered to receive 10 lashes.{KECR JS#24:326}

THE FRENCH FAMILY

1. SAMUEL FRENCH, of QA Co., d. by 23 Aug 1715.
   On 1 May 1714 Nicholas Morrey, and wife Margaret, conv. to Samuel French, cordwainer, 150 a. part of *Walton*.{QALR I(J)KA:13}
   He d. leaving a will dated 1 Dec 1714 and proved 23 Aug 1715. The heirs named were son Thomas (exec.), dau. Mary, and son Zorobabel, who was to be bound to a trade in Philadelphia,"if possible." The will was witnessed by Nich. Clouds, William Pindar, and A. Hamilton.{MWB 14:80}
   Samuel was the father of: THOMAS; MARY; and ZOROBABEL.

2. THOMAS FRENCH, son of Samuel, was named in his father's will, and m. by 30 May 1724 Ann (N).
   On 30 May 1724 Thomas and Ann conv. 150 a. *Walton* (or *Malton*) to Morris Carty of KE Co.{QALR IKB:250}

3. ZOROBABEL FRENCH, son of Samuel, d. in KE Co. by June 1715.
   He m. 1st, Sarah (N), and 2nd, on 4 Nov 1740, Elizabeth Leger.
   On 21 Jan 1748/9 Sarah Holleger, of KE Co., made her will and named her sister Elizabeth, wife of Zorobabel French, and appointed her bro.-in-law executor. She also named her nephew Samuel French.{MWB 26:75}
   Zorababel French, of KE Co., d. leaving a will dated 1 April 1749 and proved 3 June 1751. The heirs named were wife Elizabeth French to whom 100 a. was devised called *Partnership*; son Zorababel French; son Samuel French; dau. Hannah Massey; and grandson Abraham Massy. Also mentioned was son James Williamson French and dau.

Sarah French. The extx. was wife Elizabeth. The will was witnessed by Thomas Gould, Sarah Gould, and Mary Rosser.{MWB 28:146}

His estate was appraised by Benjamin Blackiston and Richard Wilson, and valued at £144.0.6. Martha Wilmer and John Eglin signed as creditors. Mary Massey and Nicholas Massey signed as next of kin. Elisabeth French, extx., filed the inventory on 6 Sep 1751.{MINV 47:137}

On 30 March 1752 his estate was appraised again by Benjamin Blackiston and Richard Wilson, and valued at £7.3.6. Elisabeth French, extx., filed the inventory mentioning Henrietta Maria Phillis Massy and Zorobabel French on 9 April 1752.{MINV 48:283}

On 6 April 1752 distribution of the estate was made by Elizabeth French, extx.{BFD 1:29}

He was the father of (by Sarah): GULLY, b. 20 Dec 1729; and SARAH, b. 10 Dec 1739.{KESH}

He was also the father of: ZORABABEL; SAMUEL; HANNAH, m. (N) Massey; and JAMES WILLIAMSON.

THE FULSTON FAMILY

1. JOHN FULSTON, was bur. 6 July 1721.{KESP} He m. Jane (N) who d. c1721.

John Fulston d. leaving a will dated 26 April 1721 and proved 26 Jan 1721/2. To son Richard he left personalty. To wife Jane, extx., he left the residue of estate.{MWB 17:74} No records of administration or inventory have been found in the Prerogative Court of MD.

Jane Fulston (Fulstone), d. leaving a nuncupative will proved 16 Feb 1721. She left personalty to Mary Horn and the residue of her estate to Richard Fulston. The will was witnessed by Mary Horn (23 years old).{MWB 17:78} No records of administration or inventory has been found in the Prerogative Court of MD.

John was the father of: RICHARD; and MARY, m. William Want of the parish of Saybridgeworth in the County of Stratford (or Hertford) in England, bricklayer; and other children, dead by 1734.

2. RICHARD FULSTON (FOULSTONE, FULLSTONE), son of John, d. by 2 Nov 1738. He m. by 8 May 1716 Sarah (Porter), widow and admx. of William Scott.{INAC 37A:111} On 14 Nov 1718 and 21 Feb 1720 Fulston admin. the estate of William Scott. On 5 July 1721 Richard and Sarah Fulston admin. Scott's estate.{MDAD 2:266 and 3:293, 463}

On 24 Dec 1716, Edward Scott and his wife Martha of KE Co., conv. to Richard Fulston and his wife Sarah, in consideration of 100 a. being part of the *Manor of Stephen Heath*, on the Bradnox Creek, 250 a.{KELR BC#1:174} On 24 Dec 1717 Richard Fulston and his wife Sarah of KE Co., conv. to Edward Scott of afsd. county, the same land which had been made over to Fulston by Edward Scott and his wife Martha, part of a tract called the *Manor of Steppen Heath* on John Jones Cove or Creek, 100 a.{KELR BC#1:193}

At November Court 1728, Richard Foulston was ordered to answer to a charge of theft.{KECR JS#22:52} At August Court 1729, Richard Foulstone of St. Paul's Parish, cooper, was found guilty of stealing property of a certain Christine Tippet, wife of Thomas Tippet. He was fined 1000 lbs. of tob.{KECR JS#WK:77}

On 25 May 1723, Richard Fulston of KE Co., cooper, and his wife Sarah, conv. land to Thomas Tyre of afsd. county.{KELR JS#W:322}

Richard Fullstone of KE Co., MD, d. by 2 Nov 1738 when William Want of the parish of Saybridgeworth in the County of Stratford in England, bricklayer, and his wife Mary, conv. land to Bedingfield Hands of Chester Town, merchant. The deed stated that Richard Falston, late of KE Co., cooper, dec., was seized of a tract called the *Manor of Stepen Heath* on the n. side of Bradnox Creek and the same Richard being so seized d. intestate whereby the same descended to afsd. Mary (Want) as sister to sd. Richard.{KELR JS#22:295}

On 26 Feb 1734 Edward Bennett of the Parish of St. John's Wapping in the County of Middlesex, mariner, under oath dep. that he knew very well John Fullstone and Anne his wife, both of the parish afsd. long since dec., and he also knew Mary Want the now wife of William Want of the parish of Saybridgeworth in the County Hertford, bricklayer, and the dau. of the sd. John Fulstone, dec., and that she was the now only surviving lawfull and reputed sister to Richard Fullstone the son of the sd. John Fullstone, dec., Richard Fullstone, as this deponent is informed, lately d. in MD, whom this sd. first deponent did also well know and was intimately acquainted with them in England, as being second cousin to the sd. Richard Fullstone and intimately acquainted and conversant in the family and doth well know that all the other children of the sd. John Fullston by Anne his wife are since dead.

Secondly, Mary Fisher, also of the Parish of St. John's Wapping, Middlesex, same place, widow, said that she knew very well the sd. Mary Want to be the only surviving lawfull and reputed sister. This deponent as a near neighbour being intimately acquainted and conversant in the Family from the childhood of the sd. Richard Fullstone and the sd. Mary his sister. (Witnessed by John Exton, of London, notary publick on 26 Feb 1734.)

On 24 April 1739, Alexander Williamson of Chester Town, conv. land to Bedingfield Hands of the same place, merchant. Whereas Alexander by his deed dated 20 June 1717 between him and his wife Anne and Richard Fulston then of the afsd. county, cooper, and his wife Sarah, paid to Richard and Sarah £50, for 150 a. called *Manor of Stepen Heath* and whereas after the execution of the deed afsd. Sarah

d. whereby the right and estate came to the same Richard by survivor-
ship and he d. intestate and the same descended to Mary wife of
William Want of the parish of Saybridgeworth in Hartford County,
England, bricklayer, sister and heir of the same Richard. And whereas
the same William Want and Mary by their deed dated 2 Nov 1738
conv. the same to Bedingfield Hands. (The sd. Alexander Williamson
further quit claims the land.){KELR JS#22:302}

THE GAMBELL FAMILY

1. JOHN GAMBALL (GAMBELL) was b. c1681/4, and d. by Oct 1759.
In Oct 1753, John Gamball, age 61, dep. regarding the bounds of a
tract called *Cornwallis's Choice;* he said that about 14 years earlier he
was upon Salters Point in company with Nathaniel Griffith and some of
the other persons that were sailors and that Nathaniel Griffith told
him that he and his father Benjamin Griffith went to Philadelphia with
Col. Codd ....{KELR JS#28:43} On 19 Aug 1755, John Gamball, age c64,
dep. regarding the bounds of a tract called *Cornwallis Choice.*{KELR
JS#28:162}

John m. Honour (sometimes given as Henrietta) (N). At November
Court 1754, James Dougherty, labourer, servant of James Calder, Esq.,
was charged with assaulting on 10 July 1754, Honour Gamball, wife of
John Gamball. He was fined 20 s.{KECR JS#25:134A}

At November Court 1732, John Gambell of St. Paul's Parish, was
found guilty of assaulting Samuel Norris on 10 Oct 1732. He was fined
200 lbs. of tob. At November Court 1739, it was presented that John
Gambell and James Meeks, on 20 Nov 1739, assaulted each other.{KECR
JS#23:29} At March Court 1741, it was presented that John Gambell, on
1 March 1741, assaulted Mary Freestone. He was fined 40 s.{KECR
JS#23:261 and JS#WK:335} At June Court 1752, it was presented that
John Gamball, assaulted Charles Pell. He was fined 1 s.{KECR JS#25:97A}

On 15 Oct 1759 his estate was appraised by ---- Bordley and John
Carvile, and valued at £652.11.4. Col. Edward Lloyd and William Rasin
signed as creditors. Ann Gamble and Lettiser Gamble signed as next of
kin. Heneritta Gamble (widow), admx., filed the inventory on 19 Feb
1760.{MINV 68:238}

Another appraisal was made 17 Nov 1760 by ---- Bordley and John
Carvile, and valued at £57.18.10. Edward Lloyd and Sarah Rasin (exec.
of William Rasin) signed as creditors. Ann Gamble and Lettiser Gamble
signed as next of kin. Stephen Kennard and Joseph Boon, admins.,
filed the inventory on 4 June 1767.{MINV 92:130}

Honor or Henrietta Gamble d. leaving a will dated 26 April 1766
and proved 13 Oct 1766. Mentioned were children Darius, Robard,
Bethein (dau.), Sarah, Cethisah(?) Boon, Rebeka Kinard, and son-in-law

Steven Kinard. The execs. were Stephen K. Kinard and Joseph Boon. The will was witnessed by Paul Whithcott and Martha Ann Whichcote. {MWB 34:300}

The estate of Honora Gambile (also Henrietta Gamble), of KE Co., was appraised by John Carvile and William Wilmer, and valued at £372.3.2. Benjamin Morgan & William Slubey, Jr. signed as creditors. Lettiser Boon and Cethier Gamble signed as next of kin. Stephen Kennard and Joseph Boon, execs., filed the inventory on 28 Feb 1768. {MINV 97:190}

On 17 Nov 1767 her estate was appraised by John Carvill and William Wilmer, and valued at £106.1.10. Benjamin Morgan & William Slubey, Jr. signed as creditors. Kettesor Boon and Cethier Gmbl (?) signed as next of kin. Stephen Kennard and Joseph Boon, execs., filed the inventory on 28 May 1768. {MINV 97:193}

On 28 Feb 1768 distribution of the estate of Henrietta Gamble, of KE Co., was made by Stephen Kennard and Joseph Boone, execs. Legatees were son Darius Gambrell, dau. Bethier Gambrell, dau. Sarah Gambrell, dau. Lethisa Boone, granddau. Rebeckar Kennard, and son-in-law Stephen Kennard. Residue to rest of children. {BFD 5:109}

John and Honor (Henrietta) Gamble were the parents of: DARIUS; ROBARD; BETHEIN (dau.); SARAH; CETHISAH(?), m.; and REBEKA, m. Stephen Kinard.

Unplaced

GAMBAL, JANE, on 9 Feb 1757, confessed to committing fornication, but refused to name the father. She was fined £3. {KECR JS#25:213A}

THE GARLAND FAMILY

1. JOHN GARLAND d. in KE Co. by May 1755. He seems to have m. 1st, by 26 April 1733, Rose (N), and 2nd, by 7 April 1755, Christiana (N).

John Garland, of KE Co., weaver, and his wife Rose, on 26 April 1733, conv. to Thomas Mahon of the same place, a moiety of a parcel of 100 a., formerly purchased by Cornelius Crowly from James Worth as part of a tract called *Queen Charleton*, which land was bequeathed by Cornelius to his daus. Elinor and Honour. {KELR JS#18:9}

John Garland, of KE Co., weaver, d. leaving a will dated 7 April 1755 and proved 20 May 1755. The heirs named were son John Garland, to whom was devised a dwell. plant. called *Ellisses Chance* (275 a.); son William Garland, to whom was devised 250 a. of a tract called *Ellisses Chance*; son Benjamin Garland; son James Garland; and wife Christiana; six other children, Mary, Jennet, Anne, Hannah, Catharine, and Sarah Garland. The extx. was wife Christiana Garland. The will was witnessed by Thos. Gould, William Clark, and Dennis Barritt.{MWB 29:455}

On 6 Aug 1755 his estate was appraised by Benjamin Hazel and Benjamin Cereston, value unknown. Christinah Garland, extx., filed the inventory on 27 Aug 1755, mentioning John Garland, Mary Anderson, John Pattison and Elias Deal.{MINV 59:177}

John Garland's estate was appraised by Benjamin Hazel and Benjamin Blakiston, and valued at £55.2.3. John Dattison and Elias Deal signed as creditors. John Garland and Mary Anderson signed as next of kin. Christopher Garland, exec., filed the inventory on 17 March 1756.{MINV 60:386}

On 1 Nov 1756 distribution of the estate was made by Christian Garland, extx. Distribution of the estate was made to Christiana Garland (widow) and to Mary, Jennett, Ann, Hannah, Catharine and Sarah, equally.{BFD 2:41}

John Garland was the father of: JOHN; WILLIAM; BENJAMIN; JAMES; MARY; JENNET; ANNE; HANNAH; CATHARINE; and SARAH.

2. JOHN GARLAND, son of John, m. Rebecca (N), who survived him.

On 28 Aug 1772 his estate was appraised by William Hazel and Samuel West, and valued at £377.3.6. Mr. Griffin Miller and Nathan Menering signed as creditors. Elias Deal and James Garland signed as next of kin. Rebecca Garland, admx., filed the inventory on 9 Dec 1772.{MINV 110:265}

On 23 Dec 1772 distribution of his estate was made by Rebecca Garland, admx.{BFD 6:195}

Unplaced

GARLAND, ANN, was bur. 9 July 1659.{ARMD LIV:130, Liber B:34}

THE GEORGE FAMILY

1. ROBERT GEORGE, weaver, and Barbara Everett of KE Co., were m. 20 da., 1 mo., 1699 at Chester Meeting House.{CEMM}

Robert d. leaving a will dated 19 da., 8 mo. (Oct) 1732 and proved 24 Nov 1732. To eldest son Robert, he left northern most half of *Stratford* bought of Thomas Garnett. To son Joseph, he left the other half of afsd. lands. To dau. Rachel Thompson, personalty. Execs. were the two sons afsd.{MWB 20:757}

Robert and Barbara were the parents of: ROBERT, b. 20 da., 11 mo., 1699{CEMM}; JOSEPH; and RACHEL, m. (N) Thompson.

2. ROBERT GEORGE, son of Robert and Barbara, was b. 20 da., 11 mo., 1699. On 9 da., 6 mo., 1727 he condemned his disorderly marriage.{CEMM} Robert George, of KE Co., age 48, on c1750, affirmed.{KEEJ: James Blake and Mary}

3. JOSEPH GEORGE, son of Robert and Barbara, was b. c1709 and was named in his father's will. On 25 March 1749, Joseph George, age c40, affirmed regarding the bounds of a tract called *Sewell* alias *Utrick*. 25 March 1749.{KELR JS#26:243}

On 13 da., 6 mo., 1729 he requested a certificate respecting affairs of marriage to be directed to the monthly meeting in TA Co.{CEMM} He m. Sarah Bartlett, dau. of John Bartlett, on 20 da., 9 mo., 1729 at Third Haven Meeting.{ESVR 1:94}

Joseph George, of KE Co., d. leaving a will dated 22 July 1756 and proved 14 Aug 1756. The heirs named were children Joseph, Bartlet, Sarah, Rachel, James, and Richard George, and son-in-law William True. The execs. were Wm. True and Joseph George. The will was witnessed by Abraham Milton, Joseph Milton, and Ann Milton (Quakers).{MWB 30:123}

On 17 Sep 1756 his estate was appraised by James Ringgold, Jr. and Lovering Merrit, and valued at £509.18.1. James Anderson and John Bordley signed as creditors. John George and Sarah Lamb signed as next of kin. William Trew and Joseph George, execs., filed the inventory on 25 April 1757.{MINV 63:366}

On 19 Nov 1757 his estate was again appraised by James Ringgold, Jr. and Lovering Merritt, and valued at £58.16.7. William Trew (Quaker) and Joseph George (Quaker), exec., filed the inventory on 23 May 1758.{MINV 64:318}

On 14 Nov 1761 distribution of his estate was made by Joseph George and William Trew, execs. Distribution was made to unnamed children. Legatee was Bartlet George.{BFD 3:106}

Joseph and Sarah (Bartlett) George were the parents of{CEMM}: JOHN, b. 12 da., 9 mo., 1731; MARY, b. 8 da., 4 mo., 1733; JOSEPH, b. 4 da., 9 mo., 1734; SARAH, b. 14 da., 9 mo., 1736; RACHEL, b. 5 da., 1 mo., 1738; THOMAS, b. 15 da., 1 mo., 1740; JAMES, b. 19 da., 6 mo., 1742; RICHARD, b. 30 da., (?) mo., 1746; and BARTLETT, b. 31 da., 11 mo., 1749 and d. 10 da., 2 mo., 1788.

4. JOHN GEORGE, son of Joseph and Sarah, was b. 12 da., 9 mo., 1731. He is probably the John George who on 8 da., 10 mo., 1755, stated that he was about to take a wife within the verge of TA Co. Monthly Meeting, and requested a certificate.{CEMM}

3-a. JAMES GEORGE, son of Joseph and Sarah (Bartlett) George, was b. 19 da., 6 mo., 1742. He is almost certainly the James George who d. by 26 April 1775.

James George of KE Co., d. leaving an estate appraised by Arthur Miller and John Rolph, and valued at £100.16.1. Morgan and Sluby and Edward Worrell signed as creditors. John George and Robert George signed as next of kin. Elisabeth George, admx., filed the inventory on 26 April 1775.{MINV 121:175}

Unplaced

GEORGE, BENJAMIN, of KE Co., was transported by 1670, and claimed land for Service in 1675.{MPL 15:311}

GEORGE, HANNAH, widow, of KE Co., d. leaving a will dated 10 Nov 1766 and proved 11 March 1767. Heirs named were Sarah Simmond, Robert George, sister Elizabeth Forkom and Joshua George. The exec. was Joshua George. The will was witnessed by John Smith (a Quaker), John Flynn, and Isaac Dolehuntee.{MWB 35:233}

GEORGE, ROBERT, m. Ann (N). They were the parents of{CEMM}: ROBERT, b. 8 da., 3 mo., 1770; JOSHUA, b. 21 da., 6 mo., 1772; SARAH, b. 2 da., 12 mo., 1775; ELISABETH, b. 18 da., 2 mo., 1778; ANN, b. 19 da., 5 mo., 1780; PRISCILLA, b. 14 da., 10 mo., 1782; and WILLIAM EDMONDSON, b. 11 da., 3 mo., 1785.

THE GIANT/GYANT FAMILY

1. JOHN GIANT d. in KE Co., leaving a will dated 4 da., 1 mo., 1719/20 and proved 17 May 1720. To his five children, John, Richard, William, Mary, and Martha, he left his estate equally. To wife Ann, co-extx., he left personalty; John Twege was the other exec.{MWB 16:38}

His estate was inv. c1720.{MINV 4:212}

John Giant was the father of: JOHN; RICHARD; WILLIAM; MARY; and MARTHA.

2. JOHN GIANT, son of John, was named as a son in his father's will. He m. Mary, widow of Andrew Tolson.

By a writ of Kent County Court of January 1747 the Sheriff was commissioned to attach the goods and chattels, lands and tenements of John Giant to the value 1968 lbs. of tob. for the use of John Wallace and Company. By virtue of the the sheriff attached the right and estate of John Giant in a plant. in the sd. county called *Middle Neck*.{KELR JS#26:106}

John and Mary were the parents of{KESH}: SARAH, b. 15 Jan 1731; RICHARD, b. 29 Sep 1734; JOHN, b. 14 Aug 1737; and WILLIAM, b. 1 April 1742.

3. RICHARD GIANT (GYANT), son of John and Mary, on 23 June 1720, was bound as an apprentice with William Mackey, carpenter, until age 21, he being 14 years old.{KEBI JS#W:70A}

4. SARAH GIANT (GYANT), dau. of John and Mary, was b. 15 Jan 1731. She may be the Sarah Giant, spinster, who, at June Court 1757, was fined 30 s. for having committed fornication; she named James Denning as the father of her base born child, Stephen.{KECR JS#25:176A}

She was charged at March Court 1762 with having committed fornication and begetting a base born child. She was fined 30 s.{KECR DD#1:16B} At June Court 1762, it was presented that Rasin Gale committed fornication with Sarah Gyant and begot a base born child. He was fined 30 s.{KECR DD#1:19B} At August Court 1762, it was presented that Sarah Gyant committed fornication and begot a base born child. She was fined 30 s.{KECR DD#1:24B}

5. WILLIAM GIANT, son of John and Mary, on 22 June 1720 was bound as an apprentice to John Beech, until age 21, he being 12 years old about this day.{KEBI JS#W:70B}

6. MARTHA GIANT, dau. of John and Mary, on 22 June 1720, was bound as an apprentice with Francis Hill, until age 16 or day of marriage, she being 7 years of age about this day.{KEBI JS#W:69A}

THE GIBBS FAMILY

1. RICHARD GIBBS, d. by 11 Aug 1713 when his estate was inv. The inventory was filed 5 Sep 1713.{INAC 34:69} His estate was admin. 17 Sep (c1715) by the admx., the unnamed widow, now wife of William Yarley.{INAC 36B:152} The estate was admin. again on 13 Jan 1715 by William Earley.{INAC 37A:105}

Mary Yearly, of KE Co., d. leaving a will dated 7 Feb 1765 and proved 8 Aug 1765. The heirs named were children John, Susanna Blackiston, Mary Summer, Patience Copper, and Silvester Gibbs. She also named her grandchildren Edward and Amelia Gibbs. No exec. was named. The will was witnessed by Richard Brice and William Grant.{MWB 33:303}

Richard and Mary (N) Gibbs were probably the parents of: JOHN; EDWARD; SYLVESTER; SUSANNA, m. (N) Blakiston; MARY, m. (N) Summer; and PATIENCE, m. (N) Copper.

2. JOHN GIBBS, of QA Co., cooper, probably son of Richard and Mary, on 16 May 1715, conv. to Renatus Smith of the same county, a parcel of land called *Gibbs Choyce* on Steelpone Creek formerly taken up by the father of the sd. John Gibbs and from him leased for 99 years to Richard Smith and his wife Rosamond, 150 a.{KELR BC#1:78}

3. EDWARD GIBBS, of KE Co., probably son of Richard and Mary, d. by Jan 1761.

Edward and his wife Mary, on 18 Jan 1733, conv. to William Yearly of the same county, a tract called *Chance* near Grays Inn Creek, 50 a., granted to Gibbs on 20 April 1715.{KELR JS#16:432} *Gibbs' Chance*, 50 a. in KE Co., was patented by Richard [sic] Gibbs on 20 April 1715.{MPL EE#6:171 and RY#1:446}

On 11 May 1734, Edward Gibbs and his wife Mary, conv. to Robert Hodges, a parcel of land ... division line of Richard Mason and Robert Hodges ... land of Thomas Ringgold called *Huntingfield* ..., 100 a. (possibly called *Prevention of Ill Conveniencys*).{KELR JS#18:16}

Edward Gibbs, of KE Co., d. by 12 Jan 1761, when his estate was appraised by Darius Dunn and Nathan Hatcheson, and valued at £80.1.4. James Dunn and George Coppen signed as creditors. Edward Gibbs and Silvester Gibbs signed as next of kin. An unnamed admin. filed the inventory on 21 March 1761.{MINV 72:115}

On 2 Aug 1761 his estate was appraised again by Darius Dunn and Nathan Hatcheson, and valued at £30.1.0. James Dunn and George Copper signed as creditors. Amelia Gibbs and Silvester Gibbs signed as next of kin. Paul Tinslaugh, admin., filed the inventory on 31 Dec 1761.{MINV 75:239}

4. SILVESTER GIBBS, probably son of Richard and Mary, and Sarah Coulson were m. 14 July 1743. They were the parents of: RICHARD, b. 3 Aug 1744; JOHN, b. 13 April 1746; and SILVESTER, b. 5 Dec 1749.{KESP}

Unplaced

GIBBS, JANE, on 16 June 1758 confessed to committing fornication and named the father. She was fined 30 s. John Wilson (Worton), acknowledged himself to be indebted for a fine of 30 s. and to pay all fees.{KECR JS#25:192B}

GIBBS, JOHN, of CE Co., m. by (c1678), Anne, relict and admx. of Edward Best of KE Co.{INAC 5:301}

GIBBS, SARAH, servant of Michael Hackett, at November Court 1753, was presented that on 1 Sep 1751 she committed fornication and begot

a bastard child. She was ordered to receive 10 lashes.{KECR JS#25:121A}
On 16 Jan 1754 John Steen and Sarah Gibbs were convicted for
fornication. They were fined.{KECR JS#25:126B}

THE GILBERT FAMILY

1. JOHN GILBERT patented 98 unnamed a. on 10 Aug 1695.{MPL
40:7} He d. 9 mo. 1706.{CEMM} He left a will dated 22 Aug 1706 and
proved 27 Nov 1707. To wife Mary, extx., he left his entire estate. Sons
John, Thomas and Efrum were to be of age at 18 years. Two daus.
were to be of age at 16. In event of remarriage of wife, John Wyatt
and Sam'll Wallis to have charge of sons, and Anthony Moris of
Philadelphia of daus.{MWB 12:192}
    His estate was admin. on 10 Dec 1707 and 7 June 1709 by Mary
Gilbert, extx.{INAC 28:55 and 29:319}
    John Gilbert was the father of: JOHN; THOMAS; EPHRAIM, and
(N), and (N), two daus.

2. JOHN GILBERT, son of John, was named in his father's will. He
was under 16 when that will was drawn up, but by April 1725 he had
married and become the father of two children.
    His will was dated 27 April 1725 and signed 19 Dec 1729. To wife
Phebe, extx., he left the dwell. plant. To son John and dau. Mary, he
left personal estate.{MWB 20:2}
    Gilbert's estate was inv. on 4 March 1729. and the inventory filed
on 3 April 1730 by Phebe Gilbert, extx. Mary Stewart and Sarah
Pearkins signed as next of kin.{MINV 15:488}
    At March Court 1730, Phebe Gilbert was fined 30 s. for having born
a child out of wedlock. She named Thomas Morsell as the father.{KECR
JS#WK:186}
    John and Phebe were the parents of: JOHN; and MARY.

3. EPHRAIM GILBERT, son of John, was living in Shrewsbury Parish,
when, at August Court 1726, he was found guilty of committing fornication on 10 March 1726 with Mary Ryle and begetting a bastard
child; he was fined 600 lbs. of tob.{KECR JS#22:187}
    Now of St. Paul's Parish, at August Court 1729, he was found guilty
of committing fornication with Rebecca West and begetting a bastard
child. He was fined 30 s.{KECR JS#WK:78}
    On 17 Aug 1737, Ephram Gilbert, age c32, dep. regarding the
bounds of the tract called *Hopewell;* he stated about 9-10 years earlier
he was overseer to Major Dowdall who showed him a bounded tree.
{KELR JS#22:19}

145

Unplaced

GILBERT, (N), m. by 29 Dec 1772, Ann, dau. of Thomas Bowers of KE Co., whose estate was distributed on that day, with dau. Ann Bowers as one of the heirs.{BFD 6:202}

GILBERT, ELIZABETH, spinster, at March Court 1747, was charged that, on 1 March 1747 she, and at diverse times as well before as since, committed fornication and begot a bastard child. She was fined 30 s.{KECR JS#25:5B}

At August Court 1748, it was presented that Dennis Shehawn, labourer, committed fornication with Elizabeth Gilbert and begot a bastard child. He was fined 30 s.{KECR JS#25:18A}

GILBERT, JOHN and THOMAS GILBERT, on 20 Dec 1745, leased from Benjamin Tasker of Annapolis, Agent and Receiver General of the Lord Proprietary, 100 a., part of *His Lordships Mannor* in KE Co., during the natural lives of sd. John Gilbert and Thomas Gilbert and Samuel Merrett, all of KE Co. (no relationships given).{KELR JS#25:339}

On 14 Aug 1760 the Agent and Receiver General of the Lord Proprietary, leased to John Gilbert of KE Co., 18 a., during the lives of sd. John Gilbert, his wife Anne and John Gilbert, son of Thomas Gilbert.{KELR DD#1:54}

THE GLASSFORD FAMILY

Refs.: A: *Wills of Chester County, Pennsylvauia, 1713-1748.* Based on the Abstracts of Jacob Martin. Family Line Publications, Westminster, MD, 1993. B: *Wills of Chester County, Pennsylvauia, 1748-1766.* Based on the Abstracts of Jacob Martin. Family Line Publications, Westminster, MD, 1994. C: *Wills of Chester County, Pennsylvauia, 1766-1788.* Based on the Abstracts of Jacob Martin. Family Line Publications, Westminster, MD, 1994.

1. HENRY GLASFORD was in Chester Co., PA, by 1 Sep 1742 when he and his wife Esther admin. the estate of Esther's former husband, Samuel Houston.{A:99 cites Chester Co. Will Book B:82}

Either he or another Henry Glasford d. leaving a will dated 5 Nov 1767 and proved in KE Co. on 13 July 1768. His will was also filed in Chester Co., PA.{B:148} He named his wife Elizabeth; bro. Joseph Glasford; cousins Henry, Elizabeth, and Sarah, children of John Glasford; nephews Henry and James Glasford, to whom land was devised in Chester Co., PA; niece Margaret Glasford, living in Ireland; Henry Culley, Michael Askins's children; Mary Page, wife of Aquilla Page;

146

Elizabeth Ory and Jane Black. The exec. was James Black. The will was witnessed by Aquilla Page, John Wallace, and Wm. Rogers. {MWB 36:533}

On 15 Aug 1768 Henry Glassford's estate was appraised by Peter Massey and W. Woodall, and valued at £430.15.11. James Black and Aquilla Page signed as creditors. Elisabeth Glassford and Elisabeth Gray signed as next of kin. James Black, exec., filed the inventory on 17 Nov 1768. {MINV 99:208}

On 13 Feb 1770 his estate was again appraised by Peter Massy and W. Woodall, and valued at £102.15.3. James Black, exec., filed the undated inventory. {MINV 106:47}

Henry Glasford's estate was appraised and valued at £19.19.8. James Black, admin. and exec., filed the inventory cont. a list of debts on 27 Oct 1770. {MINV 104:106}

On 27 Oct 1770 distribution of the estate was made by James Black, exec. Legatees were widow, Mary Page and Elisabeth Cry. Residue to Jane Black. {BFD 5:393}

Another list of debts was appraised and valued at £124.10.3. James Black, exec., filed the inventory cont. a list of debts on 18 Nov 1772. {MINV 110:253}

On 13 Nov 1772 distribution of Henry Glassford's estate was made by James Black, exec. Legatees were unnamed widow, Mary Page and Elisabeth Cry. Residue to Jane Black. {BFD 6:181}

Elizabeth Glassford, widow, of KE Co., d. leaving a will dated 8 Feb 1773 and proved 1 April 1773. The heirs named were son John Wallace, granddau. Sarah Cry and granddau. Elizabeth Baley. The will was witnessed by Mary Boyer, Margaret Stewart, and Elizabeth Fleming. {MWB 39:191}

Elizabeth Glassford of KE Co., d. by 30 April 1773, when her estate was appraised by Peter Massey and William Merritt, and valued at £243.7.6. James Black signed as creditor and James Black and Elisabeth Fleming signed as next of kin. John Wallis, admin., filed the inventory on 26 June 1773. {MINV 114:183}

THE GOODHAND FAMILY

1. CHRISTOPHER GOODHAND of Kent Island, was in MD by 1672 when he claimed land for service. {MPL 15: 379} He d. leaving a will dated 3 May 1704 and proved 4 Oct 1704. To dau. Elizabeth, he left 300 a. *Poplar Neck*, provided she married with mother's consent, otherwise tract to pass to son Marmaduke. Exec. not given. {MWB 3:654}

His estate was inv. 15 May 1705. {MWB 3:542}

Christopher was the father of: ELIZABETH; and MARMADUKE.

2. MARMADUKE GOODHAND, son of Christopher, was named in his father's will.

On 27 Feb 1718, Hannah Goodhand, seamstress, Marmaduke Goodhand and his wife Sarah, of QA Co., Gent., conv. to Nathaniel Pearce of KE Co., Gent., a tract called *Stonetone*, 500 a.{KELR JS#W:6}

THE GOODING FAMILY

1. SAMUEL GOODING was in KE Co. by 17 Aug 1735 when he made his will, which was proved 12 June 1736. To son Samuel, daus. Ann and Cotton (Katherine), and wife Elinor, he left personalty. To two sons, Samuel and Abraham, he left a tract in BA Co. bought of Thomas Long. Wife Elinor was named extx.{MWB 21:581}

The inventory of his estate was taken on 20 June 1736 and filed on 27 Sep 1736 by the extx. Elinor. Katherine Goodwin and Samuel Goodwin were next of kin.{MINV 21:494}

An additional inventory was taken 12 Jan 1736 and filed by the extx. Elinor Long on 10 March 1737. The inventory mentioned Thomas Lues and Samuel Gooding.{MINV 22:236}

Ellinor Gooden, of KE Co., d. leaving a will dated 26 Nov 1753 and proved 19 June 1754. The heirs named were son Abraham Gooden; dau. Catherine Canneday; grandson Thomas Blakesly; granddau. Joyce Lewis; dau. Ann Cannaday; son Thomas Lewis. The will was witnessed by Joseph Wickes, and John and Mary Framer (or Frances).{MWB 29:215}

On 24 July 1754 Ellinor Gooding's estate was appraised by John Wickeys and William Moore, and valued at £128.3.8. No creditors listed. Caternan Canday and Stephen Canday signed as next of kin. Abraham Gooding, admin., filed the inventory on 2 Nov 1754.{MINV 58:254}

Samuel was the father of: SAMUEL; ABRAHAM; ANN, m. (N) Canneday; and KATHERINE, m. (N) Canneday.

2. ABRAHAM GOODING, son of Samuel and Elinor, was b. c1716, and d. by 27 Nov 1762.

On 18 Dec 1761, Abraham Gooding, age c45, dep. regarding the bounds of a tract called *Waxford*.{KELR DD#1:100}

At June Court 1756, it was presented that Abraham Gooding, on 10 March 1756, assaulted John Kinslaugh. He was fined 20 s.{KECR JS#25:159A}

At March Court 1757, it was presented that Abraham Gooding of St. Paul's Parish, on 3 Aug 1756, committed fornication with Tamer Phillingame and begot a bastard child. He was fined 30 s.{KECR JS#25:168A}

Gooding d. by 27 Nov 1762, his estate was appraised by Nathaniel Miller and Thomas Miller, and valued at £64.2.2. Thomas and William Ringgold signed as creditors. Ann Canneday, Thomas Louis and Crispen Davis signed as next of kin. Abraham Gooding and John Gooding, admins., filed the inventory on 23 Feb 1763.{MINV 80:29}

On 24 Nov 1763, his estate was appraised a second time, by Nathaniel Miller and Thomas Miller, and valued at £5.7.10. C. Davis and Thomas Ringgold signed as creditors. Ann Canaday and Thomas Lewis signed as next of kin. Abraham Gooding and John Gooding, admins., filed the inventory on 15 Dec 1763.{MINV 82:236}

His estate was appraised again and valued at £0.18.0. John Gooding, admin., filed the inventory cont. a list of debts on 15 May 1764.{MINV 83:198}

Abraham was the father of{MDAD 51:73}: JOHN; and SARAH, m. Benj. Phillingham (Fillingham).

Unplaced

GOODING, AARON, of KE Co., d. by 3 June 1723, when his estate was administered by Joan Browne, wife of Thomas Browne.{MDAD 4:299}

GOODING, ANN, spinster, at June Court 1766, was charged with committing fornication on 17 June 1765, and begetting a base born child. She was fined 30 s. and was ordered to give security for the payment of her fine and to indemnify the county from any charge that might accrue by means of the afsd. bastard child called Edward.{KECR DD#1:73B}

At August Court 1766, it was presented that Edward Collins committed fornication with Ann Gooding and begot a base born child. He was fined 30 s. and ordered to give security to keep the county indemnified from any charge that might accrue by means of his bastard child called Edward.{KECR DD#1:80A}

At August Court 1772, it was presented that Ann Gooding, spinster, on 10 March 1772, committed fornication and begot a base born child. She was fined 30 s.{KECR DD#1:149B}

GOODIN, ESTHER, of Shrewsbury Parish, spinster, at November Court 1729, was found guilty of having committing fornication on 10 June 1708 and begetting a bastard child. She was ordered to receive 10 lashes. She said that Thomas Yorkson was the father.{KECR JS#WK:91}

GOODING, JACOB, m. by 14 Sep 1723, Hester, dau. of Isaac Van Bebber of CE Co.{MWB 18:187}

GOODING, JACOB, m. Sarah (N). They were the parents of: SARAH, b. 1 Jan 1728; JAMES, b. 8 Aug 1731; JACOB, b. 8 Feb 1733; and JOHN, b. 1 Aug 1736.{KESP}

GOODING, JACOB, m. by 21 April 1734, Mary, dau. of James Smith of KE Co.{MWB 21: 230}

THE GRAHAM FAMILY

1. JOHN GRAHAM, of KE Co., was b. c1719. On 25 July 1757, John Graham, age c38, dep. regarding the bounds of a tract called *Philips Choice*.{KELR JS#28:367} He m. 1st, Elizabeth (N). He m. 2nd, Mary (N), who m. by 15 Oct 1768 William St. Clair.

On 6 April 1753, Benjamin Tasker of Annapolis, Agent and Receiver General for the Lord Proprietary, leased to John Graham of KE Co., farmer, 142 a., during the natural lives of sd. John Graham, and his sons, James Graham and Andrew Graham, Jr.{KELR JS#27:277}

Graham d. leaving a will dated 25 Jan 1765 and proved 12 Dec 1767. The heirs mentioned were children Andrew, John, James, Elizabeth, Mary, and Robert Graham. Also mentioned was Sarah Cooper. The tract *Wolf Trak* was mentioned. The execs. were wife and son Andrew Graham. The will was witnessed by John Eccleston, John Comegys, and Henry More.{MWB 36:156}

On 4 Jan 1768 his estate was appraised by Robert Maxwell and W. Woodall, and valued at £966.11.9. Samuel Sloss and John Voorhust signed as creditors. James Graham and John Beazly signed as next of kin. Mary Graham and Andrew Graham, execs., filed the inventory on 1 April 1768.{MINV 97:154}

On 15 Oct 1768 his estate was appraised again by H. Woodall and Robert Maxwell, and valued at £166.5.7. John V. Boorhees & Co. and Thomas & George Gilpin signed as creditors. James Graham and John Beazly signed as next of kin. William St. Clair, Mary St. Clair, and Andrew Graham, execs., filed the inventory on 16 Nov 1769.{MINV 101:241}

On 16 Nov 1769 distribution of the estate was made by William St. Clair and his wife Mary, and Andrew Graham, execs. Distribution was made to widow and seven children, Andrew, John, Elisabeth, Mary, William, Robert, and Ann. Legatees were the widow, son Andrew, son James, son John, dau. Elixabeth, dau. Mary, son William, son Robert, and Sarah Cooper.{BFD 5:225}

John and Elizabeth (N) Graham were the parents of: JAMES, b. 7 April 1742{KESH}; and ANDREW, b. c1743. By his second wife, Mary,

John was the father of: JOHN; ELIZABETH; MARY;[15] WILLIAM; ROBERT; and ANN GRAHAM.

2. JAMES GRAHAM, son of John, was b. 7 April 1742, and d. by 12 Jan 1774. He m. Rebecca (N).

James Graham, of KE Co., farmer, he and his wife Rebecca, on 15 June 1764, conv. to William Woodall of afsd. county, farmer, part of a tract called *Smythers,* part of *Addition* and *Rumford Resurveyed,* 131 a.; also part of *Vianna,* 6 a.{KELR DD#1:539}

James Graham, of KE Co., d. by 12 Jan 1774, when his estate was appraised by Jacob Jones and Jonathon Turner, and valued at £418.1.4. Christopher Hall and Joseph Mann signed as creditors. John Beazy and Andrew Graham signed as next of kin. Rebecca Graham, extx., filed the inventory on 7 April 1774.{MINV 115:371}

On 3 April 1775 his estate was appraised by Christopher Hall and Oliver Smith, and valued at £161.10.6. No creditors listed. Jonathon Turner and Jacob Jones signed as next of kin. Rebecca Graham, admx., filed the inventory mentioning John Bearly and Andrew Graham on 25 Aug 1775.{MINV 122:78}

3. ANDREW GRAHAM, son of John, was b. c1743. He was age c21, when he dep. on 22 Aug 1764.{KEEJ: John Comegy}

4. ROBERT GRAHAM, son of John, was b. after 1749, and d. in KE Co. before 10 Oct 1770.

On 10 Oct 1770 the inventory of Robert Grayham (also Graham), "infant" (i.e., he was under 21 years of age), of KE Co., was appraised by Isaac Spencer and W. Woodall, and valued at £21.1.0. Joseph Graham, admin., filed the inventory mentioning Mary St. Clair and Andrew Graham on 20 Nov 1770.{MINV 104:223}

On 28 Nov 1770 distribution of the estate was made by James Graham, admin. Distribution was made (equally) to mother Mary and seven siblings, Andrew, John, James, William, Elisabeth, Mary and Ann.{BFD 6:17}

On 7 Aug 1774 another distribution of the estate was made by William St. Clair, admin. de bonis non. Distribution was made in eight parts to mother (unnamed); bros. and sister (five unnamed, whole blood); James Graham (bro., half-blood); Andrew Graham (bro., half-blood).{BFD 6:295}

---

[15] Mary Graham, of KE Co., d. leaving an estate appraised by Andrew Porter and William Husband, and valued at £466.4.11. John Gulton and John Craige signed as creditors. William Graham signed as next of kin. George Corry, exec., filed the inventory on 1 March 1763.{MINV 80:171}

GRAMES, ANN, of St. Paul's Parish, labourer, at November Court 1732, was found guilty of committing fornication on 10 June 1731, and begetting a bastard child. She was fined 30 s.{KECR JS#WK:319}

GRAHAME, JAMES, merchant, at March Court 1741/2, was charged with having assaulted John Robertson on 1 Nov 1741. He was fined 10 s.{KECR JS#23:255}

GRAHAM, MARY, of St. Paul's Parish, spinster, servant of James Stout, at March Court 1731, was found guilty of stealing several yards of material that were of Ann Stout but now are of James Stout on 10 Dec 1731. She was ordered to stand in the pillory ½ hour and receive 31 lashes.{KECR JS#WK:275}

THE GRANGER FAMILY

1. CHRISTOPHER GRANGER, of Kent Island, patented *Chance*, 50 a. on 19 June 1681.{MPL 24:367 and 31:188} He d. by 1704 when his estate was inv.{Inv. from MWB 3:624}
    Christopher was the father of: JOHN, b. 18 9ber 1693.{KELR GL#1:1}; WILLIAM; and CHRISTOPHER.

2. JOHN GRANGER, son of Christopher, and definitely bro. of William and Christopher, was b. 18 9ber 1693. He was living in QA Co. on 21 Oct 1723, when he and his wife Elizabeth, conv. to William Granger, of KE Co., a parcel of land in Easter Neck Island, which John Granger formerly bought of William Granger.{KELR JS#W:348}

3. WILLIAM GRANGER, son of Christopher, and defintely bro. of John and Christopher, on 21 Oct 1723, with his wife Mary, conv. to John Granger, of QA Co., a parcel of land in Easter Neck Island being ⅛ of a moiety or ½ part of a tract called *Wickliff*, which his wife has as right of her being one of the daus. of Joseph Wicks.{KELR JS#W:346}
    He d. leaving a will dated 12 Feb 1728/9 and proved 17 Jan 1732. To son William he left his dwell. plant.; to dau. Mary he left personalty; personal estate divided between wife Mary, son William and dau. Mary. Son and dau. afsd. to be brought up by bro. John, exec. He named another bro. Christopher.{MWB 20:759}
    William and Mary were the parents of: WILLIAM; and MARY.

4. CHRISTOPHER GRANGER, son of Christopher, and defintely bro. of John and William, of KE Co., d. leaving a will written 21 July 1747

and proved 4 Sep 1747. The heirs named were bro. John Granger; cousin John Granger, son of Thomas Granger; cousin Elizabeth Bryan, dau. of James Bryan; cousin William Granger; Sarah Granger, dau. "to my wife Ann Granger"; wife Ann Granger, extx. The will was witnessed by John Sudler, Emory Sudler, and Joseph Sudler.{MWB 25:151}

5. WILLIAM GRANGER, son of William (3) and Mary, d. leaving a will dated 28 Dec 1751 and proved 7 May 1752. The heirs named were wife Mary and children Elizabeth Granger, William Granger, and Thomas Granger, who were to receive the balance of the estate after wife's thirds and after Martha Smyth's and Mary Smyth's estates were satisfied. The extx. was wife Mary. The will was witnessed by Samuel Wickes, Lawrence Bolton, and Darby Hanes.{MWB 28:398}

On 11 May 1752 his estate was appraised by Samuel Tovey and Alexander Williams, and valued at £859.9.0. Ja. Smith and John Williamson for Cunliff & Sons signed as creditors. John Granger and Mary Bryan signed as next of kin. Mary Granger, extx., filed the inventory on 10 Aug 1752. (Folio 68 continued to folios 182 and 183.){MINV 50:67}

Mary Granger, widow, of KE Co., d. leaving a will dated 19 Nov 1768 and proved 28 Dec 1776. The heirs named were daus. Martha Sudler and Mary Granger; son Thomas Granger, to whom was devised the tract *Dongannor*; dau. Elizabeth Granger; son William Granger; daus. Martha Sudler and Mary Garnett; son-in-law Thomas Smyth. The execs. were son-in-law Emory Sudler and son William Granger. The will was witnessed by Thos. Ringgold, James Frisby, and Margaret Frisby.{MWB 41:496}

William was the father of: WILLIAM; MARTHA, m. 1st, (N) Smyth, and 2nd, Emory Sudler; THOMAS; WILLIAM; and MARY, m. 1st, (N) Smyth, and 2nd, (N) Garnett.

Unplaced

GRANGER, (N), m. by 23 March 1767, Mary, legatee of Jane Frisby, whose estate was distributed on that date.{BFD 5:77}

GRANGER, WILLIAM, age c43, dep. on 16 Feb 1659.{ARMD LIV:185, Liber B:73}

Elisabeth Stope recorded on 20 Nov 1661 a gift of a calf to William Granger, son of William Granger of the Isle of Kent.{ARMD LIV:206, Liber B:90}

THE GRANT FAMILY

1. JOHN GRANT, of KE Co., d. by 12 May 1718 when his estate was admin. by James Pacer and John Batson, and valued at £49.5.9. Tobias and Timothy Tolle signed as next of kin.{MINV 1:50}

On 14 Oct 1720, his estate was administered by John Twig and Ann Grant. His inventory totaled £39.17.0, and payments came to £18.9.0, leaving a balance of some £21.0.0 to be distributed to his heirs: his widow (unnamed) and son John Grant.{MDAD 3:264}

John Grant had at least one son: JOHN.

2. JOHN GRANT, son of John, is probably the John who m. Abigail (N). John and Abigail were the parents of: (possibly) JOHN; JUDAH (dau.), b. 5 Dec 1719, m. Richard Brice on 22 Jan 1740; WILLIAM, b. 9 July 1722; JONATHAN, b. 4 Jan 1725; GEORGE, b. 3 Jan 1729; and SAMUEL, b. 19 Aug 1732.{KESP}

3. JOHN GRANT, possibly son of John and Judah, and Elizabeth Richardson were m. 29 Oct 1745.

John Grant, of KE Co., d. by 17 Sep 1762, when his estate was appraised by Charles Hynson and William Hodges, and valued at £168.8.6. Alexander Hutchison and Thomas & William Ringgold signed as creditors. James Grant and William Grant signed as next of kin. Elisabeth Grant, admx., filed the inventory on 8 Dec 1762.{MINV 79:425}

A list of debts was appraised and valued at £1.1.6. Elisabeth Grant, admx., filed the inventory cont. a list of debts on 6 April 1764.{MINV 83:111}

On 6 April 1764 distribution of the estate was made by Elisabeth Grant, admx.{BFD 4:31}

John and Elizabeth were the parents of: JOHN, b. 24 Oct 1746; WILLIAM, b. 6 April 1748; JAMES, b. 18 Sep 1750; SARAH, b. 3 Oct 1752; ELIZABETH, b. 12 Sep 1756; and ANN, b. 9 Sep 1759.{KESP}

4. WILLIAM GRANT, son of John and Judah, was b. 9 July 1722, and d. leaving a will dated 16 Sep 1774 and proved 15 Nov 1774. The heirs named were bro. Samuel Grant, exec., to whom was devised the land *Grants Folley*; bro. George Grant; and nephews Jonathan and Thomas Grant, sons of bro. Samuel Grant. The will was witnessed by Jo. Page, Mary Evans, and Martha Kinslagh.{MWB 40:58}

On 13 Nov 1775 his estate was appraised by William Hodges and Thomas Slipper, and valued at £131.2.11. John Page and Thomas Catlin signed as creditors. William Grant and Judah Brice signed as next of kin. Samuel Grant, exec., filed the inventory on 16 Nov 1775.{MINV 122:89}

5. GEORGE GRANT, son of John and Abigail, was b. 3 Jan 1729. He m. Margaret Langwell on 23 Dec 1759.{KESP}

He was still living on 16 Sep 1774 when he was named in the will of his bro. William.{MWB 40:50}

6. SAMUEL GRANT, son of John and Abigail, was b. 19 Aug 1732.{KESP} He m. by 6 May 1757, Jemima (N).

On 16 Sep 1774 he and his sons Jonathan and Thomas were named in the will of his bro. William.{MWB 40:50}

Samuel and Jemima were the parents of{KESP}: JONATHAN, b. 6 May 1757; ELIZABETH, b. 22 June 1759; SAMUEL, b. 6 May 1757; THOMAS, b. 16 Aug 1764; SARAH, b. 9 Feb 1767; RACHEL, b. 28 Aug 1769; and FRANCIS, b. 24 Sep 1771.

6. WILLIAM GRANT, son of John and Elizabeth, was b. 6 April 1748, and d. in KE Co. by Aug 1770. He m. Eleanor (N), who m. 2nd, John Curry.

William Grant, of KE Co., d. leaving a will dated 25 July 1770 and proved 16 Aug 1770. Mentioned were wife Eleanor, sons William, John, James and Richard, and dau. Mary. The exec. was Oliver Smith. The will was witnessed by William Spearman, John Spearman, and John Williamson.{MWB 38:140}

On 21 Aug 1770 his estate was appraised by Bartus Comegys and Oliver Smith, and valued at £61.14.11. William Henry and James Black signed as creditors. No next of kin listed. Elisabeth Grant, admx., filed the inventory on 15 Nov 1770.{MINV 107:14}

A list of debts was appraised and valued at £69.1.6. John Curry, admin. and exec., filed the inventory cont. a list of debts on 7 March 1772.{MINV 108:100}

On 7 March 1772 distribution of the estate was made by Eleanor Curry, extx., wife of John Curry. Distribution was made to widow and residue to four sons William, John, James, and Richard. The legatee was dau. Mary.{BFD 6:165}

William and Eleanor were the parents of: WILLIAM; JOHN; JAMES; RICHARD; and MARY.

THE ROGER HAILES FAMILY

1. ROGER HAILES d. in KE Co. by 30 May 1729. He m. Ann, dau. of Edward Allibone. She may have become a Quaker convert between 1715 and 1720, since the children born after 1720 had their births recorded in Cecil Meeting. It is possible that he had two wives named Ann.

Roger Hailes (Hails), d. leaving a will dated 15 Jan 1728 and proved 30 May 1729. To dau. Jane Rickits and her husband, Philip Rickits, during his life, he left 50 a. of *Green Meddow* at the head of Farlo; to son Roger, 50 a. of *The Grange*. If son Edward would pay his bro. Roger 6,000 lbs., the land would be his. Wife Anne, extx., was to have £10 and ⅓ personal estate.{MWB 19:737}

The inventory of his estate was taken 16 June 1729, and filed 4 Sep 1729 by extx. Ann Hailes (Quaker). Next of kin were Edward Hales and Jane Hales.{MINV 15:171}

On 24 March 1737 Wm. Collins, Francis Lamb and John Davis of KE Co. gave bond that they would pay Ann, Philip, and Roger Hailes each £31.0.4 and 3 farthings due them as a filial portion of the estate of Roger Hailes, their dec. father.{KEBI JS#18:130}

On 21 Feb 1743, Ann Collins, Quaker, age c52, dep. regarding the bounds of a tract called *Brotherly and Friendly Agreement* and *Heyborns Farm;* she stated that about 25 years earlier she saw William Comegyes run a line between the land of her late husband Roger Hales and John Gale, the Elder, dec.{KELR JS#25:36} On 23 Aug 1759, Ann Collins conv. to her son Roger Hails part of two tracts called *Saint Martins* and *Allebones Addition,* now in possession of her son-in-law, David Hull, 90 a.{KELR JS#29:183}

Roger Hailes, by his wife (or wives) Anne, was the father of: EDWARD, twin, b. 29 May 1712; JANE, twin, b. 29 May 1712, m. Philip Ricketts by 15 Jan 1728; ELIZABETH, b. 2 Feb 1715{KESP}. ANN, b. 11th month called Jan 1720; ROGER, b. 9th month called Nov 1723; and PHILLIP, b. 12 da., 5 mo., 1729.{CEMM}

2. EDWARD HAILES (HALES), son of Roger and Ann, d. leaving a will dated 6 Feb 1734/5 and proved 21 Aug 1736. To bro. Philip, he left his entire estate. Hailes directed that he be bur. at discretion of his mother ———.{MWB 21.661}

Unplaced

HAILES, JOHN, and Hannah White were m. 23 May 1725.{KESP}

THE HAISLIP FAMILY

1. HUGH HAISLIP, d. by 27 Nov 1738. The inventory of Hugh Haislip's estate was taken 28 Nov 1730 and filed 4 Feb 1730. Another inventory was taken on 28 April 1731 and filed 10 March 1731. Named were William McCawley, servant, and next of kin John Murphey and Samuell Murphey. The admin. was Jeremiah Mchuffey.{MINV 16:201, 17:26}

Hugh left three sons: MATHEW; JAMES; and HUGH.{KEBI JS#18:178}

2. MATTHEW HAISLIP, son of Hugh, dec., on 27 Nov 1738, orphan, was bound to Jos. Man, brick maker, as an apprentice until age 21.{KEBI JS#18:178}

3. JAMES HAISLIP, son of Hugh, dec., on 24 June 1737, was bound as an apprentice to Thomas Horton, barber, until age 21.{KEBI JS#18:93} On 20 March 1739 he was bound to Joseph Carman as an apprentice, until age 21, to be taught the trade of mulster and brewer.{KEBI JS#18:246}

4. HUGH HAISLIP, son of Hugh, dec., on 19 June 1735, was bound to Robert Speer, until age 21, being 11 years old on 9 May.{KEBI JS#18:8}

THE BALDIN-HAZOLL CONNECTION

1. ROBERT BALDIN m. Dorothy Burman on 2 Nov 1680 at St. James, Duke Place, London (IGI). He moved to CE Co., MD, where by his last will dated 28 July 1690 he bequeathed to his wife Dorothy Baldin living in London all his estate, except £20 which he gave to his exec. Ebenezer Backiston which will the sd. Blackiston duly proved. Afterwards Blackiston gave the sd. Dorothy Baldin the ... accompts belonging to her besides what was then consigned for use. Dorothy Baldin later m. John Hazoll, citizen and weaver of London.{KELR M:29} (No will for Robert Baldin appears to have been filed in MD or in the Prerogative Court of Canterbury.)

2. WILLIAM HAZOLL, weaver, of London, and William Norman, of the parish of St. Leonards ... in the county of Middlesex, weaver, execs. of the last will of John Hazoll, late citizen and weaver of London, dec., appoint Michael Miller of KE Co. their attorney.{KELR M:29}

THE BENJAMIN HAZEL FAMILY

3. BENJAMIN HAZEL of KE Co. m. Sarah (N) who d. by 12 Feb 1769.
    As Benjamin Hazle [sic] of KE Co., on 9 May 1746 he purchased 220 a., part of *Williams Venture* from William Ellis and wife Mary.{KELR JS#25:365} Later, c1758, he purchased 50 a. part *Burrow's Addition* from William Burris, Jr. and wife Mary.{KELR JS#29:7}

157

Benjamin d. leaving a will dated 9 Sep 1764 and proved 3 Nov 1762. The heirs named were wife Sarah, sons John, William, Benjamin, Joseph and daus. Araminta, Mary, Sarah, and Martha. Tracts mentioned were *William's Venture, Hazel's Adventure, Conjunet(?), Burrous Addition* and *Clark's Addition*. The will was witnessed by John Garland, Thomas Jones, and George Cloak.{MWB 32:292}

On 30 Jan 1765, Benjamin's estate was appraised by Samuel West and Jacob Jones, and valued at £700.11.10. No creditors listed. William Hazel and Gilbert Falconer for himself and wife signed as next of kin. Sarah Hazel, extx., filed the inventory on 24 Nov 1766, mentioning Sarah Hugh, Robert Holliday, and Edward Knott.{MINV 89:253}

Sarah Hazel, of KE Co., d. by 12 Feb 1769, when her estate was appraised by Samuel West and William Blackiston and valued at £521.19.5. Samuel Ball and Benjamin Hazell signed as creditors. Benjamin Hazel and Gilbert Falconer for self and wife signed as next of kin. William Hazle, admin./exec., filed the inventory on 20 June 1770.{MINV 106:39}

Benjamin Hazle/Hasel m. Sarah (N). They were the parents of the folowing children, whose births are recorded in Shrewsbury Parish{KESH}: ARAMINTA, b. 26 Feb 1740; JOHN, b. 4 March 1742; WILLIAM, b. 2 March 1744; MARY, b. 27 Jan 1746; SARAH, b. 4 Sep 1748; MARTHA, b. 8 Jan 1751; BENJAMIN; and JOSEPH.

3-a. WILLIAM HAZEL, son of Benjamin, d. in KE Co. leaving a will dated 24 Oct 1774 and proved 5 Dec 1774. Heirs named were nephew John Gordon, to whom was devised a lot at Duck Creek Cross Roads that was his dec. father Robert Gordon's; niece Mary Gordon; her bro. John Gordon; testator's bro. Benjamin Hazel; niece Mary Currey; dau. of Molleston Currey; niece Sarah Currey; nephews Abraham and Benjamin Falconer, sons of Gilbert Falconer; and niece Precilla Falconer. Bro. Benjamin Hazel was named exec. The will was witnessed by Jas. Pearce, G. Wilson, and Ann Griffith.{MWB 40:61}

On 13 May 1775 his estate was appraised by Samuel West and George Blackiston, and valued at £1193.15.0. Davrach & Kennedy and Robert Holliday signed as creditors. Gilbert Falconer signed as next of kin. Benjamin Hazel, exec., filed the inventory on 25 Aug 1775.{MINV 122:72}

3-b. BENJAMIN HAZEL, Jr., son of Benjamin, was charged at June Court 1762 with committing fornication and begetting a base born child. He was fined 30 s. He gave security to keep his bastard child called WILLIAM from any charge on the county.{KECR DD#1}

158

THE HUGH HAZEL FAMILY

4. HUGH HAZEL (HAZLE), of KE Co., d. by 12 July 1749, when his estate was appraised by E. Comegys and W. Comegys, Jr., and valued at £19.2.6. Alexander Kelley signed as creditor. No next of kin listed. Mathew Hazle, admin., filed the inventory on 25 Sep 1749.{MINV 41:248}
   Hugh may have been the father of: MATHEW.

4-a. MATTHEW HAZEL, possibly son of Hugh, filed the inventory of Hugh's estate on 25 Sep 1749.
   At June Court 1766, it was presented that Matthew Hazell, on 19 March 1766, assaulted William Meek. Hazell was fined £4.{KECR DD#1:78A}

Unplaced

HASSELL, JOHN, m. Mary Willson on 29 May 1739 in Shrewsbury Parish, KE Co. They were the parents of{ESVR 2}: BENJAMIN, b. 29 Dec 1739; and MARY, 6 April 1741.

HAZLE, JOHN, at November Court 1743, was presented for false packing of tob. He was fined 1000 lbs. of tob.{KECR JS#24:145}

HAZLE, JOSEPH, was duly enlisted in the company of Capt. John Milboarn and received bounty money on 30 Oct 1740 (recorded 3 June 1743).

THE HENLEY FAMILY

1. CHRISTOPHER HENLEY was servant in the (c1702) inv. of Michael Miller of (KE) Co.{INAC 1:660} He d. by 31 May 1749.
   On 8 Oct 1725 John Henley made a will and left personalty to John, son of Christopher Henley.{MWB 18:422}
   He d. leaving an estate appraised by John Trew and Abraham Milton, and valued at £17.10.6. No creditors listed. Sarah Underhay signed as next of kin. James Henley, admin., filed the inventory on 31 May 1749.{MINV 40:436}
   Christopher Henly and Ezbell (also Ezebella) Smith m. 28 Dec 1704.{KESP} They were the parents of{KESP}: JAMES, b. 12 Dec 1707, bapt. 21 July 1708; ELIZABETH, b. 9 Jan 1709; WILLIAM, b. 18 Feb 1710; ANN, b. 13 Sep 171-; CHRISTOPHER, b. 3 March 1715; EZABELLA, b. 23 March 1718; SARAH, 30 Jan 1720; and JOHN, b. by 1725.

HENLY, EDWARD, m. Elenor (N), and had: ELISABETH, b. 20 June 1727.{KESH}

HENLEY, JOHN, m. Esther Ricketts on 3 Feb 1712.{KESP} He d. leaving a will dated 8 Oct 1725 and proved 18 Oct 1725. To John, son of Christopher Henley, he left personalty. To wife Hester, extx., and son-in-law William ———, the estate to be divided equally.{MWB 18:422}

On 18 May 1726 the estate was appraised by Ebenezer Blakiston and James Thomas, and filed on 28 May 1726. Nathaniel Rickets signed as next of kin. Mentioned were Ann Belrose, Jeremiah Rickett, and George Griffith.{MINV 11:532}

THE HILL FAMILY

1. THOMAS HILL was b. c1602/4. In 1652 or 1653, he dep., giving his age as c50.{ARMD LIV:21, Liber A:92} Thomas Hill, age c52, 1 July 1656.{ARMD LIV:65, Liber A:121}

He m. Christian (N), who as Christian Hill, wife of Thomas Hill, gave her age as c45, in Jan 1652.{ARMD LIV:7, Liber A:44} Thomas' widow Christiana m. 2nd, Thomas Ringgold.

On 3 May 1653, Thomas Hill demanded 1000 a. of land for transporting himself, Christian his wife and Thomas, Hassadia, Ruth, Amos, David and Joseph Hill, his children, and George Higginson and Ann Wicksham, his servants, into this province in May 1652.

Thomas Hill d. by 1 Aug 1657 when Thomas Hinson dep. that Thomas Hill, dec., "sometime last sumer Did in yor. Depts. hearing say That he had recived some goots And other Things of his dau. Rueths ...."{ARMD LIV:109, Liber B:25}

On 18 Nov 1657 Henry Morgan complained against Thomas Ringgold who m. the admx. of the estate of Thomas Hill, Sr., dec.{ARMD LIV:121, Liber B:20}

On 5 Feb 1657 Thomas Ringgold and his wife Christian, the late wife of Thomas Hill, dec., sold to Thomas Hill a parcel of land.{ARMD LIV:126, Liber B:18}

On 15 Sep 1658, Thomas Ringgold granted two cows to Ruth Hill, dau. of Thomas Hill of the Isle of Kent, dec.{ARMD LIV:143, Liber B:44}

Thomas and Christiana (N) Hill were the parents of: THOMAS, Jr.; HASIDIAH; RUTH, m. Alexander Nash on 20 Jan 1662{ARMD LIV:186, Liber B:75}; AMOS; DAVID; and JOSEPH.

2. THOMAS HILL, Jr., son of Thomas and Christiana, m. Margret Balie on 4 da., 1 mo., 1655.{ARMD LIV:38, Liber A:107} On c1 Aug 1657

John Ringgold recalled being at Thomas Hill's wedding at his father's house on 4 March 1655.{ARMD LIV:109, Liber B:26} Thomas Hill may have m. 2nd, by 28 April 1661 Elesabeth, extx. of John Deere, when they sold cattle of John Deere, dec., to James Ringgould.{ARMD LIV:217, Liber B:97} Thomas Hill may have m. 3rd, Barbery, by 31 Oct 1668 when they assigned to Richard Pether, their right to some land.{ARMD LIV:252, Liber C:12}

Thomas Hill was the father of{ARMD LIV:187, Liber B:75}: MARGRETT, b. 30 April 1658; RACHEL, b. 15 Feb 1659; PENELOPE, b. 8 March 1664; and BARBARA, b. 26 July 1667.{ARMD LIV:187, Liber B:76}

3. HASSADIA HILL, son of Thomas and Christiana, was b. c1637. He was age c19, when he dep. on 25 Aug 1656.{ARMD LIV:74, Liber A:126} Hasidia Hill m. Ann Sheares on 26 April 1659.{ARMD LIV:129, Liber B:34}

On 10 Sep 1659 Hasadiah Hill of KE Co., sold to his bro. Thomas Hill of the same place, his right to a parcel of land formerly belonging to his father, Thomas Hill, dec., called *Crany Necke*.{ARMD LIV:180, Liber B:69}

Hasadiah Hill d. by 21 Jan 1660, when Ann Hill, relict of Hasadia Hill, dec., applied as admx. of her husband's estate.{ARMD LIV:197, Liber B:83}

Unplaced

HILL, CHARLES, was b. c1722. As an orphan, son of Charles Hill, dec., on 23 March 1737 was bound as an apprentice to James Conner, shoemaker, until age 21, he being 15 years old on 28 Aug last.{KEBI JS#18:126} Earlier, on 23 Nov 1737, Charles Hill, son of Charles Hill, dec., had been bound as an apprentice to John Wright, taylor.{KEBI JS#18:106}

HILL, FARDANANDO (FERDINANDO). See HULL, FARDANANDO (FERDINANDO),

HILL, FRANCIS, d. leaving an inventory dated 8 Sep 1724 and filed 27 Oct 1724 by the admins./execs. William Mackey and John Wilson. Next of kin was Ann Hill. Mentioned were John Woodall, M. Miller, John Mackey, and John Wynn.{MINV 10:299}

Francis and Ann Hill were the parents of: MARY, b. 20 Oct 1719.{KESP}

HILL, GEORGE, and Joan Britain were m. 6 Dec 1711.{KESP} They were probably the parents of: WILLIAM, "son of George and Isaac(?)," b. 7 Aug 1712.{KESP}

On 18 March 1718 William Hill, son of George Hill and Joan his wife, was put as an apprentice to Vincent Hatcheson, until age 21, he being 7 years old on 7 Aug following. George Hill had absented himself and his wife Joan was unable to maintain the son, William.{KEBI JS#W:55B}

HILL, GEORGE, m. by 14 July 1752, Susannah, widow and admx. of Philip Hutson, late of KE Co.{MDAD 33:72}

HILL, JAMES, of KE Co., d. by 16 Jan 1761, when his estate was appraised by James Piner and James McClean, and valued at £18.12.8. Hynson Rogers for Isabella Knight signed as creditor. No next of kin listed. Thomas Ringgold, admin., filed the inventory on 14 Aug 1762.{MINV 78:227}

HILL, JOHN, of KE Co., d. and his estate was appraised by Bartin Wilkens and Charles Tilden, and valued at £23.7.1. Thomas Smyth and James McClean signed as creditors. No next of kin listed. Elisabeth Walker, extx., filed the inventory on 9 April 1773.{MINV 111:328} His estate was appraised and valued at £151.19.2. Elisabeth, now wife of Edward Woodcock, extx., filed the list of debts on 27 March 1775.{MINV 119:326} On 27 March 1775 distribution of the estate was made by Elisabeth Woodcock, extx., wife of Edward Woodcock. Legatee was Elisabeth Walker with residue to Thomas Hill in England.{BFD 7:43}

HILL, PHILIP, was b. c1698. Phillip Hill, age c66, on 1 Oct 1764, dep. regarding the bounds of a tract called *Thornton*.{KECR JW#WK:602; KELR DD#1:602}
　　Susannah Hill, wife of Philip Hill, c1728, was summoned to answer a charge that she stole thread worth 15 lbs. of tob. from William Beavans. Philip Hill, John Ashley and Thomas Ashley, were sureties. Mary Beavans, wife of Wm. Beavans, was to give evidence against her. She was acquitted.{KECR JS#WK:9, 53}

HILL, RICHARD, of London Town, AA Co., surgeon, and wife Deborah, on 10 June 1737, conv. to Wm. Woodland of KE Co., merchant, part of the tract called *Perch(?)*, originally laid out for Capt. Richard Hill, on a creek called in the patent Fendalls Creek but later known as Farly Creek, 300 a.{KELR JS#22:25}

HILL, ROBERT, of KE Co., on 15 Feb 1705 purchased from John Dowdall of CE Co. and his wife Judith, a tract called *Woller Hampton*, 200 a.{KELR GL#1:80/104}

HILL, SAMUEL, d. before 26 Aug 1740 when his widow, "old Eliza Hill," was mentioned in a deposition.{KELR JS#23:43}

HILL, THOMAS, of St. Paul's Parish, on 10 Oct 1728 was presented on charges he stole some property of Arthur Miller. He was ordered to stand in the pillory for one hour and receive 21 lashes.{KECR JS#22:43}

On 31 July 1738 Daniel Dulany of Annapolis, Esq., leased to Thomas Hill of KE Co., 100 a. of tract called *The Remains of My Lords Gracious Grant*, for the lifetime of sd. Thomas Hill, his wife Susannah and his son Daniel, the longest liver of them.{KELR JS#22:137}

On 27 Feb 1743 James Paul Heath on behalf of Daniel Dulany, leased to Thomas Hill, 100 a., part of *My Lords Gracious Grant*, for the lifetimes of Thomas Hill, his wife Susannah, and Charles Hill his son.{KELR JS#25:39}

Thomas Hill, of KE Co., d. by 4 June 1760, when his estate was appraised by Daniel Massy and John Falconar, and valued at £81.10.7. No creditors or next of kin listed. Charles Hill, exec., filed the inventory on 30 Sep 1760. Mentioned were Lau. Walsh and John Brice.{MINV 71:49}

Thomas Hill and his wife Susanna were the parents of: CHARLES; and DANIEL.

HILL, THOMAS, of KE Co., d. by 13 Feb 1748, when his estate was appraised and valued at £7.19.6. No creditors or next of kin listed. Philip Hudson, admin., filed the inventory on 9 June 1749. Mentioned were John Brisco, Robert Mansfield, and Arthur Lee.{MINV 41:6}

Thomas and Mary (N) Hill were the parents of{KESH}: THOMAS, b. 19 Dec 1739; WILLIAM, b. 11 March 1744.{KESH}

HILL, THOMAS, orphan son of Thomas Hill, dec., on 22 Aug 1746 was bound to Ferdinando Hull, as an apprentice, until age 21.{KEBI JS#20:228}

HILL, WILLIAM, d. leaving a will dated 20 June 1705 and proved 6 July 1705. To eldest son William he left all real estate. To three children (unnamed) he left all personal estate. Testator desired to be bur. according to rites of Roman Catholic Church. His exec. was to be Francis Collins.{MWB 3:731} Hill's estate was admin. on 29 Oct 1705.{INAC 25:109}

William Hill was the father of: WILLIAM; and two other children.

HILL, WILLIAM, at August Court 1733, was fined 200 lbs. of tob. because he failed to appear at the case of Dennis Long as ordered.{KECR JS#WK:438}

HILL, WILLIAM, (cordwinder). He d. leaving a will dated 30 May 1737 and proved 17 July 1741. To Chrispianns, son of Rehod Davis, he left his entire estate. Vincent Hatehison was the exec.{MWB 22:389}

HILL, WILLIAM, of KE Co., on 30 May 1745 conv. to Philip Davis of afsd. county, a tract called *Davis's Triangle* granted by patent to Philip Davis, 140 a., and bequeathed by the last will of sd. Philip Davis on 8 Aug 1735 to his daus. Tabith [sic] and Mary Davis, the former of whom d. unm., and the latter Mary m. the sd. William Hill and is since dec.{KELR JS#25:302}

THE HYNSON FAMILY

Refs.: A: Charts of the Hynson Family, Christopher Johnston Collection, MHS. B: *Old Kent on the Eastern Shore of Maryland.* By George A. Hanson. (1876). Repr.: Baltimore: Genealogical Publishing Co., for Clearfield Co., 1990.

1. THOMAS HYNSON, the earliest known progenitor, was b. c1619/20, giving his age as c35 or 36 in depositions made 1 Feb 1655, 29 Oct 1655, 29 Nov 1655, and 1 da., 7 mo., 1676.{ARMD LIV:32, 35, 70; Liber A:103, 104, 116, 124} He d. 1667. He m. Grace (N) who came to MD with him in 1651.{A}

Thomas Hynson was in Isle of Wight Co., VA by 1646. He came to MD in 1651, when, on 23 June, Thomas Hynson demanded 800 a. of land for transporting himself, his wife, and John, Ann, and Grace, his children, and three servants "this present year." In 1662 he made another claim for transporting his wife Grace, in 1651.{A}

He was a Burgess from KE Co. in 1654.{MDTP 2:289}

Thomas Hynson, Sr. conv. 200 a. his sons, Thomas and John, on 20 June 1665.{TALR 1:5}

He d. intestate in 1667, and on 20 Jan of that year administration of the estate of Thomas Hynson of "Talbot County" was granted to his sons Thomas and John.{MDTP 2:289}

Thomas and Grace (N) Hynson were the parents of five children{A}:[16] THOMAS, b. 1639; Col. JOHN, d. 1705; GRACE, m. Thomas South; ANNE, m. Maj. Joseph Wickes[17]; and CHARLES, b. 1662.

---

[16] Hanson also lists Henry as a son.

[17] Later m. Col. St. Leger Codd according to Christopher Johnston.

2nd Generation

2. THOMAS HYNSON, son of Thomas (1) and Grace, was b. 1639, and d. 1679. Thomas Hinson, Jr., age c20, dep. on 1 July 1659.{ARMD LIV:165, Liber B:58}

In 1663 Thomas Hynson m. Anne Gaine who m. 2nd, in 1680, Robert Smith of TA Co.{A}

On 9 Jan 1669 Thomas Hynson and his wife Ann conv. to Daniel Glover 200 a. on e. side of Chester River, s. side of Winchester Creek. {TALR 1:107}

On 20 June 1670 Thomas Hynson and his wife Ann of Chester River conv. to his brother John Hynson in consequence of 200 a. already delivered, land on Eastern Neck called *Wickliff*, ½ 800 a. formerly possessed by Thomas Hynson, father of Thomas (the grantor) and John, dec., also ½ 300 a. called *Partnership* and 300 a. called *Marked Place*.{TALR 1:108}

On 7 Feb 1672 Thomas Hynson of Chester River, TA Co., and his wife Ann, conv. to Henry Matthews of KE Co., 100 a. of *Hynson's Addition* laid out for his bro. John Hynson on e. side of Hynson Towne Creek.{TALR BB No.2:1}

Thomas Hynson of TA Co., d. leaving a will dated 14 Dec 1678 and proved 29 July 1679. The heirs named were eldest son Thomas at 18 years of age, plantation, "*Hynson's Town*," and 150 a. belonging thereto. To son William at 18 years of age, residue of land, 150 a., belonging to "*Hynson's Town*" afsd. To son Richard at 18 years of age, 150 a., "*Hynson's Hills*." To brother Charles, testator's portion of 200 a. on w. side of Chester River. To wife Anne, extx., 1/2 of all personalty, and privilege of remaining on plantation. To younger children (not named) residue of personalty equally. The will was witnessed by Ja: Courcey and Jas. Treahy.{MWB 9:107}

Thomas and Ann (Gaine) Hynson were the parents of: THOMAS; WILLIAM; and RICHARD,[18] and poss. others.

3. Col. JOHN HYNSON, son of Thomas (1) and Grace, was bur. in St. Paul's Parish, KE Co., on 10 May 1705. He m. 1st, on 10 Aug 1669, Hannah Jenkins. His m. 2nd, by 21 June 1670, Rachel, living in 1677, who seems to have been the mother of his children. He m. 3rd, in 1693, Ann, widow of Jonathan Grafton.{A; INAC 12:128}

---

[18] He may be the Richard Hynson who was in TA Co. and who, with his wife Esther, on 27 Nov 1705 conv. to Edward Chetham of KE Co. half of 1000 a. called *The Beginning*.{KELR GL#1:60/64} At January Court 1706, Richard Hynson's request for a license to keep an ordinary at Chester Mill was approved. {TAJU CR6399-1} On 5 Feb 1707 Richard Hynson of Talbot and his wife Hester conv. to Thomas Maclanahan of TA Co. all that belonged to them of 100 a. called *Adventure* near Matthew Read's Creek. {QALR ETA: 9}

Col. John Hynson patented the following tracts: *Bounty*, 200 a., on 10 Nov 1696{MPL 38:19}; *Hynson's Division*, 876 a., on 1 May 1701{MPL 34:380}; *Lord's Gift*, 3000 a., 10 Aug 1695.{MPL 27:362}

On 21 June 1670 John Hynson of Chester River and his wife Rachel conv. to his brother, Thomas Hynson, Hynson's *Towne Creek and Next Addition* on s. side of Chester River and 100 a. called *Hynson Towne*. {TALR 1:108}

On 14 Feb 1676 John Hinson of KE Co. and his wife Rachell conv. to Nathaniel Evetts, a parcel called *Trumpington* being part of a dividend of lands formerly belonging to Thomas South, 100 a.{KELR B:94} Some time later John Hinson of KE Co. and his wife Ann, conv. to their son and dau. William Glanvill and Mary his wife, a parcel between Graysing Creek and Langfords Bay, 300 a.{KELR M:13}

About 1701 John Hynson, Sr., conv. to his son Nathaniel Hynson, a parcel of land in KE Co., about 400 a.(?) The deed refers to land lately belonging to Maj. Joseph Wickes and now belonging to Joseph and Samuell Wickes, his sons.{KELR JD#1:25}

On 8 March 1702 John Hynson of KE Co. conv. to his sons and daus., Stephen Bordley of the same county and his wife Anne, and William Glanvill of the same county and his wife Mary, the tract called *Bounty*, 200 a.{KELR JD#1:64}

Col. John Hynson recorded on 4 July 1702 that he gave to his grandchildren John Rogers one heifer, Eliza. Rogers a heifer, Edward Rogers one heifer, Rachell Rogers a heifer, Mary Rogers a heifer, and Nathl. Rogers a heifer. He referred to the cattle marks of their grandfather Edward Rogers.{KELR GL#:1:5, 8B}

John Hynson (Hinson) d. leaving a will dated 29 Dec 1704 and proved 5 June 1705. To son John, exec., dwell. plant., at his decease to pass to grandson John. Personalty was bequeathed to dau. Sarah, grandson John afsd., dau. Elizabeth Rogers, dau. Jane Hoelger, dau. Mary Glanvill, son Nathaniell, and Stephen Bordley. Wife Ann received property which was hers when she was m., including boy John Heath and use of plant.{MWB 3:656}

Col. John and Rachel (N) Hynson were the parents of seven children{A}: JOHN, of CE Co.; Col. NATHANIEL, b. c1679, d. 1721; MARY, m. William Glanville;[19] ELIZABETH, m. (N) Rogers; ANNE, 1st, m. 14 Oct 1702, Rev. Stephen Bordley who d. in 1709 (bur. 25 Aug

---

[19] On 25 Nov 1728, John Cleaver, conv. to his wife Elizabeth, a tract, adj. a tract possessed by the heirs of Charles Hynson, dec., the tract to be called *Lords Gift*, originally surveyed for John Hynson, dec., which he conv. to William Glanvill and his wife Mary, the sd. Mary being one of the daus. of the sd. John Hynson, 300 a., and they conv. same to George Copper who conv. the same to afsd. John Cleaver.{KELR JS#X:310}

1709), and 2nd, by 31 Nov 1719, Alexander Williamson;[20] JANE, m. Philip Holleger and had a son NATHANIEL; and SARAH, m. 21 Jan 1705/6 James Smith of KE Co.

4. CHARLES HYNSON, son of Thomas (1) and Grace, was b. 1662, and d. 24 May 1711. He m. 25 March 1687 Margaret, dau. of Major William Harris of KE Co.{A; KESP} Charles Hynson, age 46, made a deposition on 30 Nov 1708 concerning a bounded tree of (N) Atchin-son.{KELR JSN:84}

Charles Hynson was a Burgess for KE Co. in 1700.

William Harris of CE Co., conv. to his dau. Margarett Hynson, wife of Charles Hynson of KE Co., and her son Thomas Hynson, a tract called *Fathers Guift*, 150 a.{KELR M:116B}

Charles Hynson d. leaving a will dated 10 July 1703 and proved 6 Nov 1711. To son Thomas, personalty, and if he married during the life of his mother he was to settle on *Father's Gift*. To dau. Dorcas, personalty. To son Charles, *Hynson's Chance* on Graysen's Creek. To dau. Margret and youngest dau. Jean, personalty. To wife Margret, extx., personalty. The testator further added "the plant. I now live upon need not be mentioned because otherwise ordered by the will of Thos. Boon and deed of gift of father Harris." To heirs of William Stanley, personal estate. The overseers were Father William Harris, John Wells, and Robert Dunn.{MWB 13:385}

Charles Hynson's estate was admin. by the extx. Margaret Hynson, widow, on 6 Oct 1712, and on 29 March 1714.{INAC 33B:118, 35A:257}

Charles and Margaret (Harris) Hynson were the parents of nine children{A; KESP}: THOMAS, b. 14 Aug 1688; DORCAS, b. 26 Aug 1690; CHARLES, b. 27 Aug 1692; JUDITH, b. 7 March 1694, d. 13 May 1703; MARGARET, b. 7 Sep 1697; JOAN (or JOAN), b. 1700, d. 1702; JANE, b. 1 March 1702; ANNE, b. 15 Dec 1705; and WILLIAM, b. 23 Dec 1708.

3rd Generation

5. JOHN HYNSON of CE Co., son of Col. John (3) and Rachel, was bur. 30 Sep 1708.{KESP} He m. Mary Stoop, dau. of John Stoop, on 1 June 1695 in St. Stephens Parish, CE Co.{CESS} She survived him and m. 2nd, Benjamin Pearce.

John Hynson of CE Co., d. leaving a will dated 20 Oct 1705 and proved 9 Oct 1708. He left all his real estate in KE Co. to his son John.

---

[20] On 31 Nov 1719, John Davis and his wife Mary, of KE Co., conv. to Thomas Slipper, of the same county, part of a tract called *Bounty* being part of 100 a. formerly given by Coll. John Hynson, dec., to his dau. Ann, the then wife of Stephen Boardly but now of Alexander Williamson, 50 a.{KELR JS♯W:88}

He named his children Nathaniel, Thomas, Jane, and Rachel and an unborn child. He also named his uncle Charles Hynson and his bro. Col. Nathaniel Hynson. Wife Mary was to be the extx. The will was witnessed by Jno. Hancock, Danll. Dusee, and Sarah Christian.{MWB 12 :Part 2: 39}

The estate of John Hynson of CE County was admin. 10 April 1714 by the execs., Benjamin Pearce and his wife Mary Pearce.{INAC 35A:129} The inventory of a John Hynson was taken 18 June 1720 and filed 22 Aug 1720. Nathaniel Hynson signed.{MINV 4:323}

John and Mary Hynson were the parents of: JOHN, bapt. 1 April 1697; NATHANIEL, bapt. 1698; THOMAS, b. 7 Aug 1700; THOMAS, b. 10 Oct 1702; JANE, bapt. 1 April 1696; RACHEL, b. 17 April 1704; ANNE, b. 26 Nov 1705; and HANNAH, b. 30 Jan 1706, bapt. 2 Oct 1708.{CESS; KESP}

6. Col. NATHANIEL HYNSON, son of Col. John (3) and Rachel, was b. c1679, and d. 1721. He m. 1st, Hannah (N), bur. 26 Nov 1713. He m. 2nd, on 6 Aug 1714, Mary Kelly, who m. 2nd, Joseph Young.{A; KESP}

On 9 March 1709 James Wessells, of KE Co., and his wife Elizabeth conv. to Nathaniel Hynson part of a tract called *Hinchingham*, formerly belonging to Walter [Tol]ley, Sr., and by him in his last will devised to his two daus. Mary and Elizabeth which sd. Mary was dec. and without issue and the same descended to the sd. afsd. Elizabeth.{KELR JSN:169}

On 19 May 1712 Edward Beck, Jr., and his wife Mary, dau. and heir of Robert Neeves, late of KE Co., dec., conv. to Nathaniel Hynson, a tract called *Rusmore*, near the head of Tavern Creek, 100 a.{KELR JSN:282}

On 25 Feb 1717 Peter Massey and his wife Sarah Massey, dau. of Daniel Toaes, Sr., of KE Co., dec., conv. to Colonel Nathaniel Hynson, Gent., 1000 a., part of a tract called *Partnership* cont. 3000 a.{KELR BC#1:283}

On 12 Nov 1718 Michael Byrne of KE Co., cordwinder, and his wife Sarah, dau. of Stephen Whetston of the county afsd., dec., conv. to Coll. Nathaniell Hynson of afsd. county, merchant, 112 a. called *Hansingham* near Tavern Creek.{KELR BC#1:346}

Col. Nathaniel Hynson, merchant, d. leaving a will dated May 1721 and proved 26 Jan 1721. To son Nathaniel, he left plant. on Eastern Neck Island, near mouth of Chester River, formerly belonging to father Col. John Hynson, dec. To dau. Hannah he left dwell. plant., 300 a. called *Suttons Underhill*. To dau. Martha he left 220 a. of *Hinchingham*, 70 a. of *Widow's Chance*, and 112 a. being part of *Hinchingham*. To dau. Rebecca he left 100 a. of *Rosmor*, 250 a. of *Fishing Pond*, 200 a. of *Widow's Right*, and 100 a. called *Hope*. To his unborn child he left *Buck Neck* on Worton Creek. To his wife Mary he left 1000 a. called *Partnership* at head of Chester River, houses and lots in Worton Town, Chester Town, Town of Battersea (called the Old Town); personalty and her thirds. To nephew Thomas and nieces Hannah and Elizabeth, personalty, some of which was in possession of Sarah Chapman. To Rev. Alex. Williamson and James Smith, care of the children and to be execs. with dau. Hannah when she arrived at age of 17. Also mentioned were nephew Thomas Bordley and niece Hannah Smith.{MWB 17:68}

The inventory of his estate was taken 22 March 1722 and filed 17 May 1722. Next of kin were Nathaniell Hynson and George Hanson. Also mentioned were John Francis, shoemaker, and his mother Elisabeth Till, and Isaac Francis and his mother Elisabeth Till. Alexander Williamson and James Smith were execs.{MINV 7:93}

Another inventory was taken 13 June 1722 and appraised 31 Dec 1722. A third inventory was taken 25 Aug 1725 and filed 1 Sep 1725. The appraisers were M. Miller and Robert Dunn.{MINV 9:68, 11:31}

On 3 June 1723 his estate was admin. by Alexander Williamson and James Smith.{MDAD 5:148}

On 9 Dec 1723 Alexander Williamson and James Smith of KE Co., acting execs. of Nathaniel Hynson, dec., conv. land to Joseph Young of KE Co. and his wife Mary. Alexander Williamson and James Smith were acting for Nathaniel's children now under age. Joseph had m. Mary, the relict and widow of afsd. Nathaniel, by which he acquired right to ⅓ of Nathaniel's land and agreed to exchange some of the lands until the time that Martha Hynson, one of the daus. of afsd. Nathaniel, arrived at age, being ⅔ of the plant. belonging to afsd. Martha which was bought of Thomas Tolley (now of BA Co.), also ⅔ in a plant. where John Robinson formerly lived belonging to Rebeckah Hynson, one of the daus. of afsd. Nathaniel which was bought of Edward Beck, Jr., and his wife Mary.{KELR JS#W:344}

Col. Nathaniel Hynson had issue by his 1st wife Hannah{B:99; KESP}: HANNAH, b. 28 July 1705, m. John Gresham, son of John and Sarah Gresham; NATHAN[IEL], b. 1709, d. 1712; MARGARET, b. 22 Dec 1712, m. Thomas Blackistone;[21] and MARY. By his 2nd wife Mary (Kelly), he was the father of{B:99; KESP}: NATHANIEL, b. 30 Oct 1714;

---

[21] On 1 Feb 1738/9, Mrs. Catharine Kelley made oath that Margret Hynson, dau. of Col. Nathall. Hynson, dec., and now the wife of Mr. Thos. Blackston, was 26 years old on the 22nd of the previous Dec, she (the deponent) being present at her birth.{KEBI JS#18:201}.

HANNAH;[22] MARTHA;[23] and REBECCA, probably m. --- Holt by whom she had a son Arthur.{KELR DD#1:558}

7. THOMAS HYNSON, son of Charles (4) and Margaret (Harris) Hynson, was b. 14 Aug 1688, and d. 1738. On 19 Oct 1710 he m. Wealthy Ann Tilden, dau. of Charles and Mary Tilden.{A}

Thomas Hynson gave his age as c38 in a deposition made 3 March 1725/6.{KELR JS#W:542} On 14 Aug 1732, Thomas Hynson, age c44 years, dep. regarding the bounds of a tract called *Fare Harbor;* he stated that about 10-12 years earlier he and his uncle, Robert Dun, dec., went over the creek to Robert Dun, Jr., and when they came ashore at the land of Robert Dun, Jr., they saw a bounded tree.{KELR JS#16:254}

On 22 Nov 1722, Thomas Hynson of KE Co. and his wife Wilthian conv. to John Grant a tract near Graysinn Creek called *Chance Addition,* 28 a.{KELR JS#W:267}

Thomas Hynson (Hinson) d. leaving a will dated 26 May 1738 and proved (cJune-Oct 1738). To wife ——, son Charles, and dau. Welthean, he left personalty. To dau. Mary Jones and her son, Thomas Jones, he left a tract of land at Whale Point, adj. Christopher Bolton's land. Bro. William and son Charles were named as execs.{MWB 21:924}

An inventory, taken 12 Sep 1738 and filed 9 Dec 1738 mentioned Mary Jones, Martha Hynson, Mary Tilden, and Charles Hynson. Charles Hynson was the exec.{MINV 23:503} Another inventory was taken 29 July 1740 and filed 14 Aug 1740. Next of kin were W. Hynson and William Hynson.{MINV 25:203}

---

[22] On 4 Feb 1722, Joseph Young, of KE Co., Gent., and his wife Mary (she being lately the widow and relict of Coll. Nathaniel Hynson, dec.) conv. land to Hannah Hynson, one of the daus. and legatees of the afsd. Nathaniel Hynson, who by his last will dated 4 May 1720 bequeathed to his dau. Hannah Hynson his then dwell. plant. being two tracts, one *Sutton Underhill* and the other *Salhill,* 550 a. Forasmuch as the afsd. Joseph and Mary in right of her dowry hath ¼ of the afsd. two tracts and whereas both parties agree to a division.{KELR JS#W:280}

[23] On 21 March 1721, Michael Miller, of KE Co., Gent., and his wife Martha, conv. to Martha Hynson, dau. of Coll. Nathaniel Hynson, of afsd. county, dec., land which William Pennington of QA Co. and his wife Elizabeth on 25 May 1721 conv. to Michael Miller, part of a tract called *Hinsingham,* 220 a., that he, Michael Miller, should convey the same to Nathaniel Hynson and whereas Nathaniel Hynson hath d. and by his last will bequeathed same to his dau. afsd. Martha Hynson, and in case she d. before coming to age of 21 years or without issue then to his son Nathan, or in default of this then to his daus. Hannah and Rebeccah, and in default of this or other children, then to his nephew Thomas Hynson or to his nephew Boardley.{KELR JS#W:209}

Thomas and Wealthy Ann (Tilden) were the parents of: CHARLES, b. 14 Jan 1713{KESP}; MARY (dau. of Thomas and Martha [sic]), bapt. 20 May 1716, m. Thomas Jones by whom she had a son THOMAS; dau. WEALTHIAN; and possibly MARTHA.[24]

8. CHARLES HYNSON, son of Charles (4) and Margaret (Harris), was b. 27 Aug 1692, and d. by 11 July 1748, having m. Francina, widow of Edward Shippen and dau. of Matthias Vanderheyden.{A}

On 21 Nov 1727 Charles Hynson made a deposition giving his age as c35.{KELR JS#X: 211} On 30 July 1730 he gave his age as c37.{KELR JS#16:41} On 12 Aug 1742 he gave his age as c50.{KELR JS#24:123}

On 10 Oct 1720 Charles Hynson of KE Co., Gent., conv. to John Huff, 100 a. *Hynson's Chance*, at the head of Graysinn Creek, which Charles Hynson, late of the county, dec., father of afsd. Charles Hynson, owned, and which he devised by his last will to his sd. son Charles Hynson.{KELR JS#W:}

On 7 April 1727 James Harris of KE Co., and his wife Augustina, conv. to Charles Hynson, a tract called *Harris's Forest*, 900 a.{KELR JS#X:59}

Col. Charles Hynson of KE Co., Gent., took the oath on 15 March 1743 as required.{KEBI JS#20:159}

Col. Charles Hynson, of KE Co., d. by 9 June 1748, when his estate was appraised by Bedingfield Hands and John Williamson, and valued at £1431.10.5. William Kenney, for Kenney & Loxson, and R. Bennett signed as creditors. W. Hynson and Charles Hynson signed as next of kin. Francina Hynson, extx., filed the inventory on 10 June 1749.{MINV 41:9}

On 11 July 1748 Francina Hynson of KE Co., widow and devisee of Charles Hynson, late of the same county, merchant, dec., conv. property to Elizabeth Chancelor of the City of Philadelphia, one of the children of William Chancelor, late of the same city, sail maker, dec., by Mary his wife, also dec. The deed stated that whereas by a certain indenture dated 18 Oct 1737 William Chancellor and his wife Mary confirmed to Charles Hynson 600 a., being the residue of a tract called *Town Reliefe* over and above the 200 a. in the same indenture mentioned to have been devised to George Lumley, the whole tract cont. 800 a.{KELR JS#26:128}

On 24 Oct 1764, Francina Hynson of the city of Philadelphia, widow and relict of Charles Hynson, KE Co., dec., conv. to James Chalmers of the City of Philadelphia, merchant, and his wife Margaret, the granddau. of sd. Francina Hynson, part of a tract called *Harriss Forest*, 680 a.{KELR DD#1:621}

---

[24] According to Hanson.

9. WILLIAM HYNSON, son of Charles (4) and Margaret (Harris), was b. 23 Dec 1708. On 21 March 1750, William Hynson, age c42, dep. regarding the bounds of a tract called *Boonly;* he recalled being present at a resurvey of his bro. Thomas Hynson who then possessed a tract taken up by John Ringgold and Henry Parker called *Bungey.* {KELR JS#27:27} On 12 June 1753, William Hynson, age c44, dep. regarding the bounds of a tract called *Broadnox.* {KELR JS#27:287} On 9 Oct 1761, William Hynson, age c53, dep. regarding the bounds of a tract called *Huntingfield.* {KELR DD#1:614}

4th Generation

10. JOHN HYNSON, of KE Co., son of John (5) and Mary, was bapt. 1 April 1697. He is probably the John who m. Frances (N), who m. as her 2nd husband Draper Lusby.

John Hynson, husband of Frances, d. by 11 Sep 1762. His estate was appraised by James Smith and William Ringgold, Jr., and valued at £268.9.4. Thomas Ringgold and Thomas William Ringgold signed as creditors. Charles Hynson and Nathaniel Rogers signed as next of kin. Francis Hynson, wife of Draper Lusby, extx., filed the inventory on 11 Sep 1762. {MINV 78:393}

On 17 June 1762, Draper Lusby of KE Co., Gent., and his wife Frances, late the widow and extx. of John Hynson, late of Easter Neck Island in KE Co., conv. land to Mathew Bryan of QA Co. Whereas the sd. John Hynson by his last will directed his extx. to sell, within three months after his decease, that part of his land in Easter Neck Island that lay to the eastward of a line drawn to the southward from a bounded red oak that stood near the main road that stood between the fresh pond and the head of Calf Pasture Creek and near where Samuel Mungar then lived, to a bounded post at the head of ... division bet-ween his bro. Charles and himself .... And whereas the sd. Frances had since m. sd. Draper Lusby. {KELR DD#1:92}

On 24 Oct 1763 his estate was appraised by William Ringgold, Jr. and James Smith, and valued at £39.2.3. Thomas Ringgold and Thomas and William Ringgold signed as creditors. William Hynson signed as next of kin. Frances Lusby (late Frances Hynson), wife of Draper Lusby, extx., filed the inventory on 10 Dec 1763. The estate was again appraised and valued at £40.12.0. No creditors or next of kin listed. Draper Lusby and his wife, Frances Hynson, admins./execs., filed the inventory on 10 Dec 1763. {MINV 82:174, 176}

11. NATHANIEL HYNSON, son of John (5) and Mary, was bapt. 1698 in St. Stephens Parish, CE Co. {CECH} He appears to have been desig-nated as Nathaniel Hynson, Sr., to distinguish him from his cousin Nathaniel Hynson, son of Col. Nathaniel. Both cousins m. women

named Mary, and Nathaniel, Jr. had a son Nathaniel who also m. a Mary.

This Nathaniel m. Mary (N), who appears to have m. 2nd, William Palmer.

Nathaniel Hynson, Sr., of KE Co., d. by 13 Nov 1755, when his estate was appraised by Thomas Smyth and Draper Lusby, and valued at £765.11.1. Thomas Ringgold and John Hynson, Jr. signed as creditors. Elisabeth Smith and John Hynson, Jr. signed as next of kin. Mary Palmer, wife of William Palmer, admx., filed the inventory on 27 Aug 1756.{MINV 61:363}

Nathaniel Hynson, Sr., of KE Co., d. by 21 July 1757, when his estate was appraised by Thomas Smyth and Draper Lusby, and valued at £167.15.5. No creditors or next of kin listed. Mary Palmer (late Mary Hynson), extx., filed the inventory on 22 Aug 1757.{MINV 63:574}

Nathaniel Hynson, of KE Co., d. before 5 May 1761. Distribution of the estate was made by Mathew Brown, admin. de bonis non, to widow (1/3) and Benjamin Hynson (2/3).{BFD 3:44}

Nathaniel m. Mary (N). They were the parents of{CESS}: JOHN, b. 10 Sep 1717; NATHANIELL, b. 3 Feb 1719; THOMAS, b. 20 Aug 1721; MARY, b. 15 July 1723; CHARLES, b. 15 March 1724; HANNAH, b. 30 Dec 1727; RACHEL, b. 10 Dec 1729; and WILLIAM, b. 30 May 1731.

12. Capt. THOMAS HYNSON, son of John (5) of CE Co., was b. 10 Oct 1702, and d. by 4 March 1748. On 22 Sep 1740, at age 35, he dep. regarding the bounds of a tract called *Postern Hole*.{KELR JS#23:135}

Thomas Hynson, of KE Co., d. leaving a will dated 17 Dec 1748 and proved 4 March 1748. He left to his eldest son Andrew *Castle Carry* and *Scotch Folly*. Second son John was to have a lot in Georgetown. Third son Charles was to have 200 a. originally called *Friendship*, but now called *Hynson's Desire*. Fourth son William was to have *Simpson's Addition*, 50 a. *Scotch Folly*, 50 a. *Manors*, and another 26 a. of *Scotch Folly*. Fifth son James was to have 250 a. *Smith's Park*. Hynson also named his daus. Hannah Freeman and Sarah Hynson, granddau. Hannah Freeman, sister Elizabeth Quiney, and cousin Sarah Holleger. Andrew Hynson, William Hynson, and Nicholas Smith were named as execs. The will was witnessed by Daniel Hull, James Brady, and Isaac Boyer.{MWB 26:81}

Capt. Thomas Hynson d. by 1 May 1749, when his estate was appraised by Richard Wilson and Edward Piner, and valued at £930.4.9. John Lovering and Richard Graham signed as creditors. Elisabeth Quinney and Abraham Freeman signed as next of kin. Andrew Hynson, exec., filed the inventory on 4 Aug 1749.{MINV 41:71}

On 24 July 1750 his estate was appraised again by Richard Wilson and Edward Piner, and valued at £185.6.0. Nathaniel Hynson and

Elisabeth Smith signed as next of kin. Andrew Hynson, exec., filed the inventory on 7 May 1753.{MINV 53:165}

On 17 April 1754, his estate was appraised again and valued at £48.12.0. (The original inventory was dated 1 May 1749.) Andrew Hynson, exec., filed the inventory on 19 April 1754.{MINV 57:119}

On 19 April 1754 distribution of the estate was made by Andrew Hynson, exec. to son Andrew Hynson, son John Hynson, son Charles Hynson, son William Hynson, son James Hynson, dau. Sarah Hynson, granddau. Hannah Freeman, sister Elizabeth Quiney and cousin Sarah Hollgier.{BFD 1:95}

Capt. Thomas Hynson was the father of: ANDREW; JOHN; CHARLES; WILLIAM; HANNAH, m. (N) Freeman; and SARAH.

13. NATHANIEL HYNSON, son of Col. Nathaniel (6) Hynson, m. Mary Smith on 29 Oct 1735.{B:99; KESP}

On 20 March 1722, Edward Beck of KE Co., and his wife Mary, conv. to Nathaniel Hynson, son and heir of Coll. Nathaniel Hynson, dec., the land which sd. Nathaniel Hynson (the father) did in his lifetime purchase of sd. Edward Beck and his wife Mary, a tract of 150 a. called *Springhill*.{KELR JS#W:287}

At March Court 1732, Nathaniel Hynson of St. Paul's Parish, Gent., was found guilty of assaulting James Kear on 23 Nov 1732. He was fined 16 s. and 8 p.{KECR JS#WK:362}

On 26 Jan 1736 Nathaniel Hynson, Jr., of KE Co., Gent., and his wife Mary, conv. to John Gresham of the same county, Gent., a tract in KE Co. but formerly in BA Co., granted to Robert Neife, lately dec., called *Spring Hill*, which tract by the death of the sd. Neife became the right of Edward Beck and Mary his wife of KE Co., which sd. Mary was the dau. and sole heir of sd. Robert Neife, and was by them conv. to afsd. Nathaniel Hynson, Jr., son of Coll. Nathaniel Hynson, late of KE Co., dec., by deed dated 20 March 1722.{KELR JS#18:349}

At March Court 1738, it was stated that Nathl. Hynson of KE Co., Gent., had agreed with the sd. court to keep a sufficient boat or scow for transporting persons over at the Narrows of Eastern Neck Island for the year ensuing for which services he was to have an allowance in the county levy of £18. It was charged that, nevertheless, Nathaniel Hynson, his duty disregarded, did not keep a sufficient boat or scow at the Narrows of Eastern Neck Island. He was fined 10 s.{KECR JS#22:126}

Nathan Hynson, Jr., of KE Co., d. by 17 Nov 1752, when his estate was appraised by Samuel Tovey and John Ringgold, and valued at £557.18.3. Edward Lloyd and Thomas Ringgold signed as creditors. Sarah Graves and —— Bordley signed as next of kin. Mary Hynson, extx., filed the inventory on 29 Nov 1753. Another inventory, appraised on 6 Oct 1753, and valued at £99.10.0, was filed by Mary Hynson, extx., on 23 Nov 1753.{MINV 56:13, 19}

Nathaniel and Mary (Smith) Hynson were the parents of{B:99; KESP}: MARY, b. 15 June 1734 [sic], d. 29 Dec 1760, m. Alexander Crabbin 4 Aug 1758 (and had issue: MARGETT and WILLIAM Hynson); and NATHANIEL, b. 24 Oct 1736.

14. CHARLES HYNSON, son of Thomas (7) and Wealthy Ann, was b. 14 Jan 1713, d. 1782. On 2 Aug 1751, Charles Hynson, age c36, dep. regarding the bounds of a tract called *Boonly;* he recalled about 16 years earlier when he was fishing with his father Thomas Hynson and his father showed him an old tree lying on the bank and told him he had heard his bro. Charles Hynson say that was a bound tree of the land called *Boonly.*{KELR JS#27:27} On 4 Oct 1756 at age c42, he dep. regarding the bounds of a tract called *Great Oak.*{KELR JS#28:291}

He m. Phebe Carvill on 30 Nov 1739.{KESP}

On 30 Oct 1747, Charles Hynson, Jr., son of Thomas Hynson of KE Co., dec., conv. to Joseph Wickes of the same county, Gent., the tract taken up by Thomas Hynson, great-grandfather of afsd. Charles, called *Hynsons Chance*, 100 a., all which sd. tract was lately the land and freehold of John Huff for and during the natural life of Charles Hynson of the county afsd., uncle to the sd. Charles party to this indenture, (by the last will of Charles Hynson, grandfather of the sd. Charles, party to these presents) of the sd. Charles, uncle to Thomas Hynson father of the sd. Charles.{KELR JS#26:85}

On 27 Feb 1755, Charles Hynson, age c42, dep. regarding the bounds of a tract called *Stanaway;* he recalled about 17 years earlier in company with his father, Thomas Hynson who was resurveying his land called *Pig Neck.*{KELR JS#28:97}

On 23 Jan 1764, Charles Hynson of KE Co., conv. to his son John Carvill Hynson, Gent., part of a tract called *Hynsons Chance*, 300 a.{KELR DD#1:480}

Charles and Phebe were the parents of{KESP}: CHARLES (twin), b. 11 Dec 1743; JOHN CARVILL (twin), b. 11 Dec 1743; MARY, b. 21 May 1746; PHEBE, b. 3 Dec 1747; and RICHARD, b. 3 Feb 1749.

5th Generation
15. NATHANIELL HYNSON, son of Nathaniel and Mary, was b. 3 Feb 1719. He may be the Nathaniel Hynson, Jr., of KE Co. who d. before 20 Aug 1767. Distribution of the estate was made by Mrs. Mary Wickes (formerly Mary Hynson), extx. Legatees named were Nathaniel Hynson, Hannah Hollis, Rachel Pritchard, Mary Robinson, William Hynson (son of John Hynson), son William, and Benjamin Hynson. Residue to widow (accountant).{BFD 5:78}

16. CHARLES HYNSON, possibly son of Capt. Thomas Hynson (5-a),[25] of Landfords Bay, was one party to an indenture tripartite made on 18 Aug 1763 between sd. Charles and Hannah Hynson, wife of sd. Charles of the first part, and Richard Hynson, son of the sd. Charles of the second part, and William Hynson of the same county, Gent., of the third part, regarding a tract called *Father's Gift*, 150 a.{KELR DD#1:419}

On 18 Aug 1763, Charles Hynson of Landfords Bay in KE Co., Gent., and his wife Hannah, late widow of James Maslin of the county afsd., dec., conv. to Thomas Maslin, Jr., her right of dower or her right by the will of her dec. husband.{KELR DD#1:410}

Charles d. by 5 Feb 1772, when his estate was appraised by Bors. Piner and Peter Massey, and valued at £314.6.8. Thomas Ringgold and Morgan & Slubey, Jr. signed as creditors. James Hynson and Sarah Wilson signed as next of kin. Mary Hynson, admx., filed the inventory on 5 May 1772.{MINV 108:304}

17. ANDREW HYNSON, son of Capt. Thomas Hynson, m. Mary, dau. of George and Mary Wilson.{BFD 2:115}

Andrew Hynson, of KE Co., d. by 21 Nov 1775, when his estate was appraised by Aquila Page and William Merritt, and valued at £336.13.8. James Pearce and Thomas Smyth signed as creditors. James Hynson and Sarah Wilson (widow of John) signed as next of kin. Mary Hynson, admx., filed the undated inventory mentioning Isaac Freeman and Robert Ford.{MINV 124:402}

Andrew and Mary were the parents of{KESB}: SARAH, b. 9 Aug 1750; THOMAS, b. 10 April 1752; and ANDREW, b. 9 Dec 1753.

18. JOHN HYNSON, 2nd son of Capt. Thomas Hynson, m. by 19 dec 1754, Rebekah (N).

John Hynson was left a lot in Georgetown by the last will of his father. On 19 Dec 1754, John Hynson of KE Co., Gent. and his wife Rebekah, conv. to George William Forester, "clark Rector" of Shrewsbury Parish, ½ of a lot in George Town, No. 36.{KELR JS#28:67}

19. WILLIAM HYNSON, 5th son of Capt. Thomas Hynson, d. in KE Co. by 10 Dec 1765, when his estate was appraised by Isaac Freeman and Robert Maxwell, Jr., and valued at £468.9.8. James McLachlan and James Black signed as creditors. Andrew Hynson and John Hynson signed as next of kin. Rachel Hynson, admx., filed the inventory on 9 Oct 1766.{MINV 89:249}

---

[25] Because of the connection to the tract *Father's Gift*.

20. NATHANIEL HYNSON, son of Nathaniel and Mary (Smith) Hyson, was b. 24 Oct 1736. He m. Mary Richardson of Wye, TA Co., and left one son{B:99}: NATHANIEL, b. 15 Jan 1781, m. Sophia Ringgold and had issue.

21. CHARLES HYNSON, possibly son of Charles (7-a) and Phebe (Carvill) Hynson, b. 1743, m. Sarah Waltham 6 Nov 176-.{KESP} They were the parents of{KESP}: CHARLES, b. 7 Dec 17--; JOHN, b. 5 Dec 17--; THOMAS, b. 22 Sep 1769; SARAH, b. 27 Dec 1771, d. 30 Jan 1772; HANNAH, b. 6 Jan 1773; and RICHARD, b. 15 Oct 1774.

Unplaced

HYNSON, ANN, age c43, dep. on 2 Feb 1656.{ARMD LIV:85, Liber B:6}

HYNSON, HENRY, d. by 2 Feb 1709. He m. Mary, widow of Andrew Price.
   On 19 Dec 1702 Henry Hynson of KE Co. and his wife Mary, dau. and heiress of Thomas Stagwell, dec., and Andrew Price, eldest son of sd. Mary, conv. to Richard Bennett, part of *Stagwell* on Wye River now called but heretofore Morgan's Creek, formerly surveyed and granted to Thomas Stagwell for 300 a. but upon resurvey found to contain 537 a., near the Long Point.{TALR 9:193}
   On 2 Feb 1709 Mary Hynson, extx. of her former husband, Andrew Price, in consideration of the sixth part of the estate which Andrew Price left to her son Thomas Price, his severall charges, debts, and legacies and her full one-third part of the same being first taken, paid and discharged out of the estate, to her son Thomas Price, one Negro man called Jack, being part of her last husband's estate.{TALR 11:107},

HYNSON, JOHN, of KE Co., on 7 April 1757, as son of Nathaniel Hynson, dec., conv. to Thomas Ringgold of Chester Town, merchant, part of a tract called *Hynsons Division*, 250 a.{KELR JS#28:344}

HYNSON, MARTHA, of KE Co., d. (date unknown), when her estate was appraised by N. Ricketts and Ebenezar Blackiston, and valued at £514.8.10. Thomas Ringgold & Son and Solomon Wickes signed as creditors. John Wickes and Samuel Wickes signed as next of kin. Joseph Wickes, Jr., exec., filed the inventory on 3 March 1772.{MINV 108:102}

HYNSON, MARY, dau. of Charles and Martha Ann Hynson, b. 3 April 1717.{KESP}

HYNSON, RICHARD, m. Anne Meredith 15 June 1732.{QALU}

Richard Hynson and wife Ann, on 1 April 1751 conv. to Rachel Duhamel 199 a., part of *Hynson's Lott.*{QALR RTC:516}

On 12 Nov 1751 Richard Hynson and his wife Ann conv. to Turbutt Bettin, 66 a., part of *Wilkinson's Addition* and part of *Waltham*. The dower of Susanna Mansfield, wife of William Mansfield, not warranted.{QALR RTD:51}

Richard and Ann were the parents of{QALU}: REBECCA, b. 15 Dec 173-; NATHANIEL, b. 10 Nov 1744, bapt 16 Nov 1744.

HYNSON, THOMAS, at November Court 1709 was bound to Richard Hursly (Thursby?) to learn the trade of weaver.{QAJU ET NO.B:4}

HYNSON, THOMAS, m. Isabelah Pearce. He and Isabalah were the parents of{KESH}: ISABELLA, b. 17 July 1725; CHARLES, b. 30 Dec 1736; WILLIAM, b. 8 May 1739; and JAMES, b. 5 Oct 1741.

Isabelah, wife of Thomas Hynson, Jr., Gent., KE Co., was dau. of Daniel Pearce and sister to Sarah Hanson, wife of Hanse Hanson.{QALR RTA:242} In his will dated 1726 and proved 4 Jan 1727, Daniel Pearce of KE Co. mentioned his son-in-law Thomas Hynson and wife Isabell to whom he left 200 a. of *Castle Carey* at head of Island Creek, bought of Wm. Chivens, 200 a. of *Friendship,* and 400 a. of *New Munster* on Elk River, CE Co.{MWB 19:361}

On 9 June 1739 Thomas Hynson, Jr., Gent., KE Co., and his wife Isabella; Hanse Hanson of KE Co. and his wife Sarah, conv. to John Dempston 498 a. called *Poplar Hill* near the mouth of Fishing Creek. Mortgaged by Daniel Pearce of KE Co., father of the said Isabella and Sarah, 19 March 1723. Pearce afterwards d. leaving a son Andrew, who soon after died, and Isabella and Sarah, his sisters, who are now heirs at law.{QALR RTB:242}

HYNSON, THOMAS, m. Sarah Joce, dau. of Thomas and Margaret Joce by 1750. Sarah was b. c1727. On 21 May 1758 Thomas and Sarah of CE Co., with John Caulk and his wife Ann of KE Co., Ann and Sarah being the daus. of Thomas Joce and co-heirs of Thomas Joce, son of Thomas Joce, dec., conv. land to Peregrine —— of the afsd. county, 20 a.{KELR JS#29:20}

HINSON, THOMAS, of KE Co., d. before 12 Nov 1770. Distribution of the estate was made by Elisha Massey and Rebeccah Gordley, admins., to Elisha Massey and Mary Gordley, dau. of Rebecca Gordley.{BFD 6:42}

HYNSON, WILLIAM, a minor, at March Court 1711 complained that he was being held by Charles Vanderford under pretext of being exec. of John Nabb late of this county contrary to law (as the petitioner is informed) as an apprentice. [Vanderford produced the indenture by which Hynson was indentured to Nabb; however the court considered the indenture insufficient to hold the petitioner as servant any longer.{QAJU ET No.B:131}

HINSON, WILLIAM, d. by 4 Feb 1716. He m. Anne, who, on 19 March 1695, joined him when he conv. to Richard Jones, Jr., land on Hinson's Creek, s. side of Chester River.{TALR 7:130}
    On 1 June 1695 John Starke conv. to William Hinson, *Bradburn's Delight,* 100 a. where his dec. father John Starke lived last and d.{TALR 7:128}
    William was the father of: THOMAS. On 4 Feb 1716 Thomas Hynson conv. to Thomas Hynson Wright 100 a., the estate of his dec. father, William Hynson.{QALR IKA:101} He may be the Thomas Hynson, of Monmouth Co., NJ, who on 28 May 1719 conv. to Thomas Hynson Wright of QA Co. 300 a. on n. side of Hynson Town Creek called Reades Back Creek known as *Shelington.*{QALR IKA:234}

HYNSON, WILLIAM, of KE Co., d. (date unknown), when his estate was appraised by James Frisby and N. Ricketts, and valued at £1085.2.4. Thomas Ringgold & Co. and Charles Groome signed as creditors. Samuel Groome, Jr. and Charles Hynson signed as next of kin. Simon Wickes, William Cowarden and John Waltham, execs., filed the inventory on 5 Jan 1768.{MINV 97:143}

HYNSON, WILLIAM, of KE Co., d. (date unknown), when his estate was appraised and valued at £7.2.0. No creditors or next of kin listed. William Sluby, exec., filed the inventory cont. a list of debts on 15 Nov 1771.{MINV 107:420}

HYNSON, WILLIAM, of KE Co., d. by March 1775, when his estate was appraised by Richard Jones and William Granger, and valued at £145.10.1. John Page, Benjamin Hynson, and Benjamin Chambers for Thomas Ringgold, Esq., signed as creditors. Mary Hynson, admx., filed the inventory on 13 May 1775.{MINV 119:326}

THE IVY FAMILY

The name has sometimes been transcribed as Irey, Ivey, and Joy.

1. ANTHONY IVY d. by 20 Aug 1717. He m. by 18 March 1706, Anne, dau. of Robert Smith, TA Co.{MWB 12:90}

On 1 July 1707, Anthony Ivy and Renatus Smith, by virtue of the will of Robert Smith, and for 4000 lbs. of tob., conv. 100 a. of *Tully's Neck* and part of *Winfield*, to John Dixon.{QALR ETA:1}[26]

On 17 Feb 1708 Anthony Ivy and wife Ann, only daughter and heiress of Robert Smith late of Talbot conv. to Richard Bennett 150 a. purchased of James Scott, son and heir of James Scott Sr. by Robert Smith.{QALR ETA: 32}

On 13 April 1709 as Anthony Ivy of QA Co., Gent., he and his wife Anne, dau. of Robert Smith, dec., conv. to Samuel Wickes of KE Co., Gent., 200 a. then in the occupation of sd. Anthony Ivy and his wife Anne.{KELR JSN:117}

At March Court 1710 Thomas Jackson charged Anthony Ivy with unpaid bills while Jackson kept an ordinary in Queens Town during the period, 6 May 1707 through 20 May 1708. The court ruled otherwise.{QAJU ET No.B:46}

On 3 July 1710 John Davis of QA Co. made a will and among other bequests, stated that Anthony Ivey was to have part of 200 a. of *Polygon*, bought from Robert Smith, "when he should pay for it."{MWB 13:109}

In 1712 Anthony Ivey and his wife Anne conv. to James Williams 100 a., part of *Salisbury* on e. side main branch Corsica Creek.{QALR ETA:112}

At August Court 1713 Anthony Ivy was summoned to answer to Andrew Imbart, apothecary of a plea of trespass for that Imbart complained that at various times of the year he prepared and delivered various medicines and physical preparations to Ivy who languished under a great and grievous malady and who promised to pay Imbart according to the account. Andrew has demanded 2000 lbs. of tob.{QAJU ET No.B:243}

On 22 Sep 1713, 775 a., called *Confusion*, was patented by Anthony Ivy.{MPL DD#5:929, PL#3:513}

Anthony Ivy was described as dec. in a deed made 20 Aug 1717 by Renatus Smith.{QALR IKA:139}[27]

Ivy's name appeared as a creditor in the 11 April 1723 administration account of George Hartshorne of QA Co.{MDAD 5:128}

On 24 March 1724 Anthony Ivy and his wife Ann mortgaged *Barbados Hall* to Richard Bennett.{QALR IKC:9}

Anthony and Ann (Smith) Ivey had one son: ROBERT.

---

[26] For other land transactions involving Anthony Ivy and wife Ann, see QALR ETA:1, 5, 6, 28, 32, 36, 39, 59, 73, 76, 78, 86, 88, 112.

[27] See also QALR IKA:241.

2. ROBERT SMITH IVEY, of KE Co., blacksmith, "only son and heir of Anthony Ivy and his wife Ann, formerly of QA Co., dec.," on 24 March 1724 released to Richard Bennett his claim to land mortgaged by Anthony and Ann Ivy.{QALR IKB:311} Robert Ivy d. by 27 Oct 1747. He m. Mary Mackey as mentioned in a deed made in 1762 by his dau. Ann. At March Court 1715/16 Robert Ivy chose as his guardian Renatus Smith.{QAJU ET NO.B:492}

Robert was listed on 13 March 1724 as a creditor in the administration account of Martha Smith of KE Co.{MDAD 6:281} However, on 22 Feb 1727 he was listed as a "runaway" debtor in the account of Maurice Carty of KE Co.{MDAD 8:520}

Mary, widow of Robert Ivy, m. 2nd, by 23 Oct 1747, (N) Powell of KE Co. On that day, as Mary Powell, she and her dau. Ann Ivy, "spinster," conv. to William Campbell, 74 a. part of *Reason*, and part of *Ditteredge*.{QALR RTC:249}[28]

He and his wife Mary were the parents of{KESP}: ANN, b. 26 Sep 1726.

3. ANN IVY, dau. of Robert and Mary, was b. 26 Sep 1726. In addition to the Oct 1747 deed mentioned above, on 26 Oct 1747, Ann Ivy, dau. of Robert Smith Ivy and his wife Mary, now Mary Powell, conv. 100 a. of *Stoke* to Thomas Shoebrook.{QALR RTC:263}

She m. by 18 Dec 1752 Daniel Hamer of KE Co., who joined her in selling 100 a. of *Triangle,* to John Wallace.{QALR RTD:160} On 28 Feb 1757 Daniel Hamer of KE Co., taylor and his wife Ann, dau. and heir of Robert Ivy, dec., and great-granddau. and heir of Robert Smith, Esq., dec., conv. to Susannah Robins of TA Co., dau. and devisee of George Robins of TA Co., Gent., dec., 600 a., *Walnut Ridge.*{QALR RTE:127}

On 19 Nov 1762 Ann Hamer of KE Co., widow and heiress to Robert Smith, formerly of TA Co., Esq., dec., conv. land to Solomon Wright. Whereas Robert Smyth left one child named Ann, who m. Anthony Ivy and had issue one child called Robert Smyth Ivy, who m. Mary Mackey and had issue, one child only, the said Ann Hamer, widow of Daniel Hamer. Daniel Hamer and his wife Ann sold certain tracts to Solomon Wright but before the deed was acknowledged Daniel Hamer died.{QALR RTF:329}

Unplaced

IVY, ALICE, widow, age 39 or more, dep. on 13 Aug 1759 that she had lived in the borough of Norfolk, VA, since she was born and was

---

[28] See also QALR RTC:311, 317, 484, 517, and RTD:160.

intimately acquainted with the family of John Britt and his wife Mary.{KELR JS#29:143}

THE JARVIS/JERVIS FAMILIES

1. EDWARD JERVIS, d. by 12 Feb 1723. He and Margrett Wade were m. 20 July 1708.{KESP}
   In 1720 Edward Jarvis, Samuel Gooden, and Richard Philligem owned Pew #34 in St. Paul's Episcopal Church.{INKE:151}
   Edward Jarvis, of KE Co., d. by 12 Feb 1723, when his estate was admin. by Margaret Jarvis.{MDAD 5:355} His inventory was signed by William Frisby and E. Beck.{MINV 8:176}
   Edward Jarvis was the father of at least two children{KESP}: ANN, bapt. 8 June 1712; and MARY (called "dau. of Edward and Mary"), b. 1 July 1715.{KESP}

2. JAMES JERVIS m. 1st, Alse, who was bur. 28 Nov 1708. He m. 2nd, Sarah Smith in Sep 1709.{KESP}

3. JOSEPH JERVES of George Town, KE Co., d. leaving a will dated 12 Jan 1759. Mentioned were wife Mary and five children (unnamed). Mary Jerves and Solomon Simmon were named as execs. The will was witnessed by Sanders Bostick, Peter Bowarm, and Solomon Jerves.{MWB 30:709}
   On 17 May 1759 his estate was appraised by Samuel Davs and Augustine Boyer, Jr. and valued at £113.3.11. Thomas Ringgold and James Louttit signed as creditors. Solomon Jervis and Caleb Jervis signed as next of kin. Solomon Semans, exec., filed the inventory on 22 June 1759.{MINV 67:137}
   An undated list of debts, appraised and valued at £319.0.5, was filed by Solomon Semans, exec.{MINV 80:228}

4. SOLOMON JARVIS, Quaker, and tavernkeeper of KE Co., d. by April 1762. He was probably a son or bro. of Joseph Jarvis, above.
   Solomon Jarvis, Quaker, and tavernkeeper of KE Co., d. by 3 April 1762, when his estate was appraised by James Piner and John Chapple, and valued at £14.17.0. Henry Semans and Daniel Semans signed as creditors. Solomon Semans and William Semans signed as next of kin. Sanders Bostick, admin., filed the inventory on 1 Dec 1762.{MINV 79:191} On 15 March 1763, a list of debts had been appraised and valued at £132.5.7. Sanders Bostick, filed the list on 15 March 1763.{MINV 80:215} Another list of debts was appraised and valued at £218.0.1. Sanders Bostick (Quaker), filed the inventory cont. a list of debts on 31 Oct 1764.{MINV 84:355} Yet another list of debts was

appraised and valued at £6.4.4. Sanders Bostick, filed the inventory cont. a list of debts on 27 April ——.{MINV 86:233}

Solomon Jarvis had at least one child: MARY, named in the will, dated 8 April 1767, of Jacob Jones, the elder, of CE Co.{MWB 36:575}

Unplaced
JARVIS, (N), m. by 25 May 1764 Hannah, dau. of Henry Semans of KE Co.{BFD 4:35}

THE JEROME FAMILY

1. THOMAS JEROME m. Sarah (N). He d. by 14 April 1743.

Thomas and Sarah were the parents of four children, whose births are recorded in St. Paul's Parish{KESP}: MARY, b. 2 Sep 1718; THOMAS, b. 10 Nov 1724; ELIZABETH, b. 15 Feb 1726; and MARTHA, b. 11 Sep 1728.

2. MARY JEROME, dau. of Thomas and Sarah, was b. 2 Sep 1718.

At June Court 1742, it was presented that Mary Jerrome, spinster, on 1 June 1741, and at diverse other times, committed fornication and begot a bastard child. She was fined 30 s.{KECR JS#24:3}

At August Court 1746, it was presented that Mary Jerom, spinster, on 1 May 1746, and at diverse times as well before as since, committed fornication and begot a bastard child. She was fined 30 s.{KECR JS#24:299} At November Court 1746, it was presented that Hugh Frazier, on 1 May 1745, and at diverse times as well before as since, committed fornication with Mary Jerom and begot a bastard child. He was fined 30 s.{KECR JS#24:323}

3. THOMAS JEROME, son of Thomas and Sarah, was b. 10 Nov 1724.

At November Court 1741, it was presented that Mathias Pooly concealed a taxable namely Thomas Jerrome. He was fined 50 s.{KECR JS#23:233}

14 April 1743: a parcel of land formerly belonging to Thos. Jerrome of KE Co., dec., now in the possession of William Slipper, guardian to Thomas Jerrome, son of Thomas Jerrome, dec., was valued at £3 per year.{KEBI JS#20:16}

4. ELIZABETH JEROME, dau. of Thomas and Sarah, was b. 15 Feb 1726.

At June Court 1763, it was presented that Samuel Tayler committed fornication with Elizabeth Jerrom and begot a base born child.{KECR DD#1:32A}

5. MARTHA JEROME, dau. of Thomas and Sarah, was b. 11 Sep 1728.

THE JOBSON FAMILY

1. JOHN JOBSON was in AA Co. by 16 Feb 1697 when he was named in the will of Edmond Duncalfe.{MWB 6:198} By 16 July 1702 he had m. Ann (N). They were the parents of: THOMAS, named as eldest son of Thomas and Ann in the will, dated 26 July 1702, of William Hopkins of AA Co.{MWB 11:212}

2. JOHN (or JOB) JOBSON, probably not the John Jobson of AA Co., d. c1713. He and Hester Holyday, widow of Samuel Holyday, were m. in St. Stephen's Parish, CE Co., on 12 July 1711.{CECH:2; INAC 33B:86}

John Jobson d. in CE Co., leaving a will dated 30 Dec 1713. He named his sons John, Philip, and Michael, his dau.-in-law Mary Holyday, and his wife Easter, extx., who was to have ⅓ of his estate. His sons were to be of age at 18. The will was witnessed by William Freeman, Benjamin Hazlehurst, and Jacob Caulk.{MWB 14:507}

John and Hester were the parents of{CECH:2}: JOHN, b. 6 May 1712 in St. Stephen's Parish; PHILIP; and MICHAEL.{CECH:18}

3. MICHAEL JOBSON, son of John, d. by April 1766. He m. Sarah (N), by whom he had issue.

On 3 April 1766, Michael Jobson's estate was appraised by J. Maxwell and John Gilbert, and valued at £50.2.2. No creditors or next of kin listed. John Jobson, exec., filed the inventory on 19 June 1766, mentioning Thomas Van Kyke and William Slubey, Jr.{MINV 89:28}

His estate was appraised again, and valued at £6.0.3. John Jobson, admin., filed the inventory cont. a list of debts on 11 Aug 1766.{MINV 89:98}

Michael and Sarah were the parents of{KESH}: JOHN, b. 27 Oct 1742; MICHAEL, b. 27 May 1745; JONATHAN, b. 7 May 1749; (probably) SARAH, b. 18 Aug 1751; WILLIAM, b. 18 Sep 1755; and MARTHA, b. 18 June 1761.{KESH}

THE JOHN JOHNSON FAMILY

1. JOHN JOHNSON d. by Dec 1731. He m. by 8 June 1722, Isabella, admx. of William Blay of KE Co.{MDAD 4:215} By 3 Jan 1728/9 he was m. to Susanna (N).

On 16 Oct 1721, Anne Anderson of KE Co., conv. to John Johnson of the same county, part of a tract called *Forrest* at the head of Churne Creek, patented to Walter Meeks.{KELR JS#W:108}

John Johnson acquired on 17 Dec 1723 a tract on Morgans Creek called *Thornton* and a tract called *Batemans Farm*, 300 a. and a tract called *Ingrams Lott*, 260.{KELR JS#W:452 (432)}

At March Court 1725, John Johnson was found guilty of assault and battery on William Brown and fined 200 lbs. of tob.{KECR JS#22:132}

John Johnson, attorney-at-law, d. leaving a will dated 21 Nov 1731 and proved 24 Dec 1731. To son Richard, he left 400 a. called *Johnson's Forrest*, also 200 a. of *Party Chance*. To dau. Mary, he left 200 a. called *Gleave's Adventure*. To son and dau., afsd. tract called *Outrange*, equally. To son John, he left personalty. To wife Susannah and children, residue of estate. Wife Susannah and son John, execs., were to live together on dwell. plant. called *Thornton and Bateman's farm*. On 24 Dec 1731 Susannah Johnson claimed her thirds.{MWB 20:432}

Another will was presented c1732 by John Jobson. This will was dated 19 Oct 1730. To eldest son John was left the dwell. plant. ———, and a mortgage on a tract in QA Co. To son Richard was left tract called *The Forrest* bought of Mr. Miller, and *Ambrosia*, adj. To dau. (intended to be called Mary), tracts called *Outrange* and *Chance*, at the head of Chester River. To wife Susannah, tract called *The Adventure* at the head of Chester River, personal estate divided with three children after a legacy to sister Phillips in England is paid. Above will recorded at request of John Johnson, eldest son of testator.{MWB 20:435}

The estate of John Johnson was taken 7 June 1732 and filed 11 Oct 1732. Next of kin were Mary Smithers and son John Johnson. The extx. was Susanna Johnson.{MINV 17:31}

Another inventory was prepared on 11 Feb 1733 and filed in July 1736. Next of kin was John Johnson. The extx. was Susanna Johnson.{MINV 21:477}

At August Court 1739, Susanna Johnson, alias Potter, was charged with having a base born child.{KECR JS#22:254}

John Johnson was the father of (by 1st wife); JOHN; MARY; (by Susanna): RICHARD, b. 3 Jan 1727/8.{KESH}

2. JOHN JOHNSON, son of John, d. by May 1737. He m. Mary (N).

The will of John Johnson was dated 7 April 1737 and proved 7 May 1737. To nephew John, son of Thomas Howard of Philadelphia, and to eldest dau. ——— of sd. Thomas he left personalty. To sister Mary was left personalty now in hands of mother-in-law Susannah Johnson; and lot in Chester Town. To wife Mary, extx., residue of personal estate.{MWB 21:790}

The inventory of John Johnson's estate was taken 16 June 1737 and filed 15 Sep 1737. Mentioned were E. Dulany and Phil. Chrisfield. Mary Johnson was admx./extx.{MINV 22:451}

3. RICHARD JOHNSON, son of John and Susannah, was b. 3 Jan 1727/8, and d. by Feb 1754.

At November Court 1740, Ebenezar Perkins was charged that on 1 June 1740 he committed waste on the land of Richard Johnson, age 12, orphan of John Johnson, dec., the land called *Batemans Farm*, did enter and carry away 10 oak trees and 2 poplar trees. Guilty.{KECR JS#23:140; KESH}

Richard Johnson, of KE Co., d. leaving a will dated 14 Dec 1753 and proved 15 Feb 1754. The heirs named were his wife, to whom he left the dwell. plant. called *Thornton and Bathan's Farm* and stock; cousins John and Phillip Brooks, sons of Phillip Brooks; cousin John Brook; cousin Phillip Brooks; sisters Susannah and Marianna Petters (or Potters - illegible), to whom he devised the plant. called, *I.U.*; and cousin John Carvil, son of John Carvil. The extx. was his wife. The will was witnessed by John Harty, Martha Hynson, and W. Hyson.{MWB29:222}

His estate was appraised by James Ringgold, Jr. and James McClean, Jr., and valued at £572.0.8. Thomas Ringgold and Hugh Wallis signed as creditors. Philip Brooks and John Carvill, Sr. signed as next of kin. Sarah Johnson, extx., filed the inventory on 3 July 1754.{MINV 57:377}

On 29 Jan 1759 distribution of the estate was made by widow, now wife of William Ringgold, Jr. Legatees were wife (unnamed), cousin John Brooks, Phillip Brooks, and John Carvil, son of John Carvil.{BFD 2:116}

THE WILLIAM JOHNSON FAMILIES

1. WILLIAM JOHNSON d. by Aug 1724. By 7 April 1720 he m. Katherine (N), who on that day joined him in conveying to Richard Bennett of QA Co., merchant, two tracts on Tersons Creek, one called *Faireall*, 200 a., and another tract called *Dunstable*, 100 a.{KELR JS#W:119}

William Johnson d. by 13 Aug 1724 when his administration was filed. Mentioned was John Brown.{MINV 10:86}

2. WILLIAM JOHNSON d. by 29 April 1740 when the estate was admin. by Elisabeth Massey; filed 2 May 1741.{MINV 25:495}

3. WILLIAM JOHNSON, and Elisabeth Massy were m. 30 March 1741.{KESH}

William and Elizabeth were the parents of: WILLIAM, b. 4 Dec 1742.{KESH}

4. WILLIAM JOHNSON and Mrs. Beatrice Pearce were m. 24 April 1747.{KESH}
William Johnson, of KE Co., d. leaving a will dated 5 March 1748 and proved 17 July 1749. The heirs named were wife and bro. Holman Johnson. The extx. was his wife (unnamed). The will was witnessed by Jeremiah Wells, Daniel Pearce, and Samuel Groome.{MWB 28:149}
The estate was appraised by John Carvill and Marmaduke Tilden, and valued at £755.7.8. John Hammer for Foster Cunliffe & Sons and Esau Watkins signed as creditors. Catharine Marcey and Hoalman Johnson signed as next of kin. Beatrice Johnson, extx., filed the inventory on 2 March 1750.{MINV 45:63}
In Oct 1753, Mrs. Batrix Johnson, age c36, dep. regarding the bounds of a tract called *Cornwallis's Choice*; she recalled her husband Gideon Pearce telling her that ....{KELR JS#28:45}
At November Court 1754, Beatrice Johnson and Esau Watkins were bound to provide maintenance support for a bastard child of Beatrice. Beatrice acknowledged she had delivered of a child since Dec last and the child had been sent to Jeremiah Cammells to be taken care of until the age of 21.{KECR JS#25:136B}

5. HOLMAN JOHNSON, bro. of the above William, d. by 1769, if not earlier.
Halman Johnson, of KE Co., d. (date unknown), when his estate was appraised and valued at £9.10.0. No creditors or next of kin listed. Hannah Parsons, admx., filed the undated inventory mentioning Mr. Samuel Matchler, Mr. William Absley, Mr. John Hild, Mr. Matthew Kennard, Mr. James Neal, and Mr. John Cannaday, and cont. a list of debts.{MINV 98:170}
On 29 Feb 1769 distribution of the estate was made by Hannah Parsons, admx., wife of Benjamin Parsons.{BFD 5:144}

THE GRIFFITH JONES FAMILY

1. GRIFFITH JONES, d. by June 1701. He m. Lucey (N), widow of Thomas Seward. She m. 3rd, Henry Green.
Griffith Jones d. leaving a will 2 Dec 1700 and proved 31 June 1701. He desired that son-in-law Thomas Seawell be paid all due him. To son Griffith, 380 a. called *Kemp* on Muddy Creek. To son Richard, 197 a., *Griffith's Delight* on Lavelly's Neck. To wife Lucy, extx., two sons afsd., dau. Mary and unborn child, personalty.{MWB 11:113} On 5 July

1701 the estate was appraised by Samuell Tovey and Edward Rogers.{INAC 23:166}

18 Aug 1702: Will of Lucey Green of TA Co., wife of Henry Green. Whereas Anth: Griffen last of TA Co., dec., by his last will bequeathed to her a parcel of land called *Kinson upon Chester*, her will is that David Jones, youngest son by Griffen Jones of KE Co., dec., hold and enjoy the same, at age 18, notwithstanding that she has several children, sons who have all land bequeathed and descended to them and from their several fathers. And whereas Thomas Seward, her former husband, bequeathed to her 150 a., part of a tract called *Sewards Hope*, she gives the same to Mary Jones, dau. of her last husband Griffen Jones, and this she does with the advice and consent of her husband, Henry Green.{KELR GL#1:new page 35}

Griffith Jones and Lucy his wife were the parents of{Recorded in KELR GL#1:7A by Lucy Green, wife of Henry Green, 3 July 1701}: GRIFFITH: b. 2 March 1688; RICHARD, b. 5 March 1692; MARY, b. 8 March 1697; and DAVID, b. 30 Dec 1700.

2. GRIFFITH JONES, son of Griffith and Lucy, was b. 2 March 1688, and d. by Nov 1748. On 18 March 1740, Griffith Jones, age c56, dep. regarding the bounds of a tract called *Gibbs Choice*.{KELR JS#23:189} On 4 June 1753, Griffith Jones, Quaker, dep. regarding the bounds of a tract called *Howells Adventure*.{KELR JS#27:317}

Griffith Jones m. 1st, Sarah, dau. of Giles Porter, on 18 Dec 1712.{KESP} He m. 2nd, by 1729, Mary, admx. of Michael Corse.{BFD 1:1, 2:71} Mary m. as her 3rd husband, Abraham Milton.

On 16 Sep 1714 payments (from the estate of Giles Porter) were made to Griffith Jones, who m. a dau. (unnamed) of Giles Porter (her portion of Giles' estate).{INAC 36B:60}

On 11 July 1715, Griffith Jones of KE Co., and his wife Sarah, conv. to Dennis Clark, a tract on Muddy Creek, 320 a.{KELR BC#1:91}

On 18 Dec 1716, Dennis Clarke, of KE Co., and his wife Mary, conv. to William Dicas of the same county, a parcel of land called *Kemps*, 320 a., which Dennis Clarke purchased of Griffith Jones, which was left to him by his father Griffith Jones, dec., who purchased the same from Simon Wilmer, dec.{KELR BC#1:169}

On 13 June 1724, Griffith Jones of KE Co., and his wife Sarah, conv. to Roger Hale, a tract called *Hales Purchase*, 50 a., being part of a tract called *The Grange*.{KELR JS#W:359}

On 26 April 1726, Griffith Jones and his wife Sarah, of KE Co., conv. to Alexander Williamson, clerk, 197 a. Griffith Jones, Sr., of KE Co., dec., on 7 Dec 1695 had surveyed a tract called *Griffiths Delight*, 197 a. due him by assignment from Simon Wilmer out of a warrant of 1100 a. granted to sd. Simon 6 Oct 1695, and whereas sd. Griffith Jones by his last will devised the same to his son Richard who d., whereby the same became the right of Griffith Jones, Jr., bro. of the sd. Richard.{KELR JS#W:529}

Griffith Jones of KE Co., d. leaving a will dated 11 July 1737 and proved 26 Nov 1748. The heirs named were wife Mary and children (unnamed). The will was witnessed by William McClean, John Gale (Quaker), and James Calder.{MWB 26:62}

On 3 May 1749 his estate was appraised by George Medford and Thomas Bowers, and valued at £334.6.6. Griffith Jones and George Medford signed as creditors. Griffith Jones and William Broscoe signed as next of kin. Mary Jones, extx., filed the inventory on 7 Sep 1749.{MINV 40:431}

Griffith Jones, of KE Co., d. before 18 Sep 1753, when distribution of the estate was made by Abraham Milton and his wife Mary, extx.{BFD 1:87}

Griffith Jones and Sarah Porter m. Dec 18, 1712.{KESP} They were the parents of{KESP}: MARY ANN, b. 19 Dec 1719; GRIFFITH, b. 25 da., 1 mo., 1725.

Griffith and Mary (N) Jones were the parents of{CEMM}: ELIZABETH, b. 28 da., 2 mo., 1729; LUCIA, b. 9 da., 4 mo., 1733; MARY, b. 31 da., 10 mo., 1734; MARGRETT, b. 1 da., 1 mo., 1737/8; and THOMAS RASIN.

3. ELIZABETH JONES, dau. of Griffith and Mary, was b. 28 da., 2 mo., 1729, and d. by Nov. 1746, evidently unm.

Elizabeth Jones, of KE Co., d. leaving a will written 9 April 1746 and proved 1 Nov 1746. The heirs named were sister Margaret Jones, bro. David Jones, and bro. Thomas Rasin Jones. The will was witnessed by Abraham Raisin, Margaret Hall, and John Raisin.{MWB 24:491}

4. DAVID JONES, son of Griffith and Lucy, was b. 30 Dec 1700. At November Court 1733, David Jones was fined £5 for saying "If they (the court afsd.) do not discharge me (for the service of Grand Juror) I will not serve and that the court might do —— the devil put in their heads to the contrary and of the sd. Lord Proprietary and his laws ...."{KECR JS#WK:441}

David Jones d. by 25 March 1740 when his estate was inv. Griffith Jones filed the inventory 10 April 1741. Next of kin was Mary Rolph.{MINV 25:477}

On 10 July 1744 Griffith Jones, Robert Lusby, and Charles Hynson, Jr., gave bond they would pay David Jones £64.10.9½, Richard Jones £64.10.9½, and Martha Jones £129.1.7 due to them as their filial portions of the estate of David Jones, their dec. father, when they were of age.{KEBI JS#20:106, 107, 109}

David and Martha Jones were the parents of{KESP}: RICHARD, b. 4 June 1735; MARTHA, b. 16 April 1737; and DAVID.

5. GRIFFITH JONES, son of Griffith (2) and Sarah (Porter), was b. 25 da., 1 mo., 1725. He m. by 16 Dec 1755, Rachel, who joined him in conv. to Charles Maccubbin of afsd. county, farmer, part of a tract called *The Grange*, originally granted to John James and formerly lying in BA Co., 176 a.{KELR JS#28:187}

On 22 March 1756, Thomas Ringgold of KE Co., Gent., and Abraham Milton of the same place, and his wife Mary, and Griffith Jones of the same place, conv. 100 a. to Thomas Jones, son of the sd. Mary, the wife of Abraham Milton, which Griffith Jones by his deed dated 22 Dec 1748 conv. to afsd. Mary by the name of Mary Jones, part of a tract called *Grange*.{KELR JS#28:250}

THE RICE JONES FAMILY

A number of references to earlier individuals named Rice Jones have been found.

Rice Jones, of Warwick River, VA, was granted 50 a., 2 Dec 1628, lying on the easterly side of Warwicksqueicke River, northly on land of Martha Key, s. to land of Phettiplace Clause, w. on sd. river and e. on the mine land. Due as his first dividend. Due unto Francis West for transfer of sd. Jones whoe came from Cannada in the *John & Francis* in 1623 and by these presents made over to him, etc.{Nugent, *Cavaliers and Pioneers*, p. 10}

Rice Jones was transported into the Province of MD between 1665 and 1669.{MPL 9:38, 12:413, and 17:415}

1. RICE JONES, the first of his family to be definitely identified, d. by 1 May 1726. He m. Elizabeth (N).

On 17 Sep 1690 William Hubbard and his wife Elizabeth, of KE Co., conv. to Rice Jones of afsd. county, a parcel of land cont. 200 a. being part of a tract of 400 a. called the *Grove*, the sd. 200 a. being purchased by William Hubbard of Cornelius Comegys, Jr., and Mary his wife on the n.e. branch of Chester River.{KELR B:252}

On 18 Jan 1714, Rice Jones, Sr., of KE Co., conv. to James Smith of the same county, a parcel of 200 a. Witnesseth that the sd. Rice Jones, Sr., for the consideration of two bonds, one for his maintenance during his natural life and the other for the purchase and making over 100 a. of land to Walter Jones, one of the sons of the afsd. Rice Jones, Sr., and by the afsd. James Smith to the afsd. Rice Jones, Sr., ... Rice Jones confirmed to James Smith, that parcel of 200 a., part of a tract of 400 a. called *The Grove*, which Rice Jones purchased of William Hubert and his wife Elizabeth.{KELR BC#1:58}

Rice Jones d. leaving an estate that was inv. on 1 May 1726, and filed 10 Sep 1726. It mentioned Hans Hanson, Elisabeth Jones, and Sarah Jones. The admin./exec. was Henry Cully.{MINV 11:552}

Rice (Rise) and Elizabeth Jones were the parents of{KESP}: RICE; JOHN, b. c1689; WALTER, b. April 1694; ANN, b. 18 Aug 1696; ELIZABETH, b. 20 (or 22) Jan 1698, bur. 21 May 1709; THOMAS, b. 10 Sep 1701; SARAH, b. 7 July 1703, bapt. 23 Oct 1704; and GRIF-FITH, b. 25 Aug 1707.{KESP}

2. RICE JONES, son of Rice, was living as late as June 1724. Rise Jones and Sarah News were m. Oct 25, 1713.{KESP}

At June Court 1724, Rice Jones of St. Paul's Parish was convicted of committing fornication with Mary Slayfoot on 1 Dec 1723 and begetting a bastard child. He was fined 600 lbs. of tob.{KECR JS#22:10}

3. JOHN JONES, son of Rice, was b. c1689.

On 22 May 1732, John Jones, age c43, made a deposition regarding the bounds of a tract called *The Dining Room*.{KELR JS#15:250}

On 13 Nov 1738, John Jones, son of Rice Jones, aged c49, dep. regarding a tract called *Dineing Room*. He stated he had a conver-sation about 6-7 years earlier with Simon Wilmer, dec., who said that the afsd. lands (*Dining Room*) were really Roberts' but that there was roguery used in the office; he had also heard John Wright say that the bounds of the afsd. land were near the head of *Fairy Meadow*.{KELR JS#22:292}

On 10 Dec 1741, John Jones, age c53, dep. regarding the bounds of a tract called *The Grove*. He recalled his bro. Rice Jones telling him ....{KELR JS#23:410}

4. WALTER JONES, son of Rice and Elizabeth, was b. April 1694, and d. by 2 June 1721.

Walter Jones d. leaving a will dated 24 Feb 1721 and proved 2 June 1722. To bro. John, 100 a. due from James Smith, clerk of KE Co., and personalty. To bro. Thomas, tob. due from Alex. Williamson. To four sisters, Margtt:, Ann, Eliza:, and Sarah, and bro. Rice, personalty. Bros. John and Rice were named as execs.{MWB 17:274}

5. THOMAS JONES, son of Rice and Elizabeth, was b. 10 Sep 1701. He may be the Thomas Jones, age c38, who, on 10 Dec 1741, dep. regarding the bounds of a tract called *The Grove*.{KELR JS#23:410}

THE ROBERT JONES FAMILY

1. ROBERT JONES d. by Oct 1719. He m. Elenor (N), who m. 2nd, James Goss.

On 16 Aug 1715, Robert Jones of KE Co., and his wife Elenor, conv. to Charles Gafutt(?) of the same county, 25 a., part of a tract called *Chester Grove* of 540 a., on Bare Branch. {KELR BC#1:87}

Robert Jones (Joanes) d. leaving a will dated 25 Oct 1719 and proved 9 March 1719. To eldest son John, he left personalty. To two sons, John and Robert, he left personalty. The sd. sons to be brought up by the exec. until 21 years of age. William Comeges was named exec. {MWB 15:349}

Jones left an inventory that was taken on 3 Nov 1720 and filed 23 April 1721. Appraisers were Samuell Wallis and William Smithers. {MINV 5:110}

On 15 Dec 1721 his estate was admin. by Elinor Goss, wife of James Goss. {A 4:97}

Robert and Elinor (N) Jones were the parents of: JOHN; and ROBERT.

2. JOHN JONES, son of Robert and Elinor, m. by 23 Feb 1735, Mary (N), who joined him in conv. to Benjamin Palmer of the same county, part of a tract called *Chester Grove*, 36 a. {KELR JS#18:230}

On 29 Jan 1746, John Jones of KE Co., and his wife Mary, conv. to Cornelius Comegys, part of a tract called *Chester Grove*, 1 a. {KELR JS#26:2}

On 20 May 1754, John Jones of KE Co., and his wife Mary, conv. to James Tilghman, of TA Co., attorney-at-law, part of a tract called *Providence*, lately in mortgage to John Tilden of the same county, Gent., 130 a., excepting 15 a. {KELR JS#27:453}

THE WILLIAM JONES FAMILY

1. (N) JONES, m. Sarah (N), who m. 2nd, by 26 Aug 1707, Thomas Webb.

On 26 Aug 1707, Joseph Trulock, of KE Co., and his wife Mary, conv. to Philip Rasin of the same county, a tract on Steelpone Creek, being part of a tract called *Forresters Delight*, 25 a., also 100 a. that Joseph Trulock bought of Thomas Webb and his wife Sarah and William Jones, son of sd. Sarah. Also 50 a., part of a tract called *Nancys Choice* which Joseph Trulock bought of Benjamin Hamblin, son of Benjamin Hamblin, dec. {KELR JSN:99}

(N) and Sarah Jones were the parents of: WILLIAM.

2. WILLIAM JONES, possibly son of (N) and Sarah (N) (Jones) (Webb), d. by March 1720. He m. Hannah (or Johanna), who m. 2nd, John Inch.

On 20 Feb 1712, William Jones of Steel Pone Creek in KE Co., heir of John Owen and Hannah the wife of sd. William Jones, conv. to Philip Raison, 60 a., part of a tract called *Leavenham* on the n. side of Steel Pone Creek.{KELR JSN:328}

William Jones, of KE Co., d. by 22 March 1720, when his estate was admin. by Hannah Inch, wife of John Inch.{MDAD 3:316}

William and Johanna were the parents of: WILLIAM, b. 31 Dec 1713.{KESP}

3. WILLIAM JONES, son of William and Johanna, was b. 31 Dec 1713, and d. by June 1761. Despite the discrepancies in ages, he may be the William Jones who made the following depositions: On 19 June 1755, William Jones, age c35, age c18-19, dep. regarding the bounds of the tract called *Williamston*.{KELR JS#28:136} On 16 March 1756, William Jones, age c35, dep. regarding the bounds of a tract called *Blays Park*.{KELR JS#28:223} On 25 July 1757, William Jones of CE Co., age c33, dep. regarding the bounds of a tract called *Philips Choice*.{KELR JS#28:366}

William Jones and Mary Spencer were m. 20 Dec 1740.{KESH}

Jonathan Woodland, guardian of William Jones, an orphan of William Jones, late of afsd. county, dec., petitioned on 7 Aug 1731 to have a commission to examine evidences of the bounds of a tract of land called *Leaven Ham*.{KELR JS#16:218}

On 12 Oct 1731, Blackledge Woodland, of KE Co., dep. regarding the bounds of a tract called *Leaven Ham*; he stated about 13 years earlier he was with his father-in-law, William Jones, going down to a Joneses Point near the mouth of Back Cove and his aged father-in-law showed him a bounded tree.{KELR JS#16:220}

At June Court 1733, Jonathan Woodland was charged with cutting, sawing and disposing of black walnut plank from the land of William Jones, an orphan of William Jones.{KECR JS#WK:370}

On 16 March 1756, Blackledge Woodland, age c49, dep. regarding the bounds of a tract called *Blays Park*. He recalled that his bro. Jonathan Woodland had a commission to settle the bound of William Jones' land about 20 years earlier, he being a guardian to the sd. Jones and at the same time he proved the sd. tree to be the beginning tree of the land formerly called *George Gown* and *New Levingham* and that he had his information from his father-in-law, William Jones.{KELR JS#28:224}

William Jones, of KE Co., d. leaving a will dated 23 March 1755 and proved 6 June 1761. The heirs named were son William Jones of N.E. [*sic*], who was to have 130 a., part of *Levenham*, and son Henry Jones, and wife Mary. Wife Mary and bros. Blackledge and Woodland Jones were named as execs. The will was witnessed by Daniel Pearce, John Grace, and John Yokley.{MWM 31:348}

On 9 Aug 1761 the estate was appraised by Joseph Raisin and John Gale, and valued at £21.5.7. G. Wilson and G. Craigg signed as creditors. John Thrift and Mary Thrift signed as next of kin. Mary Jones, admx., filed the inventory on 7 April 1762.{MINV 77:25}

William and Mary were the parents of: WILLIAM; and HENRY.

4. HENRY JONES, son of William and Mary, is almost certainly the Henry who d. by 22 June 1765, when his estate was appraised by Joseph Rasin and Abraham Rasin, and valued at £39.9.1. Bartholomew Haden signed as creditor. Mary Jones and William Jones signed as next of kin. Mary Jones, admx., filed the inventory on 16 Aug 1765.{MINV 87:275}

On 1 May 1766 his estate was appraised by Joseph Rasin and Abraham Rasin, and valued at £26.0.9. Thomas Smyth and J. Nicholson signed as creditors. Widow Mary and Mary Creadles signed as next of kin. Mary Jones, admx., filed the inventory on 18 June 1766.{MINV 89:34}

THE WILLIAM JONES FAMILY (2)

1. WILLIAM JONES d. by March 1719. He m. Anne (N) who m. 2nd, Thomas Peryn.

William Jones d. leaving a will dated 10 Dec 1719 and proved 8 March 1719. To wife Anne, use of dwell. plant., and personalty. To son Wm., ½ of land lying next to neck of —. To son Benja., the other half of sd. tract. To daus. Mary and Eliza:, personalty. To dau. Rachel, one share of personalty with her bros. afsd. Sons to live with bro. Peter. Bro. Peter and James Willson, Jr. were as named execs.{MWB 15:346}

The estate of William Jones was admin. on 15 Aug 1720. Valentine Browne and George Sanders signed as creditors. Thomas Jones signed as next of kin.{MINV 4:213}

Another inventory was prepared on 10 Aug 1720 and filed on 3 Feb 1720. Valentine Brown for Richard Bennet and Abraham Redgrave, Jr. signed as creditors. "2 infants" were listed as next of kin.{MINV 5:1}

On 3 July 1721, the estate was admin. by James Wilson, Jr. and Peter Jones.{MDAD 3:466}

On 20 Feb 1720, Thomas Peryn and Ann Peryn, his now wife formerly the widow and relict of William Jones, late of KE Co., dec., in consideration of payment by Peter Jones, agreed not to sue or demand by writ of dower any land formerly possessed by William Jones.{KELR JS#W:151}

194

William and Anne were the parents of: WILLIAM; BENJAMIN; MARY; ELIZA; and RACHEL.

2. WILLIAM JONES, son of William and Anne, may be the William who m. Margaret (N).

On 21 Jan 1737, William Jones of KE Co., and his wife Margaret, conv. to Isaac Freemon of the same place, part of a tract called *Broad Oak*, 60 a.{KELR JS#22:51}

KE Co. Debt Books show that William Jones paid taxes on *Broad Oak* from 1733 to 1769.{INKE 21}

William and Margaret were the parents of: BENJAMIN, b. 21 Jan 1741/2.{KESB}

3. BENJAMIN JONES, son of William and Anne is probably the Benjamin Jones who paid taxes on *Broad Oak* from 1738 to 1747.{INKE 20}

Benjamin Jones and Susanah Knock m. 29 Jan 1734.{KESB}

On 18 March 1746, Benjamin Jones, of KE Co., and his wife Susannah, conv. to William Stevenson of afsd. county, a tract called *Jones' Venture*, on Cyrpus Branch, 100 a.{KELR JS#25:456}

On 5 Dec 1748, Benjamin Jones and his wife Susanah, of KE Co., conv. to Isaac Freeman of the same county, part of a tract called *Broad Neck(?)*, 92 a.{KELR JS#26:178} (More likely this was *Broad Oak*.)

Benjamin and Susannah were the parents of{KESB}: BENJAMIN, b. 3 Sep 1743; and ANN, b. 27 Nov 1744.

THE DANIEL KELLY FAMILY

1. DANIELL KELLEY, d. by Aug 1707. He m. Margaret (N), who m. 2nd, Dominick Kenslagh.

Daniel Kelley d. by 5 Aug 1707 when his estate was admin.{INAC 27:193} The administration was signed by admx. Margrett Kenslagh, wife of Domineck Kenslagh, on 30 Aug 1708.{INAC 28:295}

By his wife Margaret, Daniel Kelly was the father of: KATHERINE, b. c1689; and ANNE, bapt. 19 Sep 1697{KESP}, may have m. (N) Lewis.

2. KATHERINE KELLY, dau. of Daniel, was b. c1689, and d. by 28 Jan 1739.

On 21 Nov 1727, Katharine Kelley, age c38, dep. regarding the bounds of a tract called *Bayleys Forrest;* she said that 28 years earlier she and her father Daniel Kelley were walking in the woods when they came across a bounded tree.{KELR JS#X:208}

At November Court 1726, it was presented that Katherine Kelley, St. Paul's Parish, spinster, having been admonished by the Vestrymen of the same parish, on 20 March 1725, did on 21 March 1725 and diverse other times as a fornicatrix, frequent the company of Dominick Kenslaugh, labourer.{KECR JS#22:213}

Catherine Kelly d. leaving an estate with an inventory taken 28 Jan 1739 and filed 14 June 1740. John Kinslough and Anne Lewis signed as next of kin. The admin. was Silvester Kelly.{MINV 25:79}

THE JAMES KELLY FAMILY

1. JAMES KELLY d. by 5 April 1710, a member of Cecil Monthly Meeting. He m. Charity (N), who m. 2nd, William Spearman.

On 10 Jan 1706 James Kelly patented 100 a. in CE Co. called *Kelly's Choice*.{MPL CD#4:298}

James Kelle d. 24 da., 12 mo., ——.{CEMM} He d. by 5 April 1710 when his estate was admin.{INAC 31:191} On 18 Sep 1710 the administration was filed by admx. Charity Kelly.{INAC 32A:40}

Cecil Monthly Meeting reported on 14 da., 12 mo., 1710 that Charity Spearman, widow of James Kelley, having contrary to truth taken a husband (William Spearman - see entry for Joseph Kellee below) and also run into several other evils and light actions with the testimony of truth ....{CEMM}

James and Charity were the parents of{CEMM}: JOSEPH, b. c15 da., 8 mo., 1690; BARBARA, b. 21 da., 8 mo., 1692; JAMES, b. 1 da., 2 mo., 169-; BENJAMIN, b. 15 da., 9 mo., 1696; MARY, b. 5 da., 9 mo., 1702; WILLIAM, d. 1 da., 8 mo., 1706; and ANN, b. 10 da., 1 mo., 1706/7.

2. JOSEPH KELLY (or KELLEE), son of James and Charity, was b. c15 da., 8 mo., 1690. As Joseph Kellee (schoolmaster) he d. leaving a will dated 4 da., 12 mo., 1729/30, and proved 19 March 1729. To bro. Francis, son of William Spearman of KE Co., dec., 130 a. of *Angels Lott* taken up by Bryan O'Neale. Should sd. Francis die, land to go to Benjamin, son of Benjamin Kellee.{MWB 20:5}

3. JAMES KELLY, son of James and Charity, was b. 1 da., 2 mo., 169-.{CEMM}

On 24 Nov 1721, James Kellee, of KE Co., conv. to his bro. Benjamin Kellee, of afsd. county, a parcel of land called *Kellees Choyce*, at the head of Steel Pone Creek, 100 a.{KELR JS#W:206}

On 13 da., 12 mo., 1722, Cecil Meeting reported that James Kelley had some months earlier given himself into drunkenness.{CEMM}

On 14 da., 5 mo., 1725, it was reported that the marriage of James Kelley and Jane Meade was orderly accomplished.{CEMM}

James Kellee d. by 7 June 1729 when his estate was admin. by Jane Kellee (Quaker) and filed on 4 Sep 1729. Benjamin Kellee and Joseph Kellee signed as next of kin.{MINV 15:169}

4. BENJAMIN KELLY, son of James and Charity, was b. 15 da., 9 mo., 1696.{CEMM} He m. Mary Boots on or before 10 da., 9 mo., 1724.

On 24 Nov 1721, James Kellee, of KE Co., conv. to his bro. Benjamin Kellee, of afsd. county, a parcel of land called *Kellees Choyce*, at the head of Steelpone Creek, 100 a.{KELR JS#W:206}

On 11 da., 7 mo., 1723, Benja. Kelley was accused of loose conversation.{CEMM}

On 10 da., 9 mo., 1724, it was reported that the marriage of Benj: Kellee and Mary Boots had been orderly accomplished (with consent of parents).{CEMM}

On 19 Aug 1735, Benjamin Kelley of KE Co., and his wife Mary, conv. to Charles Milward of the same, for the consideration of a tract called *Howells Adventure*, a tract called *Kelleys Choice*, near the head of Steel Pone Creek, 100 a.{KELR JS#18:177}

Benjamin d. by 23 Oct 1738 when Mary Kelly, of KE Co., widow, gave £15 to each of her children, James, Benjamin, Mary, Rachell, Sarah, and Ann Kelly, to be paid when each was of age, the girls at age 18 and the boys at age 21.{KEBI JS#18:172}

Benjamin and Mary were the parents of: JAMES; BENJAMIN; MARY; RACHEL, m. by March 1764, (N) Chapel; SARAH; and ANN.

5. JAMES KELLY, son of Benjamin and Mary, d. by 27 March 1764. He may have m. Hannah (N), admx. of Benjamin Cooley. On 23 Feb 1754 distribution of the estate of Benjamin Cooley was made by James Kelley and his wife Hannah, admx.{BFD 1:118}

James Kelly, of KE Co., d. leaving a will dated 20 Jan 1764. The heirs named were son James Kelly (Jr.), minor, to whom was devised the dwell. plant. called *Howell's Adventure* (100 a.) at age 21, and children Benjamin and Sarah Kelly. Bro. Benjamin Kelly was to have care of the three children. Bro. Benjamin Kelly was named as exec. The will was witnessed by William Gaile, John Chappel, and Abraham Raisin.{MWB 31:1078}

On 27 March 1764 the estate of James Kelly was appraised by Joseph Raisin (also Joseph Rasin) and Thomas Bowers, and valued at £124.16.3. Thomas and William Ringgold and Samuel Melborn signed as creditors. Rachel Chappel and Sarah Kelly signed as next of kin. Benjamin Kelly, exec., filed the inventory on 26 May 1764.{MINV 83:353}

The estate was again appraised by Joseph Rasin and Thomas Bowers, and valued at £36.4.9. Abram Cannel and Thomas & William Ringgold signed as creditors. Sarah Kelley and Rachel Chappel signed as next of kin. Benjamin Kelley, exec., filed the inventory on 20 Oct 1765.{MINV 88:281}

James Kelley was the father of three children: JAMES; BEN-JAMIN; and SARAH.

6. SARAH KELLY, dau. of Benjamin and Mary, d. by 12 Jan 1768, when her estate was appraised by Rasin Gale and Abraham Rasin, and valued at £7.14.3. No creditors were listed. Rachel Chappel signed as next of kin. John Chappel, admin., filed the inventory on 16 Jan 1768.{MINV 97:162}

Sarah may be the Sarah Kelly who, at March Court 1759, confessed to committing fornication. She refused to name the father. She was fined £3. John Sewell entered into security to pay the fine, fees and to keep the child called LAMBERT KELLY from becoming any charge to the county.{KECR JS#25:219B}

At March Court 1764, it was presented that Sarah Kelly committed fornication and begot a base born child. She was fined £3.{KECR DD#1:44A}

Unplaced

KELLY, ALEXANDER, m. Mary Cartey.

On 30 May 1748, William Pope, of KE Co. on Delaware, and his wife Katharine, conv. land to Alexander Kelley, of KE Co., MD. Whereas Maurice Cartey, late of KE Co., dec., was seized of a tract formerly called *Sewell*, 249 a. and 156 perches; he d. intestate whereby the land became the right of his three daus., the afsd. Katharine, Margret, the wife of Henry Ellars, and Mary, dec., lately the wife of the afsd. Alexander Kelley.{KELR JS#26:124}

Alexander Kelley, of KE Co., d. leaving a will dated 1 May 1769 and proved 24 Dec 1770. Mentioned were wife Anne, son William, and dau. Margaret Burchanall, and son-in-law William Burchanall. Tracts mentioned were *Reilys Beginning, Wilsons Beginning,* and *Utrech*. William Maxwell and wife Anne were named as execs. The will was witnessed by Francis Rutter, John Cowardin, and Joseph Ireland.{MWB 38:179}

On 27 Feb 1771, the estate of Alexander Kelley was appraised by Ebenezar Reyner and Joshua Ireland, and valued at £350.6.9. James Black and John Comegys signed as creditors. William Kelley and William Burchinall signed as next of kin. Ann Kelley, admx., filed the inventory on 18 March 1771.{MINV 106:108}

On 28 June 1771 the estate was appraised by Ebenezar Reyner and William Maxwell, and valued at £273.6.10. James Black and Abel Chandler signed as creditors. William Burchimal and William Kelley signed as next of kin. Nathaniel Comegys, admin., filed the inventory on 9 Oct 1771.{MINV 107:389}

The estate was again appraised and valued at £245.14.7. No creditors or next of kin listed. Nathaniel Comegys, admin., filed the inventory cont. a list of debts on 21 Dec 1772.{MINV 110:397}

KELLY, DENNIS, m. by 2 April 1709, Ann Kinbow, in a 1709 administration account of Edward James of Kent Island.{INAC 29:218}

KELLY, EDWARD, at Aug Court 1751, was charged with assaulting John Wroth on 10 Aug 1751. He was fined 2 s., 6 p.{KECR JS#25:81B}

KELLY, HANNAH, of KE Co., d. before 29 July 1772. Distribution of the estate was made by Mrs. Hannah Kelly, admx.{BFD 6:148}

KELLY, JOHN, of KE Co., d. by 1 Oct 1752, when his estate was appraised by Isaac Freeman and Richard Wilson, and valued at £10.5.0. James Church and P. Bryan signed as creditors. Ester Kelly, widow, signed as next of kin. Daniel Bryan, admin., filed the inventory on 9 Feb 1753.{MINV 53:61}

KELLEY, JOSHUA, d. and his estate was appraised and valued at £25.11.6. Hannah Kelley, admx., filed the inventory cont. a list of debts on 18 Aug 1770.{MINV 104:224}
On 1 Sep 1770 his estate was appraised by Nathaniel Miller and B. Miller, and valued at £136.16.9. John Page and Thomas Ringgold & Co. signed as creditors. Cristina Kelley and Peregin Kelley signed as next of kin. Hannah Kelley, admx., filed the inventory on 19 Nov 1770.{MINV 104:119}
On 18 Dec 1770 distribution of the estate was made by Hannah Kelley, admx.{BFD 6:23}

KELLY, MARGARET, widow, on 23 Feb 1704, made over to Richard Burk and Ellin his wife, her dau. Mary Kelly, to live with the sd. Richard and Ellin until she came of age of 16, being 12 years of age 27 Aug following.{KELR GL#1:28/50}

KELLEY, MARY, spinster, was charged at Aug Court 1752, with committing fornication and begetting a bastard child on 10 May 1751. She was fined £3.{KECR JS#25:100A}

KELLY, THOMAS, m. Kath. (N). They were the parents of: MARY, b. 13 Feb 1712.{KESP}

KELLY, WILLIAM, d. leaving a will dated 15 April 1723, proved 3 May 1723. To cousin Nathll. Hynson, he left a tract called *Bagley*. If he should die, the land was to go to two sisters Anne and Catherine

(Kelly), latter to have a life interest. To Joseph Young, exec., Thos. Joce and Michael Kinslagh, he left personalty.{MWB 18:112}

On 15 June 1723 the estate was admin. Elias Ringgold, attorney for Dr. Thomas Williams and James Smith (exec. of Col. N. Hynson) signed as creditors. Ann Kelly and Thomas Joce signed as next of kin.{MINV 9:297}

On 8 Aug 1724 and 31 March 1725 the estate was admin. by Joseph Young, exec.{MDAD 6:82, 295}

KELLY, WILLIAM, on 12 March 1757 was fined 30 s. for committing fornication and entered into security to pay the fine, fees and to keep the child of Beatrice Cantwell called WILLIAM from becoming a charge to the county. Beatrice was fined 30 s.{KECR JS#25:214A, 215A}

THE KENDALL FAMILY

1. WILLIAM KENDALL, d. by 28 May 1740 when his estate was inv. The inventory was filed on 11 July 1740 by Thomas Slippon, admin.{MINV 25:87} William m. Elinor (N).

William and Elinor had three children{KESP}: WILLIAM, b. 16 Feb 1729; STEPHEN, b. 5 Aug 1733; and JAMES. b. 16 May 1739.

2. WILLIAM KENDALL, son of William and Elinor, was b. 16 Feb 1729, and was living as late as 4 Jan 1754.{KESP} He m. Maryann (N).

On 11 Sep 1753, William Kindal and his wife Maryann, conv. to Isaac Melton (Milton) of afsd. county, part of a tract called *The Grange* and also called *Nossesters Habitation*.{KELR JS#27:352}

On 4 Jan 1754, William Kendall, of KE Co., and his wife Maryann, conv. to Thomas Chandler, of the afsd. county, farmer, 100 a., with 3 a. reserved for a water mill. Whereas Thomas Noster bought part of a tract called *The Grange* and by him called *Nosters Habitation*, which he sold to Francis Scott, who sold the same to Thomas Maslin, who sold the same to William Kandall, which at his death he left to sd. William Kendall, his son. Grants as well the dower right of Elenor the mother of afsd. William Kendall, the party to these presents and the wife of Thomas Slipper.{KELR JS#27:388}

3. STEPHEN KENDALL, son of William and Elinor, was b. 5 Aug 1733.{KESP} He d. by 29 Nov 1766. He m. Sarah (N), who m. 2nd, Thomas Morgan.

On 29 Nov 1766, his estate was appraised by George Presbury and James Piner, and valued at £89.13.7. William Slubey, Jr. and James Anderson signed as creditors. William Kindol signed as next of kin. Sarah Kennall, admx., filed the inventory on 10 Jan 1767.{MINV 92:7}

His estate was appraised and valued at £10.0.0. Sarah Morgan, wife of Thomas [sic] Morgan, admx., filed the inventory cont. a list of debts on 2 July 1767.{MINV 94:340}

On 5 Oct 1767, distribution of his estate was made by Sarah Morgan, admx., wife of Charles [sic] Morgan.{BFD 5:54}

Unplaced

KENDALL, THOMAS, (of Kent Island), d. leaving a will dated 9 Nov 1646 and proved (c1646/7). To the eldest son of Robert Baxter of Kent Island, he left personalty. To Thomas Youell in trust for his three children, he left the residue of estate. Test: Thos. Waggott and John Sturman.{MWB 1:33}

THE PHILIP KENNARD FAMILY

1. PHILIP KENNARD m. Mary Bally on 8 Dec 1708.{KESP} This may be an error on the part of the parish clerk because on 2 Aug 1709 he was m. to Elizabeth, widow of William Bailey, and sister of Charles James. Elizabeth m. 3rd, John Howell.

On 28 June 1709, Philip Kennard and his wife Elizabeth, conv. to Joseph Trulock, part of a tract called *Hailes* and *Drayton* adjoining Steel Pone Creek.{KELR JSN:144}

On 2 Aug 1709, Philip Kennard, of KE Co., and his wife Elizabeth, conv. to Edward Haukin (Hankin?), of KE Co., mariner, a tract where they then dwelled in that part of KE Co. that was formerly part of BA Co., 300 a.{KELR JSN:138}

On 2 Aug 1709, Philip Kennard, of KE Co., in consideration that Elizabeth ——, who was the widow and relict of William ——, dec., has sold the land which came to her by descent and whereunto she is also entitled by the last will of her bro. Charles James, dec., and in consideration of the love and good will Kennard has for William Bailey, the only issue of his wife by her former husband William Bailey, and now an infant coming of 5 years age next August, conv. to the sd. infant when age 21 all that part of the land now possessed by him, the sd. Philip Kennard, said to be formerly lying in CE Co. near the head of Worton Creek.{KELR JSN:141}

On 19 Aug 1719, Philip Kennard and his wife Elizabeth, merchant, of KE Co., conv. to John Watts, of the same county, in consideration of 200 a., part of a tract called *The Exchange*, 100 a.{KELR JS#W:40}

On 23 March 1727, William Bayley, of KE Co., bricklayer, son and heir of William Bayley, dec., conv. land to Phill. Kennard, Sr., of the same place, merchant. The deed stated that whereas the sd. Phill. Kennard and his wife Elizabeth, formerly the widow and relict of

201

William Bayley the father, on 2 Aug 1709, sold to Edward Haukin of London, merchant, a part of a tract called *Drayton*, 300 a. And sd. Edward Haukin conv. the same on 4 May 1710 to sd. Phill. Kennard. And now Phill. Kennard who m. Elizabeth, the mother of William Bayley, to prevent a dispute regarding reversion after the death of Elizabeth, purchased the sd. land.{KELR JS#X:197}

Philip Kennard, merchant, d. leaving a will dated 28 Nov 1731 and proved 17 Aug 1732. He named his son Philip Kennard, Jr., and the latter's sons John, Phil, and Joseph. He left personalty to Ruth Barney. Philip Kennard, Jr., was named exec.{MWB 20:421}

Kennard left an estate that was inv. on 5 Oct 1732. The inventory was filed 18 Nov 1732. Elisabeth Kennard, widow, signed as next of kin. Philip Kennard was named as exec.{MINV 17:38}

A list of debts was filed (c1735) by (Philip) Kennard, the exec.{MINV 21:125}

Philip Kennard was the father of a son probably b. before he m. Mary/Elizabeth James Bailey in 1708: PHILIP, Jr.

2. PHILIP KENNARD, son of Philip (1), d. by 13 Jan 1739. He m. Sarah (N), who d. by 15 April 1749.

On 27 Feb 1738, Phillip Kennard, of KE Co., merchant, and his wife Sarah, conv. to Aron Alford, of the same place, carpenter, 50 a.{KELR JS#22:366}

On 9 April 1733, Philip Kennard, of KE Co., merchant, in behalf of himself and his son John Kennard, a minor son of same Philip, conv. to John Howell, of the same county, cooper, and his wife Elizabeth, late the wife of Philip Kennard, late of the county afsd., dec., 166 a. Whereas Philip Kennard, dec., by his last will devised a tract of land called *Drayton* to the first mentioned Phillip until the afsd. John Kennard should arrive at the age of 21 years, whereas John Howell and his wife Elizabeth have a right to ⅓ of the same tract, Elizabeth's dowry.{KELR JS#16:308}

Phillip Kennard, merchant, d. leaving a will dated 12 Dec 1739 and proved 13 Jan 1739. To wife Sarah sons John, Philip and Joseph, daus. Mary and Sarah, granddau. Mary, dau. of testator's son John, John Giant, and Mary, wife of Caleb Beck, he left personalty. To son Philip, he left a plant. Wife Sarah and son John were named as execs. James Calder was appointed overseer. Note: Children to be brought up in the Church of England.{MWB 22:130}

The inventory of Philip Kennard's estate was taken Feb 1739 and filed 19 April 1740. Mary Rasin and George Rasin signed as next of kin. Sarah Kennard and John Kennard were named as execs.{MINV 24:494}

Another inventory was taken 14 Feb 1740 and filed 10 Oct 1741. Mary Rasin, George Rasin, and Henry Truelock signed as creditors and next of kin. Sarah Kennard and Philip Kennard were named as execs.{MINV 26:381}

The estate was appraised a third time by Ebenezar Blakiston and Samuel Groome, and valued at £5.12.0. Sarah Kennard, surviving extx., filed the inventory on 26 Nov 1743.{MINV 28:309}

Sarah Kennard, of KE Co., d. leaving a will dated 21 March 1748/9 and proved 15 April 1749. The heirs named were dau. Sarah Kennard and sons Phil Kennard and William Ringgold, execs. The will was witnessed by Elizabeth Craugh, Mary Bateman, and Sam Groome.{MWB 26:90} On 27 April 1749, her estate was appraised by John Carvil and Thomas Bowers, and valued at £552.18.9. C. Comegys and E. Comegys signed as creditors. Ja. Caulk and Mary Wilson signed as next of kin. Philip Kennard and William Ringgold, execs., filed the inventory on 5 Feb 1749.{MINV 43:415}

Philip Kennard, Jr., was the father of: JOHN; PHILIP; and JOSEPH; MARY; and SARAH.

3. JOHN KENNARD, son of Philip, Jr. (2), m. Mrs. Sarah Pearce on 6 March 1738/9.{KESH}

On 10 April 1742, John Kennard, of KE Co., Gent., and his wife Sarah, conv. to Richard Wethered, merchant, Lot No. 25 in George Town.{KELR JS#23:395}

John Kennard, of KE Co., d. by 8 Feb 1743 when his estate was appraised by Samuel Groome and Thomas Richardson, and valued at £719.2.5. Edward Crow and John Hammer for Forster Cunliff, Esq. & Sons signed as creditors. Mary Kennard and Oliver Caulk signed as next of kin. Sarah Kennard, admx., filed the inventory on 12 June 1744.{MINV 29:440} On 15 May 1745 his estate was appraised by Samuel Groome and Thomas Richardson, and valued at £212.10.7. No creditors or next of kin listed. Sarah Kennard, admx., filed the inventory on 25 May 1745.{MINV 31:85}

On 16 July 1746 Sarah Kennard, Matthias Harris and Simon Wilmer, Gent. of KE Co., were bound to pay Mary Kennard, Ann Kennard, and Sarah Kennard, each £174.9.8 due as the filial portion of the estate of their father, John Kennard, at age 16.{KEBI JS#20:230, 231, 232}

Sarah Kennard of KE Co., widow, d. leaving a will dated 5 March 1756 and proved 26 April 1756. Children named were Ann and Mary. Friend Wm. Ringgold, near Chester Town, was appointed to divide the estate and have care of dau. Ann until age 16. Wm. Ringgold was named exec. The will was witnessed by Aaron Alford, Moses Alford, and Jane Kennard.{MWB 30:66}

On 24 May 1764, Robert Buchanan and his wife Mary, and Ann Kennard, the sd. Mary and Ann being daus. and coheiresses of John Kennard, dec., who was son and heir of Phillip Kennard, late of KE

Co., dec., conv. to William Ringgold of Chester Town, merchant, a lot of ground and water in Chester Town, No. 7.{KELR DD#1:532}

John and Sarah were the parents of{KESH}: MARY, b. 29 Sep 1739, m. by 24 May 1764, Robert Buchanan; ANN, b. 31 Aug 1741; and SARAH, b. 9 Dec 1743.

4. PHILIP KENNARD, son of Philip (2), d. by Aug 1761. He m. Catherine (N).

On 6 Aug 1753, Philip Kennard and his wife Catharine of KE Co., conv. to Nathaniel Kennard of the same county, part of a tract called *Kennards Fancy*, 23 a.{KELR JS#27:321}

Phillip Kennard, of KE Co., d. leaving a will dated 19 Nov 1760 and proved 5 Aug 1761. The heirs named were son John Tilden Kennard (minor) to whom was devised the plant., *Kennard's Farm*, and daus. Sarah, Katherine and Mary. The extx. was testator's wife. The will was witnessed by Ann Carter, Samuel Budd, and Robert Buchanan.{MWB 31:452}

On 20 Aug 1761 the estate was appraised by William Hynson and Thomas Bowers, and valued at £719.1.0. J. Tilden and Thomas Ringgold signed as creditors. Mary Kennard and Ann Kannard signed as next of kin. Catharine Kennard, extx., filed the inventory on 2 Dec 1761.{MINV 75:232}

The estate was again appraised by Thomas Bowers and W. Hynson, and valued at £153.6.6. J. Tilden and Thomas Ringgold signed as creditors. Mary Ringgold and Ann Kennard signed as next of kin. Katharine Kennard, extx., filed the inventory on 24 Nov 1762.{MINV 79:188}

Philip Kennard was the father of: JOHN TILDEN; SARAH; KATHERINE; and MARY.

5. JOSEPH KENNARD, son of Philip, Jr. (2), was an adult in 1733.

On 15 Nov 1733, Nicholas Nixon, of KE Co. on Delaware, blacksmith, and his wife Elizabeth, conv. to Joseph Kennard, of KE Co., MD, son of Philip Kennard of the last mentioned county, merchant, a lot in the town of Chester, No. 7.{KELR JS#16:395, 396}

On 27 Feb 1738, George Read, of KE Co., and his wife Mary, conv. to Joseph Kennard, of the same county, son of Phillip Kennard, of the afsd. county, Gent., a tract called *Lynn(?)* and now commonly known as *Darnells Old Field*, on the n. side of Steel Pone Creek, which was patented on 10 Feb 1663 by John James(?) and by him devised to his son Charles, remainder to James and Humphry Tilton(?) which sd. Charles having d. without issue the sd. James and Humphrey Tilton were seized of the land and d. without issue and intestate, whereby the same land descended to the same Mary with her sisters Ellinor,

Elizabeth, and Catherine, sisters and heirs to the same James and Humphry Tilton.{KELR JS#22:355}

THE RICHARD KENNARD FAMILY

1. RICHARD KENNARD m. by c1693, Mary, widow and extx. of Nathaniel Howell, of CE Co.{INAC 10:331} Mary m. 3rd, (N) Howard, and was living on 17 Nov 1719.

Richard Kinward and Mary were the parents of{KESH}: RICHARD, Jr., b. 14 March 169-; NATHANIEL, b. 3 Dec 1696; and ANN, b. 16 March 1697.

2. RICHARD KENNARD, Jr., son of Richard (1) and Mary, was b. 14 March 169-.{KESH}

On 17 Aug 1731, Richard Kennard, age c40, dep. regarding the bounds of the tract *Williamston*.{KELR JS#16:164}

On 10 Sep 1735, Richard Kinnard, age c40, dep. regarding the bounds of a tract called *Sims Farm*.{KELR JS#18:195}

On 20 Oct 1743, Richard Kennard age c53, dep. regarding the bounds of a tract called *Beckworth*.{KELR JS#25:195}

On 31 May 1744, Richard Kennard, age c52, dep. regarding the bounds of a tract called *The Grange*.{KELR JS#25:98}

On 5 Jan 1750, Richard Kennard and his wife Mary Kennard, of KE Co., conv. to William Graves of the same county, merchant, part of a tract called *Doe Neck*, originally granted to Cosar Prince and John Powell and after several conveyances became the right of the same Richard and Mary formerly in CE Co., but now in KE Co., 27 a.{KELR JS#26:431}

On 10 May 1753, Richard Kennard, of KE Co., conv. to John Kennard, son of the sd. Richard Kennard, part of a tract called *Doe Neck*, except 27 a. sold to William Graves.{KELR JS#27:291}

In Oct 1753, Richard Kennard, age c61, dep. regarding the bounds of a tract called *Cornwallis's Choice*.{KELR JS#28:39}

On 19 June 1755, Richard Kennard, age c60, dep. regarding the bounds of the tract called *Williamston*.{KELR JS#28:137}

Richard Kennard, of KE Co., d. leaving a will dated 24 May 1752 and proved 30 Sep 1756. The heirs named were wife Mary and sons John Kennard, Richard, Steven, Thomas, Michael, Mathew, Howard, Nathaniel, and Daniel. Mary Kennard was named extx. The will was witnessed by Joshua Beck, Edward Beck, and John Younger.{MWB 30:161}

On 28 Feb 1757, the estate was appraised by William Browning and John Younger, and valued at £221.18.7. Stephen Kennard and Richard Lloyd signed as creditors. Nathaniel Kennard and Elisabeth Cully signed as next of kin. Mary Kennard, extx., filed the inventory on 16 April 1757.{MINV 63:379} On 21 Feb 1758 distribution of the estate was made by Mary Kennard, extx. Distribution was made to children (unnamed).{BFD 2:83}

Mary Kennard, widow, of KE Co., d. leaving a will dated 15 Dec 1772 and proved 15 March 1773. The heirs named were grandson Henry Thomas, son of Ebenezar (dec.), grandson William Jones, and son Daniel Kinnard, exec. The will was witnessed by Robert Buchanan and Aquilla Jones.{MWB 39:190}

Richard and Mary Kennard were the parents of: JOHN; RICHARD; STEVEN; THOMAS; MICHAEL; MATHEW; HOWARD; NATHANIEL; and DANIEL.

3. NATHANIEL KENNARD, son of Richard (1) and Mary, was b. 3 Dec 1696.{KESH} He m. Jane (N).

On 17 Nov 1719, Mary Howard, of KE Co., seamster, conv. to her son Nathaniel Kennard, 144 a., part of a tract called *Denby*, near Churn Creek.{KELR JS#W:45}

On 17 Aug 1731, Nathaniel Kennard, age c34, dep. regarding the bounds of the tract *Williamston*.{KELR JS#16:164}

At November Court 1727, it was presented that St. Leger Codd of St. Paul's Parish, having a lawful wife and having been admonished by the vestrymen of sd. parish on 6 March 1726, did on 1 July 1727 and at diverse other times, adulterously frequent the company of Jane Kennard then and yet being the wife of Nathaniel Kennard. Whereas St. Leger Codd produced a noli prosequi from his Excellency. (Proceeding ordered to cease by Leonard Calvert, asserting the case appeared to derive from prejudice and malice.){KECR JS#22:344}

At August Court 1728, Jane Kennard, wife of Nathaniel Kennard, was found guilty of assaulting Mary Codd, wife of St. Leger Codd, Esq., on 1 June 1728 at St. Paul's Parish and fined 250 lbs. of tob.{KECR JS#WK:16}

Nathaniel Kenward, KE Co., d. leaving a will dated 13 April 1742 and proved 3 Feb 1742. The heirs named were wife Jane, to whom was left personal estate and at her death it was to pass to youngest son John. To son Nathaniel was devised 75 a. of tract *Denby*; to son John was devised 141 a. of *Denby*. Wife and son John were named as execs. The will was witnessed by Caleb Beck, Joshua Beck, and Edward John Wright.{MWB 23:65}

Nathaniel and Jane were the parents of: NATHANIEL, b. 17 Nov 1718{KESH}; and JOHN.

4. JOHN KENNARD, son of Richard (2) and Mary, d. by 1772. He m. Ann (N).[29]

On 18 June 1762, Stephen Pasco, of KE Co., and bro. and heir of John Pasco, dec., conv. to John Kennard, son of Richard, part of a tract called *Cornwallis's Choice*, which John Salsbury and his wife Mary conv. to Sutton Quinney, 55 a.{KELR DD#1:83}

On 18 June 1762, John Kennard and his wife Ann, son of Richard of KE Co., conv. to Thomas and William Ringgold of Chester Town, a tract called *Doe Neck*, cont. by patent 200 a. excepting only 27 a., sold by Richard Kennard, father of the sd. John, to William Graves, and part of *Cornwallis's Choice*, 55 a., and also part of *Budds Discovery*, 20 a.{KELR DD#1:87}

John Kennard, of KE Co., d. by 1 April 1772, when his estate was appraised by James Smith and Samuel Merritt, and valued at £109.9.1. Richard Lloyd for William & James Anderson and Robert Anderson · signed as creditors. Stephen Kennard and Daniel Kennard signed as next of kin. Ann Kennard, admx., filed the inventory on 26 May 1772.{MINV 109:106}

In Nov 1772 the estate was again appraised by James Smith and Samuel Sterrett, and valued at £17.3.9. Robert Anderson and Richard Lloyd for Mr. James Anderson signed as creditors. Daniel Kennard and Stephen Kennard signed as next of kin. Ann Kennard, admx., filed the inventory on 17 Aug 1773.{MINV 113:11}

The estate was again appraised and valued at £9.2.2. Ann Kennard, extx., filed the inventory cont. a list of debts on 2 May 1774.{MINV 115:371}

On 1 April 1775, his estate was still another time appraised by Kirwan Wroth and William Apsley, and valued at £55.16.5. Richard Lloyd for Mr. James Anderson signed as creditor. Richard Kenard and Stephen Kenard signed as next of kin. William Kenard, admin., filed the inventory on 29 Dec 1775.{MINV 122:265}

5. MATHEW KENNARD, son of Richard (2) and Mary, d. by 14 May 1768. He m. Martha (N), who admin. the estate.

At June Court 1760, Mathew Kennard was fined for committing fornication on 1 April 1760 with Priscilla Dallihide. He entered into security to keep the child of Priscilla Dalluhide called HANNAH DAL-LAHIDE from becoming any charge to the county.{KECR JS#25:242A}

Mathew Kennard, of KE Co., d. by 14 May 1768, when his estate was appraised by James Smith and Richard Willis, and valued at £86.19.7. James Anderson and Thomas Ringgold & Co. signed as

---

[29] Possibly Ann Medford who m. (N) Kennard. See The Medford Family, in *Colonial Families of the Eastern Shore of Maryland*, Volume 1.

creditors. John Kinnard and Daniel Kinnard signed as next of kin. Martha Kennard, admx., filed the inventory on 6 Aug 1768.{MINV 95:285}

On 28 Jan 1769, the estate was appraised by James Smith and Richard Willis, and valued at £17.4.0. Martha Kennard, admx., filed the inventory mentioning John Kennard, Daniel Kennard, Thomas Ringgold & Co., and James Anderson on 25 Feb 1769.{MINV 99:125}

On 25 Jan 1769, distribution of the estate was made by Martha Kennard, admx.{BFD 5:138}

6. STEPHEN KENNARD, son of Richard (2) and Mary, was living in Oct 1762. He m. a dau. of Henrietta Gamble whose estate was distributed naming him a son-in-law.

On 11 Oct 1762, Richard Kennard, of KE Co. son and devisee of Richard Kennard, late of KE Co., dec., conv. to Stephen Kennard, of the same place, wheelwright, also son and devisee of the afsd. Richard Kennard, dec., the undivided 8th part of a tract called *Denby*.{KELR DD#1:167}

Henrietta Gamble, of KE Co., d. before 28 Feb 1768 when distribution of the estate was made by Stephen Kennard and Joseph Boone, execs. Legatees included her granddau. Rebeckar Kennard, and her son-in-law Stephen Kennard.{BFD 5:109}

Stephen was the father of: REBECKA.

7. THOMAS KENNARD, son of Richard (2) and Mary. d. by Sep 1771. He m. Sarah (N) who admin. the estate.

Kennard d. by 25 Sep 1771, when his estate was appraised by Charles Groome and Moses Alford, and valued at £671.2.6. Joseph Chaplin and William Ringgold signed as creditors. Stephen Kennard and Daniel Kennard signed as next of kin. Sarah Kennard, admx., filed the inventory on 30 Dec 1771.{MINV 107:275B}

The estate was later appraised and valued at £22.5.3. Sarah Kennard, admx., filed the inventory cont. a list of debts on 16 Oct 1772.{MINV 110:254}

On 16 Oct 1772, distribution of the estate was made by Mrs. Sarah Kennard, admx.{BFD 6:147}

8. HOWARD KENNARD, son of Richard (1) and Mary, d. by 27 May 1768. He m. Rachel (N) who admin. the estate.

On 27 May 1768, his estate was appraised by James Smith and Richard Willis, and valued at £76.13.0. James Anderson and Margaret Ashley signed as creditors. Michael Kinnard and Daniel Kinnard signed as next of kin. Rachel Kennard, admx., filed the inventory on 4 Aug 1768.{MINV 95:282}

The estate was again appraised by James Smith and Richard Willis, and valued at £3.1.6. James Anderson and Margaret Ashley signed as creditors. John Kennard and Michael Kennard signed as next of kin. Rachel Kennard, admx., filed the inventory on 15 March 1769.{MINV 98:279}

Later, the estate was appraised again and valued at £13.1.6. Rachel Kennard, admx., filed the undated inventory cont. a list of debts.{MINV 98:279}

9. NATHANIEL KENNARD, son of Richard (2) and Mary, d. by May 1768. He m. Mary (N) who admin. the estate.

Nathaniel Kinnard, Sr., of KE Co., d. by May 1768, when his estate was appraised by Luke Griffith and Robert Buchanan, and valued at £26.0.6. Mary Kinnard, admx., filed the inventory on 6 Aug 1768, mentioning Thomas Kinnard and Daniel Kinnard.{MINV 95:282}

The estate was again appraised and valued at £4.0.0. No creditors or next of kin listed. Mary Kennard, admx., filed the inventory cont. a list of debts on 6 Aug 1768.{MINV 97:248}

On 25 Feb 1769 distribution of the estate was made by Mary Kennard, admx.{BFD 5:144}

10. JOHN KENNARD, son of Nathaniel (3) and Jane, m. by April 1743, Jane (N).

In April 1743, John and Jane Kennard his wife, to his bro. Nathaniel Kennard, 18 a.{KELR JS#24:315}

Unplaced

KENNARD, (N), m. by 11 April 1688, Sarah, relict of Capt. Joseph Hopkins of CE Co.{INAC 9:508}

KENNARD, JANE, NATHANIEL KENNARD, and Jeremiah Covington, on 27 Nov 1744, gave bond that they would pay Ellinor and Sarah Cracknall (also given as Cracklin) each the sum of £21.16.6 due to them as the filial portion of the estate of John Cracklin [sic], their dec. father, at age 16.{KEBI JS#20:156}

KENNARD, JOHN, was b. c1720. On 20 Oct 1743, John Kennard, age c23, dep. regarding the bounds of a tract called *Beckworth;* he recalled being on the road and cutting down John March's hill when he heard ....{KELR JS#25:194}

KENNARD, JOHN, d. leaving a will dated 23 June 1769 and proved 22 July 1769. Mentioned were children Sarah, Owen, Dannis, and John.

Son John was named exec. The will was witnessed by John, Daniel and Joshua Kennard, and Alex. Cameron.{MWB 37:368}

On 20 Nov 1769, his estate was appraised by Robert Buchanan and Luke Griffith, and valued at £593.17.1. Thomas Ringgold & Co. and Thomas Smyth signed as creditors. Nathaniel Kennard and Sarah Kennard signed as next of kin. John Kennard, admin./exec., filed the inventory on 20 June 1770.{MINV 105:104}

KENNARD, MARY, of KE Co., d. leaving a will dated 30 Oct 1770 and proved 21 Jan 1774. The heirs named were sister Martha Kinnard (minor), to whom she devised ½ of the estate left by her father and now in her mother's hands, and sister Catherine Kinnard (minor). The extx. was mother Sarah Alford. The will was witnessed by Mary Sillavent and Kinvin Worth.{MWB 39:662}

On 8 June 1773, her estate was appraised by Robert Buchanan and Luke Griffith, and valued at £49.19.4. No creditors listed. Stephen Shinwood and Jean Williamson signed as next of kin. Daniel Kinnard, exec., filed the inventory on 10 June 1773.{MINV 114:236}

KENNARD, WILLIAM, was bur. 20 Oct 1698.{KESP}

KENNARD, WILLIAM, d. by 24 Dec 1714 when his estate was admin.{INAC 36B:235} Admin. William Hamstead filed the administration on 16 Aug 1715.{INAC 36C:125}

THE KENSLAGH FAMILY

1. DOMINICK KENSLAGH (KINGSLAUGH), progenitor, d. by 28 Aug 1733 when his administration was filed by exec. Dominick Kenslagh. John Kenslagh (son) signed as next of kin.{MINV 17:403}

He is probably the Dominick Kenslagh who m. by 30 Aug 1708, Margaret, admx. of Daniel Kelly of KE Co.{INAC 28:295}

At November Court 1726, Dominick Kenslaugh, of St. Paul's Parish, labourer, was charged after having been admonished by the Vestrymen, on 21 March 1725 and at diverse other times as a fornicator, of frequenting the company of Katharine Kelley, spinster. He was found not guilty.{KECR JS#22:226}

Dominick Kenslagh was the father of at least two children: DOMINICK; and JOHN.

2. DOMINICK KENSLAGH, son of Dominick, d. by April 1736.

Dominick Kenslagh (Kenslaugh), of St. Paul's Parish, d. leaving a will dated 7 March 1735 and proved 20 April 1736. To wife ———, he left 44 a., dwell. plant. called *Waxfield*, 30 a. *Bloomsbury*, and *Arcadia* beginning at the end of *New Forrest*. Should wife marry, she to have her thirds. Estate to be in hands of bro. John, exec., and divided among children. Wife to see that children are brought up in the Roman Catholic religion. To wife and children as afsd., tract called *The Second Vacation* added to *Bagley's Forrest*. The will was witnessed by Jacob Glen (Gleen), James Smith, Silvester Kelley, and John Puzey. {MWB 21:584}

3. JOHN KENSLAGH, son of Dominick, Sr., was b. c1709. On 7 March 1758, John Kenslaugh, age c49, dep. regarding the bounds of the tract called *Arcadia;* he recalled that within a short time after Morgan Hurtt, dec., was m. to the widow Brown, sd. Hurtt asked the deponent (John Kenslaugh) why he did not persuade Thomas Joce to settle the 2nd bounds of his land. {KELR JS#28:427}

John Kinslagh m. Rhoda (N).

Rhoda Kinslau, of KE Co., d. and her estate was appraised by James Dunn and James Frisby, and valued at £25.19.10. Thomas Smyth and Richard Gresham signed as creditors. Mary Whalan and Ann Kenslash signed as next of kin. Richard Kinslau, admin., filed the inventory on 13 March 1769. {MINV 98:280}

John and Rhoda Kenslagh were the parents of {KESP}: SARAH, b. 23 Aug 1741; JOHN, b. 16 Feb 1743-4; MARGRET, b. 24 July 1746; MARY, b. 20 Nov 1748; and MICHAEL, b. 12 Sep 1747.

Unplaced

KENSLAUGH, ELIZABETH, of St. Paul's Parish, spinster, at August Court 1738, was found guilty of committing fornication on 10 Oct 1737, and begetting a bastard child. She was fined £1.10. {KECR JS#22:30}

KENSLAGH, HELEN, and PAUL KENSLAUGH, were living as late as 1757.

On 15 Feb 1757, Helen Kinslaugh, of KE Co., conv. to her bro. Paul Kinslaugh of the same county, cooper, part of a tract called *Arcadia*. {KELR JS#28:324}

On 20 June 1757, Paul Kenslaugh, age c25, at the request of Healin Kenslaugh, dep. regarding the bounds of the tracts called *Arcadia* and *New Forrest*. {KELR JS#28:429}

On 18 Dec 1761, Paul Kenslaugh, age c28, dep. regarding the bounds of a tract called *Waxford*. {KELR DD#1:100}

THE STEPHEN KNIGHT FAMILY

1. STEPHEN KNIGHT m. Sarah Robinson on 24 Feb 1708 in St. Stephen's Parish, CE Co.{CECH:2} He m. as his 2nd wife, on 30 Nov 1731, Anne Seaton.{KESP}

On 2 Feb 1713, James Frisby, of CE Co., Gent., conv. to his bro.-in-law Stephen Knight of the county afsd., parcel of land called *Broad Oak*, 300 a.{KELR BC#1:5} On 9 Nov 1717, Stephen Knight, of CE Co., Gent., and his wife Sarah conv. to James Willson of KE Co., 300 a.{KELR BC#1:271}

On 25 June 1743, Stephen Knight, of KE Co., Gent., conv. to his dau.-in-law, Anne Frisby, wife of Peregrine Frisby, of CE Co., Gent., Lot no. 47 in Chester Town.{KELR JS#24:388}

On 15 Aug 1737, Stephen Knight, of KE Co., and his wife Anne, conv. to Anne Frisby of the same county, spinster, 2 lots in Chester, No. 45 and No. 46.{KELR JS#18:500}

Stephen Knight, of KE Co., d. leaving a will written 18 Oct 1742 and proved 21 March 1745. The heirs named were wife Ann Knight, extx., to whom he left real estate in KE Co. and elsewhere; grandson John Leach Knight, to whom he devised a house and lot in Chestertown; son William, his plate that is engraved with "my coat of arms," and slaves in Cecil; and slaves were bequeathed to dau. Mary Stokes, 2nd dau. Sarah Philips, and 3rd dau. Cordelia Knight. The will was witnessed by James Watson, John Watson, and Elizabeth Peavoll (Teoll?).{MWB 24:14}

Stephen Knight, by Sarah, was the father of{CECH:6, 10, 15, 18, 22}: WILLIAM, b. 9 Feb 1709; FRISBY, b. 15 April, bur. 26 April 1712; MARY, b. 11 Oct 1714, m. 31 Dec 1730 in St. Stephen's Parish, Humphrey Wells Stokes; JOHN, b. 18 Oct 1716; and SARAH, b. 1 April 1719.

By Ann (Seaton), Stephen Knight was the father of: STEPHEN, b. 27 Nov 1732, d. 15 March 1732.{KESP}

2. Dr. JOHN KNIGHT, of CE Co., son of Stephen Knight, m. Mary Thompson, dau. of Col. John Thompson, in St. Stephen's Parish, CE Co., on 15 May 1740.{CECH:8}

Dr. John Knight was the father of: JOHN LEACH, b. 27 March 174-.{CECH:47}

THE KNOWLMAN FAMILY

1. ANTHONY KNOWLMAN was transported to MD by 1674. At the same time Theophilus Knowlman, his wife Abigail, and son Theophilus were also transported.{MPL 18:150} Anthony d. by March 1715/6.

Anthony Knowlman (Knoulman) d. leaving a will dated 21 Dec 1714 and proved 9 March 1714 (1714/5). To son Anthony Knowlman, he left the dwell. plant., but if Anthony d. without issue, it was to pass to son Richard and in succession to son John Knowlman and to dau. Rachell. To (son) Richard, tract called *Knaves Choice* on Farloe Creek. To Eleanor Cole and Richard Cole, at day of freedom, personalty. The exec. was son Anthony afsd., who is to be of age at 18 years.{MWB 14:45}

Knowlman's estate was admin. by Josias Crouch on 21 April 1716. An inventory of £38/15/6 was shown. Payments were made to Rachel Knoulman (her part of her father's (unnamed) estate), John Taylar (guardian of Richard Knoulman) and to James Harris, Benjamin Griffith, and John March.{INAC 37A:111} The estate was admin. by Josias Crouch again on 16 June 1716, 20 March 1716 (1716/7), and 15 June 1717.{INAC 37A:111 and 39B:53, 70}

On 29 April 1721 his estate was admin. by Josias Crouch. Payments were made to Anthony Noteman [sic], son, and others.{MDAD 3:344}

Anthony Knowlman was the father of: ANTHONY; RICHARD; JOHN; and RACHEL.

2. ANTHONY KNOWLMAN, son of Anthony, was under 18 when his father made his will.

On 6 July 1720 Anthony Nowleman, son and heir of Anthony Nowleman, of KE Co., dec., conv. to James Harris of the same county, a tract called *Nowlemans Desire*, granted to sd. Nowleman, dec., by Michael Skidmore and his wife Judith on 10 Aug 1686, 100 a.{KELR JS#W:105}

Anthony Knowlman was the father of the following children, born in St. Paul's Parish{KESH}: ANTHONY, b. Aug 1727; and MARY, b. June 1728.

3. RICHARD KNOWLMAN, son of Anthony, was under age when his father made his will. He m. Jane, widow of George Hanson.

On 23 Feb 1730 Richard Knolman (Knoulman), of KE Co., and his wife Jane, widow of George Hanson, dec., claimed the third part of *Tolchester and Tomb* for Jane's dower, conveying land to Frederick Hanson.{KELR JS#16:120}

On 21 Nov 1737 Jane Knowlman, Nathaniel Hynson, and David Jones, of KE Co., gave bond they would pay Christina Hanson, one of the orphans of George Hanson, dec., £22.18, due her as a filial portion of the estate of George Hanson.{KEBI JS#18:104}

Richard Knowlman was listed in KE Co. Debt Books as paying taxes on *Tolchester and Tomb* in 1736 and 1737. He probably d. about the latter year as Jane Knowlman is listed as paying taxes on the same tracts in 1738 and 1739.{INKE:22}

4. ANTHONY KNOWLMAN, son of Anthony, was b. Aug 1727 in St. Paul's Parish.{KESH} He is almost certainly the Anthony Knowlman, age c39, who dep. on 16 July 1762.{KEEJ: John Carville}

On 4 Sep 1762, Anthony Knowlman, of KE Co., and his wife Prudence, conv. to Jervis James of the same place, a tract called *Niess Choice*, 100 a.{KELR DD#1:164}

THE LASSELL/LAZZELL FAMILY

1. MICHAEL LAZELL, d. c1742, having m. Martha Cook on 26 Dec 1705.{KESP}

The estate of Michael Lassell was appraised by P. Kennard and Francis Barney and the inventory filed on 16 May 1724. John James, "minor," signed as next of kin.{MINV 9:414}

Michael and Martha were the parents of: NATHANIEL; and (probably) THOMAS.

2. NATHANIEL LASSELL, orphan son of Michael, was under age in 1736, when on 19 June 1736, he was bound to Thomas Rouse, plasterer, until age 21, to the trade of plasterer.{KEBI JS#18:48}

3. THOMAS LASSELL, is placed as a son of Thomas, because Nathaniel Lassell signed his inventory as next of kin. He d. by March 1756. He m. Martha (N), who survived him.

On 23 March 1756 his estate was appraised by Paul Whichcote and James Smith, and valued at £77.6.8. Thomas Ringgold and William Wilmer signed as creditors. Nathaniel Lazzel and Ailse Reason signed as next of kin. Martha Lazel, admx., filed the inventory on 15 May 1756.{MINV 61:243}

The estate was appraised again and valued at £2.1.1. Martha Lazzel, admx./extx., filed the undated inventory cont. a list of debts.{MINV 63:376}

Distribution of the estate was made by Martha Lazell, admx. Distribution was made to widow (⅓) and the remainder equally to Mara, Martha, Hannah, John, and Thomas.{BFD 2:65}

Thomas and Martha Lassell were the parents of: MARA; MARTHA; HANNAH; JOHN; and THOMAS.

4. MARTHA LASSELL, dau. of Thomas and Martha, is probably the Martha who appeared in the following court cases:

On 19 Jan 1757 Martha Lassell confessed to fornication and proved the father. She was fined 30 s.{KECR JS#25:172A}

On 22 Jan 1757 William Smith, schoolmaster, and John Smith, offered security in the maintenance of the child of Martha Lassel.

William Smith paid the sum of 30 s. as a fine for guilt of bastardy.{KECR
JS#25:122B}

At March Court 1761, Martha Lazell was fined £3 for committing
fornication.{KECR DD#1:2B}

At August Court 1765, it was presented that Martha Lazell,
spinster, on 10 Oct 1764, committed fornication and begot a base born
child. She was fined £3 and ordered to give security to indemnify the
county from any charge that might accrue by means of this bastard
child called WILLIAM.{KECR DD#1:61B}

At November Court 1766, it was presented that John Earle, on 1
May 1765, committed fornication with Martha Lazell, Jr., and begot a
base born child. He was fined 30 s.{KECR DD#1:85B}

At November Court 1766, Martha Lazell, Jr., spinster, was charged
on 1 May 1766. She stated that she had been heretofore presented for
the same offense and hath paid her fine. The court agreed.{KECR
DD#1:86A}

At June Court 1767, it was presented that John Burk, Jr., on 1
March 1764, committed fornication with Martha Lazell and begot a
base born child. He fined 30 s.{KECR DD#1:88A}

THE LEATHERBURY FAMILY

1. THOMAS LEATHERBURY d. in Kent Co., DE, prior to 28 May
1745.

Thomas left a will dated 24 Feb 1742/3, proved on 28 May 1745. He
named his sons Charles, John, William, Jonathan, and Abel, and dau.
Mary. He mentioned his wife. Sons Charles and John were to be execs.
The will was witnessed by Jonathan Giffin, Matthew Parker, and
Thomas Parker.{Kent Co., DE, Will Book I:104-105}

Thomas Leatherbury was the father of: CHARLES; JOHN; WIL-
LIAM; JONATHAN; ABEL; and MARY, m. Luxe or Luke Miers.

2. CHARLES LEATHERBURY, son of Thomas (1), married and had
at least one son: THOMAS, named on 18 Oct 1773 in the will of
Charles' bro. William Leatherbury.{Kent Co., DE, Will Book L:144}

3. JOHN LEATHERBURY, son of Thomas (1), moved to KE Co., MD,
where he d. c1754.

John Leatherbury, bricklayer, of KE Co., left a will dated 23 Nov
1753 and proved in 1754. He named his bro. Abel Leatherbury, to
whom he devised land left him by his father, Thomas Leatherbury,
lying in Kent Co. on Delaware Bay. In his will he gave to Luke (Luxe)
Myers use of one slave woman and increase, during life of his sister
Mary Mires, wife of Luxe. He mentioned his bros. Jonathan, Abel,

William, and Charles. The will was witnessed by Solo. Wright, Sarah Porter, and Wm. Porter.{MWB 29:233}

John Leatherbury's estate was appraised by William Wilmer and James McLean, Jr. (also James McClean), and valued at £104.11.2. Abel Leatherbury and Andrew Hall signed as creditors. Abel Leatherbury and William Leatherbury signed as next of kin. Jonathon Leatherbury, exec., filed the inventory on 5 May 1755.{MINV 60:256}

4. WILLIAM LEATHERBURY, son of Thomas (1), d. in Kent Co., DE, by 17 Nov 1773. He m. Sarah (N).

William Leatherbury of Little Creek Hundred, Kent Co., DE, d. leaving a will dated 18 Oct 1773, proved 17 Nov 1773. He named his wife Sarah, sons William and Thomas, dau. Mary, and a cousin Thomas Leatherbury, son of bro. Charles. He mentioned the three children of his sister Mary Miers. Execs. were wife Sarah and John Brinckle. The will was witnessed by Christopher Deney, John McGear, and James Aaron.{Kent Co., DE, Will Book L:144}

William and Sarah were the parents of: WILLIAM; and THOMAS.

5. JONATHAN LEATHERBERRY, son of Thomas (1), settled in KE Co., MD, where he d. by May 1772. He m. Mary (N), who survived him.

Jonathan Leatherberry, farmer, of KE Co., d. leaving a will dated 14 Sep 1770 and proved 9 May 1772. Mentioned were wife Mary, son Perigrine, and bro. Able Leatherberry. The estate included a lot in Chester Town. Mary and Perigrine Leatherberry were named as execs. The will was witnessed by William Bordley, Elizabeth Bordley, and A. Bordley.{MWB 38:576}

On 23 Sep 1772 his estate was appraised by James McClean and James Claypool, and valued at £342.1.9. Smith & Ringgold and Thomas Smyth signed as creditors. Sarah Piner and Mary Leatherbury signed as next of kin. Peregrine Leatherbury, exec., filed the inventory on 8 May 1773.{MINV 111:323}

Jonathan and Mary (N) Leatherwood were the parents of: PEREGRINE, b. 1 Aug 1752 (represented KE Co. in the 6th to 8th Conventions of 1775-1776.{KESP; BDML}

Unplaced

LEATHERBURY, RICHARD, John Wickes, and William Jackson were charged at August Court 1771 with having assaulted Thomas Welch. Each was fined 1 s.{KECR DD#1:138A}

216

THE LINEGAR FAMILY

Refs.: A: Barnes; *Baltimore Co. Families, 1659-1759.*

1. JOHN LINEGAR was in BA Co. by 24 Sep 1683 when he surveyed 200 a., *John's Habitation*. The tract was later held by Stephen Bentley for Linehar's orphans.

John was the father of{A:404}: GEORGE; (N), son, who "went to remote parts and was unheard of;" (N), dau.; and (N), dau.

2. GEORGE LINEGAR, son of John, moved to KE Co., MD, and d. by 3 Nov 1758. He m. Sarah (N) who was still alive on 3 Nov 1758.{KELR JS#29:60} Sarah was b. c1697 as Sarah Linegar. She dep. cApril 1759, age c62.{KEEJ: Thomas Harris}

On 16 Aug 1739, George Leneger and his wife Sarah, being desirous to give encouragement to the Christian religion, grant to Rev. George William Forester, minister of Shrewsberry Parish, and his successors, 2 a., part of a tract called *Spring Garden*.{KELR JS#22:486}

In 1749 he purchased *Angels Lot* from Simon Wilmer.

George Linegar, of KE Co., d. leaving a will dated 11 Dec 1756 and proved 29 Oct 1757. The heirs named were children John Linegar, "now absent," Ann Frewharty (Flamarty, Flanarty), Sarah Poor, Rebecca Sappington, George Linegar, and Elizabeth Williams, whose husband John Williams was absent, having left her in distress and by report was shot in the army, gone to the northward. Mentioned was land next to the chapel called *Spring Garden* and *Back Lingan* on a branch of Gunpowder River, in BA Co., Back River. Wife Sarah Linegar and son Jacob were named as execs. Also mentioned was Rebecca Flaharty, dau. of James, and wife Ann. The will was witnessed by Adam Little, Wilson Forester (or Forrester), John Winefred, Daniel Massey, and Jacob Caulk.{MWB 30:415}

George was the father of: JOHN; ANN, wife of (N) Frewharty (Flamarty, Flanarty); REBECCA, wife of (N) Sappington; GEORGE; JACOB; and SARAH, m. by 24 March 1746, James Power of CE Co.{A:cites BALR TB#E:537}

3. JACOB LINEGAR, son of George, m. by 3 Nov 1758, Grace (N).

On 3 Nov 1758, Jacob Lineger, of KE Co., and his wife Grace, conv. to Daniel Massey, innholder, part of two tracts, one being part of *Spring Garden*, the other all that part of *Angels Lott* which was sold by Simon Wilmer to George Lineger, father to afsd. Jacob in 1749. The deed reserved the dower right to Sarah Linger, mother of afsd. Jacob Linger.{KELR JS#29:60}

On 19 June 1764, Jacob Lenegar, of KE Co., and his wife Grace, conv. to James Flaharty, another part of *Spring Garden*.{KELR DD#1:582}

Jacob Linger (Linegar), of KE Co., d. by 6 Oct 1767. His estate was appraised by William Blackiston and John Clarke, and valued at £38.14.0. Thomas Ringgold & Co. for Sedgley Hill House at Randulph signed as creditor. Sarah Wenthad and Michael Flaherty signed as next of kin. Grace Linegar, admx., filed the inventory on 6 Oct 1767.{MINV 94:96}

On 15 June 1768 a list of debts was appraised and valued at £1.1.0. Grace Linegar, admx., filed the list.{MINV 97:212}

On 15 June 1768 distribution of the estate was made by Grace Linegar, admx.{BFD 5:88}

THE EDWARD LOWDER FAMILY

1. EDWARD LOWDER was in KE Co. by 1676, and d. by Oct 1682.

On 27 June 1676, Desboro Bennet recorded a calf given by him to Charles, son of Edward and Ann Lowder.{ARMD LIV:343, Liber C:73}

On 31 Oct 1682, Isaac Winchester, of KE Co., cordwinder, conv. to Edward James of the county afsd., and after his decease, to Edward Lowder son to Edward Lowder, late of KE Co., dec., parcel called *Isaacs Chance*.{KELR R:30B}

Edward was the father of at least two children: CHARLES, v. c1671; and EDWARD.

2. CHARLES LOWDER, son of Edward and Ann, was b. c1671. As Charles Lowder, of QA Co., he gave his age as 51 in 1722.{Peden, MD Deponents, 1634-1799:120} He d. by Nov 1728. He m. 1st, Rachel (N), and 2nd, Joan (N), who survived him. She was b. c1684 and gave her age as 60 in 1724.{QALR RT#1:27}

On 30 June 1702 Edward James of TA Co. made a will. In it he left to Charles Lowder and hrs., 300 a., *"James' Camp,"* KE Co.{MWB 3:272}

On 18 March 1704, Charles Lawder, of KE Co., and his wife Rachal, conv. to Thomas Weyat, Jr., tract called *Constantinople*, 100 a.{KELR JD#1:151}

In 1706, Charles Lowder, of KE Co., and his wife Rachel, and Edward Elliott and his wife Mary, conv. to Philip Copedge of TA Co., 200 a.{KELR GL#1:116/140}

On May 24 1708 Charles Lowder and wife Rachel conv. to John Swift 50 a. called *Chance*, on the s. side of Chester River.{QALR ETA: 87}

On Apr 12 1709 Philip Copege rescinded the deed made by Charles Lowder and wife Rachel, and Edward Elliott of KE Co. and Mary his wife when they conv. him 200 a. in Kent Co. south side of Chester River called *Fork*.{QALR ETA: 36}

At June Court 1710 Charles Lowther [sic] set forth that the petitioner had a kinswoman at Doctor Thomas Goodman's. She was now of age and was still detained. He asked that she be released. The court ordered that she continue to serve until age 21, now being 17 years old.{QAJU ET No.B:75}

Charles Lowder was in QA Co. by 3 Oct 1716 when he witnessed the will of Solomon Wright.{MWB 14:330}

Lowder d. in QA Co. leaving a will dated 23 Sep 1728 and proved 29 Nov 1728. He named his wife Joan and son Charles as execs., and dau. Jane Lizenby (and her son Charles Lizinby), as well as daus. Sarah and Ann. Humphrey Wells and Daniel Newman were witnesses.{MWB 19:564}

Charles Lowder was the father of: CHARLES; JANE, wife of (N) Lizenby; SARAH; and ANN.

3. EDWARD LOWDER, son of Edward, d. by 24 Feb 1712. He left a son: EDWARD.

4. CHARLES LOWDER, son of Charles (2), was named in his father's will. He m. Anne Sutton on 2 March 1730 in St. Luke's Parish, QA Co.{ESVR 2:27}

On 7 March 1734 Charles Lowder and his wife Anne conv. to Daniel Newnam, Jr., 100 a. called *James's Choice*.{QALR RTA:370}

Charles and Anne were the parents of: SUTTON, b. 13 Jan 1738 in St. Luke's Parish.{QALU}

5. EDWARD LOWDER, son of Edward (3), was living in New Castle co., DE [then PA] on 24 Feb 1712 when as Edward Lowder of Duck Creek in New Castle Co., PA [DE], weaver, he conv. to Timothy Matthews of Kent Island, 40 a. on Kent Island called *Isaac's Chance*. Edward Lowder gave power of attorney to his uncle Charles Lowder of QA Co.{QALR ETA:142}

THE RICHARD LOWDER FAMILY

1. RICHARD LOWDER immigrated prior to 1664.{MPL 7:490} He m. 1st, Carolina (N), and 2nd, by 1690, Susannah (N).

On 20 April 1670 Richard Pether of KE Co., taylor, and his wife Mary, conv. to Jacob Jonson and Richard Lowder, both of KE Co., 300 a. of *Ruerden* on n. side of Chester River, e. side of Langford's Bay. {TALR 1:124}

On 1 Aug 1683, Richard Lowder, of KE Co., and his wife Carolina, conv. to William Young, of the afsd. county, 33 a., called *Green Branch*.{KELR K:65}

Richard Lowder d. leaving a will dated 3 Dec 1696 and proved 22 Feb 1696. To wife Susan, extx., plant. *Green Branch*. To son Richard, afsd. plant. at death of wife. To dau. Mary, 40 a. on other side of Branch.{MWB 7:278}

The estate was admin. on 30 Dec 1697.{INAC 15:306}

On 10 Aug 1702, Susanna, wife of Benjamin Ricaud, admin. the estate of Richard Louden [sic]. Assets of £84.2.6 and 6604 lbs. tob. were mentioned.{INAC 23:92}

On 12 May 1739, John Derrick, of KE Co., innholder, and his wife Susannah, conv. to Mary Hanson, dau. of afsd. Susannah, a messuage and land called ...? which Richard Lowder, late of the county afsd., dec., by his last will dated 20 Dec 1696 devised to afsd. Susannah during her natural life.{KELR JS#22:429}

Richard and Susanna were the parents of at least two children{KESP}: MARY, b. 14 Feb 1690 (may have m. (N) Hanson); and RICHARD, b. 15 Dec 1695.

Unplaced

LAUDER, ISABELLA, of St. Paul's Pariah, spinster, servant of George Copper, at June Court 1730, was charged that on 10 June 1729 she committed fornication and begot a bastard child. She was ordered to receive 21 lashes.{KECR JS#WK:127}

THE MacCATEE FAMILY

1. PATRICK MACCATEE, of KE Co., d. on 25 May 1765, He m. Eleanor (N), who survived him.

McCatee left a will dated 30 Aug 1763 and proved 6 June 1765. In his will he mentioned his wife Eleanor and children Andrew, Margaret, Elizabeth, Sarah, and George Maccatee. His wife Eleanor Maccatee was extx. The will was witnessed by Bridget Dougherty, Robert Corman, and John Calconer. On 26 May 1765 came Collen Furgeson, Patrick Craig, and made oath that in the presence of Ann Little and James Sweney they did hear Patrick Maccatee declare that every item relating to George Maccatee, dec., should be the property of his dau. Catharine Maccatee.{MWB 33:224}

Patrick McIntee [sic], of KE Co., d. by 12 March 1767, when his estate was appraised by Daniel Massy and Henry Clarke, and valued at £421.7.8. Thomas & George Gilpin and Callin Ferguson signed as creditors. James Sweney and James Gray signed as next of kin. Patt. Fowler, admin., filed the inventory on 15 Jun 1767.{MINV 92:116}

Patrick Maccatee's estate was appraised and valued at £139.3.0. Patrick Fowler, admin., filed the inventory cont. a list of debts on 25 May 1768.{MINV 97:208}

Patrick and Eleanor MacCatee were the parents of{KESH}: JAMES, b. 6 March 1749; CATHERINE, b. 20 Sep 1750; ANDREW; MARGARET; ELIZABETH; SARAH; and GEORGE.

2. ANDREW MCENTEE (MACCATEE), son of Patrick, of KE Co., d. by 28 Nov 1768, when his estate was appraised by David Massey and Henry Clark, and valued at £17.0.0. James Swaney, admin., filed the inventory on 21 Jun 1769. Mentioned were David Speer and Sarah Gray.{MINV 101:71}

Another appraisal was made and valued at £90.0.0. No creditors listed. James Sweaney and his wife, Elisabeth Sweaney, admins., filed the inventory cont. a list of debts on 3 Aug 1771.{MINV 107:114}

On 31 Aug 1771 distribution of his estate was made by James Sweeney and his wife Elisabeth Sweeney.{BFD 6:141}

3. GEORGE MCENTEE (MACCATEE), son of Patrick, of KE Co., d. by 28 Nov 1768, when his estate was appraised by David Massey and Henry Clark, and valued at £68.0.0. James Swaney, admin., filed the inventory on 21 Jun 1769. Mentioned were David Speer and Sarah Gray.{MINV 101:70}

THE MANN FAMILY

1. JOSEPH MANN d. by 2 March 1748. He m. Ann Van Sant, sister of Cornelius Van Sant. She m. 2nd, Nicholas Smith, and d. by 10 May 1776.

At August Court 1747, it was presented that Joseph Mann, on 1 May 1744, stole an iron chaine and ball of a well buckett of Walter Odogherty. He was acquitted.{KECR JS#24:394}

Joseph Man, of KE Co., d. leaving a will dated 19 Feb 1748 and proved 2 March 1748. The heirs named were eldest son Joseph, to whom was devised the dwell. plant.; 2nd son George Van Sant, to whom was devised a tract called *The Forest*, 60 a.; eldest dau. Mary; and 2nd dau. Sarah. Wife Ann and her bro. Cornelius Van Sant were named as execs. The will was witnessed by Lewis Williams (Quaker), Peter Ade, and Nichs. Smith.{MWB 26:84}

On 12 Apr 1749, his estate was appraised by C. Comegys and William Smith, and valued at £452.15.5. Wlliam Smithers and Lewis Williams signed as creditors. George Vansant and Cornelius Vansant signed as next of kin. William Man, exec., filed the inventory on 15 May 1749.{MINV 39:26}

His estate was again appraised by E. Comegys and William Smith, and valued at £123.17.7. Lewis Williams and D. Bryane signed as creditors. George Vansant and Cornelius Vansant signed as next of kin. Ann Smith, wife of Joseph Smith, admin., filed the inventory on 1 May 1750.{MINV 43:431}

His estate was again appraised and valued at £66.12.5. No creditors or next of kin listed. The undated inventory cont. a list of debts was filed on 11 April 1751.{MINV 47:116}

On 30 April 1751 distribution was made by Nicholas Smith and Ann his wife, execs.{BFD 1:1}

Ann Smith, of KE Co., d. before 10 May 1776. Distribution of the estate was made by George Vansant Mann, exec. Legatees (grandchildren) were Elisabeth Woodall, Ann Woodall, William Knock, John Blackiston, and Sarah Mann. Residue to George Vansant Mann.{BFD 7:58}

Joseph and Ann Man (Mann) were the parents of{KESB}: MARY, b. 28 April 1742; JOSEPH, b. 4 Jan 1743/4; SARAH, b. 12 Oct 1745; and GEORGE VANSANT, b. 13 Aug 1747.

2. JOSEPH MANN, son of Joseph and Ann, was b. 4 Jan 1743/4, and d. by June 1774. He m. Ann (N), who survived him.

Joseph Mann, of KE Co., d. leaving a will dated 1 May 1774 and proved 14 June 1774. The heirs named were son Joseph Mann (minor), dau. Sarah Mann, and wife Ann Mann, extx. The will was witnessed by Isaac Boyer, Th. Boyer, and Richard Peacock.{MWB 39:778}

On 5 Aug 1774, his estate was appraised by John Eccleston and Ebenezar Reyner, and valued at £523.4.11. Joseph Gilpin and William-har Beston signed as creditors. George Mann and Ann Smith signed as next of kin. Ann Man, admx., filed the inventory on 15 Sep 1774.{MINV 118:247}

On 6 May 1775, the estate was again appraised by John Eccleston and Ebenezar Reyner, and valued at £276.3.9. Gilpin & Jurey and George Mann signed as creditors. George Mann and Mary Woodall signed as next of kin. Ann Man, extx., filed the inventory on 22 Aug 1775.{MINV 122:78}

Joseph Mann and wife Ann were the parents of: SARAH; and JOSEPH (a minor in 1774).

3. GEORGE VANSANT MANN, son of Joseph and Ann, was b. 13 Aug 1747. During the Revolutionary War he was a private in the KE Co. Militia. He and George Jackson were charged with selling grain to the British in 1780. Jackson was acquitted, but Mann was sent to prison in Baltimore.{RPKE:167}

THE MANSFIELD FAMILY

1. ROBERT MANSFIELD d. by 7 May 1737. He m. and had at least five children.

Robert Mansfield d. leaving a will dated 3 Sep 1735 and proved 7 May 1737. To two sons Robert and Samuel, execs., dwell. plant. called *Seward's Hope*. To four children Robert, Samuel, Mary, and Rachel, personal estate. Dau. Rachel and her estate in be in the care of dau. Ann George.{MWB 21:788}

The inventory of the estate was made on 23 May 1737 and filed on 30 July 1737. Mentioned were Samuel Wallis, John Wallis, John Hurt, Lawrence Neal, James Cruikshank, and Robert George. The admins./execs. were Robert Mansfield and Samuel Mansfield.{MINV 22:379}

Robert was the father of: ROBERT; SAMUEL; ANN, m. (N) George; MARY; and RACHEL.[30]

2. ROBERT MANSFIELD, son of Robert, was named exec. of his father's will. He m. Jemimah Coe on 13 Nov 1740.{KESH}

Robert and Jemima were the parents of: JOHN, b. 25 Dec 1741.{KESH}

3. SAMUEL MANSFIELD, son of Robert, was named exec. of his father's will. He was b. c1715. Samuel Mansfield, age c47, dep. on 21 July 1762.{KEEJ: Christopher Bellican} Samuel Mansfield and Mary Piner m. 16 Jun 174-.{KESH}

At June Court 1756, Samuel Mansfield confessed to fornication and was fined 30 s. and entered into security with Peter Massey, Sr., to pay to keep the child of Elizabeth Stewart called LUTITIA STEWARD.{KECR JS#25:150A}

Samuel Mansfield, of KE Co., d. by 9 March 1773, when his estate was appraised by H. Maawell [sic] and Hezekiah Cooper, and valued at £206.8.3. John Lambert Wilmer and Donaldson Yeates signed as creditors. Mary Mansfield and Ann Mansfield signed as next of kin. Samuel Mansfield, admin., filed the inventory on 9 Aug 1773.{MINV 114:201}

Samuel and Mary were the parents of: SAMUEL, b. 5 Jan 1744/5; and MARY, b. 3 Jan 1746/7.{KESH}

THE McCAN FAMILY

1. EDWARD MACAN d. by May 1742. He m. by 18 Jan 1708, Elisabeth, extx. of David Murphey, of KE Co.{INAC 29:82}

---

[30] Robert Mansfeild and Saml. Mansfeild of KE Co. gave bond on 20 June 1739 they would pay Rachel Mansfeild £28.18.3 and 3 farthings as her filial portion of the estate of Robert Mansfeild, her dec. father. {KEBI JS#18:208}

Edward McCann d. leaving a will dated 7 March 1728 and proved 22 May 1742. To wife Elizabeth, extx., and children James, Edward, Ann and Eleanor, the entire estate. The will was witnessed by David Perkins and Barth Buxton.{MWB 22:488}

Edward and Elizabeth Macan were the parents of{KESH}: JAMES, b. 5 March 1709; ELIZABETH, b. 9 Feb 1712; MARGRETT, b. 23 Sep 1715; ANN, b. 28 Jan 1716/7; and EDWARD, b. 24 May 1719.

2. EDWARD MCCANN, son of Edward and Elizabeth McCann, was b. 24 May 1719. Edward McCann, age c58, on 22 Aug 1774, dep. In a second deposition he stated that John Worthington kept school and that his sister went there to school and boarded at Mr. Earl's, and it was commonly reported that Mr. Worthington was either half-bro. or bro.-in-law to Daniel Mullican.{KEEJ: John Comegys} He m. 1st, Ann (N), who d. 29 Dec 1748. Edward m. 2nd, Sarah (N), who d. 18 Jan 1765.{KESH}

At August Court 1740, it was presented that Edward McCann, Jr., on 10 Aug 1740, assaulted Benjamin Palmer.{KECR JS#23:122}

At August Court 1741, it was presented that Edward McCan, on 10 Aug 1741, stole 50 lbs. of tob. of Tarrance Grimes. He was acquitted.{KECR JS#23:211}

Edward McCann and wife Ann were parents of{KESH}: JAMES, b. 31 Nov 1743; and JERVIS, b. 16 May 1745.

By Sarah, Edward was the father of{KESH}: ELIZABETH OGLEBY, b. 13 March 1762; and EDWARD, b. 22 Feb 1764.

3. JARVIS McCANN, son of Edward and Ann, was b. 16 May 1745, and d. before 31 Jan 1775 when his inventory was filed. His estate was appraised by Vincent Heatcheson and William Maxwell, and valued at £4.5.0. Edward McCann, admin., filed the inventory on 31 Jan 1775, mentioning Andrew Hickman, Jonathon Worth, and John Nicholson.{MINV 121:258}

THE MONK FAMILY

1. HENRY MONK, d. by 24 April 1735. He m. Honour Connor on 2 Dec 1708.{KESP}

Henry was in TA Co. by 26 May 1701 when he witnessed the will of Philip Connor of Kent Island, TA Co.{MWB 11:350} By 29 Dec 1704 he had moved to KE Co., where he witnessed the will of John Hinson of KE Co.{MWB 3:656}

Henry Monk, innholder, of Chester Town, d. leaving a will dated 24 March 1734 and proved 24 April 1735. To wife Honour, extx., he left dwell. house and lot No. 47. At her decease dwell. house to son Henry and residue of lot divided among three sons Henry, James, and John, and grandson William (son of son William). Should all die, to pass to dau. Elizabeth, wife of Thomas Rouss (plaisterer). To son William, 1 s.{MWB 21:417}

Henry and Honour were the parents of{KESP}: WILLIAM, b. 9 Sep 1709; JOHN, b. 18 Dec 1711; bapt. 22 June 1712; ELIZABETH, b. 21 March 1713; m. Thomas Rouse in 1728; and HENRY, b. 31 May 1716.

2. WILLIAM MONK, son of Henery and Honour Monk, was b. 9 Sep 1709. He m. Margrett Brooks on 1728.{KESP}

He and his wife had at least one son, named in Henry Monk's will: WILLIAM.

Unplaced

MONK, ELIZABETH, spinster, was charged at November Court 1740 for assaulting Jane Davis on 1 Nov 1740. Monk was fined 10 s.{KECR JS#23:170}

MONK, GILBERT, and Margrett Bullock were m. 12 Feb 1703. He is probably the Gilbert who m. Mary Kelly on 25 May 1708.{KESP}

THE ABRAHAM MORGAN FAMILY

1. ABRAHAM MORGAN was living c1662/3.

On 8 Aug 1692 Hugh Mackgregory of CE Co. confirmed power of attorney to his wife Elizabeth, to collect debts and make sale of his property. On 5 Jan 1694 she conv. in exchange of land in Bohemia River in CE Co., 200 a. called *Mulberry Mold* which was made 29 or 30 years ago by Abraham Morgan, Sr. and his wife with James Mackgregory then of TA Co., her husband's father and also in consequence of 5500 lbs. of tobacco paid by Abraham Morgan, Jr., conveyed land in Michaells River on e. side at the mouth of Halling Creek of 100 a. and another tract on e. side of Michaells River on Harbour Rouse Creek, 110 a.{TALR 7:145}

Abraham had at least one son: ABRAHAM.

2. ABRAHAM MORGAN, son of Abraham, m. Elizabeth, dau. of Bryan Omealy. He is probably the Abraham Morgan who d. 10 Sep 1715.{TAPE} Abraham Morgan and Eliza: Jenkinson were to marry pm opr about 2 da., 5 mo., 1686.{TATH}

Abraham and wife Elizabeth, on 30 Dec 1686 conv. to Walter Quinton 150 a., part of 400 a. called *Gouldesbrough* in Tredhaven Creek.{TALR 5:73}

On 13 June 1696 Ralph Dawson, Jr. and John Dawson acknowledged to John Edmondson, Ralph Fishbourne, William Sharpe, William Dixon and Abraham Morgan, execs. of the will of Bryan Omealy, receipt for £351 and a silver tankard in the right of their wives, daus. of Bryan Omealy.{TALR 7:172}

John Edmondson of Tred Haven Creek, TA Co., d. leaving a will dated 9 Oct 1697. In his will he left 800 a. jointly to Philip, James, and Abraham Morgan, Jr. Edmondson also named his son Abraham Morgan and wife Eliza.{MWB 6:95}

Abraham and Eliza were the parents of: ABRAHAM, Jr.;[31] PHILIP; and JAMES.

3. PHILIP MORGAN, son of Abraham and Elizabeth, is probably the Philip who d. by 18 Aug 1747. He m. Sarah Jadwyn, dau. of (N) Jadwyn. on or about 31 da., 10 mo., 1707.

On 1 da., 5 mo., 1708. Third Haven Monthly Meeting noted that there was some difference between the trustees of John Jadwyn and Phillip Morgan who m. Sarah, dau. of sd. John Jadwyn, about the taking of inventory, the death of a Negro and the loss of some corn. On 28 da., 6 mo., 1712 Third Haven Monthly Meeting noted that many great and disorderly differences have a long time continued between Philip Morgan and his wife [Sarah] notwithstanding care and labour at sundry times to reclaim them. {TATH}

On 17 Sep 1719 Philip and Sarah conv. to John Sprignall 100 a. called *Chestnut Bay,* part of 100 a. which fell to Philip and Sarah Morgan by the will of her father, (N) Jadwyn's will.{TALR 12:382}

Sarah m. 2nd (N) Kindred. On 18 Aug 1747. Sarah Kindred, age 53, affirmed that it was 40 years and no more next Feb since she was married to her first husband Philip Morgan and that David Arey was m. to Elizabeth Cook some time the four part of the same winter and that their dau. Esther Arey was not born until some considerable time after David and Elizabeth were m.{TALR 17:117}

Philip and Sarah (Jadwin) Morgan had at least one son: ENOCH.

4. ENOCH MORGAN, son of Philip and Sarah, d. by 10 Oct 1767. He m. on 3 July 1742, at Tuckaho Meeting Sarah Neall.{TATH}

On 5 Nov 1762 Enoch Morgan and his wife Sarah, and Jonathan Airey of QA Co., conv. to John Jenkinson and Joseph Berry, 3 a., part of *Parrott's Lott* whereon the Tuckahoe Meeting House and graveyard now stands, for the use of the people called Quakers.{TALR 19:190}

---

[31] He may be the Abraham Morgan noted by Third Haven MM on 26 da., 12 mo., 1723, as having been removed by death. {TATH}

On 29 da. 3 mo., 1764 Tuckaho Meeting reported that Enoch Morgan has for a long time neglected attending meetings and has been guilty of drinking to excess.{TATH}

Enoch left at least one son: HENRY.

5. HENRY MORGAN, eldest son of Enock Morgan, who was heir to Phillip Morgan and his wife Sarah, dau. and legatee of John Jadwin, on 10 Oct 1767 confirmed to Henry Baker of CE Co. and Francis Baker of TA Co., merchant, power of attorney to collect rents and debts, in MD, PA (including the lower three counties).{TALR 19:448}

THE ANDREW MORGAN FAMILY

1. ANDREW MORGAN settled in KE Co. some time before 17 April 1699 when he was bur.{KESP}

Andrew Morgan and wife Mary were the parents of{KESP}: MARY, b. 11 Jan 1694; and WILLIAM, b. 27 Nov 1697, bapt. 1 Jan 1698.

THE HENRY MORGAN FAMILY

1. HENRY MORGAN was b. c1613/16, and d. in MD by 18 May 1675. Henry Morgan, age c42, dep. on 1 Feb 1655.{ARMD LIV:50, Liber A:115} Henry Morgan, age c40, dep. on 1 Nov 1656.

Henry Morgan m. Frances (N), b. c1625. Mrs. Francis Morgan, age c30, dep. on 1 Jan 1655. (Signed with the mark of Francis Morgan.){ARMD LIV:42, Liber A:110} She d. c1672, having m. 2nd, Jonathan Sybray, who d. c1684.{BDML}

Henry Morgan of the Island of Kent, transported himself into the province in 1637. He was granted 100 a. on the Island adjoining his plant. on 17 Aug 1650.{ARMD LIV:5, Liber A:44}

On 12 Oct 1658, a parcel of land called *Morgans Neck* lying on St. Michael's River was laid out for Henry Morgan of the Isle of Kent, Gent. This was in consideration that Henry Morgan, Gent., transported Edwd. Parks, John Watts, and Ann Grosse.{MPL Q:360}

Although evidently illiterate, Henry Morgan was Sheriff of KE Co., 1648-1651, and represented KE Co. in the Lower House of the Assembly, 1659/60.{BDML}

On 24 Sep 1668 William Head, of the Isle of Kent, conv. to Jonathan Sibery, land of Henry Morgan, late of the Isle of Kent, dec., "sold about 6 years ago to me," 300 a. called *Morgan St. Michells*.{TALR I:54}

The inventory of the estates of Mr. Henry Morgan and Frances Morgan was taken on 18 May 1675 by Richard Wollman and Philemon Lloyd, appraised at 772,174 lbs. tob., and filed on 22 March 1675.{INAC 1:592}

Henry Morgan was the father of (notations on the margin suggest that son Henry d. in 1674 at age 23 and that first dau., Barbary, d. in 1667 at age 13){ARMD LIV:38, 129, 130, 186, Liber A:107, Liber B:34, 74; BDML}: HENRY, b. 28 Jan 1651; BARBARY, b. 28 July 1654, bur. 5 Sep 1658; FRANCES, (dau.), b. 1 Oct 1656, d. 1698, m. Peter Sayer; MARGRETT, b. 29 March 1659, bur. 5 Sep 1659; and BARBARY, b. 5 Nov 1660, m. 1st, by 1677, John Rousby, and 2nd, Richard Smith who d. 1714.

THE JOHN MORGAN FAMILY

1. JOHN MORGAN, d. cJan 1727. He m. 1st, (N), and 2nd, Mary.
   On 5 March 1722 John Morgan and his wife Mary conv. to Charles and Samuel Morgan, his two sons by a former wife, both of TA Co., 200 a. called *Dudley's Clifts*, formerly laid out for Richard Dudley on a branch of Tuckahoe Creek.{TALR 13:49B}
   On 6 March 1722 John Morgan and his wife Mary conv. land to James Morgan, eldest son of John; James to relinquish all other rights to other lands of John Morgan reserved to his younger children, and James conv. part of two tracts: *Morgan's Neglect* and *Morgan's Addition* at the head of Brewer's Branch, Wye River.{TALR 13:50B}
   John Morgan, planter, of TA Co., died leaving a will dated 1 Jan 1727 and proved 16 Feb 1731. The heirs named were eldest son James, 120 a. of dwelling plantation ---. To sons Charles and Samuel, "*Dudley's Clifts*," bou. of Richard Dudley, Sr. To wife Mary, 1/3 personal estate absolutely and use of all lands not yet disposed of during life; at her decease to pass to sons Hugh and Robert and their hrs. To granddau. Cicelia Williams, 1s. To 6 child., viz., James, Charles, Samuel, Hugh, Elizabeth and Robert, residue of personal estate. The execs. were wife and son James. The will was witnessed by Nicholas Brown, John Rathall (Rathell) and John Karby. {MWB 20:342}
   John was the father of: JAMES; CHARLES; SAMUEL; HUGH; ROBERT; and ELIZABETH.

2. CHARLES MORGAN, son of John (1), was living as late as Nov 1737. He m. Elinor (N).
   Charles Morgan purch. 95 a. of *Chestnut Bay* on 2 Nov 1737 from Philip Jenkins (Jenkinson) and his wife Sarah.{TALR 14:280}
   On 2 Nov 1737 Charles Morgan and his wife Elinor and his bro. Samuel Morgan con. to Philip Jenkinson 16 a., part of *Dudley's Clifts*

on e. side of Deep Branch, an arm of the Tuckahoe Mill Branch near the backside of Thomas Thompson's plantation.{TALR 14:283}

Charles Morgan, of TA Co. d. leaving a will dated 18 July 1755 and proved 27 Nov 1759. Wife Ellinor. Children Charles, Hugh, Jacob, Elizabeth and Eleanor. Grandchildren: Charles and Mark Rux. Brother Samuel Morgan. Tracts: *Dudley Cliff*, purchased of Philip Jenkins, and *Chestnut Coy*. Extx. Ellinor Morgan. Wit: Abner Turner (Quaker), Wm. Lane, Thomas Tharp.{MWB 30:739}

Elinor Morgan, of TA Co. d. leaving a will dated 29 Jan 1760, proved 15 April 1760. Children mentioned were: Charles, Jacob, and Elizabeth. Exec. Abner Turner. Wit: Thomas Beall, David Kerby, Ann Evins.{MWB 30:55}

Charles and Ellinor Morgan were the parents of: CHARLES; HUGH; JACOB; ELIZABETH; and ELEANOR, m. (N) Fallowfield.[32]

3. SAMUEL MORGAN, son of John (1), was living in July 1752.

On 21 July 1752 Samuel Morgan of KE Co., PA [DE], carpenter, conv. to Charles Morgan 41 a., part of *Dudlies Cliffs*, laid out for Richard Dudley.{TALR 18:80}

4. HUGH MORGAN, son of John (1), d. by 11 March 1742/3.

On 18 July 1733 Hugh Morgan conv. land to Robert Morgan (sons of John Morgan, dec.). Reference was made to John Morgan's will written 1 Jan 1727 in which he bequeathed to his eldest son James Morgan, 120 a., part of the land he then lived on. To his sons Charles and Samuel Morgan, a tract he bought of Richard Dudley, Sr., called *Dudley's Clifts*. And the remainder of his lands at the decease of his wife Mary he left to his sons Hugh and Robert Morgan.{TALR 13:790}

On 11 March 1742/3 an evaluation was made of the land of Hugh Morgan, dec., and now commissioned to the care of James Benney as the guardian of William Morgan, son and orphan of Hugh Morgan, dec.{TALR 15:357}

Hugh was the father of: WILLIAM.

5. ROBERT MORGAN, son of John (1), was living as late as 25 Nov 1735. He m. Mary (N).

On 25 Nov 1735 Robert Morgan and his wife Mary conv. to William Michael left to him by his father John Morgan's will, bounded by a deed of partition between Hugh Morgan and Robert Morgan (18 July 1733 - Liber PF No. A:790).{TALR 14:129}

---

[32] In her will, made 27 July 1765, she named her brother Jacob Morgan as exec. {MWB 33:417}

6. CHARLES MORGAN, son of Charles (2), d. by Sep 1762.

Charles Morgan, of TA Co., planter, d. leaving a will dated 1 March 1762 and proved 11 Sep 1762. To friend Jacob Fallowfield, he left the parcel of land left the said Morgan by 3 bros., by dec. father, in which there is no division to be possessed by him, the sd. Jacob and his hrs.; 9 lbs. ten s. cash, which is due to me on account; some furniture. To friend Mark Roe (not yet 21), he left stock. To friend Charles Roe, stock. Exec. was to be friend Jacob Fallowfield. The will was witnessed by John Barwick, Jonas Fallowfield, Nathan Lain.{MWB 31:736}

7. JACOB MORGAN, son of Charles (2), was named in his father's will. He m. Hannah (N).

On 9 Feb 1768 Jacob Morgan and his wife Hannah conv. to John Jenkinson, joyner, 34 1/3 a., part of *Dudley's Clift*; also 29 a., part of *Chestnut Bay*.{TALR 19:469}

8. WILLIAM MORGAN, son of Hugh (4), d. cJune 1764. He m. Rachel (N), who was d. by 18 June 1776.

William Morgan of TA Co. d. leaving a will dated 21 June 1764 and proved 16 Oct 1764. To his wife Rachel he left a plant. near Three Bridges in TA Co., part of tracts called *Morgan's Neglect, Morgan's Addition* and *Rumsey's Forrest*. Mentioned were sons: James, John (under age 19), William, Thomas, Milcah and Elizabeth. In case of wife's death, the guardianship of children to bro. Thomas Morgan. The extx. was wife. The witnesses were James Tilghman, Chas. Leith and Samuel Cockayne.{MWB 32:296}

William Morgan was the father of: JAMES; JOHN; WILLIAM; THOMAS; MILCAH; and ELIZABETH.

9. JAMES MORGAN, son of William (6), on 18 June 1776 conv. to Thomas Spry Morgan 1/2 of part of *Morgan's Neglect, Morgan's Addition* and *Rumsey Forrest*, which had been devised by William Morgan on 21 June 1764 to his wife Rachel during her widowhood and after her death to his two sons James and John. Rachel Morgan is now dead and the undivided on account of John's minority.{TALR 20:547}

Unplaced

MORGAN, ANN, and Richard Barley, of Shrewsbury Parish, were charged at June Court 1745 with having cohabited together after receiving an admonition of the Parish Vestry. They were found not guilty.{KECR JS#24:201}

MORGAN, CHARLES, m. by 5 Oct 1767, Sarah, admx. of Stephen Kendall of KE Co. Dist. of the estate was made by Sarah Morgan, admx., on that day.{BFD 5:54}

MORGAN, DAVID, servant: At February Court 1673, Math. Payne certified that he disposed of a man servant named David Morgan for 4 years to Walter Dickison of TA Co. and on 13 da., 8 mo., 1674 they arrived in MD from which day his time began. {ARMD LIV: 600, Liber BB No.2:--}

MORGAN, EDWARD, of Antigua, m. Sarah (N).
On 24 March 1719 John Corney, now resident in TA Co., mariner, conv. to Sarah Morgan, wife of Edward Morgan of Antugua, merchant, 258 a., part of *Smith's Clifts* on Tuckahoe Creek near the mouth of Mill Creek.{TALR 12:398}

MORGAN, EVAN, d. leaving a tract, *The Fork*, to his dau. Rebecca, wife of Francis Bradley which they conv. to Andrew Price, Sr. and William Scott, on the n. side of St. Michaels River in a fork of Bugby Creek and Cold Harbour, on the n. side of the Wye River.{QALR ETA: 3}

MORGAN, HABUKUK, of Caroline Co., d. leaving a will dated 19 Feb 1775 and proved 8 March 1775. To son Habakkuk Morgan, dwelling plantation, "Addition to Goospond," 121 acres with warrant of Resurvey. To sons: James and John Morgan, tract near Marshy Hope called "Morgan's Addition to Rogues Beguiles," 228 acres, equally. To daus: Deborah and Charlotte, land where Smith Rumbley lives, part of "Edmonson's Reserve," 35 acres with the "Addition" shall be sold and money put at interest, equally divided between them. Rents from my dwelling plantation for six years to maintain my small children. To 5 children: Habakkuk, James, John, Deborah and Charlotte personal estate equally after wife's thirds are deducted. Wife, Deborah Morgan, extx. Wit: Nath'l. Potter; James Hopkins; Edward Eaton; Samuel Ireland, Jr.{MWB 40:220}

MORGAN, HERBERT, d. by 24 Sep 1714 when his estate was admin. by William Ringold.{INAC 36A:98}

MORGAN, JOB, at November Court 1740 was charged with having stolen 2 bottles of wine from the store house of William Gibbs. {KECR JS#23:167}

MORGAN, JOHN, was b. c1634. At age c27, he deposed on 1 Nov 1661. {ARMD LIV:230, Liber B:106} He m. Mary (N).

Morgan was transported into the province by Joseph Wicks in 1653.{MPL Q:66}

John and Mary (N) Morgan were the parents of: HENRY, b. 26 May 1668.{ARMD LIV:187, Liber B:76}

MORGAN, JOHN, d. by March 1667/8 when Henery Coursey claimed that John Morgan, dec., died in debt to him, 1100 lbs. of tobacco and cask.{ARMD LIV: 419, Liber BB No.2:81}

MORGAN, JOHN, d. by June 1687. He m. Elizabeth (N) who later m. Arthur Carleton.

John Morgan purchased 140 a. of *Coursey's Neck* from William Coursey on 16 Aug 1664, at the death of John Morgan to pass to Morgan's dau. Elizabeth Morgan. {TALR 1:3}

On 17 June 1687 Arthur Carleton, Sr., of CE Co., conv. to John Richards, carpenter, 400 a. called *Millford* on e. side of Tuckahoe Creek, formerly belonging to John Morgan, dec. who in his will devised to his wife Elizabeth who later m. Arthur Carleton and had issue by her one dau. The said Elizabeth d. and left the land to Arthur Carleton her husband.{TALR 5:89}

John Morgan was the father of: ELIZABETH.

MORGAN, JOHN, was b. c1647. On 30 April 1725 John Morgan, age c78, dep. he was a juryman summoned 30 years earlier for John Emerson.{TALC:29} On 3 Jan 1708, age 59, he helped to prove the will of William Hadden, tailor, of TA Co.{MWB 12:344}

MORGAN, JOHN, m. by Aug 1739, Ann, who at August Court, 1739, charged with assaulting Thomas Atkin---.{KECR JS#22:254}

MORGAN, JOHN, d. by 17 Sept 1740 when the inventory of his estate was taken. It was filed 28 Dec 1740 and mentioned Daniel Brdyand, admin., and Richard Wethered. {MINV 25:464}

MORGAN, JOSHUA, of Newcastle Co., PA, cordwinder, on 6 Aug 1700 conv. to Richard Carter, merchant, 400 a., *Poplar Ridge*, formerly laid out for Henry Parker and given by Edward Winckles to the said Joshua Morgan by his will, 16 Sep 1677.{TALR 8:45}

MORGAN, JOSIAS, son of Ellinor Husin, was named on 15 Sep 1677 in the will of Edward Winkles of TA Co., who left him 400 a. *Popler Rigg*.{MWB 10:24}

MORGAN, LABAN, TA Co., planter, d. leaving a will dated 7 Feb 1773 and proved 8 March 1773. To wife Catherine Morgan, extx., he left all of his personal estate. The will was witnessed by Daniel Clark; William Harrington; David Harrington.{MWB 39:499}

MORGAN, MARY, and Richard Evans, Jr., were charged at March Court [1739/40] that on 1 May 1739 they committed fornication and begot a bastard child. The fine was 30 shillings. Mary was ordered to receive 6 lashes. {KECR JS#23:54, 60}

MORGAN, RICHARD, m. by 26 July 1708, Mary, widow and extx. of Daniel Benching of CE Co.{INAC 28:331}

MORGAN, RICHARD, m. Phebe Skinner on 25 Feb 1730.{TAPE}

MORGAN, SARAH, of TA Co., d. leaving a will dated 7 Feb 1775 and proved 8 March 1775. To dau. Keziah Marshell, 1 shilling. To dau. Mary Morgan, stock, furniture. To son Enoch Morgan, stock, furniture, horse. To dau. and son Mary and Enoch Morgan, remainder of estate equally. Perry and Aaron Parrott to settle and divide my estate. The will was witnessed by George Parratt; Mary Parratt; Susannah Neall.{MWB 40:532}

MORGAN, WILLIAM, d. by March 1742/3, leaving a son William,\who chose James Bonner as hus guardian {TAGU A}.

MORGAN, WILLIAM, d. by 16 June 1773 when a valuation was made of the land and plant. of the orphan of William Morgan, William Morgan, Jr.; Isaac Millington, guardian - part of *Dudley's Clifts*, 65 a. referenced in the will of his father Hugh Morgan.{TALR 20:308}

THE JAMES MURPHY FAMILY

1. JAMES MURPHY was bur. Sep 1728.{KESP} He m. Margret Hynson on 1 Jan 1712.{KESP}
   James Murphey (or Murphy) d. leaving a will dated 18 Jan 1718 and proved 21 April 1729. To wife Margaret, extx., 50 a. called *Deane's Choice* (or *Chance*), bought of John Cleaver during widowhood, and 200 a. called *Churnell's Neck* s. side of Chester River, bought of John Sennott. To dau. Prys(c)illa, all sd. lands at death or marriage of mother, sd. dau. dying, lands to fall to son-in-law William Hynson, and Simon Wilmore, Jr. (son of Simon Wilmer, now sheriff of KE Co.), sd. dau. under guardianship of Simon Wilmer, Sr. Simon Wilmore, Sr. was named overseer.{MWB 19:745}

The inventory of Murphy's estate was taken 22 July 1729 and filed 29 Sep 1729 by Margaret Murphey. Next of kin were Thomas Hynson and C. Hynson.{MINV 15:183}

Margaret Murphey d. leaving a will dated 20 Dec 1732 and proved 24 July 1733. To son William Hynson, exec., personalty. Residue of estate divided equally among all children.{MWB 20:777}

The inventory of her estate was taken 1 Oct 1733 and filed 7 Feb 1733. Ja. Harris, C. Hynson, and Patrick Clarke signed as next of kin. Thomas Hynson and William Hynson signed as execs.{MINV 17:606}

James and Margaret Murphy were the parents of{KESP}: PRISCILLA, bapt. 18 June 1714, m. Stephen Bordley on 22 April 1731.

THE JOHN MURPHY FAMILY

1. JOHN MURPHY m. Mary.

At August Court 1741, it was presented that John Murphy, cordwainer, and Mark Glyn, cordwainer, servant to G. Garnett, assaulted Samuel Massey and Margret Jones. They were fined 10 s.{KECR JS#23:216}

John and Mary Murphy were the parents of{KESH}: ELIZABETH, b. 8 Nov 1727; SUSANAH, b. 1 Aug 1732; MARY, b. 21 Aug 1734; SARAH, b. 18 Feb 1737/8; JOHN, b. 20 Feb 1739/40; and MARTHA, b. 28 Feb 1742/3.{KESH}

THE SAMUEL MURPHEY FAMILY

1. SAMUEL MURPHEY m. Mary (N).

At March Court 1745, it was presented that Samuel Murphey spoke sundry treasonable words. He was taken into custody for appearance at the next Provincial Court in April next.{KECR JS#24:249}

Samuel and Mary were the parents of: SAMUEL, b. 29 Aug 1748.{KESH}

Unplaced

MURPHEY, DAVID, d. by 15 June 1708.{INAC 28:173, 29:52} His estate was admin. again on 18 Jan 1708. Elisabeth Macan, wife of Edward Macan, was extx.{INAC 29:82}

MURPHY, HUGH, was duly enlisted in the company of Capt. John Milboarn and received bounty money on 30 Oct 1740 (recorded 3 June 1743).

MURPHY, John, d. by 9 June (c1694).{INAC 13A:101}

MURPHY, JOHN, was bur. 13 March 1716.{KESP}

MURPHEY, JOHN, of KE Co., d. by 1 July 1766, when his estate was appraised by Christopher Hall and W. Caley, and valued at £82.3.10. Sarah Murphey, admnx., filed the inventory mentioning Sarah Rasin, Joannes Gleen, Frances Sinah Cole, and Elisabeth Cole on 20 Aug 1766.{MINV 90:174}

MURPHY, MARY, of KE Co., widow, aged 74, possibly c1750.{KEEJ: Isaac and Thomas Crown}

MURPHEY, ROGER, and Mary Green were m. 4 Aug 1715.{KESP}
He d. leaving a will dated 28 Nov 1730 and proved 19 April 1733. To wife Mary, extx., he left entire estate. At her decease, land to pass to Thomas, son of Thomas Cowardine.{MWB 20:862}

MURPHY, SARAH, spinster, was charged at March Court 1741 with committing fornication on 1 Feb 1740, and at diverse other times, and begetting a bastard child. She was fined 30 s.{KECR JS#23:253}
At June Court 1746, she was charged with committing fornication on 10 April 1745, and at diverse times as well before as since, and begetting a bastard child. She was fined 30 s.{KECR JS#24:274}
At March Court 1747, she was charged and fined 30 s.{KECR JS#25:4B}

MURPHY, THOMAS, and Martha Royall were m. 1 April 1706.{KESP}

THE NASH FAMILIES

ALEXANDER NASH d. in KE Co. by May 1681. He m. Ruth Hill on 20 Jan 1662.{ARMD LIV:186, Liber B:75} Ruth Hill, dau. of Thomas, was transported May 1652.{MPL ABH:348}
Alexander Nash d. leaving a will dated 30 Oct 1676 and proved 1 May 1681. To niece Thomasen Nash, home plant. To George Goldhawke, *Goldhawke and Nash's Enlargement*, at age 21. To Eliza:, Thomas and James Taylor, children of Thomas Taylor, John Spooner, and Alice Miller, dau. of Michael Miller, personalty. To Quaker church, residue of estate. Thomas Taylor and Ralph Fishborne were execs.{MWB 4:83}
His estate was admin. on 30 April 1685, 12 June 1685, 13 Sep 1686, and 15 Oct 1686. The third account mentioned Michaell Miller. Samuell Wheeler was admin.{INAC 8:360, 361, 9:108, 501}

Alexander and Ruth were the parents of: ALEXANDER, b. 16 Jan 1662 [sic]{ARMD LIV:187, Liber B:75}; and SARAH, b. 19 Aug 1664.{ARMD LIV:187, Liber B:76}

NASH, HENRY, left an estate that was admin. by George Green on 25 March 1687 and 29 March 1687.{INAC 9:218, 255}

RICHARD NASH m. by 12 Feb 1675, Anne, widow of Richard Blunt of KE Co.{MDTP 7:70; INAC 2:113}
On 28 June 1670, Ann, wife of Richard Nash, confirmed a gift in her former husband's, Richard Blunt's, life of a heifer by her given to Abell the son of John Maggisson.{ARMD LIV:289, Liber C:37}

THE CHARLES NEALE FAMILY

1. CHARLES NEALE was in KE Co. by 8 Oct 1725, when he witnessed the will of John Henley.{MWB 18:422} He d. by 1729 when his estate was inv.{MINV 15:192} He m. Margaret (N).
Charles Neale's estate was inv. by Daniel Ferrick and T. Bordley, and appraised at £35.12.3. Nicholas Neale signed as next of kin, and Nicholas Neale, admin., filed the inventory of 17 Oct 1729.{MINV 15:192}
Charles and Margaret (N) Neale were the parents of{KESP}: CHARLES, b. 23 July ----; NICHOLAS, b. 13 April 17--; and MARGRETT, b. 28 Sep 17--.

2. CHARLES NEALE, son of Charles and Margaret, was b. 23 July 17--.
He is probably the Charles Neale, labourer of St. Paul's Parish, who was charged at August Court 1726 with frequenting the company of Sarah Manning of the afsd. parish on 21 April 1725 and at diverse other times (he having been admonished), she being the lawful wife of John Manning. He was acquitted; to pay costs; John Woodall assumed payment of fees.{KECR JS#22:188}

3. NICHOLAS NEALE, son of Charles and Margaret, was b. 13 April 17--.
At November Court 1726, Nicholas Neale, St. Paul's Parish, labourer, was found guilty of committing fornication with Anne Fennen on 10 May 1726 and begetting a bastard child. He was fined 30 s.{KECR JS#22:233}
At June Court 1731, Nicholas Neal, St. Paul's Parish, was found guilty of committing fornication on 10 June 1730 with Honora Carroll and begetting a bastard child. He was fined 301 lbs. of tob. She was fined 30 s.{KECR JS#WK:211}

Nicholas Neale, of KE Co., d. leaving a will written 30 April 1746 and proved 7 June 1746. The heirs named were children Charles Neal, James Neal, Daniel Neal, Rebecca Neal, and an unborn child. Dau. Rebecca was to be brought up by Benjamin Green, son Daniel to be placed under the care of his uncle Edmund Dillhunt to learn the trade of a saddler. Wife (unnamed) and bro. Charles Neale were named as execs. The will was witnessed by Thomas Goodman, Daniel Dillihunt, and Malcum Stewart. {MWB 24:434}

On 11 Aug 1746, Nicholas Neale's estate was appraised by Morgan Brown and Edward Comegys, and valued at £115.4.5. Joseph Nicholson and Daniel Cheston signed as creditors. Mary Neil and Charles Neil, execs., filed the inventory on 5 March 1746. {MINV 35:15}

Nicholas Neale was the father of: CHARLES; JAMES; DANIEL; REBECCA; and an unborn child.

Unplaced

NEAL (?), ANN. William Morrison, mariner, were presented at March Court 1771 with having committed fornication with Ann Neal(?) and begetting a base born child. They were fined 30 s. He was ordered to give security to keep the county from any charge by means of his bastard child called WILLIAM. {KECR DD#1:127B}

NEAL(E), JACOB, d. leaving a will dated 1 Nov 1708 and proved 4 Feb 1708/9. To eldest son Barwick and son Jacob he left all his land, residue of estate to four children (not designated), they to be taken into custodianship of George Struton, exec. {MWB 12:356}

His estate was admin. by George Strutton, exec., of 27 Sep 1711 and 16 March 1712. {INAC 32C:99, 33A:153}

Jacob Neale and wife Margaret were the parents of: BARWICK; JACOB; MARGRETT, b. March 1701 {KESP}; and probably two others.

NEALE, LAWRANCE, of Shrewsbury Parish, labourer, at March Court 1733, was found guilty of committing fornication on 10 April 1733 with Jane Flanagan and begetting a bastard child. He was fined 30 s. {KECR JS#WK:476}

NEILL, MARGARET, swore at August Court 1757 that William Greenwood was the father of her base born child. She was fined 30 s. William Greenwood denied the charge of adultery. {KECR JS#25:178B}

At August Court 1767, it was presented that Margaret Neale, spinster, committed fornication on 1 May 1766. She was fined 30 s. and ordered to give security to keep the county from any charge by means of her bastard child called ANDREW MILLER. {KECR DD#1:94A}

NEAL, PRISCILLA, appeared on 1 Aug 1753 and confessed her guilt of committing fornication and having a base born child. She was fined 30 s. She identified the father as Daniel Ferrell. Daniel Ferrell confessed to being the father and was fined 30 s.{KECR JS#25:120A}

NEALE, WILLIAM, was b. c1631. Neale, age c30, dep. on 1 June 1661.{ARMD LIV:221, Liber B:100}

THE NEWELL FAMILY

1. JOHN NEWELL, d. by 19 Oct 1749. He m. Elinor Lloyd on 29 July 1711.{KESP}

John Nuell, of KE Co., d. leaving a will dated 2 Nov 1748 and proved 11 Sep 1749. The heirs named were wife Ellenor Nuell, two sons (unnamed), and two of Edward Dolin's daus., Sarah and Elizabeth Dolin. Mentioned was son John Nuell. The will was witnessed by Henry Hosier (Quaker), Wm. Haynes, and Jacob Underker(?).{MWB 27:113}

On 19 Oct 1749, his estate was appraised by Abraham Milton and Robert George, and valued at £43.1.2. Henry Hosier signed as creditor. John Nuel and Thomas Nuel signed as next of kin. Elinor Nuel, admx., filed the inventory on 5 Dec 1749.{MINV 41:286}

John and Elinor (LLoyd) Newell were the parents of at least two sons: JOHN; and THOMAS.

2. JOHN NEWELL, son of John and Elinor (Lloyd) Neale, was named in his father's will, and was living at least as late as 1755.

John Newel and Martha Collins, both of KE Co. m. with consent of parents, at Cecil Meeting House, 12/2/1752.{CFMM}

John and Martha (Collins) Newell were the parents of{CFMM}: JOHN, b. 16 da., 7 mo., 1753; and ANN, b. 6 da., 8 mo., 1755.

Unplaced

NEWELL, ANN, spinster, at August Court 1770 was presented that on 10 June 1770 she committed fornication and begot a base born child. She was fined 30 s.{KECR DD#1:119B}

NEWELL, JAMES, labourer, was charged at March Court 1747 with committing fornicaton on 10 March 1746, and at diverse times as well before as since, with Hannah Lee and begetting a bastard child. He was ordered to receive 6 lashes.{KECR JS#25:3B}

THE NICHOLSON FAMILY

Refs.: A: BDML.

1. WILLIAM NICHOLSON, of AA Co., d. by 1719, having m. Elizabeth (N), who d. c1716/7. They were the parents of{A}: JOSEPH, b. c1709, d. 1787.

2. Col. JOSEPH NICHOLSON, son of William and Elizabeth, was b. c1709, and d. 1787. He m. 1st, Hannah, widow of Edward Scott, dau. of James and Sarah (Hynson) Smith, and granddau. of John Hynson. Joseph Nicholson m. 2nd, Mary, d. c1799, dau. of William Hopper.{BDML}
   At August Court 1734, Joseph Nicholson, of St. Paul's Parish, was charged that on 10 March 1733 he broke open and destroyed a cask of cider belonging to George Moore, value of 100 lbs. of tob. He was fined 30 s.{KECR JS#WK:536}
   On 17 Sep 1739, Joseph Nicholson and his wife Hannah, of KE Co., conv. to Jonathan Evans of the same place, millwright, a grist mill on Langfords Bay now in the possession of the sd. Joseph and the Old Field adjoining the sd. mill, for 7 years. (For specific arrangements see deed.)
   Capt. Joseph Nicholson, Capt. Jacob Jones, Capt. Christopher Bateman, Insine James Ringgold, Lieutenant Willm Wilmer, and Lieutenant James More all came and took the oath of allegiance on 22 April 1740.{KEBI JS#18:278}
   On 3 Aug 1741, Joseph Nicholson, Gent., and his wife Hannah, of Chester Town, conv. to Richard Evans, Jr., and William Smith, millwright, a grist mill on Langfords Bay called Scotts Mill(?).{KELR JS#23:452}
   On 1 June 1765 William Hopper, Gent. conv. to Mary Hopper, Hugh Neil and Henrietta his wife, Joseph Nicholson the younger and his wife Elizabeth - the said Mary, Henrietta and Elizabeth, all being daus. of William Hopper and his wife Esther, tenant by courtesy for life owing to his marriage to Esther, now dec., to the land called *Green Spring*, 650 a.; also 100 a. called *Paxton's Lott*.{QALR RTG:157}
   Joseph Nicholson was the father of: JOSEPH, Jr., d. 1786; WILLIAM; JAMES, c1736-1804, Senior Officer in the Continental Navy; BENJAMIN, d. 1792; SAMUEL, 1743-1811; THOMAS, d. 1783; and ELIZABETH, m. Charles Gordon.

3. JOSEPH NICHOLSON, probably the eldest son of Joseph and Hannah (Hynson) Nicholson, was of age by 1755. On 28 July 1757 he m. Frances, dau. of William Hooper, whose will of 5 Feb 1772 named his children Elizabeth and Mary Nicholson, and grandchildren Joseph Hopper Nicholson and Mary Nicholson.{MWB 38:634} Sarah Hopper, in

her will of 25 Jan 1774 named Elizabeth Nicholson and grandson
William Hopper Nicholson.{MWB 40:267}

Joseph Nicholson, Jr., held a number of offices in the Colonial and
Revolutionary eras.{BDML}

Joseph and Mary (Hopper) Nicholson were the parents of: JOSEPH
HOPPER, 1770-1817, Member of Congress; WILLIAM HOPPER;
JAMES; ESTHER, m. 1st, Dr. John Hindman, and 2nd, William
Chambers; and SARAH, 1776-1840, m. Dr. Pere E. Niel or Noel.

4. WILLIAM NICHOLSON, son of Joseph and Hannah, was a legatee
of James Smith, whose estate was dist. by William Murray, exec.{BFD
5:122}

5. BENJAMIN NICHOLSON, son of Joseph and Hannah, was b. in
KE Co., and was of age in 1756, and d. 1792. He m. by 1771, Mary,
dau. of John and Mary (Dorsey) Ridgely.

Benjamin represented BA Co. in the 2nd-7th Conventions, 1774-
1775. He and his wife had issue.{BDML}

Unplaced

NICHOLSON (Nichallson), JOHN, servant to Robert Lamden, was
judged at March Court 1668, to serve 7 years.{ARMD LIV: 436, Liber BB
No.2:102}

NICHOLSON, JOHN, on 20 March 1682 purch. from Thomas and
Judith Wyatt 100 a., part of a tract purch. from John Lillingston.{TALR
4:185}

NICHOLSON, JOHN, at March Court 1709 petitioned to have a road
from his house to George Powell's land through Thomas Wyaetts land
to go to church and mill.{QAJU ET NO.B:19}

NICHOLSON, JOHN, and wife Sarah, on 19 July 1735 conv. to
Thomas Jackson 50 a., *Hopewell* on Devonishes Branch of the Unicorn
Branch.{QALR RTA:413}

On 6 June 1741 John Nicholson leased from James Paul Heath in
behalf of Daniel Dulany, 100 a., part of a tract called *The Remains of
My Lord's Gracious Grant,* for the lifetimes of sd. John Nichason
(Nicholson) and John Nichason, his son, and Sarah Nichason, his wife.
{KELR JS#23:245}

John and Sarah were the parents of{QALU}: THOMAS, b. 28 Jan
1737.

NICHOLSON, JOHN, m. Ann Wiggins 27 Aug 1758, by pub. of banns.{QALU}

NICHOLSON, SUSANNAH, spinster, at November Court 1752 was charged with committing fornication with John Harley on 10 Sep 1751 and begetting a bastard child. She was fined £1.10.{KECR JS#25:105B}

NICHOLSON, THOMAS, and his bro. JOHN NICHOLSON, on 19 Aug 1721 conv. to William Weyatt 100 a., part of *Tilghman's Discovery* on Double Creek.{QALR IKB:75}

On 12 Feb 1745 John Hartshorne, carpenter, and his wife Elizabeth conv. to Thomas Nickison (Nicholson) 100 a., part of *Woodhouse* on Unicorn Branch and 25 a. adj. called *Woodhouse Addition*.{QALR RTC:148}

On 24 Nov 1749 Thomas Nicholson and his wife Mary conv. to Thomas Jackson 50 a. called *Nicholson's Chance* on Devinishes Branch.{QALR RTC:407}

Thomas and Mary Nicholson were the parents of{QALU}: JANE, b. 8 Sep 1737, bapt 13 Nov ----.

NICHOLSON, THOMAS, m. Sarah Boroughs 31 Jan 1750, by pub. of banns.{QALU} They were the parents of{QALU}: LEMUEL, b. 7 Jan 1752.

NICHOLSON, WILLIAM, was bur. 15 February 1712.{KESP}

THE DANIEL NORRIS FAMILY

1. DANIEL NORRIS, was b. c1642. In June 1706 he gave his age as c64.

Formerly an inhabitant in the city of London, England, then an inhabitant of KE Co., MD, 20 June 1684.{KELR K:91}

A statement by Daniell Norris, of KE Co., age c64, was recorded cJune 1706. In it he declared that his eldest sister, Ann Norris, m. William Woodroofe at a village called Cowley in Glostershire in England, who was eldest bro. of Thomas Woodroofe who came to a place or towne called Salem in the Province of West New Jersey in America and there inhabiting near 30 years, d.

He also declared that Joseph Woodroofe, eldest son and heir of sd. dec. Thomas, in the lifetime of sd. Thomas came from Salem to visit him at his dwelling house in KE Co., MD. He was well acquainted with Thomas and Joseph in London before any of them came to America, and he said that William Woodroofe had several sons by the sd. Ann, the deponent's sister, viz., John, William, Francis, and Thomas and two daus., viz., Mary and Ann, which he was well acquainted with in England.

Norris stated that he knew of no one in America alive so nearly related to dec. Thomas Woodroofe and Joseph Woodroofe his son who d. at Salem as is the afsd. deponent.{KELR GL#1:108/132}

Daniell Norris d. leaving a will dated 13 Jan 1706 and proved 23 March 1707. To son-in-law William Bently and granddaus. Mary and Patience, children of sd. Wm. Bently, personalty. To son Daniell and Eliza:, residue of estate, including three tracts and 120 a. left to testator by his bro. Thomas Norris; land bought of Richd. Tighman, and land bought of Michael Miller. Dau. afsd. and her children to occupy dwell. house during minority of son and dau., and then to occupy log house for 20 years. To son Daniell log house, graveyard, &c. Should children of sister ———, arrive from England, their passage to be paid by devisee. Testator desires to be bur. by dec. wife Eliza:. William Trew, Sr., and Henry Hosier were named as execs.{MWB 12:242}

Daniel Norris' estate was admin. on 4 May 1707, 16 Aug 1709, 18 Nov 1709, and 30 Oct 1710 by Daniel Norris, the exec.{INAC 28:186, 30:178, 31:60, 32C:20}

Daniel Norris was the father of: DANIEL; and ELIZA, m. William Bentley.

2. DANIEL NORRIS, son of Daniel, admin. his father's estate in 1709. He d. by Nov 1725.

Daniel Norrice, of St. Paul's Parish, d. leaving a will dated 19 Oct 1725 and proved 16 Nov 1725. He left his entire estate to his bro. John Ball, exec.{MWB 18:424}

THE PERKINS FAMILY

Elsie Clements, widow of S. Eugene Clements, has furnished some of the following information. She cites, "A Sketch of Intercolonial Migration" by the late Emily Ritchie Perkins in a folder titled "Perkins Family of Chestertown, Maryland" held by the Library of the Daughters of the Revolution, Washington, D.C. We will refer to this source as {A} in the following paragraphs.

1. ISAAC PERKINS, b. London, England, c1612, d. 13 Nov 1685, m. Susanne Wise. They were the parents of the following children: LYDIA, BENJAMIN, ISAAC, SUSANNE, JACOB, HANAH, REBECCA, MARY, DANIEL, EBENEZER, CALEB, JOSEPH.{A}

2. EBENEZER PERKINS, son of Isaac, was b. 9 Dec 1659, d. at New Castle on the Delaware, Sep 1703, leaving a will dated 27 July 1703

and proved 16 Oct 1703. He named children Isaac, Ebenezer, Daniel, David, Jonathan, Abigail, and Elizabeth. Wife Mary was the extx. The will was witnessed by Derek Janson and Teunis Keunders.{A; Phila. Will Book B:456}

Ebenezer Perkins was the father of the following children (who evidently moved to KE Co., MD): ISAAC; EBENEZER; DANIEL; DAVID; JONATHAN; ABIGAIL; and ELIZABETH.

3. EBENEZER PERKINS, son of Ebenezer (2), was named in his father's will. He m. Mrs. Sarah Barney on 14 May 1740.{KESB}

He is probably the Ebenezer Pearkins, of KE Co., who d. leaving a will dated 6 Nov 1746/7 and proved 10 Nov 1748. He mentioned his son-in-law Francis King, son Ebenezer, and wife (unnamed). The execs. were Friends, Samuel Wallis, Thomas Bowers, and William Reason. The will was witnessed by Alexander Kelly (Quaker), John Askin, and Milner Herring.{MWB 26:60}

On 1 May 1749, his estate was appraised by W. Comegys and C. Comegys, and valued at £706.19.2. Thomas Perkins and Daniel Perkins signed as next of kin. Margrett Perkins, admx., filed the inventory on 19 June 1749.{MINV 41:21} On 13 April 1750, his estate was appraised and valued at £158.3.6. William Murray signed as creditor. Ebenezar Perkins and Sarah Reyner signed as next of kin. Margaret Randall, wife of Theophilus Randall (Quakers), admx., filed the inventory on 26 April 1750.{MINV 43:430}

Ebenezer Perkins was the father of: EBENEZER; and possibly (N), dau., m. Francis King.

4. DANIEL PERKINS, son of Ebenezer (2), was b. June 1685 in Hampton, New Hampshire. On 26 Feb 1733/4, Daniel Perkins, age c46, dep. regarding the tract *Shads Hole*.{KELR JS#18:2} He d. by 20 Feb 1748. He m. Susannah Stanton by 1 May 1715.{KESP} Susanna Perkins d. by 20 Feb 1764.{A}

On 2 March 1730, Daniel Perkins, of KE Co., millwright, and his wife Susanna, conv. to Francis Belluss(?), part of a tract called *Rayley*, 38 a.{KELR JS#16:313}

On 28 April 1730, Daniel Perkins, of KE Co., and his wife Susannah, conv. to Gideon Pearce, a tract called *Shaws Chance*, 100 a.{KELR JS#X:443}

On 24 March 1732, Daniel and his wife Susannah, conv. to John Gresham, of KE Co., Gent., land which was granted to Christian Geist, late of AA Co., dec. and afsd. Daniel, called *Unity*.{KELR JS#16:335}

On 24 April 1739, Daniel Pearkins, of KE Co., millwright, and his wife Susanna, conv. to Moses Tennant, of the City of Philadelphia, boat builder, ½ or moiety of messuage, tenements and lot in Chester, No. 9, which was sold to Daniel Pearkins by Patrick Mullen, late of Chester Town.{KELR JS#22:310}

On 20 March 1740, Daniell and Susanna conv. to George Reason, of the same county, part of a tract called *Drayton*, 12 a., on Churn Creek, where a grist mill lately stood.{KELR JS#23:154}

Daniel Perkins had several court appearances. At November Court 1725, Daniel Pearkins was fined 100 lbs. of tob. for using indecent language in court.{KECR JS#22:117} At March Court 1725, he was found guilty of shooting with a hand gun a mare worth 900 lbs. of tob., property of John Johnson, Gent., from which wound the mare d. He was fined 100 lbs. of tob.{KECR JS#22:118, 126} At June Court 1727, he was found guilty of assaulting Thomas Shearman on 19 June 1727 and fined 600 lbs. of tob.{KECR JS#22:300} At June Court 1729, he was found guilty of assaulting Thomas Gresham on 10 Oct 1728, and fined 500 lbs. of tob.{KECR JS#WK:73} At November Court 1739, he was charged with assaulting Stephen Sturgeon on 20 Aug 1739.{KECR JS#23:33} At November Court 1740, Daniel Perkins was charged that, on 1 June 1740, he cut down and carried away 70 oak trees off the lands of Henry Augustus Bodein, an orphan, under the age of 21, to wit, of the age of 18, commonly called the *Horn Bridge Plantation.*{KECR JS#23:138}

On 24 Oct 1743, Daniel Perkins gave his son Thomas Perkins 22 head of cattle, 9 horses, 36 sheep, 50 hoggs, 8 beds and furniture, a Negro man named Peter, a negro woman named Dinah, a white servant man named Arthur McDannel, 18 chairs, two black walnut tables, two desks, a chest of drawers, a looking glass, 10 pewter dishes, 2½ dozen pewter plates, and other items.{KEBI JS#20:36}

At March Court 1746, Perkins was accused of refusing to grind John Briscoes(?) corn.{KECR JS#24:340}

Daniel Pearkins, of KE Co., d. leaving a will dated 28 Nov 1742 and proved 20 Feb 1748. The heirs named were wife (unnamed) to whom he left ⅓ of his estate, including a saw mill and a grist mill, son Ebenezer Pearkins, son Thomas Perkins, and son Daniel Pearkins. The exec. was son Thomas. The will was witnessed by John Stevenson, Jannet Stevenson, and John Watson.{MWB 26:73}

In 1749, his estate was appraised by Samuel Walles and John Walles, and valued at £1250.13.4. (The inventory was done on the 19 da., 3 mo., 1749.) Richard Coley and Charles Harrison signed as creditors. Daniel Perkins and Ebenezar Perkins signed as next of kin. Thomas Perkins, exec., filed the inventory on 3 July 1749.{MINV 41:35} On 10 June 1750, his estate was appraised again and valued at £320.7.7. Thomas Perkins, exec., filed the inventory on 22 Feb 1757.{MINV 62:234}

Susannah Perkins, of KE Co., widow of Daniel Perkins, late of KE Co., d. leaving a will dated 22 Oct 1753 and proved 20 Feb 1764. The heirs named were son Daniel Perkins, dau. Sarah Perkins, dau. Susan-

nah Day, dau. Elizabeth, dau. Martha, and son Thos. Perkins. The
exec. was son Daniel Perkins. The will was witnessed by Cooter
Griffith and Abraham Haines.{MWB 31:1080}

On 26 March 1764, her estate was appraised by Ebenezar Reyner
and Samuel Mansfield, and valued at £158.4.2. James Anderson and
Hugh Wallis signed as creditors. Thomas Perkins and Sarah Weikers
signed as next of kin. Daniel Perkins, exec., filed the inventory on 15
Sep 1766.{MINV 90:346}

Daniel and Susanna Perkins were the parents of{KESH}:
EBENEZER, b. 7 April 1717; ELINOR, b. 16 March 1718; THOMAS,
b. 12 March 1720; SUSANAH, b. 3 Dec 1723, m. 1st James Corse, m.
2nd John Day;[33] DANIEL, b. 27 Oct 1725; ELIZABETH, b. 11 April
1728; SARAH, b. 16 Oct 1739; and MARTHA (named in mother's will).

5. DAVID PERKINS, son of Ebenezer (2), was named in his father's
will and evidently moved to KE Co., MD, where he d. by 18 Oct 1748.
He m. 1st, Sarah Reding on 18 Feb 1723.{KESH} He m. 2nd, Rebeckah
Taylor on 11 da., 3 mo., 1743.{CEMM}

David Perkins d. leaving a will dated 10 Aug 1749 and proved 18
Oct 1748. The heirs named were wife Rebekah, dau. Sarah to whom
was devised land in New Castle Co., PA, and son David Perkins to
whom the remainder of the land descended. The execs. were wife
Rebekah (Quaker) and son David Perkins (Quaker).{MWB 25:434}

On 10 Nov 1748, his estate was appraised by John Wallis and
Nicholas Smith, and valued at £529.19.6. Anthony Camron and John
Gleaves signed as creditors. Daniel Pearkins and Thomas Perkins
signed as next of kin. Rebecca Perkins and David Perkins, execs., filed
the inventory on 9 Jan 1748.{MINV 38:236}

On 1 June 1752, his estate was appraised again by Nicholas Smith
and John Wallis, and valued at £8.7.1. John Marwell and John Gleaves
signed as creditors. Thomas Perkins and Ebenezar Reyner signed as
next of kin. Rebecca Perkins, extx., filed the inventory on 13 June
1752.{MINV 50:56} On 13 June 1752, his estate was admin. by Rebecca
Perkins, surviving extx., a Quaker. Payments were made to Daniel and
Ebenezer Perkins.{MDAD 33:46} On 13 June 1753 distribution of the
estate was made by Rebecca Perkins.{BFD 1:64}

David Perkins had one son, by his 1st wife, Sarah: DAVID, may
have d. by 1 June 1752; SARAH.

---

[33] John Day, son of Mathias, who d. 1762. Wife Susannah is
mentioned in his will.{MWB 31:689} Also see Day Family Bible at the
Archives of Delaware.

6. EBENEZER PERKINS, son of Daniel (4) and Susanna, was b. 1 April 1717.{KESH} He d. by 10 Nov 1748. He m. Margaret (N). (NB: He m. Sarah, dau. of Francis Barney, according to BDML.)[34]

At November Court 1740, it was presented that Ebenezar Perkins, on 1 June 1740, committed waste on the land of Richard Johnson, age 12, orphan of John Johnson, dec., the land called *Batemans Farm*, where he did enter and carry away 10 oak trees and 2 poplar trees. He was found guilty.{KECR JS#23:140}

At November Court 1740, Ebenezer Perkins, son of Daniel Perkins, was charged on 12 June 1740, at the request of William Seale, of KE Co., mariner, that he counterfeited the figures on a Bill of Loading. (Apparently this case was referred to the Provincial Court.){KECR JS#23:142}

At March Court 1744, Ebenezer Perkins, Jr. [sic], was presented for not maintaining a bridge in repair. Whereas he erected a mill dam on Morgans Creek, over the branch whereof a main road led, to wit the main road from Chester Town to Sassafras Ferry as also to the head of Chester River, by the erecting of which mill dam the road was greatly annoyed and made dangerous to all the good subjects, and further Joshua George gave the court here to understand that the sd. dam was a publick nuisance and that not withstanding the sd. Ebenezer refused to keep up, maintain and repair the bridge "against the peace and against the laws of Great Britain and this Province." He was found not guilty.{KECR JS#24:187}

Ebenezer Perkins, of KE Co., d. leaving a will dated 14 May 1750 and proved 26 Feb 1750. The heirs named were son Isaac Perkins, to whom he devised two grist mills and and a saw mill, and daus. Arminta and ----. The extx. was wife Sarah. The will was witnessed by Thomas Bowens, Thomas Perkins, and James Hackett.{MWB 28:12}

On 23 May 1751, his estate was appraised by John Wallis and Henry Bodien, and valued at £498.15.1. Theophilus Randall and Thomas Chandler signed as creditors. Thomas Perkins and Ebenezar Perkins signed as next of kin. Sarah Perkins, extx., filed the inventory on 25 May 1751.{MINV 47:120}

On 22 Jan 1754, his estate was appraised by John Wallis and Henry Bodien, and valued at £369.3.0. Theophilus Randall and George Medford signed as creditors. Daniel Perkins and Susanna Perkns signed as next of kin. Thomas Perkins, admin., filed the inventory on 1 June 1754. (Original administration by Sarah Perkins.){MINV 57:388} On 1 June 1754 distribution of the estate was made by Thomas Perkins, admin. de bonis non.{BFD 1:118}

---

[34] Mrs. S. Eugene Clements gives date of marriage as 14 May 1740.

Ebenezer Perkins was the father of (perhaps by Margaret, as he did not name this first son in his will): EBENEZER, d. c1763.

Ebenezer and Sarah were the parents of: ARIMENTI, b. 22 April 1741; ISAAC, b. 5 Aug 1743;[35] and MARY.{KESH; MWB 25:189}

7. THOMAS PERKINS, son of Daniel (4) and Susanna, was b. 12 March 1720.{KESH} He d. by 13 April 1768, having m. Ann or Hannah (N).

At August Court 1750, Thomas Perkins was charged with assaulting Theophilius Randolph on 1 Aug 1750. He was fined 30 s.{KECR JS#25:64B}

Thomas Perkins, of KE Co., d. leaving a will dated 16 Feb 1768 and proved 13 April 1768. Mentioned were wife Hannah, children Frederick (eldest son), Thomas, Mary, and Ann Perkins, an unborn child, and bros.-in-law Jonathan Turner and Ebenezer Beyner. Guardians appointed were Jonathan Turner and Ebenezer Reyner, for Frederick, Thomas, Mary, and Ann. Also mentioned was Francis Haynes. Tracts mentioned were *Broad Neck, Covington's Marsh, Perkins' Adventure, Lordship's Manor* and *Cammels Worth More,* on Morgan Creek. The will was witnessed by Bartus Piner, Isaac Jenkins, and John Foreman.{MWB 36:418}

On 19 Feb 1768, his estate was appraised and a list of debts valued at £597.2.1 was compiled. Ebenezar Reyner, exec., filed the inventory cont. a list of debts and mentioning Jonathon Turner on 10 July 1770.{MINV 10} On 30 March 1768, his estate was appraised by John Maxwell and John Eccleston, and valued at £1460.9.7. Sarah Rasin and James Anderson signed as creditors. Susannah Piner and Sarah Wickes signed as next of kin. Ebenezar Reyner and Jonathon Turner, execs., filed the inventory on 26 Sep 1768.{MINV 96:265, 106:44}

Thomas Perkins was the father of: FREDERICK (called eldest son); THOMAS, b. 1 Feb 1754; MARY; ANN; and (N), unborn child (named in Thomas' will).

8. DANIEL PERKINS, son of Daniel (4) and Susanna, was b. 27 Oct 1725 and d. by 25 June 1768.

Daniel Perkins, of KE Co., d. leaving a will dated 16 March 1768 and proved 25 June 1768. Mentioned were wife Mary and 6 children, unnamed. The extx. was Mary Perkins. The will was witnessed by Simon Wickes, David Sine, and Jonathan Turner.{MWB 36:464}

On 27 Oct 1768, his estate was appraised by John Wickes and Samuel Frisby, and valued at £480.19.7. Thomas Smyth and Thomas

---

[35] Probably the Col. Isaac Perkins who served in the 4th Battalion of the Flying Camp during the Revolutionary War.

Ringgold signed as creditors. Isaac Perkins and Frederick Perkins signed as next of kin. Mary Perkins, extx., filed the inventory on 2 Oct 1770.{MINV 104:107}

Daniel Perkins and his wife Mary were the parents of six children (unnamed in their father's will).

9. EBENEZER PERKINS, son of Ebenezer (6), perhaps by his first wife Margaret, was not named in his father's will. He is probably the Ebineazer Perkins, of KE Co., who d. leaving a will dated 30 Nov 1763 and proved 14 Jan 1764. The heirs named were dau. Margaret, son Ebineazer Perkins, Jr., and dau. Margaret. The will was witnessed by John Johnson, Rebecca Dixon, and Sophiah Johnson.{MWB 31:1062}

On 30 March 1764, his estate was appraised by John Eccleston and Isaac Willson, and valued at £440.9.7. John Johnston and Hugh Walles signed as creditors. Isaac Perkins and Thomas Perkins signed as next of kin. Margaret Perkins, admx., filed the undated inventory.{MINV 83:360}

On 18 Jan 1765, his estate was appraised again and valued at £73.2.0. Thomas Smith and D. Hands signed as creditors. Margaret Perkins, admx., filed the inventory on 23 Jan 1765.{MINV 86:127} On 30 Dec 1767 distribution of the estate was made by Margaret, admx. and wife of John Eccleston.{BFD 5:51}

Ebenezer Perkins was the father of: MARGARET (possibly the eldest, as she may have been the admnx. of her father's estate), m. John Eccleston; and EBENEZER.

10. ISAAC PERKINS,[36] son of Ebenezer (6) and Sarah, was b. 5 Aug 1743 and d. 1791.[37] By 16 Nov 1765 he m. Ann, dau. of Hugh Wallis.{BDML}

He represented KE Co. in the Lower House of the Assembly, 1777 and 1786-1787, and was a Captain of the Fourth MD Battalion of the Flying Camp.{BDML}

Isaac and Ann were the parents of: ARAMINTA, b. 1765, m. Josiah Johnson; EBENEZER, b. 1767, m. Sarah Jenkins; ANN, m. by 1791, George Jackson; WILLIAM, b. c1780; SARAH, m. by 1798, James Groome; and MARY, b. c1781, m. John Black.

11. FREDERICK PERKINS, eldest son of Thomas (7), was so named in his father's will.

---

[36] See William Frederick Perkins, Twelve Generations of a Branch of the Perkins Family in Maryland since 1790. {MHS Shelf #CS71-P448-1966.}

[37] Mrs. S. Eugene Clements gives date of death as 1794.

On 2 April 1773, his estate was appraised by John Eccleston and Charles Groome, and valued at £848.9.5. Thomas Ringgold, Peregrine Frisby, and Macal Medford signed as creditors. Susannah Piner and Jonathon Turner signed as next of kin. Isaac Perkins, admin., filed the inventory on 12 June 1773.{MINV 115:200}

On 11 March 1774, his estate was again appraised by Nathaniel Reding and Mr. Thomas Gresham (dec. by 8 Jan 1776), and valued at 305.0.0.{MINV 122:266}

On 8 Jan 1776, the estate was appraised a third time, by J. Maxwell and Nathaniel Reading, and valued at £961.8.10. Macall Medford and A. Frisby signed as creditors. Jonathon Turner and Susannah Pinor signed as next of kin. Isaac Perkins was admin. The second and third inventories were filed on 26 Jan 1776.{MINV 122:267}

12. THOMAS PERKINS, son of Thomas, was b. 1 Feb 1754 and d. by 11 March 1771.

On 11 March 1771, his estate was appraised by John Eccleston and J. Maxwell, and valued at £1.11.6. Sarah Rasin and James Anderson signed as creditors. Sarah Wicks and Susannah Piner signed as next of kin. Ebenezar Reyner and Jonathon Turner, execs., filed the inventory on 3 Sep 1771.{MINV 107:297}

On 27 Aug 1773, his estate was appraised again and valued at £138.13.9. Jonathon Turner and Ebenezar Reyner, execs., filed the inventory cont. a list of debts on 1 Sep 1773.{MINV 114:235}

A third appraisal was made on 13 March 1774 by Joshua Lamb and Hezekiah Cooper, and valued at £306.7.4. Susannah Piner and Sarah Wickes signed as next of kin. Ebenezar Ryner and Jonathon Turner, admins., filed the inventory on 25 June 1774.{MINV 115:423}

Unplaced

PERKINS, ELIZABETH, m. William Wilson on 18 Aug 1745.{KESH}

PERKINS, ELIZABETH, m. 1st Ebenezer Reyner on 31 July 1746 and had children: AMELIA, b. 8 May 1747; MARGARET, b. 14 Oct 1749; REBECCA, b. 7 Sep 1751; SARAH, b. 14 July 1753; HANNAH, b. 15 April 1756; EBENEZER, b. 11 Feb 1758; and MARGARET, b. 10 Aug 1760.

PERKINS, GEORGE, of KE Co., d. leaving a will dated 22 May 1770 and proved 9 Aug 1770. In it were mentioned wife Mary and son William, with reference to other children (unnamed). A house in Chester Town was mentioned. The will was witnessed by William Bordley, Thomas Kensey, and Thomas Crane.{MWB 38:137}

On 8 Nov 1770, his estate was appraised by Thomas Crane and James Piner, and valued at £52.14.1. John Bolton and James Anderson signed as creditors. William Perkins signed as next of kin. Richard Harding and his wife, Mary Harding, execs., filed the inventory on 12 June 1772.{MINV 109:108} Another appraisal was made and his estate was valued at £297.16.6. A list of debts was filed on 12 June 1772.{MINV 109:123}

On 12 June 1772 dist. of the estate was made by Mary Harding, extx., wife of Richard Harding.{BFD 6:165}

PERKINS, JACOB, d. leaving an estate that was appraised 4 Jan 1733 and filed 11 May 1734. Isaac Perkins (bro.), John Perkins (bro.), and "children not of age" were listed as next of kin. Admins. were Evan Lewis and his wife Sarah Lewis.{MINV 18:26}

PERKINS, JOHN, d. by 17 March 1744, when his estate was appraised by George Medford and John Briscoe, and valued at £141.19.9. No creditors or next of kin were listed. The unnamed admin. filed the inventory on 29 May 1745.{MINV 30:270}

Another appraisal was made by George Medford and John Binss, and valued at £293.2.6. David Hull signed as creditor. Wright Perkins signed as next of kin. The admx. filed the inventory on 4 May 1744.{MINV 29:30}

PERKINS, JOSEPH, d. leaving a will dated 20 June 1765 and proved 6 July 1765. The heirs named were housekeeper Elizabeth Henry and dau. Sarah Perkins. Mentioned was Mary Kennard, widow. The exec. was Richard Frisby, who was to have the care of dau. Sarah. The will was witnessed by Philip and John Hill, and Wm. Smith.{MWB 33:228}

On 25 July 1765, his estate was appraised by William Hynson and John Carvill, and valued at £135.5.3. James Anderson and Nathaniel Kennard signed as creditors. No next of kin listed. Richard Frisby, admin., filed the inventory on 23 Aug 1766.{MINV 89:99}

An appraisal of debts, valued at £106.9.0, was filed by Richard Frisby, exec., on 3 March 1767.{MINV 92:82}

On 3 March 1767 his estate was distributed by Richard Frisby, exec. Legatees were Elisabeth Henry (housekeeper) and dau. Sarah. Residue was given to Sarah Perkins.{BFD 5:63}

PERKINS, SARAH, of Shrewsbury Parish, spinster, at March Court 1748, was charged with assaulting Ebenezer Perkins on 10 March 1748. She was fined 10 s.{KECR JS#25:31B}

PERKINS, WRIGHT (or RITE), d. (date unknown), when his estate was appraised by George Medford and Francis Lamb, and valued at

£223.3.3. Thomas Cooper and Jacob Jones signed as creditors. Elisabeth Wilson and Isaac Fonch signed as next of kin. Rebecca Perkins, admx., filed the inventory on 2 Oct 1749.{MINV 41:249}

On 14 April 1750, his estate was appraised again by George Medford and Frances Lamb, and valued at £40.15.0. Rebecca Perkins, admx., filed the inventory on 14 April 1750.{MINV 43:430}

THE RASIN FAMILY

The compilers thank Mr. Chris Christou of Baltimore for generously making his material on the Rasin family available for this work.

1. THOMAS RASIN was b. c1640 in England, and d. 1687 in SM Co., MD. He m. Elizabeth (N), b. c1650, d. after 1696.

Some 90 rebels sailed on the ship *Happy Return*, under Capt. Washam, after the Monmouth Rebellion of 1685. The prisoners were put on board at Weymouth. They were delivered to John Browne and Company for Sir William Booth of Barbadoes. Thomas Rason was sold to Col. John Simpson.

Thomas Rasin, of SM Co., d. leaving a will dated 18 April 1687 and proved 23 April 1688. He mentioned his wife and five children, and appointed them as joint execs. and legatees of his estate. The sons were to be of age at 18, and the daus. at 16. All were to be brought up as Roman Catholics. Mr. Penington and Col. Darnall were named as overseers. The will was witnessed by Kenelm Cheseldyne, Alice Bramble, and Eliz Smithson.{MWB 4:301}

Elizabeth Rasin, widow, was in TA Co. when she bought 1 a. from Mr. Wilson 1696. She was probably the mother of Philip and Thomas.

Thomas and Elizabeth had 6 children (Fresco; Marriages and Deaths of St. Mary's County, MD): PHILIP, Sr., b. c1675, d. 31 Jan 1717; MARY, b. c1677; THOMAS, b. c1680, d. 20 Oct 1731; JOHN, b. c1682; ELIZABETH, b. c1684, m. 1st, Richard Carter, who d. by 22 Feb 1715[38], and 2nd, by 1731, (N) Kirby; SARAH, b. c1685 (she is supposedly a dau. of Thomas also; some records say she m. George Warner); and FRANCIS.[39]

---

[38] On 22 Feb 1715 Elizabeth Carter, widow and relict of Richard Carter, dec., granted to her bro. Thomas Rasin of KE Co., MD, power of attorney to recover debts owed to her or to the estate of her dec. husband. {TALR 12:371}

[39] On 20 March 1716, Philip Rasin and his wife Elizabeth, of KE Co., appointed his brother Francis Rasin, of the county afsd., as their attorney to acknowledge a deed of sale to William Reding.{KELR BC♯1:208}

2. PHILIP RASIN, Sr., son of Thomas (1), was b. c1675, possibly in England. He d. 31 da., 1 mo., 1717 in Cecil Meeting, and was bur. at the Friends Meeting. He m. Elizabeth Thackston, dau. of Thomas Theckston. She was b. c1685, and d. by Dec 1719. She m. 2nd, Abraham Redgrave, Jr.,[40] c1717 in KE Co., MD. Elizabeth inherited the land called *Devitt* (per deed 17 July 1710, #2, p. 130).

At the time of his death, Phillip Reasin was overseer of the Cecil Monthly Meeting.{CEMM}

Joseph Trulock, of KE Co., and his wife Mary, conv. to Philip Rasin, of the same county, a tract on Steelpone Creek, being part of a tract called *Forresters Delight*, 25 a., also 100 a. that Joseph Trulock bought of Thomas Webb and his wife Sarah and William Jones, son of sd. Sarah on 26 Aug 1707, and 50 a., part of a tract called *Nancys Choice* which Joseph Trulock bought of Benjamin Hamblin, son of Benjamin Hamblin, dec.{KELR JSN:99}

On 17 July 1710, Phillip Rasin and his wife Elizabeth, of KE Co., conv. to Elizabeth Bowdy a parcel of land called *Drevite* on the s. side of the Sassafras River.{KELR JSN:214}

On 20 March 1716, Philip Rasin and his wife Elizabeth, of KE Co., appointed his bro. Francis Rasin, of the county afsd., as their attorney to acknowledge a deed of sale to William Reding.{KELR BC#1:208}

On 21 March 1716, Philip Rasin and his wife Elizabeth, of KE Co., conv. to Nathaniel Pearce, of the same county, part of two tracts, one called *Drevite* and the other *St...ton*, 120 a.{KELR BC#1:217}

On 22 Nov 1716, Philip Rasin and his wife Elizabeth, of KE Co., formerly CE Co., conv. to John Hambline, of the same county, in exchange for 100 a. on Jacobus Creek, 20 a., part of a tract called *Drevitt*(?) and also an adj. parcel, formerly a part of 100 a. in the occupation of George Harris, of KE Co., dec., and purchased of sd. George Harris by Henry Eldersly and sold by him to James Wroth, who sold same to Thomas Theckston, (the father of Rasin's wife), formerly of KE Co.{KELR BC#1:159}

Philip d. leaving a will dated 29 March 1717 and proved 24 May 1717. He left to his three sons land in Kent on Jacob's Creek, son Philip the dwell. house, son Thomas land next to Wm. Jones, son John, "daus. to be," wife Elizabeth, bro. Thomas Rasin, burial at Friends' burying place, Scisell (Cecil) Meeting House. Philip, Sr., d. 31 Jan 1717 in KE Co., MD, and was bur. in Friends Burying, KE Co., MD.

---

[40] He was b. 4 Aug 1696 in Shrewsbury Parish, KE Co., MD, the son of Abraham Redgrave, Sr., and Margaret. Elizabeth would have been much older than Abraham. Abraham Redgrave, Jr., made an oath 17 Dec 1719 about sums paid "by his deceased wife." /s/"Abraham Redgrave, who intermarried with Elizabeth Rasin, who was the admin. of Philip Rasin.

Philip Rasin's estate was inv. on 12 June 1717. Thomas Rasin was next of kin.{INAC 38B:105} The estate of Phillip Rasin was admin. on 17 Dec 1719 by Thomas Rason and Elisabeth Rason, now wife of Abraham Redgrave, Jr.{MDAD 2:407} On 4 April 1720, his estate was admin. by Abraham Redgrave, Jr., and Thomas Rayson.{MDAD 3:36}

On 17 Nov 1720 Abraham Redgrave, Jr., Gideon Pearce, and Thomas Gideons of KE Co., gave bond they would pay Elizabeth Rasin, at 16 or day of marriage, and John Rasin, at age 21, orphans of Philip Rasin, dec., each £44.18.11 from their father's estate.{KEBI JS#W:86A, 86B} On the same day Thomas Thackston, Francis Harney, Jr., and Robert Meeks of KE Co., gave bond they would pay Philip Rasin, one of the orphans of Philip Rasin, dec., to pay him £44.18.11 from his father's estate, at the age of 21.{KEBI JS#W:86A}

On 12 Aug 1742, Charles Hynson, age c50, dep. regarding the bounds of the tract, *Standley's Hope* and part of another tract called *Grange*. He stated that about 20 years earlier he was called by Thomas Rasin, Thomas Thaxton, John Haley, and Abram Redgrave to divide the lands of Philip Rasin between his three sons.{KELR JS#24}

Philip and Elizabeth had 5 children{CEMM}: PHILIP, Jr., b. 6 da., 8 mo., 1703, at Cecil Monthly Meeting, d. 1733; ELIZABETH, b. 21 da., 11 mo., 1706, in KE Co., MD, at Cecil Monthly Meeting, and m. John Gale;[41] THOMAS, b. 13 da., 8 mo., 1708, d. Jan 1737 in KE Co., MD;[42] MARY, b. 25 da., 12 mo., 1710, m. Griffith Jones; and JOHN RASIN, b. 30 da., 7 mo., 1713, at Cecil Monthly Meeting.[43]

---

[41] John Gale, b. c1706, d. leaving a will dated 4 Dec 1775 and proved 30 Jan 1776, naming wife Bersheba, son Rasin, John Gale, grandchildren Malachi, James, Mary, Catherine, and Rosamond.

[42] Thomas Rasin d. leaving a will dated 1 Jan 1737 and proved 21 Jan 1737. To bro. John he left *Partnership*, naming dec. bro. Philip (in case of a dispute over above land, it may belong to Philip's children Joseph and Benjamin, under 21), sister Mary Jones and her daus, Elizabeth, Mary, and Lucea Jones, and sister Elizabeth Gale and her sons John and Rasin Gale.{MWB 21:867}
Thomas Rasin's estate was inv. on 9 Aug 1737 and recorded 2 Sep 1737. Samuel Groome and Francis Barney were appraisers. John Rasin and Thomas Rasin signed as next of kin. Mary Rasin was the admx./extx.{MINV 22:386} The estate was inv. again on 2 Feb 1737 and recorded 2 Aug 1738. Griffith Jones and John Gale signed as next of kin. John Raisin was the exec.{MINV 23:393} A list of debts was filed c1739 by John Rasin, exec.{MINV 24:391} Another inventory was filed 5 Jan 1739 by John Rasin.{MINV 24:393}

[43] He d. cMarch 1761. On 30 Jan 1717, Roger Wild, of KE Co., conv. land, 50 a., to John Rasin, of the same place, son of Philip Rasin, dec.{KELR BC#1:263}

3. THOMAS RASIN, son of Thomas (1), was b. c1680 in MD. Thomas Rasin, a member of Chester and Cecil Monthly Meetings, d. 20 da., 8 mo., 1731, in KE Co., MD.{CEMM} He m. Mary Warner c1714. She was the dau. of George Warner and Anne Hopkins (or Hoskins), b. 1697 in MD, d. cSep 1761 in KE Co., MD. Evidently the marriage was contrary to the discipline of the Quakers, because on 9 da., 4 mo., 1714, a committee was appointed to visit Thomas Rasin concerning his disorderly marriage.{CEMM}

On 25 Nov 1707, Joseph Trulock, of KE Co., and his wife Mary, conv. to Thomas Rasin part of a tract called *Bares Grime* on Steelpone Creek, 25 a.{KELR JSN:17}

On 2 May 1718, Thomas Rasin, of KE Co., and his wife Mary, conv. to Thomas Theakston, and his wife Mary, 140 a.{KELR BC#1:280}

On 19 Aug 1721, Nathaniel Pearce, of KE Co., and his wife Sarah, conv. to Thomas Chandler part of two tracts, *Drevite* and *Stanston*, 120 a., which was by Philip Rasin, of KE Co., and his wife Elizabeth, conv. to sd. Nathaniel Pearce.{KELR JS#W:185}

On 11 da., 4 mo., 1729, a committee of members of Cecil Meeting was appointed to appear at court in order to prevent Thoms. Maslin's children from being taken from among Friends. (The son named Thomas Maslin chose Thomas Rasin as his guardian, but the court kept the other children as the being too young to choose a guardian.){CEMM}

He d. leaving a will dated 18 da., 10 mo., 1731, and proved 3 March 1731. To wife Mary, extx., dwell. plant. ———, being the first purchase from Thomas Thackstone, land where sd. Thackstone now lives. To son George, afsd. tracts after his mother's decease. To son William, 300 a. called *Forrester's Delight* bought of Thomas Thackstone, with part of *Hillen's Adventure*. To son Abraham, 150 a. of tract called *Fair Promise* bought of George Warner, and land bought of Andrew Riddle, with 100 a. adj. thereto, being part of *Friendship*. To four sons George, William, Abraham, and Joseph, residue of personal estate. Mentioned Friends of Chester and Cecil Meetings, and sister Elizabeth Kirby, not to be pressed by extx. for money due testator.{MWB 20:426}

On 21 Nov 1745, George Rasin, William Rasin, John Rasin, and John Gale, of KE Co., gave bond they would pay Abraham and Joseph Rasin each £115.5.6 as their filial portions of the estate of their father, Thomas Rasin, at age 21.{KEBI JS#20:204, 205}

Mary (Warner) Rasin d. leaving a will dated 17 Dec 1759 and proved 1 Sep 1761. To her son William Rasin, she left part of Warner's Marsh as was devised by my father George Warner. To son Abraham Rasin, 300 a. *Friendship*, 200 a. *Pool*, and 100 a. *Standly's Hope*, and son George Rasin was to have £20. Abraham, exec., was to have the remaining part. The will was witnessed by John Rasin (nephew of husband).{MWB 31:449}

On 15 Jan 1762, the estate of Mary Razin, Quaker, of KE Co., was appraised by Joshua Lamb and Henry Bodain, and valued at £156.14.0. William Razin and Mary Razin signed as next of kin. Abraham Razin, exec., filed the inventory on 17 Aug 1762.{MINV 78:374}

Thomas and Mary (Warner) Rasin had 8 children{CEMM}: THOMAS, b. 27 da., 7 mo., 1715, in KE Co., MD, d. 1729 at Cecil Monthly Meeting in KE Co., MD; GEORGE, b. 6 da., 7 mo., 1718, in Cecil Monthly Meeting, d. cOct 1761; JOSEPH, b. 9 da., 12 mo., 1720, in KE Co., MD, d. 1729 at Cecil Monthly Meeting in KE Co., MD; WILLIAM, Esq., b. 12 da., 7 mo., 1723, in Cecil Meeting, d. 13 Feb 1762;[44] ABRAHAM, b. 21 da., 11 mo., 1725, at Cecil Meeting, d. 26 Sep 1777; ISAAC, b. 4 mo., 1728, in KE Co., MD, d. 1729 at Cecil Monthly Meeting in KE Co., MD; JESSE, b. c1729 and d. 1729 in Cecil Meeting, KE Co., MD; and JOSEPH, b. 15 da., 10 mo., 1731, in KE Co., MD.

4. PHILIP RASIN, Jr., son of Philip, Sr. (2), was b. 5 da., 8 mo., 1703, in KE Co., MD, at Cecil Quaker Meeting. Philip m. Mary (N), b. c1703.

Phillip Rasin (Rason) d. leaving a will dated 9 Nov 1732 and proved 22 Nov 1732. To eldest son Joseph, dwell. plant. ———. To son Benjamin, one a. and dwell. house in Chester Town, and £20 above his third part of personal estate. To wife Mary, extx., personalty. Test. were Thomas Rasin and Griffith Jones.{MWB 20:557}

Philip Rasin's estate was inv. 14 May 1733 and recorded 15 June 1733. John Gale and John Rasin signed as next of kin. Mary Rasin was extx.{MINV 17:393}

When his estate was admin. on 14 May 1733, four children were named.

On 24 May 1737, Mathew Manlove, Benjamin Palmer, and David Hall gave bond they would pay Benjamin Rasin £37.18.9 due him as his filial portion of the estate of Philip Rason, his dec. father, at the age of 21, and they would pay Joseph Rasin, £57.18.9 and 1 farthing.{KEBI JS#18:67, 68}

Philip and Mary had 2 children: JOSEPH, Sr., b. c1730, d. c1781; and BENJAMIN, b. c1727.

5. JOHN RASIN, son of Philip, Sr. (2), was b. 30 da., 7 mo., 1713, at Cecil Meeting in KE Co., MD. John d. cMarch 1761 in KE Co., MD. He m. 1st, by 1735, Margaret Spalden. She was b. c1715, and d. 15 da., 11 mo., 1749, in KE Co., MD.{CEMM}

---

[44] On 10 da., 6 mo., 1752, William Rasin (son of Thomas and Mary Rasin) was disowned because he had taken the oath to government in order to qualify himself for a legislative member.{CEMM}

John m. 2nd, c1750, Rosamand Blackiston, b. c1730, d. by 1772, dau. of William and Ann (Park) Blackiston. She m. 2nd, c1762, Abraham Rasin, b. 21 Jan 1725 in KE Co., MD, the son of Thomas and Mary (Warner) Rasin.

John Rasin, age c30, Quaker, on 21 Feb 1743, affirmed regarding the bounds of a tract called *Brotherly and Friendly Agreement* and *Heyborns Farm;* he recalled John Heyborn laying out some land for Elizabeth Noble.{KELR JS#25:30}

On 20 March 1743, John Rasin, of KE Co., and his wife Margaret, and John Watts, of the same county, and his wife Elizabeth, daus. and co-heirs of Andrew Spaulden, late of the same county, dec., to Levring Merrit, of the same county, 100 a.{KELR JS#25:58}

Abraham Rasin, Quaker, and Rosa Rasin his wife, posted administration bond on 17 March 1761.{KE Admin. Bonds 5:282}

On 21 May 1761, his estate was appraised by Samuel Groome, Jr., and Thomas Bowers, and valued at £915.14.8. James Louttett and Edward Drugan signed as creditors. Joseph Raisin and Philip Raisin signed as next of kin. Rosa Razin, admx., filed the inventory on 27 May 1762.{MINV 77:194}

The estate of John Rasin, Quaker, of KE Co., was appraised again, and valued at £7.15.0. Abraham Rasin, admin., filed the inventory cont. a list of debts on 2 Aug 1764.{MINV 84:252}

John Rasin's estate was admin. by Rosa Rasin, admx., on 17 July 1762. The account listed debts and credits, and cash due to William Rasin, £27.{KEAD 6:277-9, 377-8}

On 2 Aug 1764, distribution of the estate was made by Rosa Rasin, admx., wife of Abraham Rasin.{BFD 4:53}

John and Margaret (Spalden) Rasin were the parents of{CEMM}: LAWRENCE (transcribed as LAURINA), b. 11 da., 12 mo., 1736; PHILIP, b. 2 da., 12 mo., 1740, d. cMarch 1771; THOMAS, b. 5 da., 12 mo., 1742; ELIZABETH, b. 28 da., 12 mo., 1744; JOHN, b. 23 da., 12 mo., 1746, d. 1784, m. Araminta Brooks (b. c1745); and MARGARET, b. 5 da., 8 mo., 1749.{CEMM}

John and Rosamond (Blackiston) Rasin were the parents of: MARY, b. c1755 in KE Co., MD, d. cDec 1805 in KE Co., MD; SARAH, b. c1755; ANN. b. c1757; and WILLIAM BLACKISTON, b. c1760, d. c1810.

6. GEORGE RASIN, son of Thomas (3), was b. 6 July 1718 in KE Co., MD, and d. cOct 1761 in KE Co., MD. He m. Sarah Powel, b. c1720. On 9 da., 11 mo., 1744, George Reason had an intention of marriage

with Sarah Powel of TA Co. and requested a certificate.{CEMM} She m.
2nd, Isaac Whitelock of the Borough of Lancaster in PA on 8 da., 7
mo., 1767, at Cecil Meeting House.{CEMM}

On 16 June 1741, George Rasin petitioned to examine the evidences
of the bounds of his tract *Drayton*.{KELR JS#23:260}

George Rasin, of KE Co., d. leaving a will dated 1 da., 4 mo., 1761,
and proved 20 Oct 1761. The heirs named were daus. Mary and Ann
Rasin, wife Sarah, the unborn child, eldest son William Rasin, second
son George Rasin, and dau. Sarah Rasin. The exec. was son Abraham.
The will was witnessed by John Rasin, Peregringe Brown, and
Margaret Hall.{MWB 31:449}

The estate of George Raisin (also George Razin), Quaker, of KE
Co., was appraised on 12 Nov 1761 by N. Ruxton Gay and Nicholas
Jones, and valued at £889.13.10. James Loulett and Sarah Razin signed
as creditors. Abraham Razin and Mary Razin signed as next of kin.
Sarah Razin, extx., filed the inventory on 27 Aug 1762.{MINV 78:370}

His estate was again appraised and valued at £8.17.2. No creditors
listed. Sarah Rasin, extx., filed the inventory cont. a list of debts on 5
July 1764.{MINV 84:5}

His estate was again appraised and valued at £136.12.4. Sarah
Rasin, extx., filed the inventory cont. a list of debts on 26 May
1764.{MINV 84:9}

On 6 July 1764 distribution of the estate was made by Sarah Raisin,
extx. Distribution was made to pregnant widow.{BFD 4:37}

George and Sarah had 7 children{CEMM}: MARY, b. 15 da., 10 mo.,
1746; ANN, b. 28 da., 2 mo., 1748; WILLIAM, b. 22 da., 5 mo., 1750;
GEORGE, b. 15 da., 5 mo., 1752; GEORGE II, b. 1 or 7 da., 9 mo.,
1756; SARAH, b. 20 da., 2 mo., 1758; and ABRAHAM, b. 22 da., 5 mo.,
1761.{CEMM}

7. WILLIAM RASIN, Esq., son of Thomas (3), was b. 12 July 1723 in
KE Co., MD, and d. 13 Feb 1762 in KE Co., MD. He m. Sarah Savage,
b. c1723.

It was reported to the Cecil Monthly Meeting on 10/6/1752 that
William Rasin (son of Thomas and Mary Rasin) had taken the oath to
government in order to qualify himself for a legislative member. He
was disowned.{CEMM}

William was an Anglican, Gent. As a merchant he owned a gristmill
and pond from 1759 to death. He resided in Georgetown, KE Co. His
wife and parents were Quakers. He served in Lower House from KE
Co. from 1751-1753 and 1757-1758 and Sheriff from 1753-1756. He in-

herited 300 a. from his father c1731, and purchased 155 a. He purchased 2,245 a. in KE Co. between 1754-61, inherited 62 a. from his mother in 1760, purchased 7 lots in KE Co. (5 in Georgetown) between 1752-61, held lease on land, 6 lots in Georgetown, and ¾ lots in Chestertown in 1760, sold 1,127 a. in Kent 1754-60, and d. Feb 13, 1762. He had 2 servants, 26 slaves, 1,635 a., and 7 lots in KE Co.{BDML}

William Rasin, of KE Co., d. leaving a will dated 10 Feb 1761 and proved 22 Feb 1762. The heirs named were son Thomas Rasin, to whom was devised a tract called *Margarett's Delight* and part of tract called *The Gift*, son William Rasin, to whom was devised land lying near head of Steel Pone Creek, which testator's father devised to him, wife Sarah, son Joseph Rasin, dau. Sarah, dau. Susanna, and dau. Rebecca. The will was witnessed by Ann Eliza. and John Chapple and James Piner.{MWB 31:536}

The inventory of William Rasin, Quaker, of KE Co., was appraised on 13 May 1762 by Daniel Mosey (also Daniel Massey) and Alexander Baird, and valued at £2364.17.10. Thomas Ringgold and William Murray, as execs. of James Smith, signed as creditors. Abraham Rasin and Mary Reasen signed as next of kin. Sarah Rasin, extx., filed the inventory on 17 March 1763.{MINV 80:177}

The estate was again appraised and valued at £880.17.0. No creditors or next of kin. Sarah Rasin, extx., filed the inventory cont. a list of debts on 24 Feb 1764.{MINV 83:1}

Later his estate was appraised and valued at £16.8.11. No creditors or next of kin. Sarah Rasin, Quaker, extx., filed the inventory cont. a list of debts on 30 April 1767.{MINV 92:145}

Distribution of the estate of Ann Richardson was made on 22 Aug 1766 by Mrs. Sarah Rasin, extx. of William Rasin.{BFD 5:6}

William and Sarah were the parents of: THOMAS; WILLIAM, b. 6 Oct 1750; JOSEPH; SARAH; SUSANNAH; and REBECCA.

8. ABRAHAM RASIN, son of Thomas (3), was b. 21 da., 11 mo., 1725, and d. 26 da., 6 mo., 1777.{CEMM} He m. 1st, Rosamand Blackiston, c1762 in KE Co., MD. She was b. c1730, and d. by 1772, the dau. of William and Ann (Park) Blackiston. Abraham m. 2nd, c1770, Jane (N), b. c1740, d. after 1798. She m. 2nd a Mr. Gale.

Abraham d. leaving a will dated 4 May 1777 and proved 14 Nov 1777. He named his wife Jane, daus. Mary and Sarah Rasin, and sons Thomas and Warner Rasin (minors), to be in care of Joshua Lamb, Thomas Bowers, Samuel Wallis, and George Lamb, they to give a yearly account to Cecil Meeting. He mentioned tracts called *Stanley's*

Hope, Pool, Howard's Lot, Friendship, Fair Promise, Camel's Farm, and *Fish Hall*. He named his wife Jane as extx. Will was witnessed by Joseph Rasin, Thomas Corse, and Daniel Lamb.{KEWB 6:38}

Abraham and Rosamond had two children: WARNER, b. 23 da., 9 mo., 1763, d. 4 da., 11 mo., 1804{CEMM};[45] and THOMAS, b. c1765.

Abraham and Jane were the parents of{CEMM}: MARY, b. 17 da., 1 mo., 1772; SARAH, b. 1 da., 5 mo., 1774; and THOMAS, b. 28 da., 4 mo., 1776.

9. JOSEPH RASIN, Sr., son of Philip (4), was b. c1730 in KE Co., MD, and d. c1781. He m. Mary Medford, b. c1731.

On 11 Dec 1738, it was recorded that James Moor and Jeremiah Coventry had appraised a lott in Chester Town belonging to Joseph Raison, son of Phillip Raison, dec., now in possession of David Hull, guardian of sd. orphans. Valued at £2 annually.{KEBI JS#18:188}

On 19 Dec 1738, John Williams and George Medford, of KE Co., appraisers of the estate in land of Joseph Raison, son of Phillip Reason, dec., now in possession of David Hull, the appointed guardian - gave the annual value of the sd. land as £8.{KEBI JS#18:187}

Joseph and Mary (Medford) had one child: JOSEPH, Jr., b. 15 da., 8 mo., 1765.{CEMM}

10. PHILIP RASIN, son of John (5), was b. 2 Feb 1740 in KE Co., and d. March 1771. He m. c1769 Hannah Freeman, b. c1755, d. after 1821, dau. of Isaac and Martha (Scott) Freeman, Jr. Hannah m. 2nd John Gleaves after 1780, and 3rd (N) Burneston.

Hannah was young when she m. Philip Rasin who d. 1771. She was one month pregnant when Philip d. and his son Philip is not mentioned in the will. He may have d. without knowing he had any children. She may have m. a Mr. Gleaves since she is referred to as Hannah Gleaves, then Burneston, in later deeds.

Philip Rasin, of KE Co., d. leaving a will dated 4 Feb 1771 and proved 5 March 1771. Mentioned were wife Hannah and bros. Thomas, John, and William. The execs. were his bros. Thomas and John. The will was witnessed by Roger Halls, Barney Corse, and Rasin Gale.{MWB 38:220}

---

[45] Warner m. 1st, Ann Miflin, b. c1763, and d. 19 da., 12 mo., 1799, age 28.{CEMM} He m. 2nd, Margaret Wilkerson, b. c1765.

On 12 March 1771, his estate was appraised by J. Maxwell and John Duyer and valued at £441.14.1. No creditors or next of kin listed. John Rasin and Thomas Rasin, execs., filed the inventory on 7 June 1771, mentioning Joseph Rasin, Abraham Rasin, and Donaldson Yeats. {MINV 106:213}

Philip and Hannah had 1 child: Capt. PHILIP FREEMAN, b. 4 Oct 1771, d. 23 Oct 1820.

11. WILLIAM BLACKISTON RASIN, son of John (5), was b. 1760 in KE Co. and d. c1810 in Worton, KE Co., MD. He m. Martha Wroth, widow of William Apsley, c1786/1788 in KE Co. She was b. c1760 in KE Co., MD, dau. of Kinvin Wroth, Jr., and Frances Beck. Martha d. after 1827 in KE Co., MD, and was bur. in KE Co., MD.

The couple were m. after 16 Oct 1786, when her father's will called her Martha Apsley, and before Jun 1788 when she posted an administration bond as Martha Rasin, extx. of her dec. husband William Apsley. On 12 April 1799, the account of Capt. William Rasin and Martha his wife, extx. of William Apsley of KE Co., dec., mentioned distribution to his son George Apsley and Daniel Kennard, who m. a dau. of William Apsley. {KEAD 10:202-204}

William Raisin was a sergeant 5th Regiment on 12 Feb 1779, and a 2nd Lieut. in the 5th Regiment on 26 Jan 1780. He transferred to the 1st Regiment on 1 Jan 1781, and retired 12 Apr 1783. {Rieman Steuart, The Maryland Line in the Rev. War, 1969, p. 121} William was an Ensign at the Battle of Camden, SC, Aug 10 1780. He was a Capt. of the Light Infantry.

William B. Rasin, of KE Co., late a lieutenant in the Revolutionary War, or his order, was granted by the State of MD a sum of money equal to half pay as a lieutenant, annually in quarterly payments, during his life, "as a further reward to those meritorious services which he rendered his country in establishing her liberty and independence." {Nov 1804 Session of Laws of MD Resolutions, Vol. 7}

William Raison or Rasisin was included in a List of Officers and soldiers entitled to lots westward of Ft. Cumberland. In April 1787, in lots of 50 a. each, Lt. William Raison was granted lots 2405, 2406, 2407, and 2408. On 4 Oct 1800, by a Federal Bounty Land Grant, Lt. William Raisin received 200 a. {Warrant number 1,844}

After William B. Raisin's death, his heirs were included in a List of the Tracts and lots of land in KE Co. charged for the payment of taxes. Includes in Second District: persons charged Rasin, William Capt.'s heirs, names of tracts and number of lots "Part of *Hermitage* and

260

Towns Relief, amount due $1.36.{*Republican Star* Oct 15 1811; also published in the Baltimore *Whig*}

On 13 June 1832, Elie Ridgely petitioned for a patent to be recorded agreeable to an act of the General Assembly of MD passed at the November session 1788, that a certain William Raisin, a Lieutenant of the MD line, was entitled to the following lots, viz. No. 2405, 2406, 2407, and 2408, lying contiguous to each other to the westward of Fort Cumberland, in Allegany County, and cont. 50 a. each, making in all two hundred a. of land, that two of sd. lots, No. 2405 and 2406, were on the 28 Aug 1826, exposed to public sale to the highest bidder by William McMahon, collector of the county charges, as the property of sd. William Raisin for payment of the county charges, when the petitioner became the purchaser and fully paid the purchase money for the same, that William McMahon, collector afsd., has since by his deed bearing date the 3 Jan 1827, conv. sd. land to the petitioner.{MPL GGB#2:308}

On 10 May 1838, the heirs of William Raisin sold 200 a. of land that William Rasin received from commission agreeable to the act of Assembly passed at November session 1788 designated as lot Nos. 2405, 2406, 2407, and 2408, land was w. of Fort Cumberland and this land descended to his four children upon his decease, Philip Rasin, Cyrus Rasin, Rachel Rasin, now Rachel Duyer, and Ann Rasin, now Ann Denning. Philip Rasin and Sarah his wife, Cyrus Rasin and Wilamina Rasin his wife, Philip Duyer and Rachel his wife, and Daniel Denning and Ann his wife signed.{Allegany Co. Land Record DB#W:184-7}[46]

---

[46] William Rasin was mentioned in the wills of his bro. Philip Rasin in 1771 and of his sister Mary in 1798.

Town Relief was land that belonged to the Wroth family since their earliest days in KE Co. An application through the Children of the American Revolution was accepted May 1995 for John Barnhouser as his, William Rasin's, 5th great grandson. He is the only descendant accepted in the CAR on Capt. Rasin's service in the Revolution. National #142106.

An article in the *Maryland Genealogical Society Bulletin*, June 1995, by Christos Christou, Jr., provides a history of Capt. Rasin and proofs of this line and corrects mistakes in older histories. *Worton Gleanings* by Cooper, 1983, says William served in the Revolutionary War during his in teens.

Index 49 at Annapolis Archives, Box 3, Folder 21, Lt. Wm. Rasin, Oct 11 1781, pay receipt. Box 3, Folder 18, Lt. Wm. Rasin, paid 1st Regt. troops, Oct 24 1781. Index 50 at AA 1794, Capt. of KE Co. Militia. Index 51, Capt. Wm Rasin, Jun 18 1794, Capt of KE Co. Militia. Militia Appointments, No. 1, p. 52, No. 2, p. 29. Aug 5-7 1783, Lt. Wm Raisin, Intendent's Ledger A, No. 9, p. 30, 44, No. 15, p. 24, A No. 10, p. 8, 62.

William B. and Martha (Wroth) had four children: PHILIP REED, b. c1790, d. 1 April 1841; CYRUS, b. c1794, d. 13 March 1865; RACHEL, b. c1795; and NANCY ANN, b. c1797.

12. WILLIAM RASIN, Esq., son of William (7), was b. 6 Oct 1750, and d. c1803 in Georgetown, KE Co., MD. He m. Sarah Freeman on 20 March 1776 in KE Co., MD. She was b. c1753, and d. after 1794, dau. of Isaac Freeman, Jr., and Martha Scott.

William Rasin has often been confused with his cousin, William Blackiston Rasin, who was a Lieutenant during the Revolution and later made Captain, but other records show this is incorrect. This erroneous service has been included in DAR records.

William and Sarah (Freeman) Rasin had one child: THOMAS, b. 11 July 1777, d. 5 Sep 1785.

Unplaced

RASIN, SARAH, at June Court 1768, was charged with committing fornication, on 10 May 1767, and begetting a base born child. She was fined 30 s. and ordered to give security to keep the county from any charge by means of her bastard child called SOPHIA WILMER.{KECR DD#1:101A}

RASIN, THOMAS, Quaker, of KE Co., d. by 11 June 1772, when his estate was appraised by Peter Massy and John Wilson, and valued at £473.8.4. John Voorhees and Gavin Murray for Jamison Johhnstone & Company signed as creditors. Abraham Rasin and Sarah Rasin signed as next of kin. William Rasin, admin., filed the inventory on 24 Dec 1773.{MINV 115:360}

His estate was again appraised and valued at £15.8.0. William Rasin, admin., filed the inventory cont. a list of debts on 24 Dec 1773.{MINV 115:364}

On 26 Aug 1773 his estate was again appraised by Peter Massy, and valued at £203.16.9. John Voorhees and Gavin Murray for Jamison Johnstone & Company signed as creditors. Abraham Rasin and Sarah Rasin signed as next of kin. William Rasin, admin., filed the inventory on 24 Dec 1773.{MINV 115:365}

RASIN, WILLIAM, was b. c1727. He was age c32 cApril 1759 when he dep.{KEEJ: Thomas Harris}

THE RICAUD (RICHAUX-RICAND) FAMILY

1. (N) RICAUD was the father of at least two sons: BENJAMIN, settled in MD; and THOMAS, living in London in 1684.

2. BENJAMIN RICAUD, son of (N), and bro. of Thomas, settled in KE Co., and m. by 26 June 1678, Elizabeth, widow of Thomas Hall, and extx. (and mother) of Christopher Hall of KE Co.{ARMD 51:267; AALR WH#4:306}

Christopher Hall, of KE Co., d. leaving a will dated 29 Jan 1674 and proved 7 July 1678, naming his mother Elizabeth Ricaud, and sisters Sarah, Eliza, and Mary Ricaud. William Bateman and Abraham Childs were witnesses.{MWB 9:99}

Benjamin Richand d. leaving a will dated 24 Jan 1684 and proved 24 March 1684/5. He named his wife Eliza, extx., she to have a life interest in his plant., sons Benjamin and Thomas, and daus. Mary (actually Sarah) Deane, Elizabeth Rowles, and Mary Edwin. He also mentioned the heir of his bro. Thomas Ricand in London.{MWB 4:80}

The inventory of Benjamin Ricord's estate was appraised 29 April 1685 by Henry Hosier and Charles Tilden, and valued at a total of £3030.0.11.{INAC 8:366}

Benjamin and Elizabeth were the parents of: BENJAMIN, b. by 1684, d. 1713; THOMAS, b. by 1684, living 18 Sep 1687 in KE Co.; ELIZABETH, b. by 1674, m. 1st, by 1684, Christopher Rowles, and 2nd, Joseph Hawkins; MARY, b. by 1674, m. by 1684, (probably William) Edwin; and SARAH, b. by 1674, named as sister in will of Christopher Hall, m. 1st, William Dean, and 2nd, Stephen Whetstone.{MWB 4:80, 7:115, 13:82; INAC 36:17}

3. BENJAMIN RICAUD, son of Benjamin, was bur. in St. Paul's Parish, KE Co., on 11 Dec 1712.{ESVR 1:32} He m. by 10 Aug 1702, Susannah, extx. of Richard Louden (or Lowder).{INAC 23:92}

He was living in KE Co. on 18 Sep 1687 when he and bro. Thomas witnessed the will of Henry Kenett.{MWB 4:298} On 16 Aug 1710, Benjamin Ricaud signed the inventory of Stephen Whetstone of KE Co.

as one of the next of kin.{INAC 31:420} On 23 Oct 1710 Benjamin and Thomas Ricaud signed the inventory of Jacob Young, whose estate also made a payment to Elizabeth Ricaud. Mary Young was the extx.{INAC 32C:62}

On 23 Feb 1712 (1712/13?), his estate was appraised by M. Miller and William Ringgold. John Ingram and William Edwin signed as next of kin. Personal property was valued at £207.6.8.{INAC 36B:323}

The estate of Benjamin Ricaud was filed on 14 April 1713 by admx. Susannah Ricaud. There were two inventories totalling £28.15.3 and £207.6.8. William Edwin received a payment from the estate.{INAC 33B:227} His estate was admin. by Mrs. Susanna Ricaud on 21 Sep 1714. There were assets totalling £203.11.5 and £115.0.6. Payments were made to the admx. (Susanna Ricaud) as extx. of Richard Lowder, and his children (unnamed), John Ingram who m. Mary Bruinton (a niece), Michael Byrne for Elizabeth Dean (niece) & dau. of Sarah Whetstone, William Dean (nephew), Tabitha Dean (niece), Roger Canaday who m. Jane (N), a relation of the dec., Edward Davis who m. (N), widow of Thomas Ricaud, Thomas Ricaud (son of Thomas), John Maxwell who m. Elizabeth Ricaud (dau. of Thomas), Mary Edwin (child of Mary, sister of dec.), William Edwin (child of Mary, sister of dec.), Robert Hodges m. Tamar (child of Mary, sister of dec.), and Margaret Edwin (child of Mary, sister of dec.).

Ricaud's estate was admin. again on 16 March 1715 by the admx. Susannah, now wife of John Darick.{INAC 37A:12} Susannah Rickard m. John Derrick on 17 Dec 1713 in St. Paul's Parish.{ESVR 1:20; KESP}

4. THOMAS RICAUD, son of Benjamin and Elizabeth, was b. by 1684, was living 18 Sep 1687 in KE Co. He was bur. 29 Dec 1699 in St. Paul's Parish.{KESP; ESVR 1:31} He m. Mary (N).

Thomas and Mary were the parents of the following children, named in the 1714 administration account of the estate of Benjamin Ricaud{ESVR 1:31; KESP; INAC 36B:17, and 37A:12; INAC 36B:17}: ELIZABETH, b. 24 Jan 1696 in St. Paul's Parish, KE Co., m. John Maxwell; THOMAS, b. 28 Jan 1698 in St. Paul's Parish; BENJAMIN, b. 6 June 1700 in St. Paul's Parish, he may be the Ben Rickard who was bur. 11 Dec 1712{KESP}; MARY, m. William Edwin;[47] and SARAH, b. by 1674, named as sister in will of Christopher Hall, m. 1st, William Dean, and 2nd, Stephen Whetstone{MWB 4:80, 7:115, and 13:82; INAC 36:17}.[48]

5. THOMAS RICAUD, son of Thomas and Mary, d. in KE Co. by 3 June 1722. He m. Mary (N), who may have m. 2nd, (N) Cooper.
On 27 July 1721, Thomas Ricand, of KE Co., and his wife Mary, conv. to Benjamin Ricand, of the same county, a parcel of land near Swan Creek called *Deprived Mischief* formerly laid out for Benjamin Ricand, dec., uncle to the sd. Thomas Ricand, for his service performed within the Province of MD, 100 a.{KELR JS#W:103}

Thomas Ricaud d. leaving a will dated 5 April 1722 and proved 3 June 1722. Bequests were made to son Benjamin, plant. whereon mother Mary Davis now dwells, personalty, he was to be free at 18 years. To unborn child, 100 a. called *Ricand's Addition*, and personalty. To wife Mary, extx., tract called *Middle Spring* at head of Swann Creek.{MWB 17:174}

Thomas Ricaud's estate was inv. on 25 July 1722 by M. Miller and George Hanson, who valued the personal estate at £122.11.6. Benjamin Ricaud and Elizabeth Maxwell signed as next of kin.{MINV 5:242 and 9:82} Another inventory, totalling £12.8.11, made by the same appraisers on 14 Sep 1724, was filed on 20 Dec 1724.
Benjamin Ricaud and Mary Cooper signed as next of kin. Mary Ricaud filed the inventory.{MINV 10:298}

Mary, widow of Thomas Ricaud, may be the Mary Ricaud who signed the inventory of John Maxwell on 22 Nov 1722 as one of the next of kin.{MINV 9:73}

On the petition of Mary Rickand (c1724), widow, at June Court, to establish the bounds of her land, a tract called *Middle Spring*, a

---

[47] William and Mary (Ricaud) Edwin were the parents of{INAC 37A:12}: MARY; WILLIAM; TAMAR, m. Robert Hodges; and MARGARET.

[48] William Dean d. in KE Co. leaving a will dated 1 June 1695 and proved 30 Aug 1695. Wife Sarah named as extx. Named children WILLIAM; TABITHA (to have 200 a., *The Forest*, in BA Co.); ELIZA (not yet 16); and JANE (not yet 16).{MWB 7:113}
Stephen Whetston, of KE Co., d. leaving a will dated 12 Nov 1710 and proved 29 June 1710. Named wife Sarah, extx., and her daus. Jane and Tabitha.{MWB 13:82}

commission was appointed. The following depositions were annexed: Mary Cooper, aged c48, that when she walked with her dec. husband Thomas Rickand, he referred to a bounded tree; Susanna Derrick, aged c53, said that her dec. husband, Benjamin Ricand referred to a boundary; Ralph Page, aged c44 years, said he put in two posts for the bounds; William Breward, aged c50 years, said he helped put up some posts; William Brown, aged c45 years, said he was living at Stephen Wheatstones when he was shown a boundary post.{KELR JS#W:372}

Thomas Ricaud, Jr., and Mary were the parents of: BENJAMIN.

6. BENJAMIN RICAUD, son of Thomas and Mary, was b. 6 June 1700 in St. Paul's Parish.{ESVR 1:31} He is placed as the Benjamin who m. Jane Cooper on 4 Feb 1730, since his nephew Benjamin, son of Thomas, would be too young.{KESP; ESVR 2:26}

Benjamin and Jane were the parents of three children, b. in St. Paul's Parish, KE Co.{KESP; ESVR 2:26}: SARAH, b. 22 June 1732; THOMAS, b. 2 Nov 1734; and MARY, b. 28 July 1736.

7. BENJAMIN RICARD, son of Thomas and Mary, was not yet 18 when his father made his will on 5 April 1722.{MWB 17:174} He d. in St. Paul's Parish, KE Co., by 9 May 1774, having m. Mary (N), who d. 15 Feb 1772.{ESVR 3:15}

Benjamin Ricand, of KE Co., d. leaving a will dated 12 Jan 1773 and proved 9 May 1774. The heirs named were dau. Mary Worrell, son-in-law John Hatchison, dau. Martha Hatchison, dau. Rachel Bradsha, son Richard Ricand, and grandsons Richard Hatchison, Benjamin Hatcheson, and Richard Blackston. The exec. was son Richard Ricand. The will was witnessed by Edward Beck, Robert Greenfield, and Edwd. Slipper.{MWB 39:827}

Benjamin and Mary were the parents of: RICHARD, b. 28 Nov 1753 in St. Paul's Parish, m. Sarah (N). Sarah Ricaud and Martha Miller signed the inventory of Thomas Page, of KE Co., on 14 Feb 1775 as next of kin.{MINV 122:242} (Richard and Sarah had one dau.{ESVR 3:15}: 7-a. MARY, b. 8 Sep 1773); [BENJ]AMIN, b. 5 Sep 1776{ESVR 4:3};

[ELIZAB?]ETH, b. 25 Dec ----, d. 26 Dec 1778; (N), m. by 1773, (N) Brackiston{MWB 39:827}; MARTHA, m. by 1773, John Hutchinson; and MARY, m. by 1773, (N) Worrell.

Unplaced

RICAUD, MARTHA, and Sarah Tayler signed the inventory of John Cooper on 28 Feb 1754 as next of kin.{MINV 57:399}

RICAUD, MARY, was bur. 14 April 1716.{KESP}

RICAUD, MARY, wife of Benjamin Ricaud, d. 15 Feb 1778.{ESVR 4:3}

THE RINGGOLD FAMILY

Refs.: A: Christopher Johnston, Charts of the Ringgold Family, Johnston Gen. Collection, MHS. Thanks also to the aid given by Ray Ringgold.

1. THOMAS RINGGGOLD, progenitor, was b. c1609/11 and d. c1672. At age 43, he dep. at November Court 1652.{ARMD LIV:10, Liber A:57} Thomas Ringgold, age c44, dep. on 29 Oct 1655.{ARMD LIV:33, Liber A:103}
He settled first in Lower Norfolk County, VA, but by 1654 had settled in KE Co., MD. His first wife, the mother of his two sons, has not been identified; his second wife was Christian, dau. of Thomas Hill.{A}
On 27 Jan 1654, Thomas Ringold, of KE Co., acknowledged to have sold to his son John Ringold a cow and a steer, and to his son James Ringgold two heifers.{ARMD LIV:106, Liber B:28}
On 18 Nov 1657, Henry Morgan complained against Thomas Ringgold who had m. the admx. of the estate of Thomas Hill, Sr., dec.{ARMD LIV:121, Liber B:20}

On 5 Feb 1657, Thomas Ringgold and his wife Christian, the former wife of Thomas Hill, dec., sold to Thomas Hill a parcel of land.{ARMD LIV:126, Liber B:18}

On 2 Dec 1661, Thomas Ringgould, of Isle of Kent, acknowledged bequeathing to his sons, John Ringould and James Ringgould ½ of his land called *Huntingfield*, 1200 a., beginning at a marked locust being the northern most bounds of Mr. South's land, the ½ that is 600 a.{ARMD LIV:207, Liber B:91}

Thomas Ringgold and his first wife were the parents of{A}: Maj. JAMES; and JOHN.

Second Generation

2. Maj. JAMES RINGGOLD, son of Thomas Ringgold (1), lived at Huntingfield, KE Co., and was b. c1636 and d. 1686. James Ringgold, age c23, dep. on 20 Dec 1660.{ARMD LIV:190, Liber B:79}

Like his father, he was twice m. but his first wife has not been identified. His second wife, and mother of most of his children, was Mary, widow of Edward, dau. of Capt. Robert Vaughn.{A}

James Ringgold established a town in KE Co. near Grey's Inn Creek in 1675.{MPL 19:599}

On 22 Aug 1676, an indenture was made between James Ringgold, of KE Co., MD, Gent., and Samll. Tovey, late of the City of Bristoll in England, merchant, and now of Kent, afsd.{KELR A:381}

On 20 Nov 1678, James Ringgold, of KE Co., and his wife Mary, of the one part for 5 s. were conv. by Samuel Tovey, of afsd. co., of the other part land in Great Neck on Grays Inn Creek in Chester River and is part of a tract of 100 a. granted and intended to be granted by the sd. James Ringgold to the sd. Samuel Tovey ... part of a tract of 1200 a. formerly granted by patent to Thomas Ringgold, father of the sd. James and called *Huntingfield* ... .{KELR A:514}

James Ringgold d. leaving a will dated 18 May 1686 and proved 28 Sep 1686. To sons William and John, 600 a. called *The Plaines*. To youngest son Charles, 150 a. called *Ringgolds Fortune* at mouth of Anake. To son James, dwell. plant., provided son Thomas refuse to give him 300 a. of northern portion of 600 a. of land given by dec. father, Thomas Ringgold, to sd. son Thomas. If son James by reason of being the eldest son of the now only dau. of Capt. Robert Vaughan, dec., inherit lands of sd. Vaughan, then testator gives to son Thomas the entire tract of 600 a. together with plant. To dau. Barbara Lanham and to William Williams, personalty. To children afsd. and dau.-in-law Rebecka Borten, personalty. To wife Mary, ⅓ personalty and ½ dwell.

plant. She to administer estate jointly with Col. Henry Coursey.{MWB 4:232}

The estate of Maj. James Ringgold was admin. on 22 Oct 1686 and 9 Sep 1687. It contained a list of debts.{INAC 9:224, 457} An account was filed on 8 May 1694 by extx. Mary Speares.{INAC 13A:213}

James Ringgold was the father of two children by his first wife{A}: Maj. THOMAS; and BARBARA, m. 1st, Josias Lanham, and 2nd, Edward Blay.

By his second wife, Maj. James Ringgold was the father of{A}: JAMES, b. c1675; CHARLES, d. by 1723; WILLIAM, b. 1677, d. 1754; and JOHN.

3. JOHN RINGGOLD, son of Thomas Ringgold (1), was b. c1636 and d. 1672. John Ringgold, age c20, dep. on 9 da., 7 mo., 1656.{ARMD LIV:71, Liber A:124}

John Ringgold's will named his father Thomas, his bro. James, and his "cousins" (nephew and niece) Thomas and Barbara Ringgold.{A}

John Ringold d. before 12 Feb 1674 when his estate was admin. Legatees were Elisabeth Cooke, now wife of Samuel Wheler, Thomas Ringold (father), and William Savidge. James Ringold and Richard Hill were execs.{INAC 1:178}

Third Generation

4. Maj. THOMAS RINGGOLD, son of Maj. James Ringgold (2), lived at Huntingfield, KE Co. He was bur. 10 Oct 1711 having m. three times; 1st, Sarah (N) who was bur. 20 April 1699;[49] 2nd, on 7 Sep 1699,[50] Mary Tilden, who was bur. 9 Sep 1709; and 3rd, Frances (N), who m. 2nd, on 12 Feb 1712, Jos. Crafford.{A; KESP}

Thomas Ringgold patented *Ringold's Chance*, 200 a., on 15 April 1696.{MPL 40:497}

On 22 Aug 1696, Thomas Ringgold and his wife Sarah, of KE Co., conv. to Thomas Smith, of the same county, part of a tract called *Trumpington*, 200 a.{KELR M:61B}

Thomas Ringgold d. leaving a will dated 18 Jan 1710 and proved 16 Oct 1711. To son Thomas, he left ½ of his dwell. plant. To sons Elias and James, he left plant. *Hunting Field* and land between *Cattail Marsh* and the part of *Prevention of Inconveniency*, sold by father

---

[49] Christopher Johnston's charts state she d. 20 Nov 1699.
[50] Hanson gives date as 17 Sep 1699 and states she was the dau. of Marmaduke and Rebecca Tylden.

269

———, to William Hodges. To youngest son Josias, he left 200 a., part of *The Plains*, bought of bro. William Ringgold. To unborn child, he left personalty. To wife Frances, he left ½ of the dwell. plant., &c. Thomas Smith, bro. William, and son Thomas were execs.{MWB 13:394}

The estate of Maj. Thomas Ringgold was admin. by execs. William and Thomas Ringgold and filed on 20 Dec 1712.{INAC 33B:166}

The account of the estate of Maj. Ringgold, of KE Co., was filed 12 March 1712. The approvers of the inventory were William Ringgold and Thomas Ringgold. Widow (unnamed), two children (unnamed), Elias Ringgold, and James Ringgold were mentioned.{INAC 34:71}

The administration of the estate was also filed on 22 June 1713. Legatees were widow (unnamed) and William Ringold.{INAC 34:194} It was filed again on 23 Feb 1714 when reference was made to widow (unnamed). William Ringgold was exec.{INAC 36B:142, 243}

On 12 Oct 1721, his estate was again admin. by William Ringgold and Thomas Ringgold. Sir Robert Dunkley, merchant in London, was mentioned.{MDAD 4:37}

On 16 Aug 1722, his estate was admin. by William Ringgold and Thomas Ringgold. Bro. William was mentioned.{MDAD 4:234}

On 8 March 1722, the estate of Maj. Thomas Ringgold, of KE Co., was admin. again by William Ringgold and Thomas Ringgold.{MDAD 5:44}

The estate of Maj. Thomas Ringold, of KE Co., was admin. yet again on 3 Nov 1723 by William Ringold.{MDAD 5:245}

By his first wife, Sarah, Maj. Thomas was the father of{A}: THOMAS, bur. 1728.

By his second wife, Mary (Tilden), he was the father of{A}: SARAH, bapt. 29 April 1700; JAMES, d. 1767; and ELIAS, b. 6 Sep 1702.{KESP}

By his third wife Frances, he was the father of{A}; JOSIAS, b. 1710; and MARY ANN, bapt. 18 April 1712, m. Thomas Smythe.{A; KESP}

5. JAMES RINGGOLD, eldest son of Maj. James Ringold (2) by his 2nd wife, was b. c1675, and d. 1704. He m. Mary, dau. of Moses Harris. After Ringgold's, death she m. 2nd, Thoms Godman.{A}

James Ringold, of Kent Island, d. leaving a will dated 27 Oct 1704 and proved 15 March 1704/5. To wife Mary, extx., he left ⅓ of personalty and ⅓ of real estate during life. To his three children: Moses, Mary and James, he left the residue of estate.{MWB 3:660}

The list of debts was filed c1704/5.{KI Inv. from Wills: 3:546} Admin. was filed on 28 Feb 1711 by extx. Mary Godman, wife of Thomas Godman.{INAC 33A:202}

Moses Harris of TA Co. d. leaving a will dated 16 Feb 1712. He named the two child. of dau. Mary Godman, wife of Thomas Godman, by former marriage with James Ringgold: granddau. Mary Ringold and hrs., who was to have 400 a., *Harris' Range* where Bowling Green now lives, and her brother, James Ringold.{MWB 13:455}

James and Mary (Harris) Ringgold were the parents of{A}: MOSES; MARY, m. Robert Blunt{QALR RTB:121}; and JAMES, of Kent Island, d. 1740.

6. CHARLES RINGGOLD, son of Maj. James (2) and Mary (Vaughn) Ringgold, d. by 1723. On 17 Jan 1705, he m. Elizabeth Parke, who m. 2nd, Philip Davis.

Charles Ringold, of KE Co., d. by 8 Sep 1723, when his estate was admin. by Elisabeth Davis, wife of Phillip Davis.{MDAD 5:240}

Charles and Elizabeth were the parents of{A; KESP}: JAMES, b. 30 June 1709; MARY, bapt. 14 Dec 1712;[51] CHARLES, b. 27 April 1713; and VINCENT, b. 12 Aug 1716.

7. WILLIAM RINGGOLD, son of Maj. James (2) and Mary (Vaughn) Ringgold, was b. 1677 and d. 1754.{A} William Ringgold, age c51, dep. in Aug 1726 regarding the bounds of a tract called *Arcadia*.{KELR JS#X:43} On 25 June 1743, Mr. William Ringgold, age c66, dep. regarding the bounds of a tract called *Fancy*.{KELR JS#24:439} William Ringgold of KE Co., age c71, dep. April 1747 that when his grandfather, Thomas Ringgold, came out of England, he purchased a tract called *Crawford* (QAEJ: Barnes, Elizabeth v. Frisby).

William m. Martha (N).{A}

On 13 Nov 1699, William Ryngold and his wife Martha, of TA Co., conv. to Thomas Smith, of KE Co., 108 a., being part of 670 a. called *The Plaines*.{KELR M:105B}

On 13 Nov 1699, William Ringgold and his wife Martha, of TA Co., conv. to Thomas Ringgold, of KE Co., 200 a., taken up by his father Maj. James Ringgold in 1677, called *The Plaines*.{KELR M:109B}

On 11 Oct 1715 William Ringgold of KE Co., Gent., and his wife Martha conv. to Rowland White 106 a., part of *Grantham* in Wye River adj. *Lobb's Crooke*.{TALR 12:238}

---

[51] The parish register states she was a dau. of Charles and Mary Ringgold.

At November Court 1731, it was presented that William Ringgold of St. Paul's Parish, with many others unknown, on 29 Aug 1729 broke 20 panels of a fence made with rails, of the value of 100 lbs. of tob., erected to enclose the corn growing of Thomas Ambrose, owner of the tract *Queen Charlton*, allowing horses, steers and bulls to eat and consume the corn to the great damage of Thomas Ambrose. Ringgold was acquitted.{KECR JS#WK:261}

William Ringgold, of KE Co., Gent., on 24 Aug 1739 conv. to his son-in-law Essau Watkins and his dau. Sarah, wife of afsd. Essau, part of a water lot in Chester Town, No. 11.{KELR JS#22:392}

On 25 April 1743, William Ringgold, of KE Co., Gent., conv. to his son James Ringgold, of the county afsd., part of a tract called *The Plaines*.{KELR JS#24:319}

William Ringgold d. leaving a will dated 10 Nov 1753 and proved on 1 April 1754. The heirs named were son James Ringgold, to son Thomas Ringgold one seat in a pew in the addition to St. Paul's Parish Church, to dau. Robena Ringgold one seat in the addition to St. Paul's Parish Church where she now sits, and son John Ringgold. The exec. was son John. The will was witnessed by Chas. Scott, Ann Scott, and Samuel Wickes.{MWB 29:221}

On 17 Feb 1756, the estate was appraised by William Hynson and John Wickes, and valued at £50.9.5. No creditors or next of kin listed. John Ringgold, exec., filed the inventory on 9 April 1756.{MINV 60:476}

Mr. William Ringgold, of KE Co., d. by 1754, when his estate was appraised by W. Hynson and John Wickes, and valued at £297.8.6. James Ringgold and Thomas Ringgold signed as creditors. Thomas Ringgold and Rebecca Ringgold signed as next of kin. John Ringgold, exec., filed the inventory on 2 July 1754.{MINV 57:381}

William and Martha were the parents of{A}: SUSANNA, bapt. 26 Oct 1712, m. Benjamin Wickes; JAMES, d. 1766; JOHN; THOMAS, living in 1753; REBECCA; and SARAH, m. Esau Watkins.{KESP}

Fourth Generation
8. THOMAS RINGGOLD, son of Maj. Thomas (4) and Sarah, d. and was bur. Aug 1728. On 1 Aug 1712, he m. Rebecca, dau. of Simon Wilmer, b. 27 July 1696, d. 1750.{KESP}

On 24 May 1722, Samuel Wicks and his wife Frances, Edward Norrest and his wife Mary, and Thomas Ringold and his wife Rebecca, of KE Co., conv. to Charles Baker, surviving heir of Charles Baker, of the same county, a tract called *Chigwell*, between Langfords Bay and Chester River, 200 a.{KELR JS#W:233}

The estate of Capt. Thomas Ringgold was admin. on 17 Dec 1728 and filed on 17 May 1729 by admx./extx. Mrs. Rebecca Ringgold. Charles Ringgold and James Ringgold listed as next of kin.{MINV 14:73, 235}

Rebecca Ringgold, Eastern Neck of KE Co., d. leaving a will dated 20 Nov 1746 and proved 12 Jan 1750. The heirs named were son William Ringgold, to whom was devised land upon which he lived, being part of a tract called *Tilghman* and *Fox Grove*, son Thomas Ringgold, dau. Sarah Williamson and her husband Alexander Williamson, to whom was devised the tract called *Pine Grove*, dau. Rebecca Ringgold, to whom was devised land in Chestertown and land from her uncle James Ringgold, grandson Alexander Williamson, grandson Thomas Ringgold, and bro.-in-law James Ringgold. The exec. was James Ringgold. The will was witnessed by Darby Hands, William Nickerson, and Rose Cunningham, Sr.{MWB 28:6}

Thomas and Rebecca were the parents of{A; KESP}: THOMAS, b. 5 Dec 1715, bur. 23 Sep 1717; THOMAS, b. 5 Dec 1718, m. Anna Maria Earle; WILLIAM, b. 1723; REBECCA, bapt. 4 June 1727; and SARAH, m. Alexander Williamson.

9. JAMES RINGGOLD, son of Maj. Thomas (4) and Mary (Tilden) Ringgold, d. 1767. Johnson states he d. s.p., but he may have had at least one dau. He may have m. Mary, dau. of Mary Brown of KI, QA Co.

On 22 Nov 1728, James Ringgold, of KE Co., and his wife Mary, conv. to Rebecca Ringgold, of the same county, 50 a., part of a tract called *Hinchin Field* originally granted to Thomas Ringgold as 1200 a.{KELR JS#X:307}

On 17 June 1729, James Ringgold (bro. of Elias), of KE Co., Gent., conv. to Elias Ringgold, of afsd. county, Gent., and his wife Mary, 225 a. of a patent granted to Thomas Ringgold in 1659 for a tract called *Hunting Field*, 1200 a. which descended to his eldest son James Ringgold, and from him descended to his eldest son Thomas Ringgold, father to the afsd. Elias and James. Sd. Thomas by his last will dated 1710 devised to his wife Frances ½ of his dwell. plant. and the other ½ to his eldest son.{KELR JS#X:367}

On 28 Jan 1734 Mary Brown of KI, QA Co., made her will, naming dau. Mary Ringgold, and granddau. Sarah, dau. of James Ringgold.{MWB 21:560}

On 23 Dec 1749 Nathan Samuel Turbutt Wright, Gent., heir of Thomas Hynson Wright and Dorcas wife of Nathan Samuel Turbutt

Wright; and Thomas Wright, his bro., conv. to James Ringgold of
Eastern Neck in KE Co., Gent., 800 a., part of *Coursey's Point* alias
Smith's Mistake, Bishop's Addition, Bishop's Outlett and *Bramton's
Addition*. {QALR RTC:399}

On 30 Aug 1751 Samuel Austin and his wife Mary conv. to James
Ringgold of Eastern Neck in KE Co., Gent., 78 a. called *Coursey's
Point* alias *Smith's Mistake* on n. side of Corsica Creek that William
Bishop and his wife sold to John Austin, father of said Samuel
Austin. {QALR RTD:32}

On 30 Aug 1751 Jacob Bayley conv. to James Ringgold of Eastern
Neck, KE Co., 200 a. on n. side of Corsica Creek called *Bishop's
Outlett*, sold by William Bishop to Jacob Bayley, father of the grantor;
also 50 a. adj. {QALR RTD:34}

James Ringgold, of KE Co., d. leaving a will dated 5 Sep 1767 and
proved 19 Dec 1767. Heirs named were bros. Josias and Elias Ringgold;
bro. Josias Ringgold's children Sarah, Mary, Ann, Hannah and Rebecca
Ringgold; nephews Thomas Smith, Elias Ringgold, and James Ringgold;
nephews Thomas and Wm. Ringgold, children of bro. Thomas, dec.; to
nephew Josias Ringgold, land in QA Co.; nieces Sarah and Mary Ann
Ringgold and Sarah Williamson; nieces Hannah and Rebecca Ringgold;
niece Sarah Williamson's children Ann Tomson, and Rebecca and Sarah
Williamson; and cousins William Frisby, Rebecca and Anna Maria
Frisby, Ann Tomson, James Frisby, and Thomas Ringgold, son of
nephew Thomas. Also named were James Williamson, Henrietta
Williamson, and James Stenson. {MWB 36:149}

Tracts named were *Hunting Field*, near Bushups Cove, and
Coursey's Point, on Corsica Creek. The exec. was nephew Thomas
Ringgold. The will was witnessed by Joseph and Samuel Wickes, and
James Hynson. {MWB 36:149}

10. ELIAS RINGGOLD, son of Maj. Thomas (4) and Mary (Tilden)
Ringgold, was b. 6 Sep 1702 and d. Oct 1737. On 15 April 1725 he m.
Mary Bordley. {KESP}

Elias Ringgold d. leaving a will dated 19 Oct 1737 and proved 21
Nov 1737. To wife Mary, extx., he left a lot in Chestertown, No. 97, at
her decease it was to pass to child not yet born, also dwell. plant. part
of *Hunting Field*. If both wife and unborn child die, it was to pass to
bro. James. Should bro. die, to nephew Thomas, son of bro. Thomas
(dec.). To bro. James, he left part of *Hunting Field* during life. {MWB
21:803}

Elias and Mary were the parents of{A; KESP}: THOMAS, b. 30 Oct 1726, bur. 25 Aug 1729; and ANN, b. 29 Sep 1728, bapt. 17 Nov 1728, bur. 25 Aug 1729.

11. JOSIAS RINGGOLD, son of Maj. Thomas (4) and Frances, was b. c1710, and d. 1770. On 11 Aug 1730 he m. Rachel Smith.{KESP}

Josias Ringgold, of KE Co., d. leaving a will dated 4 May 1769 and proved 23 Feb 1770. Mentioned were children Thomas, Sarah, Mary, Ann, Hannah, and Rebecca, and grandchildren Josias and Sarah, children of Josias. Mentioned were the tracts *The Plains, Green Charlton, Coopers, Ringalos* and *Poplar Farm*. The extx. was dau. Sarah. The will was witnessed by Robt. Reade, Thos. Smythe, and John Frisby.{MWB 37:494}

The estate was appraised on 1 March 1770 by James Dunn and Samuel Griffith, and valued at £901.11.7. Thomas Ringgold and Smyth & Sudler signed as creditors. Thomas Ringgold and Joseph Ringgold signed as next of kin. Sarah Ringgold, extx., filed the inventory on 17 July 1770.{MINV 107:9}

The estate of Josias Ringgold, of KE Co., was dist. by 4 Nov 1772. Distribution of the estate was made by James Smith, Jr., and his wife Sarah Smith, execs. Distribution was made to five daus., Sarah, Mary, Ann, Hannah, and Rebecca.{BFD 6:178}

Josias and Rachel were the parents of{A; KESP}: THOMAS, b. 14 Dec 1732, d. in infancy; THOMAS, b. 25 March 1734; JOSIAS, b. 28 Sep 1735; SARAH, b. 6 Oct 1738; MARY ANN; ANN; REBECCA; and HANNAH.

12. JAMES RINGGOLD, son of James (5) and Mary (Harris), was b. c1710, d. 1740. He m. Mary (N).{A}

On 14 Aug 1732, James Ringgold, Jr., age c22, dep. regarding the bounds of a tract called *Fare Harbor*; he stated he was in company with Arthur Miller, Jr., to Robert Dunn's Landing and when they came to the land Michael Miller told him in the water lay the bounded tree of Gibs land.{KELR JS#16:254}

James Ringgold of Kent Island, QA Co., died leaving a will dated 24 Oct --- and proved 17 April 1740. The heirs named were son Thomas and hrs., upper part of *Coxes Neck*; in event of his death without hrs. land to pass to son William and hrs. and failing such to male hrs. of testator's daus. Sarah, wife of John Carter, Jr., and Mary. To son William and hrs., residue of *Coxes Neck*. Should he have no hrs. sd. land to pass to hrs. of Thomas or male hrs. of daus. afsd. To wife

Mary, extx., 1/3 estate. To child., viz.: Thomas, Sarah Carter, Mary, Rachel and Susana, personalty. The will was witnessed by William Elliott, Robert Wilson, Henry Carrill and Elizabeth Wilson.{MWB 22:161}

James and Mary were the parents of{A}: THOMAS; WILLIAM; SARAH, m. John Carter; MARY; RACHEL; and SUSANNA.

13. JAMES RINGGOLD, son of Charles (5) and Elizabeth, was b. 30 June 1709.{A}

At June Court 1733, James Ringgold, of St. Paul's Parish, son of Charles Ringgold, was found guilty of committing fornication on 10 June 1732, with Dorcas Cleaver and begetting a bastard child. He was fined 30 s.{KECR JS#WK:385}

14. JAMES RINGGOLD, son of William (7) and Martha, was b. c1705 and d. 1766. On 4 Dec 1735, James Ringgold, age c30, dep. regarding the bounds of a tract called *The Plains*.{KELR JS#18:199}

James m. Mary Tovey (or Lovey) on 2 Dec 1726.{A; KESP}

William Ringgold (18) stated that some time after his bro. Thomas' death, James Ringgold, son of Wm., who had m. Mary Tovey, offered the land to Rebecca Ringgold.{KELR DD#1:615}

James Ringold, Jr., of KE Co., d. leaving a will dated 30 Dec 1765 and proved 3 June 1766. Mentioned were children William, James, John, Anne, Martha, Mary, and Sarah, and Sarah Porter, dau. of Richard Porter, dec. Tracts mentioned were *Timely Discovery*, *The Plains*, and *Pontridge*. The exec. was son James Ridgely. The will was witnessed by John Moore, Will Hinds, Henry Thomas, and James Strong.{MWB 34:43}

James and Mary were the parents of{KESP}: MARTHA, b. 16 Nov 1727 (elsewhere it states she was bapt. 4 June 1727); WILLIAM, b. 19 July 1729; MARY, b. 5 March 1732; JAMES, b. 22 Aug 1734, bur. Sep 1735; and ANN, b. 23 Dec 1736; JOHN; and SARAH.

15. JOHN RINGGOLD, son of William (7) and Martha, m. Mary (N) and had one child{A; KESP}: ANN, b. June (probably c1735), m. (N) Carvil.

16. THOMAS RINGGOLD, son of William (7), was living as late as 1753.{A}

Thomas Ringgold, son of William, was presented at June Court 1747 for cutting and selling five timber trees and 200 fence logs from the land of Philip Davis. He was fined 2 s. and 6 pence.{KECR JS#24:378}

On 13 May 1755, Thomas Ringgold, of Chester Town, attorney-at-law and heir of his grandfather James Ringgold, formerly of Eastern Neck, Gent., dec., conv. to John Ringgold, Gent., son and devisee of William Ringgold, dec., part of a tract called *The Plains* which his father William by his last will devised to him, 200 a.{KELR JS#28:144}

Fifth Generation

17. THOMAS RINGGOLD, son of Thomas (8) and Rebecca (Wilmer) Ringgold, was b. 8 Dec 1715 and d. 1 April 1772. On 24 Oct 1743, he m. Anna Maria, dau. of James and Mary (Tilghhman) Earle, b. 1725, d. 1794.{A; KESP}

At March Court 1745, it was presented that Thomas Ringgold assaulted John Leith(?) on 21 Nov 1745. He was fined 40 s.{KECR JS#24:244}

On 31 Dec 1757 John Woodal of KE Co., son and heir of John Woodal, late of QA Co., dec., conv. to Thomas Ringgold of Chester Town, merchant, 27 a., part of *Crompton*, which remained unsold by his father to Henry Callister.{QALR RTE:189}

On 6 June 1760 Thomas Ringgold of Chester Town, merchant, conv. to John Hughes of Philadelphia, merchant, 20 a., part of *Crompton* near Red Lyon Branch.{QALR RTF:88}

On 25 May 1762 Thomas Ringgold of Chester Town, merchant, and his wife Anna Maria conv. to Robert Evans, 75 a. called *Friendship Addition*.{QALR RTF:212}

On 29 Dec 1763, Thomas Ringgold, of Chester Town, merchant, great-grandson and heir of James Ringgold, dec., who was patentee of a tract of 600 a. called *The Plains* have remised, released and confirmed to John Ringgold all that part of afsd. tract contained in a deed of exchange from Josias Ringgold conv. to the sd. John Ringgold cont. 19 a.{KELR DD#1:462}

Thomas Ringgold, of Chester Town, d. leaving a will dated 8 Feb 1768 and proved 15 April 1772. Mentioned were wife Anna Maria, child Thomas Ringgold, nephews James Williamson and William Frisby, nieces Rebecca, Sarah and Henrietta Maria Williamson, cousins Lambert Wickes and Richard Wickes, bro. William, and his sister's children. The estate included a plant. in Eastern Neck which descended to him from his father and lots in Chester Town, including a house and lot bought of Dr. Wm. Murray where his son was living. The exec. was son Thomas. The will was witnessed by Samuel Thompson, William Granger, and B. Brice.{MWB 38:624}

Thomas and Anna Maria (Earle) Ringggold were the parents of{A}:
THOMAS, b. 1744, d. 1776, m. Mary Galloway.

18. WILLIAM RINGGOLD, son of Thomas (8) and Rebecca (Wilmer)
Ringgold, was b. c1723. On 9 Oct 1761, William Ringgold, age 38, dep.
regarding the bounds of a tract called *Huntingfield*; he refered to his
bro. Thomas' death. He stated that some time after, James Ringgold,
son of Wm., who m. Mary Tovey, offered the land to Rebecca
Ringgold.{KELR DD#1:615}

19. JOSIAS RINGGOLD, son of Josias, was living in 1768. He m.
Sarah (N).
   On 3 May 1768 Josias Ringgold [and his wife Sarah], son of Josias
Ringgold of KE Co., Gent., and devisee of James Ringgold of Eastern
Neck, KE Co., dec., conv. to William Ringgold of Kent Island, 206 a.,
part of *Smith's Mistake* on Corsica Creek.{QALR RTH:245}

Sixth Generation
20. THOMAS RINGGOLD, son of Thomas (17) and Anna Maria, was b.
1744, and d. 1776. He m. Mary Galloway.{A}
   Thomas Ringgold, merchant, of Chester Town, KE Co., d. leaving a
will dated 15 Feb 1774 and proved 6 Dec 1776. To his mother
(unnamed), he left a yearly allowance of £600, a house and lot in
Chester Town and other property including all that his father left on
the plant. at Eastern Neck. To his wife (unnamed), he devised the
house where he lived in Chester Town, the piece of ground called
Scotch Point, £600 yearly, slaves and servants (all named) and other
items. He left his sons, Thomas, Samuel, and Benjamin, a large number
of a. in KE Co., QA Co., and FR Co. (*Conegocheague Manor* and other
tracts). To his dau. Anna Maria, he left £6,000. The execs. were
Michael Earle, William Hamsley, and John Galloway. Other heirs
named were Thomas Ringgold Tilghman, son of James Tilghman, Esq.,
of Philadelphia, Tench Tilghman, James Williamson, John Calloway,
and Wm. Hamsley, Jr., cousins Rebecca Thompson, Rebecca Hemsley,
and Henrietta Maria Williamson, cousins James and William Ringgold
sons of Uncle Wm. Ringgold, sons and daus. of Uncle Richard and
James Earle, cousins Mary Hemsley and Charlotte Hemsley, and bro.
and sister-in-law Benja. and Anne Galloway. The will was witnessed by
James Nicholson, Jos. Galloway, Nicholson, Jno. Combs, Samuel
Harrison, Jr., and Robt. Pemberton.{MWB 41:301}

Thomas and Mary (Galloway) Ringgold were the parents of:
THOMAS; SAMUEL; BENJAMIN; and ANNA MARIA.

Unplaced

RINGGOLD, (N), m. by 29 Oct 1768, Sarah, dau. of James Smith of
KE Co.{BFD 5:122}

RINGGOLD, CHARLES, at June Court 1767, was charged with having
assaulted John Devonish on 10 Aug 1766. He was fined 6 pence.{KECR
DD#1:89B}

RINGGOLD, CHARLES, of KE Co., d. by 28 May 1768, when his
estate was appraised by John Wickes and James Dunn, and valued at
£113.1.7. Thomas Ringgold & Company signed as creditors. Rebecka
Crouch and Ann Ringgold signed as next of kin. Joice Smith, admx.,
filed the inventory on 24 June 1769.{MINV 101:73}

RINGGOLD, CHARLES, at Aug Court 1771, was charged with having
neglected his duties as road overseer. Included were the roads leading
from Herrin Pone (pond?) to Swan Creek Bridge over the bridge to
Thomas Jerrom's plant. and a publick main road leading from the
bridge to a place called Joce's Lane, and another publick main road
leading from the bridge afsd. to another bridge in the county called
Tavern Bridge, over which sd. bridge and road afsd. the leige subjects
of our sd. Lord the King with their horses, carts and carriages go pass
and ride at their pleasure, and Charles Ringgold was appointed overseer of the roads and bridges afsd., but the roads have been in great
decay and on which one could not ride without great danger and
damage. He was fined 50 s.{KECR DD#1:133A}

RINGGOLD, CHARLES, of KE Co., d. leaving a will dated 8 March
1771 and proved 25 Nov 1773. The heirs named were wife Rachel, dau.
Rachel Ringgold, dau. Sarah Ringgold, and dau. Mary Hynson. Sarah
Ringgold was extx. The will was witnessed by Thos. Slipper, Edwd.
Gibbs, and Mary Hynson.{MWB 39:494}
  The estate of Charles Ringgold, Jr., of KE Co., was appraised by
James Dunn and John Caulk, and valued at £37.19.10. Thomas
Ringgold for self and Sedgely Hillhouse signed as creditors. Randolph
(no surname given) signed as next of kin. Thomas Slipper, admin., filed
the inventory on 17 March 1774.{MINV 115:341}

279

On 10 Jan 1774, his estate was appraised again by John Hatchem and James Glenn, and valued at £488.11.2. Philip Smith signed as creditor. Mary Hynson signed as next of kin. Sarah Ringgold, extx., filed the inventory on 10 March 1774.{MINV 115:342}

On 23 Sep 1775, his estate was appraised by Jacob Glenn and John Hutchison, and valued at £43.9.6. No creditors or next of kin listed. Sarah, wife of Christopher Driver, extx., filed the inventory on 6 Jan 1777.{MINV 125:47, 48}

RINGGOLD, Ensign JAMES, took the oath of allegiance on 22 April 1740.{KEBI JS#18:278}

RINGGOLD, JAMES, and others, at March Court 1770, were each fined 1 s. for not attending a jury of inquest.{KECR DD#1:113B}

RINGGOLD, JAMES, of KE Co., d. by 4 June 1744, when his estate was appraised by John Tilden and Charles Scott, and valued at £220.15.9. Hugh Campbell and Robert Maine signed as creditors. Charles Ringgold and William Ringgold signed as next of kin. Elisabeth Ringgold, admx., filed the inventory on 14 Aug 1744.{MINV 30:1}

The names of the children of James and Elizabeth Ringgold are obliterated in the church register (St. Paul's Parish). The dates of birth are: 23 Sep 1735; 28 June 1738; 15 Dec 1741; and 10 March 1743.{KESP}

RINGGOLD, JAMES, was bur. Jan 1743/4.{KESP}

RINGGOLD, JAMES, and wife Mary, were the parents of two children, whose birth dates, but not their names, were recorded in St. Paul's Parish: one b. 11 Nov 1740, the other b. Feb 1746.{KESP}

RINGGOLD, JOICE, d. (date unknown), and her estate was appraised by James Dunn and Nathaniel Miller, and valued at £57.14.2. Thomas Smith (admin. for Richard Gresham) and Thomas Ringgold signed as creditors. Lewis Atkinson signed as next of kin. Thomas Slipper, admin., filed the inventory on 21 Jan 1775.{MINV 121:255}

RINGGOLD, THOMAS, m. Rebecca Ringgold m. on 11 May 1741.{KESP} They were the parents of children whose names are obliterated in the register of St. Paul's Parish. The dates of birth are: 21 April 1742; 21 Dec 1743; 31 Jan 1745; 26 April 1748; and Sep 1750.{KESP}

RINGGOLD, WILLIAM, and wife Mary were the parents of an unnamed child, b. 7 March 1738.{KESP}

RINGGOLD, WILLIAM, Jr., m. Sarah Jones on 9 Jan 1750.{KESP}

RINGGOLD, WILLIAM, m. by 29 Jan 1759, (N), widow of Richard Johnson of KE Co.{BFD 2:116}

THE ROLPH/RALPH FAMILY

1. JOHN ROLPH, progenitor, was bur. 29 Aug 1723.{KESP}
   The inventory of his estate was taken on 10 Oct 1723 and filed on 23 April 1724. Next of kin were Thomas Rolph and Glavill Rolph.{MINV 9:357}
   On 19 Aug 1724, his estate was again admin. by John Rolph. Payments were made to son Glanvill Rolph, to Phil. Jones who m. a dau. of the dec., and to Thomas Rolph.{MDAD 6:75}
   John Rolph was the father of: JOHN; GLANVILLE; (N), dau., m. Phil. Jones; and THOMAS.

2. JOHN RALPH, son of John (1) and Mary, d. by 9 June 1739. He is probably the John Rolph who m. Mary Jones on 20 July 1721.{KESP}
   On 18 June 1728, Nathan Berry, of KE Co., taylor, and his wife Jane, and Elinor Dyars(?), co-heir with Jane Berry, conv. land to John Rolph of afsd. county, a tract of 100 a.{KELR JS#X:240}
   On 20 Aug 1728, John Rolph, of KE Co., and his wife Mary, conv. to Francis Ludolph Bodien, of the same county, ½ of a tract called *Sewards Hope* on the main branch of Morgans Creek, 150 a.{KELR JS#X:292}
   John Ralph d. leaving a will dated 15 April 1739 and proved 9 June 1739. To son William, he left 100 a. called *Broadway*. To son John, he left 100 a. called *Meconnakin* purchased of Eleanor Dyer (widow) and Jane Berry, wife of Nathaniel. To wife Mary, extx., he left ⅓ of personal estate. The residue of his estate was to be divided between sons afsd. and daus. Mary and Martha.{MWB 22:103}
   On 13 Aug 1739, his estate was inv. It was filed on 17 Feb 1739 by Mary Rolph, extx. Next of kin were G. Rolph and Sarah Atcheson.{MINV 24:478}

John and Mary (Jones) Rolph were the parents of{KESP}: MARY, bur. 9 April 1729; JOHN, bur. 11 Sep 1729; WILLIAM; JOHN; MARY; and MARTHA.[52]

3. GLANVIL ROLPH, son of John (1) and Mary, d. by 23 Oct 1742. He m. Margaret, widow of William Shield.

Rolph d. leaving a will dated 10 July 1740 and proved 23 Oct 1742. To wife Margaret, extx. and son Glanvil, personalty. To Mary Shield, £10. Testator willed that in event of his wife's remarriage or abuse of his son in any manner he was to be put under the guardianship of his uncle, Mitchel Hult.{MWB 22:509}

On 22 Aug 1743, his estate was appraised by Edward Worrell and Benjamin Wickes, and valued at £409.14.6. George Copper, Jr., and Jacob Glen signed as creditors. Sarah Hatcheson and John Jones signed as next of kin. (Name not given), extx., filed the inventory on 20 Oct 1743.{MINV 28:214}

Glanville was the father of: GLANVILLE; and JOHN.

4. THOMAS ROLPH, son of John (1) and Mary, was named in his father's will, and d. by 25 Jan 1732/3. He m. Margaret (N).

Thomas Rolph d. leaving a will dated 8 Nov 1732 and proved 25 Jan 1732. To wife Margrett, extx., entire estate and care of all children. The will was witnessed by Elias Ringgold, Mary Ringgold, and Elizabeth Holadgr (Hollager).{MWB 20:562}

He was the father of: THOMAS, bapt. 15 April 1725.{KESP}

5. WILLIAM RALPH, son of John (2) and Mary (Jones), d. by 3 June 1767.

William Rolph, of Chester Town, KE Co., d. leaving a will dated 20 Aug 1755 and proved 13 Aug 1755. The heirs named were son John Rolph, dau. Francis, and sister Martha. Personal estate to be divided between his three children. Bro. John Rolph was appointed to act, under direction and advice of friend Thomas Ringgold, of Chester Town, as exec., and also guardian to children and their estate. The will was witnessed by Moses Chepley and Mary Smith, of KE Co.{MWB 29:508}

---

[52] At March Court 1765, it was presented that Martha Rolph committed fornication and begot a base born child. She was fined £3. John Rolph entered into security for her.{KECR DD#1:55B}

His estate was appraised by John Trew and Arthur Miller, and valued at £244.12.5. Thomas Ringgold and William Murray signed as creditors. Joseph Warrell and Simon Worrell signed as next of kin. John Rolph, exec., filed the inventory on 15 Feb 1756.{MINV 60:381} His estate was appraised again and valued at £346.12.4. No creditors or next of kin listed. John Rolph, exec., filed the inventory on 12 Nov 1761.{MINV 76:240}

The estate of William Rolph, of KE Co., was appraised again and valued at £35.0.4. No creditors or next of kin listed. John Rolph, exec., filed the inventory cont. a list of debts on 26 Nov 1761.{MINV 76:239}

On 3 June 1767, distribution of William's estate was made by John Ralph, exec. Legatees were John Ralph, dau. Nancy, dau. Frances, and sister Martha. Residue to three children (unnamed), equally.{BFD 5:78}

William was the father of: NANCY; FRANCES; and one unnamed child.

6. JOHN ROLPH, son of John (2) and Mary (Jones) Rolph, is probably the John Rolph, Jr., who was charged at August Court 1772, that on 15 Aug 1772 he committed fornication with Milcah Jackson and begot a base born child. He was fined 30 s. and ordered to give security to keep the county from any charge by means of his bastard child called AMINTA.{KECR DD#1:151A}

7. JOHN ROLPH, son of Glanvill (3) Rolph, late of KE Co., d. leaving a will dated 28 Feb 1760 and proved 31 March 1760. Mentioned were mother Margaret Copper, and bros. and sister John Shield, George Hanson, and Ann House Hanson. The exec. was John Shield. The will was witnessed by Gustavus Hanson, John Waltham, and John Page.{MWB 30:804}

8. THOMAS ROLPH, son of Thomas (4), was bapt. 15 April 1725.{KESP} He is probably the Thomas who d. by 10 Aug 1761.

Thomas Rolph, of KE Co., carpenter, d. by 10 Aug 1761, when his estate was appraised by John Carville and —— Bordley, and valued at £15.1.0. B. Hands and Alexander McClean signed as creditors. Thomas Rolph and William Rolph (bros.) signed as next of kin. Andrew Hall, admin., filed the inventory on 26 Feb 1763.{MINV 80:26}

<u>Unplaced</u>

RAFFE, EDWARD, and Ufley Veale were m. 6 Nov 1705.{KESP}

ROLPH, SARAH, was bur. 3 Dec 1719.{KESP}

ROLPH, WILLIAM, was bur. 22 April 1721.{KESP}

THE SHAWN FAMILY

The name appears in the records with a variety of spellings: Shawhan, Shawhawn, Shawhorn, Shehawn, and Shohan.

1. DARBY SHAWN was b. c1673, and d. by 3 April 1736. He m. Sarah Meeks on 20 Nov 1707.{KESP}
   On 26 Feb 1733/4, Darby Shawhorn, age c60, dep. regarding the tract *Shadshole*.{KELR JS#18:2}
   Darby Shawhawn d. leaving a will dated 16 Oct 1735 and proved 3 April 1736. To his wife Sarah, extx., he left entire estate, except following legacies. To sons Daniel, John and Dennis, and dau. Sarah, wife of Edward Dier, and dau. Elizabeth, personalty. To sons Darby and David, 110 a. dwell. plant. called *Shad's Hole*.{MWB 21:572}
   Sarah Shawhawn d. leaving a will dated 20 Oct 1735 and proved 10 April 1736. To son Dennis and dau. Sarah Diah, personalty. Sons Darbe, David, and William to be in the care of Edward Diah until age of 21, or during life of his wife Sarah. To Elizabeth and William Shawawn, £10.{MWB 21:583}
   Darby and Sarah (Meeks) Shawn were the parents of: SARAH, m. Edward Diar; ELIZABETH; DANIEL; JOHN; DENNIS; DARBY; DAVID; and WILLIAM.

2. DANIEL SHAWN, son of Darby and Sarah, was named in his father's will. By 18 March 1735/6 he m. Jennett (N).
   On 14 Oct 1740, Daniel Shawhan, of KE Co., cordwainer, and his wife Jennett, conv. to John Shawhawn part of a tract called *Shads Hole*, beginning at a post by the w. side of a road which leads from Thomas Creek to Daniel Perkins' mill ... 50 a.{KELR JS#23:145}
   Daniel and Jennet (N) Shawn were the parents of{KESH}:
   MARGARET, b. 18 March 1735-6; and DANIEL, b. 17 Dec 1738.

3. JOHN SHAWN, son of Darby and Sarah, was named in his father's will but not in his mother's. He and Elizabeth Peach were m. 8 Oct 1730.{KESH}

John and Elizabeth were the parents of{KESH}: JOHN, b. 13 Sep 1732; DANIEL, b. 12 April 1735; and JOSEPH, living in 1767.

4. DENNIS SHAWN, son of Darby and Sarah, was named in both parents' wills.

At August Court 1748, it was presented that Dennis Shehawn, labourer, committed fornication with Elizabeth Gilbert and begot a bastard child. He was fined 30 s.{KECR JS#25:18A}

He d. leaving a will dated 16 April 1770 and proved 24 April 1770. Mentioned were children Isaac and Bathsheba. The exec. was Nicholas Jobson. The will was witnessed by John March, Isaac Briscoe, and Wm. Walters.{MWB 37:527}

On 25 April 1770, his estate was appraised by Roger Hales and John March, and valued at £64.19.9. Thomas Ringgold & Company and Donaldson Yeates signed as creditors. John Shawn, Sr., and John Shawn, Jr., signed as next of kin. Michael Jobson, exec., filed the inventory on 4 Sep 1770.{MINV 106:21}

On 29 March 1771, his estate was appraised by Roger Hales and John March, and valued at £92.16.0. Donaldson Yeates and Thomas and William Ringgold signed as creditors. John Shawhan and John Shawhan, Jr., signed as next of kin. Michael Jobson, exec., filed the inventory on 18 April 1771.{MINV 108:25}

On 10 June 1773, a list of debts was appraised and valued at £20.0.0. Michael Jobson, admin./exec., filed the inventory cont. a list of debts on 10 June 1773.{MINV 114:213}

On 16 June 1773, distribution of the estate was made by Michael Jobson, exec. Legatees were dau. Batsabe and Isaac Shehawn, with residue to eleven children (unnamed).{BFD 6:291}

Dennis Shawn was the father of: ISAAC; BATHSHEBA; and at least 9 others.

5. DARBY SHAWN, son of Darby and Sarah, was under age when his mother made her will in 1735.

Darby Shawn, of KE Co., d. leaving a will dated 28 Sep 1767. The heir named was nephew Joseph Shawn, exec., son of bro. John. The will was witnessed by Wm. March, John Turner, and Gideon Hayne.{MWB 36:229}

285

Derby Shawn's estate was appraised on 7 Oct 1767 by John March and Jonathon Turner, and valued at £110.19.0. James Black and James Anderson signed as creditors. John Shawn and Shadrack Shawn signed as next of kin. James (Joseph?) Shawn, exec., filed the inventory on 11 Jan 1768.{MINV 97:168}

6. DAVID SHAWN, son of Darby and Sarah, was under age when his mother made her will in 1735. He d. by 20 Oct 1766.

At March Court 1761, David Shawn, a single man, was charged that on 7 Dec 1759 he committed fornication with Jane Greenwood and begot a bastard child. He was fined 30 s.{KECR DD#1:4A}

On 20 Oct 1766, his estate was appraised by James Piner and Thomas Wilkins, and valued at £127.4.4. Thomas Ringgold and William Slubey, Jr., signed as creditors. Dennis Schawn and Darby Shawhawn signed as next of kin. —— Shawhawn, admin., filed the inventory on 13 Nov 1766.{MINV 90:352}

On 24 April 1767, his estate was appraised by Jacob Carter and Isaac Winchester, and valued at £6.2.0. No creditors or next of kin listed. John Shawn, admin., filed the inventory mentioning Thomas Ringgold, Darby Shawhawn, Benjamin Morgan, William Slubey, Jr., and Shadrack Shawn on 11 Nov 1768.{MINV 99:83}

7. JOHN SHAWN, Jr., son of John and Elizabeth, was b. 13 Sep 1732. He d. by 26 Feb 1774, when his estate was appraised by Hezekiah Cooper and John Gilbert, and valued at £11.13.7. J. Maxwell and Isaac Spencer signed as creditors. Aves Shehawn and Edward Blackston signed as next of kin. John Shehawn, admin., filed the inventory on 8 March 1775.{MINV 120:417}

THE SHIELD/SHEILD FAMILY

Refs.: A: Research by Mrs. William S. Bavis of Gaithersburg, MD, who has generously shared the results of her researh.

1. WILLIAM SHEILD, d. and was bur. on 13 May 1717.{KESP} He m. Mary, dau. of Thomas and Eliza Parker some time before 17 July 1695 when Thomas Parker, of KE Co., made his will, naming his son-in-law William Shields.{MWB 7:117} Mary Parker m. 2nd, Richard West.{A}

William was transported to MD in 1676 by Capt. Peter Pagan on the *Elizabeth Katherine*.{Skordas}

Eliza, widow of Thomas Parker, m. 2nd, Thomas Smyth. As Elizabeth Parker Smyth, of Lankford Bay, widow, she made a will dated 20 Dec 1713 and proved 28 July 1714. She left personalty to her son Thomas Parker and gave to dau., Mary Sheele, William Sheele, and Richard West, joint execs., all her goods and chattels in return for her care during her natural life.{MWB 14:3; INAC 36B:139}

Wm. Sheild d. in 1717.{KESP} Richard West m. William's widow, Mary Parker Sheild.

In 1712, Richard West bought 200 a. in KE Co., MD., part of a 1,000 acre land grant called *Pentridge,* from Marmaduke Tilden, for 10,000 lbs. of tob.{KELR JS#N:291}

Just before Richard West d. in 1732, he made two wills. In both, after paying his debts and providing for Mary's thirds, he devised the remainder to the sons of his friend, William Sheild, dec., namely William and John.

On 21 June 1732, he gave the plantation to William alone and it is witnessed by Fred Hanson and John Evans.{KELR JS#16:229}

West made a second will dated 22 June 1732 and proved 16 Jan 1732/3. He gave his plant. and 100 a. to John, but says, "In case William wants it, he can have it but he must make over a feasible portion to John." This second will, he said, revoked all previous wills and is witnessed by Elias Ringgold, Glanville Rolph, and Morgan Huff.{MWB 20:61}

William and Mary (Parker) had three children in all, but William and Mary d. in their minority without heirs.{A: cites KE Admin. Accts., 1749, Box 8, Folder 6; MSA}

William Shield was the father of: WILLIAM; JOHN, d. young; and MARY.

2. WILLIAM SHIELD, son of William and Mary (Parker), d. in 1733. He m. 1st, by Oct 1712 Rhoda Dammes, sister of John Dammes, and dau. of Jane Blackwell. William m. 2nd, Margaret Huff on 17 Feb 1723.{KESP} Margaret Huff m. 2nd, Glanvill Rolph (a month after William's death), (possibly 3rd, Richard Evans, d. 1743), 4th Hans Hanson, and 5th (N) Copper.

On 20 Oct 1712 William Shields the younger and his wife Rhoda conv. to Jane Blackwell, widow, their interest in 137 a., part of *Hambleton's Park* in Wye River, devised to grantors for life, Rhoda being one of the sisters and heirs of John Dammes, late of TA Co.{TALR 12:140} On 8 Aug 1717 William Shield and his wife Rhoda conv. to

James Barnwell 100 a., part of *Bedworth* on e. side of Woodenhawk Branch.{TALR 12:297}

Jane Blackwell, widow, of TA Co., died leaving a will dated 17 Oct 1720 and proved 21 Jan 1723. The heirs named were grandchild Rachel Shield and hrs. (dau. of dau. Rhoda), 1/2 of *"Hambleton's Park,"* cont. 137 a. To 4 child., viz., John, Abednego, Rhoda Shield and Sarah Saunders, residue of personal estate. The exec. was son-in-law William Shield. The will was witnessed by Cha. Stevens, Wm. Cole and John Barwick. {MWB 18:247}

On 21 June 1732, Richard West, of KE Co., for love and affection that he bears, left to his friend William Sheild, son to William Sheild, late of KE Co., dec., the upper ⅓ of the tract where he lives; his mother was to have her thirds of sd. land during her natural life.{KELR JS#16:229}

William Shield d. by 19 April 1733, when his estate was inv. by Edward Worrell and Joseph Sutton. His personal property was valued at £50.0.4. Glanvill Ralph and wife Margaret, admins., filed the inventory on 11 May 1733.{MINV 17:390}

Glanvill Rolph, guardian to Wm. and John Sheild, orphans of Wm. Sheild, of KE Co., dec., sought to have a commission view the plant. of the orphans."{F. Edward Wright, "Excerpts from Kent County Court Records, 1731-1735," BMGS 34 (4) (Fall 1993) 406}

On 21 July 1737, Glanvill Rolph, Thomas Hatcheson, and Benj. Weeks, of KE Co., gave bond they would give Mary Sheild £9.18.6 due her as her filial portion of the estate of William Sheild, her dec. father, at age 16 or day of marriage. They also promised to pay William and John Sheild each £9.18.6 due them as their filial portion of the estate of William Sheild, their dec. father, at age 21.{KEBI JS#18:77, 78, 79}

Glanvil Rolph d. leaving a will dated 10 July 1740 and proved 23 Oct 1742. He named his wife Margaret as extx., and also named son Glanvil, and Mary Shield, who was to have £10. Testator willed that in event of his wife's remarriage or abuse of his son in any manner, he was to be put under the guardianship of his uncle, Mitchel Hult.{MWB 22:509}

William Shield and Rhoda were the parents of{TAPE}: WILLIAM, b. 9 Nov 17--; and RACHEL, m. by 19 Aug 1751, John Pitts.[53]

---

[53] Rachel Shield m. by 19 Aug 1751 John Pitts, late of TA Co., but now of SO Co., conv. to Edward Lloyd, Esq., 400 a. called *Hambleton's Park* which belonged to Rachel Sheild, wife of John Pitts. {TALR 18:8}

3. JOHN SHIELD, son of William and Margaret, d. by 15 Feb 1775. He m. Martha Ann Evans, who m. 2nd (N) Jones.

The following wills establish that he was living as late as 1760. Richard Evans, of KE Co., d. leaving a will dated 19 Sep 1743 and proved 15 Oct 1743. The heirs named were father, bro. Jonathan, dau.-in-law Martha Andrews, son-in-law John Shield, and wife Margaret, extx. The will was witnessed by George Clark and Hannah Huff.{MWB 23:231}

John Shield is listed in the Debt Books of KE Co. from 1747 to 1769 as owning *Pentridge.*{INKE:33}

On 21 Feb 1755, Margaret Hansen willed (or conv.) 225 a., *Tolchester & Tombs* (adj. land) to John Sheild. This land she had acquired from H. Hansen.{A: cites KELR JS#28:77}

John Rolph, son of Glanvill Rolph, late of KE Co., d. leaving a will dated 28 Feb 1760 and proved 31 March 1760. Mentioned were mother Margaret Copper, and bros. and sister John Shield, George Hanson, and Ann House Hanson. The exec. was John Shield.{MWB 30:804}

John Shield's estate was appraised by George Pressbury and James Ringgold, and valued at £693.8.3. Morgan & Sluby and William Ringgold signed as creditors. Martha Ann Shield and Margaret Shield signed as next of kin. Martha Shield and Richard Jones, admins., filed the inventory on 15 Feb 1775.{MINV 121:250}

A list of debts was compiled and valued at £29.4.0. Richard Jones and Martha Shield, admins., filed the inventory cont. a list of debts on 15 Feb 1775.{MINV 121:257}

John Shields, of KE Co., d. before 3 Aug 1776. Distribution of the estate was made by Richard Jones and his wife Martha Jones, admins.{BFD 7:67}

On 14 Feb 1764 William Pitts, shoemaker, conv. to John Pitts, 137 a., a moiety of *Hambleton's Park* in the branches of Wye River lately in the tenure of John Dames Saunders, dec. and now in the possession of John Pitts - which moiety William Pitts claims in the right of his grandmother Jane Blackwell and his mother Rachel Shield. {TALR 19:252}

On 3 Aug 1773 John Pitts, formerly of TA Co., but now in BA Co., conv. to John Gibson, the elder, of TA Co., a moiety of 137 1/2 a., part of *Hambleton's Park,* devised by Jane Blackwell to her granddau. Rachel Shields, mother of said John Pitts. {TALR 20:310}

John and Martha were the parents of{A}: MARGARET; and (possibly) WILLIAM.

Unplaced

SHIELD, (N), m. by 8 Feb 1723, Elizabeth, dau. of Elizabeth Ross.{MWV 18:280}

SHIELD, BRYAN, d. by March 1731. He m. Jane Curtis 24 Sep 1711.{TAPE}
At June Court 1712 he paid the fine of Mary Gibson, spinster of QA Co., who had a child by Thomas Wallis.{QAJU ET No.B:190}
At March Court 1731 John Clayland and Roger Clayland of TA Co., planters, were bound to pay the following children of Bryan Shield each £20.7.8: James Shield, Sarah Shield, Elizabeth Shield and Benjamin Shield.{TAGU A}

SHIELDS, JAMES, m. Elizabeth Griffin 1 Aug 1746.{QALU} James Sheild, of TA Co. d. leaving a will dated 2 Feb 1759 and proved 27 Feb 1759. Mentions Son Griffith. Also Elizabeth Plummer, dau. of Christopher Plummer. Brother Benjamin Shield and his dau. Elizabeth. Exec. Somon Stevens Miller. Wit: Benjamin Stank, Ann Saunders.{MWB 30:667}

SHIELDS, JOHN, d. by c1701.{INAC 21:93}

SHIELD, LAMBERT, m. Mary Merchantt 25 Apr 1737.{TAPE} On 14 Jan 1741 Lambert and Mary conv. to Thomas Matthes 50 a., part of two tracts, *Rich Farm's Addition and Bedworth.*{TALR 15:125} On 11 Dec 1746 Lambert Shields and his wife Mary, and John Dames Saunders and his wife Rachel, conv. to James Barnwell, Jr., 50 a., part of *Rich Farm's Addition.*{TALR 17:7}

SHIELD, MARGARET, m. Michael Hussey on 20 May 1735.{QALU}

SHIELDS, MARY, was bur. 24 Feb 1714.{KESP}

SHIELD, REBECCA, m. William Stacey.{TAPE}

SHIELD, SUSANNAH, of KI, QA Co., died leaving a will dated 12 Aug 1735 and proved 24 Sept 1735. The heirs named were Morrice and

Susannah, son and dau. of James Silney, exec., personalty. To two brothers James and Darby Sliney, residue of estate, divided equally between them. The will was witnessed by Ralph Elston, John Rawles and Mary Raunsbeary. {MWB 21:460}

N.B.: Probate shows James Sliney to be eld. brother of the whole blood to the testatrix.

THE CASPARUS SMITH FAMILY

1. CASPAR (or CASPARUS) SMITH was b. c1679, giving his age as 52 in 1731.{Cecil Co. Land Commissions, 1:200} He m. Ann Robinson in St. Stephen's Parish, CE Co., on 11 Oct 1703.{CECH:2} She was the widow of James Robinson, Jr., of CE Co.{MWB 3:378}

Anne was a dau. of Thomas Kear, whose extx. m. William Dixon, in Dixon's admin. account of 7 July 1708.{INAC 28:160}

Casparus Smith, of QA Co., d. leaving a will dated 31 July 1732 and proved 14 Sep 1732. He named his three sons Daniel, Benjamin, and Casparus, who were to have 160 a., *Jones' Fancy*. Daus. Mary, Sarah, and Ann were to have 1 s. each, and dau. Rebecca was to have personalty. Son Daniel was named exec. and was to have care of sons Benjamin and Daniel and dau. Rebecca until they came of age. The will was witnessed by James Horsely, John Weekes, and Andrew Findley.{MWB 20:596}

Casparus and Ann were the parents of several children, b. in St. Stephen's Parish{CECH:15, 16}: DANIEL, b. 20 Jan 1705; MARY, b. 27 Jan 1707; SARAH, b. 2 April 1709; ANNE, b. 10 Aug 1713; BENJAMIN; CASPARUS; and REBECCA.

2. DANIEL SMITH, son of Casparus and Ann, was b. in St. Stephen's Parish, CE Co., on 20 Jan 1705. He settled in QA Co., where he m. Isabel (N).

Daniel and Isabel Smith were the parents of the following children, b. in St. Luke's Parish, QA Co.{ESVR 2:32, 38}: SARAH, b. 1 June 1738; and MARGARET, b. 25 Feb 1740.

1-a. BENJAMIN SMITH, son of Casparus, was named as cousin in the will, made 2 Dec 1737, of James Keare, of KE Co.{MWB 21:865} He is probably the Benjamin who d. by 5 Oct 1759 in QA Co. He m. Hannah (N), who survived him.

Benjamin Smith, of QA Co., d. leaving a will dated 4 Oct 1758 and proved 5 Oct 1759. He named his wife Hannah and sons James and Benjamin. His will mentioned the tracts *Jones Ferry* and *Mary's Chance*. No exec. was named. The will was witnessed by Daniel and Isabella Smith and James Roberts.{MWB 30:680}

Benjamin was the father of: JAMES; and BENJAMIN.

1-b. CASPARUS SMITH, son of Casparus and Ann, settled in QA Co., where he m. Joan Lowther on 13 Feb 172-.{ESVR 2:47}

THE NICHOLAS SMITH FAMILY

1. NICHOLAS SMITH, bro. of William, was of age in 1724, and d. by 24 Dec 1770. He m. 1st, by 1738, Rebecca, dau. of John Wyatt. He m. 2nd, on 14 April 1749, Ann, dau. (or widow?) of Joseph Mann.{A; KESB}

Nicholas Smith may have been b. c1702. Nicholas Smith, age c57, dep. on 3 April 1759.{KEEJ: Thomas Harris}

Nicholas Smith resided on his plant. made up of three tracts: *Vienna, Reserve,* and *Tanfield More.* He represented KE Co. in the Lower House from 1749-1751.{A}

On 12 May 1732, Nicholas Smith, of KE Co., and his wife Rebecca, conv. to William Smith, of the same county, 100 a., part of a tract called *Viana.*{KELR JS#16:204}

On 26 Dec 1738, Nicholas and wife Rebecca conv. to William Bootes, of the same county, 55 a., part of a tract called *Tanfield Moore* near Prickle Paire Branch.{KELR JS#22:231}

On 12 Aug 1758, Nicholas Smith, Sr., conv. to his son Nicholas Smith, Jr., part of a tract called ——, 175 a.{KELR JS#29:27}

Nicholas Smith, of KE Co., d. leaving a will dated 15 Jan 1770 and proved 24 Dec 1770. Mentioned was wife Anne. The children named were Oliver Garfield Moore Smith, Lambert, Rebecca Burgin, Hannah Blackiston dau. of wife Ann Smith, and John and Elizabeth Stoop. Also mentioned was George Van (Sant?) Mann. Wife Anne was extx. The will was witnessed by Jesse Cosdon, Joseph Boots, and David Burk.{MWB 38:180}

On 22 April 1771, Smith's estate was appraised by John Eccleston and Peter Massy, and valued at £8.9.11. William Rogers and Ann Calder signed as creditors. William Smith and Isable Denning signed as next of kin. Ann Smyth, extx., filed the inventory on 11 June 1771.{MINV 105:291}

On 3 Jan 1771, his estate was appraised again by John Eccleston and Peter Massy, and valued at £830.1.2. William Rogers and A. Calder signed as creditors. William Smith and Isabel Denington signed as next of kin. Ann Smith, extx., filed the inventory on 18 March 1771.{MINV 106:111}

A list of debts was appraised and valued at £88.12.1. Ann Smyth, extx., filed the inventory cont. a list of debts on 21 Aug 1771.{MINV 107:113} Another list of debts was appraised and valued at £75.17.6. Ann Smith, extx., filed the inventory cont. a list of debts on 13 June 1772.{MINV 109:125}

Nicholas Smith, of KE Co., d. before 13 June 1772. Distribution of the estate was made by Mrs. Ann Smith, extx. Distribution was made to widow (⅓) with residue equally to Elisabeth Stoopes, Rebecca Burgan, Hannah Blackiston, Lambert Smith, and Oliver Smith. Legatees were Hannah Blackiston, Oliver Smith, Lambert Smith, Rebecca Burgan, James Smith, and widow.{BFD 6:208}

On 13 June 1772, distribution of the estate was made by Ann Smith, extx., to the widow with residue equally to Elisabeth Stoops, Rebecca Burgin, Hannah Blackiston, Lambert Smith, and Oliver Smith.{BFD 6:125}

Ann Smith, of KE Co., d. leaving a will dated 6 Feb 1775 and proved 1 March 1775. The heirs named were granddau. Elizabeth Woodall and her sister Ann Woodall, their mother Mary Woodall, son George Vansant Mann, grandson William Knock, grandson John Blackeston, dau. Hannah Blackeston, son George V. Mann, and granddau. Sarah Mann and her bro. Joseph Mann. The exec. was son George V. Mann. The will was witnessed by Thos. Seegar, Matthew Smith, and Hester Newcomb.{MWB 40:202}

On 2 March 1775, her estate was appraised by Isaac Spencer and William Smith, and valued at £525.10.11. Mary Woodall and Hannah Blackiston signed as next of kin. George Vansant Man, exec., filed the inventory on 13 Dec 1775.{MINV 122:272}

A list of debts was appraised and valued at £35.13.9. George Vansant Mann, exec., filed the inventory cont. a list of debts on 13 Dec 1775.{MINV 122:277}

On 10 May 1776, distribution of the estate was made by George Vansant Mann, exec. Legatees were (grandchildren) Elisabeth Woodall, Ann Woodall, William Knock, John Blackiston, and Sarah Mann. Residue to George Vansant Mann.{BFD 7:58}

Nicholas and Rebecca (Wyatt) Smith were the parents of{A; KESH}: NICHOLAS; JOHN, b. 2 Nov 1724; OLIVER, b. 21 Jan 1737;

293

LAMBERT, b. 15 March 1744; REBECCA, b. 24 May 1746, m. (N) Burgis; and ELIZABETH, b. by 1749, m. (N) Stoops.

Nicholas and Ann were the parents of{A}: ISABELLA, b. 28 Oct 1750; and HANNAH, b. 1753, m. (N) Blakiston.

2. WILLIAM SMITH, bro. of Nicholas, d. by 13 April 1767, when his estate was appraised by John Eccleston and Isaac Spencer, and valued at £451.12.7. J. Nicholson and John Basts signed as creditors. Nicholas Smith and Nicholas Riley signed as next of kin. William Smith, admin., filed the inventory on 22 June 1767.{MINV 92:91}

Smith's estate was appraised and valued at £182.15.10. William Smith, admin, filed the inventory cont. a list of debts on 21 June 1768.{MINV 96:193} The estate was again appraised by John Eccleston and Isaac Spencer, and valued at £60.4.2. John Bools and J. Nicholson signed as creditors. Nicholas Smith and Nicholas Riley signed as next of kin. William Smith, admin., filed the inventory on 21 June 1768.{MINV 97:201}

On 18 Aug 1768, distribution of the estate was filed by William Smith, admin.{BFD 5:87}

3. NICHOLAS SMITH, son of Nicholas and Rebecca (Wyatt) Smith, d. by 1762. He m. Mary (N).{A}

Nicholas Smith, Jr., of KE Co., d. leaving a will dated 5 March 1762 and proved 30 March 1762. Son George was given part of the tract *Grantham* (175 a.), with the balance of the estate to be divided amongst the rest of children. The extx. was wife Mary Smith. The will was witnessed by John and James Woodall and Edward Clements.{MWB 31:566}

Nicholas Smith, of KE Co., d. by 21 May 1762, when his estate was appraised by John Watson and Matthew Smith, and valued at £131.13.1. Thomas Gilpin and Phillemon Pratt signed as creditors. John Smith and Nicholas Smith signed as next of kin. Mary Smith, extx., filed the inventory on 24 June 1762.{MINV 78:170} His estate was again appraised by Mathew Smith and W. Haley, and valued at £22.3.0. Thomas Gilpin signed as creditor. Philemon Pratt, John Smith, and Jonathon Smith signed as next of kin. Mary Welsh, wife of Lewis Welsh, extx., filed the inventory on 3 July 1764.{MINV 84:6} Distribution of the estate was made by Mary Welsh, extx., wife of Lewis Welsh. Distribution was made to widow and children (unnamed). Legatee was eldest son George.{BFD 5:106}

Nicholas and Mary Smith were the parents of: GEORGE; and others.

THE ROBERT SMITH FAMILY

Refs.: A: BDML, 2:748.

1. (N) SMITH, perhaps of Penryn, Cornwall, England, was the father of at least two sons{A}: ROBERT, d. c1706/7; and RENATUS, d. 1719.

2. ROBERT SMITH, son of (N), and bro. of Renatus, d. c1706/7. He m. c1680, Ann (possibly Ann Gaines, widow of Thomas Hynson who d. 1679).{A}
Robert Smith immigrated by 1677 and settled on the s. side of Chester River, in that part of TA Co. that later became QA Co.{A}
Smith was a member of the TA Co. Associator's Convention, 1689-1692, a delegate to the Lower House of the Assembly from TA Co. from 1692-1693, 1694-1697, 1698-1700, 1701-1704, and 1704-1706. He was also a Chief Justice of the Provincial Court from 1694-1699.{A}
On 2 June 1696, Robert Smith, of TA Co., and his wife Ann, conv. to Richard Dawson, of KE Co., a parcel of land called *Fresh Rum*, 100 a.{KELR M:41A} On 22 June 1697, Robert Smith, of TA Co., and his wife Anne, conv. to Thomas Usher, of KE Co., a parcel of land called *New Harbour*, 100 a.{KELR M:66A}
On 11 June 1697, Robert Smith and his wife Anne, of TA Co., conv. to Marcy Sedley, of KE Co., and her heirs, 100 a. part of *Mount Pleasure*.{KELR M:66B}
On 24 Nov 1702, Guy Williams and his wife Mary conv. land to Robert Smith, all of TA Co.{KELR JD#1:88}
On 24 Nov 1702, Charles Hollinsworth, Jr., and his wife Allice, of KE Co., conv. land to Robert Smith of TA Co.{KELR JD#1:91}
On 16 Aug 1703, William Carsey (Coursey), of TA Co., and his wife Elizabeth conv. land to Robert Smith. Whereas Vincent Lowe of afsd. county, dec., by his last will devised several tracts to be sold by his execs. - 3,000 a. which was paid for by sd. Robert Smith.{KELR JD#1:145}
Robert Smith, of TA Co., d. leaving an undated will which was proved 18 March 1706. To every one of the children and heirs of his bro. in England he left 1,000 a., to be taken out of *Long Adventure*, *Gloster*, *The Square*, and another tract, and if necessary, out of part of *Walnut Ridge*. Bro. Ranatus was to have lands adj. to the afsd. John

Jordan and land in *Bishop's Addition*. Charity Jordan was to have a plant., and the residue of his estate was to go to dau. (N) Ivy (misread as Joy). Bro. Renatus and Anthony Ivy were named execs. Thomas Phillips and Richard Hollingsteed were witnesses.{MWB 12:90}

On 13 April 1709, Anthony Ivy, of QA Co., Gent., and his wife Anne, dau. and heiress of Robert Smith, dec., conv. to Samuel Wickes, of KE Co., Gent., 200 a. then in the occupation of sd. Anthony Ivy and his wife Anne.{KELR JSN:117}

Robert Smith was the father of: ANNE, m. Anthony Ivy.

3. RENATUS SMITH, of QA Co., son of (N), and bro. of Robert, d. c1719.{A}

On 20 March 1716, Renatus Smith, of QA Co., Gent., conv. to William Reding, of KE Co. (later acknowledged by Eleanor, wife of William Reding), part of a tract called *Gibbses Choyce* on Jacobus Creek, 150 a.{KELR BC#1:197}

On the last day of Feb 1717, Renatus Smith, conv. to his dau. Mary Cole, a tract called *Chesterfield*.{KELR BC#1:270}

On 29 June 1722, James Earle, of QA Co., Gent., and William Turbutt, of the sd. county, commissioners appointed by the Assembly for the sale of land, late the estate of Robert Smith, of TA Co., dec., to John Johnson, of KE Co., to pay Richard Cole of QA Co. and his wife Mary, dau. of Renatus Smith, dec., surviving exec. of Robert Smith, dec., what the sd. Renatus Smith paid on account of the sd. Robert Smith and other debts - a tract called *Outrange*.{KELR JS#W:250}

On 20 Dec 1722, William Clayton, of TA Co., and William Turbutt, of QA Co., Gent., conv. to Richard Cole, of QA Co., carpenter, and his wife Mary, dau. of Renatus Smith, late of QA dec., by virtue of an act of assembly on 27 Oct 1720, the land of Robert Smith.{KELR JS#W:284}

On 25 March 1724, William Clayton, of TA Co., and James Earle, of QA Co., conv. to Richard Cole, of QA Co., carpenter, and his wife Mary, dau. of Renatus Smith, dec., surviving exec. of Robert Smith, in the sale of the land of Robert Smith, TA Co., dec., a tract formerly called *Sewell* now called *Uterick* at the mouth of Middle Creek - by act of Assembly.{KELR JS#W:365}

Renatus Smith was the father of: MARY, m. Richard Cole.

THE THOMAS SMITH FAMILY

<u>Refs.</u>: A: BDML, 2:730 ff.

1. THOMAS SMITH, the progenitor, was b. c1656 and d. 1719. On 28 Sep 1706, he gave his age as c50.{KELR C:202} He immigrated c1680, and settled in TA Co. and then in KE Co.{A} Col. Thomas Smith was bur. 21 May 1719.{KESP}

He m. 1st, by 1684, Elinor (N), widow of Nathaniel Evitts, of KE Co.{INAC 9:199} He m. 2nd, c1708, Martha (c1680-1739), dau. of Tristram and Anne (Coursey) Thomas.{A}

Smith represented KE Co. in the Lower House from 1681-1682, 1694-1697, 1697/8-1700, 1701-1704, and 1716-1718. He was also a Justice of the Provincial Court.{A}

Col. Thomas Smith (Smyth) d. leaving a will dated 30 June 1718 and proved 4 Aug 1719. To son Thomas, he left a dwell. plant., being part of *Trumping, Smyth's Meadow, Ratcliff Cross, The Addition* in s. side of Davies' Creek, and *Smyth's Venture*, also a lot in New Yarmouth on Grasin Creek. To dau. Martha, he left land being part of *Hinchingham*, and *Smyth's Desert*, except 100 a. given to John Griffith and Mary, his wife. To son Thomas and dau. Martha, a pew in St. Paul's in KE Co. To Jane Coursey, part of *Smyth's Meadows*. To wife Martha, extx., dwell. plant., and *Smyth's Meadow*, or ½ of *Ratcliff Cross*. Mentions plant., 150 a. *Langford's Bay*, being part of *The Plaines*. Overseers were Thomas Bordley, James Harris, and Col. Edward Scott.{MWB 15:159}

On 8 March 1719, Martha Smith, extx. of Thomas Smith, named David Macbride as her attorney against Peter Green, in a plea of debt.{KEBI JS#W:62A}

His estate was inv. on 9 Sep 1719. Mentioned were servants David Reed (taylor), Robert Linch, and Morgan Rice. Madam Martha Smith was named extx.{MINV 4:11}

Mrs. Martha Smith d. leaving a will dated 22 Jan 1723 and proved 3 March 1723/4. To children Thomas and Martha, she left her entire estate; should children die before being of age according to their father's will, estate to children of bro. William Thomas. Both to be instructed in faith of Church of England. To Bro. William Thomas, exec. and guardian of children, £100, now in England.{MWB 18:245}

Her estate's inventory was taken 11 May 1724 and filed 6 Aug 1724. Henry Hosier signed as next of kin. William Thomas was named exec.{MINV 10:31} Another inventory was taken 10 March 1724/5 and filed 13 March 1724. William Thomas was named exec.{MINV 10:288}

Martha Smith, of KE Co., widow of Col. Thomas Smith, d. by 13 March 1724/5, when her estate was admin. by William Thomas, exec. Payment was made to James Thomas.{MDAD 6:281}

Thomas and Eleanor Smith may have been the parents of{A}: JAMES, c1683-1760.

By Martha he was the father of: THOMAS, b. 21 Feb 1710; and MARTHA, b. 2 Dec 1712, m. Richard Gresham.{A; KESP}

2. JAMES SMITH, b. c1683, and d. c1760, is placed by Papefuse as possibly having been a son of Thomas and Eleanor.{A}

James Smith m. Sarah Hynson, dau. of John Hynson, on 21 Jan 1705.{A; KESP}

Smith represented KE Co. in the Lower House of the Assembly from 1719-1721/2, and was also a Clerk of the KE Co. Court from 1707-1760.{A}

On 3 Aug 1710, James Smith, of KE Co., and his wife Sarah, conv. to Thomas Joce of the sd. county, 100 a. part of a tract called *Stepney*.{KELR JSN:221}

James Smith, of KE Co., d. leaving a will dated 2 Feb 1760. The heirs named were children James, William, Hannah Nicholson, Sarah Ringgold, Mary Wickes, and Ann Murry (Murray), grandchildren William Nicholson, son of Joseph, Mary Sterling wife of Rev. James Sterling, and son-in-law Wm. Murray, Hannah Nicholson's husband, who "has had ⅓ profits of my clerk's office." Mentioned were Dr. John Scott and John McCrocon. Tracts mentioned were *Smith's Port of Worth's Folly Grove*. The exec. was Wm. Murray. The will was witnessed by Alexander Williamson, Jr., Elizabeth Calder, and Thomas Bickersteth.

Mentioned in the codicil were Richard Tilghman and Peregrine Tilghman. It was witnessed by George Garnett.{MWB 30:808}

Smith's estate was appraised on 26 March 1760 by William Ringgold and John Chapple, and valued at £993.13.1. John Eccleston and Thomas Perkins signed as creditors. James Smith and William Smith signed as next of kin. William Murray, exec., filed the inventory on 5 May 1761.{MINV 75:40}

On 29 Oct 1768 distribution of the estate was made by William Murray, exec. Legatees were Ann Murray and William Nicholson son of Joseph Nicholson. Residue equally to Hannah Nicholson, Sarah

Ringgold, son James, Mary Wicks, Ann Murray, son William, and granddau. Mary Sterling.{BFD 5:122}

James and Sarah were the parents of{KESP}: JOHN, b. 12 Oct, bapt. 15 Oct 1706; HANNAH, b. 14 March 1708, m. (N) Nicholson; SARAH, b. 23 Sep 1711, m. (N) Ringgold; JAMES, b. 2 April 1714; WILLIAM; MARY, m. (N) Wickes; and ANN, m. (N) Murray.{KESP}

3. THOMAS SMITH, son of Thomas and Martha, was b. 21 Feb 1710.{KESP} He d. by 9 Jan 1741/2. He m. 1st, on 14 Feb c1728, Mary Ann (c1712-c1734) Ringgold, dau. of Thomas and Frances Ringgold. Thomas Smith m. 2nd, on 20 June 1734, Mary, b. 1713, dau. of William and Jane (Thompson) Frisby.{A; KESP}

Thomas Smith represented KE Co. in the Lower House in 1738, and about the same time was a captain.{A}

Thomas Smith of KE Co., d. leaving a will dated 6 Nov 1741 and proved 9 Jan 1740 [sic]. The heirs named were wife Mary, extx., to whom was devised the dwell. plant., *Ratlif Cross*. At her decease it was to pass to daus. Mary and Martha, they to be under the care of wife during their minority. To son Thomas, was devised ½ of *Trumping Town*, formerly granted to his grandfather, Thomas Smythe, also *Smythes Meadows*, and 300 a. of *Smith's Range*, formerly called *Smyth's Venter*. To son William, was devised 300 a., part of *Smith's Range* and 108 a., part of *The Plains*. Son Thomas was to be bound to Mr. James Calder, lawyer, and son William, to Capt. William Hopkins, mariner, during their minority. The will was witnessed by Richard Gresham, Robert Lusby, and Alex. Williamson.{MWB 22:458}

The estate of Capt. Thomas Smith, of KE Co., was appraised on 2 June 1742 by John Gresham and Samuel Tovey, and valued at £1140.7.7. Robert Maine and William Murray signed as creditors. Martha Gresham and William Thomas signed as next of kin. Mary Smith, admx., filed the inventory on 30 July 1742.{MINV 27:11}

On 20 March 1744, Mary Smith, widow, Robert Lusby, and Alexander Williamson, Gent., of KE Co., gave bond they would pay Mary, Martha, Thomas, and William Smith each £197.0.11 due them as their portion of the estate of their father Thomas Smith, dec., at age 21.{KEBI JS#20:163, 169, 170, 171, 172}

Thomas Smith was the father of{A}: THOMAS; WILLIAM, apprenticed to William Hopkins; MARY; and MARTHA, m. 1st, by May 1770, Emory Sudler, and 2nd, Thomas Garnett.

4. JAMES SMITH, son of James, was b. 2 April 1714. James Smith, age c47, dep. on 16 July 1762.{KEEJ: John Carville}

5. THOMAS SMITH, son of Thomas and Mary Ann (Ringgold) Smith, was b. c1730, and d. 1819. He m. 1st, Sarah (1730-1761), dau. of Richard Gresham, and 2nd, on 11 Oct 1764, Margaret (1745-1794), dau. of Thomas Bedingfield and Sarah Hands.{A}

Thomas Smith represented KE Co. at the Conventions of 1774, 1775 and 1776.{A}

Thomas Smith was the father of{A}: THOMAS, b. c1757; RICHARD GRESHAM, d. by 1795; WILLIAM, b. c1777; JAMES; HENRY; MARIA, m. Dr. Thomas Wilson; ELIZABETH, m. (N) Nichols; and SARAH, m. 1788, Matthew Tilghman.

THE WILLIAM SMITH FAMILY

1. WILLIAM SMITH was bur. 30 Jan 1707.{KESP} He m. Sarah (N), who survived him.

William Smith d. leaving a will dated 21 Sep 1701 and proved 11 March 1707. To four sons, viz., William, Charles, James and Thomas, he devised the plant. and 250 a. on Langford's Bay. Wife Sarah to have use of the plant., also all personalty. If she m., personal estate was to be divided between her and sons afsd. and three daus. Sarah, Eliza: and Mary.{MWB 12:258}

William Smith's estate was admin. on 17 May 1708 and 28 Aug 1709.{INAC 28:265, 30:182}

William and Sarah were the parents of: WILLIAM; CHARLES; JAMES; THOMAS, b. 7 Feb 1700, d. young{KESP}; SARAH; ELIZABETH; and MARY, m. William Dicas.

2. WILLIAM SMITH, son of William and Sarah, was named in his father's will, and was living as late as 1715.

On 30 Aug 1708, William Smith, KE Co., conv. to Charles Smith, of the same county, and Mary his wife, all his right to land left to him by his father, being part of a tract of 200 a. where Abraham Ambrose lived, and which his father, William Smith, purchased of William Coursey by patent.{KELR JSN:108}

On 18 April 1715, William Smith, of KE Co., conv. land to William Dicas, of afsd. county. The deed stated that William Smith, of afsd. county, dec., by his last will had devised his plant. and land which lies in Langfords Bay and where the sd. William dwelt, being 200 a. to four of his sons, viz., William, Charles, James, and Thomas Smith, but the sd. Thomas Smith d. before he came to full age and assuming that his portion belonged to the afsd. William Smith, son of afsd. William Smith, dec., now the sd. William Smith for the love and affection which he bears for William Dicas who m. Mary the sister of afsd. William Smith, conveys to them the land that might have been laid out for afsd. Thomas Smith, dec.{KELR BC#1:65}

3. JAMES SMITH, son of William and Sarah, m. Joyce Quinney 6 Dec 1708.{KESP}

On 8 March 1710, James Smith, of KE Co., and his wife Joyce, conv. to Charles Smith, of afsd. county, 50 a., the right of James Smith to a parcel of land purchased by his father Wm. Smith, late of KE Co., of Wm. Coursey, of TA Co., on 27 March 1680.{KELR JSN:253}

On 19 March 1727, James Smith, of KE Co., Gent., and his wife Sarah, conv. to their son John Smith, part of a tract called *Hinchingham*.{KELR JS#X:183}

On 29 Dec 1741, Joyce Smith, of KE Co., conv. to her son James Smith, part of a tract called *Conney Warren*.{KELR JS#23:424}

James Smith d. leaving a will dated 21 April 1734 and proved 29 May 1734. To wife Joice, extx., entire personal estate. To dau. Joice tract called *Providence* bought of Daniel and Timothy ——, at her decease to be divided among three sons James, Sutton, and William. To sons Samuel, Joseph, and Daniel, or to the survivor, tract called *Holyland*. To sons John and Thomas, dau. Sarah, late wife of Cornelius Hurley, and dau. Mary, now wife of Jacob Gooding, 1 s. each. Test: Charles Smith.{MWB 21:230}

Smith left an estate that was inv. 27 Aug 1734 and filed 4 Oct 1734 by John Smith, the exec. Next of kin were John Smith and Sarah Hurley.{MINV 20.1}

Joyce Smith, of KE Co., (c1738), conv. to her sister Mary Hull, wife of Daniel Hull, the remaining part of a tract called *Cunney Warren*, formerly belonging to her father Sutton Quiney, conv. to him from Anthony Wilkinson by the name of *Wilkinsons Chance*, 100 a.{KELR JS#22:225}

James and Joyce Smith were the parents of{KESP}: JOHN; MARY, b. 16 Dec 1712, m. Jacob Gooding; SITTON (SUTTON), b. 5 March 1717; JOYCE, b. 9 Aug 1719; WILLIAM, b. 27 Feb 1722; JAMES, b. 20 April 1714; SAMUEL; JOSEPH; DANIEL; THOMAS; and SARAH, m. Cornelius Hurley.

4. SUTTON SMITH, son of James and Joyce Smith, d. by 21 Jan 1758.

At March Court 1740, it was presented that Sutton Smith, on 10 Jan 1740, assaulted Mary Read.{KECR JS#23:193}

Sutton Smith, of KE Co., d. by 21 Jan 1758, when his estate was appraised by N. Ricketts and Henry Heart, and valued at £142.2.10. John Grant and Thomas Quinney signed as creditors. James Smith and Samuel Smith signed as next of kin. Joseph Smith, admin., filed the inventory on 7 Feb 1758.{MINV 65:130}

Distribution of the estate was filed by James Smith and John Quinny, admins. de bonis non on 3 March 1762.{BFD 3:119}

5. JAMES SMITH, son of James and Joyce, was b. 20 April 1714, and d. by 28 June 1775, having m. and left issue. On 9 Oct 1761, Mr. James Smith, age c46, dep. regarding the bounds of a tract called *Huntingfield*.{KELR DD#1:615}

At November Court 1733, James Smith, Jr., of St. Paul's Parish, son of James Smith, tanner, was found guilty of committing fornication on 10 Aug with Sarah Lewis and begetting a bastard child. He was fined 30 s.{KECR JS#WK:452}

James Smith, of Worton, KE Co., d. leaving a will dated 29 April 1775 and proved 28 June 1775. The heirs named were son Samuel Smith, to whom was devised part of tract *Cunney Warran*, son Simon Smith, dau. Rachel Smith, son Richard Smith, son James Smith, and Ann Falconar. Wm. Dawson, exec., was to have care of son Samuel until he was of age. The will was witnessed by Thomas Jones, Martha Jones, and Alex'r. Glenn, Sr.{MWB 40:494}

On 7 Aug 1775, his estate was appraised by Mar. Tilden and Charles Groome, and valued at £173.11.7. Eleazer McComb and Richard Graves signed as creditors. Simon Smith and Richard Smith signed as next of kin. William Dawson, exec., filed the inventory on 11 Feb 1776.{MINV 122:270}

On 22 Feb 1776 his estate was appraised again by Mar. Tilden and Charles Groom, and valued at £159.0.0. Eleazer McComb and Morgane Ruby signed as creditors. Simon Smith and Richard Smyth signed as next of kin. James Smith, exec., filed the inventory on 13 Dec 1776.{MINV 125:46}

His estate was appraised again and valued at £163.4.7. William Dawson, exec., filed the inventory cont. a list of debts on 13 Dec 1776.{MINV 125:46} Another appraisal was made and a list of debts was valued at £80.10.0. William Dawson, exec., filed the inventory cont. a list of debts on 12 Dec 1776.{MINV 125:49}

James Smith was the father of: SAMUEL; SIMON; RACHEL; RICHARD; JAMES; and ANN, m. (N) Falconar.

6. JOSEPH SMITH, son of James and Joyce, may be the Mr. Joseph Smith who d. by 10 Aug 1761, when his estate was appraised by William Copper and Paul Hitchcock, and valued at £16.8.3. John Gooding and Samuel Smith signed as creditors. James Smith and Mary Meeks signed as next of kin. John Bourk, admin., filed the inventory on 11 Feb 1762.{MINV 75:229}

His estate was appraised again and valued at £9.5.7. John Burk and Michael Wilson, admins., filed the inventory cont. a list of debts on 8 Jan 1763.{MINV 80:15}

His estate was appraised a third time and valued at £ 1.11.0. John Burk and Michael Wilson, admins., filed the inventory on 3 Nov 1763.{MINV 82:38}

7. DANIEL SMITH, son of James and Joyce, was named in his father's will. He is probably the Daniel Smith who d. by 12 Jan 1767.

The land called *Holey Land*, 50 a., belonged to Daniel and Joseph Smith, minors, under the tuition of appointed guardians John Smith and James Smith. There were six very old houses about to fall down.{KEBI JS#20:158}

Daniel Smith, of KE Co., d. by 12 Jan 1767, when his estate was appraised by Thomas Perkins and Henry Bodien, and valued at £197.10.2. The inventory mentioning James Black, William Hull, Samuel Smyth, and James Smyth was filed by the admx. on 17 March 1767.{MINV 91:210}

The estate of Daniel Smith, of KE Co., was appraised again and valued at £23.17.2. Isaac Cannel, admin., filed the inventory cont. a list of debts on 21 July 1773.{MINV 114:214}

Another list of debts was appraised and valued at £187.12.7. Isaac Cannel, admin., filed the inventory cont. a list of debts on 27 July 1773.{MINV 114:216}

On 27 July 1773 distribution of the estate was made by Isaac Cannel, admin. de bonis non.{BFD 6:266}

1. CHARLES TILDEN, progenitor, immigrated 1677.{MPL 15:423} He m. Mary (N) by 1681.

Charles Tilden received a patent for the tract *Bishford*, 200 a., on 26 June 1686.{MPL 25:226, 33:221}

Charles Tilden had at least two sons, as evidenced in the land record of 24 May 1717 in which Edward Scott and his wife Martha and Marmaduke Tilden, all of KE Co., conv. land to John Tilden of afsd. county. In the deed it was stated that Elias King and Charles Tilden, Gent., late of KE Co., had granted to them 200 a. in a fork of the n.w. branch of Langford Bay, and since by the last will of Elias King did devise his lands to Edward Scott, and by heirship the sd. Marmaduke Tilden came to the right of his father Charles Tilden's lands. That sd. Edward and Martha his wife and Marmaduke Tilden "for the good will and brotherly love and natural affection which we have for John Tilden" and for 10 s., granted him a tract called *Bishford*.{KELR BC#1:249}

Charles Tilden was the father of: MARY (dau. of Charles and Mary), b. 21 July 1681{KELR K:1}; MARMADUKE; JOHN; and ANN, m. —— Wilson.

2. MARMADUKE TILDEN, son of Charles, d. in 1726, m. Tabitha (N).

On 28 May 1712, Marmaduke Tilden and his wife Tabitha, of KE Co., conv. to Richard West 200 a. called *Pentridge* in Langfords Bay.{KELR JSN:291}

Marmaduke Tilden d. leaving a will dated 24 May 1726 and proved 19 Oct 1726. To wife, extx., ⅓ of estate and use of dwell. plant. To sons Marmaduke and Charles, and daus. Jane, Mary, and Martha, personalty and residue of estate. James Harris and bro. John were appointed overseers.{MWB 19:20}

The estate of Capt. Marmaduke Tilden was inv. by 21 Jan 1726. John Tilden and Jo. Harris signed as next of kin. Thomas Hynson was admin./exec.{MINV 12:471} The estate was again inv. by 26 Aug 1728. John Tilden signed as creditor. Elisabeth Ringold signed as next of kin. James Ringold and Patrick Clark were mentioned.{MINV 14:57}

---

[54] Hanson, in *Old Kent*, states that there was an earlier Marmaduke Tilden, but to date no record of that Marmaduke has been found.

Marmaduke and Martha were the parents of: MARMADUKE; CHARLES; JANE; MARY; and MARTHA.

3. JOHN TILDEN, son of Charles (1), d. by 4 Oct 1746. He m. Cathrine Blay, dau. of William Blay.{Chancery 25 May 1734, p. 661}

On 22 Aug 1737, Richard Wethered and his wife Isabella and John Tilden and his wife Catharine, all of KE Co., conv. to George Douglass, of the sd. county, a tract called *Mill Fork*, originally laid out for 800 a. out of which sd. tract was heretofore sold 3 parcels, 500 a. to Isaac Ingland, another part to John Clayton, and another parcel to Alexander Mackey, of KE Co., with now a remainder of 200 a. to Douglass.{KELR JS#22:28}

On 21 July 1741, Richard Wethered, of KE Co., merchant, and his wife Issabella, conv. to Daniel Dulany, Esq., of Annapolis, ¼ of a tract called *Partnership*, originally granted to the sd. Issabella by the name of Issabella Blay, John and Catherine Tilden, and Rachell Brown in fee which as yet remains undivided.{KELR JS#23:267}

John Tilden, of KE Co., d. leaving a will written 5 Aug 1746 and proved 13 Oct 1746. The heirs named were son John Tilden to whom was devised the dwell. plant. *Bishford Resurvey*, dau. Catharine Tilden, son William Blay Tilden, to whom was devised tracts called *Blay's Range* and *Blay's Addition* and a lot in Georgetown, cousin John Thomas, sister Ann Willson, friend William Hynson, and cousin Mrs. Sarah Kennard. The exec. was son John Tilden. The will was witnessed by Henry Hart, John Read, and Cornelius Hurt.{MWB 24:489}

On 12 Nov 1746, the estate of John Tilden was appraised by John Carvill and Joseph Wickes, and valued at £811.15.2. Isabella Wethered and Mary Williams signed as creditors. Catharine Tilden and Isabella Wethered signed as next of kin. John Tilden, exec., filed the inventory on 14 Jan 1746.{MINV 34:177}

On 2 May 1749 the estate was again appraised by John Carvill and Ja. Wickes, and valued at £244.5.6. Catharine Kinnard and Isabella Wethered signed as creditors. Isabella Wethered signed as next of kin. John Tilden, admin./exec., filed the inventory on 24 Oct 1753.{MINV 55:191}

John and Catherine were the parents of: JOHN; CATHERINE; WILLIAM BLAY; and MARY, b. 10 March 1727/8.{KESH}

4. MARMADUKE TILDEN, son of Marmaduke (2), was b. c1714/5. On 9 Oct 1761, Marmaduke Tilden, age c47, dep. regarding the bounds of

a tract called *Huntingfield*.{KELR DD#1:612} Marmaduke Tilden, age c47, dep. on 16 July 1762.{KEEJ: John Carville}

He m. Sarah (N), who survived him until 1774.

Marmaduke Tilden, of KE Co., d. leaving a will dated 29 Oct 1767 and proved 17 Feb 1767. Mentioned were wife Sarah, children Marmaduke, Charles, Mary Worril, Tabitha, Martha, and Ann, and son-in-law Edward Worril, husband of dau. Mary. The extx. was wife Sarah Tilden. The will was witnessed by John, John, Jr., and Ann Carvill.{MWB 36:428}

On 25 Feb 1768, his estate was appraised by John Wickes and N. Ricketts, and valued at £960.10.3. Thomas Ringgold and Company and William Murray signed as creditors. Mar: Tilden and Mary Worrell signed as next of kin. Sarah Tilden, extx., filed the inventory on 11 May 1768.{MINV 96:186}

Distribution of the estate was made on 28 June 1770 by Mrs. Sarah Tilden, extx., to widow (⅓) and children, equally. Legatees were Marmaduke Tilden, Charles Tilden, dau. Ann, dau. Martha, Tabitha Tilden, widow (unnamed), and dau. Tabitha.{BFD 6:12}

The estate was appraised for the last time and valued at £3.0.0. Sarah Tilden, extx., filed the inventory cont. a list of debts on 11 Feb 1772.{MINV 108:92} On the same day distribution was made by Mrs. Sarah Tilden, extx., to herself with residue to children, equally. Legatees were Marmaduke Tilden, Charles Tilden, Anna Tilden, dau. Martha, Tabitha Tilden, and widow. Marmaduke Tilden and Mary Worril were mentioned.{BFD 6:72, 216}

Sarah Tilden, of KE Co., d. leaving a will dated 16 Oct 1773 and proved 10 May 1774. The heirs named were son Charles Tilden, dau. Martha Tilden, dau. Tabitha, grandson John Waltham, dau. Sarah Hynson wife of Charles Hynson, and grandson Joseph Kennard, son of John Kennard. The three youngest children were Charles, Martha, and Tabitha Tilden. The exec. was Charles Tilden. The will was witnessed by Rachel Smith and Alexr. Glenn.{MWB 39:775}

On 31 --- 1774 her estate was appraised by Charles Groome and Lake Griffith, and valued at £367.9.0. Morgan and Stubey and Thomas Ringgold signed as creditors. Martha Loram and Tabitha Tilden signed as next of kin. Charles Tilden, exec., filed the inventory on 1 Nov 1774.{MINV 118:253}

Marmaduke and Sarah were the parents of: MARMADUKE; CHARLES; MARY, m. Edward Worril; TABITHA; MARTHA; and ANN.

5. JOHN TILDEN, son of John (3), d. by 23 Feb 1764. He m. Elizabeth (N).

John Tilden, of KE Co., d. leaving a will dated 4 Jan 1764 and proved 23 Feb 1764. The heirs named were William Blay Tilden, to whom was devised land called *Blayes Range* and *Blays Addition*, son John Tilden, wife Elizabeth Tilden, Sarah Kennard, and William Mitchell. The extx. was wife. The will was witnessed by Joseph Rasin, Thomas Knock, and Sarah Pearce.{MWB 31:1079}

The estate of John Tilden, Quaker, of KE Co., was appraised on 23 March 1764 by Abraham Rasin and Thomas Bowers, and valued at £884.13.8. John Wethered and Thomas Smyth signed as creditors. William Wethered and William Blay Tilden signed as next of kin. Elisabeth Tilden, extx., filed the inventory on 8 June 1764.{MINV 84:21}

The estate of John Tilden, Quaker, of KE Co., was again appraised by Thomas Bowers and Abraham Rasin, and valued at £67.12.9. John Wethered and Thomas Smyth signed as creditors. William Blay Tilden and William Wethered signed as next of kin. Elisabeth Tilden, extx., filed the inventory on 18 Aug 1766.{MINV 90:170} His estate was again appraised and valued at £280.0.0. Elisabeth Tilden, extx., filed the inventory on 8 May 1767.{MINV 94:5}

John and Elizabeth were the parents of: JOHN.

6. WILLIAM BLAY TILDEN, son of John m. Sarah (N). They were the parents of{KESH}: WILLIAM BLAY, b. 20 da., 2 mo., 1764; JOHN, b. 24 da., 12 mo., 1765; KATHERINE, b. 26 da., 10 mo., 1767, m. —— Hynson; and CHARLES, b. 31 da., 8 mo., 1769.

Unplaced

TILDEN, ELISABETH, d. by 18 Dec 1707 [sic] when the estate was appraised by John Tilden and Thomas Midford. The inventory was filed on 8 March 1727. Francis Bodien and Michael Corse signed as creditors. Elenor Earle and Mary Read signed as next of kin. George Reed, Quaker, filed the inventory.{MINV 13:3}

THE ALEXANDER WILSON FAMILY

1. ALEXANDER (SANDER) WILSON was in KE Co. by 30 Aug 1699 when he wit. the will of John Lewin.{MWB 11:111} He d. by 20 March 1707 when as "Sander Wilson" his estate was administered.{INAC 28:182}

His estate was administered again on 21 May 1708 by the admin., Michael Miller.{INAC 28:227}

Alexander m. Rebecca (N), and had at least one son: MICHAEL, b. 6 Dec ----.{KESP}

2. MICHAEL WILSON, son of Alexander, d. by 24 Nov 1722. He m. and had at least one son.

On 15 Nov 1720, Thomas Wilson, son of Michl. Wilson, an orphan, was bound as an apprentice to John Knowles, weaver.{KEBI JS#W:87A}

On 24 Nov 1722, the estate of Michael Wilson was appraised by Josias Lanham and John Brown, and proved by John Wilson, Margaret Wilson, and Sarah Jones.{MINV 9:67}

Michael Wilson, of KE Co., d. by 24 Nov 1722, when his estate was admin. by Samuell Weeks. The account mentioned Michael's dec. wife.{MDAD 5:27}

Michael may have had a son: MICHAEL.

3. MICHAEL WILLSON, possibly son of the Michael who d. in 1722, m. Anne (N).

Michal and Ann Willson were the parents of{KESH}: RACHEL, b. 25 Oct 1734; MICHAEL (twin), b. 22 Jan 1735; and WILLIAM (twin), b. 22 Jan 1735.

THE GEORGE WILSON FAMILY

Refs.: A: Christopher Johnston, Chart of the Wilson Family, Johnston Genealogical Collection, MHS.

1. GEORGE WILSON d. by 1 March 1675/6. He m. Winifred (N).

George Wilson d. leaving a will dated 24 May 1675 and proved 1 March 1675/6. He named sons Peter, James, John, and dau. Eliza. The execs. were sons Peter and James. William Peerce, Abraham Strand, Richard Thornton, and William Southbee were named overseers. The will was witnessed by Thos. Barton and Jeffrey Tomson.{MWB 5:13}

On 25 Oct 1677 George Wilson's estate was dist. by William Pearce, admin., to the children (unnamed) and relict (unnamed).{INAC 4:503}

George Wilson was the father of: PETER; JAMES; JOHN; and ELIZA.

2. PETER WILSON, son of George (1), d. in CE Co. by 27 April 1695.

He left a will dated 11 April 1695 and proved 27 April 1695. To his eldest son Peter he left the plant. To his bro. John he left 100 a., part of *Varyna*. To his youngest son Peter [sic] he left the residue of his lands. No exec. was named. The will was witnessed by James Wilson and Thomas Windell.{MWB 7:61}

Peter was evidently the father of two sons: PETER, the Elder; and PETER, the Younger.

3. JAMES WILSON, son of George (1), Oldfield Point, KE Co., was b. c1664. On 13 April 1731, James Wilson, age c67, dep. regarding the bounds of a tract called *The Adventure*. He recalled one Dawson coming up here from TA Co. about 30 years earlier to see a tract of land that was Bryan Omely's which he was about to buy of one of his sons who m. one of Brian Omely's daus.{KELR JS#16:128}

He may be the James Wilson who m. by 3 May 1695, Mary, admx. of William Jones, of CE Co.{INAC 13A:307} If he is the James who m. Mary Jones, then the Catherine named in his will was a second wife.

James d. testate in 1732.{A}

On 20 April 1726, James Wilson, of KE Co., conv. to his son James Wilson, part of a tract called *Broad Oak* and part of a tract called *Margaretts Delight*, 220 a.{KELR JS#W:532}

On 20 April 1726, James Wilson, of KE Co., merchant, conv. to his son-in-law William Woodland and his dau. Mary his wife, a part of a tract called *Margaretts Delight*, 102 a.{KELR JS#W:519}

On 20 April 1726, James Wilson, Sr., of KE Co., merchant, conv. to his son John Wilson, part of a tract called *Verrinia*, 73 a.{KELR JS#W:521}

On 20 April 1726, James Wilson, of KE Co., Sr., merchant, conv. to his son George, part of a tract called *Broad Oak*, 200 a.{KELR JS#W:534}

James Wilson, merchant, d. leaving a will dated 23 July 1732 and proved 18 Aug 1732. To wife Catherine he left dwell. plant., &c. To grandson James he left 30 a. adj. land formerly given to son John. To son George he left dwell. plant. with remaining part of *Verina*, except the graveyard, also residue of *Broad Oak*. To grandson John, son of son John, he left 120 a. of *Margrett's Delight*. To grandson Wilson Woodland he left residue of last named tract, including part where Christopher Ry lives. To granddau. ———, dau. of son John, and grandsons James and John, £10 each. To son-in-law Thomas Jones, £5. To son George and dau. Mary Woodland, residue of personal estate.

The execs. were wife Catherine, son George, and son-in-law William Woodland.{MWB 20:423}

James was the father of{A}: JAMES; MARY, m. William Woodland; JOHN; and GEORGE.

4. JOHN WILSON, son of George (1), d. 1732. He may be the John Wilson whose dau. Sarah was named in the 9 June 1687 will of Robert Crooke, of CE Co.{MWB 7:309} He m. (perhaps as a second wife) Hannah (N).

John Wilson was living on 27 Sep 1708 when Peter Willson, of KE Co., conv. to John Willson, of the same county, couper, part of a tract called *Varina* on the s. side of Sassafras River, adj. land in the possession of James Willson, bro. to the afsd. John Willson.{KELR JSN:80}

John Wilson, of KE Co., on 12 July 1729 conv. to his dau. Alice Redgraves, wife of Abraham Redgrave, of KE Co., part of a tract called *Margrets End*, 104 a.{KELR JS#X:444}

John Wilson d. leaving a will dated 23 Dec 1732 and proved 27 July 1733. To son Richard he left the tract called *Verina*, 100 a. called *Peter's Field*, and 100 a. of *Margaret's End*. To dau. Rebecca Vansant he left 50 a. adj. the last mentioned tract to son Richard. To granddau. Hannah Redgrave he left 50 a. adj. George Vansant's, being part of *Margaret's End*. To daus. Elizabeth Stapley, Rebecca Vansant, and Alce Redgrave, personalty. Residue of personal estate to son Richard, exec. Sister Alce Wilson, John Redgrave (son of dau. Alce Redgrave), grandsons Abraham Redgrave and William Redgrave, and granddau. Elizabeth Redgrave were mentioned. The will was witnessed by Thomas Gould, Isaac Freeman, Daniel Hull, and Michael Wilson (Willson).{MWB 20:778}

John Wilson had issue{KESB}: SARAH, b. by 9 June 1687; JOHN, b. 25 April 1705; RICHARD, b. 10 Nov 1707; JOSEPH, b. 30 jn 1709; REBECCA, b. 1 April 1711, m. (N) VanSant; ELIZABETH, m. (N) Stapley; ALCE, m. (N) Redgrave; and JOHN, d. v.p.

Third Generation

5. PETER WILSON, probably one of the sons of Peter (2), who d. 1695, was living on 27 Sep 1708, when he conv. to John Willson, of the same county, couper, part of a tract called *Varina* on the s. side of Sassafras River, adj. land in the possession of James Willson, bro. to the afsd. John Willson.{KELR JSN:80}

He d. by June 1721.

He may have had at least two sons: PETER; and JAMES.

6. JAMES WILSON, son of James (3), d. 11 May 1728.{KESH}

James Wilson (Willson), Jr., d. leaving a will dated 9 May 1728 and proved 5 July 1728. To father James Wilson, Sr., exec., he left entire estate. After his decease all lands, part of *Board Oak* and part of *Margaret's Delight,* to nephew James, son of James ([sic], could this be John?) Wilson, dec., and to George, son of George Wilson, Sr., to enjoy same at age 21. Should father die before nephews afsd. are of age, sd. lands to be in the care of bro. George during their minority.{MWB 19:550}

7. JOHN WILSON, son of James (3), d. before his father. He m. Mary (N), and had several children, named in the wills of his bro. James and father James, Sr. After his death, Mary m. 2nd, Laughlin O'Bryan of Newtown, KE Co.

On 19 Nov 1723, John Wilson, of KE Co., taylor, and his wife Mary, conv. to William Yearly, of afsd. county, a parcel of land called *Prevention of Inconveniency,* 150 a.{KELR JS#W:337}

On 19 Nov 1723, John Wilson, of KE Co., taylor, and his wife Mary, conv. to Robert Hodges, of the same county, 150 a. called *Grays Inn* on w. side of Graysin Creek.{KELR JS#W:338}

At August Court 1724, John Wilson, innholder, and his wife Mary Wilson were ordered to answer charges that they assaulted Andrew Guyer and his wife Joan. Christian Cully, wife of Henry Cully, innholder, of KE Co., was to give evidence against John Wilson.{KECR JS#22:26}

At August Court 1726, John Wilson, innholder, St. Paul's Parish, was ordered to answer the charge that on 27 Sep 1726, he, being a victualler and keeper of a public house, unlawfully without leave or license from the Commander, entertained and harbored three sailors belonging to the ship called the *Thomas and Mary* then riding at anchor in Chester River, of which ship and sailors Thomas Apleby was commander and master, to the great delay and hindrance of the business of the ship and commander. He was found not guilty.{KECR JS#22:206}

At March Court 1727, Mary Wilson, St. Paul's Parish, wife of John Wilson, innholder, was found guilty of assaulting on 1 March 1727 Mary Sherman. She was fined 200 lbs. of tob.{KECR JS#22:362}

At August Court 1727, Mary Wilson, wife of John Wilson, St. Paul's Parish, was charged with stealing property of Mary Cully on 10 July 1727. She was acquitted.{KECR JS#22:318}

On 20 Sep 1727, John Wilson, of KE Co., and his wife Mary, conv. to Thomas Jerrum, the tract called *Graysen*, on w. side of Graysin Creek, 150 a.{KELR JS#X:135}

At November Court 1727, Mary Wilson was ordered to answer the charge of stealing two geese and one gander. She was acquitted.{KECR JS#22:335}

At November Court 1727, Mary Wilson, wife of John Wilson, was found guilty of assaulting Henry Cully on 10 Nov 1727 and fined 2 s. and 6 pence.{KECR JS#22:334} At the same court she was found guilty of assaulting Thomas Pool on 10 Nov 1727 and fined 5 s.{KECR JS#22:333}

On 11 Feb 1731, John Wilson, of Chester Town, in KE Co., innholder, and his wife Mary, conv. to Richard Bennett, of QA Co., Lot No. 69 in the town.{KELR JS#16:182}

John Wilson d. leaving a will dated 1732 and proved 19 Jan 1732. To wife Mary, extx., two lots in Chester Town, Nos. 41 and 49, and entire personal estate. To sons James and John, lot No. 53. To son George Augusta, 50 a. purchased from William Dicas.{MWB 20:563}

Laughlin O'Bryan, of Newtown, KE Co., joyner, and his wife Mary, conv. land to John Conner of sd. town, merchant. Whereas John Willson, late of Newtown afsd., taylor, dec., was seised of an estate in Chester Newtown on Chester River called lot No. 41 by virtue of a deed of 22 Nov 1723 from Simon Willmer of New Town, Gent., and his wife Darcas, and John Willson by his last will dated 1732 devised to his wife Mary, one of the parties to this indenture, afsd. lot and house, along with lot No. 49. Mary later m. Laughlin O'Bryan.{KELR JS#18:294}

The inventory of John Wilson's estate was appraised 6 June 1727 and filed 14 Oct 1731 by the admx., Mary Wilson.{MINV 16:517}

John and Mary (N) Wilson were the parents of: JAMES (probably the James named in the will of his uncle James Wilson, Jr.); JOHN; GEORGE AUGUST; CHRISTIAN;[55] and SARAH, b. 23 Dec ---- .{KESP}[56]

---

[55] On 20 Nov 1739, Christion Wilson, dau. of John Wilson, dec., was bound as an apprentice to Simon Wilmer, until age 16 or day of marriage.{KEBI JS#18:234}

At August Court 1750, it was presented that Christian Willson, spinster, on 1 June 1749, committed fornication and begot a bastard child. She was fined £3.{KECR JS#25:62B}

At March Court 1752, it was presented that Christian Wilson, spinster, on 10 April 1751, committed fornication and begot a bastard child. She was fined £3.{KECR JS#25:88B}

[56] On 19 June 1740, Sarah Wilson, dau. of John Wilson, dec., an orphan, was bound to Nathaniel Kennard until age 16 or day of marriage.{KEBI JS#18:261}

8. **GEORGE WILSON**, son of James (3), was b. c1699. On 13 April 1731, George Wilson, age c32, dep. regarding the bounds of a tract called *The Adventure*. He recalled hearing his father, James Wilson, 8 to 10 years earlier, speak about an enquiry by one Dawson, of TA Co., concerning a tract that belonged to Brian Omely.{KELR JS#16:127} On 21 Jan 1740, George Wilson, age c43, dep. regarding the bounds of a tract called *Adventure*. He recalled his father, James Wilson, telling him that a certain Dopson who m. Bryan Omealy's dau. came up to this deponent's father's house and ... .{KELR JS#23:182} On 17 Sep 1740, Mr. George Wilson, age c43, dep. regarding the bounds of a tract called *Postern Hole*. He recalled hearing John Cole, of KE Co., dec., tell his father, James Wilson, dec., ...{KELR JS#23:134}

George d. 1748, having m. Mary Kennard.{A}

On 9 May 1728, his son George was named in the will of James Wilson, Jr., as a nephew.{MWB 19:550}

George Wilson was a Burgess in the Assembly for KE Co. from 1728 to 1746.{A}

George Wilson, of KE Co., d. leaving a will dated 5 Nov 1748 and proved 4 March 1748. The heirs named were son George Wilson, to whom he left the plant. "where my father James Wilson formerly dwelt" and the tract called *Cerena*, wife Mary Wilson, to whom he devised his dwell. plant. which would pass to son George at her death, and payments were to be made to daus. Mary, Sarah (Bodeen), Frances, Rachel, Araminta, and Millisan Wilson. Also mentioned were niece Mary Hasel, wife of John Hasel, and nephews James and John Wilson, sons of bro. John. The execs. were son George and wife Mary. The will was witnessed by Levrs. Williams, Daniel Hull, and Thomas Smith.{MWB 26:74}

On 1 May 1749, his estate was appraised by Nicholas Smith and C. Comegys, and valued at £847.17.11. No creditors or next of kin listed. George Wilson and Mary Wilson, execs., filed the inventory mentioning John Baine, Henry Bodien, Andrew McKittrick, Mary Wilson, Frances Wilson, and John Wilson on 3 June 1749.{MINV 40:440}

The estate of Mr. George, of KE Co., was appraised on 4 May 1758 by Nicholas Smith and Peter Massey, and valued at £255.15.2. No creditors or next of kin listed. Mary Willson and George Willson, execs., filed the inventory mentioning John Barrie (?), Arramintee Willson, and Miligion Willson on 18 May 1758.{MINV 64:320}

On 9 May 1759, distribution of the estate was made by Mary Wilson and George Willson, execs. Distribution was made to widow and remainder equally to George, Mary wife of Andrew Hynson, Sarah wife of Henry Bodion, Frances wife of William Woodland, Rachel wife of William Downes, Araminta Wilson, and Millison Wilson.{BFD 2:115}

Mary Wilson, widow of George Wilson, KE Co., d. leaving a will dated 2 March 1768 and proved 29 May 1771. Mentioned were children Rachel Downs and Mary Hynson, grandsons John Wilson, George Wilson, William Woodland, James Wilson, and William Wilson, and granddaus. Sarah Wilson and Mary Wilson. The exec. was grandson George Wilson. The will was witnessed by William Henry and John Wilson.{MWB 38:301}

On 3 June 1771, the estate of Mary Wilson was appraised by James Pearce and Abraham Freeman, and valued at £793.3.0. Archibald Wright and Peregrine Browne signed as creditors. Milicent Rogers and Rachel Downes signed as next of kin. George Downes, exec., filed the inventory on 4 Sep 1771.{MINV 106:394}

Her estate was again appraised and valued at £13.2.5. No creditors or next of kin listed. George Wilson, exec., filed the inventory cont. a list of debts on 17 June 1773.{MINV 114:200}

On 30 Oct 1771, her estate was again appraised by Abraham Freeman (dec. by 11 May 1773) and Jame Pearce, and valued at £160.11.5. William Rogers and Archibald Wright signed as creditors. Melicent Rodgers and Rachel Downes signed as next of kin. George Wilson, exec., filed the inventory on 17 June 1773.{MINV 114:207}

Distribution of the estate was made on 17 June 1773 by George Wilson, exec., to dau. Millicent and grandchildren George Wilson, James Wilson, John Wilson, William Wilson, and Sarah Wilson.{BFD 6:286}

George and Mary (Kennard) Wilson were the parents of{A}: GEORGE; MARY, m. Andrew Hynson; SARAH, m. Henry Bodeen; FRANCES, m. William Woodland; RACHEL, m. William Downes; ARAMINTA; and MILLISAN (MILLICENT).

9. JOHN WILSON, Jr., son of John (4), d. by 12 Dec 1726, when his estate was appraised by Abraham Redgrave and Thomas Hepbourn. The inventory was filed on 10 Jan 1726, by Mary Wilson, admx. J. Boden and Elisabeth Jones signed as creditors. John Willson and George Willson signed as next of kin.{MINV 11:843}

10. RICHARD WILSON, son of John (4), d. by 30 Oct 1765. He m. 1st, Johanna, by whom he had at least three children, and 2nd, Frances (N).

Richard Wilson, of KE Co., d. leaving a will dated 20 Jan 1762 and proved 30 Oct 1765. Mentioned were wife Frances and children John (eldest son), James, Richard, Simon, Lambreth and Samuel Wilson, Hannah Smith, Ann Smith, and Mary Wilson. The tracts *Virginia* and *Margaret's End* were mentioned. The execs. were Frances Wilson and son John Wilson. The will was witnessed by John Wilson, Wm. Downes, Jacob Spendlove, and Wm. Hubbard.{MWB 33:403}

On 12 Nov 1765, his estate was appraised by W. Haley and Peter Massy, and valued at £546.16.4. Lewis Dromgoole and James McLachlan signed as creditors. James Stavely and Alice Fosster signed as next of kin. John Willson, exec., filed the inventory on 4 June 1766.{MINV 89:31}

By Johanna, Richard was the father of{KESP}: JOHN, b. 14 Oct 1727; —— , b. 17 Sep 1729; and JAMES, b. 28 Oct 172-.

By Frances, Richard was the father of{KESB}: ANN MATTHEW, b. 8 Jan 1735; JOHN, b. 31 Oct 1737; LAMBERT, b. 31 Nov 1739; RICHARD, b. 1 Sep 1742; SAMUEL, b. 10 April 174-; GEORGE, b. 29 Jan 174-; and JAMES, b. 15 March 1749.

Fourth Generation

11. JAMES WILSON, son of Peter (5), of CE Co., dec., on 20 June 1721 acquitted and discharged his bro. Peter Wilson from any claim he had to any land which belonged to his father.{KELR JS#W:163}

He may be the James Wilson who d. c1722 when his estate was appraised, and signed by next of kin James Wilson and Sarah Linger (Lineger).{MINV 7:67}

On 17 June 1724, his estate was admin. by Peter Wilson, admin.{MDAD 6:14} Another account was filed 17 June 1724 by Peter Wilson. Payment was made to John Willson.{MDAD 6:330}

12. PETER WILSON, son of Peter (5), m. by 20 June 1721, Mary (N).

On 20 June 1721, Peter Wilson and his wife Mary, of KE Co., conv. to John Wilson, of sd. county, a tract called *Peter Town* on the upper side of Muddy Cove, 43 a.{KELR JS#W:163}

On 15 May 1727, Peter Wilson, of KE Co., and his wife Mary, conv. to John Wilson, part of a tract called *Verrina*, 82 a.{KELR JS#X:102}

On 14 April 1729, Peter Wilson and his wife Mary, of KE Co., conv. to John Brown, of the same county, 50 a., on the w. side of Doggs Branch.{KELR JS#X:363}

On 30 March 1730, Peter Wilson and his wife Mary, of KE Co., conv. to William Woodland, of the same county, carpenter, 100 a., being part of a tract called *The Forrest.*{KELR JS#X:448}

On 2 Sep 1730, Peter Wilson, of KE Co., conv. to John Wilson, of the same place, a tract called *Veryna,* formerly in 1663 granted by patent to Thomas Cornwalys, Esq., and by him on 20 July 1669 conv. to George Wilson, of BA Co., now KE Co., who left part of the tract to his eldest son Peter, who thereafter left part of the same to his son Peter Wilson, one of the parties of these presents.{KELR JS#16:66}

13. JAMES WILSON, son of John (7) and Mary, was still a minor on 28 April 1734 when John Haily and Isaac Freeman, appointed by the court, made a return of the orphan's land and building, that of James Wilson, son of John Wilson, dec., now in the possession of Daniel Hull. The property contained by estimation 100 a. having one new dwell. house of very worth 20' and 18, one old log dwell. house, one old 40' tob. house, one decayed log tob. house 25' and 20', one old log corn house, one out house 12' and 8', a young orchard about 80 apple trees, and between 300 and 400 panels of old fence. Daniel Hull was given free privilege to clear ... a. of ground.{KEBI JS#18:41}

On 20 Nov 1739, James Wilson, son of John Wilson, dec., was bound to Thomas Williams as an apprentice until age 21.{KEBI JS#18:232}

On 1 June 1745, an agreement was made between George Wilson, Sr., of KE Co., and James Wilson, of the afsd. county. The agreement stated that forasmuch as James Wilson, predeseser of the sd. George and James Wilson, in his last will dated 23 July 1732 gave to his grandson, the present James Wilson, 30 a., part of a tract called *Verina,* and also gave to his son, the present George Wilson, all the remaining part of the afsd. tract, and whereas the sd. 30 a. hath not been laid out, therefor to prevent any controversies the above George Wilson and sd. James Wilson agree to lay out and bound the sd. 30 a. {KELR JS#25:264}

14. JOHN WILSON, son of John (7) and Mary, on 20 Nov 1739, was bound as an apprentice to Hugh Hern until age 21 in the trade of a tanner.{KEBI JS#18:233}

15. GEORGE WILSON, son of George (8) and Mary (Kennard) Wilson, was b. c1725. George Wilson, age c34, dep. on 3 April 1759.{KEEJ: Thomas Harris}

He m. Margaret Hall. She was at one time the wife of Gen. St. Clair by whom she had a son, Dr. Campbell St. Clair of Sussex Co., DE.{A}

Mr. George Willson (also George Wilson), of KE Co., d. by 10 March 1761, when his estate was appraised by Nicholas Smith and W. Comegys, and valued at £919.5.0. William Salisbury and Joseph Sweory signed as creditors. No next of kin were listed. Margaret Wilson, admx., filed the inventory on 2 May 1761.{MINV 75:33}

On 6 March 1762 his estate was again appraised by Nicholas Smith and William Comegys, and valued at £272.12.8. William Salisbury and James Storney (?) signed as creditors. Rachel Davis and William Wilson signed as next of kin. William St. Clair and his wife Margaret, admins./execs., filed the inventory on 24 June 1762.{MINV 78:168} His estate was again appraised and valued at £31.5.3. No creditors or next of kin listed. William St. Clair and his wife Margaret, admins., filed the inventory cont. a list of debts on 24 June 1762.{MINV 78:169}

His estate was dist. on 17 Oct 1763 by William St. Clair, admin. Distribution was made to widow (⅓) with residue to six children George, Mary, James, John, William, and Sarah.{BFD 4:17}

George and Margaret (Hall) Wilson were the parents of{A}: GEORGE; JOHN, m. Mary Perkins; WILLIAM; MARGARET, m. Col. William Henry; and SARAH, m. a George Wilson.

16. ARAMINTA WILSON, dau. of George (8) and Mary (Kennard) Wilson, d. leaving a will dated 3 April 1760 and proved 10 June 1760. In it were mentioned her mother, Mary Willson, bro. George Wilson, sister Mary Hynson, cousin Henry Auguston's Bodein, cousin William Woodland son of Frances Woodland, sister Rachel Downs, sister Milleson Willson, and Ann Prowl. The extx. was her mother Mary Wilson. The will was witnessed by John Wilson, Wm. Husbands, and Elizabeth Stanton.{MWB 31:30}

The estate of Araminta Wilson, of KE Co., was appraised and valued at £61.18.6. No creditors or next of kin were listed. Mary Wilson, extx., filed the inventory cont. a list of debts on 12 Oct 1762.{MINV 79:76}

The estate was dist. on 12 Oct 1762 by Mary Wilson, extx. Distribution was made to Mary Wilson. Legatees were Mary Wilson, Henry Augustine Bochen (Bodien?), William Woodland.{BFD 3:152}

317

Fifth Generation

17. JOHN WILSON, son of George and Margaret (Hall) Wilson, m. Mary Perkins, dau. of Thomas and Anne (Harrison) Perkins, of The White House, KE Co.{A}

John and Mary (Perkins) Wilson were the parents of{A}: Capt. FREDERICK, m. Sarah L. Stewart (dau. of Dr. Alexander Stewart and his first wife, Sally Rasion); WILLIAM ROGERS; THOMAS; and MARGARET, m. Dr. James Black.

Unplaced

WILLSON, (N), m. Hannah Creswell on 13 July 1724.{KESP}

WILSON, (N), m. by 28 May 1756, Ann, dau. of John Halley, of KE Co.{BFD 2:30}

WILLSON, DAVID, of (New) Castle upon Tyne, labourer, age 26, unm., gave bond on 6 July 1698 to William Mason of St. Clements ... London, merchant. David apprenticed himself to sd. William to serve him in the plant. of VA for 4 years ensuing the arrival.{KELR M:92B}

WILSON, ELIZABETH, at March Court 1761 was charged with having had a base born child.{KECR DD#1:2B} At August Court 1763, it was charged that Elizabeth Wilson committed fornication and begot a base born child. She was fined £3. She gave security to indemnify the county from and charge for the maintenance of the child called GEORGE.{KECR DD#1:35B}

WILLSON, GEORGE, of KE Co., d. by 21 Aug 1723, when his estate was admin. by Peter Willson (admin. of James Willson, exec. of dec.).{A 5:228}

WILSON, GEORGE: His wife Elinor was a witness at March Court 1738, in the case of Ann Grimes, spinster, who was found guilty of committing fornication and begetting a bastard child.{KECR JS#22:135}

WILSON, ISAAC, m. by 1 June 1752, Sarah, admx. of William Butcher, of KE Co.{MDAD 33:51}

WILSON, ISAAC, of KE Co., d. by 10 Oct 1769, when his estate was appraised and valued at £56.4.9. No creditors or next of kin listed.

Rachel Wilson, now wife of Andrew Hickman, admx., filed the inventory mentioning cash received on 23 July 1771.{MINV 107:114}

On 30 Aug 1770, his estate was appraised by John Eccleston and William Maxwell, and valued at £59.3.7. Samuel Wallis and James Black signed as creditors. James Wilson and William Hull signed as next of kin. Andrew Hickman, admin., filed the inventory on 24 May 1771.{MINV 108:35}

Distribution of the estate was made on 22 July 1772 by Andrew Hickman and his wife Rachell Hickman, admins.{BFD 6:151}

WILSON, ISBELLA, spinster, at March Court 1745 was charged that on 10 May 1745, and at diverse times as well before as since, she committed fornication and begot a bastard child. She was fined 30 s.{KECR JS#24:269}

At March Court 1747, it was presented that Isabella Willson, spinster, on 1 March 1747, and at diverse times as well before as since, committed fornication and begot a bastard child. She was fined 30 s.{KECR JS#25:5B}

WILSON, JAMES, a "Scot" and servant of Capt. Thomas Bradnox, d. on 19 Aug 1652 from an "intermitting fever joined with the dropsy or scurvy ... It was stated that the stripes given him by his Master not long before his death were not material."{ARMD LIV:8, Liber A:47}

WILSON, JAMES, d. by 10 May 1704.{KE Inv. from Wills: 3:352}

WILSON, JAMES, merchant, at March Court 1758, was charged that on 10 May 1756, he assaulted Elizabeth Couzins. He was fined 20 s.{KECR JS#25:185B}

WILSON, JOHN, and Ann Jones were m. 16 Jan 1704.{KESP}

WILLSON, JOHN, of KE Co., d. leaving a will dated 27 Nov 1748 and proved 24 April 1749. The heirs named were wife Elizabeth, sons James and Thomas, dau. Mary, dau. Sarah wife of James Roberts, and son John who was to be under the care of his mother until age 18. The execs. were wife Elizabeth and son James. The will was witnessed by R. A. Page, Benjamin Ricard, and Daniel Canady.{MWB 26:93}

On 4 May 1749, his estate was appraised by W. Hynson and John Wickes, and valued at £114.18.2. James Roberts and James Jones signed as creditors. Thomas Maswitson (?) and Sarah Roberts signed as next of kin. Elisabeth Wilson and John Willson, execs., filed the inventory on 22 July 1749.{MINV 41:53}

On 2 Oct 1749, his estate was appraised by W. Hynson and Jo. Wickes, and valued at £31.9.7. Jacob Jones and James Roberts signed as creditors. Sarah Roberts signed as next of kin. Elisabeth Wilson and John Wilson, execs., filed the inventory on 21 July 1750.{MINV 43:449}

Distribution of the estate of John Wilson, of KE Co., was made on 21 July 1758 by Elisabeth Wilson and James Wilson, execs. Distribution was made to widow and remainder equally to James, Thomas, John, Mary, and Sarah.{BFD 2:86}

John and Elizabeth Wilson were parents of{KESP}: THOMAS, b. 12 June 1711; ——, b. 9 July ----; —MES, b. 17 May 1724; THOMAS, b. 17 Sep 172-; SARAH, b. 1 July 1730; and MARY, b. 25 April 17--.{KESP}

WILLSON, JOHN, and Eloner Dasha were m. 10 Sep 174-.{KESH}

WILLSON, JOHN, age c31, in Oct 1753 dep. regarding the bounds of a tract called *Cornwallis's Choice*.{KELR JS#28:47}

WILLSON, JOHN, m. by 16 April 1767, Sarah, dau. of Richard Gibson, of TA Co. The latter made his will on the afsd. date, naming the children of John and Sarah as John, Margaret, Aminta, Sarah, and Ann.{MWB 35:426}

John Wilson, of KE Co., d. by 23 Nov 1773, when his estate was appraised by Peter Massy and Christopher Hall, and valued at £681.1.3. William Rogers and William Henry signed as creditors. James Wilson and Rachel Wilson signed as next of kin. Sarah Wilson, extx., filed the inventory on 12 Feb 1774.{MINV 115:355}

Distribution was made on 9 July 1775 by Mrs. Sarah Wilson, admx.{BFD 7:8}

John and Sarah (Gibson) Wilson were the parents of: JOHN; MARGARET; AMINTA; SARAH and ANN.

WILSON, MARY, widow, age 55, dep. in April 1759 that 43 years earlier she heard her father-in-law Daniel Pearce, say ... .{KEEJ: Thomas Harris}

WILSON, MERIDETH, of KE Co., d. by 10 March 1767, when the estate was appraised by Ebenezar Blackiston and William Wilmer, and valued at £7.6.5. William Busby and Martha Brown signed as creditors.

No next of kin listed. William Crabbin, admin., filed the inventory on 6 May 1767.{MINV 94:8}

The estate was appraised and valued at £9.3.6. No creditors or next of kin listed. William Crabbin (also William Crabin), admin., filed the inventory cont. a list of debts on 6 May 1767.{MINV 94:8}

WILLSON, PETER, and Cathrine Henry were m. 1 Sep 1737.{KESH} They were the parents of{KESH}: JOHN, b. 6 Feb 1740/1; and JAMES, b. 21 March 1742/3.

WILSON, ROBERT, labourer, at November Court 1732, was charged with stealing a wallet and two glass bottle of James Kann. He was acquitted.{KECR JS#WK:329A}

WILSON, SARAH, at November Court 1758, confessed to committing fornication and named the father. She was fined 30 s. William Wilson, shoemaker, entered into security for the sum of £10 for fine and fees.

WILSON, THOMAS, and Ann King m. 29 Aug 1745.{KESH}

WILSON, THOMAS, and wife Mary, were the parents of: JAMES, b. 15 May 1747.{KESH}

WILSON, WILLIAM, m. Rebecca, dau. of Pierce and ... .{CEMM}

WILSON, WILLIAM, on 20 Nov 1682 was conv. by Henry Williams and Febe his wife, of KE Co., a parcel of 50 a. called *The Eastern Island*.{KELR K:30A}

William was the father of: SARAH. Alexander Walters of Kent Isle gives to Sarah Wilson, dau. of William Wilson, of sd. Island, c1682, a heifer with her mark ... .{KELR K:2}

WILSON, WILLIAM, d. by 17 April 1738 when his estate was inv. It was filed by Sarah Wilson, admx., on 17 March 1738. William Young signed as next of kin.{MINV 24:67}

William Wilson and Sarah Young m. 20 Jan 1732.{KESP} They were the parents of{KESP}: WILLIAM, b. 28 Feb 17--; MARY, b. 8 Aug 1733; and ELIZABETH, b. 1 Jan ----.

WILSON, WILLIAM, and Elisabeth Perkins were m. 18 Aug 1745.{KESH}

WILSON, WILLIAM, at June Court 1763, was charged with having committed fornication and begetting a base born child. He was fined 30 s.{KECR DD#1:33A}

THE JOSEPH YOUNG FAMILY

1. JOSEPH YOUNG, son of Samuel Young, of AA Co., whose will of 2 Jan 1722/3, named his son Joseph and Joseph's daus. Mary and Milcah.{MWB 21:707} Joseph d. by 24 June 1737, having m. Mary, widow of Col. Nathaniel Hynson.

On 4 Feb 1722, Joseph Young, of KE Co., Gent., and his wife Mary, conv. land to Hannah Hynson, of afsd. county. Whereas Joseph Young m. the afsd. Mary, she being lately the widow and relict of Coll. Nathaniel Hynson, dec., and the above Hannah Hynson is one of the daus. and legatees of the afsd. Nathaniel Hynson who by his last will dated 4 May 1720 bequeathed to his dau. Hannah Hynson his then dwell. plant. being two tracts, one *Sutton Underhill* and the other called *Salhill*, 550 a. Forasmuch as the afsd. Joseph and Mary in right of her dowry hath ⅓ of the afsd. two tracts and whereas both parties agree to a division.{KELR JS#W:280}

On 26 Aug 1728, Joseph Young, of KE Co., and his wife Mary, conv. to Margarett Blackistone (formerly Margarett Hynson) and dau. of afsd. Mary and now the wife of Thomas Blackistone of KE Co., a tract which Col. Nathaniel Hynson, of KE Co., dec., by his last will gave to above sd. Mary, 1,000 a. of a tract called *Partnership* cont. 3000 a.{KELR JS#X:277}

On 1 May 1736, Joseph Young, of KE Co., Gent., gave to his dau. Mary Young one silver tankard weighing about £18.8 [sic] and the sum of £20 sterling in plate, and to his dau. Milcah Young he gave £30 in plate.{KEBI JS#18:30}

Joseph Young, Esq., of CE Co., d. leaving a will dated 9 Feb 1736/7 and proved 7 May 1737. Dau. Mary was to have tracts *New York* and *Garnett's Meadows*. Dau. Milcah was to have *Holland's Lot* and *New Stadt*. Joseph also named his bros. Richard and Samuel. There may have been a third dau. His wife was appointed extx. The will was witnessed by Susan and Thomas Jobson, Sarah Budd (later m. to Edward Fottrell), and Moses Rawlings.{MWB 21:752}

Joseph Young, Esq., of CE Co., d. by 24 June 1737 when his inventory was signed by next of kin Edward Fottrell, Sarah Fottrell, and Richard Young.{MINV 23:151, 23:144}

William Frisbey, Ebenezer Blakistone, and William Harris, of KE Co., Gent., are bound to the guardianship of Milcah Young, dau. of Joseph Young, dec., and received of the admx. of the Rev. Mr. Arthur Holt sundry Negroes, viz., Simon, Peter, Sarah, Guy, Ann, Hannah, Pegg, Phill, Ruth, Marshall, Charles, Lydia, Reyna, Ruth, Moll, Guy, Nell, Jutine, and Phillis, amounting to the sum of £397 by appraisement. Mr. William Frisby who m. the sister of the sd. Milcah prayed that the court appoint him guardian to sd. orphan and deliver sd. Negroes into his hands. 23 Nov 1743.{KEBI JS#20:42}

Joseph Young was the father of: MARY; MILCAH; and possibly a third dau.

2. MARY YOUNG, dau. of Joseph, was living on 15 May 1738, when George Garnett, of Chester Town, cordwinder, conv. land to Mary Young, of the same place, dau. and devisee of Joseph Young, late of KE Co., dec. Whereas Joseph Young purchased from the same George a tract called *Garnetts Meadow(?)* and paid George £20 the sd. George by his writing obligatory made the same Joseph in his lifetime dated 2 Feb 1733 oblige himself to convey same to sd. Joseph. Joseph afterwards made his last will dated 9 Feb 1736 by which he devised the above mentioned land, 41 a., to afsd. Mary his dau. and d. before any conveyance was made.{KELR JS#22:71}

On 10 June 1738, John True, of KE Co., conv. land to Mary Young, dau. and devisee of Joseph Young, dec., of the same county. Whereas the sd. John for the purchase of that part of a tract called *New York*, which sd. John had in possession unsold, and also that parcel of land thereto contiguous between the dwell. house of the sd. John and the branch called John Trues Branch, having actually paid sd. John £200, he the same John by his writing obligatory made to the sd. Joseph dated 21 May 1733 obliged himself to convey the afsd. parcel of land to the same Joseph.{KELR JS#22: between 100 and 105; JS#22: 324}

THE WILLIAM YOUNG FAMILY

1. WILLIAM YOUNG, d. by 31 May 1687. He m. Frances --- on 14 April 1670.{court.VR}

At March Court 1672 Simon Clymer claimed that Willm. Young owed him for work he had done by agreement in building a church. {ARMD LIV: 556, Liber BB No.2:--}

On 21 Sep 1675 William Young, carpenter, and his wife Frances, conv. to John Sergeant and Richard Webb, 200 a. called *Carpender's Square* on Thomas' Branch of Wye River.{TALR 1:340}

On 21 Nov 1676 William Young, carpenter, and his wife Frances, conv. to John Greene, 200 a., *Carpender's Square*, in Wye River.{TALR 3:31}

Richard Webb in his will dated 4 Sep 1678 left 200 a. Middle Plantation to Sarah Young, eld. dau. of William Young of TA Co.{MWB 10:22}

On 11 June 1680 William Young, carpenter, and his wife Frances, conv. to John Serjeant, cooper, 200 a. near the head of Wye River called *Hopewell*, adj. land of Peter Sides.{TALR 3:340}

On 18 Oct 1680 William Young, planter, and his wife Frances, conv. to Nememiah Covington, planter, the dwell. plant. were Covington resided near the head of Wye River, and other land.{TALR 3:371}

On 12 Aug 1682 William Young, carpenter, and his wife Frances, conv. to John Browne, part of the land laid out for Thos. Williams called *The Addition* on Williams' Branch, Back Wye River and adj. called Partnership, total 350 a.{TALR 4:139}

On 15 June 1683 William Young, carpenter, and his wife Frances, conv. to Richard Jones, smith, 100 a. *Young's Chance* on Back Wye River.{TALR 4:199}

He was in KE Co. by 1 Aug 1683 when Richard Lowder of KE Co. and his wife Carolina conv. to him 33 a., called *Green Branch*.{KELR K:65}

On 17 June 1684 Jacob Seth and his wife Barbara conv. to William Younge, carpenter, 33 a., part of *Mt. Mill* on w. side of Thomas' Branch.{TALR 4:304}

William Young d. leaving a will dated 12 Jan 1686 and proved 31 May 1687. To wife (unnamed), extx., he devised a tract called *Stanford*. To sons William and John, the plant. at death of wife. To eldest dau. Sarah, 200 a. called *Middle Plantation*. To second dau. Eliza, the plant. in event of death of Sarah.{MWB 4:278}

His estate was admin. on 16 July 1687.{INAC 9:494}

William was the father of: WILLIAM; JOHN; SARAH, m. William Scott; and ELIZABETH, m. James Gould.[57]

---

[57] The men who m. William Young's daus. Sarah and Elizabeth are identified in TALR 13:675.

2. WILLIAM YOUNG, son of William (1), d. in KE Co. by Nov 1754. he may have m. 1st, Cornelia, dau. of Cornelius Mulrain[58], and 2nd, by 7 Aug 1750, Elizabeth (N).

On 16 Feb 1696 William Young conv. to William Scott a parcel called *Standford,* bought by his father, William Young of Jacob Seth, 60 a., part of *Mt. Mill* in Wye River.{TALR 7:223}

On 18 June 1710 William Young and his wife Cornelia of QA Co. conv. to Peirce Welsh of TA Co., innholder, all his rights to 250 a. in 4 tracts: *Cornelius Garden, Salem, Stepton* and *Colien,* all adj., on n. side of Great Choptank River.{TALR 12:2}

On 7 Aug 1750 William Young and his wife Elizabeth conv. to Thomas Lee 52 a., part of *Stratton* adj. his bro. John Young's land.{QALR RTC:452}

On 14 Nov 1754, when his estate was appraised by W. Hynson and Samuel Miller, and valued at £200.10.2. Benjamin Richards and William Murray signed as creditors. Lidia Flynn signed as next of kin. Anne Webber, extx., filed the inventory on 24 Jan 1755.{MINV 60:191}

3. JOHN YOUNG of William (1), d. by Aug 1742. He m. Elizabeth (N).

At March Court 1726/7, John Young, taylor, was fined 7 s. and 6 pence for being drunk and swearing one oath.{KECR JS#22:266}

At June Court 1727, Elizabeth Young, of St. Paul's Parish, wife of John Young, was charged with assaulting Ester Weller on 10 June 1727. Elizabeth Young was ordered to pay fines and fees of 2,268 lbs. of tobacco.{KECR JS#22:293}

On 25 Nov 1735 Nathaniel Scott gave to John Young, son of William Young, late of QA Co., 50 a., part of *Partnership.*{QALR RTA:449}

John Young, tailor, St. Paul's Parish, KE Co., d. leaving a will dated 26 Jan 1741/2 and proved 25 Aug 1742. The heirs named were wife Elizabeth, to whom was left the entire estate, and servant Wm. Brown who received personalty. The will was witnessed by Lawrence Atkinson, Stephen Ingram, and Elizabeth Ingram.{MWB 22:507}

John Young's estate was inv. by 27 July 1744, appraised by —— Bordley and William McClean, and valued at £58.15.10. No creditors or next of kin. Lambert Wilmer, exec., filed the inventory on 4 Aug 1744.{MINV 29:453}

---

[58] In a deed dated 30 Jan 1737 John Angley mentioned Cornelius Mulrain of TA Co. who left three daus., including Cornelia, wife of William Young. {TALR 14:317}

Elizabeth Young, widow, KE Co., d. leaving a will dated 22 Oct 1742 and proved 8 Nov 1742. The heirs named were mother Ann Windell and Rebecca, wife of Jacob Glan, Jr., leaving personalty. Dau. Elizabeth Hanson was given the residue of the estate, and in the event of her death without heirs, the estate was to pass to Lambert Wilmer, exec. Slaves were to have their freedom at marriage of dau., afsd. exec. Lambert Wilmer, was to have care of Elizabeth Hanson during her minority. The will was witnessed by James Read, Archibold Boyde, and Geo. Garnett.{MWB 22:510}

Elizabeth's estate was appraised by William McClean and T. Bordley, and valued at £300.15.1. Thomas Clay and Charles Hynson signed as creditors. Hans Hanson and Edward Windle signed as next of kin. Lambert Wilmer, exec., filed the inventory on 25 April 1744.{MINV 28:489}

John and Elizabeth Young were the parents of: JOHN.

4. JOHN YOUNG, son of John (3) and Elizabeth, was living in Oct 1754.

On 21 Oct 1754 John Young (son of John Young) and his wife Mary conv. to Nathaniel Scott, Jr., part of *Stratton*, conv. from Richard Stratton, 54 1/2 a.{QALR RTD:264}

He may be the John Young to whom, on 18 Feb 1764, Charles Murphy and his wife Mary conv. 99 1/2 a. called *Murphy's Chance Resurveyed*.{QALR RTG:35}

On 31 Dec 1770 John Young and his wife Mary conv. to Robert Goldsborough, son of Robert Goldsborough, attorney at law, part of *Bantry*, devised by Samuel Sample Atwell, dec. to said Mary, wife of John Young, by the name of Mary Atwell.{TALR 20:135}

John Young, of St. Michaels Parish, TA Co., d. leaving a will dated 27 Nov 1774, and proved 3 Jan 1775. One hundred a. including dwelling house and orchards to be sold to pay debts, except ½ acre to be used as graveyard for my family. To wife Mary Young, extx., remainder of lands during life and use of above 100 acres until sold then to son Samuel Young; also to son Samuel tract of land *Fishing Bay* to be purchased but wife Mary Young to have use of tract during life. To 6 children: Samuel, Ann, Margaret, Elizabeth, Mary and John Young, personal estate equally after purchase money for above tract and wife's thirds are deducted. To sons: Samuel and John Young, to be bound out at trades and daus. to be in care of my wife. The will was witnessed by John Skinner; Richard Start; Archibald McInnis.{MWB 40:523}

John and Mary Young were the parents of: SAMUEL; ANN; MARGARET; ELIZABETH; MARY; and JOHN.

Unplaced

YOUNG, (N), m. by 10 Feb 1708, Mary, dau. of Richard Jones of QA Co.{MWB 12:355}

YOUNG, CHARLES, at March Court 1713/4 was named by Sarah Hopwood as the begetter of her bastard child.{QAJU ET No.B:268} However, at June Court 1715 he was charged that on 20 Oct 1713 at St. Paul's Parish he committed fornication with Sarah Hopwood. He was acquitted.{QAJU ET No.B:404}

YOUNG, CHARLES, m. Margaret Marsh on 23 Dec 1750, by pub. of banns.{QALU}

YOUNG, DAVID, d. leaving a will dated 20 Aug 1715 and proved 7 Sep 1715. To Edward Crew, he left personalty. To wife Sarah, extx., he devised the residue of estate.{MWB 14:70}

YOUNG, DAVID, of QA Co., died leaving a will dated 24 Oct 1728 and proved 29 Nov 1728. The heirs named were 2 daus. Eliza. and Sarah, entire estate; care and tuition of sd. daus. to sister Christiana Barnett until 16 yrs. of age; shd. sd. sister die during their minority, child. to care of bro. Edward. The execs. were Thomas Barnett and Edward Young. The will was witnessed by Otho Coursey, george Jackson and John Smith.{MWB 19:563}

YOUNG, EDWARD, m. Hannah (or Anne) Hamer on 26 Jan 1736.
    He may be the orphan boy brought into court by George Jackson at March 1715/6, and bound to Jackson to age 21, to learn the trade of carpenter.{QAJU ET No.B:489}
They were the parents of{QALU}: JOSEPH (twin), b. 3 Nov 1737; and BENJAMIN (twin), b. 3 Nov 1737; CHRISTIAN (dau.), b. 24 Sep 17--, bapt -- Oct 1741; SARAH, b. 2 Oct 1743.

YOUNG, JOHN, of Queen Anne's Co., age 53, dep. April 1730.{QAEJ: Hawkins, Ernault}.

YOUNG, JOHN, m. Mary (N). They were the parents of{QALU}: ALICE, b. 20 Nov 1730; NATHANIELL, b. 18 March 1739, bapt 14 Sep 1740.

YOUNG, JOHN, Jr., m. (N) Atkinson (date not given).{QALU}

YOUNG, JOHN, m. Frances Sexton, dau. of Patrick Sexton of QA Co., whose will dated 26 Dec 1763, named dau. Francis Young and also John Young.{MWB 31:1094}
   Yohn Young, of QA Co., d. leaving a will dated 3 Jan 1768, and proved 22 Jan 1770. He named his wife Frances, and children: William, Solomon, John, Benj., Mary, Lewcrecy and Suffian. Son John was the exec. The will was witnessed by Richard Mason, Chas. Murphey, and Philzmon Murphy.{MWB 37:611}
   John and Frances were the parents of{QALU}: GIBSON, b. 23 March 1736; WILLIAM; SOLOMON; JOHN; BENJAMIN; MARY; LUCRETIA; and SUFFIAN.

YOUNG, JOSEPH, m. (N) Beal, on 27 Aug 1758, by pub. of banns.{QALU}
   Joseph Young, of QA Co., planter, d. leaving a will dated 7 Jan 1774, and proved 17 March 1774. To son Samuel Young, Negro boy, Richard. Residue of personal estate after debts are paid to sons Benjamin Young, Joseph Young, John Beal Young, Samuel Young and my two daus. Mary Young and Sarah Young. Friend James Ruth was exec. The will was witnessed by Thos. Ruth, Senr., Thos. Thomson, Solo. Sparks.{MWB 39:889}
   Joseph Young was the father of: SAMUEL; BENJAMIN; JOSEPH; JOHN BEAL; MARY; and SARAH.

YOUNG, MARY, at March Court 1757 confessed fornication and was fined 30 s. She stated that Cornelius Robertson was the father of her base born child called JAMES.{KECR JS#25:172B}

YOUNG, THOMAS, of TA Co., d. leaving a will dated 7 Jan 1687/8 and proved 20 June 1688. The heirs named were William Burton, William Carman and his sister, Susan Carman, personalty. The will was witnessed by Jno. Holt, Margaret Holt and Wm. Cowell.{MWB 6:21}

YOUNG, WILLIAM, m. Elizabeth (N). They were the parents of{QALU}: PRESTON, b. 28 Oct 17--, bapt 8 Nov 1741[59]; WILLIAM, b. 8 May 1744, bapt 17 Nov 1744; NOAH, b. 23 --- 1745; ELIZABETH, b. --- Jan 1749; JOHN, b. 17 Jan 1751; DANIEL, b. 8 Sep 1753; JAMES, b. 20 Sep 1755; and BENJAMIN, b. 24 July 1757.

---

[59] On 6 Dec 1775 he was named as son-in-law in the will of Katherine Sherwood of KI, QA Co. {MWB 41:97}

INDEX

331

BATHURSELL,
Henry, 7
BATSON, John, 154
BATTERSHALL,
Henry, 8
John, 8
Mary, 8
Rachel, 8
Rachell, 8
William, 8
BATTERSHELL,
Henry, 8
Rachell, 7
William, 8
BATTERSHILL,
Elizabeth, 8
Henry, 8
John, 8
Mary, 8
Rachel, 8
William, 8
BAUD, Alexander,
25
BAVIS, William S.,
286
BAXTER, Mary, 106
Robert, 201
BAYARD, James, 27,
28
BAYLEY, Jacob, 274
William, 201, 202
BAYLEYS FOR-
REST, 195
BEALE, Elizabeth,
72
BEALL, Thomas,
229
BEARD, Rachel, 11,
13
Richard, 11
BEARLY, John, 151
BEAVANS, Mary,
162
William, 162
BEAZLY, John, 150

BEAZY, John, 151
BECK, Ann, 75, 87,
88
Anne, 90
Aquilla, 105
Caleb, 87, 202, 206
E., 182
Edward, 87, 168,
169, 174, 205, 266
Frances, 260
George, 120
Hannah, 120
John, 60
Joshua, 205, 206
Mary, 168, 169,
174, 202
Vivian, 20
BECKWORTH, 87,
205, 209
BEDING, Nathaniel,
35
BEDINGFIELD,
Margaret, 300
Sarah, 300
Thomas, 300
BEDWORTH, 288,
290
BEECH, John, 143
BEEDLE, Ann, 96
Henry, 96
BEGINNING, 14,
165
BELLICON, Chris-
topher, 6
Mil., 6
BELLSHER, 4
BELLUSS, Francis,
243
BELROSE, Ann, 160
BELSHEW, 33
BENCHING, Daniel,
233
BENNET, Desboro,
218
Rachel, 83

Richard, 194
BENNETS BRIDGE,
14
BENNETS HOPE,
38
BENNETT, Edward,
137
Elizabeth, 98
George, 84
R., 171
Richard, 7, 98, 99,
177, 180, 181,
186, 312
BENNETTS HOPE,
38
BENNEY, James,
229
BENTHAME,
Richard, 113
BENTLY, Eliza., 242
Mary, 242
Patience, 242
Stephen, 217
William, 242
BEORE, Roger, 112
BERRY, Jane, 281
Joseph, 226
Nathan, 281
BEST, Edward, 144
Merty, 28
BESTON, William-
har, 222
BETTIN, Turbutt,
178
BEYNER, Ebenezer,
247
BICKERSTETH,
Thomas, 298
BINSS, John, 250
BIRCHFIELD,
Maurice, 38
BISHFORD, 304
BISHFORD
RESURVEY, 305
BISHOP, Elijah, 118

333

BOON, Cethisah,
138
Joseph, 138, 139
Kettesor, 139
Lettiser, 139
Thomas, 167
BOONE, Joseph,
139, 208
Lethisa, 139
BOONLY, 101, 172,
175
BOOT, Joseph, 27
BOOTES, William,
292
BOOTH, William,
251
BOOTS, Joseph, 292
Mary, 197
William, 28
BORDLEY, A., 216
Agnes, 9, 10
Ann, 10, 11, 12
Anne, 12, 13, 14,
166
Anthony (Arthur),
15
Ariana, 12, 14
Arthur, 12
Beal, 14
Beale, 14, 51
Bridget, 10
Elisabeth, 14
Elizabeth, 9, 10, 11,
14, 216
Hannah, 14, 15, 16
Harry, 9
Henry, 15
Isabella, 9, 13, 14
J., 12
Jane, 9
Johannes de, 9
John, 9, 10, 11, 13,
14, 141
John Beale, 12, 14
Margaret, 9, 10, 14

Margarett, 14
Margrett, 11, 13
Martha, 12
Mary, 9, 10, 11, 12,
274
Mathias, 12, 14
Priscilla, 13, 234
Prissilla, 13
Rachel, 11, 13
Richard, 9
Sarah, 12, 13, 14
Stephen, 9, 10, 11,
12, 13, 14, 15, 16,
17, 166, 234
Susanna, 10
Susannah, 9
T., 236, 326
Thomas, 9, 10, 11,
12, 13, 14, 20, 78,
169, 297
William, 9, 10, 11,
12, 13, 14, 15, 16,
17, 86, 216, 249
BORDLEY'S, 14
BORDLEYS GIFT,
14
BORDLY, Ariana, 11
BOROUGHS, Sarah,
241
BORTEN, Rebecca,
268
BOSTICK, Rachel,
27
Sanders, 182, 183
BOUDY, Elisabeth,
15
Henry, 15
Katherine, 15
Richard, 15
Rosamond, 15
Solomon, 15
BOUNTY, 11, 83,
107, 166
BOURK, John, 303
Thomas, 58

BOWARM, Peter,
182
BOWDAY, Elizabeth,
15
BOWDIE, Henry, 16
John, 16
Mary, 16
Rachel, 16
Sarah, 16
BOWDY, Elizabeth,
15, 252
Henry, 15
Kath., 15
Richard, 15
Rosamond, 16
Solomon, 15
BOWENS, Thomas,
246
BOWER, Thomas, 16
BOWERS, Ann, 16,
17, 146
Elisabeth, 17
Hannah, 14, 15, 17
Isabella, 16, 17
James, 18
Jane, 18
John, 17
Martha, 16, 17
Mary, 17, 18, 91
Pearce, 16, 17
Thomas, 3, 16, 17,
73, 89, 90, 92,
146, 189, 203,
204, 243, 256,
258, 307
William, 14, 16, 17,
18
BOWLES, Ann, 19,
20
Elinor, 20
Isaac, 18, 19, 20
James, 18, 19, 20
Jane, 20
John, 18, 19
Margrett, 19

336

338

Morres, 48
Morris, 135
Susannah, 48
William, 46
CARVELL, Ann, 51
CARVIL, Ann, 51
John, 51, 186, 203
Thomas, 50
CARVILE, John,
138, 139
CARVILL, Ann, 13,
51, 306
Jane, 13, 50
John, 13, 51, 63,
84, 139, 186, 187,
250, 305, 306
Phebe, 175, 177
CARVILLE, Anne,
51
Avarilla, 50
Blanche, 50
Jane, 51
Johanna, 49
John, 50, 283
Margaret, 49
Mary, 50, 51
Phoebe, 50
Robert, 49
Susanna, 49, 50
Thomas, 49, 50
CARWARDING,
Ann, 104
John, 103, 104
Thomas, 103
CASTLE CAREY,
178
CASTLE CARRY,
173
CASTLE CARY, 38
CATLIN, Thomas,
154
CATTAIL MARSH,
269
CAULK, Ann, 178
Ja., 203

Jacob, 184, 217
James, 27
John, 178, 279
Oliver, 203
William, 24, 42
CERENA, 313
CERESTON, Ben-
jamin, 140
CHADBOURN,
Richard, 131
Susannah, 132
William, 131, 132s
CHADDOCK,
Elizabeth, 126
Richard, 126
CHALMERS, James,
171
Margaret, 171
CHAMBERS, Ben-
jamin, 179
Esther, 240
Micle/Michael, 24
William, 240
CHANCE, 30, 31,
42, 107, 123, 127,
144, 152, 185,
218, 233
CHANCE AD-
DITION, 170
CHANCELLER,
Mary, 52
Salome, 52
William, 52
CHANCELLOR,
Elizabeth, 52
Mary, 51, 52
William, 51, 52
CHANCELOR,
Elizabeth, 52, 171
CHANDLER, Abel,
54, 198
Hannah, 52, 53, 54
Jane, 54
Mary, 52, 54
Michael, 52, 53, 54

Michal, 53
Nathaniel, 52, 53,
54
Phebe, 53
Rachel, 53
Sarah, 53, 54
Spencer, 53
Tahpenah, 54
Tahponah, 53
Tapenah, 53
Thomas, 52, 53, 54,
91, 200, 246, 254
CHANGE, 134
CHAPLIN, Joseph,
208
CHAPMAN, Sarah,
169
CHAPPEL, John,
197, 198
Rachel, 197, 198
CHAPPELL, John,
101
CHAPPLE, Ann
Eliza., 258
John, 14, 40, 182,
258, 298
CHEPLEY, Moses,
282
CHESELDINE,
Kenelm, 20
CHESELDYNE,
Kenelm, 251
CHESTER, 99
CHESTER GROVE,
192
CHESTERFIELD,
296
CHESTNUT BAY,
226, 228, 230
CHESTNUT COY,
229
CHESTON, 98, 99
D., 12
Daniel, 237

340

CHETHAM, Edward, 165
CHEW, Henrietta
  Maria, 14
  Margaret, 14
  Samuel, 14
CHIGWELL, 272
CHILDS, Abraham, 263
CHILDS HARBOR, 38
CHILDS HARBOUR, 38
CHIN, Thomas, 64
CHIVENS, William, 178
CHOICE, 233
CHRISFIELD, Absalom, 55
  Anton, 55
  Arthur, 55
  Benjamin, 27, 56
  Edward, 56
  Ellinor, 55
  Mary, 55
  Phil., 186
  Philip, 55
  Richard, 55
  Rosamond, 55
  Rossamond, 55
  Sarah, 55
CHRISTFIELD, Ann, 55
  Phil., 118
CHRISTIAN, Ann, 56
  Anne, 20, 56
  Christian, 57
  Elizabeth, 56
  James, 56, 57
  Laurance, 56
  Lawrence, 56
  Mary, 20, 56
  Rachell, 56
  Rebecca, 26, 56

Sara, 21
Sarah, 168
Thomas, 20, 56, 57
CHRISTOU, Chris, 132, 251
  Christos, 261
CHURCH, Elizabeth, 58
  James, 199
  Jane, 58
  Katherine, 57
  Margaret, 57, 58
  Mary, 57
  Philemon, 57
  Samuel, 57, 58
  Sarah, 58
  Tabitha, 57
  Thomas, 57
  William, 58
CHURNELL'S NECK, 233
CLARK, Ann, 65
  Benjamin, 63
  Charles, 60, 61
  Daniel, 61, 233
  Dennis, 58, 66, 188
  Eleanor, 63
  Elizabeth, 61, 62, 63, 64
  Esabella, 63
  Esther, 66
  George, 61, 62, 64, 289
  Gilbert, 64
  Henry, 63, 221
  James, 62, 64
  Jane, 63
  John, 58, 60, 62, 63, 64, 66
  Joseph, 65
  Joshua Foster, 61
  Margaret, 63
  Martha, 59, 60, 61
  Mary, 58, 59, 60, 61, 63, 65, 66

Mathew, 59, 60
Patrick, 65, 304
Peter, 65
Rachel, 59, 60, 108
Rachele, 60
Rebecca, 58, 60
Rebeccah, 65
Robert, 66, 71
Samuel, 58, 66
Samuell, 66
Sarah, 58, 60
Thomas, 61, 62, 65
William, 58, 59, 60, 61, 140
CLARKE, Alexander, 63
  Daniel, 61
  Dennis, 58, 59, 188
  Elinor, 62
  Elizabeth, 64
  Esther, 66
  George, 61
  Hannah, 65
  Henery, 64
  Henry, 62, 63, 64, 220
  Jane, 62
  John, 59, 60, 62, 63, 65, 218
  Margrett, 62
  Martha, 59
  Mary, 58, 59, 62, 66
  Mathias, 60
  Patrick, 65, 234
  Rachell, 60
  Rebecca, 59
  Samuel, 66
  Samuell, 59
  Sarah, 59, 64
  William, 63, 66
CLARK'S ADDITION, 60, 158
CLARKS CONVENIENCY, 59

341

342

Nathaniel, 81
Rebecca, 81
Richard, 79, 80,
    244
Solomon, 81
Spencer, 81
Wolmon, 81
COLIEN, 325
COLLIER, Alice, 47
COLLINS, Ann, 156
  Bartholomew, 64
  Edward, 149
  Francis, 28, 40, 163
  John, 43
  Martha, 238
  William, 156
COLLY, Daniel, 79,
    80, 81
COLSTON, Mar-
    garet, 10, 11
  William, 10
COMAGES
    CHOICE, 32
COMBS, John, 278
COMEGES, William,
    192
COMEGGYS FARM,
    18, 19
COMEGYS, Bartus,
    155
  Boullay, 126
  C., 63, 203, 221,
    243, 313
  Cornelius, 1, 18,
    19, 24, 25, 32, 40,
    58, 111, 190, 192
  E., 1, 159, 203
  Edward, 33, 59,
    237
  Hannah, 132
  John, 150, 198
  Maj., 126
  Mary, 132, 190
  Nathaniel, 198, 199
  Rebecca, 18

W., 28, 29, 159, 243
William, 82, 132,
    156, 317
COMEGYS
    CHOICE, 32
COMEGYS FARM,
    111
COMEGYS FARM
    ADDITION, 111
COMPTON, Henry,
    10
CONEGOCHEAGU
    E MANOR, 278
CONELL, Jerom, 61
CONER, Peter, 80
CONFUSION, 180
CONJUNET, 158
CONN---DY,
    Elizabeth, 38
CONNER,
  Catherine, 77
  Charles, 76, 77
  Hannah, 77
  Isabella, 13, 14, 78
  James, 6, 13, 76,
    77, 78, 161
  Jane, 76
  John, 14, 78, 312
  Mary, 76
  Nathaniel, 77
  Philip, 75, 76, 77
  Phillip, 75
  Sarah, 75, 76, 77
  Susanna, 78
CONNEWAY, Mor-
    gan, 75
CONNEY WARREN,
    301
CONNOLIN, John,
    28
CONNOR, Charles,
    76
  Elinor, 77
  Elisabeth, 78
  Elizabeth, 77

Elynor, 77
Honor, 78
Honour, 224
Isabella, 77, 78
James, 76, 77, 78
Jane, 76
John, 77
Nathaniel, 76
Philip, 4, 224
Thomas, 78
CONNWAY, Dennis,
    35
CONN[ER], Charles,
    76
  Nathaniel, 76
  Philip, 76
CONSTAN-
    TINOPLE, 218
CONVINTON,
    Jeremiah, 102
  Thomas, 102
COOK, Elizabeth,
    226
  Martha, 214
COOKE, Elisabeth,
    269
  Giles, 21, 133
COOLEY, Anne, 79
  Benjamin, 78, 79,
    80, 81, 82, 197
  Daniel, 78, 80, 81,
    82
  Daniell, 79
  Edward, 78, 79
  Elizabeth, 78, 80,
    81, 82
  Frances, 81
  Hannah, 80
  Jane, 81
  John, 79, 80, 81
  Mardy, 79
  Martha, 79, 80, 81,
    82
  Mary, 79, 80
  Nathaniel, 79

343

Richard, 79, 80, 81
Samuel, 82
COOLLEY, Daniel, 78
Elizabeth, 78
COOLY, Daniel, 79
COOPER, Alexander, 85
Henry, 94
Hezekiah, 223, 249, 286
Jane, 266
John, 267
Joseph, 85
Martha, 85
Mary, 265, 266
Nathaniel, 85
Sarah, 150
Thomas, 251
COOPERS, 275
COP, Elisabeth, 74
COPARTNERSHIP, 44
COPEDG, Edward, 82
Elizabeth, 82
COPEDGE, John, 82, 117
Mary, 82
Philip, 218
COPEGE, Philip, 218
COPING, John, 82
COPPDEGES RANGE, 43
COPPEDGE, Edward, 82
Elizabeth, 82
John, 82
Philip, 82
Sarah, 82
COPPEIDG, Edward, 82
COPPEN, George, 144

COPPER, Benjamin, 85
Charles, 67, 68, 83, 84, 85, 86
Cyrus, 84, 85
George, 69, 83, 84, 86, 166, 220, 282
Gustavus, 85
Joseph, 83, 85, 132
Margaret, 283, 287, 289
Margret, 84
Martha, 132
Mary, 83, 84, 85, 86
Norris, 85
Patience, 86, 143
Philip, 84, 85
Rachell, 83
Rebecah, 85
Rebecca, 84, 85
Samuel, 85, 86
Sarah, 83, 84
Thomas, 86
William, 41, 83, 84, 85, 86, 113, 303
COPPIDGE, John, 82
Mary, 82
COPPING, Edward, 82
CORBETT, Alexander, 107
CORMAN, Robert, 220
CORNELIUS GARDEN, 325
CORNER'S NECK, 76
CORNEY, John, 231
CORNINE, John, 6
CORNWALLIS CHOICE, 129, 138, 320

CORNWALLIS HIS CHOICE, 105
CORNWALLIS'S CHOICE, 50, 87, 129, 205, 207
CORNWALYS, Thomas, 316
CORRY, George, 151
CORSE, Ann, 17, 87, 91, 92, 93
Anna, 87
Anne, 16, 90
Barbara, 88
Barney, 259
Casandra, 92
Daniel, 90, 92, 93
David, 16, 17, 87, 91, 92
Elisabeth, 90, 92, 93
Elizabeth, 87, 88, 90
George, 92, 93
Hannah, 31, 87, 89
Hannah Leaburn, 89
Isaac, 90, 91
Jacob, 90
James, 16, 17, 86, 87, 89, 90, 91, 92, 93, 115, 245
James Rigby, 92
Jane, 92
Jennett, 88
John, 86, 87, 88, 89, 91, 92, 93
Martha, 89
Mary, 16, 17, 89, 90, 91, 188
Michael, 87, 88, 89, 90, 91, 188, 307
Michall, 86
Michel, 90
Michl., 90
Offley, 87

Rachel, 87, 88, 90
Rebecca, 90
Rebeccah, 89
Rebekah, 90, 92
Samuel, 89, 91, 93
Sarah, 92
Susanah, 245
Susanna, 90
Susannah, 89, 91
Thomas, 16, 17, 92, 259
Thomas Hynson, 89
Timothy, 89
Welthy, 92
William, 86, 87, 88, 89, 91, 92, 93
Withyann, 89
CORSE'S
  MEADOWS, 90
CORSEY, Elizabeth, 100
  Frances, 100
  Henry, 100
  William, 100
CORWARDING,
  Ann, 104
COSDEN, Asell, 29
COSDON, Jesse, 292
COSENS, Edward, 101
  Elizabeth, 101
COSTYNE, Henry, 45
COURCEY, Ja., 165
COURSE, Ann, 88
  David, 91
  Elizabeth, 92
  James, 88, 89
  John, 89
  Michael, 89
  Welty Ann, 34
COURSEY, Ann, 93, 96
  Anne, 95, 100
  Araminta, 97

Arraminta, 96
Catherine, 93
Edward, 99
Elisabeth, 96
Elizabeth, 93, 94, 95, 96, 97, 98, 99, 100
Henery, 232
Henry, 93, 94, 95, 96, 97, 99, 118, 269
James, 93, 94, 95, 96, 97
Jane, 34, 93, 94, 95
John, 93, 94, 95, 96, 97, 100
John C., 95
Juliana, 93, 95, 96, 97
Katherine, 93
Margaret, 100
Mary, 93, 94, 95, 96, 97, 98, 99, 100
Otho, 96, 97, 99, 327
Rachel, 97, 99
Sarah, 98, 99
Thomas, 94, 95, 96, 97, 98, 100
William, 93, 94, 95, 96, 97, 98, 99, 232, 300, 301
COURSEY UPON
  WYE, 98
COURSEY'S AD-
  DITION, 99
COURSEY'S
  CHOICE, 34, 94
COURSEY'S NECK, 232
COURSEY'S
  POINT, 274
COURSEY'S
  RANGE, 94, 97

COURSEY'S
  TOWNE, 97
COUSANS, Edward, 101
  Elizabeth, 101
COUSANS'S LOTT, 101
COUSINS, Edward, 100, 101
  Elizabeth, 68, 100, 101
  William, 101
COUTES, Hercules, 4
COUZANS, Edward, 101
COUZENS, Edward, 78, 79, 101
  Elisabeth, 79
  Elizabeth, 78, 101
COUZEN'S
  CHANCE, 101
COUZEN'S LOTT, 101
COUZINS,
  Elizabeth, 319
COVENTON, Ed-
  ward, 103
  Henry, 103
  Jerom, 43, 102
  Mary, 103
  Rachael, 103
  Rachel, 103
  Rebecca, 103
  Sarah, 103
  Thomas, 103
COVENTREE, Han-
  nah, 102
  Jeremiah, 102
  Mary, 102
  Priscilla, 102
  Rachell, 102
  Thomas, 102
COVENTRY, 109
  Jeremiah, 259

Thomas, 103
COVINGTON, Cassandra, 102
Jacob, 98
Jeremiah, 102, 103, 209
Mary, 103
Nehemiah, 102, 103
Nememiah, 324
Phillip, 103
Rachel, 102, 103
Sarah, 98
Thomas, 102, 103
COVINGTON'S MARSH, 247
COWARDEN, Abraham, 104, 105, 128, 129
Ann, 129
Dorcas, 105
Edward, 103
Elenor, 104
Frances, 104, 106
John, 104, 105, 106
Martha, 105
Mary, 104, 105, 106
Pasco, 105
Sarah, 105
Thomas, 104, 105
William, 16, 106, 122, 179
COWARDIN, Ambrose, 104
Elenor, 106
Frances, 105
John, 198
Mary, 106
Peter, 106
Thomas, 104
COWARDINE, Abraham, 104
Edward, 105
Frances, 104, 105
Thomas, 105, 235

COWARDING, Ann, 104, 105
Anne, 105
Ebenezar, 104
Ebenezer, 104
Edward, 104, 105
Elinor, 106
Frances, 104
John, 104, 105, 106
Martha, 104
Peter, 106
Rebecca, 105
Thomas, 103, 104
COWELL, William, 328
COWRSEY, Henry, 93
COX, Andrew, 44
Ruth, 44
COXES NECK, 275
COZENS, Edward, 79, 80, 81
Mary, 102
Rebecca, 40, 102
CRABBIN, Alexander, 175
Mary, 175
William, 35, 321
CRABIN, William, 321
CRACKNALL, Elinor, 209
John, 209
Sarah, 209
CRACKNELL, John, 15
Thomas, 15
CRAFFORD, Frances, 269
CRAIG, Patrick, 220
CRAIGE, John, 151
CRAIGG, G., 194
CRAMP, Elizabeth, 112

CRANE, Thomas, 249, 250
CRANNY NECK, 43
CRANY NECKE, 161
CRAUGH, Elizabeth, 203
CRAWFORD, 271
John, 132
CREADLES, Mary, 194
CRESWELL, Hannah, 318
CREW, Edward, 39, 327
Samuel, 39
Thomas, 81
CROMPTON, 277
Mary, 27
CROOKE, Robert, 310
CROOME, Thomas, 122
CROUCH, Ann, 108
Blanch, 108
Catherine, 107
Elizabeth, 109
George, 106
James, 108
Joan, 109
John, 109
John Wedge, 107
Josias, 109, 213
Judith, 107
March, 109
Martha, 109
Mary, 55, 106, 107, 108, 109
Nicholas, 107, 109
Rachell, 108
Rebecca, 108
Rebecka, 279
Richard, 107, 108, 109
Samuel, 85

DILLHUNT, Edmund, 237
DILLIHUNT, Daniel, 237
DINEING ROOM, 126, 191
DINING ROOM, 102, 191
DINNAN, Mary, 114
DISTANCE, Anne, 7
Mary, 7
Ralph, 7
DITTEREDGE, 181
DIXON, John, 180
Rebecca, 248
William, 19, 226, 291
DOE NECK, 105, 205, 207
DOLEHUNTTE, Isaac, 142
DOLIN, Edward, 238
Elizabeth, 238
Sarah, 238
DOLLINGTON, 125
DONGANNOR, 153
DONN'S HAZARD CORRECTED, 44
DORAN, Elizabeth, 117
James, 117
Jane, 117
Margaret, 117
Mary, 117
Sarah, 117
William, 117
DORSEY, Mary, 240
DOUGHERLY, Walter, 33
DOUGHERTY, Bridget, 220
James, 138
DOUGLAS, Thomas, 117

DOUGLASS, George, 305
DOWDALL, John, 162
Judith, 162
Major, 145
DOWNES, George, 314
Margaret, 100
Rachel, 314
William, 314, 315
DOWNS, Mary, 99
Rachel, 314, 317
William, 103
DOYN, Ann, 113
DRAPER, Judith, 107
DRAYTON, 201, 202, 244, 257
DRECUTE, 124
DREVITE, 252, 254
DREVITT, 15, 252
DRIVER, Christopher, 280
Sarah, 280
DROMGOOLE, Lewis, 315
DRUGAN, Edward, 256
DUDDLESTONE, Elizabeth, 37
DUDLEY, Richard, 228, 229
DUDLEY CLIFF, 229
DUDLEY'S CLIFT, 230
DUDLEY'S CLIFTS, 228, 229, 233
DUDLIES CLIFFS, 229
DULANY, Daniel, 163, 305
Darby, 117, 118
E., 186

Edmond, 118
John, 118
Katherine, 117
Mary, 118
DULLAHUNTEE, Thomas, 68
DUN, Robert, 82, 170
DUNAHOW, Catherin, 49
DUNAVAN, Mary, 44
Timothy, 44
DUNCALFE, Edmond, 184
DUNCAN, James, 123
DUNHAMEL, Rachel, 178
DUNKLEY, Robert, 270
DUNLOP, John, 129
DUNN, Darius, 144
Das., 8
Hezekiah, 67, 68
James, 51, 81, 86, 211, 275, 279, 280
John, 87
Robert, 42, 116, 167, 169, 275
William, 8
DUNNAHOW, John, 49
DUNNAVON, Mary, 44
Timothy, 44
DUNSTABLE, 186
DURDEN, Rebecca, 33
DUSEE, Daniel, 168
DUYER, John, 52, 53, 54, 260
Philip, 261
Rachel, 261
DYARS, Elinor, 281

DYER, Edward, 55,
101, 110
Eleanor, 281
John, 53

-E-
EADES, 25
EADS, Kath., 15
EARECKSON, Charles, 82
Dorothy, 82
Matthew, 82
EARICKSON, William, 6
EARL, John, 77
Mr., 224
EARLE, Ann, 94
Ann Maria, 273
Anna, 95
Anna Maria, 277,
278
Anne, 95
Carpenter, 94
Elenor, 307
Elizabeth, 94
James, 94, 95, 277,
278, 296
John, 215
M., 94
Mary, 277
Michael, 95, 278
Richard, 65, 278
EARLEY, William,
143
EARUKSON,
Elizabeth, 43
EAST HUN-
TINGTON, 12
EASTERN ISLAND,
321
EATON, Edward,
231
ECCLESTON, John,
123, 150, 222,
247, 248, 249,

292, 293, 294,
298, 319
Margaret, 248
EDMONDSON,
James, 123
John, 123, 226
William, 123
EDMUNDSON,
John, 5
EDWARD, Francina,
171
EDWIN, Margaret,
264, 265
Mary, 263, 264, 265
Tamar, 265
William, 263, 264,
265
EGLIN, John, 72,
134
ELDERSLY, Henry,
252
ELDRIDGE,
Elizabeth, 39
ELGIN, John, 49,
136
ELINA, Andrew,
118, 119
ELINOR, Annecke,
118
ELIZABETH
KATHERINE,
286
ELLARS, Henry, 48,
198
Margaret, 48
Margret, 198
Mary, 48
ELLENOR, Andrew,
3, 118, 119
Ann, 3, 119
Sarah, 119
ELLIOT, Elizabeth,
42
ELLIOTT, Edward,
218

John, 44
Mary, 218
Susanna, 43
William, 276
ELLIS, Mary, 62, 63,
157
Thomas, 26, 72
William, 56, 62, 63,
157
ELLISE'S CHOICE,
60
ELLISSES
CHANCE, 139
ELMES, William,
109
ELSTON, Catherine,
117
Ralph, 291
William, 117
EMERSON, John,
232
EMORY, Arthur, 98
John, 97
Sarah, 98
ENGER, Elizabeth,
42
ENGLAND, Ann, 87
Isaac, 90
Mary, 90
ERICKSON, John,
33
Mary, 33
ESSEX, 3
EVANS, Elizabeth,
67
Evan, 104, 105
Henry, 3
James, 4, 42, 47
Jane, 98
John, 42, 287
Jonathan, 239, 289
Margaret, 287
Martha, 289
Martha Ann, 289
Mary, 4, 154

350

FISHING POND,
168
FITZGÁRRET,
Charles, 94
William, 94
FITZGARROLL,
Patrick, 64
FLAHARTY, James,
217
Rebecca, 217
FLAHERTY,
Michael, 218
FLAMARTY, Ann,
217
FLANAGAN, Elinor,
77
Jane, 237
FLANARTY, Ann,
217
FLEMING,
Elisabeth, 147
Elizabeth, 147
FLENTON,
Clemons, 28
FLING, John, 97
FLINTHAM, Ben-
jamin, 123
Clement, 123
John, 123
Margaret, 123
Sarah, 123
William, 123
FLINTKEM, Clem-
mons, 29
FLINTON, Clement,
29
John, 123
FLYNN, John, 142
Lidia, 325
FOARD, Richard,
124
FOLLY LAND, 107
FONCH, Isaac, 251
FORBES, Alexander,
42

FORD, Ann, 124
Charles, 73, 123
Elizabeth, 123, 124,
125
Fardenando, 124
Ferdinando, 123
George, 124
James, 123
John, 123
Martha, 73, 123
Mary, 123, 124
Rachel, 123
Rachell, 30
Rebekah, 123
Richard, 124
Robert, 30, 123,
124, 176
Thomas, 124
William, 123, 125
FORDUM, Ann, 94
FOREMAN, Arthur,
126, 127, 128
Beatrice, 128
Benjamin, 128
Charles, 125, 126,
128
Deborah, 129
Elizabeth, 4, 125,
126, 127, 128, 130
Francis, 127, 128
Frederick, 128
Fredrick, 128
Honnor, 126
Honour, 126, 127
James, 128
John, 125, 126,
127, 128, 129, 247
Margaret, 125, 126,
129
Margarett, 125, 129
Mary, 119, 126,
127, 128, 129
Milderatt, 125, 126
Mildred, 125, 126
Priscilla, 129

Rebecca, 128
Richard, 127
Robert, 119, 125,
127
Sarah, 127, 128,
129
Temperance, 129
Walter, 127, 128
William, 125, 126,
127, 129, 130
FOREST, 221, 265
FOREST LODGE,
82
FOREST OF DEAN,
39
FORESTER,
Elisabeth, 130
George William,
130, 176, 217
Mary, 130
Rev. Mr., 130
Wilson, 217
FORK, 218
Evan, 231
FORKOM,
Elizabeth, 142
FORREST, 25, 123,
132, 185
FORREST OF WIN-
SOR, 44
FORRESTER, Anna,
130, 131
Catherine, 130
Catherine Mar-
garetta, 131
Charlotta, 130, 131
Elizabeth, 130, 131
Frances Dorcas,
131
Francis Dorcas, 130
George William, 58,
130, 131
Mary, 130, 131
Mary Elizabeth,
130, 131

Mary Wilmer, 131
Temperance, 131
Wilson, 217
FORRESTER'S
 DELIGHT, 254
FORRESTERS
 DELIGHT, 192,
 252
FOSSTER, Alice,
 315
FOSTER, Elizabeth,
 9
Richard, 9
Thomas, 94
FOTTRELL, Ed-
 ward, 322
Sarah, 322
FOULSTON,
 Richard, 137
FOULSTONE,
 Richard, 136
FOUNTAIN,
 George, 75
FOUR SQUARE, 97
FOUSLTONE,
 Richard, 137
FOWLE, William,
 109
FOWLER, Benjamin,
 60
Edward, 5
Jonathon, 123
Patrick, 220
Rachel, 60
FOX, Daniel, 6
FOX GROVE, 273
FOXEN, George, 132
Martha, 132
FOXON, Ann, 131
George, 85, 131,
 132
John, 131
Martha, 85, 131,
 132
Rachel, 131

Richard, 131
Susanna, 131
FRAMER, John, 148
Mary, 148
FRANCES, John,
 148
Mary, 148
FRANCIS, Isaac, 169
John, 42, 169
Mary, 70
FRAZIER, Ann, 67,
 68
Hugh, 183
John, 67, 68
FREEMAN,
 Abraham, 133,
 134, 173, 314
Ann, 132, 134, 135
Avarilla, 134
Edward, 134
Hannah, 132, 133,
 134, 173, 174, 259
Isaac, 79, 122, 132,
 133, 134, 135,
 176, 199, 259,
 262, 310, 316
Jacob, 132, 133,
 134
James Wilmer, 134
Jemima, 133, 134
Jemimah, 134
Judith, 135
Martha, 134, 259,
 262
Mary, 132, 133, 134
Richard, 132
Sarah, 134, 262
Thomas, 132
W., 134
William, 132, 133,
 134, 184
FREEMON, Isaac,
 195
FREESTONE, Mary,
 138

Walter, 65
FRENCH, Ann, 48,
 135
Elisabeth, 136
Elizabeth, 135, 136
Gully, 136
Hannah, 135, 136
James Williamson,
 135, 136
John, 48
Mary, 135
Samuel, 135
Sarah, 135, 136,
 136s
Thomas, 48, 135
Zorobabel, 135, 136
FRESH RUM, 295
FREWHARTY, Ann,
 217
FRIENDSHIP, 40,
 90, 103, 129, 130,
 173, 178, 254, 259
FRIENDSHIP AD-
 DITION, 277
FRISBEY, William,
 323
FRISBY, A., 249
Anna Maria, 274
Anne, 212
James, 36, 153,
 179, 211, 212, 274
Jane, 153, 299
John, 275
Margaret, 153
Mary, 299
Peregrine, 36, 212,
 249
Rebecca, 274
Richard, 250
Samuel, 247
Thomas, 36
William, 182, 274,
 277, 299
FULER, Henry, 94

FULLSTONE, Anne,
137
John, 137
Richard, 136, 137
FULSTON, Jane,
136
John, 136
Mary, 136
Richard, 136, 137,
138
Sarah, 136, 137
FULSTONE, Jane,
136
FURGESON, Collen,
220
FURTHERGILL,
Anne, 10

-G-
GAFUTT, Charles,
192
GAILE, William, 197
GAINE, Anne, 165
GAINES, Ann, 295
GAITSKILL, Jane,
81
Ruth, 81
GALE, Bersheba,
253
Catherine, 253
Charles, 54
Elizabeth, 253
James, 253
Jane, 258
John, 87, 93, 156,
189, 194, 253,
254, 255
Malachi, 253
Mary, 56, 253
Phebe, 54
Rasin, 89, 91, 128,
143, 198, 253, 259
Rosamond, 253
GALLOWAY, Anne,
278

Benjamin, 278
John, 278
Joseph, 278
Mary, 278, 279
GAMBAL, Jane, 139
GAMBALL, Hen-
rietta, 138
Honour, 138
John, 138
GAMBELL, John,
138
GAMBILE, Hen-
rietta, 139
Honora, 139
GAMBLE, Ann, 138
Bethein, 138
Cethier, 139
Cethisah, 138
Darius, 138
Henrietta, 138,
139, 208
Lettiser, 138
Rebeka, 138, 139
Robard, 138, 139
Sarah, 138
GAMBRELL,
Bethier, 139
Darius, 139
Lethisa, 139
Sarah, 139
GARLAN, James, 60
GARLAND, Ann,
140
Anne, 139
Benjamin, 139, 140
Catharine, 139, 140
Christiana, 139,
140
Christinah, 140
Christopher, 140
Hannah, 139, 140
James, 139, 140
Jennet, 139
Jennett, 140
John, 139, 140, 158

Mary, 139, 140
Rebecca, 140
Rose, 139
Sarah, 140
William, 139, 140
GARNETT, G., 234
George, 4, 14, 120,
121, 298, 323, 326
Jonathan, 121
Martha, 120, 299
Mary, 153
McGeorge, 58
Sophia, 120
Thomas, 14, 140
GARNETTS
MEADOW, 323
GARNETT'S
MEADOWS, 322
GATSKILL, Ruth,
81
GATTERY, Caleb, 4
GAY, N. Ruxton, 257
GEIST, Christian,
243
GEORGE, Ann, 142,
223
Barbara, 140, 141
Bartlet, 141
Bartlett, 141
Benjamin, 142
Elisabeth, 142
Hannah, 142
James, 141, 142
John, 141, 142
Joseph, 121, 140,
141, 142
Joshua, 142, 246
Mary, 141
Priscilla, 142
Rachel, 140, 141
Richard, 141
Robert, 140, 141,
142, 223, 238
Sarah, 141, 142
Thomas, 141

355

Jacob, 149, 150, 301
James, 150
John, 149, 150, 303
Katherine, 148
Mary, 150, 301
Samuel, 18, 148
Sarah, 150
GOODINGS, Ellinor, 148
GOODMAN, Edmond, 117
Thomas, 218, 237
GOODSON, William, 56
GOODWIN, Elinor
Katherine, 148
Samuel, 148
Sarah, 18
GOOSE HAVEN, 7
GORDLEY, Mary, 178
Rebeccah, 178
GORDON, Charles, 239
Elizabeth, 239
John, 158
GOSS, Elenor, 192
Elinor, 192
James, 192
GOTT, Henry, 4
GOULD, Elizabeth, 324
James, 324
Sarah, 136
Thomas, 136, 140, 310
GOUL-DESBROUGH, 225
GRACE, Catherine, 118
John, 194
GRAFTON, Ann, 165

Jonathan, 165
GRAHAM, Andrew, 150
Ann, 150, 151
Elisabeth, 150
Elizabeth, 150, 151
James, 150, 151
John, 41, 114, 115, 150, 151
Mary, 150, 151, 152
Rebecca, 151
Richard, 173
Robert, 150, 151
William, 150, 151
GRAHAME, James, 152
GRAMES, Ann, 152
GRANCE, 52
GRANGE, 156, 188, 190, 200, 205, 253
GRANGER, Ann, 153
Christopher, 152
Elizabeth, 152, 153
John, 152, 153
Mary, 152, 153
Sarah, 153
Thomas, 153
William, 152, 153, 179, 277
GRANT, Abigail, 154, 155
Ann, 154
Eleanor, 155
Elisabeth, 154, 155
Elizabeth, 154, 155
Francis, 155
George, 154
James, 154, 155
Jemima, 155
John, 154, 155, 170, 302
Jonathan, 154, 155
Judah, 154
Margaret, 155

Mary, 155
Rachel, 155
Richard, 155
Samuel, 154, 155
Sarah, 154, 155
Thomas, 154, 155
William, 143, 154, 155
GRANTHAM, 20, 271, 294
GRANTS FOLLEY, 154
GRAVES, Richard, 14, 302
Sarah, 107, 174
W., 120
William, 57, 65, 105, 205, 207
GRAY, Elisabeth, 147
James, 220
Jane, 63
Joseph, 127
Sarah, 221
GRAYHAM, Robert, 151
GRAYS INN, 311
GRAYSEN, 312
GREAT OAK, 50, 175
GREEN, Ann, 19
Benjamin, 237
Bowles, 19
Bowling, 271
Catherine, 19
Elizabeth, 101
George, 236
Henry, 187, 188
Lucey, 187, 188
Martha, 131, 132
Mary, 235
Mathew, 132
Peter, 19, 297
Robert, 8, 80, 101
GREEN BANK, 19

356

GREEN BRANCH,
219, 324
GREEN
CHARLTON, 275
GREEN MEDDOW,
156
GREEN OAK, 30, 73
GREEN SPRING,
239
GREENE, John, 324
GREENFIELD,
Robert, 266
GREENWOOD,
Jane, 286
William, 237
GREERES RANGE,
86
GREER'S RANGE,
89
GRESHAM, Han-
nah, 169
John, 23, 169, 243
Martha, 298, 299
Richard, 107, 113,
211, 280, 298,
299, 300
Sarah, 169, 300
Thomas, 244
GRIFFEN, Anth.,
188
GRIFFIN, Anthony,
5
Elizabeth, 290
GRIFFITH, Ann,
158
Benjamin, 138, 213
Blanche, 50
Cooter, 245
Coter, 122
David, 106
Elizabeth, 13
George, 13, 105,
160
John, 66, 297
Lake, 306

Luke, 50, 209, 210
Mary, 297
Nathaniel, 138
Samuel, 13, 17,
111, 275
GRIFFITH'S
DELIGHT, 187
GRIFFITHS
DELIGHT, 188
GRIFFTH, Samuel,
81
GRIMES, Tarrance,
224
GROERS RANGE,
89
GROOM, Charles, 16
Samuel, 107
GROOME, Charles,
16, 123, 128, 179,
208, 249, 302, 306
James, 248
Samuel, 108, 179,
187, 203, 253, 256
Sarah, 248
GROSSE, Ann, 227
GROVE, 190, 191
GROVES, Elizabeth,
125
GRUMBLE, 14
GUDSON, William, 2
GULTON, John, 151
GUY, Robert, 91
GUYER, Andrew,
311
Joan, 311
GWINN, Thomas,
127
GYANT, Richard,
143
Sarah, 143

-H-
HACKET, Mary, 19
Michael, 19

HACKETT, James,
246
Michael, 20, 144
Michaell, 57
William, 125
HACKITT, Michael,
102
HADDEN, William,
232
HADEN, Bar-
tholomew, 194
HAILES, 201
Ann, 2, 155
Anne, 156
Edward, 2, 156
Hannah, 156
Jane, 2, 156
Philip, 156
Roger, 2, 155, 156
HAILS, Roger, 156
HAILY, John, 316
HAINES, Abraham,
245
HAISLIP, Hugh,
156, 157
James, 157
Matthew, 157
HALE, Christopher,
113
Roger, 188
HALES, Edward,
156
Jane, 156
Roger, 31, 91, 285
HALES PUR-
CHASE, 188
HALEY, John, 114,
253
W., 294, 315
William, 114
HALL, Andrew, 216,
283
Blanche, 50
Chris., 114

357

Christopher, 27, 38,
151, 235, 263,
265, 320
David, 91, 255
Elizabeth, 263
George, 71
Hugh, 65
Margaret, 189, 317,
318
Mary, 38
Parker, 50
Thomas, 263
HALLEY, Ann, 318
John, 318
HALLS, Roger, 259
HAMBLETON'S
PARK, 287, 288
HAMBLIN, Ben-
jamin, 192, 252
HAMBLINE, John,
252
HAMER, Ann, 181
Anne, 327
Daniel, 181
Hannah, 327
HAMILTON, A., 135
Catherine Mar-
garetta, 131
Isabella, 47
John, 131
HAMLIN, William,
36
HAMLINS LOTT,
36
HAMMER, John,
187, 203
HAMMOND,
Catharine, 61
HAMPSHIRE, 38
HAMSHORE, 38
HAMSLEY, William,
278
HAMSTEAD, Wil-
liam, 210

HANCOCK, John,
168
HANDS, B., 8, 31,
49, 78, 283
Bedingfield, 137,
138, 171
D., 118, 248
Darby, 273
Sarah, 300
HANES, Darby, 153
HANKIN, Edward,
201
HANNAH, Rachel,
102
HANSEN, H., 289
Margaret, 289
HANSINGHAM, 168
HANSON, Andrew,
118
Anicake, 118
Anikeck, 118
Ann House, 283,
289
Catherine, 118
Christina, 213
Elizabeth, 326
Fred, 287
Frederick, 49, 69,
112, 118, 213
George, 169, 213,
265, 283, 289
Gustavas, 132
Gustavus, 283
Hance, 83, 118
Hans, 69, 96, 191,
287, 326
Hanse, 178
J. C., 51
Jane, 213
Margaret, 118, 287
Margarett, 118
Mary, 69, 108, 220
Sarah, 178
Thomas, 132

HAPPY RETURN,
251
HARBSON, William,
1
HARDCASIN, Mark,
117
HARDING, Mary,
250
Richard, 250
HARLEY, John, 241
HARMAN, Rachel,
102
Robert, 102
HARMON, Henriet-
ta, 21
HARNEY, Francis,
253
HARPER, Mary,
113, 114
HARRINGTON,
David, 233
George, 55
William, 233
HARRIS, Ann, 96
Augustina, 171
Edward, 69
Elizabeth, 78
George, 252
Ja., 234
James, 20, 50, 105,
171, 213, 297
Jane, 50, 76
Jo., 304
John, 48
Margaret, 167, 170,
171, 172
Mary, 93, 96, 270,
275
Matthias, 203
Moses, 270, 271
Richard, 93
Sarah, 13
Susanna, 48
Thomas, 316

William, 56, 101,
109, 167, 323
HARRIS' FOREST,
171
HARRIS' RANGE,
271
HARRISON, Anne,
318
Charles, 244
Samuel, 278
HARRISS FOREST,
171
HART, Elizabeth, 92
Henry, 305
James, 74
HARTSHORNE,
Elizabeth, 241
George, 180
John, 241
HARTY, John, 186
HASEL, John, 313
Mary, 313
HASKELL, Michael,
126
HASSELL, Ben-
jamin, 159
John, 159
Mary, 159
HASSITT, Robert,
97
HASTENS, George,
19
Mary, 19, 20
HASTINGS, George,
19, 20
James, 61
HATCH, David, 94
HATCHEN, John,
280
HATCHESON, Ben-
jamin, 266
Nathan, 144
Sarah, 282
Thomas, 288
Vincent, 162

HATCHISON, John,
266
Martha, 266
Richard, 266
HATECHISON,
Vincent, 164
HAUKIN, Edward,
201, 202
HAWKINS, Cor-
nelius, 66
Elizabeth, 264
John, 98
Joseph, 263
Judith, 98
HAWKINS PHAR-
SALIA, 98
HAWLYN, Richard,
106
HAYLING,
Elizabeth, 115
HAYNE, Gideon, 285
HAYNES, Francis,
247
William, 238
HAYWOOD, Wil-
liam, 2
HAZEL, Araminta,
158
Benjamin, 65, 140,
157, 158
Hugh, 159
John, 158
Joseph, 158
Martha, 158
Mary, 158
Mathew, 81
Sarah, 158
William, 140, 158
HAZELL, Mathew,
62
William, 158
HAZEL'S ADVEN-
TURE, 158
HAZLE, Hugh, 159
John, 159

Joseph, 159
Mathew, 159
HAZLEHURST,
Benjamin, 184
HAZOLL, John, 157
William, 157
HEAD, William, 227
HEADING, 16
HEADINGS, 22
HEART, Henry, 302
HEATCHESON,
Vincent, 224
HEATH, Hannah,
111, 112
James, 23, 41, 111,
112
James Paul, 163
Mary, 41
HEATH'S CHANCE,
86, 93
HEBRON'S FARM,
86
HEITHS RANGE,
25
HEMSLEY, Char-
lotte, 278
Mary, 278
Rebecca, 278
Vincent, 99
William, 1
HENDRICKSON,
Milderatt, 125,
126
Mildred, 125, 126
HENGHES, Francis
Dorcas, 130
HENLEY, Ann, 159
Christopher, 159,
160
Edward, 160
Elenor, 160
Elisabeth, 160
Elizabeth, 159
Esther, 160
Hester, 160

HUME, William, 7
HUNT, John, 5
HUNTER, Samuel,
    43
HUNTING FIELD,
    269, 273, 274
HUNTINGFIELD,
    108, 144, 172,
    268, 278, 302, 306
HURLEY, Cornelius,
    301
    Sarah, 301
HURLOCK, James,
    60
HURSLY, Richard,
    178
HURT, Cornelius,
    305
    Henry, 110
    John, 223
    Martha, 81
HURTT, Mary, 107
    Morgan, 211
HUSBAND, William,
    39, 151
HUSBANDS,
    Elizabeth, 113
    William, 317
HUSIN, Ellinor, 232
HUSSEY, Margaret,
    290
    Michael, 290
HUTCHINGS, Mar-
    tha, 47
HUTCHINSON,
    Ann, 132
    John, 267
    Martha, 267
    William, 132
HUTCHISON,
    Alexander, 154
    John, 280
    Nathan, 67
HUTHCESON,
    Vincent, 83

HUTSON, Philip,
    162
HYDE, Bryden
    Bordley, 8
    Samuel, 117
HYDE PARK, 81
HYNSON, Andrew,
    122, 173, 174,
    176, 313, 314
    Ann, 11, 164, 166,
    177, 178, 295
    Anne, 12, 13, 164,
    165, 166, 167, 177
    Benjamin, 173, 179
    C., 234
    Charles, 50, 51, 52,
    66, 67, 83, 85,
    131, 154, 164,
    165, 166, 167,
    168, 170, 171,
    172, 173, 174,
    175, 177, 178,
    179, 189, 253,
    306, 326
    Dorcas, 167
    Elizabeth, 169
    Esther, 165
    Frances, 172
    Francina, 52, 171
    Grace, 164, 165,
    167
    H., 85
    Hannah, 165, 168,
    169, 170, 173,
    177, 322
    Henry, 177
    Hester, 165
    Isabelah, 178
    Isabella, 178
    J. C., 51
    James, 173, 174,
    176, 178, 274
    Jane, 167, 168
    Joan, 167

John, 3, 11, 35, 66,
    76, 109, 164, 165,
    166, 168, 172,
    173, 174, 177,
    239, 298
John Carvill, 175
Judith, 167
Katherine, 307
Margaret, 167, 169,
    170, 171, 172
Margarett, 167, 322
Margett, 175
Margret, 233
Martha, 168, 169,
    170, 177, 186
Martha Ann, 177
Mary, 166, 167,
    168, 169, 170,
    171, 172, 173,
    174, 175, 176,
    177, 179, 279,
    280, 313, 314,
    317, 322
N., 200
Nathan, 174
Nathaniel, 166,
    168, 172, 173,
    174, 175, 177,
    178, 213, 322
Nathaniell, 169,
    175, 199
Phebe, 175, 177
Phoebe, 50
Rachel, 167, 168,
    173, 176
Rebecca, 168, 170,
    178
Rebeckah, 169
Rebekah, 176
Richard, 51, 165,
    175, 177, 178
Sarah, 166, 167,
    173, 174, 176,
    177, 178, 239,
    298, 306

362

JEAPPON, Marthar,
110
JENKINS, Hannah,
165
Isaac, 247
Philip, 228, 229
Sarah, 248
JENKINSON, Eliza.,
225
Emanual, 17
John, 226, 230
Martha, 17
Philip, 228
JEROM, Mary, 183
JEROME, Elizabeth,
183
Martha, 183, 184
Mary, 183
Sarah, 183, 184
Thomas, 183, 184
JERROM, Elizabeth,
183
Thomas, 279
JERROME, Mary,
183
Thomas, 183
JERRUM, Thomas,
312
JERVES, Solomon,
182
JERVIS, Alse, 182
Caleb, 182
Edward, 182
James, 182
Joseph, 182
Margrett, 182
Mary, 182
Sarah, 182
Solomon, 182
JOANES, John, 192
Robert, 192
JOBSON, Ann, 184
Easter, 184
Job, 184
John, 184

Jonathan, 184
Martha, 184
Michael, 184, 285
Nicholas, 285
Philip, 184
Sarah, 184
Susan, 322
Thomas, 322
William, 184
JOCE, Ann, 108
Margaret, 178
Mary, 105
Sarah, 178
Thomas, 178, 200,
211, 298
JOHN'S
HABITATION,
217
JOHNSON, Aramin-
ta, 248
Batrix, 187
Beatrice, 187
Elisabeth, 187
Hoalman, 187
Holman, 187
Isabella, 184
John, 50, 184, 185,
186, 244, 246,
248, 296
Josiah, 248
Katherine, 186
Mary, 185, 186
Phillips, 185
Richard, 51, 185,
186, 246, 281
Sophiah, 248
Susanna, 184
Susannah, 185, 186
William, 186, 187
JOHNSON'S FOR-
REST, 185
JOHNSTON, Chris-
topher, 164, 267,
308
John, 248

JOHNSTONE,
Jamison, 262
JONES, Ann, 191,
195, 319
Anne, 194, 195
Aquilla, 206
Benjamin, 194, 195
Blackledge, 194
David, 188, 189,
213
Elenor, 192
Elisabeth, 191, 314
Elizabeth, 189, 190,
194, 195, 253
Griffen, 188
Griffith, 7, 58, 89,
90, 93, 187, 189,
190, 191, 253, 255
Hannah, 193
Henry, 193, 194
Hugh, 130
Jacob, 151, 158,
183, 239, 251, 320
James, 134, 319
Jane, 62
Johanna, 193
John, 61, 191, 282
Lucea, 253
Lucey, 187
Lucia, 189
Lucy, 187, 188, 189
Margaret, 189, 195
Margett, 191
Margret, 234
Margrett, 189
Martha, 171, 189,
302
Martha Ann, 35,
289
Mary, 73, 79, 90,
170, 187, 188,
189, 190, 192,
193, 194, 195,
253, 281, 282,
309, 327

364

Mary Ann, 31, 189
Nehemiah, 79
Nicholas, 257
Peter, 194
Phil., 281
Rachel, 194, 195
Rice, 190, 191
Richard, 35, 179,
  187, 188, 189,
  289, 324, 327
Rise, 191
Robert, 192
Sarah, 45, 188, 189,
  190, 191, 192,
  193, 281, 308
Susanah, 195
Thomas, 62, 158,
  170, 190, 191, 302
Thomas Rasin, 189
Walter, 190, 191
Wealthian, 171
William, 45, 192,
  193, 194, 195,
  206, 252, 309
Woodland, 194
JONES' FANCY,
  291
JONES FERRY, 292
JONES HIS PLOTT,
  43
JONES NEGLECT,
  55
JONES' VENTURE,
  195
JONSON, Jacob, 219
JORDAN, Charity,
  296
John, 296
Martha, 16, 17
JOYNER, Sarah, 119
William, 119
JUMP'S CHOICE, 6

-K-

KANDALL, William,
  200
KANN, James, 321
KARBY, John, 228
KEAR, Ann, 291
  Mary, 19
  Thomas, 19, 291
KEARE, James, 291
KEARLY, John, 15
KELLE, James, 196
KELLEE, Benjamin,
  196, 197
James, 197
Jane, 197
Joseph, 196, 197
KELLEES
  CHOYCE, 196,
  197
KELLEY, Alexander,
  48, 159
Ann, 200
Anne, 195, 198
Benjamin, 197, 198
Catharine, 169
Cristina, 199
Daniell, 195
Hannah, 80, 199
James, 80, 198
Jane, 196
John, 114
Joshua, 199
Katharine, 210
Katherine, 195
Margaret, 195
Margart, 198
Mary, 48, 197, 198,
  199
Peregin, 199
Sarah, 198
Silvester, 211
William, 198
KELLEYS CHOICE,
  197
KELLY, Alexander,
  198, 243

Ann, 196, 197, 199
Anne, 7, 199
Barbara, 196
Benjamin, 196, 197
Catherine, 196, 199
Charity, 196, 197
Daniel, 210
Dennis, 199
Edmund, 7
Edward, 199
Ester, 199
Hannah, 197, 199
James, 196, 197
John, 199
Joseph, 196
Kath., 199
Lambert, 198
Margaret, 199
Mary, 169, 197,
  198, 199, 225
Rachell, 197
Sarah, 197
Silvester, 196
Thomas, 199
William, 196, 199,
  200
KELLY'S CHOICE,
  196
KEMP, Thomas, 187
KEMPS, 188
KEMP'S BEGIN-
  NING, 58
KENARD, Nathl., 69
  Phil., 69
  Richard, 69
KENDALL, Elenor,
  200
Elinor, 200
James, 200
Maryann, 200
Sarah, 200
Stephen, 200, 231
Thomas, 201
William, 200

KENETT, Henry,
263
KENNALL, Sarah,
200
KENNARD, Ann,
203, 204, 207
Catherine, 204
Daniel, 205, 206,
207, 210, 260
Dannis, 209
Elisabeth, 202
Elizabeth, 201, 202
Henrietta, 208
Howard, 205, 206,
208
Jane, 69, 203, 206
John, 202, 204,
205, 206, 207,
209, 210, 306
John Tilden, 204
Joseph, 202, 203,
204, 306
Joshua, 210
Martha, 207, 208
Mary, 201, 202,
203, 204, 205,
206, 207, 209,
210, 250, 313,
316, 317
Mathew, 205, 206,
207
Michael, 205, 206,
209
Nathaniel, 69, 204,
205, 206, 209,
210, 250, 312
Owen, 209
P., 214
Phil, 202
Philip, 201, 202,
203
Phill., 201, 202
Phillip, 46
Rachel, 208, 209
Rebecka, 208

Rebeckar, 139, 208
Richard, 205, 206,
207, 208, 209
Sarah, 202, 203,
204, 208, 210,
305, 307
Stephen, 138, 207,
208
Steven, 205, 206
Thomas, 205, 206,
208
William, 210
KENNARDS FAN-
CY, 204
KENNARD'S
FARM, 204
KENNARDY, Ed-
ward, 18
KENNEDY,
Elizabeth, 38
John, 42
KENNETT, Wh., 37
KENNEY, William,
80, 171
KENSEY, Thomas,
249
KENSLAGH,
Dominick, 195,
210
Elizabth, 211
Helen, 211
John, 210, 211
Margaret, 195, 210,
211
Margrett, 195
Mary, 211
Michael, 211
KENSLASH, Ann,
211
KENSLAUGH,
Dominick, 196
Healin, 211
Helen, 211
Paul, 211
KENT, William, 99

KERBY, David, 229
KERSEY, James, 48
John, 117
KERSLEY, John, 15
KEUNDERS,
Teunis, 243
KEY, Elizabeth, 9
Martha, 190
Richard, 9
KEYS, Liney, 86
KILLINGSWORTH,
82, 110
KILLINS WORTH
MORE, 64
KILLY LONGFORD,
119
KILNER, Tho., 37
KINARD, Rebeka,
138
Stephen, 139
Stephen K., 139
KINBOW, Ann, 199
KINDAL, Maryann,
200
William, 200
KINDNESS, 11, 12
KINDOL, William,
200
KINDRED, Sarah,
226
KING, Ann, 321
Elias, 2, 304
Francis, 243
John, 98
KINGSLAUGH,
Dominick, 210
KINHEAD, Peter,
114
KINNARD,
Catharine, 305
Catherine, 210
Daniel, 206, 208,
209
Jane, 209
John, 208

367

LAZZEL, Martha,
214
Nathaniel, 214
LEATHERBERRY,
Able, 216
Jonathan, 216
Mary, 216
Perigrine, 216
Thomas, 216
LEATHERBURY,
Abel, 215, 216
Charles, 215, 216
John, 215, 216
Jonathan, 215
Jonathon, 83, 216
Mary, 83, 85, 215,
216
Peregrine, 85, 216
Richard, 216
Sarah, 216
Thomas, 215, 216
William, 215, 216
LEAVAN HAM, 193
LEAVENHAM, 193
LEE, Arthur, 163
Ester, 66
Hannah, 238
Thomas, 325
LEGER, Elizabeth,
135
LEGG, John, 44
LEITH, Charles, 230
John, 277
LENEGAR, Grace,
217
Jacob, 217
LESAGE, David, 99
LETCHWORTH,
Thomas, 135
LEWELLIN, Audry,
12
LEWELLIN
RESIDUE, 12
LEWIS, Anne, 196
Evan, 250

John, 307
Mary, 17
Robert, 112
Sarah, 250, 302
Thomas, 17, 97,
148
LEYBURN, George,
91
LIDLE, William, 94
LILLINGSTON,
Carpenter, 94, 95
Frances, 94
James, 94
Jane, 94, 95
John, 240
Mary, 94, 95
LINCH, Robert, 297
LINEGAR, Ann, 217
Elizabeth, 217
George, 217
Grace, 217, 218
Jacob, 75, 217, 218
James, 217
John, 217
Rebecca, 217
Sara, 217
Sarah, 217
LINEGER, George,
217
LINGER, Jacob, 217,
218
Sarah, 217, 315
LITTLE, Adam, 217
Ann, 220
LITTLE NECK, 76
LIZENBY, Charles,
219
Jane, 219
LLOYD, Edward, 4,
12, 70, 138, 174,
288
Elinor, 238
Henrietta Maria,
14
James, 13

Philemon, 228
Richard, 13, 15,
102, 107, 205, 207
LOBB'S CHOICE,
271
LOCKEET,
Elizabeth, 113
LODGE, Walter, 125
LONDON
BRIDGES, 63
LONG, Dennis, 163
Elinor, 148
Thomas, 148
LONG ADVEN-
TURE, 295
LONG BRANCH, 44
LONG NECK, 98
LONG WEEK, 98
LORAM, Martha,
306
LORD'S GIFT, 94
LORDS GIFT, 66, 83
LORDSHIP'S
MANOR, 247
LOUDEN, Richard,
220, 263
LOUIS, Thomas, 149
LOULETTE, James,
257
LOULITT, James,
114
LOUTTET, James,
256
LOUTTIT, James,
58, 182
LOVELIN, William,
133
LOVERING, John,
173
LOWDER, Ann, 218,
219
Anne, 219
Carolina, 219
Charles, 218, 219
Edward, 218, 219

368

Jane, 219
Joan, 218, 219
Mary, 219, 220
Rachel, 218
Richard, 219, 220,
263, 264, 324
Sarah, 219
Susan, 219
Susannah, 219
LOWE, Vincent, 98,
295
LOWTHER, Charles,
218
Joan, 292
LOYD, Edward, 51
Hannah, 111, 112
John, 111, 112
LUES, Thomas, 148
LUMLEY, Elizabeth,
11
George, 10, 11, 52,
171
Margaret, 10
LUSBY, Draper, 35,
172, 173
Frances, 172
Robert, 189, 299
LYNCH, Ann, 105
Anne, 105
Thomas, 105
LYNN, 204

-M-
MAAWELL, H., 223
MACAN, Ann, 224
Edward, 223, 224,
234
Elisabeth, 223, 234
Elizabeth, 224
James, 224
Margrett, 224
MACBRIDE, David,
297
MCCABE, James,
113

MCCANN, Ann, 224
Edward, 224
Eleanor, 224
Elizabeth, 224
Elizabeth Ogleby,
224
James, 224
Jarvis, 224
Jervis, 224
Sarah, 224
MCCARTY, Dennis,
23
MACCATEE,
Andrew, 220
Catharine, 220
Eleanor, 220
Elizabeth, 220
George, 220
Margaret, 220
Patrick, 220
Sarah, 220
MCCAWLEY, Wil-
liam, 156
MCCAY, Alexander,
28
Rebecca, 22
MCCENTEE,
Andrew, 221
Patrick, 221
MCCLEAN,
Alexander, 283
James, 12, 15, 49,
162, 186, 216
William, 189, 325,
326
MCCLURE, James,
74
MCCOMB, Eleazer,
302
MCCROCON, John,
298
MACCUBBIN, Char-
les, 190
MCDANIEL, John,
114

MCDANNEL, Ar-
thur, 244
MACDONALD,
Margaret, 34
MCDOUGALL,
Mary, 63
MCENTEE, George,
221
MCGEAR, John, 216
MACHLIN, Richard,
95
MCHUFFEY,
Jeremiah, 156
MCINNIS, Ar-
chibald, 326
MCINTEE, Patrick,
220
MCINTOSH,
Alexander, 113
Margaret, 113
MACKEY,
Alexander, 305
John, 161
Mary, 181
William, 8, 143, 161
MACKGREGORY,
Elizabeth, 225
Hugh, 225
James, 225
MCKINNIE, Hugh,
26
MACKINTOUCH,
Hannah, 28
MCKITTRICK,
Andrew, 313
MACKLIN, Richard,
94
MACKLYN, Richard,
94
MACKRACKIN,
John, 131
Judith, 131
MACKRILL, Ben-
jamin, 128

369

371

MILL FORK, 24, 25,
305
MILLER, Abraham,
40
Alice, 235
Andrew, 237
Ann, 12
Arthur, 6, 8, 12, 15,
17, 142, 163, 275,
283
B., 199
Griffin, 140
Honour, 126
Honur, 127
John, 126, 131
M., 161, 169, 264,
265
Margrett, 41
Martha, 170, 266
Michael, 46, 82,
157, 159, 170,
235, 242, 275, 308
Michaell, 3
Nathaniel, 149,
199, 280
Richard, 108
Samuel, 18, 83, 325
Somon Stevens,
290
Thomas, 149
MILLFORD, 232
MILLINGTON,
Isaac, 233
MILTON, Abraham,
6, 121, 123, 141,
159, 188, 189,
190, 238
Ann, 141
Isaac, 200
Joseph, 141
Mary, 188, 189, 190
Phi., 12
Philip, 80
MILWARD, Charles,
197

MITCHELL,
Elizabeth, 121
John, 73, 74
William, 307
MOHONE, Thomas,
120
MOLL, John, 36
MONK, Elizabeth,
225
Gilbert, 225
Henery, 225
Henry, 76, 224, 225
Honour, 224
James, 225
John, 225
Margrett, 225
William, 225
MONTGOMERY,
Mary, 26
MOOR, George, 43
James, 259
John, 119
MOORE, George,
239
James, 76, 129
John, 66, 276
William, 120, 148
MOOTH, Thomas,
117
MORE, Henry, 150
James, 239
John, 120
MORETON, 56
MORGAN, Abraham,
225, 226
Andrew, 227
Ann, 230, 232
Barbary, 228
Benjamin, 286
Catherine, 232
Charles, 201, 228,
229, 230, 231
Charlotte, 231
David, 231
Deborah, 231

Edward, 231
Eleanor, 229
Elinor, 228, 229
Elizabeth, 229, 230,
232
Ellinor, 229
Enoch, 226, 227,
233
Evan, 231
Frances, 227, 228
Habukuk, 231
Hannah, 230
Henry, 108, 227,
228, 232, 267
Herbert, 231
Hugh, 228, 229,
230, 233
Jacob, 229, 230
James, 226, 229,
230, 231
Job, 231
John, 5, 228, 230,
231, 232
Joshua, 232
Josias, 232
Laban, 232
Margrett, 228
Mary, 80, 227, 228,
229, 231, 232, 233
Milcah, 230
Philip, 226, 227
Rachel, 230
Rebecca, 231
Richard, 233
Robert, 228, 229
Samuel, 228, 229
Sarah, 200, 201,
226, 227, 228,
231, 233
Thomas, 200, 201,
230
Thomas Spry, 230
William, 227, 229,
230, 233

375

376

378

379

380

182, 186, 190,
197, 199, 204,
207, 208, 210,
214, 248, 249,
258, 267, 268,
269, 270, 271,
272, 273, 274,
275, 276, 277,
278, 279, 280,
282, 283, 285,
286, 299, 306
Thomas William,
172
William, 8, 35, 49,
111, 128, 149,
172, 186, 197,
203, 204, 207,
208, 264, 268,
269, 270, 272,
273, 274, 276,
277, 278, 280,
281, 285, 289, 298
William T., 134
RINGGOLDS FOR-
TUNE, 268
RINGGOULD,
James, 115
Thomas, 268
RINGOLD, Anne,
276
Charles, 271
Elisabeth, 304
James, 269, 270,
271, 276, 304
John, 267, 269, 276
Martha, 276
Mary, 270, 271, 276
Moses, 270
Sarah, 276
Thomas, 269
Vincent, 271
William, 231, 276
RINGOLD'S
CHANCE, 269

RINGOULD, James,
268
John, 268
RISER, 58
ROBERT, Robert,
126
Sarah, 18
ROBERTS, James,
18, 292, 319, 320
Sarah, 18, 319, 320
ROBERTSON, John,
152
ROBINS, George,
181
Susannah, 181
ROBINSON, Ann,
291
David, 47
Elizabeth, 115
James, 291
John, 169
Mary, 175
Sarah, 212
RODGERS,
Melicent, 314
ROE, Charles, 230
Mark, 230
Rachel, 103
ROGERS, Ann, 79
Cassandra, 35
Edward, 166, 188
Elizabeth, 166
Hynson, 162
John, 21, 23, 62,
166
Mary, 166
Milicent, 314
Nathaniel, 35, 166,
172
Rachell, 166
W., 27, 134
William, 147, 292,
293, 314, 320
ROLPH, Francis,
282

G., 281
Glanvil, 282, 288
Glanvill, 281, 283,
287, 288, 289
Glanville, 282, 287
Glavill, 281
John, 142, 281,
282, 283, 289
Margaret, 282, 287,
288
Martha, 282
Mary, 189, 281, 282
Sarah, 284
Thomas, 281, 282,
283
William, 282, 283,
284
RONALD, Andrew,
31
ROSMOR, 168
ROSS, Elizabeth,
290
George, 70
Gertrude, 70
ROSSER, Mary, 136
ROUND STONE, 56
ROUSBY, Barbary,
228
John, 228
ROUSE, Elizabeth,
225
Priscilla, 129
Thomas, 214, 225
ROUSS, Elizabeth,
225
Thomas, 225
ROWLES, Chris-
topher, 263
Elizabeth, 263
ROYALL, Martha,
235
RUBY, Morgane, 302
RUERDEN, 219
RUMBLEY, Smith,
231

RUMFORD RESUR-
VEYED, 151
RUMSEY'S FOR-
REST, 230
RUSH, Susannah, 8
Thomas, 8
RUSK, Rachell, 7
RUSMORE, 168
RUSSELL, John, 39,
93, 95, 96
Juliana, 93, 95
Michaell, 4
Rachel, 39
RUSSENDALL, 96
RUSSH, Susannah,
7
Thomas, 7
RUTH, James, 328
Susannah, 7
Thomas, 7, 328
RUTTER, Francis,
198
RUX, Charles, 229
Mark, 229
RY, Christopher, 309
RYLE, Mary, 145
RYLEY, Mary, 69
Richard, 1
RYNGOLD, Martha,
271
William, 271

-S-
ST. ANDREWS
CROSSE, 57
ST. CLAIR,
Campbell, 317
Gen., 317
Margaret, 317
Mary, 150, 151
William, 150, 317
ST. JOHNS
FIELD(S), 113,
114, 115

SAINT MARTINS,
156
ST...TON, 252
SALEM, 325
SALHILL, 170, 322
SALISBORY, Wil-
liam, 72
SALISBURY, Jane,
116, 117
William, 117, 317
SALSBURY, Jane,
117
John, 105, 207
Mary, 105, 207
William, 1, 31
SALST, Jane, 117
William, 117
SALTER, John, 97,
118
SANDERS, George,
194
SAPPINGTON,
Rebecca, 217
Thomas, 114, 115
William, 114
SAPPINTON,
Thomas, 115
SATTERFIELD'S
LUCK, 100
SAUL, Mary, 112
SAUNDERS, Ann,
290
John Dames, 289,
290
Rachel, 290
Sarah, 288
SAVAGE, Sarah,
257
SAVIDGE, William,
269
SAVIN, William, 40
SAVORY, William,
105
SAYER, Frances,
228

SCHAWN, Dennis,
286
SCHEE, Capt., 8
SCILLA, 33
SCOTCH FOLLY,
173
SCOTCH POINT,
278
SCOTT, Ann, 272
Charles, 78, 272,
280
David, 134
Edward, 37, 52,
119, 136, 137,
239, 297, 304
Francis, 200
Hannah, 239
James, 180
John, 80, 133, 298
Martha, 134, 136,
137, 259, 262, 304
Nathaniel, 325, 326
Rachel, 37
Roger, 117
Sarah, 324
William, 37, 98,
136, 231, 324, 325
SCUSE, James, 113
SEALE, William, 246
SEATON, Anne, 212
SEAWELL, Thomas,
187
SECOND
VACATION, 211
SEDLEY, Marcy,
295
SEEGAR, Thomas,
293
SEMANS, Daniel,
182
Hannah, 183
Henry, 27, 182, 183
Solomon, 26, 112,
113, 182
William, 26, 72, 182

382

SENNOTT, John, 233
SERGEANT, John, 324
SERJEANT, John, 324
SETH, Barbara, 324
Jacob, 99, 324, 325
SEWARD, Lucey, 187
Lucretia, 125
Lucy, 125
Thomas, 125, 128, 187
SEWARD'S HOPE, 223, 281
SEWELL, 33, 48, 59, 141, 198, 296
John, 198
Mary, 26, 99, 123
SEXTON, Frances, 328
Patrick, 328
SHADS HOLE, 243, 284
SHAHAWN, John, 74
SHARPE, William, 226
SHAW, John, 24, 76
Sarah, 76
SHAWHAN, Daniel, 284
Jennett, 284
John, 74, 285
SHAWHAWN, Daniel, 284
Darbe, 284
Darby, 284, 286
David, 284
Dennis, 284
Elizabeth, 284
John, 284
Sarah, 284
William, 284

SHAWHORN, Darby, 284
SHAWN, Bathsheba, 285
Daniel, 74, 284, 285
Darby, 284, 285, 286
David, 286
Dennis, 285
Derby, 286
Elizabeth, 285, 286
Isaac, 285
James, 286
Jennett, 284
John, 285, 286
Joseph, 285, 286
Margaret, 284
Sarah, 284, 285, 286
Shadrack, 286
SHAWS CHANCE, 243
SHEARES, Ann, 161
SHEARMAN, Thomas, 244
SHEATH, 99
SHEELE, Mary, 287
William, 287
SHEGS, Mary, 114
SHEHAWN, Aves, 286
Batsaba, 285
Dennis, 146
Isaac, 285
Jhn, 286
SHEILD, John, 287, 289
Mary, 288
Mary Parker, 287
William, 287, 288
SHELINGTON, 179
SHEPPARD HOOK, 99
SHERMAN, Mary, 311

SHERVIN, George, 61
SHERWOOD, Daniell, 6
Katherine, 329
SHERWOOD FOREST, 113, 114
SHEWEL, Mary, 26
SHEWELL, Mary, 26
SHIELD, Abednego, 288
Benjamin, 290
Bryan, 290
Elizabeth, 290
Griffith, 290
James, 290
Jane, 290
John, 55, 283, 287, 288, 289, 290
Margaret, 282, 287, 289, 290
Martha, 290
Martha Ann, 289
Mary, 282, 286, 287, 288
Rachel, 288, 289
Rhoda, 287, 288
Sarah, 290
Susannah, 290
William, 282, 286, 287, 288, 289, 290
SHIELDS, Lambert, 290
Mary, 290
Rebecca, 290
Rhoda, 287
William, 287
SHINWOOD, Stephen, 210
SHIP NECK, 83
SHIPPEN, Francina, 171
Margaret, 66
SHIRKY, Neal, 41

384

SPOONER, John,
235
SPRIGNALL, John,
226
SPRING GARDEN,
217
SPRINGHILL, 174
SQUARE, 295
STACEY, Rebecca,
290
William, 290
STAGWELL, 177
Thomas, 177
STALKER, Martha,
79, 80
Thomas, 79, 80, 81
STANAWAY, 67,
108, 175
STAND OFF, 64
STANDFORD, 325
STANDLEY'S
HOPE, 253
STANDLY'S HOPE,
254
STANFORD, 324
STANK, Benjamin,
290
STANLEY, William,
167
STANLEY'S HOPE,
259
STANSTON, 254
STANTON,
Elizabeth, 317
Susannah, 115, 243
STAPLEY,
Elizabeth, 310
STARKE, John, 179
START, Richard, 326
STAVELY,
Elisabeth, 31
James, 315
STEDMAN,
Abraham, 52
Elizabeth, 52

STEEL, James, 1
STEEN, John, 145
STENSON, James,
274
STEPNEY, 298
STEPNEY FIELDS,
1
STEPNEY HEATH
MANNER, 37, 67
STEPTON, 325
STERLING, James,
298
Mary, 298, 299
STERRETT, Samuel,
207
STEVENS, Charles,
288
John, 4
Margaret, 117
Peter, 47
STEVENSFIELDS,
44
STEVENSON,
Isabella, 13, 14
Jannet, 244
John, 244
William, 13, 14, 195
STEVENTON, 11,
13
STEWARD, Lutitia,
223
STEWART,
Alexander, 318
Elizabeth, 223
Malcum, 237
Margaret, 147
Mary, 145
Sally, 318
Sarah L., 318
STOKE, 181
STOKES, Humphrey
Wells, 212
John, 212
Mary, 212
STONETONE, 148

STOOP, Elizabeth,
292
John, 167, 292
Mary, 167
STOOPES,
Elisabeth, 293
STOOPLEY GIB-
SON, 119
STOOPS, Elizabeth,
294
STOPE, Elisabeth,
153
STORNEY, James,
317
STOUT, Ann, 69, 70,
152
James, 69, 70, 152
STRAHAM, James,
113
STRAND, Abraham,
308
STRATFORD, 140
STRATFORDS
MANNOR, 121
STRATTON, 325,
326
Richard, 326
STRONG, Ann, 104
James, 104, 276
STRUTON, George,
237
STRUTTON,
George, 237
STURGEON,
Stephen, 244
STURMAN, John,
201
SUDLER, Emory,
15, 153
James, 43
John, 153
Joseph, 43, 153
Martha, 153, 299
SULLIVAN, Sarah,
55

386

387

John, 7, 37, 192, 280, 304, 305, 307
Katherine, 37, 307
Mar., 302
Marmaduke, 187, 287, 304, 305, 306
Martha, 304, 305, 306
Mary, 170, 269, 270, 273, 274, 304, 305
Mary Worril, 306
Sarah, 306, 307
T., 204
Tabitha, 304, 306
Wealthy Ann, 170, 171
William Blay, 305, 307
TILGHHMAN, Mary, 277
TILGHMAN, 273
James, 192, 230, 278
Matthew, 300
Peregrin, 298
Richard, 5, 94, 95, 298
Sarah, 300
Tench, 278
Thomas Ringgold, 278
TILGHMAN'S DIS-COVERY, 241
TILGHMAN'S FARM, 123
TILL, Elisabeth, 169
Gertrude, 70
Thomas, 70
William, 70
TILLARD, John, 84
Kezia, 85
TILTON, Catherine, 205
Elinor, 204

Elizabeth, 46, 205
Humphrey, 46, 205
Humphry, 204
James, 204, 205
Mary, 204
TIMBER LEVEL, 132
TIMBER LEVELL, 134
TIMELY DIS-COVERY, 276
TIMMS, John, 67, 132
TINSLAUGH, Paul, 144
TIPPET, Christine, 137
Thomas, 137
TISDELL, Chris-topher, 45
Mary, 45
TITTLE, Richard, 124
TOAES, Daniel, 168
Sarah, 168
TOALSON, Andrew, 52
TOBENS FOLLY, 130
TOBIN, Margaret, 117
TOBIN'S FOLLY, 130
TOLCHESTER & TOMBS, 289
TOLCHESTER AND TOMB, 213
TOLLE, Timothy, 154
Tobias, 154
TOLLEY, Elizabeth, 168
Mary, 168
Thomas, 11, 169
Walter, 168

TOLSON, Andrew, 142
Mary, 142
TOMSON, Ann., 274
Jeffrey, 308
TORE, John, 26
TOVEY, Mary, 276, 278
Samuel, 33, 153, 174, 299
Samuell, 188, 268
TOWN RELIEF, 51, 52, 127
TOWN RELIEFE, 52, 171
TOWNE CREEK, 166
TOWNS RELIEF, 261
TRAMPINGTON, 94
TREAHY, Jas., 165
TREGGO, William, 109
TREW, John, 59, 65, 159, 283
William, 32, 59, 141, 242
TRIANGLE, 181
TRIGGS MAR-GARET, William, 1
TRUE, John, 59
William, 59, 141
TRUELOCK, Henry, 202
TRULOCK, Henry, 128
Joseph, 192, 201, 252, 254
Mary, 252, 254
William, 77
TRUMPERTON, 96
TRUMPING, 297
TRUMPING TOWN, 299

388

389

Samuell, 145, 192
Thomas, 290
William, 117
WALLS, Elizabeth,
89
WALNUT RIDGE,
295
WALSH, Lau., 163
WALTER, Flower,
44
WALTERS, William,
285
WALTHAM, 178
John, 179, 283, 306
Sarah, 177
WALTON, 135
Thomas, 93
WANNELL, Henry,
34
WANT, Mary, 136,
137, 138
William, 136, 137,
138
WARCOPE, Thomas,
63
WARD, Henry, 71
James, 123
John, 123
WARNER, Anne,
254
Edward, 50
George, 251, 254
Mary, 254, 255, 256
WARRELL, Joseph,
283
WASHAM, Capt.,
251
WATERS, Alex., 118
Margaret, 118
WATKINS, Esau, 80,
187, 272
Essau, 272
Mary, 70
Sarah, 272

WATKINSON,
Elizabeth, 134
WATSON, Elisabeth,
79
Elizabeth, 74
James, 26, 74, 78,
125, 212
John, 60, 212, 244,
294
William, 74
WATTS, Elizabeth,
256
John, 201, 227, 256
WAXFIELD, 210
WAXFORD, 148, 211
WEBB, Richard, 324
Robert, 24
Sarah, 192, 193,
252
Thomas, 192, 252
WEBBER, Anne, 325
WEBBY, 29
WEDGE, John, 107
Judith, 107
WEDGE'S
RECOVERY, 84
WEDGES
RECOVERY, 107
WEDGES
RECOVERY
RESURVEYED,
107
WEDGES RESUR-
VEY, 107
WEEKES, Ann, 69
John, 291
Joseph, 69
WEEKS, Benjamin,
288
Joseph, 109
WEIKERS, Sarah,
245
WEIR, James, 128
John, 16
WEITMAN, John, 16

WELCH, Thomas,
216
WELLER, Ester, 325
WELLS, Ann, 96
Anne, 96
Humphrey, 219
Jeremiah, 187
John, 96, 167
Ruth, 43
WELSH, Alse, 120
Lewis, 294
Mary, 294
Peirce, 325
WENTHAD, Sarah,
218
WESSELLS,
Elizabeth, 168
James, 168
Margrett, 57
WEST, Francis, 190
Mary, 286
Mary Parker, 287
Rebecca, 145
Richard, 286, 287,
288, 304
Samuel, 140, 158
WETHERED, Isabel-
la, 305
John, 307
Richard, 203, 232,
305
William, 307
WETHERILL,
Thomas, 118
WEYAT, Thomas,
218
WEYATT, William,
241
WHALAN, Mary,
211
WHALAND, John,
13
WHEATSTONES,
Stephen, 266

Samuel, 315
Sander, 307
Sarah, 176, 310,
  312, 313, 314,
  317, 318, 319,
  320, 321
Simon, 315
Thomas, 300, 308,
  318, 320, 321
William, 249, 314,
  317, 321, 322
William Rogers,
  318
WILSONS BEGIN-
  NIG, 198
WINCHESTER,
  Isaac, 218, 286
Jacob, 43
John, 116
WINCKLES, Ed-
  ward, 232
WINDELL, Ann, 326
Thomas, 309
WINDLE, Edward,
  326
WINEFRED, John,
  217
WINFIELD, 180
WINKLES, Edward,
  232
WINN, Thomas, 126
WINSOR'S FOR-
  REST, 44
WISE, Susanna, 242
WOLF TRAK, 150
WOLLER
  HAMPTON, 162
WOLLMAN,
  Richard, 228
WOOD, Joana, 97
William, 113, 133
WOOD YARD, 76
WOODAL, John, 277
WOODALL, Ann,
  222, 293

Elisabeth, 222
Elizabeth, 293
James, 294
John, 59, 161, 236,
  294
Mary, 59, 60, 222,
  293
W., 147, 150, 151
William, 151
WOODCOCK, Ed-
  ward, 162
Elisabeth, 162
WOODHOUSE, 241
WOODHOUSE
  ADDITION, 241
WOODLAND, Black-
  edge, 193
Frances, 314, 317
James, 111
Jonathan, 193
Mary, 309
Sarah, 38
William, 162, 309,
  310, 314, 316, 317
WOODROOFE, Ann,
  242
Francis, 241
John, 241
Joseph, 241, 242
Mary, 242
Thomas, 241, 242
William, 241
WOODWARD, John,
  39
WOODYARD
  THICKETT, 75,
  76
WOOLFORD, Roger,
  69
WORREL, William,
  80
WORRELL, Edward,
  13, 142, 282, 288
Mary, 81, 266, 267
Simon, 80, 81, 283

WORRIL, Edward,
  306
WORTH, James, 139
Jonathan, 224
WORTHINGTON,
  John, 224
WORTON, 56, 57
John, 144
WORTON MANOR,
  70
WRIGHT, Archibald,
  314
Charles, 2
Dorcas, 273
Edward, 70
Edward John, 206
John, 75, 77, 127,
  161, 191
Katharine, 2
Mary, 75, 98, 99,
  100
Nathan Samuel
  Turbutt, 273
Nathaniel, 100
Samuell, 37
Solomon, 123, 132,
  181, 216, 219
Solomon Coursey,
  100
Thomas, 274
Thomas Hynson,
  98, 99, 100, 179,
  273
WRIGHTSON, J., 12
Ja., 12
John, 57
WROTH, Frances,
  260
John, 199
Kinum, 61
Kinvin, 210, 260
Kirwan, 207
Martha, 260, 262
Priscillah, 102
Richard, 102

WYAETTS, Thomas,
240
WYATH, Cassandra,
102
WYATT, John, 145,
292
Judith, 240
Rebecca, 292, 293,
294
Thomas, 240
WYNN, John, 161

-Y-
YAPP, 31, 86, 88
YARDSLEY,
Elisabeth, 62
YARLEY, William,
143
YATES, Donaldson,
53, 54
YEARLY, Mary, 143
William, 101, 144,
311
YEATES, Donaldson,
32, 53, 54, 73,
223, 285
YEATS, Donaldson,
260
YEWELL, Thomas,
45
YOKLEY, John, 194

YORKSON, John, 56
Thomas, 56, 149
YOUELL, Thomas,
201
YOUNG, Alice, 328
Ann, 326, 327
Anne, 327
Benjamin, 327, 329
Charles, 97, 327
Christian, 327
Cornelia, 325
Daniel, 329
David, 40, 327
Edward, 327
Elizabeth, 324, 325,
326, 327, 329
Frances, 323, 324,
328
Hannah, 327
Jacob, 264
James, 328, 329
Jo., 23
John, 103, 324,
326, 327, 328, 329
John Beal, 328
Joseph, 18, 168,
170, 200, 322,
323, 327
Lewcrecy, 328
Lucretia, 328
Margaret, 326, 327

Mary, 168, 169,
170, 264, 322,
323, 326, 327, 328
Milcah, 322, 323
Nathaniell, 328
Preston, 329
Richard, 322
Samuel, 322, 326,
327, 328
Sarah, 324, 327
Solomon, 328
Suffian, 328
Thomas, 328
William, 219, 321,
323, 324, 325,
328, 329
YOUNGE, William,
324
YOUNGER,
Elizabeth, 128
John, 128, 205
YOUNG'S
CHANCE, 324
YUNG, Joseph, 169

-Z-
ZUILLE, Elisabeth,
78
Mathew, 91
Matthew, 78

394

Heritage Books by Robert W. Barnes and F. Edward Wright

Colonial Families of the Eastern Shore of Maryland, Volumes 1–3

Heritage Books by Robert W. Barnes:

1783 Tax List of Baltimore County
Robert W. Barnes and Bettie S. Carothers

Index of Baltimore County Wills, 1659–1850
Robert W. Barnes and Bettie S. Carothers

Baltimore and Fell's Point Directory of 1796

Baltimore County, Marriage References, 1659–1746

Baltimore County, Maryland Deed Abstracts, 1659–1750

Colonial Families of Anne Arundel County, Maryland

Gleanings from Maryland Newspapers, 1776–85

Gleanings from Maryland Newspapers, 1786–90

Gleanings from Maryland Newspapers, 1791–95

Index to Marriages and Deaths in the
Baltimore County Advocate, 1850–1864

Heritage Books by F. Edward Wright:

18th Century Records of the German Lutheran Church at Philadelphia, Pennsylvania
(St. Michael's and Zion): Volume 1, Baptisms, 1745–1769
Robert L. Hess and F. Edward Wright

18th Century Records of the German Lutheran Church at Philadelphia, Pennsylvania
(St. Michael's and Zion): Volume 2, Baptisms, 1770–1786
Translated by Robert L. Hess, Ph.D. Edited by F. Edward Wright

18th Century Records of the German Lutheran Church of Philadelphia, Pennsylvania
(St. Michael's and Zion): Volume 3, Baptisms, 1787–1800
Translated by Robert L. Hess, Ph.D. Edited by F. Edward Wright

18th Century Records of the German Lutheran Church at Philadelphia, Pennsylvania
(St. Michael's and Zion): Volume 4, Marriages and Confirmations
Robert L. Hess and F. Edward Wright

18th Century Records of the German Lutheran Church at Philadelphia, Pennsylvania
(St. Michael's and Zion): Volume 5, Burials
Robert L. Hess and F. Edward Wright

Abstracts of Bucks County, Pennsylvania, Wills, 1685–1785

Abstracts of Cumberland County, Pennsylvania, Wills, 1750–1785

Abstracts of Cumberland County, Pennsylvania, Wills, 1785–1825

Abstracts of Philadelphia County, Pennsylvania, Wills:
Volumes: 1682–1726; 1726–1747; 1748–1763; 1763–1784; 1777–1790;
1790–1802; 1802–1809; 1810–1815; 1815–1819; and 1820–1825

Abstracts of South Central Pennsylvania, Newspapers, Volume 1, 1785–1790

Abstracts of South Central Pennsylvania, Newspapers, Volume 3, 1796–1800

Maryland Calendar of Wills:
Volume 9: 1744–1749; Volume 10: 1748–1753; Volume 11: 1753–1760;
Volume 12: 1759–1764; Volume 13: 1764–1767; Volume 14: 1767–1772;
Volume 15: 1772–1774; and Volume 16: 1774–1777

Maryland Eastern Shore Newspaper Abstracts
Volume 1: 1790–1805; Volume 2: 1806–1812;
Volume 3: 1813–1818; Volume 4: 1819–1824;
Volume 5: Northern Counties, 1825–1829
F. Edward Wright and Irma Harper;
Volume 6: Southern Counties, 1825–1829;
Volume 7: Northern Counties, 1830–1834
Irma Harper and F. Edward Wright;
Volume 8: Southern Counties, 1830–1834

Maryland Eastern Shore Vital Records:
Book 1: 1648–1725, Second Edition; Book 2: 1726–1750; Book 3: 1751–1775;
Book 4: 1776–1800; and Book 5: 1801–1825

Maryland Militia in the War of 1812:
Volume 1: Eastern Shore; Volume 2: Baltimore City and County;
Volume 3: Cecil and Harford Counties; Volume 4: Anne Arundel and Calvert Counties;
Volume 5: St. Mary's and Charles Counties; Volume 6: Prince George's County;
and Volume 7: Montgomery County

Maryland Militia in the Revolutionary War
S. Eugene Clements and F. Edward Wright

Middlesex County Virginia, Marriage References and Family Relationships, 1673–1800

Middlesex County, New Jersey, Records of the 17th and 18th Centuries

New Castle County, Delaware, Marriage References
and Family Relationships, 1680–1800

Newspaper Abstracts of Allegany and Washington Counties [Maryland], 1811–1815

Newspaper Abstracts of Cecil and Harford Counties [Maryland], 1822–1830

Newspaper Abstracts of Frederick County [Maryland], 1811–1815

Newspaper Abstracts of Frederick County [Maryland], 1816–1819

Northampton County, Virginia, Marriage References
and Family Relationships, 1634–1800

Northumberland County, Virginia, Marriage References
and Family Relationships, 1645–1800

Orphans' Court Proceedings of New Castle County, Delaware, 1742–1761

Quaker Minutes of the Eastern Shore of Maryland: 1676–1779

Quaker Records of Henrico Monthly Meeting and Other Church Records
of Henrico, New Kent and Charles City Counties, Virginia

Quaker Records of South River Monthly Meeting, 1756–1800

Richmond County, Virginia, Marriage References and Family Relationships, 1692–1800

Sketches of Maryland Eastern Shoremen

St. Mary's County, Maryland, Marriage References and Family Relationships, 1634–1800

Stafford County, Virginia, Marriage References and Family Relationships, 1661–1800

Supplement to Maryland Eastern Shore Vital Records, Books 1–3

Sussex County, Delaware, Marriage References, 1648–1800

Sussex County, Delaware, Wills: 1800–1813

Tax List of Chester County, Pennsylvania, 1768

Tax List of York County, Pennsylvania, 1779

The Maryland Militia in the Revolutionary War
S. Eugene Clements and F. Edward Wright

Vital Records of Kent and Sussex Counties, Delaware, 1686–1800

Washington County [Maryland] Church Records of the 18th Century, 1768–1800

Western Maryland Newspaper Abstracts, Volume 1: 1786–1798

Western Maryland Newspaper Abstracts, Volume 2: 1799–1805

Western Maryland Newspaper Abstracts, Volume 3: 1806–1810

Wills of Chester County, Pennsylvania, 1766–1778

York County, Pennsylvania, Church Records of the 18th Century, Volume 1
Marlene S. Bates and F. Edward Wright

York County, Pennsylvania, Church Records of the 18th Century, Volume 2
Marlene Strawser Bates and F. Edward Wright

York County, Pennsylvania, Church Records of the 18th Century, Volume 3

York County, Virginia, Marriage References and Family Relationships, 1636–1800

York County, Virginia, Wills Inventories and Accounts, 1760–1783